# THE PRIVATE JOURNAL OF
# HENRI FRÉDÉRIC AMIEL

**THE MACMILLAN COMPANY**
NEW YORK · BOSTON · CHICAGO · DALLAS
ATLANTA · SAN FRANCISCO

**MACMILLAN & CO., Limited**
LONDON · BOMBAY · CALCUTTA
MELBOURNE

**THE MACMILLAN COMPANY**
OF CANADA, Limited
TORONTO

HENRI FRÉDÉRIC AMIEL, 1852

# The Private Journal of
# HENRI FRÉDÉRIC AMIEL

TRANSLATED BY
## VAN WYCK BROOKS
AND
## CHARLES VAN WYCK BROOKS

INTRODUCTION BY
BERNARD BOUVIER

*Enlarged and Revised Edition*
*Conforming to the Original Text*

NEW YORK
## THE MACMILLAN COMPANY
1935

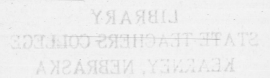

# INTRODUCTION

AMIEL wrote in 1876: "If five hundred of the fourteen thousand
pages of my Journal are preserved, this would be a good deal,
enough, perhaps." Immediately after his death, the first editors of
the *Fragments du Journal intime* fulfilled this timid ambition. In
1883 and in 1884, they published the two slight volumes, revised in
the fifth edition of 1887, upon which Amiel's renown is based and
which, since reprinted to the number of thirty thousand, have been
translated into many languages. Thanks to the severely guided choice
of the editors, this renown has slowly carried the author of the
*Journal intime* to the first rank among the moralists of the French
tongue. No one today questions that he is entitled to this eminent
position. Among the various critics, whose judgment faithfully reproduces the feeling of countless readers, scattered through every
land, opinions indeed differ, but the conclusion is unanimous. In
that long discourse which, as the ages pass, registers the continuous
thought of humanity, Amiel uttered words that endure, with the
meaning, the accent, the turn of phrase which his genius imparted
to them; and recently, on the occasion of the hundredth anniversary
of his birth, he was hailed as one of the boldest explorers, one of
the greatest discoverers of the human soul.

But has not the time come for him to speak anew, the time for
us to enrich, if not by several volumes, at least by a few hundred
more pages, the confession that has been borrowed from the enormous manuscript? This is the task which I proposed to myself
when I received this precious trust, guarded jealously from all eyes
during forty years. An undertaking that was easy only in appear-

v

ance. In the simple methods that scholarship applies to all sorts of texts, conscience, love and aesthetic feeling play little part. They do not therefore assist an editor who wishes and is indeed bound to choose with a sometimes painful anxiety. The editors of 1883 knew this quite well. In order to surmount the difficulty, they adopted the principles that gave their work its original character. I am following other principles today; and it is simply to explain them, by describing the manuscript of the *Journal intime* and telling its story, that I address myself to those readers who may be curious to compare this new text with the consecrated text. They will not look here for the biography of Amiel that Edmond Scherer himself did not choose to write when he presented the first *Fragments*, nor any further judgment concerning a man who spent his life judging himself. They will, no doubt, however, wish to be more completely informed about a work that has grown dearer to them in proportion as it has grown more familiar. An authoritative biography of Amiel should be preceded by his correspondence. I now possess a part of this, and I am endeavouring to collect whatever may still remain in other hands. After this new collection of *Fragments*, I hope to have the time and strength to publish it.

I trust that I may be pardoned for speaking deliberately in the first person. I should be glad to imitate the admirable reserve of the lady who wrote the preface to the edition of 1883, but this would require artifices of language that seem to me unnecessary. Noble scruples restrained this noble woman, to whom the *Journal intime* owes its revelation to the public. Herself the legatee of the manuscript, she wished me to inherit it after her. This responsibility seemed formidable to me, and it has been my wish to accept only the moral obligation of improving my acquaintance with the *Journal intime*, freed at last from its captivity, in order, in turn, to make it better known. I tell simply what I have learned from these papers, which for a time were entrusted to the safe-keeping of two others and myself, and which were bequeathed to me. My one endeavour is to serve Amiel's none too certain thought and will.

# INTRODUCTION

## II

The "regular *Journal intime*" opens with the end of the year 1847. This date reappears inscribed upon each of the one hundred and seventy-three note-books of which the manuscript consists. Amiel was then, at twenty-six, a student at the University of Berlin, in a period of full self-possession, security and equilibrium, which was to find its precise expression in a daily writing of notes on his labours, his reading, his scientific and social relations, as well as on his inner life. "I am now full of hope; this restless melancholy, this dark moodiness that have been preying upon me for so long, seem to be about to disappear. The future no longer frightens me now that I see the possibility of realizing my dreams, now that my doubts are diminishing and my powers increasing, now that I am becoming a man." (*Antécédents du Journal intime*, February 6, 1846.[1])

But before making the Journal the essential work of his life and finding in it, outside and above, or rather at the heart of every social and professional activity, the *raison d'être* of his mind, he was to hear confusedly and follow gropingly and, as it were, in spite of himself, the inner call. One finds attempts, often abandoned and resumed, to note down his daily reflections and experiences, between the ages of eighteen and twenty-five. These youthful experiments fill one or two note-books, the first of which, set apart under the rubric "reserved," runs from June 24, 1839 to August 27, 1841. This is the most characteristic of the preliminary series and permits one to catch an early glimpse of the innermost feelings, the conflicts of ideas and sentiments which were to lead this exceptional soul, always more and more willingly, to observe, judge and describe itself in a confidence of thirty-five years, while yielding to a ruinous liberty, in point of any solid, strong and definitive work.

The following is the first of these reflections: "The way to learn nothing at all, even while working, is to flit about from one work to

[1] Amiel himself groups under this general heading the juvenile note-books which he also calls, sometimes the *Premier Journal*, sometimes *Notes et réflexions, ou Journal*.

another, or to read too much at a single sitting. I skim, I turn twenty times the pages of a book of history, when I might have read it attentively. In this way I have found the recipe for always having to begin anew. We shall have to regulate this." And this eighteen-year-old student continues: "I should like to read and learn so many things at once that I am paralyzed with discouragement, and, confronted with my work, I remain powerless to make up my mind to limit myself to a single subject, and not daring to begin. This is a serious fault: one more thing to be corrected . . ." (*Premier Journal*, June 24, 1839.)

In response to the tireless curiosity of a mind which was already half aware that the complete was to be its need and its dream, that nothing finite would ever satisfy it, he yielded, in the time that was left from his courses, which do not seem to have captivated him greatly, and along with the distractions of friendship and the family, which never really engrossed him, to an eager and especially discursive reading. Here, for instance, is what he read between June 24 and October 17 of this year 1839: Béranger, *Chansons;* Mignet, *Napoléon;* Victor Hugo, *les Orientales; les Voix intérieures;* Mme. de Staël, *Corinne;* Michelet, *Introduction à l'Histoire universelle;* J.-J. Rousseau, *Lettres sur la botanique;* de Saintines, *Picciola;* Balzac, *La Peau de chagrin, Physiologie du Mariage;* G. Sand, *La dernière Aldini;* Ch. Nodier, *Mlle. de Marsan;* Jules Janin, *Chemin de traverse;* Grégoire de Tours, *Histoire des Francs;* Montaigne, a few books of the *Essais;* Villemain, *Eloge de Montaigne;* a few chapters of the *Perfectionnement moral;* Charles Didier, *Rome souterraine,* and I think there are some that I have forgotten! But he soon came to "feel what is false in the life of books," as opposed to real life: "I recognize with a sort of terror the enormous illusion under which I have lived without examining it, that everything is in books, and that one learns there more quickly and better." (*Antécédents du Journal intime,* Berlin, April 8, 1845.)

Is not this the supreme temptation of the intelligence, the mischievous disorder that intellectual curiosity induces, the forbidden attraction of the tree of good and evil? "We shall have to regulate this." The phrase reappears like a refrain through these early note-books. And this sketch of a journal was indeed a refuge from the increasing embarrassment of the young man, abandoned without rule or measure to the thirst for knowledge. "We shall have to regulate this": one must find and impose on oneself a discipline of work, a rigorous control of these multiple intellectual adventures, the wisdom, in short, and the persevering line of conduct that can alone trace out for him the conclusive plan of a vocation.

"For a long time, I have been concerned about my vocation. This is the planet, as Goethe says, about which gravitate for the moment my readings and my reflections. I have periods of cruel uncertainty. Perhaps it is because pride blinds me and I never believe that I shall find a sufficiently high and remote place for myself. Where will all this end? *Qui vivra verra.*" (*Premier Journal*, October 14, 1840.)

Meanwhile, Amiel strove by means of "principles" to stabilize a quest that was at times sadly disturbed by a feeling of the flight of time ill-spent. Here are two of them: "In order to group one's studies, one must set oneself a definite aim, and on the whole rather a spacious one, in one's efforts and one's labours."—"Each special branch must be fecundated and inspired by the idea of this vast whole to which it belongs. This is the only way to study it fruit-fully." (*Premier Journal*, October 8, 1840.)

I continue my citations. On March 6, 1840, he had written: "Spent almost all my free time draughting this little four-inch card, containing all the rules that I have adopted for my conduct. I have belaboured my brain to make the three that concern study complete. I have found a framework in which I have been able to include everything. How to remember what one has learned;—how to learn anew;—how to be sure that one knows." (*Premier Journal*, March 6, 1840.)

But discouragement, infidelity to this discipline were soon to re-appear and render more pressing the appeal to this singular aid, the

Journal; "Oh, these days I am really weary of myself: I see how small are the results of my two and a half years of Auditory[1]; I feel my life slipping from me without bearing fruit, without being put to use. I am frittering my forces away on a little disconnected reading, and even of this the traces are soon gone. Indolence has overrun everything. It is destroying me. But no, it is I who mean to destroy it. I am going to busy myself, from this evening, with an examination of my life. I shall carry it out and put it all into writing. From the past, I shall turn towards the future, and, humbled by this past, I shall form my life anew; in fine, I shall make a clear choice of my vocation, I shall determine the work I wish to accomplish, and I shall construct accordingly my plans for next year and the years following, directing all of them towards this single aim. I shall not too strictly circumscribe my liberty, because, by so doing, I should gain nothing; but I shall trace out a general itinerary. Yes, I shall have to come back often to the goal which I set myself; and every month, every week indeed, there must irrevocably be an examination of my progress, intellectual, moral and even physical."

Order in his reading, the choice of a career, a method and plan of work, examination of conscience, such are the first stages in the exercise of his will through which the author of the *Premier Journal* passed.

Not, however, without hesitation, even a certain resistance, did Amiel decide upon this periodic dialogue with himself. He very soon perceived the danger in it: "There is a certain pleasure in moralizing to oneself, spouting fine resolutions, and a foolish melancholy in feeling that one is incapable of following them." (*Premier Journal*, October 14, 1839.)—"These journals are a delusion. They do not contain the tenth part of what one thinks in half an hour on this subject. If they could be simply a table of contents, they would be valuable." (*Premier Journal*, October 13, 1840.)

[1] "Auditory" was the name given to the three years of general studies in science and literature passed by the students of Geneva before they entered the professional schools.

# INTRODUCTION

But how, on the other hand, when one has the instinct, the need and the dream of the complete, how consent to lose anything of oneself, to renew oneself, to undergo metamorphoses, to die every day and be reborn something else, without gathering the lessons of these successive experiences? "An idea that strikes me is this: Every day we leave a part of ourselves behind us on the road. Everything around us disappears, faces, relatives, fellow-citizens, the generations pass away in silence, everything falls and is gone, the world slips through our fingers, our illusions are dispelled, we behold the ruin of everything, and, as if this were not enough, we fall into ruin ourselves. We are as alien to the self that has lived as if it were not ourself; what I was a few years ago, my pleasures, my feelings, my thoughts, I no longer know; my body has passed away, my soul has passed away also, time has carried everything off. I am a witness of my metamorphosis, I no longer know what I was, the things I enjoyed as a child I can no longer understand, my observations, my hopes, my creations as a young man are lost; what I have thought, what I have felt (my only precious possessions), the consciousness of my former existence, I possess no more: it is a past that has been swallowed up. For melancholy, this thought has no parallel. It recalls the words of the Prince de Ligne: *If one remembered all that one had observed and learned in one's life, one would be a savant indeed.* This thought should suffice to make one keep an assiduous journal." (*Premier Journal,* October 8, 1840.)

As we shall see, during his year in Italy, little moved by the spectacle of the scenes, the architecture or the works of art, and constantly prone to transpose all his sensations to the plane of moral or philosophical reflection, Amiel, even in his adolescence, was able to find a charm and interest in things only through an act of the intellect. He was unwilling to attack anything until he was master of its principle. That which is, for others, the recompense of labour was for him its condition. His first perception was a perception of the plurality of things, his ambition strained towards the totality of knowledge, his instinctive method of learning was synthesis.

Let us hear what he says, at the end of one of his self-examinations, several of which the *Premier Journal* already contains: "I think I am well-endowed, but my natural state is one of rest. All the faculties I possess require, to be aroused, an express act of the will. Will is more necessary to me than to others, for my faculties have no power of impulsion in themselves. They are absolutely devoted and passive servants. An energetic will could go a long way with my instruments, for it would be richly served. If I do not acquire a will, I shall be nothing.

"The consciousness of success doubles my strength; I do not begin if I do not hope to succeed. I am quickly discouraged: I need to triumph, I need to have confidence in myself. Without faith in myself, I shall never undertake anything great." (*Premier Journal,* June 18, 1841.)

Deep, humble words, revealing the secret tragedy of a young manhood that is in other ways so rich, outwardly so lively and sometimes so brilliant. Constantly borne back upon itself, the thought of the twenty-year-old Amiel revolves, as in a circle, in this agony, apparently without issue, of the choice of a vocation.

This mind, already open to universal things, dreaded to be dependent on anything, to give itself to any particular truth, to sacrifice any of the magnificent gifts that each fresh meditation caused it to discover in itself. He would have liked, at once, and even though it were necessary to renounce the whole individual man, to attain to the knowledge and definition of the absolute man. "Everything is in everything," he was to write a few years later, "and if the eye could ever penetrate to the bottom of a single object, the universe would become transparent for it. One man represents man; man contains the animal, the animal the vegetable, the vegetable the mineral, the mineral algebra and geometry. Thoroughly to understand a man would be to find the universe an open book." (*Premier Journal,* Berlin, February 4, 1845.)

A piercing vision, bold as an epitome in which all the sciences are assembled! A conquest and occupation of the unknown! The very struggle that Amiel had early undertaken to know himself and realize peace in himself, through an equilibrium of his mind and heart, was to guide him to his true vocation.

"At nightfall, today, I set myself to reflecting on a system of life, an immense plan of work, such as one might be tempted to undertake if one forgot that only human forces are at one's disposal. Nature, humanity, astronomy, the natural sciences, mathematics, poetry, religion, the fine arts, history, psychology, everything should be comprehended in philosophy, as I conceive it . . . Then I was assailed by scruples. To study that which is, to understand and even find the reason for that which has happened, would this be of any use? To have extended my intelligence, to have comprehended everything; when I succeeded in this, would it not be a personal goal, a selfish enjoyment? How can one be of use to the world? Is it not by finding a new idea rather than by rummaging among all the ideas that have been created?— To this my answer was: Once the idea of God is understood, and the role of humanity is determined, my part would be to make them known, my duty would summon me to say to the poet, to science, to music, to philosophy, to everything that men do: there is your task, there is your objective . . ." (*Premier Journal,* October 8, 1840.)

No one will smile at these transports of an encyclopædic imagination, at this impassioned intellectual romanticism, if he reflects that Amiel at the age of twenty was thus tracing the immense horizon of his life-work, the *Journal intime,* the forces of which were already stirring obscurely within him.

I take as a proof of this the noble and spacious confession, astonishing in its audacity, touching in its humility, which he was to pen in his solitude at Fillinge, in Savoy, on September 14, 1841, in a letter to his Aunt Fanchette:

"Last evening, I returned to my room, and there, under the gaze of the stars that thronged the heavens, I reflected earnestly. I asked myself what I have asked twenty times before, what should the thought be about which I am to order my life, the dominant idea, the aim, the motive that should ensphere all the other motives, dominate over all the others and give unity to my career. One of the things that causes me most pain is the feeling that I am being disintegrated and dissipated by life: one's forces are scattered, one does not know precisely what one is doing, and, after one has gone through all sorts of troubles and toils, one has not advanced a step towards happiness. One must therefore centralize one's activity, ascertain clearly the end one has in view and how one is to reach it . . .

"As for the end, it lies in that which does not pass away, in that which eludes everything, set-backs and tyrannies alike, in that which belongs to us and will belong to us, in our soul. Our soul is a solemn trust; it is the only eternal thing amid all the things that surround us, these mountains, this globe, these suns. It is the divine breath that has more value than all these worlds; we owe it everything. It should be conscious of itself, of its goal, its inner life; we should bring before its judgment every day our actions, our feelings, our acquisitions; and it must judge of all that pertains to its true culture, and judge all that lacks roots and fruits that are immortal. One must tell oneself that this soul is destined to an endless and limit-less increase, that, if we have been cast upon this planet, we are to outlive it and pass elsewhere . . . But this eternal education we have to begin upon this earth; the world, our career, our friends, our relatives, our religion are the instrumentalities of God. The true relations are those between God and ourselves. The love of created beings is a pious love, hallowed by the law of heaven, but it is still an education, a means for mounting higher. Charity is the greatest ladder by which to attain to the supreme love.—Our soul has many different faculties, many powers, seemingly opposed, but they all rally about its centre; they are only the radii which, although divergent, spring from a single source, emanate from the one central point. All that the earth can provide us we must take. The faculties should all be cultivated together, in order to maintain equilibrium and not bring about the hypertrophy of one at the expense of some other. Music and geometry, astronomy and aesthetics, philosophy and poetry, the moral sciences and the industrial arts, nothing is superfluous, nothing is to be rejected. The end does not change, but the means are alterable and flexible. If scientific cultivation is lacking, if sickness fetters us, well, the inner life still profits by learning to suffer; it grows strong, it is tutored by a detachment from the world, it studies its impressions, it is purified and becomes resigned. If books are lacking, one has the human heart to explore; if society is lacking, one has works of art or those of nature. If all these harvests of life are unavailable, if one has not the means to procure them for one's soul, the table of the inner life will yet not be empty; God and ourselves will still remain, ourselves, our faculties, the play of our passions and our ideas, the structure and the action of the understanding, especially the moral study of our heart, and all this that we may make it an offering to our soul, while offering our soul itself to God.

"The inner life should be a Vestal altar, and its fire should be kept burning night and day. Our soul is the holy temple of which we are the Levites. All things should be brought before the altar, illumined and passed through the fire of examination; and the soul owes itself the consciousness of its action and its will . . ."

It is easy to recognize certain of the thoughts, certain of the accents of the *Antécédents,* written at the same time as this vibrantly enthusiastic confession, which responds to the agonies of adolescence by a sort of prophecy, a swift and sweeping vision of the writer's destiny.

The *Journal intime* was indeed to realize Henri Frédéric Amiel's "vocation". It has been misjudged, I think, in being taken for a sort of disillusioned confidant, a companion in despair, a vulture tearing at the vitals of this chained Prometheus; or rather in being represented as a kind of bill of indictment against a world to which Amiel had never been able to adjust himself, a sort of revenge which the martyr of the ideal wreaked, day after day, on an ungrateful fatherland, a hostile social life and an abortive career. No, the Journal is anything but a work of this cruel and sterile kind. "I had no comforter, no friend superior to myself to understand me and give me strength during my adolescence." So speaks Amiel at twenty-four. But by the time he was twenty he had unwittingly discovered the remedy for his trouble, for this privation from which he suffered with his whole being: namely, to give himself this superior friend, this guide, this stimulator, this counsellor and this judge, whose words were to fill his solitude and vindicate his courage. This was to be the *Journal intime*.

And yet, if many pages of this work, pursued to the final obliteration of every hope and every disappointment, seem to justify the severity of certain moralists, if Amiel himself at times condemned it, this was because it submitted, in turn, to the "law of irony" which he defined as the "unconscious dupery, the refutation of oneself by oneself, the concrete realization of the absurd."—"The philosopher, too, falls under the law of irony, for after having mentally ridded himself of all his prejudices, impersonalized himself from top to bottom, he is obliged to come back to his body and his rags again, eat and drink, be hungry, thirsty, cold, and do as all other mortals do, after having for a moment done as no one does." Yes, like all other mortals, yield to the hungers and thirsts of the heart, seek after glory, groan over disappointments, lapse into envy, dream of domestic happiness and comfort, foil the inquisitive, unmask the wicked, appeal for sympathy and admiration, assert his merits, demand his rewards, in fine, surpass others in claiming all his rights.

All these human frailties enter and cross the stage of the *Journal intime*. But their momentary and shifting combination does not celebrate any victory or any conquest. The law of duty and sovereign intelligence annul the law of irony. In the depths of the soul of Amiel there was neither defeat nor despair; there was heroism, as the *Antécédents du Journal* already announced. All the dissonances were to be effaced in the supreme accord of the moral conscience and the mind.

## III

The manuscript of the regular *Journal intime* consists of 173 quarto note-books—in reality, 174, if one allows for an error in pagination—which Amiel sewed together himself and assembled in thirteen volumes bound in boards with parchment backs. The whole runs to about 16,900 pages, while the four note-books of the *Antécédents* number something less than two hundred.

During the first years, the author followed a fairly regular practice of paragraphing, logically distinguishing the units by means of subtitles, which he underscored, and marginal notes added afterwards.

In reality, he was still groping: the diversity as well as the abundance of facts and reflections to be stored away embarrassed him. Nor could he keep to the rule of devoting to the Journal the last hour (from nine to ten o'clock in the evening) of a day of work that was rigorously partitioned. He did not follow the plan that he had outlined of a journal divided into five books of intimate notes: "1, Moral; 2, Intellectual; 3, Physical; 4, Inner life, impressions; 5, Projects, plans." (*Antécédents,* October 30, 1840.)

This was the time when he proposed to elucidate "the art and the method of life".—"The principle is the will: to will what one knows; the aim is the vocation: to know what one ought to do; the method is the plan of life: to determine how one ought to do it." But he was soon to weary of this pedantry of the catechism: "Spent several hours rereading and garnishing with annotations one of the volumes of my *Journal intime,* in order to make references and comparisons. It is rather tiresome, with its everlasting personal and moralistic preoccupation. The absence of facts is due to the division of the work; I meant to reserve the facts for other parallel volumes . . . It is therefore necessary to improve the Journal by making a place in it for people and things. Being now psychological and moral, it should become more picturesque. Or should this be the work of another note-book? Should not the whole subjective life, more directly grasped in the consciousness of it than recounted in its acts, be entered in the Journal? The three concentric spheres of the subjective life, namely, the facts and the actions;—the ideas that are perceived;—the feelings that are experienced, should form and compose the matter of the Journal." [1]

And Amiel draws up this curious table:

A. ACTA:    a) Use of time and hours (*statistics*);
            b) Details (*hopes*).
B. COGITATA: a) Acquired knowledge (*museum*);
            b) Ideas occurring and discovered (*arsenal*).
C. SENTITA: a) The transitory; fugitive apperceptions (*poetry, drama*);
            b) The abiding, fundamental feeling (*religion, confessional*).

But he soon abandoned all pedagogical intentions in regard to the division of work. In connection with the scheme above, a subsequent marginal note puts this question: "Does a private Journal express life?" It was from life that the Journal was in fact ever more spontaneously to draw its inspiration. "If I continue it," Amiel wrote in 1852, "it will assume another aspect . . . For the moment, this Journal is still a mystical, hybrid being, a letter-rack, a memorandum-book, a minute of proceedings, an inquisitor, a confidant, a notary, in which, however, two roles dominate, that of the clerk of the court who records, and that of the Nestor who sermonizes. Statistical or monitory, it is a bore in either case. And so it is far from amusing to reread. But if to write it has been useful, it has its excuse." One sees, little by little, merely by the arrangement of the writing and the character of the note-books, how the Journal ceases to be a discipline and becomes a diversion, a relaxation, before the day arrives when it becomes an indispensable companion, and some-

[1] *Journal intime,* December, 1849. All the citations made in the course of this Introduction are taken from unpublished portions of the manuscript.

times an imperious master. After this, it becomes more like its author, it appears to model itself on his nature and accommodate itself to his humour. If it does not as yet receive his first morning greeting, still he summons it more constantly to him; and the weeks, even the days, grow more and more rare in which Amiel has consigned nothing to it:

"Journal neglected, journal wearisome; for it records only a few clumsy facts and few or no impressions; it preserves the matter and loses the spirit of the days that roll by. Instead of a bouquet, I have a mere herbarium, and even the flowers in it are pressed ones, without scent or freshness. And a dried flower is no longer true, it is a lie. A journal that does not keep up with life is not a journal at all, and its very fidelity may be deceptive. A witness who does not tell the whole truth is as much a false witness as one who perverts it, and more so than one who tells nothing. Therefore write every day, or return only with misgivings to the days that have been forgotten." (*Journal intime,* April 22, 1851.)

After the autumn of 1852, there were to be, save for a few exceptions, at very long intervals, no more blank days. And it was at this time also that the type of entry was established, a type that was almost uniform during the periods of physical and moral calm. Amiel inscribes under the date a list of his readings, the letters he has written and the calls he has received; and then develops, in paragraphs long or short, first the analysis and criticism of the articles and the works he has read, then observations on his meetings with people, his conversations and experiences of the day.

From one day to another, from one year to another, the number of pages may vary considerably. On the cover of the 144th notebook, which ends with the year 1876, Amiel inscribes this observation: "14,000 pages in 25 years, amounts to 482 pages a year, or one and three-tenths pages a day for 10,480 consecutive days." As a matter of fact, his changeable humour did not bind itself to any calculation. "I have scribbled quite enough today (11 pages); at this rate, this would come to 3700 pages in one year, as much as in the ten years from 1848 to 1858.—Assuming four pages a day of durable work: in three months this would be a volume. Allowing nine months for preparation and meditation: this would still make one volume a year." (*Journal intime,* April 7, 1866.)

The years were thus to be very unequal. The average for the first ten is 293 pages; for the ten following, 528 pages; for the ten following these, 635 pages. The three fullest years are 1870 (813 pages), 1871 (841 pages), and 1880 (809 pages).

Facing the date (March, 1868) of its inscription, the reader will find a facsimile of the cover of one of these note-books of the Journal, the eighty-ninth. I might have reproduced that of the second volume (1848), which bears the following inscription, a curious programme, still very confused, in fact, and drawn up in the style of a Berlin student, of the work that he had just undertaken: "General bird's-eye view. Review of the whole, and of the course of my development. Headquarters of operations. A glance over the inner harmony or dissonance, over lacunæ, defects and embarrassments, over the simultaneous and organic evaluation of my physical, intellectual and moral forces.—Thermometer of my psychological condition.— My most central, most secret, most self-collected life.—Relations with the sphere of the eternal.—Inner experience. Self-consciousness. Balance, proportion, measure, harmony, eurhythmy. *Lebenskunst.* Infinite education.—States of the soul and guiding or consoling principles.—Character. Inclination. Impressions."

Not all the covers of the unlined note-books are thus encumbered. Among the earliest, a few bear the epigraph, *Specula, speculum.* Others, later, contain mottos that are admonitions: TO THE POINT. WATCH OUT. NOTHING WITHOUT A REASON. FOR OTHERS. *NULLA DIES SINE LINEA. NE CRAS. CAVE CASSUM.* "BE FAST." Sometimes they are citations borrowed from his reading at the moment, among which one finds Seneca, Martial, Montaigne, Fénelon, Voltaire, Rousseau, Goethe, Heine, George Sand, Sainte-Beuve, Vinet, Emerson, to mention only the most illustrious names or those that are most frequent. Or, again, sometimes stanzas, couplets, quatrains, occasionally signed with Amiel's initials. The following are a few examples:

> *Nul ne fait bien que ce qu'il fait sans trêve;*
> *Tout vrai talent s'exerce chaque jour;*
> *Plus verdit l'arbre, et plus il prend de sève;*
> *Plus le cœur aime, et plus il tient d'amour.*
>
> (Volume 35, March, 1858.)

> *Nature, en ma faveur tu fus en vain prodigue:*
> *Pour moi, vouloir, agir, vivre est une fatigue.*
>
> (Volume 37, March, 1859.)

> *Crois, et tu peux agir; doute, et tu restes coi;*
> *Pour oser quelque chose et vaincre, il faut la foi.*
>
> (Volume 70, January–March, 1865.)

> *Dans cette existence qu'oppresse*
> *Le malheur de l'humanité,*
> *Il n'est de bon que la sagesse*
> *Et de sage que la bonté.*
>
> (Volume 107, September–November, 1870.)

> *Obtenir la paix, tu le peux;*
> *Presque le bonheur, si tu veux:*
> *Fais ton devoir, et rends heureux.*
>
> (Volume 111, February–April, 1871).

## DAPHNIS ET CHLOÉ

> *Unis par le cœur, sans prêtre ou notaire,*
> *Avant d'être époux, ils furent conjoints;*
> *Le code civil vient après Cythère:*
> *Pour aimer plus tôt, s'en aime-t-on moins?*
>
> (Volume 117, January, 1872.)

> *De l'idéal disert amant,*
> *Contemplatif à l'âme fière,*
> *Tout ce qu'il veut, il peut le faire,*
> *Mais il voulut bien rarement.*
>
> (Volume 159, May–July, 1879.)

> *Fallait-il qu'on le dit ou qu'on me le cachât?*
> *Ainsi je dois mourir noyé dans mon crachat:*
> *Mon âme, hélas! la devinait cette fin lamentable,*
> *Et n'est pas résignée.*
> *Quoi! rien pour mon salut, quoi! rien pour mon rachat?*
> *Ignoble et dure destinée!*
>> (Volume 164, January–March, 1880.)

In the course of the Journal itself, Amiel's reflections turn very often into proverbs in verse, couplets, quatrains, and even short poems, sometimes humorous, for the most part gnomic. The published *Fragments* retain a few of these, although, as a rule, the editors of 1883 suppressed them. Most of them are doubtless commonplace, though still characteristic of the turn of mind of a moralist who was too often enamoured of the pretty, even of the precious. From the cover of the one hundred and thirty-first volume, which dates from 1874, I take this significant note: "A necessary supplement to this Journal is the collection of *Pensives,* an assemblage of more than 700 gnomic fragments, jotted down from day to day for a few years and gathered together separately. These trifles render actual moral situations, or situations through which I have passed. They may have no literary value, but they are a psychological commonplace-book." The collections of the *Penseroso* and *La Part du Réve* are the most successful examples of this sententious poetry.

Certain periods of the Journal abound more in poetry than others; for instance, the years 1868–1872, many of the pages of which present a continuous medley of prose and verse. The author wrote a little later: "I observe that the rhymeless days are those when I allow myself to be most dejected." Here is one of the days of high courage and an alert freedom:

*November 8, 1861 (9 a. m.)*

> *Sirocco, sol mouillé, vent tiède, ciel couvert,*
> *La terre est de feuilles jonchée;*
> *Oublions! l'arbre nu sait-il qu'il était vert?*
> *Le nid froid, qu'il eut sa nichée?*
> *Vivons, marchons front haut, fêtons même l'hiver,*
> *A quoi bon la tête penchée?*

*Va, ne sois point ingrat et savoure les biens*
  *Dont le ciel pour toi fut prodigue:*
*Si chaque homme a ses maux, sache porter les tiens,*
  *Aux mauvais pensers fais la figue.*
*Un cœur joyeux, voilà le meilleur des soutiens,*
  *C'est le cœur triste qui fatigue.*

*Tes longs abattements viennent de ton ennui,*
  *Et ton ennui de ta faiblesse;*
*Trop vite tu t'assieds, trop tôt l'espoir t'a fui,*
  *Trop aisément ton cœur se blesse;*
*Sois homme, prends courage et dis-toi qu'aujourd'hui*
  *Ton ennemi, c'est la mollesse.*

"All these eighteen lines have sprung involuntarily out of the first line, which had taken the shape of an Alexandrine, and from an impulse of gratitude that I felt this morning when I thought of the freedom that Providence had granted me. The verse gave rise to the thought, and the thought to the verse. When the two are accomplices, the damage is done all by itself, and the strophes can multiply themselves without intention and without a single erasure."

Most of these improvisations in verse are filled with erasures and corrections. The prose text, on the other hand, is almost wholly free from them and written straight off. The finest parts of the Journal seem to have been written at a single sitting, and some of these extend over several pages. Too self-conscious in the notebooks at the outset, often relaxed and difficult in the last, the writing is at these times singularly firm, rapid, docile to the thought, soberly free from any over-refinement, rather logical than artistic and with a noble intellectual elegance. The mind arranges all, pervades, illumines. It is sovereign contemplation, rendered with the graphic beauty of a condensed power and going straight to the mark.

Thus, in itself, the manuscript speaks to the eye and conveys, by its changing form, the evolution of its inner life. From the position of a clerk, it is promoted to that of private secretary, from that of a witness to that of a confidant, of a counsellor to that of a liberator. The agitations of the soul of Amiel are revealed in the mere appearance of these pages. Often before daybreak, scarcely out of bed, he lights his lamp to write. "It is always when I awake that the thoughts of the previous day come back to me. The night somehow sifts them and disengages them from the insignificant or indifferent facts that contained them." At intervals of a few hours, continually on days that are most troubled, he comes back to it "like a bird in a cage beating the bars". Or, on the other hand, when some great spectacle of nature fills his vision and exalts his mind, he marks the phases of it by notations spaced according to the rhythm of the incidents. This may be some conflict of light and darkness, a storm among the mountain-tops, the symphony of a sunset over the lake and the beloved shores of Clarens. Seven o'clock, eleven o'clock in the morning, noon, three o'clock, five, eight, eleven in the evening: strophes in prose, fragments detached from a scenario, the Journal at these times sings or builds up a work of poetry.

Did Amiel reread later these dramatic tableaux and these inspired monologues? He rarely reopened the note-books he had finished; more rarely still, once or twice only, did he lend some volume or other to friends of whom he felt certain. And each of these experiments he seems to have regretted, except, indeed, the day when, for two hours, he read selected pages from the one hundred and fifty-sixth volume (January–February, 1879) to her whom he called Fida, or Seriosa, the lady to whom, four years later, the manuscript in its entirety was to be disclosed: "I was more than rewarded. My poor little Stoic, who was sadly depressed at the beginning, was quite radiant at the end. She said to me: On this 2nd of April I have been carried away. You could not possibly imagine the good you have done me. I feel as if I were a soul already and were seeing the things of this world as one sees them from the world beyond." (*Journal intime,* April 2, 1879.)

Amiel was quite unable to turn this manuscript to any account, for there was no table of contents, no index to guide him. His countless papers accumulated in his cases, not exactly disdained, for he preserved them all, but collected in bundles, at random, and never touched again. "What would be still better would be a general index to my papers, courses, notes, memoranda, correspondence, *allerley,* and especially a table of contents for my *Journal intime:* for this vast hotch-potch cannot be of use to anybody, even to its proprietor and author. As I am never able to find anything in it, I might as well not possess it. It is of no use to me at all." (*Journal intime,* April 22, 1876.)

## IV

As to the instructions which he left regarding the disposition of his "personal papers", Amiel hesitated for a long time. He drew them up first in 1874, altered them in 1877, and finally rewrote them, three weeks before his death, on April 22, 1881. They concerned essentially the correspondence, the manuscripts of his courses, his unpublished poems and the *Journal intime.* "In the hope that my labours, my experiences and my meditations may not be entirely lost but may be of use to others, whether or not they cause my name to survive, I wish, and this is the desire which I suggest most urgently to my heirs, that means may be found to make a posthumous publication of whatever I may have written that is useful and good." (*Instructions,* July 23, 1877.) He was looking forward at that time to an edition of his works in six volumes, reserving from his funds the sum that was necessary for its publication. Of these volumes the first was to contain a selection from the unpublished manuscripts of the *Méandres,* together with reprints of the collections represented by the *Grains de Mil, Penseroso, La Part du Rêve* and *Jour à Jour;* the fifth, his critical articles and studies; the sixth, his scientific works in literary history and in the history of philosophy. The second, third and fourth volumes, under the title *Pensées d'un Contemplateur,* were to have been reserved for a selection of letters and "reflections and fragments of every kind drawn from the 12,000 pages of the Journal, the first thousand of which furnished the prose portions of the *Grains de Mil*".

Certain friends were designated to "be consulted regarding the substance, form and conduct of the undertaking", among them Marc Monnier, Victor Cherbuliez, Auguste Bouvier, Joseph Hornung and Edmond Scherer.

Without returning to this project of a general edition, the subsequent instructions seem to discharge the testamentary executor of a part of his task. "He is to deliver the collection of unpublished poems to Mlle. Berthe Vadier, whose approval shall be final in regard to whatever is to be published. He is to deliver the collection of the *Journal intime* to Mlle. Fanny Mercier, whose approval shall be final in regard to whatever is to be used in the publication. These two devoted friends, who are likewise my pupils, are to be considered as authoritative in the details and general prosecution of the whole undertaking." (*Instructions*, July 23, 1877.)

More precisely still, the "additional instruction" of April 22, 1881, stipulates, among other matters: "I bequeath to Mlle. Fanny Mercier: first, my correspondence; secondly, my *Journal intime* (nearly 16,900 pages); thirdly, the manuscripts of my lectures, to be set in order first of all; fourthly, the souvenirs of my youth and student days."

Amiel thus pursued to its final consequences the principle upon which he had resolved in 1874: "To my family, all that I have received from them; but to myself, to those, that is, whom I have chosen as my spiritual family, my creation, my thought."

## V

It was through Fanny Mercier, the unassuming Genevan school-mistress, the "dear Calvinist", the "little saint", the "Christian", the "Sensitive-plant", the "Seriosa", the "Fida", the "Stoica" of the *Journal intime,* that this desire of Amiel, his deepest and most sa-

cred, was fulfilled, the desire that the best of his thought should
be safe-guarded and transmitted to others.

Marie-Françoise Mercier (1836–1918), with her sister Pauline,
whom Amiel liked to call Perle or Perline, directed a day-school for
girls. The two sisters, in perfect accord, Pauline's lively grace harmonizing with Fanny's virile and passionate seriousness, lived with
their mother, for whom they cared with tender solicitude to her
ninety-fourth year. Together they made up the "Trèfle", the "Ile d'
azur", the "Passerine", the household in which the author of the
Journal spent so many hours of trustful friendship. "Coming home
last night, and again this morning on awaking, mused on the Passerine. Would not this cordial, honest, intelligent, affectionate atmosphere be salutary for one's daily life? Does it not seem as if
Providence had offered it to me? Simplicity, virtue, reverence for
duty, the love of wholesome and pure delights, what is lacking
there?" (*Journal intime*, July 5, 1875.)

One understands better the meaning of these words, added by
Amiel to his *Instructions* of 1881, directed to Fanny Mercier: "You
have said to me sometimes that you would be my widow. I leave
you the rights of a widow, my correspondence and my Journal."

During the years 1882 and 1883, this admirable woman, broken-
hearted by the death of the master, her confidant and friend, over-
burdened with work, with her strength exhausted, sorted out, night
after night, the riches of the immense confession, grasped its ampli-
tude and depth, responded to the infinite suffering in it, dwelt on its
moral beauty and lived anew, assailed as she was by memories, luminous and sad, tormented with scruples, sometimes consumed with
anguish, all its grandeurs and all its weaknesses. "It is a debt of
loyalty towards a soul that suffered greatly . . . I must confess,—is
it because I am a woman?—the idea of survival through one's
name, through renown, is one that rarely occurs to me—relatively
to myself, never, this goes without saying,—but even when thinking
of others, even in thinking of our friend, it is very little in my mind.
What haunts me all the more is the idea of living again through the

xxvii

spirit. That whatever was best in our dear ones who are gone should not vanish with their presence, that their work should not be lost, that it should be gathered together, that it should be a treasure accessible to all, enriching those who need it in their sorrows,—this is my desire . . . To see that justice is rendered to our friend, and, as he wished, to save for others the legacy of his unhappy life, the harvest of experiences and thoughts that ripened in the very depths of his sufferings and his struggles . . . A posthumous publication is such a difficult thing, and that of a *Journal intime* such a delicate thing! It is, in a way, to surrender a soul, and this may well be a betrayal, if the work is not one of intelligent loyalty. This responsibility for a work in which the right of truth and the right to protection must be reconciled is a very serious one, and it often troubles me; all the more because my personal interest—is this perhaps a feminine instinct?—would have led me only to shelter, to embalm these intimate confidences in quiet seclusion . . . The last sheet, that is, the third of our volume has been printed this afternoon. I suppose this should give me a certain feeling of happiness, but I must confess to the friend of our friend that I have not the strength for this now. My reading and rereading has been too painful, it has stirred up too many questions, opened too many abysses, given birth to too many regrets. My heart has been rent by the recital of our friend's sufferings, too moved by his words, too wounded by his errors and his defeats, too indignant at the spitefulness and hypocrisies of men . . . The last thing which the testamentary executor always said to me was, Make haste. I could not make him understand that to choose one shade of feeling among hundreds of others like it requires a certain amount of study and leisure, and that one cannot extract two hundred and fifty pages out of seven thousand without a certain hesitation, when one is seeking for the true and yet wishes not to miss the beautiful and the good. In short, I have spent my nights in bewilderment in the presence of these seven thousand pages without a single landmark (no table of contents, not a marginal note), stirred by a thousand thoughts, yet wishing only

one thing, to discover the true features under so many fleeting profiles, to fulfil the last wish . . . My only desire is that everything we
are to give about him and in connection with him may be such as
will do good, render the soul loftier, initiate others into a higher,
purer life, in short, a more salutary life." (Letters of Fanny Mercier
to Edmond Scherer, August–September–October, 1882.)

All the nobility of soul of Stoica, the "dear Calvinist", so reserved
in her admissions, so austere in her dignity, so passionate in her
faith and her affections, she revealed thus, unwittingly and in spite
of herself, to "the friend of our friend", that proud, remote man,
the permanent senator, the master-critic, Edmond Scherer, whom
she as yet knew only through a few of Amiel's judgments, but who,
she surmised, would alone be able to comprehend at once the *Journal intime*, to welcome and aid her in her heroic enterprise, her
doubts and qualms, her sacrifices and her immovable resolution.

If it was to Fanny Mercier, his "guardian angel", that Amiel finally decided to entrust the manuscript of his Journal, that she
might know it in its entirety and be the first to choose the portions
to be published, it was because he could rely unreservedly upon her
intelligence and her heart. Over his correspondence and his confessions, he left her the "widow's rights". The last note he wrote to her
was signed, "Your old friend for twenty-four years". "Is she not my
very special friend, she who has taken me for her master and guide,
and whom I call my little saint? . . . If she lacks the creative verve
and overflowing gaiety of heart, she has intelligence, will, especially
conscience, purity, a rare moral sense. She is loyalty itself, courage,
charity, fidelity. She is deeply attached to me. Her discretion and
her delicacy are perfect, her power of devotion has amply proved
itself. Does there exist a more truthful woman, a woman more incapable of evasions? Can self-forgetfulness go further, submission
to the law of life, self-discipline, scrupulousness of every kind?
Does anyone love the good more absolutely or seem more made for
heroism than this humble, unpretentious little Calvinist whose inner
being is a flame, a divine flame?" (*Journal intime*, July 5, 1875.)

"I always marvel as I read in this deep, pure soul." (*Journal intime*, September 14, 1874.) "Error, evil, the ugly, the false, the mediocre grieve and perturb her . . . In her need for perfection, she cannot understand the *laisser aller* of other people; her delicacy cannot adjust itself to indelicacy; her purity is disconcerted by vice, crime, wickedness, and even by images of them. She is an aesthetic ermine, a moral sensitive-plant. *Lauter Gold*. A hidden spring, deep and clear, with which no mire mingles and which reflects only the stars. I am stirred and touched to wonder by this child-like ingenuousness in a strong intelligence and a valiant character. This friend is my conscience. And when I feel her trembling, silently weeping like some poor, simple woman, my heart is wrung for her. Her moral beauty fills me with respect and her sensibility fills me with wonder. There is certainly something rare and even extraordinary about her. Truly, she edifies me, for she gives me back my faith in sainthood. And in this austere being, this stoic soul, this impalpable creature, there is a loving, even a passionate woman, who would gladly resign herself to being only a soul and cannot succeed in doing so. It is piety itself. It is a religious drama." (*Journal intime*, December 8, 1872.)

When Edmond Scherer came to know this exceptional woman, at the very moment when he was discovering, in the pages transcribed from the Journal, the unrecognized genius of his friend, he joined with her in the work of justice which she suggested to him. It was not without some hesitation at first. It was I myself, a young student, who placed in the hands of the author-senator the first fragments copied out for him by Fanny Mercier. A cousin of my father, she had charged me with this mission, together with a letter, and anxiously awaited the reply. This was in the spring of 1882. Edmond Scherer read the letter, but he did not wish to open the big yellow envelope in which Fanny Mercier had gathered together the revealing copies. "Take these papers back, young man," he said to me. "I knew Amiel, and I have read his works. He was never successful in anything. We should let his memory sleep. Do not let us stir up his ashes." But as I insisted without reserve, encouraged by the thought of this kinswoman whom I loved as much as I respected her, and who in my eyes could not be mistaken, he consented to keep the envelope and return it directly. She had chosen these pages, however, so happily, to win and persuade the disillusioned critic that he wrote to her the following day: "Send me as much of the Journal as you can."

Thus began between Fanny Mercier and Edmond Scherer a correspondence, lasting for eight years, which, as a sequel to the correspondence between herself and Amiel, will some day present an example of everything that is rarest and most beautiful in the friendship that may unite a superior woman and a superior man.

Other collaborators indeed assisted in the first edition of the *Fragments*: Marc Monnier, and especially Professor Joseph Hornung, an old friend, a colleague of Amiel's at the University, a man of high culture and devoted heart whom he had designated as one of his testamentary executors. But it was to Scherer at first, and soon to him exclusively that Fanny Mercier went for advice, criticism and support. "I should have liked to ask you about everything, day after day, submitting everything to you . . . My wish was to realize the intentions of our friend, to fulfil his desire, and without you, dear friend, I should not have been able to do so. Without you, the longing, the duty, desire, promise, memory, loyalty and all these cherished and unique relics could never have proved to be stronger than death." (Fanny Mercier to Edmond Scherer, October, 1882.)

By obtaining at last from Scherer that "philosophical and moral study", that "psychological biography", which opens the first volume of the *Fragments* of 1882, the editor of the Journal, always anxious to efface herself and withhold her name from publicity, followed the actual indications of her master and really "fulfilled his desire". She had often encountered Scherer's name in the pages of the manuscript. "He has the scientific and the literary mind, open at once to poetry and to philosophy, acute, searching, analytical. There are great similarities between us and we understand one another at a word, closely related as we are by our studies as well as our cast of mind." (*Journal intime,* October 15, 1850.)

"Edmond Scherer has responded, and his response astonishes me as much as it touches me. Coming from a mind as keen, as critical and severe as his, a judgment on myself like that which he addresses to me is the most unexpected and the most precious testimony that I have ever received." (*Journal intime,* December 27, 1861.)

"If all other traces of my passage are effaced, these six thousand pages will be a testimony of my secret life and will provide the lines for the portrait of an individual. This would doubtless have no value for literature or science, but a psychological biography is not without interest. Some chosen friend (Edmond Scherer . . .) might perhaps make a book of it, perhaps a book of *pensées.*" (*Journal intime,* October 26, 1864.)

Before he decided to write his *Study,* Scherer found it necessary to overcome a good many scruples, the strongest of which had even disposed him at first to decline altogether: "They [the volumes of the Journal committed to him] contain judgments on France and the French which our friend, as I acknowledge, had the right to make, in which I even find an element of truth, but which I could never permit myself to appear to sanction or commend by taking part in the publication of a volume containing them."

The entreaties of Fanny Mercier, the reading of a greater number of extracts from the manuscript finally persuaded Scherer; and he composed the sketch that opens the series of the great articles devoted to the *Journal intime* by Renan, Caro, Bourget, Matthew Arnold, Gaston Frommel, etc. Among those of the men of his generation, the testimony of Amiel's old friend remains the most penetrating and the truest. His pages on optimism and pessimism, on the "intermediary position" of the author of the Journal, sum up perfectly the moral history of a generation that was at first enthusiastic and then gradually disillusioned with the ambitions of positivism. But the truth, or the truths, which the Journal brings to bear on the knowledge of human nature outstrip this experience, while, on the other hand, the essays in racial psychology which it contains remain circumscribed by the political events and the social evolution of a period. Its earliest commentator would no doubt have recognized this later.

Fanny Mercier and Edmond Scherer were, indeed and in truth, the labourers in the vineyard of Amiel's glory.

## VI

The *Fragments* were at first to have appeared under the title, *Caractéristique du Penseur,* which would have answered perfectly to Fanny Mercier's idea of the selection she was arranging. The title was abandoned, but the work of the editor realized her intentions, with all the preferences, in regard to choice and exclusion, of which these consisted. "Omitting whatever is local and private in character," she said in the preface dated October, 1882, "the editors, in choosing their extracts, have striven to reproduce the intellectual and moral physiognomy of their friend, to bring out his lofty thoughts, his spacious views of life, men and things . . . confidences of a contemplative spirit, a philosopher for whom the things of the soul were the sovereign realities." They had thus resolutely distinguished among the diverse, but not disparate, elements which the manuscript presents. In her choice, Fanny Mercier obeyed that instinct of moral perfection which constituted the always unrelaxed spring of her will. The astonishment, the anguish, the terror, the "inexpressible grief" which the reading of certain pages of the Journal had inspired in her vibrant, Puritan soul, these she had accepted for herself. "To have read these things is in a way to have lived them. I come forth matured from this experience." But she was resolved to let nothing of them appear in the extracts she was giving to the public. All the energy of a conscience that suffered from whatever lay outside the sublime and the perfect, all this she applied to the service of the ideal image which she had kept of the master and friend and which she sought to rediscover in his long confessions. This, it appeared to her, was the truth, this was piety, this was duty; the yawning abysses, the errors and defeats, the failures of will, the radical abdication of faith, those experiences of sin seemed to her abolished by death. Therefore let silence enshroud them . . . "She would always like to have a perfect friend, one who is not as I am. She has formed a picture of me in her dreams and cannot be consoled because I do not fit into this ideal." (*Journal intime*, October 5, 1879.)

Ephemeral realities devoid of educative value, sad contradictions of the natural man, enigmas to the uninstructed delicacy of an unmarried woman, heresies even of moral judgment and religious thought, all such confidences she considered vain, harmful or untrue. She felt that it was necessary to establish the momentarily obscured image of the "thinker", in all its purity. Was it not the mission of the *Journal intime* "to render the soul loftier, initiate others into a higher, purer life, in short, a more salutary life"? And what more faithful application of the principles of her author.—"Whatever is mediocre and bad should be allowed to perish. How would it be if everyone's private journal and correspondence were to see the light? Too much is published already; only the excellent and the beneficent has a right to survive." (*Journal intime*, July, 1875.)

In fact, as, during the master's lifetime, Fanny Mercier had constantly desired that he should compose a powerful and well-arranged book, a book of disinterested thought and learning, some fine work in which all his faculties should be combined and exalted, she wished in some way to achieve, after him, indeed through him and for him, this work for which she had hoped in vain. The *Caractéristique du Penseur* would reveal the unknown Amiel, the true Amiel, for whom the things of the soul were the sovereign realities.[1]

[1] "The great maxims of the Gospel still seem the surest pillow, when the wearied soul wishes to rest on something. They give one courage. Woe unto those who corrupt, dishearten and desolate their brothers. The work they do is evil. With this in mind, I should not wish to have doctrines of pessimism published. To sow despair is a thing that weighs upon the conscience, even if one has truth on one's side. Would it not

This explains, even to the details, the method pursued by the first editors of the Journal.

It would be tedious to describe this at length. Those who are curious about it may compare the texts of 1883–4 and 1887 with the present edition.[1] They will soon perceive how an over-purified cult of the true, the good and the beautiful could lead to a literary and moral purism, impairing that truth, in the end, which the editors wished to be surpassingly beautiful and good. Fanny Mercier, sending Scherer the copies of the pages that she had chosen, asked him how he felt "about the publication of these various passages or their elimination, and, in the text, her corrections of style and words here and there, if need be, and whatever suppressions were desirable". Scherer acquiesced, although he protested his respect for a writer "whom one should touch only with fear and trembling". They did not justify or even explain their method of work, feeling answerable, as they did, only to a very dear memory, whose errors they thought they had a right to correct. The image which they had formed of Amiel seemed to them a better likeness than that which he freely displayed in the changing pages of his Journal. Thus their work, relieved of any exact reproduction of the manuscript, was to give it an ideal concentration and unity. The spontaneous, the fa-

---

be a barbarous and reprehensible cruelty to acquaint a child gratuitously with a crime of his father, supposing that oneself alone possessed this terrible secret? No, all truths are not such as one should utter, and those that render life unbearable should be kept secret. Besides, who knows whether they are absolutely true? To kill hope is murder, and even a superstition should be treated with consideration until one has a better faith to oppose to it." (*Journal intime,* January 12, 1872.) Comment of Fanny Mercier: "This is food for thought, is it not, for the editors of the Journal? They would not wish anything that is *evil*." Scherer's reply: "Good heavens, yes: it is true, quite true, but how much one would also have to say in favour of absolute sincerity, and of the right of the truth, the whole truth, in order to express it! In any case, however, it is clear that this passage, in spite of its eloquence, should be withheld."

[1] The earliest text is available to American and English readers in the translation by Mrs. Humphry Ward, Macmillan, 1885.

(Translators' note.)

miliar, the unpolished or the trivial in the unrevised confidences was systematically sacrificed. The thinker was relegated to a state of mind that was purely scientific and contemplative. And while the story and the poetry of this life were certainly impoverished, even the thought itself suffered. Alert readers have indeed surmised that certain parts, certain aspects of the original have been concealed from them. This is doubtless the cause of the invariable incompleteness, the frequent inadequacy and the occasional contradictoriness of the verdicts of even illustrious critics on the *Journal intime*.

The writer of the *Fragments* almost always appears robed in ceremony, when he is not in the priestly attitude of the thinker. In order to detach the daily meditation from the individual occasion, the insignificant fact, the passing experience, its interpreters choose only the general, central part, and they usually suppress, on the one hand, the adventitious opening and, on the other, the final return from the general to the particular, from the "philosophy" to the poetry. In order to give a fragment a composition that is better balanced, more academic in a sense, they sometimes find occasion to combine under a single date parts taken from different days, sometimes even to complete a fragment with borrowings from Amiel's letters written at the same date. Thus, for instance, the impressionism of a series of sensations candidly noted in the Journal gives place to a skilfully composed landscape, the plein-air study to an easel-piece (April 11, 1868).

Elegance condemned terms of local usage. *"Retaconner"*, for instance, is replaced by *"refaire* a dozen hemistiches" (June 4, 1860 [1]); *"rêvassé . . .* until I fell asleep" by *"rêvé,* with my head in my hands" (July 21, 1856).

"This world of wolves and foxes", a somewhat too violent expression, disappears. So also the "Good-night to the bridal bed" of August 8, 1865; the "shabby and monotonous manhood" of April 28, 1852; this phrase of August 1, 1853: "From Catholicism, as from

[1] This passage was omitted in Mrs. Ward's version.

(Translators' note.)

Epicureanism, one can no more return than from a mutilation of one's virility". Bold figures had to be toned down; such frequent expressions of emphasis as *quite, very, much* had to be avoided, together with such vehement epithets as *furious, horrible.* "The absolute doubt of thought" becomes "the doubt of thought"; "detest all the churches" becomes "disapprove of all the churches". When the manuscript says, "the socialist democracy", Scherer adds "and not socialist", no doubt to humour this democracy, which Amiel did not like. "There is honey in the jaws of the lion", "the *que sais-je?* of the dead", "the disappearance of God" are struck out. "To know how to be ready is at bottom to know how to die" (August 15, 1851) is an ingenious arrangement, inasmuch as the manuscript says, "To know how to finish is at bottom the same thing as knowing how to die". Amiel is authorized to say neither "my attic" nor "my carcass". "I am writing in my shirt-sleeves beside my open window", "the vagabond and bohemian", and "a tortoise drawing his paws under his shell", referring to himself, are removed. More classic than Chateaubriand, the editors erase "Does a crocodile lurk, perhaps?" (April 5, 1864). They contrive to suppress and emasculate his loving and passionate nature, when, apropos of his budding inclinations, they bar these expressions: "the roll of the infanticides of my former life", "the fertile embrace" and "an intellectual onanism". At the very least, they take the risk, by omitting the preliminary words in certain cases (August 3, 1856, August 9, 1862, January 29, 1866, August 26, 1868, April 15, 1870, April 28, 1871), of falsifying the tone, the turn, sometimes the meaning of the whole passage. A "so to speak" will be introduced that checks the audacity of a metaphor. "The German is not of the noble breed" seems to the editors preposterous; "Is individual immortality likely?", imprudent; "I have a crab in my bronchial tubes", ignoble . . . These are examples enough, surely, of this industrious and disastrous piety!

## VII

"There is", wrote the inheritor of the *Journal intime,* "a piety towards the dead, a piety that divines intentions and dictates respect for them; there is such a thing as divination, delicacy, absolute loyalty." For him to whom, after her, the manuscript was entrusted, with the mission of publishing new fragments from it, one obligation unites all the others, subordinating them to it, absolute loyalty. Loyalty to the manuscript, loyalty to the reader. This signifies, first of all and above all, to forbid oneself any modification in the text that is reproduced from the manuscript; then, since one is obliged to choose among these thousands of pages, to choose with such freedom that the Journal recovers its natural character, its diversity in monotony, rather than a variety that is contrived to produce an artificial unity; more than this, to choose from among the neglected or forbidden parts of the manuscript, not to change for the worse the familiar figure of its author, but to enrich this; to strive, by this constant and strict exactitude, for a harmony with the model, more changeable, perhaps, but also truer and more living; and finally, not to be unmindful that everything that has been known for forty years about the *Journal intime* should have its place in an edition that is intended to be authentic and, within the limits imposed, definitive.

In order to present a more expressive image of the "thinker", the editors of the *Fragments* inserted various detached maxims and reflections, most of them extracted from the Journal, but grouped arbitrarily at the end of every year. Undated sentences without any order, interrupting the chronological succession of the passages and impeding the natural flow of the confession. Without failing to appreciate the originality, grace, power and beauty of these more or less developed thoughts, I suppress them in the present edition, holding them in reserve for a special collection in which others will be added, in order to form with them a varied and harmonious whole, such as Amiel often dreamed of but did not bring to pass.

As the reader may be aware, the fifth edition of the *Fragments,* which appeared in 1887, differs from the first and has been invariably reprinted since. While a dozen erroneous dates were rectified in it, twenty-one fragments disappeared to be replaced by thirty new fragments.[1] In this second choice, the scruples and predilections of the editors had not changed. When I took up their work, it seemed to me at first that the edition of 1922, since it restored the familiar texts to the letter of the manuscript, should reproduce them all. I have therefore reinstalled the fragments that were suppressed in 1887, notwithstanding their inferior value, beside those that had replaced them. Both indeed are frequently modified, inasmuch as I give them in a more complete form, if not always in their entirety, as they are in the Journal. Readers who are familiar with the *Fragments* and those who enjoy little philological problems will easily distinguish them, if they compare the editions. They may, if they choose, inform themselves in detail, in regard to the procedure of the first editors. For my own part, deeply sensible, as I am, of the gratitude that is due to them, I shall not attempt to bury them under an apparatus of critical notes, in which the reader would find neither pleasure nor profit.

For the second volume alone of the editions previous to my own, that is, for the years 1867–1881 of the Journal, I count seventy-seven fragments that have been renovated in this way. These complete passages are truer because they convey the essential and uniform rhythm of Amiel's thought, which follows the Hegelian progression: thesis, antithesis, synthesis. First, the particular, individual, local fact, or the spontaneous notations of the artist; then the generalization, in which come into play the bold invention, the unexpected comparisons, the power of synthesis, and at the same time the wide culture of the philosopher; finally, the "conclusion", as it often occurs to himself to call it, which is sometimes a return from the thought to the thinker, a lyrical effusion or a melancholy refrain, sometimes a clarified, disinterested reflection, a firm resolution, an idealism that is realizable. Amiel would not unwillingly have defined

[1] Most of these new passages were inserted by Mrs. Ward in the second edition (1888) of her version, while those that had been deleted were largely retained.

(Translators' note.)

these three phases of the intellectual process of so many of the pages of his Journal as history, dreams and free science, philosophy.

Accordingly, I have taken much less pains than my predecessors to avoid repetitions. The immense manuscript abounds with them, repetitions of maxims, images and comparisons, repetitions of ideas and judgments, especially repetitions of confidences of the heart, complaints about his health, his isolation, his weakness of will, his apathy, his deprivations. Only on rare occasions did Amiel reread what he had written, and then it was always capriciously and at random. These repetitions, however, did not escape him. But he saw that they had a useful aspect, as a verification and check. One who wishes to please, he said, avoids them, but one who is concerned only with the truth tolerates them. Art strives to do something new, for fear of satiety; observation notes the real as it presents itself. "Perhaps there are one or several constants in these daily variations of thought and feeling . . . Are there seasonal or yearly variations, variations from period to period?" He leaves the question open. If there is no scientific profit to be drawn from these innumerable jottings, well! they will have helped him to live, like other hygienic habits, like bathing, rubbing oneself down, sleeping, eating, walking. If a Journal is instructive or diverting, well and good; if it serves as a memorandum of one's life, so much the better; if it sharpens the analytical temper and keeps the art of expression in good repair, better still; but its principal function, whatever the repetitions, is to "establish the integrity of the mind and the equilibrium of the conscience, that is, one's inner health."

The new edition of the *Journal intime* offers, in fine, two hundred and sixty-three entirely unpublished fragments. Those who have borne the expenses, considering this proportion already rather large, have obliged me, in order to keep to it, to reduce by a third the choice I had made, preferably from the years 1876–1881, among a great number of pages all of which appeared to me interesting and worthy of publication. These successive eliminations have cost me many anxious and painful hours. I have felt at times the tribulations through which Seriosa passed, hesitating, however, where she decided at once and irrevocably. The psychological and moral truth compelled me to set aside the commands that she imposed on herself, at least with regard to certain brief extracts which Amiel's unfettered sincerity would not have disavowed. The painter of landscapes was already known, the religious and literary critic, the psychologist of nationalities, the architect of the world of the mind; but if the man was to be discerned more clearly in the thinker, it seemed necessary that one should hear a few of his bitter and exasperated disclosures on the family, the city, teaching and the academic life, on the constraints of the unmarried man and his relations with women.

In connection with the *Fragments* of 1883, the malady of the ideal has been discussed. Certain unpublished fragments permit us to diagnose the malady of modesty. This is always a force thwarted in its expansion, one that turns back upon the man of imagination, thought and desires, tormenting, scourging and wearing him cruelly. The earliest manifestations and some of the disorders of puberty had filled the author of the youthful Journal, this young man of eighteen, ardent, pure and true, first with astonishment, then with apprehension, clouding his vision and paralyzing his will. This secret difficulty never knew either long respites or a complete cure. More than fifty years went by before Amiel, examining himself on the subject, uttered the word "repression" and analyzed the symbolism of dreams. In this long lease of suffering, from which he derived only a keener clairvoyance and a more complete renunciation, he remained generous, heroic and proud. And in this struggle, which destroyed all the joy of living, the mind won the final victories.

"How hard it is to live, O my tired heart!" is not the last sigh of the *Journal intime,* as the work of its first editors would give us to believe. Amiel's end, if it did not resemble the *decrescendo,* the diminishing *lamento* of a great organ-piece, was clear, noble and simple. Between the crises of suffocation, he continued to follow

xli

the course of events in the world and to nourish his mind with copious reading. He was keenly sensible of the pressing anxieties of friendship. "Love and be in accord," that is, accept the universal law and give your heart to all who, like yourself, submit to it, this maxim, inscribed on his tombstone, was really the ultimate reason of his life and the lesson of his death. The reader will understand why I have wished to reproduce in its entirety the authentic conclusion of the manuscript. Many years before, when he had just lost a dear friend, far away, Amiel had written: "How I have understood that ardent longing to have the last words, the last glance of those whom one has loved! It seems as if a dying man spoke to us from beyond the grave."

# VIII

"I have never confessed the depths of my grief except to my Journal." This simple avowal of the tortured months of 1868 perhaps brings the interminable confession back to its essential *raison d'être* and its final significance. For all things are a grief to the man who dreams of perfect justice and perfect truth; and the perpetual dialogue, beyond and above the world's agitations, between the conscience, the mind and the heart, is, in the last analysis, the pastime of an exile from the ideal.

The Journal is too close a likeness of Amiel to be defined by any plain or comprehensive formula. It oscillates unceasingly between a striving for the complete, for a cold objectivity and lyrical abandon. It is altogether, and at all times, a book of reason and a book of passion. At the moment when he began to write, Amiel strove no doubt to free himself from a wholly egotistical contemplation, an irksome pietism and asceticism. He dreaded, very early, the fatal spell and the price of introversion. Now as a friend, now as an enemy, the Journal recounted thenceforward a long struggle and a reconciliation, constantly renewed, between the man and the soul of the writer. "I am beginning to weary of this sterile and merely curious study and to wish for profit, progress, action. The function of a mirror is no longer enough for me; I wish to realize . . . The intuition of the good that does not lead to heroic effort is a form of cowardice." (*Journal intime*, October 15, 1850.)

It would be useless to attempt to follow any logical curve in describing the relation between his mind and his written words. There was no logical evolution in Amiel's moral history, nothing but a long effort, interrupted only by brief relapses, towards the certitudes of the absolute. Nothing did more to sustain this constant aspiration than the confession of his profound griefs, for this, day after day, gave him inner light, if not peace; and, in the most critical hours, peace, if not strength; and, when the cycle of the years was fulfilled, the strength at last to die like a sage.

When he reached the last third of his career, and the manuscript already filled ninety-six books, Amiel again put to himself the question: "What purpose does the *Journal intime* serve?" And he replies with a note written on the cover of the ninety-seventh book, with the date May 23, 1869: "1., To disburden one's heart; 2., To become aware of one's life; 3., To clarify one's thought; 4., To interest one's old age, if one reaches old age; 5., Perhaps to interest the friends to whom it will be left; 6., Perhaps to provide with a few useful thoughts various unknown friends who exist among the public."

He has thus ceased to demand that his confidant should school him, correct him. The examination of conscience has lost its critical rigour. He lingers over the curiosities of the inner life, and even the complacencies of biography. It is Montaigne, as he says, substituted for Pascal, psychology substituted for morality. The inevitable egoism of these daily conversations assumes a more general and in some degree a more impersonal character. The Journal has accomplished the negative work from which Amiel long shielded himself. The writer has detached the man from the ambition to create and severed him from social activity. Whether by the asperity of the inward analysis or, on the other hand, by the attraction of solitary

xliii

reflection and a monologue that is unchecked and unending, the habit of the Journal has slowly destroyed the will. "To dissect your heart as you are always doing", he wrote once, "is to kill your life. Eternal and foolhardy chemist of yourself, when will you cease to dissolve your feelings from mere curiosity? You have already succeeded in clipping your wings, drying up all your sap, terrifying your instincts." (*Journal intime,* February 24, 1851.)

Again, when his resistance relaxes, when his courage gives way: "With what lively pleasure do I return to my Journal after a day of separation; it is like seeing a friend again. It is a necessity to me and it rests me. I speak to it and it answers me . . . It is the book of memories, and the hour when I pay it a visit is the hour of self-communion." (*Journal intime,* December 30, 1851.)

All these silent pages, "landmarks of the past, funeral crosses, pyramids of stone, stalks that have grown green again, white pebbles, medals", help the pilgrim to recover the track of his thoughts, his tears and his joys. Or rather they mark his moments of relief from the anxieties of his inner life. To analyze his suffering, to penetrate to its cause, or merely to determine it in words is to dissipate it and to find calm. Pure and impersonal contemplation, indifferent to will and desire, brings the thinker back to the universal law, to duty and God. Little by little, everything in everyday reality that can be disengaged by the consciousness, that can be formulated in the mind and take shape in the imagination will belong to the Journal. "The object to be assigned to it is to have no particular object, but to serve in every way . . . A little caprice does no harm, the unforeseen is not necessarily a fault. Thus conceived, the Journal is the model confidant, dreamed of by the comic and the tragic poets: it knows nothing, it is ready for everything, it listens admirably, and yet it is able to console, to reprimand and counsel." (*Journal intime,* May 10, 1855.)

If the Journal permitted Amiel to withstand a world that seemed to him hostile, the danger was that it might have swept him off, year after year, into those lofty regions of moral isolation where the soul no longer encounters any temptations save pride. But in these regions he never tarried. A natural humility, a tireless curiosity about life, awakening again after every abdication, led him back to the spectacle of things and ideas. "Why should I continue this Journal? Because I am alone. It is my conversation, my society, my companion, my confidant. It is also my consolation, my memory, the bearer of my burdens, my echo, the reservoir of my inner experiences, my psychological itinerary, my protection against the mildew of the mind, my excuse for living, almost the only useful thing that I can leave behind me." (*Journal intime,* September 20, 1864.)

Was this Journal to give a perfectly just idea of its author? To succeed in this, he would have had to study himself as a philosopher and paint himself as an artist, all of which might have troubled his modesty and ultimately turned into a thankless and ridiculous task. In point of fact, the writer, by passing over in silence his good impulses and his best moments, magnifies his offences and his griefs. He sins by omission and paints in black, quite without meaning to do so, but through the unequal distribution of the lights and shadows. It is just as with writers of sermons, satirists and crime-gazettes that convey a false idea of an epoch by dwelling on the evil it contains . . . "I am a little happier, a little less bad, a little less weak than my Journal says and believes." (*Journal intime,* June 16, 1866.)

From this time forward, Amiel's judgments on his work, as it increased by nourishing itself on his intellectual and moral substance, alternated, to the end, between a desolate melancholy and a gently gay quietism, between complaint and gratitude. "This eating oneself away in solitude springs from the suicidal instinct. The *Journal intime* is the cage in which we keep this fox that is devouring our heart, this vulture that is tearing our liver. The corrosive that may have served us in criticizing people and things outside ourselves is thus turned against us. The chemist has allowed the *aqua regia* to run over his hands, and it burns him to the bone."

(*Journal intime,* March 31, 1879.) But from evil itself, and this is the experience attested by the long meditation of the Genevan thinker, something good may spring: "To live is to be healed and renewed every day; it is also to rediscover and reconquer oneself. The Journal . . . restores our equilibrium. It is a kind of conscious sleep, in which, ceasing to act, to will, to strain, we return to the universal order and seek our peace. Thus we escape the finite. Self-communion is like a bath of the soul in contemplation, and the Journal is only self-communion, pen in hand." (*Journal intime,* January 28, 1872.)

The man is disseminated in the work, but he is not dissolved in it, as he seems to believe and fear. He finds himself in it again, on the contrary, only he finds himself transfigured. It is the Journal that gives the key to the thought and conduct of his life which Amiel, in his moments of despair, felt that he had lost. The Journal reveals to him his own secret, unveils to him the mystery of his apparent failures and reaps the magnificent harvest of his long privation. By a phenomenon of disentangling and re-entangling himself, to use his own language, his Journal, the note-books of that immense manuscript, have become his own individuality, the present, palpable and indestructible reality of a multiple and transitory self, capable of all metamorphoses. "These thousands of pages have value only for me and for those, who, after me, can find something of interest in the itinerary of a soul, in an obscure state of life, far from report and renown . . . My Journal is my principal idol, perhaps, the thing to which I am most devoted." (*Journal intime,* December 21, 1860.)

*
* *

It was the Journal that realized Amiel's vocation. Does it tell the worst and the best about his soul? Do those who have analyzed themselves the most know themselves the least? I cannot say. It may be that "the conscience cannot unveil its uttermost depths to anyone but God". But the *Journal intime* certainly represents the activity, sustained for more than thirty years, of a strong and subtle mind that conceived the entire life of the universe as matter for thought, and the gift of a profound heart of which "the most tenacious and perhaps the only passion" was inner liberty. His mind strained towards the absolute, his heart towards the infinite. In the eternal conflict between the real and the ideal, the greatness and the suffering of Amiel were born of the vast expanses and unfathomable depths into which this mind and heart, forever driven back into their prison, still ventured forth. The whole Journal recounts and describes the impulses, the ambitions, the thirsts of a cramped character, a straitened condition of life, an oppressed temperament. No system sufficed to fill the empty places that analysis had hollowed in it and all about it. Therefore, the thinker accepts a religion, a faith and a morality that are very human. Pascal and Montaigne are reconciled in the pages of the Journal. All the dignity of man is to be found in the man who knows himself and faithfully dedicates himself. To him who confesses, in the truth of the inner light, peace and strength are given, and, in addition, the admiration and sympathy of those who are moved by a sincerity so humble and so proud and an art so disdainful of artifice.

In opening the sanctuary of his secret life, Amiel performed an act of heroic resolution. Fastidious and just as he was, he opened himself to malice, stupidity and injustice. He offered a hostage to fate. But the divine light which, at times, bathes these Elysian Fields of the soul envelops him who enters there with piety, with love and gratitude. If to know oneself is sovereign wisdom, if to conquer oneself is the perfection of duty, to confess oneself may be the supreme goodness.

The man who has created a form of thought cannot finally doubt himself. A magnificent recompense was in store for the humble author of the *Journal intime*. Possibly he surmised this when he said, "To unbosom oneself is to expose and surrender oneself. But this courage touches magnanimous hearts."

BERNARD BOUVIER.

Geneva, February, 1922.

# THE PRIVATE JOURNAL OF
# HENRI FRÉDÉRIC AMIEL

# AMIEL'S JOURNAL

*Berlin, December 16, 1847.*[1]—Poor journal! Here you have been waiting for seven months, and only in December am I applying the resolution that I formed in May. Poor me, rather! I am not free, for I lack the strength to carry out my will. I have just read over my notes for this year. I saw it all, foresaw it, I made myself the finest promises, had glimpses of the most enticing vistas, and nothing has come of it all. I have let things go. It is not intelligence that I lack but character. When I appeal to my inner arbiter, it sees clearly and speaks truly enough. I understand myself but I do not make myself obey. At this very moment I feel that, without gaining strength to conquer my faults, I delight in discovering them and the reasons for them. I am not free. Who more than I ought to be so? No outer constraint, the enjoyment of all my time, the power to set myself any goal whatever.—But for weeks, for whole months, I run away from myself; I yield to the whims of the moment, I follow every fancy.

Terrible thought: every man makes his own destiny.

The Indians said that destiny is not a judgment but the consequence of actions performed in another life. One does not have to go back so far. Every life makes its own destiny.—Why are you weak? Because ten thousand times you have yielded. Thus you have become the toy of circumstances; it is you who have made them strong, not they that have made you weak.

I have just marshalled before the eyes of my conscience my whole previous life, childhood, school, family, adolescence, travels,

[1] Extract from the note-book that bears the number 1, with the title, added later, *Beginning of a regular private journal.*

games, inclinations, pains, pleasures, the good and the bad. I have tried to separate the parts played by nature and by free will, to recover in the child and young man the lineaments of my present self. I have considered myself in my relations with things, books, relatives, sisters, comrades, friends. The ills against which I struggle are the same old ills. It is a long story, one that I shall have to write some day.—If antagonism is the condition of progress, I was born to advance.

You are not free, why? Because you are not in harmony with yourself, you are ashamed of yourself, you yield to your curiosity and your desires. What would cost you the most would be to renounce your curiosity.

You were born to be free, you were born to realize your ideas bravely and fully. You know that peace lies in that. Equilibrium, harmony; to know, to love, to will; idea, beauty, love; to live by the will of God, by the eternal life; to be at peace with yourself, with destiny; you know very well, you have often recognized and felt that all this was your duty, your nature, your vocation and your happiness. But aside from the larger question of your general duty, you have not sufficiently determined your special vocation, or rather you have not seriously believed that matters stood where they did; you have turned this way and that. To give up this diversion, to concentrate, in your will, on a conception—that is the most difficult thing for you.

\*

\* \*

To express, to realize, to perfect, to produce: fill your mind with this idea. This is art. Discover the proper form for each thing. Follow your thought to its conclusion, let your word express your thought; finish your phrases, your acts, your readings. Half-thought, half-words, half-knowledge are a sad business. This means to define, to circumscribe, exhaust, or else give up your curiosity. Order, energy, perseverance, I have asked for these before.—Dissipation is the morass of your inner life. You lose sight of yourself and your intentions; nothing interests you more than that which does not really interest you. But to yield to this laziness is to give the tempter all the more strength, it is to sin against your liberty and fetter yourself for the morrow. Physical strength is acquired only through graduated exercises, sustained and energetic. Gradation, energy, continuity are the conditions equally of the intellectual and the moral life.

*

*   *

Whence comes this strange fault of always attacking things in the longest way, preferring the less important to the more important, undertaking what is least urgent—this zeal for the accessory, this dread of the straight line? Whence, among several letters to be read, this pleasure in opening the least interesting; among several visits, preferring the least necessary; among several studies, choosing precisely the furthest from the natural course; among several purchases, the least pressing? Is it only the tendency to eat one's black bread first? A refinement of taste? Is it the desire for completeness, the haste to profit by an occasion that may escape, since one can always count on the necessary? A fine zeal, this! Is it not really avoiding duty, an ingenious ruse for dismissing what is important and what is ordinarily most painful, a trick of the perverse and lazy self? Or is it mere irresolution, want of courage, the postponement of effort to some other time?

The last two explanations, which come to the same thing, seem to me the truth of the matter. "Time gained, everything gained", say the diplomats. The heart, a shrewd diplomat, does likewise. It does not refuse, it merely postpones. Unless it is deliberate, postponement is a defeat of the will. One should only put off till tomorrow what cannot be done today.

Considering all these things, the heart decrees, first, as a guarantee, to keep a journal, a few words every evening; on Sunday, review the week; on the first Sunday of the month, review the month; and at the end of the year, review the year.—Secondly, as a practical conclusion, to plan here what I must do, with the time and means allotted me. This point to be taken up again.

*Berlin, December 31, 1847.*—I need affection. To have the appearance of a friend and not the reality is an offence to my candour. I am always repelled by an absence of seriousness.—I do not yet know how to get on with men, especially with those of my own age. Why? Because you are despotic. You are jealous of your equals. No, it is not that. You grant superiority only to those whom you love. In order not to be jealous, you must love. Yet justice must come before love. To one who would be grateful to you, you would give gladly, but you have nothing to offer the man who asks you for nothing.—You must do justice to others. The way to do this is always to think that everyone is in some point your superior, and to acknowledge his superiority by willingly effacing yourself in yielding him this position. Really interest yourself in others; that is the way to inspire interest in them. No haughtiness, stiffness, pride. Apply yourself to the good in every man, to his superiority and not to his weaknesses. Seek to give pleasure and happiness to others; make people like to be with you; lovableness is a reflection of love.

Be just. That is, respect everyone's individuality; respect his opinions, his lights; listen to him with deference, consider him and do not impose yourself.—Be good. Seek to do good, to enlighten, interest, comfort, help, etc. . . .—Be flexible. Do not ask anyone for what he does not possess. Take everyone as he is: do not ask friendship of him who has only wit, or wit of him whose forte is information. Learn to yield to other people's natures. That is the art of living. Resign yourself, learn to be supple. The pliancy that springs from goodness and not deceit is not a fault but a quality.— Be true. You are rather exclusively that already. You cannot hide your dislikes. But be true in your manners, that is, simple. Be, instead of appearing. Try not to seem either stupider or more scornful than you are. Measure, unaffectedness, propriety are very important qualities; propriety, above all,—but the real propriety which is based on the true relations of things. Propriety in style, language, actions is a constant sense of proportion with regard to places, times, age, sex, circumstances, etc. It is the expression of the true, the feeling for the suitable.

*Berlin, March 15, 1848.*—I must put a stop to this life of exclusive receptiveness, and produce. To make up my mind, to realize, which means to produce and specialize: that is urgent. You will soon be twenty-seven. Your youth, your strength should serve you. If your life is not to evaporate in futility, you must concentrate without delay. You must impose a task on yourself. A task: let this be your daily thought. Work while you have the light. You are responsible for the talent that has been entrusted to you.

Every man has his task. We all labour at the task of our race, to determine the mission of humanity and realize it. The cobbler who soles a shoe serves, through a multitude of connecting links, to magnify the life of God in man. The ascending metamorphosis of life, progressive spiritualization: this is our duty. Help man to become always more divine, in his intellect, in his feeling, in his acts. This is the goal.—Among all the vocations, which is the one that you ought to choose? That in which you can best be yourself? And which you can best fill? The science of unity, philosophy, the philosophy of life.

*Berlin, July 16, 1848.*—But one thing is needful: to possess God. All the variable forms into which this possession is divided ought to be possessed as if one did not possess them. All the senses, all the powers of soul and mind, all external resources, are so many portals opening on the divinity, so many ways of tasting and adoring God. Thence comes their value, infinite but relatively infinite. Nevertheless, one must be able to detach oneself from all that can be lost, to bind oneself absolutely only to the absolute and the eternal, and to enjoy the rest as a loan or usufruct, merging one's time in one's eternity, one's partial loves in one's supreme love, one's human variety in one's divine unity.—To adore, to comprehend, to receive, to feel, to give, to act: that is your law, your duty, your happiness, your heaven. Come what may, even death. Be in accord with yourself, have nothing with which to reproach yourself, live in the presence and the communion of God, and let your existence by guided by those general forces against which you are powerless. —If death allows you time, so much the better, but you must account for your days. If it removes you, better still: your life has been pleasant, and you have been carried off before you have known bitterness. If it half kills you, still better: this closes for you the way of success and opens that of heroism, resignation and moral greatness. Every life has its greatness; and as one cannot be out-side of God, it is best consciously to find one's dwelling in him.

*Berlin, July 20, 1848.*—To judge our epoch from the point of view of universal history, history from the point of view of the geological periods, geology from the point of view of astronomy, liberates the mind. When the duration of a man's life, or of a peo-ple's, seems as microscopic as a gnat's, and, reciprocally, the life of an ephemera as infinite as that of a celestial body, with all its dust of nations, one feels very small and very large, and one surveys from the height of the spheres one's own existence and the little whirlwinds that stir our little Europe.

*Berlin, November 15, 1848.*—Many times you have dreamed, as this journal bears witness, of a fine activity at Geneva. Our life lacks a centre, and our studies also. To inject into it the craving for science, the impulse for poetry and philosophy, to prepare for the religious metamorphosis of the future, to enter into communion with Germany, rouse the Swiss-Latin originality, work towards a centre for the intellectual life, having for its base French Switzer-land and Savoy, after the plan that I have already thought of; to provide a foundation for our theology, for the natural sciences, literary criticism, literary production; to show the genesis and inter-dependence of the sciences.—An encyclopædia; propædeutics.—To divert these incessant political quarrels, and give them more substance by making the study of man more popular—to create a living and active school that would shed lustre on the Genevese name. To find out where our originality lies and develop it (*Letters on Geneva*); for only at this price can we preserve ourselves. One must be strong to have the right to exist; we are disappearing because our principle of life is failing.—The Calvinistic life . . . Beware, there you touch the burning question. If the basic and characteristic element in Genevese nationality is Protestantism, it is only in a revolution of Protestantism, a restoration, that is, or a metamorphosis, that the rejuvenation of Geneva is possible. The question is whether Protestantism is not a school, lasting three centuries, in the history of Geneva, and whether a Geneva is not possible before and after this brilliant period. Protestantism has been a virile graft which has borne all our fruits; but its influence is no longer exclusive and is even in its decline. The Protestant State is conclusively at an end, since Geneva is a mixed population.—The new Geneva cannot be the old any longer. What will its religion be? Its principle?—Let us not indulge in day-dreams! It is always on the frontiers of religions that one meets with intolerance; the necessity for self-preservation makes the attitude more polemical. To hope for a reconciliation in Geneva between Catholicism and Protestantism would be to delude oneself.—But the Protestant wing is itself in a state of schism. There are the immovable, the indifferent, the lukewarm, the national Church and the dissenters, the Freethinkers and the orthodox. To transform our Protestantism, which is no longer in harmony with our life and our science, that is the point. Only through education, and through its axis, philosophy and theology, can this result come about.

But watch your plan, study your forces, and do not cut down all the trees of the forest at once.

Light, therefore, the sacred flame in the hearts of young men. Gather their talents about a standard. Exert an influence over preaching and journalism—through teaching, over the young; through the talented, over literature and life; form alliances with Lausanne and Neuchâtel. Create in this way a public and a public opinion.

Encourage, at the same time, a learning that is independent and superior to specialization, and its realization in original forms; see that the national aim lies in the human aim, the political in the national. Preserve in each particular effort the feeling for the whole.[1]

*Geneva, March 3, 1849.*—Are you not wasting your life? Are not indolence, timidity, distraction destroying your future? You disregard God's gift which is within you. You do not dare to see what you should be and be it. You confuse intention with strength, that is, your own will with the will of God.—You must at all costs acquire a superiority; this means a specialty. In what field have you more talent than anyone else? Where do you find satisfaction, intellectual peace? In the serene majesty of great thoughts and wide horizons; in the philosophy of history and the religions. For long periods, in lower regions, I forget myself, and it is only on the high mountain of contemplation that I feel what I am. Pontiff of the infinite life, Brahman adoring the ways of destiny, the calm flood reflecting and condensing the rays of the universe; in a word, contemplation, that is what draws me.—"To be master of myself as of the universe", to be the consciousness of the whole and of myself, and to symbolize it in words for others in some imposing and solitary work. In trying too hard to do justice to the particular, the finite, the contingent, you lose yourself, and fall back from the eternal heights.

*April 20, 1849.*[2]—It is six years today since I last left Geneva.[3] How many journeys, what impressions, observations, thoughts, how many forms, things and men have since then passed before me

[1] Here Amiel sums up in advance the ideas which he developed, in the following year, in his candidate's thesis for the chair of aesthetics, to which he was appointed, at the Academy of Geneva: *Du mouvement littéraire de la Suisse romane.* Geneva, 1849.

[2] When no other place is indicated, it is understood that the author is writing at Geneva.

[3] Between April, 1843, and December, 1848, the author had taken a journey in France, followed by a stay of five years in Germany.

and in me! These last seven years [1] have been the most important of my life: they have been the novitiate of my intelligence, the initiation of my being into being.

Dense flurries of snow three times this afternoon. Poor flowering peach and plum-trees! What a difference from six years ago, when the gay cherry-trees, decked in their green spring mantles, laden with their festive bouquets of flowers, smiled for my departure through the whole Vaudois countryside, and the lilacs of Burgundy wafted their gusts of perfume over my coach-box!

*May 3, 1849.*—My poor friend, you are downcast. Why? Because you cannot quite see how to live and are not yet resigned to impotence and death. You must look this future in the face and accept it. Your weak chest will undoubtedly force you to renounce the career of a professor, for you are still exhausted from a single lecture you gave yesterday; but how to make a living if speaking fails you?—a life cut short, probably no marriage, for want of health and money, a career impossible, no outer activity. In short, you are a condemned and useless being if you do not win health for yourself.

You have never felt the inner assurance of genius, the presentiment of glory or happiness. You have never seen yourself as great or illustrious, or even as a husband, a father, an influential citizen. This indifference to the future, this utter lack of confidence are no doubt significant. What you dream is vague, indefinite, ethereal; you are not meant to live, for you are now scarcely capable of it.— Take hold of yourself; let the living live; expect nothing more from your damaged carcass, but formulate your ideas, let your thought and heart give testimony: in that way you will be most useful.— Renounce yourself and accept your cup with its honey and its gall, no matter which. Bring God down to yourself, bathe yourself in his fragrance in advance, let your breast be the temple of the Holy Ghost; do good works, make others happy and better.—Have no

---

[1] The stay in Germany had been preceded by a year spent in Italy (1841–1842).

more personal ambition; then come what may, you will be consoled for living and for dying.

*May 27, 1849.*—To be rejected even by those one loves is the real cross; it is this that sets that sad and melancholy smile on the lips of superior men; it is the keenest bitterness felt by men who devote themselves; it is this that must oftenest have wrung the heart of the Son of Man; it is the cup of suffering and resignation. If God could suffer, this is the grief that we should cause him, indeed every day. He also, he, in fact, above all, is the great rejected, the sovereignly misunderstood. Alas! alas!—Not to tire, not to grow cold; to be happy with what exists, and not concern oneself with what is lacking; to be indulgent, patient, sympathetic, kind; to watch for the blossoming flower and the opening heart; always to hope, like God; always to love—that is duty.

*June 3, 1849.*—Delicious weather, fresh and clear. A long morning walk. Surprised the hawthorne and wild rose in blossom. Vague and wholesome odours from the fields. The Voirons hedged with a border of dazzling mist, the Salève robed in lovely velvety tints. Work in the fields. Two charming donkeys, one greedily browsing on a barberry hedge. Three young children: I had a boundless desire to take them in my arms. To enjoy leisure, the peace of the countryside, fine weather, a carefree mind; to have my two sisters with me; to rest my eyes on fragrant meadows and full-blown orchards; to be so sweetly happy—is this not too much? Do I deserve it? Oh! let us enjoy without questioning the kindness of heaven; let us enjoy it gratefully. The evil days come quickly and plentifully enough. I have no expectation of happiness. Let us profit the more from the present. Come, good Nature, smile and delight me. Veil from me for awhile my griefs and those of others; let me see only the draperies of your queenly mantle, and hide the troublous things under your splendour.

*October 1, 1849.*—Yesterday, Sunday, read over and made extracts from the whole Gospel of St. John. It confirmed me in my belief that Jesus was not a Trinitarian, that one needs only to believe in him and discover the true image of the founder behind all the prismatic refractions through which it reaches us, and which more or less alter it. A luminous and heavenly beam of light fallen upon the world of men, the word of Christ has been broken into iridescent colours and deflected in a thousand directions. The historic task of Christianity is, from age to age, to rid itself of shell after shell, to undergo new metamorphoses, ever more and more to spiritualize its understanding of Christ, its understanding of salvation.

I am astounded at the incredible amount of Judaism and formalism that still exists, nineteen centuries after the Redeemer's proclamation that it was the letter which killed and that symbolism was dead.—The new religion is so profound that it is not understood even now, and so bold that even now it would seem blasphemous to the majority of Christians.—The person of Christ is the centre of that revelation; revelation, redemption, eternal life, godhead, humanity, propitiation, incarnation, judgment, Satan, heaven, hell, all this is materialized and coarsened, and presents that strange irony, a deep meaning carnally interpreted, a kind of counterfeit money, in an inverse sense, which is worth more than its face value. The Christian hardihood and freedom must be reconquered; it is the Church that is heretical, the Church whose sight is obscured and whose heart is timid. Whether one likes it or not, there is an esoteric doctrine, not a yoke but a living force.—There is a relative revelation: everyone enters into God as much as God enters into him, and, as Angelus,[1] I think, says, the eye with which I see God is the same eye with which he sees me.

Christianity, if it means to triumph over pantheism, must absorb it; for our faint hearts of today, Jesus would seem tainted with an odious pantheism, for he confirmed the word of the Bible, *Ye are*

[1] Johann Scheffler, called *Angelus Silesius,* 1624–1677, born and died at Breslau, author of mystical religious poetry, very well known in Germany.

*gods;* and St. Paul likewise, who tells us that we are the *race of God.*

Our age needs a new doctrine, that is, a deeper explanation of the nature of Christ and the light that it flashes on heaven and mankind.

*December 14, 1849 (8 a. m.).*—Virile virginity, you deserved a temple for your rarity; and if the ancients forgot you, they made a mistake. At twenty-eight years of age, not yet, as Pythagoras says, to have betrayed one's strength to any woman, or, as Goerres says, not to have tasted, or, as Moses says, not to have known, or, as the French novelists say, not yet to have possessed, is a phenomenon, or rather a curiosity, of which none of my acquaintance of my own age can offer a second example. Is it a good thing? Is it a misfortune? Is it a stupidity? Is it a virtue? I have often debated this question. To have slept in all the beds of Europe from Upsala to Malta, from Saint-Malo to Vienna, in châlets and hotels, among the shepherdesses of Brittany and a step from the girls of Naples, and to know sexual pleasure only in imagination; to have had the most precocious temperament and read the most provocative books; to have had even the most seductive chances, and all this before twenty; curious even about crime, and, with greater reason, curious about love, inflammable, always blundering, by what miracle did I bring home the innocence of my childhood? There are many reasons, some to my credit, though I give the credit to my good angel, to my better self.—*Puber, liber; liber, miser,* that is the gist of two letters which I wrote once, while travelling, to B. . . .—What has restrained me? Regard for others: I have always had a horror of doing wrong, of leading others into evil; the idea of corrupting was unbearable to me, and the girl or woman whom I should not have injured would for that very reason have been unworthy of me. This dilemma I have never been able morally to resolve.—Sincerity: as I have had to give advice to two young sisters, I have remained pure in order not to be a hypocrite, for I abhor hypocrisy. Incapable of the effrontery of vice, or of concealing it, I have never been able to yield to it.—Imagination: by magnifying a hundred-fold both the pleasure and the remorse, this has always restrained me through terror even while tempting me through allurement.—A fourth guardian has been my fabulous and even stupid timidity. I have never been able to utter an immodest word to a woman, and even now it is an effort for me not to blush when others utter these words. I have blushed more often for others, on account of others, than on my own account. The witness was embarrassed for the guilty. I still regret this stupid timidity; I regret more a few kisses that I might have taken, indeed should have taken, at Stockholm, Cherbourg and other places, than various acts that were reprehensible. These recollections of a chaste pleasure are dear to me; they have more fragrance for me than complete possession probably has for a libertine.—Another powerful guardian has been my self-distrust. I always felt that the spark might become a fire, that it was easier to repress the madness of passion than to restrain it once it was let loose. I was afraid of myself, and I never dared let myself go. I remember having refused G——, who was leading me on, whom I was holding in my arms, both of us nearly beside ourselves. I feared the tiger of passion: I did not dare to unmuzzle the ferocious beast, to give way to myself. I am almost sorry I did not, especially as I have learned since that my scruples on her behalf did her too much honour and showed an excess of delicacy. I repressed rather than destroyed the temptation. It was a folly, perhaps: one is not completely a man as long as one is ignorant of woman. I have preferred ignorance to remorse; and this for me has been a sacrifice which others, less consumed with the desire for knowing, could scarcely understand.—On the other hand, I had sworn to myself to be as heroic as the pure woman who only surrenders her flower of chastity, her virgin's crown, to him who in return gives her the marriage wreath. I had sworn to myself to give to her who should win my heart an offering that was exquisite and rare, the virginity of my senses, with the first-fruits of my soul, a great, complete, flawless and stainless love, so that, without shame,

I could accept an equal gift, uncover my whole life before her eyes
and let her plumb my depths without finding anything base in my
recollections, any rivalry even in my dreams. If this is folly, God,
I thank thee for it. The ideal is also a dream, but a dream that
prevails over all the poverty of the real. For a son of Eve, to renounce the apple of knowledge is to be better than one's mother;
but it is not I who deserve the credit, it is my good angel, my instinct, God within me. I have wished to bite the apple, and it was
he who paralysed my lips; I have wished to sin and I have sinned,
and it was he who preserved me. Therefore I cannot be proud;
only touched, full of thanks and humble.

*Sunday, April 7, 1850.*—Much disturbed with dreams last night,
I have a somewhat muddled head, and I rose late. After breakfast,
carefully explored all our spring shoots, from the parsley to the
rose-bushes, from the lilacs to the peach-trees: trellises, slips, grass,
clumps, buds—nothing was forgotten. The air is as mild as possible,
softly humid, breathing of vegetation, soothing, fertile.

I find that the diurnal consciousness is different from the nocturnal, as Kerner and the mesmerists say. In the nocturnal mood, I
am more collected, less distracted, more serious; in the former,
the prejudices, allurements and illusions that come from without
resume their sway. It is the opposition between the inner and the
outer worlds, between concentration and projection, between the
religious and the mundane man, the essential man and the changing
man; thus we see alternately *sub specie aeterni et temporis,* to
speak with Spinoza. The nocturnal consciousness brings us into the
presence of God and ourselves, in a word, unity: the diurnal consciousness places us again in rapport with others, with the outside
world, in a word, diversity.

Consequently a project must be examined by these two lights;
life must appear before this double tribunal. Consciousness has its
rotation as the planet has, its dark side where appear the stars,
the thought of the infinite and contemplation, its luminous side
where everything shines, where colours and objects, intercrossing,

dazzle and stupefy us.—The complete life has these two aspects: the human soul turns in God like the planet in the heavens, and the succession of the infinite and the finite, of totality and detail, of contemplation and action, night and day are its ascending initiation.—Neither one tendency nor the other is to be blamed or regretted; they must be harmonized, for they are both in the divine path, and both, in so far as they aid each other, are good.

This explains why the ideas that pursued me on awaking appear to me now, some hours later, in a totally different light. I am already immersed in the diurnal dispersion.—These ideas concerned marriage. And this is how it seemed to me then: everything that is indissoluble must be contracted only in fullest consciousness, *sub specie aeterni.*—Everything that is transitory, therefore, considerations of beauty, pride, vanity, wealth, external advantage, must be recognized, examined, repulsed as a directing motive: remorse would follow sooner or later.—To deceive or to be deceived, to yield to a temptation leads to cruel results. Happiness is necessarily reciprocal and is found only in being given.

A marriage that would make you forget your vocation and your duties, that would prevent you from constantly looking within, that would not improve you, in short, is a bad marriage.

The marriage that seems to you like a chain, like slavery, like suffocation, is worthless.—Slavery disappears only if there is love, and love is true only if it is central and can see itself as eternal; only that is eternal which can forever grow, develop, increase.— The marriage that cannot be an infinite aspiration, upborne on double wing, the temporal marriage, would offer you no happiness; it would not be worth your independence, it would bring you constant anxiety, regret, reproach, endless suffering.—The true marriage should be really a pilgrimage, a purgatory, in the exalted sense of the Catholic dogma. It should be a path to the true human life; the religious point of view is the only one worthy of it. Therefore, as long as you do not feel that marriage is a need of your manly vocation, or until some definite union offers you a contrary perspective—abstain. One thing only is needful, to be what we ought to be, to accomplish our mission and our work.

In my instability and my desire to understand all points of view, I pass through a thousand temptations and let myself drift. So I return, after many detours, to the point I have reached so many times before.—I have a double good fortune: the leisure that permits me to collect my thoughts, and this private journal, which enlightens me at will, and which I can consult as a sibyl, for we have in ourselves an oracle that is always waiting, conscience, which is nothing else than God in us.

*September 9, 1850.*—My strength lies especially in criticism: I wish to be aware of everything, to understand everything. My salient trait is elasticity, aptitude for learning, receptiveness, the power to assimilate and penetrate. My proper state, as I have found again today, is to feel the universe living in me, to feel a personal progress in all the progress of science and the arts, to feel that every talent and every genius, that every man is my deputy, my organ and my function, to live in the universal life and, in consequence, forget myself. I am objective and not subjective, I am more contemplative than ambitious; for me understanding is the end, and to produce is only a way of understanding better. Consciousness is more marked in me than will. My proper title is thinker. Encyclopædic curiosity, *homo sum, nihil humani,* etc.—A psychologist, studying the metamorphoses of mind, before and in humanity. My limited being I multiply by the infinitude of equivalent forms, rising or descending.

And yet I have my doubts. This Proteanism, so dear to me, which seems to me a privilege, is yet itself a captivity, for I have become a critic although I have had an aptitude for production. Long habit has thus imposed on me a form, on me, so multiform or rather form-evasive. I am the prisoner of the critical tendency, the analytical, the reproductive. It is a limiting, a petrifaction, a privation, a diminution of myself. Should I not seek to free myself from it? Yes, from the point of view of my harmonious growth, my individual culture; perhaps no, from the point of view of strength, a career, success, for one achieves something only by limiting oneself, one acquires authority only by taking a form, one carries an activity far only by becoming a specialist. Is it not best to throw one's intellectual weight on the side of one's inclination?

*October 23, 1850.*—This evening glanced over the complete works of Montesquieu. I cannot yet properly render the impression made on me by this singular style, coquettishly grave, concise in its fluency, refined in its strength, malicious in its coldness, detached while yet so curious, abrupt, irregular, like so many notes thrown off at random, and yet deliberate. I seemed to see a severe, impassive intelligence clothing itself in sprightliness, wishing to pique as well as to instruct. The thinker is also a wit, the jurisconsult savours of the coxcomb; and a whiff of the perfumes of Cnidos has penetrated the sanctuary of Minos. It is a beautiful, serious book, as far as it could be in the eighteenth century.—The artificiality, if there is any, resides not in the words but in the matter. The style runs on without constraint or ceremony, but the thought is self-conscious.

*December 30, 1850.*—The relation of thought to action greatly preoccupied me, as I awoke, long before I got up, and this odd formula, half nocturnal, caught my fancy: action is only condensed thought, thought that has become concrete, obscure, unconscious. It struck me that our slightest actions, eating, walking, sleeping, are the condensation of a multitude of truths and thoughts, and that the wealth of buried ideas is in direct proportion to the commonness of the action (as dreams are the more active the deeper we sleep). We are besieged by mystery, and what we see and do every day conceals the greatest number of mysteries. Through spontaneity we reproduce analogically the work of creation: when we are unconscious, it is simple action, when we are conscious, it is intelligent and moral action. At bottom this is Hegel's observation,[1] but it had never seemed to me more evident, more palpable. All that is, is thought.

[1] *Alles Wirkliche ist vernünftig und alles Vernünftige wirklich.*

but not conscious and individual thought. Human understanding is only the consciousness of being.—This is what I once formulated as follows: Everything is a symbol of a symbol, and a symbol of what? Mind.

*February 17, 1851.*—For six or seven hours without stopping I have been reading the *Pensées* of Joubert. I felt at first the liveliest attraction, the strongest interest, but it has already largely cooled. This desultory, fragmentary thought, falling relentlessly like drops of light, fatigues me, not my head, but my reason. Joubert's merits are grace of style, the vivacity and delicacy of his perceptions, the charm of the metaphors. But his faults are: 1., The philosophy is only literary and popular.—2., The originality is only in the detail and the turns of thought. He poses many more problems than he solves, notes and asserts more than he explains. In short, he is a thinker rather than a philosopher, a critic remarkably organized, with an exquisite feeling for sensation, but an intelligence without the capacity for coördination, a writer without flow, choked, only emitting, through fissures, so to speak, little jets of marvellous transparency and brilliance, but without force or range, like jets of liquid glass. He lacks concentration and continuity; he is a philosopher and an artist who is imperfect rather than abortive, for he thinks and writes marvellously in miniature; he is an entomologist, a lapidary, a jeweller, a coiner of maxims, adages, flashes, aphorisms, counsels, questions, and his collection (extracted from the notes in his journal, accumulated during fifty years of his life) is a collection of insects, butterflies, brilliants, medals and carved stones. The whole is nevertheless more ingenious than strong, more poetic than profound, and leaves the reader rather the impression of a great wealth of precious little curios than of a great intellectual existence and a new point of view.—Joubert's place therefore seems to me below and very far from that of the true philosophers and poets, though honourably among the moralists and the critics. He is one of those men who are greatly superior to their works, who have in their persons what their works lack, unity.—This first judgment is however, incomplete and severe. I shall have to modify it later.

*February 20, 1851.*—I have almost finished these two volumes of *Pensées,* at any rate read about twenty of the thirty-one chapters, and the greater part of the Correspondence. This latter especially charmed me; it is remarkable for grace, delicacy, atticism and precision. One sees that the author loved and followed Mme. de Sévigné. The chapters of metaphysics and philosophy are the least significant. Whatever concerns the whole, large views, are scarcely in Joubert's province; he has no philosophy of history, no speculative intuition. He is the thinker of details, and his domain is psychology and matters of taste. In this sphere of the niceties and delicacies of imagination and feeling, in the circle of private affections and preoccupations, education, social relations, he abounds in ingenious sagacity, witty observations and exquisite touches. He is a bee going from flower to flower, a zephyr that amuses itself by snatching and pilfering here and there, an Æolian harp, a furtive beam trembling through the foliage. There is something impalpable in this writer, something immaterial, disembodied, which I should not venture to call effeminate, but which is not virile. He lacks bones and body; he flutters about, timid, clairvoyant, dreaming, far from reality. He is a spirit, a breath, rather than a man. He has a woman's mind in the character of a child, so that he inspires less admiration than tenderness and gratitude.

*February 27, 1851.*—Reread the first book of *Émile.* I was shocked beyond all expectation, for I opened the book with a lively craving for style and beauty. I had an impression of heaviness, hardness, a strained and painful magniloquence, something violent, hot-headed and stubborn, devoid of serenity, nobility, grandeur. I found, in the qualities as in the defects, a want of good tone; the flame of talent, without grace, distinction or the note of good breeding. I understood for the first time the repugnance that Rousseau inspires, the repugnance of good taste. I recognized how dangerous this model is for style, just as this sophisticated and adulterated truth is dangerous for thought. The true and the strong in Rousseau did not escape me, and I admired him still, but his mischievous aspects struck me with a force that was relatively new.

*(Same day.)*—The pensée-writer is to the philosopher what the dilettante is to the artist.—He plays with thought and makes it produce a great many pretty details, but he is more concerned about truths than the truth, and the essential in thought, its consistency, its unity, escapes him. He handles his instrument agreeably, but he is not the master of it, and still less does he create it. He is a horticulturist and not a geologist; he works the earth only as much as is necessary to make it bear flowers and fruits, he does not dig it deep enough to know it. In a word, the pensée-writer is a superficial, fragmentary, curious philosopher; he is the literary philosopher, the oratorical, talking and writing philosopher; the philosopher is the scientific pensée-writer. The pensée-writers serve to arouse the philosophers and to popularize them. They have thus a double usefulness, aside from their charm. They are the scouts of the army of readers, the mobilizers, the doctors of the mob, the changers of thought, which they mint into current coin, the lay-priests of knowledge who go from the clergy to the laity, the interpreters of the Church to the flock and of the flock to the Church. The pensée-writer is a serious man of letters; that is why he is popular. The philosopher is a particular kind of savant (through the form of his science, not through its basis), that is why he cannot be popular.—In France, for one philosopher (Descartes) there are thirty pensée-writers; in Germany, for ten pensée-writers there are twenty philosophers.

*March 12, 1851 (3 p. m.).*—Why do I feel like weeping? Or drowsing? Languor of springtime, need of affection. I have come back from a sweet afternoon's walk through this warm sun, which penetrates to the marrow. Everything in us seems empty, vain, poor, when nature speaks of love. Books repel us, action makes us smile disdainfully. Music, poetry, prayer alone are tender enough to correspond with our secret longing. They are the only nest of down in which the bruised and sensitive soul can rest without being bruised. Science is too hard, diversion too unfeeling, thought too hasty.

Happy they who know how to sing; they lull their suffering to sleep, they collect their tears in a crystal prism. My walking companion has gone to his piano, I have opened my journal. He will be consoled sooner than I.

Is it our ordinary life that is false, or its impressions that deceive us? Neither the one nor the other.

Spring is good, as winter is. The soul must be tempered and hardened, as it must also open and relax. Respect every new need that appears in your heart; it is a revelation, the voice of nature, rousing you to a new sphere of existence; it is the larva, trembling in the presentiment of the butterfly. Do not suppress your sighs or stifle your tears, for they promise some great thing that you do not suspect, a treasure forgotten, a faculty that is drowning and calls for help. Pain is good, for it brings knowledge of the good; dreaming is salutary, for it presages a more beautiful reality; aspiration is divine, for it prophesies the infinite, and the infinite is Maya, the smiling or the sombre form of God.

The greatness of a being is proportional to his needs. Tell me what you desire, and I will tell you what you are. And yet, you will say, there is something greater than aspiration, which is resignation. True, but not the passive, sad resignation, which is enervating, but the serene, determined resignation, which is a strength. The one is a privation, for it is nothing but regret; the other is a possession, for it is hope. And if you look you will see that this resignation is only a higher aspiration. Thus the law holds.

*March 26, 1851.*—How many of the illustrious men whom I have known have already been reaped by death: Steffens, Marheineke, Dieffenbach, Neander, Mendelssohn, Thorwaldsen, Œhlenschlaeger, Geijer, Tegner, Œrsted, Stuhr, Lachmann,[1] and, among ourselves,

[1] Steffens, disciple of Schelling; Marheineke, theologian of the school of Hegel; Neander, celebrated professor of exegesis and ecclesiastical history, at Berlin; Geijer, historian, and Tegner, poet, were both Swedes. Œrsted, the physicist, published a volume entitled *Spirit in Nature*. Stuhr is the author of a history of religions, and Lachmann is the illustrious philologist, Germanist and editor of the *Niebelungen*.

Sismondi, Tœpffer, de Candolle, savants, artists, poets, musicians, historians. The old generation is passing. What will the new one give us? What will we give? A few great old men, Schelling, Humboldt, Schlosser, still link us with a glorious past. Who is preparing himself to bear what is to come? Who among the dwarfs of the present are to be the giants of the future, the heroes of the second half of the century? A chill seizes us when the ranks grow thin, when we feel our own age pressing, when we approach our zenith and fate says to us: Show what is in you, this is the moment, the time, or else fall back into nothingness, be accursed, forgotten, despised. You have the floor! Take your turn! Give your measure, say your word, reveal your nullity or your capacity. Emerge from the shadow. It is not a question of promise and hope any longer but of fulfilment and reality. The time for apprenticeship has passed, the sowing-time, the time of germination; let us see your harvest. Servant, bring forth your talent and show us what you have done with it. Speak now; or forever hold your peace.—This is a solemn summons in the life of every man, this call of the conscience, solemn and fearful as the Last Trump, asking, "Are you ready? Give your account. Render account of your years, your times of leisure, your powers, your studies, your gifts and your works! Are you prepared for your mission? Or have you frittered away your hours, lived from hand to mouth, a faint-hearted epicure, without greatness, without foresight, without devotion?—This is the hour of the great of heart, withdraw,—the hour of the heroes and the geniuses, return to the dust, away."

*April 2, 1851.*—What a lovely walk! Clear sky, rising sun, all the tints vivid, all the contours distinct, save the softly misty and infinite lake. A sheen of hoar-frost powdered the meadows, gave the green box-hedges a charming vivacity and all the countryside a tone of vigorous health, youth and freshness.—"Bathe, O disciple, your earthly breast in the flush of dawn!" Faust tells us, and he is right. Every dawn signs a new contract with existence; the morning air breathes a new and joyous energy into the veins and marrow; every day is a microscopic repetition of life. All is fresh, flowing, light in the morning as in childhood. Like the atmosphere, spiritual truth is more transparent. Like the young leaves, the organs absorb the light more eagerly, breathe in more ether and less of the terrestrial elements.

To the contemplative soul, the night and the starry sky speak of God, eternity, infinity. Dawn is the time for projects, for the will, for budding actions. The sap of nature is diffused in the soul and urges it to live, as silence and the "morne sérénité de la voûte azurée" incline it to collect itself.—Spring is here. Primroses and violets have celebrated its arrival. The peach-trees are opening their imprudent corollas; the swelling buds of the pear-trees and the lilacs announce the burst of bloom that is to come; the honeysuckle is already green. Sing, poets, for nature is singing already her song of resurrection. Through all the leaves she is murmuring a hymn of gladness, and the birds must not be the only ones to raise a clearer voice.

*April 6, 1851.*—In what respect am I not vulnerable? If I were a father, what a host of vexations a child could cause me! As a husband, I should find a thousand ways of suffering, for my happiness requires a thousand conditions. My heart has too thin an epidermis; I have an uneasy imagination, I yield too readily to despair, my feelings have prolonged reverberations.—What might be spoils for me what is; what ought to be consumes me with sorrow. So, too, reality, the present, the irreparable, necessity repel or even frighten me. I have too much imagination, too much consciousness and penetration, and not enough character. The speculative life alone has enough elasticity, immensity, reparability; the practical life repels me.

And yet it attracts me; I need it. Family life especially, in its delightful elements, its moral depth, solicits me almost as a duty. The ideal of it even persecutes me at times. A companion of my life, my labours, my thoughts, my hopes; a cult of the family, the good it does to others, the education of others it leads one to undertake, etc., etc., the thousand and one moral relations that unfold around the first: all these images often intoxicate me. But I put them aside, because every hope is an egg out of which may come a serpent instead of a dove, because every joy that miscarries is a knife-blow, because every seed entrusted to destiny contains an ear of sorrows, which the future may raise from it.

I distrust myself and happiness because I know myself. The ideal poisons for me all imperfect possession. Everything that compromises the future, destroys my inner liberty, subjects me to things, or obliges me to be something else than what I should wish and ought to be, everything that attacks my idea of the complete man, wounds me to the heart, contracts me, wrings me, even mentally, even in advance. I abhor useless regrets and repentances.—The fatality of consequences involved by every one of our acts, that chief idea of the drama, that sombre, tragic element of life, arrests me more surely than the arm of the Commander. I act only reluctantly, and almost only by force.

To be dependent is for me an insupportable thought; but to be dependent on the irreparable, the arbitrary, the unforeseen and especially dependent through my own fault, to be dependent on an error, I mean, to alienate my liberty, my hope, to kill sleep and happiness, that would be hell!

All that is necessary and providential, that cannot be imputed to someone else, I could endure, I think, with strength of mind. But responsibility mortally envenoms grief. And an act is essentially voluntary. So I act as little as possible.

The final plunge of self-will, rearing its head, though in dissimulation, the search for repose, satisfaction, independence! Is there not some residue of egoism in this disinterestedness? In this fear? In this idle susceptibility?

You would like to fulfil your duty, but where is it? What is it? Here inclination comes again and interprets the oracle. The final question is this: Is it one's duty to obey one's nature, even the best and the most spiritual, or to overcome it? Goethe and Schiller, the

human point of view and the religious, realizing oneself and abandoning oneself, having for a centre one's *idea* or, on the other hand,
God, are equivalents of the same debate. To avoid unhappiness as a
shackle, or to seek it as a purification.

Is life essentially the education of the mind and intelligence or
that of the will? And does the will consist in force or in resignation?—If the object of life is to bring us to renunciation, then
welcome sorrows, fetters, sufferings of every kind!—If the object
is to manifest the complete man, then guard one's integrity! To test
the question is to tempt God. When all is said, the God of justice
veils from me the God of love. I tremble and do not trust.

Any double, divided, opposed voice in the conscience is not yet
the voice of God. Descend still deeper into yourself, till you hear
only one simple voice, a voice that removes all doubt, that brings
with it persuasion, light, serenity. Happy, says the apostle, are those
who are at peace with themselves, and do not condemn themselves
in the part they take. This inner identity, this unity of conviction,
is the more difficult the more the mind discerns, analyzes, foresees.
It is very difficult for freedom to return to the frank unity of
instinct.

Alas! one must therefore reascend a thousand times the heights
that one has scaled already, reconquer the points of view one has
attained, one must πολε μεῖν πόλεμον. The heart, like a king, under
the form of perpetual peace, does nothing, therefore, but sign truces.
The eternal life is thus eternally to be won afresh. The river of
days sweeps us far from the mountains of our homeland, and we
must return in clouds to visit their summits, an infinite circle, a fatal rotation, the labour of Sisyphus. Alas, yes, peace itself is a struggle, or, rather, struggle, activity is the law. We find no rest save in
effort, as the flame finds existence only in combustion. O Heraclitus,
the image of happiness is thus the same as that of suffering; anxiety
and advance, hell and heaven are equally inconstant. The altar of
Vesta and the torment of Beelzebub blaze with the same fire.—Yes,
that is life, life two-faced and two-edged. The fire that gives light is

also the fire that consumes; the element of the gods may become that of the accursed.

*April 7, 1851.*—Read in part Ruge's volume,[1] *Die Academie* (1848), in which Humanism, the point of view of the young Hegelians, in politics, religion and literature, is represented by correspondence or direct articles (Kuno Fischer, Kollach, etc.).—They recall the party of the Encyclopædists of the last century, supremely able to dissolve anything by reasoning and reason, incapable of constructing; for construction rests on feeling, instinct, will. The philosophic consciousness is taken here for the power of realizing, the redemption of the intelligence for the redemption of the heart, that is to say, the part for the whole, and the last in chronological order for the first. They impress me with the radical difference between *intellectualism* and *moralism*. They wish to supplant religion with philosophy. The principle of their religion is man, and the summit of man is thought. Thus their religion is the religion of thought.

Here are the two worlds: Christianity brings forward and preaches a salvation through the conversion of the will, Humanism preaches a salvation through the emancipation of the mind. One seizes upon the heart, the other upon the brain. Both wish man to attain his ideal; but the ideal differs, if not in its content, at least in the disposition of this content, in the predominance and sovereignty that is given to this or that inner force: for the one, the mind is the spokesman of the soul; for the other, the soul is an inferior state of the mind; the one wishes to enlighten while making better, the other to make better while enlightening. It is the difference between Socrates and Jesus.

The capital question is that of sin. The question of immanence,

[1] Arnold Ruge, born in 1803, died at Brighton in 1880, chief editor of the *Hallische,* then of the *Deutsche Jahrbücher* (1838–1843), to which Strauss, Bruno Bauer, Ludwig Feuerbach contributed. He was a member of the Parliament of Frankfort.

On the margin of this fragment, Amiel wrote later, when he reread it: "The *Humanists* (Ruge, Feuerbach, etc.), Philosophy and Religion, Intellectualism and Moralism."

dualism, is secondary, for this can be resolved while the other remains. The Trinity, the life to come, heaven and hell may cease to be dogmas and spiritual realities, formalism and literalism may vanish, the human question remains: What is it that saves? How is man brought to be truly man? Is the ultimate root of his being responsibility, yes or no? Is it to do or to know the good, to act or to think, which is the final end?—If knowledge does not give love, it is insufficient. And what it gives is only the *amor intellectualis* of Spinoza, light without warmth, a resignation, contemplative and grand, but inhuman because it is hardly transmissible and remains a privilege, indeed the rarest of all. *Moral love* places the centre of the individual at the centre of being; it has at least salvation in principle, the germ of eternal life; thought describes its circles around the centre, more and more extended and unlimited in their increase.—Cherubim and seraphim: there is the dilemma already, or rather the distinction. To love is virtually to know, to know is not virtually to love: there is the relation of these two modes of man. Redemption through knowledge, or through intellectual love, is thus inferior to redemption through will, or through moral love. The first can liberate from the self, it can enfranchise one from egoism. The second urges the self outside of itself, renders it active and efficient. The one is critical, purifying, negative; the other is vivifying, fecund, positive. Knowledge, however spiritual and substantial it may be in itself, is yet formal relatively to love. Moral force is therefore the vital point.

And this force is attained only through moral force. Like alone acts on like. One does not improve through argument but through example; one does not touch except through emotion; one does not hope to excite love except through love. Be what you wish to make others become. Make yourself, not your words, a sermon.

Therefore, to return to the subject, philosophy cannot replace religion; the revolutionaries are not apostles, although the Apostles were revolutionaries. To save from without inward—and by the "without" I mean also the intelligence relatively to the will—is an error and a danger. The negative part of the work of the Humanists is good; it will strip from Christianity a whole shell that has grown to be external; but Feuerbach and Ruge cannot save humanity. We must have saints and heroes to complete the work of the philosophers. Knowledge is the power of man, and love his strength; man *becomes* man only by the intelligence, but he *is* man only by the heart. To know, to love, to be able: that is the complete life.

*June 15, 1851.*—This evening, walked up and down a little on the Pont des Bergues, under a beautiful moonless sky. I marvelled at the freshness of the waters, streaked with the lights from the two quays and shimmering under the sparkle of the stars. Meeting those various groups of young people in phalanx, families, couples, children, singing or talking on their way back to their homes, their garrets or their drawing-rooms, I had a feeling of sympathy for all these passers-by; I opened my eyes and ears like a poet and a painter, or merely as a curious well-wisher; I felt content to live and to watch others living. Perhaps I could have wished for some young girl on my arm, with love in her eyes, to share this poetry a little. Sometimes this vision dances before me, but I turn my eyes away from it. It is too charming and intoxicating for me to abandon myself to it. The *all or nothing* is the cause of my stoicism. To seek is odious to my pride; not to seek leads to nothing, and no one can seek for me, neither mother, nor aunt, nor sister, nor friend. So I gird my loins and carefully button my hair-shirt. And the thirtieth year approaches. Blow out your lamp. It is growing late, and tomorrow has its task to be done.

*August 15, 1851.*—To know how to be ready is a great thing! A precious faculty, and one that implies calculation, clear-sightedness, decision. For this one has to be able to cut the knots, for not all knots can be untied; one has to be able to disengage the essential, the important from the endless minutiæ; in a word, to simplify one's life, one's duties, one's affairs, one's impedimenta, etc.

It is astonishing how entangled and wound up as a rule we are in a thousand and one obstacles and duties, which are not real duties and which yet shackle us in our movements. To know how to finish is at bottom the same thing as knowing how to die; it means distinguishing the truly necessary things and putting the others back in their place. To be as free as possible at every moment, one must have a great deal of order. It is disorder that makes slaves of us. The disorder of today takes its toll from the freedom of tomorrow.

The things we allow to trail along behind us rise up in front of us later and obstruct our road. When each of our days regulates that which concerns it, liquidates its affairs, respects the day that is to follow, we are always ready. Whatever encumbers us destroys all ease, all liberty, all clarity; and encumbrance is the fruit of procrastination.

Do not put off to the morrow what can be done at once. Nothing is done while something remains to be done. To finish is the mark of the master.

*Aix-les-Bains, September 2, 1851.*—Venturing into Tocqueville *(De la Démocratie en Amérique).* My impression is still mixed. A fine work, but I feel it is a little too imitative of Montesquieu. Then this abstract, sharp, refined, sententious style is a little stiff, over-nice and monotonous. It has too much wit and not enough imagination. It is fragmentary, clipped, sparkling, and yet it is fatiguing with its abrupt changeableness. It makes one think rather than charms one, and although it is grave it is jerky in style. This method of parcelling out thought, illuminating the subject by successive facets, has serious disadvantages. One sees the details too clearly, to the detriment of the whole. This multitude of sparks gives out a very poor light.—Altogether, I find this style sprightly, subtle, even profound, but a little dry, broken and wearisome. The author is evidently a serious, mature, penetrating mind, who surveys his subject from aloft and analyzes acutely its thousand convolutions.

*Aix-les-Bains, September 6, 1851.*—Tocqueville's work has a calming effect on the mind but leaves a certain distaste behind it. One recognizes the necessity of all that happens, and the inevitable is quieting; but one sees that the era of mediocrity is at hand in every sphere of life, and the mediocre freezes all desire. Equality gives birth to uniformity, and it is in sacrificing the excellent, the remarkable, the extraordinary, that one gets rid of the bad.—Low spirits will become the malady of the equalitarian age. The useful will replace the beautiful, industry will replace art, political economy will replace religion, and arithmetic will replace poetry.

The time of the great men is passing; the epoch of the ant-hill, of the multiple life, arrives. By continual levelling and the division of labour, society will become everything and man will be nothing.

Statistics will register great advances, and the moralist a gradual decline; the average will rise like the bottom of the valleys by the denuding and sinking of the mountains. A plateau less and less undulating, without contrasts, without oppositions, monotonous, such will be the aspect of human society. Extremes meet, and if the march of creation consists at first in endlessly disengaging and multiplying differences, it afterwards retraces its steps, effacing them one by one. May equality, which, in the beginning, is torpor, inertia, death, become in the end the form of life?

Is it not purchasing universal well-being at too great a price, to pay with the highest faculties, the noblest tendencies of the human species? Is this indeed the fatal lot reserved for democracies? Or rather, above the economic and political equality towards which socialistic democracy tends, will there form a new kingdom of the mind, a church of refuge, a republic of souls, in which, beyond simple right and gross utility, the beautiful, the infinite, admiration, devotion, sanctity, will have a cult and a city? Are utilitarian materialism, barren, egoistic legality, the idolatry of the flesh and the self, of the temporal and Mammon, the issue of our efforts? I do not believe it.—The ideal of humanity is far too lofty. But the animal is the first to protest, and the suffering that is superfluous and of social origin must first be banished before there will be a return to spiritual goods. Everyone has to live, before he can occupy himself with religion.

*Aix-les-Bains, September 7, 1851 (10 p. m).*—A strange, tranquil moonlight, with a fresh breeze and a sky traversed by clouds, makes our terrace at this hour enchanting. These beams, soft and pale, shed from the zenith a resigned peace that penetrates the heart. It is the calm joy, the pensive smile of experience, with a touch of stoical vigour. The stars shine, the leaves shiver beneath the silvery reflections; not a sound of life in the countryside; the great shadows lose themselves in the alleys and at the turning of the steps. Everything is mysterious, secret, solemn.

Nocturnal hour, hour of silence and solitude, you are full of grace and melancholy, you sadden and you console; you speak to us of all that is no more and of all that must die; but you say to us; Courage! and you promise us rest.

*November 9, 1851 (Sunday).*—Second address of Adolphe Monod at Saint-Gervais, less imposing perhaps, but almost bolder and for me more edifying than that of last Sunday. The subject was Saint Paul, or the active life, as that of the other day was Saint John, or the inner life of the Christian. I felt again the golden chains of eloquence; I hung on his lips and was enraptured by his audacity and his grace, by his fire and his art, his sincerity and talent. I realized that, for the strong, difficulties are a source of inspiration, and that what would make others stumble is the occasion of their highest triumphs.—He made Saint Paul weep for an hour and a half, he made a sort of old nurse of him, hunted out his old cloak, his prescriptions of water and wine to Timothy, the sailcloth that he mended, his friend Tychicus, in short everything that could make one smile, and from this he drew the most constant pathos, the most austere and striking lessons. In the tears of pain, charity and tenderness, he brought to life the whole Saint Paul, as martyr, as apostle and as man, with a grandeur, an unction, a warmth of reality, such as I had never seen before.

The apotheosis of suffering in our century of well-being, when pastors and flocks are benumbed in Capuan languors; the apotheosis of an ardent, militant charity in our epoch of coldness and indifference to the soul; the apotheosis of Christianity, human, natural, become flesh and life, in our epoch when some place it, so to speak, above man and the rest beneath him; and finally, in the peroration, the necessity for a new people, a stronger generation, to save the world from the storms that threaten it. People of Saint Paul, rise, to your work! Paul wept, but he triumphs. Today like him, tomorrow with him!

Diction, composition, resources, delivery, images, it was all instructive, striking, precious to receive. What an infinite thing is such an hour's study! What treasures of skill to marvel over, even while one weeps.

*November 18, 1851.*—That energetic subjectivity which asserts itself with full assurance, not afraid to be something particular and definite, unconscious and unashamed of its subjective illusion, is unknown to me. In the intellectual order I am essentially objective, and my distinctive speciality is the ability to share all points of view, to see through all eyes, that is to say, not to be shut up in any individual prison. From this comes an aptitude for theory and irresolution in practice, from this comes critical talent and constraint in spontaneous production, from this came also a long uncertainty in convictions and opinions, while my aptitude remained on the instinctive level. But now that it is conscious and self-possessed, it is able to come to conclusions and assert itself in its turn, so that, after having given nothing but anxiety, it finally brings peace. It says: There is no peace of mind save in the absolute, no rest for the feelings save in the infinite, no rest for the soul save in the divine. Nothing finite is true, or interesting, or worthy to arrest me. All that is particular is exclusive, all that is exclusive repels me. There is nothing non-exclusive but the Whole; it is in communion with Being and through all being that I find my end. Thus, in the light of the absolute, every idea becomes worthy of study; in the infinite, every existence worthy of respect; in the divine, every creature worthy of love. The complete and harmonious man, the Christ-man: that is my credo. Love, with understanding and strength; that is my aspiration.

*December 2, 1851.*—The law of secrecy. Do as the plant does; protect with obscurity everything that germinates in you, thought or feeling, and do not expose it to the light of day until it is already formed. Every conception should be enveloped in the triple veil of modesty, silence and shadow. Respect mystery, for its profanation leads to death. Do not bare your roots, if you wish to grow and live. And if possible, even at the day of birth, do not invite witnesses, as queens do, but open like the gentian of the Alps under the eye of God alone.

*February 1, 1852 (Sunday).*—Spent part of the afternoon reading the *Monologues* of Schleiermacher. This little book made almost as great an impression on me as it did the first time, twelve years ago. It plunged me back into that inner world to which I return with joy, when I have strayed from it. I was able, moreover, to measure the progress that I have made since then by the transparency which all these thoughts had for me, by the crowd of analogies with my own which I recognized in them, by the freedom with which I entered into this point of view and also judged it. It is grand, powerful, profound, but it is still proud and even egoistical. The centre of the universe is still the Self, the great *Ich* of Fichte.

Indomitable liberty, the apotheosis of the individual expanding to contain the world, emancipating itself to the point of recognizing that nothing is foreign to it, that there is no limit: that is the point of view of Schleiermacher. The *inner life:* 1., in its emancipation from time; 2., in its double end, the realization of the species and of individuality; 3., in its proud domination of all hostile circumstances; 4., in its prophetic security as regards the future; 5., lastly, in its immortal youth. Such is the content of the five *Monologues.*

We enter upon a life that is monumental, typical, profoundly original and impervious to every outside influence; a fine example of the autonomy of the Self, a fine model of character. Stoicism;

but the motive of this life is yet not religious; it is rather moral and philosophical.—I see in it not a model, but an example; not a result to be imitated but a precious subject for study.

This ideal of absolute liberty, inviolable, unshatterable, developing in accordance with its own laws, self-respecting, disdaining the world and practical activity, is also the ideal of Emerson. Here man rejóices in himself, and, finding refuge in the inaccessible sanctuary of his personal consciousness, he becomes a God. He is his own principle, the motive and end of his destiny; he is himself, and that is enough. The pride of life is not far from a kind of impiety, a displacement of adoration. In discarding humility, this superhuman point of view runs a grave risk, the very temptation to which Adam succumbed, that of becoming one's own Master in having become like the Elohim. The heroism of the *Monologues* borders on temerity, the liberty seems too like independence and not enough like submission; the whole side of duty is left too much in the shade; the soul is too alone and too emancipated from God; in short, the right and the worth of the individual are too exclusively overemphasized, and in the individual the unity of life does not sufficiently disclose the discord and the struggle beneath it, peace is bought too cheaply, serenity is too much a thing of nature and not enough a conquest.

Ontologically, the position of man in the world of mind is poorly indicated. The individual soul, not being unique, cannot, unless it goes outside of itself, conceive itself alone. Psychologically, the force of spontaneity in the self is conceived too exclusively. In actual fact, in the evolution of man, it is not everything. Morally, evil is scarcely mentioned; anguish, the condition of true peace, does not appear. Peace is neither a victory nor a salvation, it is good fortune, rather.

*February 2, 1852.*—Still the *Monologues*. Yesterday I defended myself well enough against them by criticism. Now, without scruple or danger, I can abandon myself to the sympathy and admiration they inspire in me. This essentially free life, this sovereign conception of human dignity, this actual possession of the universe and the infinite, this enfranchisement from everything transitory, this powerful feeling of superiority and strength, this invincible energy of will, this perfect self-penetration, this autocracy of the unswayed consciousness, all these signs of a magnificent and indomitable personality, a nature that is consistent, complete, profound, harmonious, indefinitely perfectible, have filled me with joy and gratitude. What a life, what a man! These perspectives opening into the interior of a great soul do much good. One is fortified at the contact, refreshed and invigorated. The spectacle restores our courage. When one sees what has been, one no longer doubts that it can be. Seeing a man, one says to oneself: Yes, let us be men.

*March 3, 1852.*—Public opinion has its value and even its power; to have it against one, erroneous though it may be at every point, is painful if it means the opinion of our friends, harmful if it means the opinion of other men.—Public opinion must not be flattered or courted; but, if possible, we should not oblige it, we should not even permit it to follow a false scent with regard to ourselves. The first course is base, the second imprudent. We should be ashamed of the one; we may regret the other.—Be careful, you are strongly inclined to this latter fault, and it has already caused you a good deal of harm. With your scornful rigidity, you count on the justice of time; if you were wiser, you would ease its task and hasten its coming.—Living in society, it is not enough to have your conscience with you; it is good and possibly necessary to win public opinion to your side. Bend your pride, abase yourself even to the point of expedience. This world of wolves and foxes, crafty egoism and active ambitions, enormous vanities and Lilliputian merits, this world of men in which one must lie by smiles, conduct, silence as well as speech, a world that is distasteful to the upright and proud soul; this is your own world. You must know how to live in it. It makes success necessary,—succeed. It recognizes strength alone,—be strong. Public opinion tries to bend all necks beneath its law. Instead of defying it, one should overcome it. I understand the anger of scorn and the desire that one feels to crush things, which is irrepressibly aroused by everything that crawls, everything tortuous, oblique, ignoble . . .

But I cannot remain long in this state of mind, which is one of vengeance. This is a world of men; these men are brothers. Let us not banish the divine breath. Let us love. Evil must be overcome with good; one must preserve a pure conscience. But even from this point of view, one can still prescribe prudence. Be innocent as the dove and wise as the serpent, said the apostle.—Have a care for your reputation, not from vanity, but in order not to prejudice your work, and from love for the truth. There is always an element of self-seeking in this refined disinterestedness which, in order to feel superior to public opinion, will not justify itself. The expedient thing is to appear to be what one is; the humble thing is to feel that one is little.

And now, thanks to you, Journal, my excitement has passed. I am calm and full of kindly feelings. I have just read over this notebook, and my morning has flown away in this monologue. For the rest, I have found these pages monotonous; the same sentiment reappears three or four times. Well, these pages are not written to be read, they are written to tranquillize me and remind me. They are landmarks in my past, and sometimes, in place of the landmarks, funeral crosses, pyramids of stone, stalks that have grown green again, white pebbles, medals; all this helps one to retrace one's path in the Elysian Fields of the soul. The pilgrim has marked his stopping-places; he can retrace his thoughts, his tears, his joys. This is my travelling-diary; if a few passages are useful to others, and if I have sometimes even communicated them to the public, these thousand pages in their entirety are good only for me and for those who, in after times, may interest themselves in the itinerary of a soul, an obscure existence, as remote from the sounds of the world as from renown. These pages will be monotonous when my life has been so, they will repeat themselves when feelings repeat themselves; they always tell the truth, and the truth is their only muse, their only pretext, their only duty. As a psychological and biographical register, they will have some value later in my old age, if I grow old; they already have a value for me as confidants, as a sympathetic pillow.

*(Later.)*—. . . There are not many young people of my age who, without material cares, are more, and more often, than myself the victim of inner torments. When I think of my sombre, solitary walks, the sad and senseless rages that I feel under the midday sun, on certain days of spring, the evenings and the mornings that I waste wringing my heart, the tears I recall in Berlin and other places; when I think of my Faust-like vigils, the moral solitude in which I have grown ever since my childhood, save for the happy chances of friendship, precious but episodic; when I reflect on what I would be without the distractions of study, without self-forgetting, without the life of thought, without the tranquil refuge of knowledge, I cannot help seeing that my life is founded on sadness, because I have lived alone, abandoned to myself, driven inward, and that it is not good for man to be alone. These are sufferings that make others laugh, when one has leisure and independence, when one can study, travel, loaf as one pleases; and yet, although I cannot say so, I have suffered and even suffered enough. Thank God, I am not such a fool as to pride myself on it, but I find the phrase, "the fortunate man of the time", curious by the contrast. In other respects, it expresses something true, I mean my present state and external life. I have the attitude and exterior of a man who desires nothing and has made his place in the world. But the world too often takes your armour for your epidermis, your appearance for your reality and thinks you are insensible because you contain your feelings.

*April 26, 1852.*—This evening, feeling empty, I retired into myself: the future, solitude, duty, all these solemn and pressing ideas came to visit me. I took up my credo again, reorganized (this time in a separate note-book) the catechism of my life, my plan of conduct, the unity of my chequered and capricious existence.—I

collected my thoughts, reviewed, assembled, concentrated and arranged myself; and this is very necessary amid all the dispersion
and distraction which the day and its details bring with them.

Read part of Krause's book *(Urbild der Menschheit, 1811)*,[1]
which responded marvellously to my thought and my need. Almost
always this philosopher has a beneficent effect upon me; his deeply
inward religious serenity wins and pervades one. He gives peace and
the feeling of the infinite.

Still, I miss something: worship, a piety that is positive and
shared. When will the Church arise to which my heart belongs? I
cannot, like Scherer, content myself with being right alone. I need
a less solitary Christianity. It must be more practical, too: often as
I pray, I did not take communion at Easter. So my religious needs,
like my social needs and my need of affection, are not satisfied.
When I cease to be torpidly oblivious of them, they awake with a
sort of aching bitterness. My life is tepid, it lacks energy, substance,
greatness and joy. Why? For want of reagents, stimulants, circumstances. I sleep like the dormouse because winter surrounds me.
Winter is the medium in which I am plunged, an atmosphere that
is inert, torpid and full of ghosts, paltry, commonplace, wearisome
cares that envelop and oppress me. I waver between languor and
ennui, dissipation in the infinitely little and nostalgia for the unknown or far-away.—A singular moral strength is necessary to
resist these circumambient influences, to regenerate oneself perpetually amid all this injurious wastefulness. It is the story of the
*provincial* life, so often treated by the French novelists; only that
the province is all that is not the fatherland of the soul, every place
where the heart feels a stranger, unsatisfied, restless, dry. Alas!
truly seen, this place is the earth, and the fatherland one dreams of
is heaven. This suffering is the eternal nostalgia, the thirst for happiness.

*In der Beschränkung zeigt sich erst der Meister,* says Goethe.—

[1] Karl Christian Friedrich Krause,. 1781–1832, German philosopher,
leader of a school; he gave his system the name *panentheism.*

Manly resignation is also the motto of the masters of life: manly, that is, courageous, active, resolute, persevering; resignation, that is, renunciation, abnegation, concentration, limitation. Resigned energy, this is the wisdom of the sons of earth, this is the serenity that is possible in a life of struggle and combat; it is the peace of the martyr and the promise of triumph.

*Lancy,*[1] *April 28, 1852.*—Languors of spring, once again return-ing. You are visiting me after a long absence. Last evening the theatre, this morning poetry (Ch. Reynaud, Heine), the song of the birds, the tranquil sunlight, the air of the verdant fields all mount up in my heart and my eyes are moist. O silence, you are frighten-ing!—frightening as the calm of the ocean which allows one to plunge one's eyes into its unfathomable abyss; you allow us to see in ourselves vertiginous depths, inextinguishable, infinite needs, long-cherished sorrows and regrets. Let the storms come! At least they ruffle the surface of these waters with their terrible secrets. Let the passions blow! By stirring up the waves of the soul, they veil its bottomless gulfs. In all of us, children of earth, sons of time, eternity inspires an involuntary anguish and infinity a mysterious terror. We feel as if we were entering the realm of death.—Poor heart, you long for life, you long for love, you long for illusions, and you are right, after all, for life is sacred.

In these moments of intimacy with the infinite, what a different aspect life assumes! How all that occupies, preoccupies, impassions and fills us suddenly becomes, before our eyes, puerile, frivolous and vain. We seem to ourselves marionettes, playing in earnest a fantastic pageant and taking baubles for treasures. How different at such times everything is; reality seems less true than fable and art. The end of all this is the development of the soul, all the rest is shadow, pretence, figure, symbol, dream; the soul is the only reality, the rest is the sublime phantasmagoria that is destined to form and enliven it. Berkeley seems true, Fichte and Emerson also. Fairy-tales and legends are as unerringly true as natural history, truer

[1] A village near Geneva.

indeed, at least they are more transparent emblems. Immortal, enduring, alone perfectly real is consciousness; the world is only a firework. Consciousness is a universe and its sun is love.

Ah, already I am falling back into the general, objective life of thought, which delivers me (shall I say?), no, deprives me of the inward life of feeling. The savant kills the lover; reflection dissolves revery and burns its delicate wings.—That is why science does not make men: it makes entities of them, abstractions. Ah, let us feel, let us live and not always analyze. Let us be natural, first, before we reflect. Let us give ourselves before we take back. Let us experience before we study. Let us go out to life:

> *Enivrons-nous de poésie,*
> *Nos cœurs n'en aimeront que mieux!*

Spring languors, you speak of love. It is sweet to share one's life that one may double it. Shall I never have the heart of a woman to rest upon? A son in whom to live again? A little world where I can allow all that I hide in myself to come to flower? I draw back in dread for fear of shattering my dream; I have staked so much on this card that I dare not play it. Let us still dream. . . .

Do no violence to yourself, respect in yourself the oscillations of feeling: they are your life and your nature; a wiser than you made them. Do not abandon yourself entirely either to instinct or to will; one is a siren, the other a despot. Be the slave neither of your impulses and your sensations of the moment nor of an abstract and general plan. Be open to what life brings, from within and without, to the unforeseen; but give your life unity, bring the unforeseen back to the lines of your plan. Lift nature to mind, and let the mind again become nature. It is on this condition that your development will be harmonious and the serenity of Olympus, the peace of heaven, will shine on your brow;—always on condition that you have made your peace and that you have climbed your Calvary.

*(Afternoon.)*—Shall I never recover any of those prodigious reveries, such as I have had at times,—at dawn, one day in my

boyhood, as I sat among the ruins of the château of Faucigny; once, under the midday sun, on the mountain above Lavey, lying at the foot of a tree and visited by three butterflies; one night on the sandy shores of the North Sea, with my back on the beach and my eye wandering in the Milky Way;—those lofty reveries, immortal, cosmogonic, when one bears the world in one's breast, when one touches the stars and possesses the infinite? Divine moments, hours of ecstasy when thought flies from world to world, penetrates the great enigma, breathes large, tranquil, deep draughts, like the diurnal breathing of the Ocean, serene and limitless as the blue sky; visits of the muse Urania, who traces on the brows of those she loves the phosphorescent nimbus of the contemplative power, and pours into their hearts the tranquil intoxication of genius, if not its authority: moments of irresistible intuition when one feels great like the universe and calm like a god?—From the celestial spheres to the moss or the shells I was resting upon, the whole creation was subject to me, lived in me and in me accomplished its eternal work with the regularity of fate and the impassioned ardour of love. What hours, what memories! The ruins of them that remain with me are enough to fill me with respect and enthusiasm, as if they were visits of the Holy Ghost. And to fall back from these heights, with their unbounded horizons, into the muddy ruts of triviality! What a fall! Poor Moses, you also saw, rolling in the distance, the pleasant slopes of the Promised Land, and you had to stretch out your tired bones in a pit dug in the desert.—Which of us has not his promised land, his day of ecstasy and his end in exile? But what a pale counterfeit of this life one glimpses is the life of actuality, and how these radiant flashes of our prophetic youth dull yet more the twilight of our shabby and monotonous manhood!

*Lancy, April 29, 1852.*—Marked the progress of our lilacs, spiræas, etc. A charming surprise: the bursting of one of our small-leafed shrubs, which had broken into bloom overnight at all its extremities —coquettish, dainty, fresh as a wedding-garland, with all the graces of a half-unclosing. What a graceful and chaste beauty these white flowerets had, discreetly open like a morning's thoughts, and poised like bees or drops of dew on the young leaves, so delicate and so virginally green! Mother of marvels, mysterious, tender nature, why do we not live in you? Tœpffer's poetic idlers, Jules, Charles, all those sensitive friends and lovers of nature, those delighted and dazzled observers, came to my mind like a reproach or a lesson. The modest garden of a pastor's house, the narrow horizon of a garret offer as much instruction as a library for him who knows how to look and understand. Yes, we are too occupied, too busy, too encumbered, too active. We should be able to toss overboard all our baggage of cares, pedantry, erudition, to make ourselves simple and childlike again, to live in the present, thankful, ingenuous, happy. Yes, one must know how to be idle; in attentive and meditative inaction the soul smoothes out its wrinkles, relaxes, unfolds itself, revives like the trodden grass or the pruned hedge or the crumpled leaf, again becomes natural, spontaneous, sincere, original; revery, like the dew, refreshes and renews talent; a source of joy and thoughts, it accumulates, while at play, materials and images; it is the Sunday of the mind, and who knows if the repose of idling is not as important and not more fecund than the tension of work? Idling, so gracefully sung and vaunted by Tœpffer, is not only delightful but useful. It is a health-bath that gives elasticity to body and soul: it is the token and festival of liberty; it is a joyous feast, the feast of the butterfly fluttering, pilfering its way through the meadows. And the soul is a butterfly also.

*Lancy, May 2, 1852 (Sunday).*—This morning read the Epistle of St. James and the exegetical volume of Cellérier [1] on this epistle, then a good many of Pascal's *Pensées*, after having passed, however, more than an hour in the garden with our two little rascals. I made them examine at close hand the flowers, the shrubs, the cockchafers, the snails, to exercise them in observation, admiration and kindliness.

How important are the first talks of earliest childhood! How I

[1] Jacob Elysée Cellérier, Professor of Theology at the Academy of Geneva, born 1785, died 1862.

have felt the sanctity of this mission! I enter upon it only with a sort of religious fearfulness. Innocence and childhood are sacred. The sower who scatters the seed, the father who scatters the fertile word perform a pontifical act, and should do it only with religious feeling, with prayer and gravity, for they are working for the kingdom of God. All semination is a mysterious thing, whether the seed falls into the earth or into souls. Man is a husbandman; his whole work, rightly understood, is to develop life, to sow it everywhere; this is the task of humanity, and this task is celestial. The influence of a word uttered at the proper moment is incalculable. We forget too easily that speech is a revelation and a seed-sowing *(sermo-serere)*. Language! What a profound thing! But we are obtuse, for we are material and materialistic. We see the stones and the trees; we do not distinguish the armies of invisible ideas that people the air and perpetually beat their wings about each one of us!

*May 3, 1852.*—Men, like the masculine costume, are vulgar, ugly or uniform among all classes; it is the women who, like the mountain flora, mark with the most characteristic precision the gradation of the zones superimposed on society. The moral hierarchy is plainly and visibly apparent in one of the sexes; it is confused in the other. Among women, it has the regularity of averages and nature; among men it has the unforeseen caprices of freedom. This is because man rather forms himself by his will and woman is rather moulded by her lot; because the one modifies circumstances with his energy, while the other submits to them and reflects them in her gentleness; briefly, because woman is rather of the species and man the individual.

*May 6, 1852.*—Oddly enough, women are the sex that is at once most one and most different; the most alike from the moral point of view, the most different from the social point of view. Women are a sisterhood in the first case, in the second a hierarchy. All the degrees of culture and condition are sharply marked in their exterior, their manners and their tastes; the inner community is found in their feelings, their instincts and desires. The feminine sex thus represents the equality of nature and the inequality of human history; it maintains the unity of the species and separates the categories of society. Woman has therefore an essentially conservative mission. She preserves, on the one hand, the work of God, that which is permanent in man, the beautiful, the great, the human; she preserves, on the other hand, that which is the work of circumstances, the usages, absurdities, prejudices, pettinesses—the good and the bad, the serious and the frivolous. How could one wish it otherwise? Accept the smoke, if you would have the fire. This is a law that is providential and consequently good.—Woman is tradition, as man is progress; without both there would be no life. History, like all that has life, is the product of two forces; if its father is progress, tradition is its mother. Each sex has its part to play in the common work of the race.

*Lancy, May 14, 1852.*—Yesterday I was full of the philosophy of joy, gladness, youth, the smiling spring and the intoxicating roses; I preached strength and forgot that it was a pæan to good luck, that if I were tried and afflicted like the two friends with whom I was walking, I should have reasoned and talked as they did.

Our systems, it has been said, are the expression of our character or a theory of our situation. That is to say, we like to think that what has been given has been acquired, we take our nature for our own work and our fate for our conquest. An illusion born of vanity and also of the craving for liberty; we are loath to be the product of circumstances or the flowering of an inner germ; and yet we have received everything, and the part that is truly ours is very small, for it is mainly the negation, the resistance, the faults and the errors that make up this part. We receive everything, life and happiness, but the way in which we receive it is what remains to us. Let us receive with confidence, without blushing, without anxiety; let us also accept our nature from God, let us be charitable with it, and firm and solicitous for it; let us not accept the evil and sickness in ourselves but accept ourselves in spite of the evil and sickness. And let us not be afraid of pure joy; God is good, and what he does is well done.—Let us be resigned to everything, even to happiness; let us perfume with the incense of prayer the thorny paths of trial and the flowering roads of felicity. The truly saintly man, one of the mystics says, Bœhme or Angelus, would preserve the freshness of heaven even in the flames of hell. Peace of conscience is the incorruptible diamond that nothing external is able to mar. If it did not seem a savage and merciless paradox, I should say: Suffering is our own fault, holiness is serene. The apostle dared to say, "Be ye joyful"!

*

\*     \*

Saw the first glow-worm of the season, in the grass beside the little winding road that goes down from Lancy to the town. It was creeping furtively through the turf, like a timid thought or a newborn talent.

*June 17, 1852.*—All despotisms have a shrewd and superior intuition for whatever maintains human independence and dignity, and it is curious to see our radicals laying down the law just like Louis Napoleon, strange to see realistic teaching everywhere serving to smother under a mass of facts the freedom to examine moral questions. Materialism is the auxiliary doctrine of every tyranny, whether of a single man or of the masses. To crush the spiritual, moral, general, human man, if I may say so, by specializing him; to create, not complete human beings but wheels for the great social machine, to give these not conscience but society for a central principle, to enslave the soul to things, to depersonalize man, is the dominant tendency of our epoch. Moral atomism and social unity, the substitution of the laws of dead matter (gravitation, number, mass) for the laws of the moral nature (persuasion, adherence, faith); equality, the principle of mediocrity, becoming dogma; unity through uniformity (the Catholicism of a badly apprehended democracy); number becoming reason; always quantity instead of quality; a negative liberty that has no rule in itself, and is limited only

45

by force, everywhere taking the place of positive liberty, which is
the possession of an inner rule, a moral authority and check,—this
is the dilemma posed by Vinet, socialism and individualism.—I
should rather call it the eternal antagonism between the letter and
the spirit, between form and substance, between the outer and the
inner, between appearance and reality, which recurs in every conception and every idea. Materialism dulls and petrifies everything,
renders everything gross and falsifies every truth. There is a materialism in religion, politics, etc., that spoils everything it touches,
liberty, unity, equality, individuality. And so there are two ways of
understanding democracy.

To return to our starting-point, the Bœotianism that threatens us,
or rather the gross realism against which our teaching must struggle,
is not a momentary and personal thing but a tendency of the age,
a propensity of our degenerate national spirit. What is really
threatened is moral liberty, the conscience, the very nobility of man,
the respect for the soul. To defend the soul, its interests, rights and
dignity, is the most pressing duty for everyone who sees the danger;
to defend the humanity in man is the work of the writer, the pastor,
the teacher, the philosopher. Man, the true man, the ideal man, this
should be their motto, their watchword and their rallying-cry. War
on everything that defiles him, demeans him, shackles him, distorts
him; protection for everything that strengthens him, ennobles him,
elevates him! The touchstone for every system, religious, political
or pedagogical, is the man that it forms, the individual that comes
from its hands. If the system does harm to the intelligence, it is
bad; if it does harm to the character, it is vicious; if it does harm
to the conscience, it is criminal.

*July 20, 1852.*—Marc Monnier spent the morning with me. We
talked about Germany, Paris, travel, Hegel, the present and the future. He is always the same good fellow, flexible, strong, easy,
happy, full of verve, spring, gaiety and imagination, with his polar
star and his pair of scales, his sure taste and abounding facility. I
could not be a week in his company without becoming a poet again,

or at least a writer. He is going to settle in Paris in October. He is
ten years older than his age. We discussed the *Revue suisse* and my
plans. I went as far as Carouge with him. There is the "fortunate
man of the time", a title that I scarcely deserve, although it was
given to me. Today I was particularly sad.

*Lancy, August 12, 1852.*—Every sphere of being tends to a more
elevated sphere, of which it already has revelations and presentiments. The ideal, under all its forms, is the symbolic anticipation of
an existence higher than our own towards which we tend. As volcanoes reveal to us the secrets of the interior of the globe, so inspiration, enthusiasm, ecstasy are the passing explosions of the inner
world of the soul. Human life is only the advent of the spiritual
life, and there are innumerable degrees in one as in the other. Therefore keep watch and pray, disciple of life; chrysalis of an angel,
prepare for the unfolding that is to come; for the divine ascension is
only a series of ever more ethereal metamorphoses, in which every
phase, the consequence of those that have gone before, is the condition of those that follow. The divine life is a series of successive
deaths, wherein the spirit casts off its imperfections and its emblems
and yields to the growing attraction of the ineffable centre of gravitation, the sun of the intelligence and love. Created spirits, recognizing their mission, tend to form constellations and Milky Ways in
the empyrean of the divine; becoming gods, they surround with a
sparkling and incommensurable court the throne of the sovereign.
Their grandeur is their homage. The divinity with which they are
invested is God's most radiant crown. God is the father of spirits;
the vassalage of love is the constitution of the eternal kingdom.

*August 13, 1852 (noon).*—I have spent the whole morning in deep
meditation. What voyages and what flights! I took up the problem
of Mejnour and Zanoni.[1] What is the true life? Surveyed, sounded,
traversed all knowledge in its three dimensions, cleared the bounds
of time and space, reviewed mysteries, initiations, evocations, in-

[1] Mejnour and Zanoni, characters in a symbolic romance by Edward
Bulwer-Lytton, 1840.

vocations of every kind. Described circles round every activity, every individuality. I had an extraordinary feeling of ubiquity, clairvoyance and intellectual power. Around myself I recaptured spiritual space, the horizon, the ether . . . The result was that I all but reproduced, with the intensity of a dream, the life with which Bulwer must have been saturated when he wrote his book; then, after dilating in it, having enlarged and found myself in it, I also traced my own circle round it, detached myself from it, feeling that I was pinched for room. I passed back from Plotinus to Jesus Christ, and from Tyana to Nazareth. On mornings like these one lives ages, and ages of humanity, for one sees and feels anew and reproduces that which has made races and religions, civilizations and divinities live and die.—I was almost surprised that my hair had not turned white when I came back to myself.

*August 23, 1852.*—My afternoon has been taken up with visitors, two of my students first, . . . then Marc Monnier and Victor Cherbuliez, with whom we discoursed on Germany, Molière, Shakespeare, the style of the French writers, and played several rounds of bowls. Cherbuliez was the winner; he has grown rosier, younger, gayer, his eye is gentle and keen, his brow high and meditative, his mouth malicious, his voice alone is a little old and broken. He is a very distinguished fellow. These two youthful souls, so gifted, so full of warmth, ardour, hope, made me melancholy. Besides, I have never known Victor well: he is too reserved, too circumspect, too coldly clever for that. I am haunted by an involuntary thought.

*Lancy, September 27, 1852 (10 a. m.).*—Today I complete my thirty-first year. . . .

Be pure, constant, faithful to yourself, master of your instincts; be energetic, believe in yourself, do not wait for the approval, the sympathy, the gratitude of others. Reflect that you have a work to do, that time wasted is a theft from God, that discouragement is a weakness, and that peace of conscience is the only peace, won only by courage and devotion.—Be devoted to your family, your friends, your country, all men; fight against your inconstancy and womanish weakness; be brave, be strong, be a man.

Be the champion of the truth, defend the soul and freedom, minister to the birth of the new humanity, the future society; despair neither of yourself nor of others, love, believe, work, fight, hope.—Do not let yourself be seduced by trifles, minutiæ, frippery, the shells along the road. Do not forget your goal; gird up your loins, concentrate your forces, simplify your life, collect your intentions together, tie up your bundle, economize, not your heart, but your time and your hours. The time for dispersion and dreams in the fields is past. Leave to adolescence the joyous, disorderly course, the pursuit of all the flowers. One has to think of the harvest now, of binding up one's sheaf and giving one's fruits. . . .

The most beautiful of poems is life: life which is read and composed at a single breath, in which fancy and conscience are allies and aid each other, life that knows it is a microcosm and rehearses in miniature, in the presence of God, the universal, divine poem.—Yes, be man, that is, be nature, be Spirit, be God's image, be what is greatest, most beautiful, most elevated among all the spheres of being, be an idea and an infinite will, a reproduction of the great Whole. And be all by being nothing, by effacing yourself, by letting God enter into you as air enters a vacant space, reducing your selfish ego until it is only a vessel that contains the divine essence. Be humble, composed, silent, that you may hear in the depths of yourself the voice that is subtle and profound; be spiritual and pure, that you may enter into communion with the pure spirit. Withdraw often into the last sanctuary of your innermost consciousness, re-enter your atomic *punctuality*, that you may be freed from time, space, matter, temptation, dispersion, that you may escape from your organs and your own life; die often, in other words, and question yourself in the presence of this death, as a preparation for the last death. He who can confront, without a shudder, blindness, deafness, paralysis, disease, betrayal, want,—he who, without trembling, can face the sovereign Justice, he only can say that he is

49

prepared for death, whether partial or total. How far from this am I, how far my heart is from this stoicism! But at least to detach oneself from everything that can be taken from one, to accept everything as a loan and a gift, to cling only to the imperishable, this is something that must be attempted.—To believe in a good and fatherly God, a God who educates us and tempers the wind to the shorn lamb, who punishes only when it is necessary and takes away our joys with regret: this thought, or rather this conviction, gives courage and security. Oh, how we need love, tenderness, affection, kindness, and how vulnerable we are, we immortal, sovereign sons of God! Strong as the world, or weak as the worm, according as we represent God or represent nothing but ourselves, according as we rest on Being or stand alone.

Only the religious point of view, that of an active and moral religion, spiritual and profound, gives life its full dignity and energy. It renders one invulnerable and invincible. Spiritual baptism is the true water of the Styx; no earthly arm can give us a mortal wound, no resistance can weary one who has been dipped in its flood. Only in the name of heaven can earth be conquered. All good things were given to him who asked for wisdom only. It is when one is disinterested that one is strongest, and the world lies at the feet of him whom it cannot tempt. Why? Because the spirit is lord of matter, and the world belongs to God.—"Be of good cheer," a heavenly voice said; "I have overcome the world."

Thanks, leisure; thanks, retirement; thanks, Providence! I have been able to return to myself, able to give audience to my good angel. I have renewed myself in the feeling of my vocation and my duty, in the remembrance of my frailty. Come, new year, bring what you will, but do not take my peace from me; leave me a clear conscience and hope in God!

Lord, lend thy strength to the weak who are yet of good will! (*Noon.*)

*Lancy, October 31, 1852.*—A half hour's walk in the garden in a fine rain.—Autumnal landscape. The sky hung with various shades of gray, mists trailing over the mountains on the horizon; nature melancholy; leaves falling on all sides like the last illusions of youth under the tears of incurable sorrows. A flock of chirping birds pursued one another in the thickets, sporting among the branches like schoolboys huddled together and hiding in some pavilion. The ground strewn with leaves, brown, yellow and reddish; the trees half stripped, some more, some less, with patches of russet, lemon-yellow, amaranth (the order of spoliation: first the catalpas, then the mulberries, acacias, planes, walnuts, lindens, elms and lilacs); clumps and shrubbery turning red; a few flowers still, roses, nasturtiums, red, white, yellow and streaked dahlias, shedding their petals, withered petunias, mesembrianthemums of a deep carnation, eclipsing the mignonettes with their crown-like leafage in tints of mauve and rose; dried maize, bare fields, impoverished hedges.—The fir, alone vigorous, green, stoical in the midst of this universal sickliness, eternal youth braving the decline.—All these countless and marvellous symbols, which the forms and colours, the vegetation, which all living things, the earth and the sky offer every moment to the eye that can see them, charmed and thrilled me. I held the wand of poetry and had only to touch one of these objects for it to tell me its moral significance. I had a scientific curiosity also. I took notes and I asked questions. Why does the red dominate? What makes one kind of leaf last longer than another? Etc., etc.

Every landscape is a state of the soul, and he who reads in both marvels at the likeness in every detail. True poetry is truer than science, because it is synthetic and grasps at once what the combination of all the sciences can only attain at best some day in the future. The poet divines the soul of nature, the scientist only serves to accumulate the materials for its demonstration. The one rests in the whole, the other lives in a particular region. The one is concrete, the other abstract.

The soul of the world is more open and intelligible than the individual soul; it has more space, time and strength to manifest itself.

*November 6, 1852.*—I am still susceptible to all the passions, for I have them all within me; like an animal-tamer I keep them in their cages and on leash, but I hear them growling sometimes. I have stifled more than one budding love. Why? Because with that prophetic certainty of the moral intuition, I felt that they were unlikely to live and less durable than myself. I stifled them for the future benefit of the decisive affection. I have sounded and rejected the loves of the senses, the imagination and the sensibility; I wished for a love that was central and profound. I still believe in this, and so much the worse for the honour of the female sex if I am mistaken. I will have none of those twopenny passions that dazzle, consume and wither; I invoke, I await, I still hope for the great, the holy, the grave and serious love that lives in every fibre and in all the powers of the soul. The woman who does not understand this is not worthy of me. And if I must remain alone, I prefer to carry away my hope and my dream rather than mismate my soul.

*November 8, 1852.*—Responsibility is my invisible nightmare. To suffer through one's own fault is a torment of the damned, for one's grief is envenomed by the absurdity of it, and by the worst absurdity, that of being ashamed of oneself in one's own eyes. I have strength and energy only against evils that come from without, and it drives me mad merely to think of an irreparable evil committed by myself, something that would destroy my peace and freedom for life.—I pay for my privilege. My privilege is to look on at the drama of my life, to be conscious of the tragi-comedy of my own fate, to be aware, moreover, of the secret of the tragi-comic itself, that is, to be unable any longer to take my illusions seriously, to see myself, so to speak, from the theatre, on the stage, from beyond life, in existence, and to have to pretend a particular interest in my individual role, whilst I live in the confidence of the poet who is playing with all these very important actors and knows everything that they do not know. This is an odd position, and one that becomes cruel when pain forces me back into my little role, to which it authoritatively binds me, warning me that I have let myself go too far in supposing, after my little gossip with the poet, that I am exempted from my modest role as the valet in the play.—Shakespeare must often have had this feeling, and Hamlet, I think, must express it somewhere. It is the condition of the Doppelgänger, quite peculiarly German, which explains the distaste for real life and the repugnance for public life that is so common among the German thinkers. It is as if there were a degradation, a Gnostic fall, in folding the wings of genius and returning into one's own coarse, particular shell.—Without pain, which is the string of this bold kite, the umbilical cord by which this sublime thought is attached to its humanity, man would soar too quickly and too high, and the chosen individuals would be lost for the race, like balloons which, but for gravitation, would never return again from the empyrean.

How, then, find the courage for action? By slipping a little into unconsciousness, spontaneity, instinct, which holds one to the earth and dictates the relatively good and useful.

By believing more practically in Providence, which pardons and permits one to make amends.

By accepting the human condition more simply and candidly, by dreading trouble less, calculating less, hoping more; in short, by lessening, with our clearsightedness, our responsibility, and, with our responsibility, our timidity.

By acquiring more experience through losses and lessons.

*November 10, 1852.*—Felt, on awaking, all the grandeur of the gods of the Greek Olympus; filled with contempt, too, for the barbarous rantings of the ignorant men who have treated them like wicked toys. I understood their nobility, their ideal depth, and for an hour I was a pious Greek.—How could the finest of the human races have debased itself in its divinities? As men are, so are their gods. This reflection alone should make us modest. . . .

Greek mythology is the religion of the ideal. Each entity, great or small, city or individual, bears within itself unawares an idea, its own idea. To extract this, recognize it, fix it, is to have found the beacon, the religion, the god of this particular life. The god of each existence is the ideal graven in it. Every life has thus but one god . . .

How much we have to learn from the Greeks, our immortal forbears! And how much better than ourselves they solved their problem!—Their man was not our man, but how much better they revered, cultivated, ennobled the man they knew!—In a thousand other respects, we are barbarians beside them, as Béranger said to me, with a sigh, in 1843.—Barbarians in education, in eloquence, in public life, in poetry, in matters of art, etc. With us it requires millions of men to produce a few élite; a thousand sufficed in Greece. If the measure of a civilization is the number of accomplished men it produces, we are still a long way from this model people. We no longer have slaves beneath us, but they are among us. Barbarity is not at our frontiers, it lives next door to us. We bear within us much greater things, but we are a good deal smaller. This is a very strange result: the objective civilization created great men, without seeking to do so; the subjective civilization creates shabby and imperfect men, quite to the contrary of its desire and mission. Things become majestic and man grows mean. Why?

1. We have too much blood in our veins that is barbarous and coarse. We lack harmony, measure and grace.

2. Christianity, by breaking man into the outer and the inner, breaking the world into earth and heaven, hell and paradise, has disintegrated human unity, in order to reconstruct it, to be sure, more deeply and more truly; but Christianity has not yet digested this potent leaven. It has not yet attained the true humanity; it still lives under the antinomy of sin and grace, the world below and the world above.—It has not reached to the bottom of the heart of Jesus; it is still in the narthex of penitence; it is not reconciled, and even the churches still wear the livery of servitude and lack the joy of the daughters of God, baptized with the Holy Ghost.

3. Excessive division of labour.

4. Bad and stupid education, which does not develop the whole man.

5. The problem of poverty.—We have abolished slavery, without having solved the question of labour. Legally, there are no more slaves; actually, there are. And as long as the majority of men are not free, one cannot conceive of the free man, one can scarcely even realize him. Reasons enough, heaven knows.

*November 12, 1852.*—St. Martin's summer lingers on and all the days begin with mist. Trotted about the garden a few minutes to limber my joints and warm myself. Marvelled over the last buds of the roses, the delicate crimping of the strawberry leaves, embroidered with hoar-frost, and especially the ravishing tapestries of the village-spiders, hanging in the green branches of the firs, tiny ball-rooms for the fairies, light as moonbeams, carpeted with pearl-dust, which a thousand imperceptible threads, trembling with dew, held from above like the chains of a chandelier and from below like the anchors of a vessel. These airy little structures had all the fantastic lightness of the elves and the vapoury freshness of the dawn. They brought back to me the poetry of the North. I felt, as it were, a breath from Sweden, from Iceland and Caledonia, Frithiof and the Edda, Ossian and the Hebrides, all that world of cold and mists, of spirits and reveries, where warmth comes not from the sun, but from the heart, where man is more in relief than nature, that chaste, vigorous world, where the will plays a greater part than sensation, and thought a greater part than instinct,—in short, the romantic, Germanic poetry, northern poetry, gradually stirred in my sympa-thetic memory. A bracing poetry, having the effect of a moral tonic. Strange charm of imagination: a sprig of fir and a few spider-webs can make countries, epochs and nations live for it again.

*(Same day.)*—Topped off the evening with a little literary read-ing. A few bits of the *Chrestomathie française,* and Vinet's remark-able letter, at the head of the second volume, have given me a de-lightful hour or two. This letter struck me; it seemed to me that I was writing it myself. Never have I felt as today the intellectual kinship I have with Vinet, the moralist-psychologist, the critical augur and judge. I think I could write a continuation of him, for

my most apparent aptitude is of the same nature and perhaps not less in degree. It even seems to me that I have resources and a reach and horizon that are possibly greater. My travels, the variety of my studies, the multitude of things and men with which I have come in contact, are quite equal to his. A less constant and clearly-defined vocation, a life less devoted to duty, but much the same aptitude, a talent of the same kind, a broader culture and perhaps a superior flexibility: these would be the elements for the comparison. As a Christian, I shall always rank below him; as a thinker, as a writer, I can perhaps hope for more.

The man will remain a model; his philosophy, his theology, his aesthetics, in short, his objective work will be or is now surpassed at all points. Vinet is a great soul and a fine talent, though not well served by circumstances, a personality worthy of all veneration, a man of great goodness and a distinguished writer, but hardly a great man or a great writer. He has depth and purity, but not greatness. Too much meditation and reflection, and not enough power. He is too refined, subtle, analytical, he is too ingenious, he gives too much thought to detail and has not enough flow, eloquence, imagination, warmth or largeness. Casuistry of conscience, grammatical casuistry, eternal self-suspicion, perpetual moral self-examination, these describe his talent and his limits. He lacks fire, movement, popular feeling, infectiousness; individualism, his title to glory, is also the cause of his weakness. Everywhere one finds in him the solitary and the ascetic. His mind is always in church, continually testing itself. Hence that scrupulous, anxious, discreet air that sets the tone of his style. Moral energy, but over-squeamish, a fine organization, but poor health, as it were, this is what one feels about him. All the force is bent back on itself, against itself; if I dare to invent the phrase, an over-constant reflexivity,—whether in praise or reproach, this is the term that I should apply to him.—More spontaneity, I mean more dash in his bearing, more objectiveness, more body in his mind, more circles of life around his individual circle: this is what he leaves to be desired, and this is what, if he had it, would make his style, rich as it is in substance and full of ideas, a great style. Vinet, as man and writer, is conscience personified.—Happy the literature and the society that could have two or three such men!

*November 16, 1852 (5 a. m.).*—I awoke today only three hours later than I went to sleep last night. My equilibrium establishes itself like a see-saw. But what different sensations, although everything seems as it was. How unlike are the men illumined by the evening and the morning lamp! And how different are the vigils that end and begin the day! The late vigil is full of excitement, expansion, imagination, the soul in its multiplicity and vivacity; with the morning watch comes calm, meditation, concentration, the soul in its simplicity and composure. One is heated, the other cool. In the one, we produce; in the other, we receive. In the first we live, in the second we feel ourselves living.—I hear my heart and my watch marking the flight of the seconds, and in the distance reverberates the muffled sound of the threshers' flails. This is the hour when the soul listens, the hour of prayer and lofty thoughts, the hour of the infinite and the eternal; and it shows a perfect psychological wisdom that the voice of the muezzin, the bells of all the convents and the various calls of all the religions should, at this morning hour, bid men raise themselves to God. At this moment, the voice of the conscience speaks alone; later, other voices awake in turn. The eternal life (depth), the particular life (activity), the universal life (extension) —I was right: this is indeed the regular rhythm of the day between two sleeps, that is, of life itself, conscious, spiritual, responsible. To curtail one of these periods would be a mutilation. To extend, in turn, one over the two others is a right and oftentimes a duty.

*November 17, 1852.*— . . . Day is at hand; it is a quarter to seven. Between the cold daylight piercing through the mist on the panes and the warm lamplight shining on my paper there is but one slight, transparent curtain. Strange, symbolic struggle: it is the heart, tranquil in its solitude and self-communion, which the outer world is coming to assail, snatching away its peace, imposing duties, vexations, trifles, dispersion in any case. We have been living quite in ourselves, we have to live in the outer world! . . . Here is the day, one has to lie, Delphine said, in her fine poem, *La Nuit:* a woman's phrase. Let us say: Here is the day, one has to act.—Night, day; solitude, society; truth, lies: such is the equation of the woman of Paris. I will say: the lamp and the daylight are the self and the non-self, calm and movement, meditation and action, consciousness and will.—Let us draw the curtain. Out, lamp!

*December 26, 1852 (Sunday)*.—If I cast away many of the rags and tatters of our theology and our Church, it is to reach Christ himself better. My philosophy permits me to do this. It does not pose the dilemma of religion or philosophy, but that of a religion that is understood or a religion that is accepted. For me, philosophy is a way of grasping things, a mode of perceiving reality. It does not create nature, man, God, but it finds them and seeks to comprehend them. Philosophy is the ideal reconstruction of consciousness, consciousness comprehending itself together with everything it contains. It may contain a new life, as in the case of regeneration and salvation; consciousness may be Christian. An understanding of the Christian consciousness is an integral part of philosophy, just as the Christian consciousness is a capital form of the religious consciousness, and as religious consciousness is an essential form of consciousness.

*January 6, 1853*.—Self-control with tenderness is the condition of authority over childhood.—Let a child never discover any passion in you, any weakness that he can make use of, let him feel he cannot deceive you or disturb you, and he will feel you are naturally superior to him, and your sweetness will have for him a very special value, for it will inspire him with respect. A child who can stir you to anger, impatience, agitation feels that he is stronger than you, and a child respects nothing but strength. The mother should think of herself as her child's sun, immovable and always radiant, to which the restless little creature, always ready for tears and bursts

of laughter, heedless, inconstant, passionate, stormy, comes to re-
charge himself with warmth, electricity and light, to find his level,
to be calmed and strengthened. The mother represents the good, virtue, Providence, Law, that is to say, the Divinity, in the form that
childhood can approach. If she yields to passion, she reveals a capricious, despotic God, or even several gods that are in discord. A
child's religion depends on what its mother and father are and do,
not on what they say. Everything and especially every being tends
to transform others in its image. The inner, unconscious ideal that
guides your life is precisely what reaches the child; your words,
your remonstrances, your punishments, even your outbursts are only
thunder and comedy to him; your mode of worship—that is what
he instinctively divines and feels.

If you are silly, violent, impatient, unjust, morose, soft, weak,
stingy, nothing you say or do will be able to mask the fundamental
impression. Through everything that we wish to be, the child sees
what we are; hence his reputation as a physiognomist. He extends
his power as far as he can over each one of us; he is a shrewd diplomat. He feels, without knowing it, everyone's influence, and he reflects it by transforming it according to his own nature: he is a
magnifying mirror.—This is why a child is a critic and chastisement for the shortcomings of his parents; it is the sin punishing itself.—This is why the first principle of education is, Bring up yourself. The first rule to follow in mastering a child's will is, Become
the master of your own!

*February 5, 1853 (7 a. m.).*—I am always astonished at the difference between one's inward mood in the evening and the morning.
In the evening I see everything in black, in the morning in rose.
The passions, which give their tone to the evening, leave the morning free for the contemplative part of the soul. What seemed impossible in the first case seems easy in the second. Our whole being,
hated, irritated, strained by the nervous excitement of the day,
reaches in the evening the culminating point of its human vitality;
the same being, refreshed, assuaged, rested by the calm of sleep, is

nearer heaven in the morning, more benevolent, better. I feel that one should weigh a resolution in both balances, examine an idea in both lights, in order to diminish the chance of error by taking the average of our diurnal oscillations. Our inner life describes every day the regular barometric curves, independently of the accidental upheavals which the various storms of the feelings and the passions may raise in us. Every soul has its climate, and is a climate; it has its own meteorology in the general meteorology, and psychology will never be perfected before the physiology of the planet, which, quite inadequately, today, we style the physics of the globe.

I have prayed, I have longed for the spirit of forbearance, gratitude and forgiveness in place of the spirit of retaliation, vengeance, impatience. I have recognized that what seems to us impossible is often only an impossibility in a quite subjective sense. Our soul, under the action of the passions, produces through a strange mirage gigantic obstacles, mountains and abysses that stop us short; quench the passion, and this phantasmagoria will vanish. Wonderfully symbolized in the poems of chivalry, in the form of enchanted forests through which none but heroes pass, how worthy of attentive study, as a moral phenomenon, is this power of mirage and fascination, which almost reaches the point of hallucination! Thus we ourselves produce our own spiritual world, our monsters, our chimæras and our angels; we objectify everything that ferments in us. Everything is marvellous for the poet, everything is divine for the saint, everything is great for the hero, everything is paltry, mean, ugly, bad for the base and sordid soul. The evil man creates about himself a pandemonium, the artist an Olympus, the elect a paradise, which each of them sees alone. We are all of us visionaries, and what we see is our own soul in things. We reward ourselves and punish ourselves unawares.—So also everything seems to change when we change.

The soul is essentially active, and the activity of which we are conscious is only a part of our activity, and voluntary activity is only a part of our conscious activity.

Here is the basis for a psychology and an ethics. Man reproducing the world, enveloping himself with a nature which is the objectification of his spiritual nature, rewarding and punishing himself; things being the divine nature; the nature of the perfect spirit comprehending itself only according to the measure of our perfection; intuition the reward of inner purity; science (objective) arising out of goodness (subjective); in short, a new phenomenology, more complete and more moral, in which the total soul becomes spirit.—There, perhaps, is the subject for my summer course. The whole domain of inner education, the mysterious life (the unconscious, religion, apparitions, inspiration), the relation of nature to mind, of God and all beings to man, the repetition in miniature of the cosmogony, theogony, mythology and universal history; the evolution of mind; in a word, the problem of problems into which I have often plunged, but from which finite things, details, minutiæ have turned me aside a thousand times; that is what this question contains. I return to the brink of the great abyss, self-collected, however, without pride, without fanaticism, with the clear feeling that here lies the problem of science, that to sound it is a duty, that God conceals himself only in his light and his love, that he summons us to become spirits, to possess ourselves and to possess him in the measure of our powers, that our incredulity, our spiritual cowardice, is our infirmity and our weakness.

On the brink of this great abyss, I feel the shiver of sublimity running through my veins, but without freezing my heart. Æneas on the brink of Avernus undertook a less daring journey; Dante, gazing into the three worlds, with their various skies, glimpsed in the form of images what I wish to grasp in its purer form. But he was a poet, and I shall be only a philosopher. The poet makes himself understood by human generations and the crowd; the philosopher addresses himself only to a few rare minds. . . .

Day has come, and with it comes the dispersion of the mind in action. I feel demagnetized, pure clairvoyance gives place to observation, and the ethereal depths of the heaven of contemplation vanish before the glitter of finite things. Is this to be regretted? No, but it proves that the hours most apt for phenomenology are those that precede the dawn. From these heights, let us come back to earth. *(8:15.)*

*February 10, 1853.*—This afternoon I made an excursion to the Salève with my four best friends, C[harles] H[eim], E[rnest], N[aville], E[lie] L[ecoultre], E[dmond] S[cherer], the cronies of our little group. . . . The conversation was very brisk and kept us from noticing the deep mud that obstructed our steps. Naville, Scherer and I especially kept it well supplied, and I was the one who kindled it. Liberty in God (Are the age of our globe and the laws of nature fixed? Are the natural sciences certain? Does science end in atheism? God as caprice, God as causality? The one deducing from nature, the other from history;—that each oracle answers only according to the question that is put;—that everyone makes his God in his own image;—that every science determines an attribute of God); the essence of Christianity (Can it be determined? Historically or directly? Does it imply the supernatural? Is the supernatural only the measure of our ignorance, or is it the essence of revelation? Miracles? Are the rationalists and the sects within Christianity? Is religious truth a question of the majority and tradition? Supernatural and divine Christology in opposition, etc., etc.), and, on the way back, the new publications in philosophy (Strauss-Durkheim, Hollard, the Lotus of the Law, Humboldt, etc.), both in polemics and individualities (Secrétan, Vinet, Baudry, the *Revue de Théologie*),—these were the three subjects of conversation. The principal results for me were:

1. An excellent exercise in dialectics and argumentation with solid adversaries.

2. Personally I learned nothing, but I saw many of my ideas confirmed, and I penetrated better and better into the minds of my friends, while becoming myself more detached. I am much nearer to Scherer than to Naville, but I follow another path even than his.

3. A very striking fact, analogous to the changing of swords in *Hamlet,* is that abstract minds (which proceed from ideas to facts)

are always fighting in behalf of concrete reality, while concrete minds (which proceed from facts to ideas) usually fight for abstract notions. Everybody pretends to what he is least strong in. Everyone sets his heart on what he aspires to, and aspires instinctively to what he lacks. This is an unconscious protest against the incompleteness of every nature. Everyone strives towards what he has the least of, and the point of arrival is precisely opposite to the point of departure. The Promised Land is the land where one is not. The most intellectual nature takes ethicism for its theory; the most moral nature has an intellectualist morality. I could observe this throughout our three or four hours' discussion. Nothing is more completely hidden from us than our own everyday illusion, and our greatest illusion is to think that we are what we think we are.

4. The mathematical intelligence and the historical intelligence (the two classes of intelligence) can never understand each other. When they manage to grasp each other verbally, they differ over the things which the words mean. At the bottom of every detailed discussion between them reappears the problem of the origin of ideas. If they do not think about this, confusion results; if they do think about it, they are poles apart. They agree only in regard to the goal, truth; never in regard to the road, the method or the criterion.—The thought of thought, the consciousness of consciousness, to this the philosopher's critical faculty should attain, and few minds rise so far; accordingly, most of the best remain dupes of their thought, imprisoned in their consciousness.

5. Heim was the impartiality of consciousness, Naville the morality of consciousness, Lecoultre the religion of consciousness, Scherer the intelligence of consciousness, and I the consciousness of consciousness. A common ground, but different individualities. *Discrimen ingeniorum.*

The chimes of St. Pierre are ringing midnight . . . What most delighted me in this long discussion was the feeling of my freedom. To discuss the greatest questions without being fatigued, to be greater than the world, to play with one's strength,—that is the well-being of the intelligence and the Olympic festival of thought. *Habere, non haberi.*—There is an equal joy in the feeling of mutual confidence, the sense of esteem and friendship in the battle; like athletes, one embraces before and after the combat, and the combat is only a deploying of the forces of free and equal men.

*March 20, 1853.*—Sat up alone . . . and took the place of the mistress of the house. Paid two or three visits to the children's alcove. Young mothers, I understood you. Sleep is the mystery of life; there is a deep charm in this darkness illumined by the calm glow of a night-lamp, in this silence measured by the rhythmic breathing of these young sleeping creatures. One feels that one is a witness of a marvellous operation of nature, and it did not seem to me I was profaning it. I watched and listened noiselessly, rapt, touched, discreet, by this poetry of the cradle, the ancient and ever new benediction of the family, this image of creation, asleep under the wing of God, this image of our consciousness immersed once more in the darkness in order to rest from thought, and of the grave, too, that divine couch where, in turn, the soul comes to find rest from life.

*April 27, 1853.*—This evening I read the treatise by Nicole, so much admired by Mme. de Sévigné, on the means of maintaining peace among men and on rash judgments. This gentle, insinuating, shrewd, piercing, humble wisdom, which so well unfolds the secrets and *arrière-pensées* of the heart, and subjects everything to the sacred rule of the love of God and man, is singularly benign. Everything in it is on the same level, simple, well-assembled, well thought out, but without pomp or brilliance or any worldly ornaments of style. The moralist effaces himself and addresses only the conscience in us. He is a confessor, a friend and a counsellor.

"Peace must be maintained, as much for ourselves through wisdom as for others through charity. Without peace, we cannot accomplish our task, or be useful to others.—The way lies in giving no offence to others and in taking offence at nothing. In order not to give offence, one must examine and treat with respect other people's opinions and divine and respect their passions. In order not to take offence, we must uproot from our hearts all attachments that cause us to depend on others (the desire for consideration, authority, gratitude, affection), we must in humility and detachment demand and expect nothing."—Such is the gist of this treatise of one hundred and thirty pages.

One or two chapters touched me directly, the whole work indeed. I give offence and I take it. I have a certain inflexibility and pride. I wish to force error to bend to the truth and to force the passions of others to bow to what is right. When I am in the right, I hold out and keep my colours flying. I do not think enough about not shocking people, or about pleasing them, or making them listen to me in a friendly spirit. Consequently, even in the best circumstances, I mean when I am disinterested, when I am not seeking to make my own opinion or inclination triumph, I still make two mistakes, namely, in wishing to make others bow, as I bow myself, before impersonal things, before ideas.—I am not considerate, patient, helpful.—I make it a point of conscience to persist instead of yielding, to conquer by main force instead of conquering by address; to subdue instead of winning over. I have no regard for the self-esteem of others, I treat their egos without ceremony. I deal with men as if they were neither fools nor knaves, or as if it were not in their power to cease to be one or the other. I cannot take or accept men as they are; respecting man as I do, I wound men as if conscientiously, forbidding myself tact, address, flexibility; and although I am able to withhold my thoughts, I am not able to disguise them. In short, I am a porcupine of principles.—What Nicole teaches me is that, with a good conscience, one can act differently; that it is more important to save souls than principles; that I lack charity, ardent love for my neighbour, the patience to suffer, the patience to endure. I have known this for a long time, but I forget it.

*May 11, 1853.*—Psychology, poetry, the philosophy of history in its moral aspect, through all these spheres of thought I have passed swiftly on the wings of the invisible hippogriff. But the general impression has been one of tumult and anguish, temptation and unrest.

I love to plunge into the ocean of life, but sometimes I lose all sense of the axis and the pole, lose myself and feel the consciousness of my vocation wavering. The whirlwind of the Wandering Jew carries me away, snatches me out of my little familiar close and sweeps me through all the empires of men. In my wilful abandonment to the general, to the universal and the infinite, my own particular self evaporates like a drop of water in a furnace; it does not condense again until the cold returns, until after enthusiasm has died away, and the feeling of reality comes back. Expansion and condensation, abandonment and self-recovery, the conquest of the world and the sounding of one's consciousness: such is the play of the inner life, the progress of the microcosmic mind, the marriage of the individual soul with the universal soul, the fertile embrace of the finite and the infinite, out of which is born the intellectual advance of man; another betrothal unites the soul with God, the religious consciousness with the divine. This is the history of the will. And that which precedes will is feeling, preceded itself by instinct. Man is only what he becomes, a profound truth; but he becomes only what he is, a truth still more profound. What are you? The problem of predestination, birth, freedom: there is the abyss. And yet one must plunge into it, and I have plunged; but not today, that would lead too far.

The prelude of Bach (arranged by Gounod for the violin, piano and organ) had predisposed me to it, for it pictures the soul, tormented and appealing, and at last seizing upon God and possessing itself of peace and the infinite with an all-prevailing fervour and embrace.

*May 14, 1853.*—The third concert was the shortest: variations for piano and violin by Beethoven, and two quartettes; nothing else. The quartettes were perfectly limpid and easy to grasp in their unity. The one of Mozart (the 18th) was quite Attic and Socratic: I., Elegant drawing-room conversation, full of grace and urbanity; II., Boudoir conversation, more intimate, a confession of sorrowful experiences, confidences, but always with dignity; III., Return to the world, distraction; IV., Gaiety, vivacity.—In Beethoven's there was less talking and more dancing: I., Quadrille, animation; II., Resistance to dissipation in the name of duty; one thinks of staying at home, but the voices of pleasure are too infectious and one ends by going to the ball; III., Dance; IV., Whirlwind of merriment. —I was able to compare the two masters; their individualities stood out clearly—Mozart, all grace, freedom, ease, a sure, clear, fluent form, an exquisite and aristocratic beauty, serenity of soul, health and talent on a level with his genius; Beethoven, more pathetic, more passionate, rent with feeling, more intricate, more profound, less perfect, more the slave of his genius, more carried away by his fancy and passion; more moving and more sublime than Mozart, who is all beauty. Mozart refreshes you like Plato's dialogues; he respects you, reveals to you your strength, gives you freedom and equilibrium. Beethoven grips you, he is more dramatic, tragic, oratorical, violent, while Mozart is more disinterested and poetic. Mozart is more Greek, and Beethoven more Christian. One is serene, the other serious. The first is stronger than destiny, because he takes life less profoundly; the second is less strong, for he has measured himself against greater sorrows. His talent is not always equal to his genius, and the pathetic is his dominant trait, as perfection is that of Mozart. In Mozart, everything is in equilibrium and art triumphs; with Beethoven, feeling carries the day, and emotion disturbs art while deepening it.

*July 26, 1853.*—Why do I write short verses better and more easily than Alexandrines, the difficult things more easily than the easy? Always for the same reason: I do not dare to move without shackles, to show myself without a veil, in short, to act on my own account and seriously, to believe in myself and assert myself, whereas a little badinage, diverting attention from myself to things, from feeling to skill, puts me at my ease: to sum it all up, timidity. —There is another reason also: I am afraid of being great, I am not afraid of being ingenious, and besides, uncertain as I am of my talent and my instrument, I like to reassure myself by surrendering to virtuosity. Thus all my published literary essays are scarcely more than studies, exercises, games, for the purpose of testing myself. I play scales, I run up and down my instrument, I train my hand and assure myself that I am capable of execution, but the work does not come. My effort expires, I am satisfied with the power and do not reach the point of using my will. I am always preparing and never achieving. To sum this up, it is curiosity.— Timidity and curiosity—there are the two obstacles that bar me from the literary career. Nor must I forget procrastination: I am always reserving the important, the great, the grave things for the future, and wish meanwhile to settle with what is trifling, with the slight and amusing. Sure of my attraction to the vast and profound, I linger in everything that is opposite to them, lest I should fail to do these latter proper justice. My tastes are all for genius, and my productions are clever. Serious at bottom, I am frivolous in appearance. A lover of thought, I seem especially to court expression; I keep the substance for myself and reserve the form for others. And so the effect of my timidity is that I never treat the public seriously and show it only my amusing side, all that is enigmatic and capricious in me, while the effect of my curiosity is that everything tempts me, a shell as well as a mountain, and I never come to the end of my studies. The effect of my procrastination is that, always busy with the preliminaries and antecedents, I am never able to begin to produce.

For me there are never any conclusions, I am unwilling to bind myself, and so I remain for the public problem and form, talk, poetry, the indeterminate, freedom. Even in print, I am intangible. No one can enclose me in a circle, after the fashion of Emerson. The *Deus absconditus* of Mme. L. was not a bad hit, at least as an epithet. But if this is the fact, the fact might be better. I understand myself, but I do not approve of myself . . .

*July 29, 1853 (11.30 p. m.).*—This evening I had an experience that may be summed up thus: In a kiss, can one steal away a soul? [1]

I snatched a kiss, and as the blood flowed back to my heart I felt, I saw in advance how such a trifle might be a betrayal or might decide a destiny. The impulse, as a matter of fact, was spontaneous and irresistible. Sympathy, a feeling of pity and tenderness and attraction, and the thing was done, the cheek pressed against my lips, and the cheek had given itself. The kiss, almost brotherly at the beginning, had, in the act, almost turned to passion.—The swift rapture, the transformation of feeling under the influence of sex, the power and the intoxication of a kiss, a woman's astonishing capacity for dissimulation, the promptness of regret, all this struck me with the rapidity of thought at the contact with the satiny skin, or rather in the second afterwards. And all this without any bitterness, for I feel that I really did no harm. What I felt was the harm that I might have done, if the circumstances or the characters had been different.

A charming recollection remains with me, that of an electrical emotion and a very tender and very artless kiss. It did not have the ardour of fever, but it had the perfume of the rose. Innocent, loving, quick, it does not reproach me, and I shall embalm it in my memory, like those rare treasures which the pilgrim, returning from his travels, ranges among his precious objects.

*August 1, 1853.*—I have just finished Pelletan's work (*Profession de foi du XIX^e siècle*). It is a fine book. It lacks one thing only: the notion of evil. It is Condorcet's theory supported by additional props: indefinite perfectibility, man essentially good, life, conceived physiologically, dominating virtue, duty, sanctity; in short, a view of history that owes little to ethics, an identification of liberty with nature, the natural man taken for the whole man. Fine, generous, poetic aspirations, but dangerous because they lead to an implicit confidence in the instincts, and rather naive, too, because their man

[1] Amiel adds on the margin, with the date August 15, 1852: *Und ach! dein Kuss!* (*Gretchen*).

is a daydream and they gloss over reality, past and present. The book is a theodicy of a progress that is fated and irresistible, an enthusiastic hymn of the triumph of humanity. It is earnest, but superficial morally, lyrical but fanciful; it confuses the progress of the race with the progress of the individual, the progress of civilization with inner improvement. Why? Because its criterion is quantitative, or purely external (the wealth of life), and not qualitative (the goodness of life). Always the tendency of the French to take the appearance for the thing itself, the form for the substance, the law for the essence; always this absence of true seriousness, of the moral personality, always the outside for the inside; this obtuseness of conscience which does not recognize the sin that is present in the will, which places evil outside of man, moralizes from the outside and remodels all history. This is the philosophic superficiality of France, which she owes to her fatal notion of religion, the fruit of a life fashioned by Catholicism and absolute monarchy. No profound responsibility or freedom.

Catholic thought cannot conceive of the personality as master of itself and self-conscious. Its boldness and its weakness spring from the same cause: non-responsibility and the vassalage of the conscience, which knows only slavery or anarchy, which proclaims the law but does not obey it, because the law is outside itself, not within itself. Another illusion (that of Quinet, Michelet, etc.) is to leave Catholicism without passing into a positive religion; to struggle against Catholicism with philosophy, a philosophy quite Catholic at bottom, being an anti-Catholic reaction. The mind and conscience fashioned by Catholicism are powerless to rise to another form of religion. From Catholicism, as from Epicureanism, one can no more return than from a mutilation of one's virility.

*Genoa, October 6, 1853.*—The sky is grey and dreary. The rain has fallen all day but has stopped now for a moment. It is four o'clock in the afternoon. I have not been out of doors yet. What have I been doing? I have written to Mme. —— at Naples; then, delighted that I was not obliged to live and trot about as a tourist, and after reading my guide-book and making my plans for tomorrow, I gave the day over to revery. I have been living with the poets. How inwardly refreshing is this Germanic breeze, speaking of faith, the ideal, purity, love, the spiritual life! It is like a memory of another world that comes to visit me in this. I needed it, I lose myself so quickly, I become demagnetized, I abdicate, I deindividualize myself so easily! Schiller and Julius Hammer have brought me back to my native air, for, if my mind is cosmopolitan, my heart is Germanic at bottom, or rather, if I am able to forget myself in all the regions of the soul, I find peace only in the depths of consciousness.—All these lives with which I came in contact, yesterday, for example, in the garden of the Concordia (dilettantes, men of pleasure, etc.), drew me into their orbit, transformed me as if by the philtres of Circe. To become myself again, I must cure myself of all the alien forms which the outer world imposes on me; to recover my nature, I must undergo the painful operation of a daily moulting. What subsists of me, after these discharges, is the memory of my metamorphoses, no reality, but a capacity for all; no matter, but the form, the mould, the method, the image of particular substances and monads; in short, no productive, bold, spontaneous originality, but passive reproductiveness, illimitable impressibility.

Other people influence me not by their wills, which I absolutely resist, nor by their faculties, for I free myself from these and dominate them, in the act of understanding them, but rather by their nature and their instincts, precisely because instinct does not force itself upon me and because I lack it. Whatever in others already exists in myself has little effect upon my nature, but everything they have that is foreign to me invades me at once. My nature has a horror of ignorance and is ashamed of incompleteness. It craves universality, and does not dare to make up its mind to be anything that is finite. It aspires to make itself all to all, it longs for omnicompetence and ubiquity. What it fears above everything is being confined and duped, duped by itself or by others. It strains towards all-awareness, which implies the possession of unity in the experience of infinite diversity. That is why the unknown is for me an enemy, a menace, a humiliation, even while it is a joy and a discovery. It diminishes me in order to enlarge me; it is an iceberg to melt, a sphinx to subdue.

Subtle perception, tenacity of thought, a faculty of combining, classifying, distinguishing and analyzing to a rather high degree, a great need for construction and totality, a slothful and too exacting talent for expression and representation, an imagination exerted only in the interests of thought, a timid, diffident, arbitrary character, a soul that is tender to the point of mysticism: there is my inventory. This is the nature of a writer who is more earnest than amusing, more critical than inventive, more a philosopher than a poet, above all a moralist, psychologist and literary judge, indicating at once what is and what ought to be, the reality and the ideal, in human things. Why not accept myself as I am? Assert myself in my own nature? Win recognition for my own special power and gifts? Console myself by the acquisition of an aptitude and the feeling for a new way of life, instead of always measuring my present inferiority with everyone else?

*Turin, October 11, 1853.*—My third day at Turin has slipped away . . . I have penetrated further into the peculiar genius of this town and people; I have felt it living and emerging slowly in more distinct impressions. This is what especially occupies me: to grasp the soul of things, and the national soul; to live the objective life, to open for myself a new moral fatherland, to win the freedom of this unknown world and enrich myself with this other form of existence; in short, to feel it from within, to unite myself with it and reproduce it sympathetically. This is the goal and the recompense of my effort.

The problem began to clear for me today, on the terrace of the military hospital, facing the Alps, in the fresh, transparent air, under a stormy sky.—But this intuition is only a synthesis wrought by instinct, to which everything, streets, houses, landscape, accent, dialect, physiognomies, history, habits, etc., etc., all contribute their atoms.—I might call it the ideal integration of a people, its reduction to the generative point, its entrance into consciousness.—This point explains the rest, arts, religion, history, politics, customs, and without it nothing can be explained. The ancients realized their consciousness in the national god; the modern nationalities, more complicated and less artistic, are more difficult to decipher.—It is always the δαίμων, the gift, the fatum, the horoscope, the inner genius, the mission, the primitive nature—what people want and what they are able to do; their strength and its limits, in quality and quantity.

The wholesome, chaste, tonic air of thought and the spiritual life bathed me with the wind blowing down from the Alps: I breathed the atmosphere of inner freedom. I hailed with emotion and rapture the mountains whence came to me this feeling of strength and purity. I seemed to emerge from the heavy, sensual realm of passion and mount into a more ethereal sphere of the soul. Beatrice held out her hand to me.—The spell broken, Rinaldo leaving Armida, the poetry of the North, Maya overcome, the Brahman victor over all seductions, the flesh, Satan and nature as symbols of the Middle Ages, the freedom of the Alps; a thousand sensations, analogies and thoughts assailed me.—The history of the subalpine regions, too, from the Ligurians to Hannibal, from Hannibal to Charlemagne, from Charlemagne to Napoleon, rose before my mind.—All the points of view, picturesque, topographical, ethnographical, historical, psychological, ideal, superimposed themselves on one another, yielding glimpses of each through the others, as it were concentrically. I was alive objectively and subjectively: I rejoiced and my mind drank it in. Sight passed into vision without any touch of hallucination, and the landscape was my instructor, my Virgil.

I could also perceive the difference between myself and the majority of travellers, all of whom have a special object and content themselves with one or with several things, while I desire everything or nothing and strain perpetually towards the whole, whether of all objects brought together or all the elements of the thing before me. In other words, I desire the sum of all desires and I wish to know the sum of the different parts of knowledge. Always the complete, the absolute, the *teres atque rotundum,* sphericity, non-resignation. In short, always the aspiration that outruns one's power and therefore attains only the outline, the presentiment, the provisional.—Well, today at least, I accepted myself and even felt a kind of satisfaction in my nature and a measure of pride in myself.

*October 27, 1853.*—I thank thee, God, for the hour I have just passed, kneeling, in thy presence. Thy will was clear to me; I have measured my faults, reckoned up my griefs, felt thy goodness towards me. I have tasted my nothingness. Thou hast given me thy peace. In bitterness there is sweetness, in affliction joy, in contrition strength, in the God who punishes the God who loves; there is honey in the jaws of the lion. To lose one's life that one may find it, to give that one may receive, to possess nothing that one may conquer all, to renounce oneself that God may give himself to us,— what an impossible problem but what a sublime reality! Without suffering, one cannot really know felicity; the redeemed are happier than the elect, and the converted sinner knows a bliss more divine than the felicity of Jove.

The apotheosis of grief, the transfiguration of evil by good: this is the divine marvel *par excellence.* Through love to bring back the free creature to God, and the evil world to the good; this is the summit of the creative effort, this is the eternal will of the infinite mercy. Every converted soul is a symbol of the world's history. To be happy, to possess eternal life, to be in God, to be saved are all the same thing: this is the solution of the problem, the end of existence. And felicity increases just as wretchedness may. Eternal growth in immutable peace, a deepening that is ever more profound, a possession of celestial joy that is ever more intense, more spiritual, this is happiness. Happiness has no bounds, for God has no bottom, no shores; and happiness is the conquest of God through love.

The centre of life is not in thought, or in feeling, or in will, or even in consciousness, in so far as this thinks, feels or desires, for a moral truth may still escape us, although it has been grasped and possessed in all these ways. Deeper than consciousness there exists a being which is our very substance, our nature. Only the truths that have entered this last region, that have become ourselves, that have become spontaneous and involuntary, instinctive and unconscious, are really our life, something more than our property. So long as we can distinguish the least space between the truth and us, we are outside of it. Thought, feeling, desire, the consciousness of life are not yet quite life. And we can only find our peace and rest in life, in the eternal life. And the eternal life is the divine life, it is God. To be divine is thus the end of life: then only can truth no longer be lost by us, for then it is no longer outside of us, or even in us; we are it and it is we. We are a truth, a will, a work of God. Freedom is nature at last, the creature is one with its Creator, one through love; it is what it was meant to be. Its education is accomplished, and its final happiness begins. The sun of time sets, the light of eternal beatitude appears.

Our carnal hearts may call this mysticism, but it is the mysticism of Jesus: "I am one with my Father. Ye shall be one with me. We shall be one with you."

*January 31, 1854.*—A walk: the air incredibly pure, delights for the eye, a warm and gently caressing sunlight, one's whole being joyous. A spring-like charm. Felt to my marrow this purifying, moving influence, laden with poetry and tenderness; had a strong religious feeling of gratitude and wonder. Seated motionless on a bench in the Tranchées, beside the ditches with their garb of moss, carpeted with grass, I felt intensely, delightfully alive, and let the great, buoyant waves of the music of a brass band that reached me from the Terrace of Saint-Antoine surge through me, opening my eyes again and again to absorb the feeling of universal life, the plants and the hillsides. Rejoiced as a lizard might, as a blind or a deaf man might, a painter, a poet. But I had to rejoice alone.— Forgotten impressions came back from my childhood and school-

days and those indescribable effects that colours and shadows, sunlight, hedges, birdsongs have on the soul that is opening to poetry.
I was young again, full of wonder, simple as candour and innocence
itself, I gave myself up to life and nature; they lulled me with an
infinite gentleness; I was touched by the fairy's finger and understood the language of things and beings.

To open oneself in purity to nature, which is ever pure, to permit this immortal life to pass into us is to listen to the voice of
God. Sensation may be a prayer, and self-abandonment may also be
self-communion.

*February 18, 1854.*—To substitute the verb for the adjective is to
kill scholastic psychology, for it is to substitute the activities of
the soul for that mosaic of pieces and fragments which we call faculties and sub-faculties; it is to put organology in the place of anatomy, life, flexible, rich, all one, in the place of the fibres of the
cadaver, the creative and durable force in the place of the created
and uncertain tool, in short, the spirit in the place of matter.—The
substantive is the natural form of French thought, and that is why
it is not philosophical: philosophy is the consciousness of mystery,
and the mystery is genesis, becoming, appearance, in other words
the emergence from nothingness, generation and birth, in short, the
verb. German philosophy thinks with the verb.

Everything congeals and solidifies, everything crystallizes in our
language, which seeks form and not substance, the result and not its
formation, in short, what is seen rather than what is thought, the
outer rather than the inner.—We like the attainment of the aim, not
the pursuit of the aim, the goal, not the road, the idea that is ready-
made, the bread that is ready-baked; just the opposite of Lessing.
We desire conclusions. This clarity of the ready-made is a superficial clarity, a physical, outward, solar clarity, so to speak; but,
lacking the sense of genesis, it is the clarity of the incomprehensible,
the clarity of the opaque, of the obscure. We are always frolicking
on the surface, our mind is formal, that is, frivolous and material,
or rather artistic and not philosophical, for what it desires is the

figure, the fashion, the manner of being of things, and not their deeper life, their soul, their secret.

*From Vevey to Geneva, March 16, 1854.*—Dreamed for a long while, following the lines of the shores and the ripples of the wake of the boat.—There is a poignant melancholy in feeling one's decline, and every power that leaves us is a foretaste of the decay which is bitterer than death. What makes this pain so keen is that one feels one has been struck in one's very soul, diminished in one's humanity. To climb down again in the scale of beings: is not this the most frightful of all things?—Yes, unless one has placed one's dignity and happiness in that which cannot perish, in the consciousness of self, the immortal element of the soul. To detach oneself from everything that is mortal, within us as well as outside us, is the way to save our peace.

What does this lake say to me with its serene sadness, level, dull and calm, reflecting the mountains and the clouds, with all their monotony and their cold pallor? That the voyage through life with all its disenchantments is still possible to duty inspired with the remembrance of heaven.—I had a clear and very deep feeling of the flight of all things, the fatality of every life, the melancholy that lies beneath the surface of everyone's existence, but also of the sure foundation that lies under these restless waves.

Bear witness to the truth you have received, help others to live and live well, do not grieve any heart or soul, dare oftener to be earnest, true, simple, loving; be less circumspect, more good-natured, more open, and you will have more occasion to do good; and to do good is the sweetest satisfaction that a man can feel. To be understood, appreciated and loved comes after this, for the satisfaction of the conscience is even more intense than that of the heart.

*March 29, 1854 (morning).*—Hygiene of the soul.—Place yourself in harmony with the outer world; do not strive or cry. There is nothing more hostile to one's inner freedom than to break off communication with nature. Bathe yourself in the calm of the morning light till you feel the rapport is reëstablished, till forms and colours, distant objects and the plasticity of things are clearly, peacefully, vigorously reproduced in you.

Felt this morning (from seven to half-past seven) all the notes of the nervous tonality succeed one another in myself.—Had a good deal of trouble recovering objectivity, that is, forgetting myself, and growing calm. The body, sick, irritated, thrusts itself between things and us.

*Entre la joie et moi toujours passe quelque ombre.*

I am approaching steppes that are foreign to me in the psychic life. What was the strongest in me is becoming the weakest.—Observe them, without putting my heart into them, without being irritated, without being troubled.

The means of education change, even if the end remains the same: contentment through effort yields to contentment through patience. Be content in spite of everything; remain calm: this is the strongest strength. To liberate oneself from one's nerves, from one's visible and corporeal soul, to retire into a more inward region, this is the needful thing.

*(Evening.)*—With my habit of observing myself coldly and as a not-myself, I felt the various regions of my brain living under my skull; I felt a sort of dull, sickly vibration, like that which heat produces in a soft substance which it penetrates, then light contractions, superficial or internal, affecting the whole or certain parts (the temples and the back of the head), then a painful tension in the very centre of the encephalon. A slight effort at composition which I had to make between four and six o'clock gave me as it were a contusion, completely floored me; my nervous fibre, having no elasticity, could not resume its play and its normal state.—A painful emotion, an over-strong sensation, a tension of the will, of sight or hearing is more than I have power for at present. I walk, eat and sleep well, I do not feel any muscular lassitude, and yet I

have no energy. Anything vital and virile in the way of action seems remote and almost beyond my reach. I envy children, young men and men and look at them as they pass as if they were images of what I am no longer. All the superfluities of life have been withdrawn from me, and even much of what is necessary. This feeling of impoverishment, decrepitude, impotence is singularly depressing. The harvest time comes, and the reaper sinks in his furrow, overcome with malaria. I have loved the life of thought over-much, I have made it too much my refuge, my asylum, my stronghold; it was in a way my secret idol, and it is shattered. The hand of God is upon me and searches me. God leaves me all the rest, ease, leisure, independence, the family circle, position; he forbids me only one tree in the garden, the tree of knowledge. Happily, the tree of life remains. Renounce, take your cross, detach your heart from everything that can be lost, learn to be satisfied with little, to enjoy the fruits of the tree of life, the one thing needful; do this and you will recover your calm again. Acquiesce, bend, submit; no agitation, resistance, anger, bitterness, dejection. What God does is well done and his will is your good.—You have not been able to simplify your heart, curb your desires, circumscribe your plans, and now you are forced to do so; you wished to know your true limits, and here are limits that admit of no dispute; you were restless, turbulent, changeable, ambitious, and here is something that will make humility and moderation easier for you.

Even from evil one can extract good: one can learn first of all to know, then to endure affliction; one can receive instruction and benefit from it, discover one's true duty, one's true strength and support. Is the religion of sickness truer than that of health? Yes, if it bears the test where the other breaks down. A faith that preserves our peace in health and sickness is truer than one that is troubled at the passing of health, just as a substance that is proof against water and fire is firmer than one that is proof against water only.

*July 27, 1854 (5 p. m.)*.—I have finished the *Histoire hollandaise* [1] of Mme. d'Arbouville with a feeling of being gripped as powerfully as I was the first time I read it, with my eyes full of tears and my forehead bathed in perspiration. This story pierces me to the marrow. It is terrifying in its truthfulness. I felt this in the intoxication of calm, the infinite impassibility that pervaded me. The poetry of the cloister, tranquil to a degree that makes one shiver, that slow destruction of all the mortal fibres, all the loves of earth, that deep, funereal peace have filled my soul as the shadows fill a valley at the fall of day. The nostalgic longing for heaven possessed my heart. The thirst for eternity, which time exasperates, the great silence of the world and the soul, when one hears God, all this life of privation, of waiting and immutability, this drama of solitude, this languor, ineffable and ascetic, this prodigious pathos of Catholicism so overwhelmed me that I shuddered. Is it sublime? Is it monstrous?— This is one of the religious forms, one of the states of consciousness that nothing can replace. It is the abstract, the pure form of the love of God, of sanctity. The soul retires into its divine generality, fearing to lose God in the details of a dispersive life and dull the divine sense by the touch of worldly souls. The cloister is a simplification of life, the refuge of exile, the peristyle of paradise, the haven of weak or broken souls, who need the irrevocable, the harbour of rest and silence where one can sleep in God and be healed of life or escape it. He who has never had or has no more faith in life and happiness, who expects nothing of time or the affections, nothing of men and things, who has felt all desire perish in him, he can seek and find opening for him the doors of a monastery. For him the world has nothing more to give.

*(7.30 p. m.)*.—I have been carried far away on trains of revery. I caught glimpses of what a serious passion might make of me, I have dreamed of forgotten persons and circumstances, and sounded the depths of my heart. I have realized sadly how vulnerable I am;

[1] The works of Mme. Sophie d'Arbouville (1810–1850) have been collected in three volumes: *Poésies et Nouvelles,* Paris, 1855.

irony, mockery, sneers, even the coldness of others have a lamentable power over me. I do not dare to act, love or produce without
the approval of my circle. I have a timid, fearful, pusillanimous
will. I dare to assert only my ideas, only things that concern me outwardly, not my own personality. Having no faith in myself, I am, as
it were, ashamed of my individuality and afraid of anything that
affirms it, pins it down, determines it. Other people are unable to
make me do anything, but they are able to paralyze me completely.
By wounding my vanity or my feelings, which are terribly susceptible, they disgust me and discourage me with everything.—Deep
down in my timorous self, I am filled with passionate desires, and
I have a longing for independence without having the strength for
it. Distrustful, fearful, sensitive, with an immense faculty for suffering and enjoying, I am afraid of love, life and men, because I need
them so intensely. I dread all my instincts, and my life is a perpetual
constraint and reticence. I yield to one instinct only, that of treating all my passions icily and fearfully. I have a terror of destiny,
and every impulse appals me.—I always recognize in this the effect
of my orphaned childhood and the derisive atmosphere of Geneva.
The organ of sensibility never grew robust enough in me to brave
the inclemencies of the outer world, and, in order not to be wounded
in its over-refinement, it has grown used to living only within. I am
not equipped to beat my path through circumstances, and I have
never enjoyed anything except in imagination. I shall have dreamed
all the lives, to console myself for not having lived one. I shall have
watched all the realities pass, lest I should give men any hold over
my happiness. I shall have dared nothing, in order to be less dependent and suffer less. I shall have lived as little as possible, in
order not to invite the blows of fate. This is a gloomy oracle. But
unless conscience and the voice of God cause me to hear some
other, I shall be obliged to submit to it.—My nature, timid before
the unknown, discouraged and mistrustful, ardent and passionate,
must have God as an ally, clear proof as a consort, duty as a stay.

—As God sees best! This is a soothing thought to set at rest the pangs of responsibility.

*November 5, 1854.*—Today, for five hours, thoroughly exercised my dexterity of eye and hand, with the children as a fascinated and applauding audience (dominoes, toys, cards, chairs, glasses of water, decanters, knives, brooms, puzzles, a variety of games). Dashed about like a goblin among all these possessions of the house, bobbing and tossing about and balancing everything, setting everything dancing and turning somersaults. It was mechanics in fun, involving the sense of weight and space, the sense of combinations and the unexpected, that I brought into play, and this is by no means useless. All this childish nonsense develops the initiative of the imagination, precision in the organs, while resting the mind and rejuvenating the character, and gives amusement while it gives pleasure. Conquering any difficulty always gives one a secret joy, for it means pushing back a boundary-line and adding to one's liberty; every victory magnifies us, even the most imperceptible victory, even over a toy. Why? Because every victory is at bottom a victory over oneself and consequently an enlargement of oneself. When I make a pyramid stand on end, it is not so much that I am subduing matter as that I am diminishing some incapacity in myself. Thus every limit I extend is a power that I acquire, a bondage that I break, an augmentation of knowledge and strength. To struggle, that is life: to grow is its reward.—This is the philosophy of play; everything hangs together.

*November 19, 1854.*—Read the last two volumes of *David Copperfield* . . . Agnes bound me again with her magic charm and filled my eyes with tears. I think she is my favourite heroine, or rather my dearest feminine ideal: perfect devotion, serene and heavenly purity, a deep, sweet calm, invincible fidelity, a beautiful, great, simple, tender soul, religious and spotless, whose influence soothes and fortifies one, makes one better and larger. Ah! how well I know that I could love to distraction, when I meet these characters in fiction that answer to my dreams.—If I have been cold all these years, it

is because reality has not offered me anything complete, and because every rent in the ideal lacerates love within me. Not yet, in
any order of things, have I known how to renounce anything, or
how to content myself with the less than perfect; the ideal has prevented me from living, and my ambition has never been able to find
a satisfaction on a level with its secret hopes.—If I could only see
my own life poetically! But it seems to me the merest bauble, the
most prosaic jest; my poetry is all outside of me. That is my
trouble. Diffidence and irony with myself have caused my weakness;
I have kept up against myself the deadly warfare that circumstances
made on me in youth. I cannot see myself either historically or
heroically, and so I do not take myself seriously; I remain insignificant to myself, and I play with my nature as with a child's toy.—It
is the same with the affections and the characters I encounter on my
path; I never believe in a piece of good luck, in a favour of Providence, and I tell myself that it cannot be anything much, since it is
given to me. Benefits are proportionate to those who receive them.
One who mocks himself becomes too easily ungrateful and offensive
to others.—It was a keen instinct in —— to forbid me to scoff
at myself! She was certainly right.—Not to take yourself seriously
is to affront God, who permits his holy spirit to dwell in you and
places as high a value on your soul as upon the most greatly privileged. This irony is an irreverence to the gift that is in you; this
lack of respect is an ingratitude for the worth of an individual; in a
word, this trifling is irreligious as well as injurious; and, if the fear
of God is the beginning of wisdom, the feeling of personal dignity
is the beginning of strength.—The strong man, the man of genius, is
one who gives to his private experiences a universally representative
value, one, that is, who can see in things everything they contain
and can extract their typical significance. Jean Paul and Emerson
say that the great authors are men who have dared to affirm themselves. Well, to dare to affirm oneself, one must feel that one is a
legitimate spokesman of Providence; therefore, one must think
nobly of oneself and greatly of one's task, one must renew, in one's

heart, through contemplation, the ideal of human majesty and the feeling of the infinite worth of every soul.

A very lively sense of caricature, of the contrast of things with the ideal, has made you ironical; dig deeper into reality and its richness will compel you to take it less lightly.—Only God cannot become ridiculous, and everything is laughable that is not God or of God, but, as God is everywhere, everything can become serious again. *(Midnight.)*

*December 17, 1854.*—It is when we are doing nothing in particular that we are living through all our being, and we cease to augment ourselves only to possess and ripen ourselves. The will is in suspense, but nature and time are always at work; and although our life is no longer our work, the work goes on none the less. With us, without us, or in spite of us, our existence travels through its appointed phases, our invisible Psyche weaves the silk of its chrysalis, our destiny fulfils itself, and all the hours of our life labour together towards that flowering-time which we call death. All this activity is fated; neither sleep nor idleness interrupts it, but it may become free and moral, a joy instead of a terror.

*February 2, 1855.*—Like a bubble of air bobbing for an instant on the surface of a restless ocean, our life wanders, heedless, unquiet, over the grave towards which it gravitates. Tossed between life and death, between Vishnu and Siva, we are but ephemeras whose years are seconds in the weeks of nature. Never have I felt more clearly the inanity of our existence, in the presence of the eternal and the infinite. Our greatness lies in reducing this life to the point where it can be offered to the Being, in tearing ourselves away from time, the finite, the changing, to become citizens of the eternal, the infinite and the permanent, in passing from space to spirit, from selfishness to love, from evil to good, from the world to God. This unstable and fleeting life still suffices to yield us the possession of eternal life: it is therefore great enough. Nothing is small when it contains the infinite in germ; and God is in us and asks only to live in us . . . To open oneself to God in order to cease to die, to escape what passes away by taking refuge in the soul's centre, to feel oneself immortal, greater than Sirius or Aldebaran, to resume one's dignity with gratitude, to glorify human life, the cradle of the supreme life, to recognize in oneself the portion of nothingness and the portion of being: this is the great art of living, nowhere better summarized than in religion, or better realized than in Christianity. Mortal life is the apprenticeship of the eternal life, and the eternal life begins the moment one ceases to be the egoistic self and becomes God dwelling in us.

*March 28, 1855.*—There is not a blade of grass that has not a story to tell, not a heart that has not its romance, not a face whose smile does not mask a sorrow, not a life that does not hide a secret, its goad or its thorn. Everywhere grief, hope, comedy, tragedy; and even under the petrifaction of age, as in the tortured forms of certain fossils, one finds the agitations and torments of youth. This thought is the magic wand of the Andersens and Balzacs, the poets and preachers; it strips the scales from our carnal eyes and gives us a clear vision of human life; it opens to the ear a world of unknown melodies and makes us understand the thousand tongues of nature. The sorrows of love give us the gift of tongues; grief makes us seers and sorcerers.

*April 16, 1855.*—Felt this morning the prodigious effect of climate on one's state of mind. I was Italian and Spanish in this clear, blue air and this southern sun. The very walls smile at one. And I was in love with all nature. The chestnuts were in full bloom; with their glossy buds, shining like little flames at the curved tips of every branch, they represented the candelabra of spring in the eternal dance of nature. How young everything was, how kindly, how gracious!—The moist freshness of the tufts of grass, the transparent shadows in the courtyards, the vigour of the russet towers of St. Pierre, the white curbstones of the streets. I felt that I was a child. The sap of life mounted again in my veins as in the plants. All my sensations were gay once more; I seemed to have shaken off a whole outworn chrysalis, wrinkled with cares and vexations, and to have been reborn a butterfly. Oh! how sweet a thing is a little simple happiness, a little pure, childlike joy!—And now a brass band that has stopped in the street makes my heart leap as it did at eighteen. It is the perpetual intoxication, the sparkling of hope in the rosy champagne of the present, the state of the young girl entering the enchanted garden of life, the state of one in love. Oh! I am still young. Thanks be to God, there have been so many weeks and months when I thought myself an old man. Come, poetry, nature, youth, love, mould my life anew with your fairy hands, begin your immortal songs in me again, sing your siren melodies, let me drink from the cup of immortality, lead me back to the Olympus of the soul. Or rather, away with this paganism! God of joy and pain, do with me as thou wilt; sorrow is good and mirth is also good. Thou fillest my cup with joy. I accept it from thee and give thee thanks for it.

*April 17, 1855.*—The weather continues incredibly pure, bright and warm. At ten o'clock in the evening, I am writing in my shirt-sleeves, beside my open window. July at the heels of February . . . The day is filled with the singing of birds and the night with stars. Nature has grown benign, and her graciousness clothes itself in splendour.

For almost two hours I have been contemplating this magnificent spectacle, feeling myself in the temple of the infinite, in the presence of the worlds, the guest of God in this immense nature. How all these stars wandering in the pale ether drew me far from earth; and what inexpressible peace, what a dew of the eternal life they shed upon the soul in ecstasy! I felt the world floating like a skiff in this blue ocean. It is good to feed oneself with this deep, calm delight; it purges and enlarges the whole man. I gave myself up to it gratefully and submissively.

*April 21, 1855.*—A good deal of reading. My mind has been vigorous, a rare thing for the last two years, since my severe hemorrhages.—Exact analysis of moral synonymies, erudition, ethnography, comparative anatomy, the cosmic system: this is the way I have filled my time. I have been reading Prichard, Hollard, Carus (*Erdenleben*), Liebig (*Animal Chemistry*).—I have run through the universe, from the deepest depths of the empyrean to the peristaltic motions of the atoms in the elementary cell; I have dilated in the infinite, mentally liberated from time and space, reducing the boundless creation to a point without dimensions, and seeing in this point the multitude of suns, Milky Ways, stars and nebulæ.

I tried to trace the curve which the point of my lifted finger described in space, relatively to the absolute fixed point, and I found an integral exceeding any capacity of mathematics at its two extremities. The pulsation of the capillary vessels, the plastic molecular action, the conflict between muscle and terrestrial gravity (unconscious factors), the voluntary movement (human factors), then the circular curve around the earth's axis, with a velocity relative to the latitude, and to the radius of the little circle described by this parallel, then the cycloid due to the displacement of the earth, rising to the second degree because it turns around the sun, and to the third because this orbit is an ellipse; then the movement of our sun, which is perhaps a double and conjugate sun; and this system itself in motion in our stellar crystalline heaven, which without doubt moves in its turn in the measureless depths of the celestial abyss: such is this integral of integrals.

And on all sides mysteries, marvels, prodigies boundlessly stretching out, numberless and bottomless. I felt this unfathomable intuition alive in me; I touched, felt, tasted, embraced my nothingness and my immensity, I kissed the hem of the garment of God and gave him thanks for being mind and for being life. These moments are glimpses of the divine, when one grows conscious of one's immortality, when one realizes that an eternity is not too much for the study of the thoughts of the Eternal and his works, and when one adores in stupefied ecstasy, in the ardent humility of love.

*May 23, 1855.*—Irresolution, sloth, fickleness, despondency, pusillanimity, all my old enemies assailed me this morning . . . You surrender your liver to the dark vulture of gloom, and with a frantic stupidity spend your time eating out your heart. This is the slow suicide of one who hangs himself. You rest on the points of all the most painful ideas, then when they have pierced their holes in you, you turn and turn until they become drills, and you take no rest that does not transpierce you in every direction. This bitter, senseless pleasure becomes a mania . . . All the harmful passions attract us, as chasms do, by vertigo. Weakness of will leads to weakness of mind, and the abyss, for all its horror, fascinates one as a refuge. Frightful danger! This abyss is within us; this gulf opens like the vast jaws of the infernal serpent that is intent on devouring us, it is the depths of our being; our freedom as it were swims over this void, which forever aspires to swallow it up. Our only talisman is the moral force assembled around its centre, the conscience, a tiny, inextinguishable flame whose light is known as Duty and whose heat is called Love. This little flame must be the star of our life, it alone can guide our shivering ark through the tumult of the great waters, give us escape from the temptations of the sea, from the monsters and tempests vomited forth by the night and the flood. Faith in God, in a holy, merciful, fatherly God, is the divine ray that kindles this flame. Oh, how I feel the deep and terrible poetry of primitive terrors, from which the theogonies came forth; how the history of unchained forces, savage chaos and the nascent world becomes my own life and substance; how all grows light and becomes a symbol of the great, unchanging thought, the thought of God throughout the universe! How present to me, how sensible and inward is the unity of everything! I seem to perceive the sublime theme which, through the infinite spheres of existence, under all the modes of space and time, all created forms reproduce and sing in the breast of the eternal harmony. I feel like Dante reascending from the infernal shades to the regions of light, and, as with Milton's Satan, my flight across chaos carries me to paradise. Beatrice and Raphael, the messengers of eternal love, have shown me the path. Heaven, hell, the worlds are within us. Man is the great abyss.

*July 27, 1855.*—So life wears away, tossed like a boat by the

waves, from right to left, up and down, drenched with the bitter
spray, now sullied by the foam, now cast upon the shore, then seized
again by the caprice of the tide. Such at least is the life of the heart
and the passions, the life that Spinoza and the stoics reproved, the
opposite of that serene and contemplative life, always even as the
light of the stars, wherein man lives in peace and sees all things
under the eye of eternity; the opposite also of the life of conscience,
wherein God speaks alone and all self-will abjures itself before his
will made manifest.

I pass from one to another of these three existences, which are
equally familiar to me; and this very mobility deprives me of the
advantages of each. My heart is gnawed with scruples, the soul cannot crush the needs of the heart, and the troubled conscience cannot well distinguish any longer, in the chaos of contradictory inclinations, the voice of duty or the supreme will. The want of simple
faith, the indecision that springs from versatility and self-distrust,
almost always throws into doubt and uncertainty everything that
concerns only my personal life. I am afraid of the subjective life
and recoil from every enterprise, desire, demand or promise that
might involve me in the world of reality; I have a terror of action
and only feel at ease in the impersonal, disinterested, objective life
of thought. Why is this? Because of timidity. Whence comes this
timidity? From the excessive development of the reflective power,
which has almost destroyed my spontaneity, my impulse and my
instinct, and so even my assurance and confidence. When the time
for action comes, I see on all sides snares and pitfalls, causes for
error and repentance, hidden threats and troubles ill-concealed, and
naturally I dare not budge. Irony early overtook my childhood; and,
not to be vanquished by destiny, my nature, I believe, armed itself
with a circumspection that was sufficiently strong not to be surprised by any solicitations. This strength makes my weakness. I have
a horror of being deceived, especially by myself, and I deprive myself of everything in order not to beguile myself or to be beguiled:
humiliation is the pain I most dread, and therefore pride should be

the deepest of my vices. This is logical, but it is not true: it rather seems that distrust, an incurable doubt of the future, a sense of the justice but not of the goodness of God, incredulity, in a word, is my misfortune and my sin. Every act is a hostage delivered into the hands of an avenging fate. This instinctive persuasion freezes one. That every act is a pledge confided to a fatherly Providence is the faith that brings calm with it.

To me, pain is a punishment and not a mercy, that is why I have a secret horror of it. And feeling that I am vulnerable at every point, open to affliction everywhere, I remain motionless, like a timid child who, left alone in his father's laboratory, dares not touch anything for fear of the springs, explosions and catastrophes that might start up and burst from any corner at the least movement of his inexperienced hands. I trust God, directly and in nature, but I distrust all agents, free and evil, man and men, the inconstancies and the deeds of society; I feel or foresee evil, moral and physical, as the consequence of every error, fault or sin, and I feel that suffering is a reproach.

In essence, is it not a vast self-love? Is it not the purism of perfection, the refusal to accept the human condition, a tacit protest against the order of the world that lies at the root of your faint-heartedness? It is the all or nothing, titanic ambition, idle from distaste, a longing for the ideal driven inward, the retreat of Achilles into his tent, offended dignity and wounded pride refusing themselves to whatever seems beneath them; it is an irony that takes neither itself nor reality seriously, in comparison with the infinite that is glimpsed and dreamed of. It is the state of mental reservation that yields to circumstances for form's sake, but does not acknowledge them at heart because it does not see the divine order and necessity in them. It is perhaps disinterestedness through indifference, which does not complain at what is, but cannot say that it is satisfied. It is philosophic legitimism encamped in a *de facto* society that is not *de jure;* it is the weakness that cannot conquer and yet does not wish to be conquered; it is the spite that breaks with whatever can do without its co-operation; it is the isolation of the disappointed soul which has abjured even hope.

But all this is only a test to which one has to submit. Its providential purpose is no doubt to lead one to the true renunciation, the sign of which is charity. It is when we no longer expect anything for ourselves that we are able to love. To do good to men through love for them, to turn one's talent to account to please the Father from whom we hold it for his service: this is the sign and the means of the healing of this inner discontent, which conceals itself under indifference.

*September 4, 1855.*—In the internal government of oneself, the parliamentary form succeeds the monarchical. Good sense, conscience, desire, reason, the present and the memory of the past, the old man and the new man, prudence and generosity take the floor in turn, the reign of the barristers begins; chaos replaces order and the twilight the light. The simple will is the autocratic regime, interminable discussion is the deliberative regime of the soul. The first is plain, clear, quick and strong, the second confused, indecisive, slow and weak; the result is that the latter settles by exhausting them the questions which the former settles by a single thrust; the one is preferable from the theoretical point of view, the other from the practical point of view. To know and to act are their two respective advantages.

As a better course, one should bring into action the three powers in the soul, superimposing the executive on the legislative and co-ordinating the judiciary. In addition to the man of counsel, there should be the man of action and the man of justice. Reflection, with you, comes to no conclusion because it returns upon itself, wrangling and disputing; you lack the general who commands and the judge who decides. Will and decision of mind are indispensable in order to limit the critical force of reflection. A prolific mother of evasions, scruples, objections of every kind, the critical faculty, like a refracting prism, breaks the light-rays into a seven-coloured spectrum; like the magic word of a bungling conjuror, it raises twenty goblins that it cannot quell or revoke; it substitutes anatomy for the living creature and cannot see the forest for the trees.

Analysis is dangerous, if it dominates the synthetic power.—Reflection is a formidable thing, if it destroys the faculty of intuition. —Inquiry is fatal if it supplants faith.—To decompose is deadly unless one has, in more than equal strength, the vital energy for combination. The separate action of any of the inner spheres becomes a destructive play when these spheres cease to have the power to return to united action.—The moment the sovereign abdicates, anarchy begins. The moment a body ceases to live, the worms set to work in it.

And just there is the danger that threatens you. You are losing the unity of life, strength, action, the unity of self; you are legion, a parliament, anarchy; you are division, analysis, reflection; you are synonymy, yes and no, dialectics; hence your weakness. The passion for the complete, the abuse of the critical faculty, the mania for anatomy, the distrust of the first movement, the first word, the first idea, this explains the point you have reached. The unity and simplicity of being, confidence, spontaneity, are vanishing out of your life. This is the reason why you cannot act, why you have no character at all.

One must give up the hope of knowing all, desiring and embracing everything; one must confine oneself to some one region, content oneself with some special thing, satisfy oneself with a definite work, dare to be what one is, resign with a good grace what one has not, cleave to one's own person, believe in one's individuality. As Rückert says,

> *Ne pas se plaire seulement aux plus belles choses du monde,*
> *Mais trouver la plus belle du monde la chose qui vous plaît.*

Self-distrust consumes you; trust, abandon yourself, surrender yourself, believe, and you will be on the road to recovery. The proof that this tendency is evil is that it makes you unhappy and prevents you from acting. Incredulity is death; and irony, turned against self, like dejection, is a form of incredulity. It is easier to condemn oneself than to sanctify oneself, and self-disgust springs more from pride than from humility . . . True humility is contentment.

*November 12, 1855.*—When it is changed in its population, its customs and its spirit, is a country still one's fatherland? Our parties have disgusted me with political life; I cannot give my heart to any of them, for I feel no respect or enthusiasm for any, and self-interested conflicts have always been nauseous to me. But whence comes this complete detachment? Everything, alas, induces it in me: my antipathy for our national character, and for our climate; the isolation in which I have been left among my equals; the want of any point of civic attachment. I love my relatives and my friends, our Church and our schools, but I do not like our political life or our social life. Geneva gives me no joy, and I have never permitted it to cause me pain. I have not found a mother in it, and the filial sentiment has slowly died in my soul. In a word, I am still a voter, but I am no longer a citizen.

This is the fact, and it is an evil, a fault and a misfortune. It is a lowering of one's life, a lowering of one's duty. Poor is the life that does not extend far enough for one to love one's country; a conscience is a mutilated thing when patriotism is stricken from its list of duties. One must give one's heart. The habit of critical detachment has separated you from Geneva. Struggle against this habit, revive the civic feeling by studying the history of your country and by sharing in the common life. The aerostatic existence which you ordinarily lead contributes to this indifference; by seeking to be useful, by associating yourself with works of which you approve, you will create ties for yourself, you will become interested. Between egoism and human sympathy you will reëstablish an essential sphere, that of the civic life.

But can we cleave to those who do not cleave to us? Yes. There is such a thing as disinterested love, the most beautiful of the loves, which gives and offers itself unwearyingly and without expectation of return, which is never ridiculous, even in its own eyes, for it has no bargains to drive and therefore is never cheated.

*January 21, 1856.*—Yesterday seems as remote to me as last year; the past is only an outline for my memory, as the starry sky is for my eye. I can no more recover one of my days in my memory than a glass of water poured into a lake; it is not so much lost as melted away; the individual has returned to the mass; the divisions of time are categories that cannot any more shape my life than compartments traced by a stick in water can leave a lasting imprint. I am fluid, I must resign myself to it.

How true it is that our destinies are decided by nothings, and that a slight imprudence, coinciding with one insignificant chance, like a raindrop falling on an acorn, may raise the tree upon which we and others may be crucified! What happens is quite different from what we intend. We intend something good, and it leads to disaster. The serpent of fatality, or, to speak more truly, the law of life, the very force of things, once intertwined with one or two very simple facts, cannot then by any effort be cut away; the logic of situations and characters inevitably produces some fearful denouement. This is the fascination of destiny, which obliges us to feed our misfortune with our own hand, to prolong the existence of our vulture, to cast into the holocaust of our chastisement, one after another, our powers, our qualities, our very virtues, in expiation of some negligence; in a word, which brings home to us our nothingness, our dependence and the implacable majesty of the Law. The sense that a Providence exists softens the punishment, but does not cancel it. The wheels of the divine chariot crush us first, in order to satisfy justice and give an example to men; then a hand is held out to us, to raise us, or at least to reconcile us with the love concealed beneath the justice. Pardon can never precede repentance, and repentance begins only with humility. And as long as any fault seems a trifle, as long as imprudence or negligence strikes us in its excusable aspect and not in its enormity, its culpability, as long as Job complains, as long as Providence seems too severe, as long as one

inwardly protests against fate, or has any doubt of the perfect justice of God, one has not yet entire humility, or any true repentance. The expiation can only be spared after one has accepted it;
when one submits sincerely, then is the time that grace can be accorded. Only when pain finds its work done can God dispense us
from it. The ordeal only comes to an end when it has lost its usefulness; therefore it almost never comes to an end.—Faith in the
justice and the love of the Father, who lets us live to teach us to
live in holiness, is therefore the best and the only support against
the sufferings of this life. The root of all our ills is unbelief; we
doubt that what happens to us should have happened; we fancy that
we are wiser than Providence, because at bottom, to avoid fatalism,
we believe in chance. Freedom in subjection, what a problem! And
yet it is to this one always has to return.

*January 26, 1856.*—Philosophy, talk, emotions, pleasures of the
eye, friendship, a few new facts acquired, a good deal of give-and-
take: such has been my day. Epicurean enough, which is to say
pleasant but unfruitful.—Then the heart's complaint became audible
in the far reaches of the inner life, the voice of regret and censure.
How much time lost for loving! What a false shame of one's true
needs! What restlessness in this outward freedom from care! And
what a feeling of emptiness in this existence without a centre, without substance, or any fixed point! You need marriage, an attachment, something to place you, root you, settle and nourish you. And
you blush at this dependence and armour yourself with pride and
raillery against yourself and others. You are afraid of being cheated,
you distrust the world and life and do not wish to expose yourself
to their malignity or seek for what might be refused you. You are
tender, loving, eager for sympathy, but in your timidity you assume
a mask of indifference; you are a mock stoic, a mock egoist, a mock
mute. You turn yourself to stone, as the redskin makes himself appear insensible, in order not to rejoice the enemy; your instinct
seeks to maintain, for want of better, your solitary dignity and impassive serenity. Not daring to suffer, you repress, in the presence of

men, all tears, all complaints and all desires. You are frivolous from an insurmountable timidity, a moral suicide from bashfulness.—You wish to be divined like a woman, and to make demands for yourself or offer yourself revolts you like an act of harlotry, like a baseness, an indecency of the soul.—It is your bad luck, my poor fellow, to have for defects the qualities of the other sex. For what is a grace in woman is a fatal silliness in man.

*May 7, 1856.*—All day long continued Rosenkranz's [1] *History of Poetry,* and did nothing else. All the great names of Spain, Portugal and France, up to Louis XV, have passed before me. It is good to take these rapid surveys; the point of view renovates the subject and modifies all one's old ideas, and this is always agreeable and liberating. For one of my natural tendency, this philosophical and genetic manner of embracing and expounding literary history has a lively attraction. But it is precisely contrary to the French way of proceeding, which scarcely considers anything but the peaks of the subject, linking them together by triangulation and theoretical outlines, and then gives these lines out for the actual high-relief of the landscape. The real formation of public opinion, the public taste, of an established *genre,* cannot be discovered by this abstract method, which suppresses the period of growth in favour of the final fruit, fullness in favour of line, the preparation in favour of the result, the multitude in favour of the chosen type. Thus one obtains an apparent clarity, the clarity of the fact; but a real obscurity remains, the obscurity of the cause. This method is characteristic; it is bound by invisible ties to the respect for usage and fashion, to the Catholic and dualist instinct, which admits two truths, two contradictory worlds, one as substantial as the other, and accepts quite naturally magic, miracles, the incomprehensible, the arbitrary in God, the king, language, etc. It is the philosophy of Chance which has become a habit, an instinct, a belief, second nature. It is the religion of caprice.

[1] *Geschichte der Poesie,* by Rosenkranz, disciple and biographer of Hegel.

By one of those eternal contrasts that redress the balance of things, the Romance peoples, who excel historically in the practical matters of life, have no philosophy of it, while the Germanic peoples, who are lost in the practical side of life, have the philosophy of life. The German, abstract in his life, is concrete in his thought, the reverse of the Frenchman.—By instinct, every being seeks to complete himself outwardly and inwardly; and it is by this same secret law that man seeks woman, that the terrorist loves the pastoral, that women love emotions, that the man of the study admires the man of action, that the most living of peoples is attracted to the most mathematical theory, that every defect a man has gives him a keen perception of any similar defect in his neighbour, etc., etc.—Substance and form are thus contrasted and mathematical intelligences are often attracted by the facts of life, as lively minds are attracted to the study of abstract laws.—Thus, oddly enough, what we think we are is just what we are not, what we would like to be is sometimes the least suited to us; our theory condemns us, and our practice gives the lie to our theories. And this contradiction is a good thing, for it is a source of conflict and movement, a condition of progress. Every life is an inward struggle, every struggle supposes two contrary forces; nothing real is simple, and that which thinks itself simple is the furthest from being so.—The consequence is that every state is a moment in a series, every being is a compromise between contraries, a plexus of contrasts; concrete dialectics is the key that opens to us the understanding of beings in the series of beings, and of states in the series of moments: dynamics is the explanation of equilibrium. Every situation is an equilibrium of forces; every life is a struggle of opposing forces acting within the limits of a certain equilibrium.

I have recognized these two principles a thousand times, but I have never sufficiently applied them.

And to apply is to fecundate, and one only possesses what one fecundates (an idea, a piece of ground, a woman, etc.). To fecundate is to infuse life into a thing, to give inner movement, metamorphosis, growth. A true religion is one that transforms life, a true thought is one that renovates our views and even the things we are thinking about. Truth proves itself by its effects; a truth that changes nothing is sterile, and sterility is death. The sign of life is metamorphosis, and the proof of true life is procreation. What begets nothing is nothing.

*May 9, 1856.*—A historical study that is isolated leads to nothing. The complete and concrete history of the human spirit and of the genius of nations in the integrality of their energy, blossoming in their religion, their literature, their entire destiny: this is the question, this is the thing, this is what is needful. The natural totality, the organic growth, the life, in a word, of individuals, societies, nations, the race, that is what satisfies me and attracts me. Every abstraction is factitious and is only a means, a method, an artifice of study; actually, one must come back to the evolution of the whole, for nothing in nature or history exists apart. Solidarity is the formula of every real existence. Philosophic history, what a splendid subject!

*Pressy,*[1] *June 8, 1856.*—Day of happiness. Gave my heart to everything, to nature, which has been marvellously beautiful today, to the whole family, all of whom I have seen, to the friends I met, to the wild roses in the hedges, to the crickets in the ditch, to the blue sky, dancing with all the enchantments of the hours of day and night, like a rondo of genii with immortal graces, to the good Providence whom I blessed for the joy that flooded me and for the poetry that bathed my soul and pervaded my senses, more and more almost with every moment. When at last I closed the shutters of my little room, blue with the dreamy moonbeams that filtered mysteriously through the trees in the orchard upon which my window opens, and, like a child going to sleep on its mother's breast, closed my eyes to the rocking of our globe in its circular voyage through the ocean of the heavens, the emotion that filled me had reached its most thrilling intensity. The warm, yellow light through

[1] A village near Geneva.

which the green Salève thrust its rounded crests brought back to me sensations of Sicily; the purity of the distant objects, the sharp contours of buildings and foliage, the splendour and the gaiety of the festive landscape, the limpidity of the air awakened in me a thousand memories of happy times; how many ravishing suggestions of similar days and like impressions in all the latitudes! Especially in the evening, with the murmur of the waves on the lake, turning white under the northern breeze, while the tints of the great sunset gradually melted into the rugged peaks of the bluish Jura; and the Mediterranean, the Ocean, the Baltic, Greece, Brittany, Norway, the known and the unknown, and all the plans and backgrounds of a wanderer's life were visible in an infinite perspective. Magnificent frame for the sweetest of reveries!

My head uncovered, the map hung to my shoulder by a cord, I climbed, saturating myself with all these pictures, all this intoxicating music, from Geneva to Pressy, from the town to the village.

*July 1, 1856.*—A man, and still more a woman, always betrays something of his or her nationality; and the women of Russia, like the lakes and rivers of their country, seem to be subject to sudden and even prolonged rigidities. In their undulating mobility, caressing as water, there is always the threat of the ice that one cannot foresee. Their humour freezes or thaws at a puff of wind that passes in the morning, a thought sets them bristling with sharp crystals or smooths out a brow already freezing. The way they suffer or punish is to turn to stone. The Northern nature, a swift mobility, a centre that is always prepared to harden, winter, the frosts, are present, under the smiles and the ermine, at the bottom of the Russian soul. The high latitudes, the difficulty of life, the inflexibility of their autocratic system, the gloomy, austere sky, the inexorable climate,—all these harsh gifts of fate have left their stamp on the race of the Muscovites. A certain sombre obstinacy, a sort of primitive ferocity, a background of savage harshness, which, under the sway of circumstances, might become implacable and even ruthless; a coldly indomitable force, will, resolution, that would rather wreck the world than yield; the indestructible instinct of the barbarian horde persisting in a half-civilized nation,—are recognizable, to the attentive eye, even in the harmless extravagances and superficial caprices of a young woman of this powerful race. Even in their nonsense they betray that fierce, headstrong genius which burns their own towns and keeps on their feet battalions of dead soldiers.

What terrible masters would the Russians be if ever they should spread the night of their rule over the Southern countries! A polar despotism, a tyranny such as the world has not yet known, silent as the darkness, keen as ice, unfeeling as bronze, outwardly lovely as snow and as coldly brilliant, a slavery without compensation or relief: this is what they would bring us. But probably they will gradually lose the virtues and the defects of their semi-barbarity.

Time and the sun will ripen these sirens of the North, and they will enter the concert of the peoples in some other way than as a menace or a dissonance.—If they can convert their hardness into firmness, their cunning into grace, their Muscovitism into humanity, they will cease to inspire aversion or fear and will make themselves loved; for, aside from their inherited characteristics, the Russians have many strong and engaging qualities.

*July 3, 1856.*—The German conceives and pursues the ideal, but he is never an artist, spontaneously, of himself; he is not of the noble breed, he admires but does not possess the genius of form; he is the opposite of the Hellene, he has the critical faculty, desire and aspiration, not the serene command of beauty. He cannot therefore do what he wishes to do, although he can play with his wish. The South, more artistic, more self-satisfied, more capable of execution, lazily rests in the feeling of its equilibrium. On one hand, the idea, on the other the talent. The realm of Germany is beyond the clouds, that of the Southern peoples on this earth. The Germanic race ponders and feels; the Southerners feel and express; the Anglo-Saxons will and do. To know, to feel, to act, this is the trio of Germany, Italy, England. France formulates, speaks, decides and laughs.

Thought, talent, will, speech, or, in other words, science, art, action, proselytism: thus are the roles assigned in the great quartette.

*July 21, 1856.*—*Mit Sack und Pack,* here I am back again in my town lodgings. I have said good-bye to my friends and my country joys, to the verdure, the flowers and the joy of living. Why did I leave them all? The pretext was anxiety for my poor uncle; this was the reason I gave to myself and others. But were there not really other reasons? I rather think there were. There was the fear of making myself a burden upon the two or three families of friends who surrounded me with kind attentions for which I could make no return. There were my books, which undoubtedly called me back, and perhaps the wish to keep my own word. But all this would have counted for nothing, I think, were it not for another instinct, the instinct of the Wandering Jew, which snatches away the cup when I have moistened my lips, forbids me any prolonged enjoyment, and cries: On! on! do not sleep, do not form attachments, do not stop! This unquiet feeling is not a need of change, it is rather the fear of what I love, the mistrust of that which charms me, the unrest of happiness. What an odd nature, and what a strange propensity!— not to dare to enjoy anything naturally, simply, without scruple, to leave the table for fear the repast may end. A contradiction and a mystery!—not to use, for fear of abusing; to think that one is obliged to go away, not because one has had enough, but because one has stayed for a while; to play towards oneself the part of Sancho's doctor. I am indeed always the same; the being that wanders needlessly, the voluntary exile, the eternal traveller, the man who never rests, the vagabond and bohemian who, driven onward by an inner voice, builds nowhere, buys and labours nowhere, but passes, looks, sets up his tent and goes his way.—Is not a kind of emptiness also the cause of this nomadic restlessness? The unceasing pursuit of something that I lack? The aspiration towards a truer peace, a satisfaction that would be more complete? Neighbours, friends, kindred,—I love them all; and these affections, when they are active, leave me with no sense of deficiency. But they do not fill

my heart; that is why they do not stabilize me. I am always awaiting the woman and the work that will be able to possess my soul
and become my object in living.

> *Promenant par tout séjour*
> *Le deuil que tu cèles,*
> *Psyché-papillon, un jour*
> *Puisses-tu trouver l'amour*
> *Et perdre tes ailes!*

I have not given away my heart; hence my restlessness of spirit.
I will not allow it to be taken captive by that which cannot fill it;
hence my pitiless instinct of detachment from all that charms me
without permanently binding me. My variableness, so like inconstancy, is really therefore only a seeking, a hope, desire, anxiety: it
is the malady of the ideal, which causes one to taste things, then to
judge them, and attempts the unknown, not from attraction but as
a sort of duty.—Thus my life is a game, trying to take itself curi-
ously, if not seriously; I trifle because I have to do so, because it is
a habit and the part of prudence, in order not to soften and despair;
I force myself to be frivolous, heedless, detached, in order not to
suffer or break my heart over the merest trifles. In other words, I
hold myself in reserve.

> *Jeu, pudeur ou dédain, on peut prendre le masque*
> *Et pour de meilleurs jours se réserver le casque,*
> *Plus fort, plus sûr.*

The question is therefore always one between the ideal and common sense, the one never abating its demands, the other adjusting
itself to whatever is expedient and real.—This common-sensible notion of marriage and love, at a reduction, so to speak,—is it not
profane, even absurd? But what is one to say of an ideal that prevents life from completing itself, destroys the family in the germ?
Is not that a vicious thing? Is there not in my ideal a measure of

pride, an unwillingness to accept my destiny? An inner protest against superiorities that are artificial and arbitrary? A horror of undeserved humiliations? To be humiliated in my love would drive me to distraction. And I prefer deprivation to such a risk. All of which leads to nothing, ends only *in statu quo;* and that is why I think of something else and do not occupy my mind with that which can only bring me trouble.

*(Noon.)*—Dreamed, with my head in my hands, till I fell asleep —of what? Of happiness. It was as if I were slumbering on the fatherly breast of God. His will be done!

*August 3, 1856.*—A delightful Sunday afternoon at Pressy. Rode on the box of the diligence with V. G., an old comrade who is now a doctor. Received with open arms by everybody, covered with kisses by the children (the triad, G., M. and C.), kept for dinner and tea by these good friends who united their households so they could all have me at once. Frolicked with this nestful of children, who clung to me as if I were the queen-bee, and whom I love as my benefactors. Loulou was more bewitching than ever and insisted that she would be my little wife, when she was grown-up like her mother. Blindman's buff, races, climbing in the fir-trees, a visit to the flower-beds, apricot-picking. The new Berquin. Talk under the great oak. The little ones in the apple-trees. In the evening, the piano, fragments of airs from Haydn's *Four Seasons*. Returned late, under a magnificent spread of stars, with a blaze of heat-lightning behind the Jura. Drunk with poetry, staggering with my sensations. I walked home slowly, blessing the God of life, overwhelmed with an infinite beatitude. Only one thing was lacking, a soul to share it with, for in my enthusiasm and emotion I was like a cup running over. The Milky Way, the great black poplars, the rippling of the waves, the shooting stars, the singing in the distance, the lighted town, everything spoke in the ideal tongue; I felt poetic and almost a poet. The furrows of knowledge disappeared under the magic breath of wonder; my elasticity came back to me, a free and living confidence of mind; I was young again, capable of abandonment and love. All my dryness of heart had disappeared. The dew of heaven had fertilized the gnarled, dead staff; it began to grow green and flower again. If we had not beauty, dear God, how wretched we should be! With it, everything is reborn in us; the senses, the heart and imagination, the reason and will assemble like so many bones at the word of the prophet and unite in a single, self-same energy. What can happiness be if it is not this plenitude of existence, this intimate accord with the universal life and the divine? For a whole half day I have been happy, and I have wrapped myself in this joy, steeping myself in it to the very depths of my consciousness.

I could see clearly, too, by the contrast, what harms me so at Geneva, the general character of the population which polarizes and shrinks me. The moment I find myself in an atmosphere of sympathy, art, poetry, good-fellowship, kindliness, I am a different being. Ugliness, harshness, malice, mockery, vulgarity, banality, coarseness of imagination and language, dull eyes, low thoughts hurt me and make me evil myself.

*Dès que nous aimons moins, nous cessons d'être en Dieu.*

And I lapse here at every turn into coldness, indifference and aversion.

*August 7, 1856.*—Publications . . . On all hands my friends complain of me. They keep repeating: concentrate, write, produce, do something, apply yourself, think of some work, bring your own stone to the pile . . . Unfortunately, unanimous as they are in demanding something of me, they no longer agree about what they wish me to do. A dictionary, a critical work, a psychological work, a public course, verses, history, travels, etc., they counsel me to do this or that, advising me to give up all the rest. Yesterday Scherer said to me, "Quadruple your *Grains de mil* and make a volume of it. It would be very pleasant for you and for us, too. You can be as varied and flexible there as you wish. It was a good vein, follow it up." Get married and write your book; everything turns about these two demands, and I have myself been making them for a long while. But to choose is what I have not been able to do, and these two things mean a choice.

*August 31, 1856 (Sunday, 11 a. m.).*—I cannot find any voice for what I feel. The street is silent, a sunbeam falls in my room, I am wrapped in profound self-communion; I hear my heart beating and my life passing. I know not what solemnity invades me, penetrates and subdues me, the peace of the graves over which the birds sing, the still immensity, the infinite calm of repose. It is as if I had become a statue on the shores of the river of time, as if I were present at some mystery, from which I shall come forth old and ageless. I feel no desire, no fear, no impulse, no special exaltation; I feel anonymous and impersonal, as if my eye were fixed like a dead man's, my mind vague and universal like the void, like the absolute: I am in suspense, I am as if I were not.—At such times as these it seems to me that my consciousness withdraws into its eternity: it observes its stars and its nature, with all its seasons and its myriads of individual things, circling within it, perceives itself in its very substance, superior to all form, containing its past, its present and its future, a void all-comprehending, a medium invisible and fertile, a universal virtuality, detaching itself from its own existence in order to regain its self-possession in the purity of its inwardness. At these sublime moments the body disappears, the mind is simplified and unified; passion, griefs, intentions, ideas are reabsorbed into being, like raindrops in the ocean whence they were born. The soul goes back into itself, into the indeterminate; it is *reimplicated* beyond its own life; it returns into its mother's womb again, becomes once more a divine embryo. Everything is effaced, the days one has lived, the habits one has formed, the traits that have stamped themselves upon one, the individuality that one has fashioned; everything relaxes and dissolves, resumes its original state, subsides into its primal fluidity, without shape, angle or pattern. It is the spheroidal state, undivided and homogeneous unity, the state of the egg out of which life is to spring. This return to the seed is a phenomenon well-known to the Druids and the Brahmans, the neo-Platonists and the hierophants. It is contemplation and not stupor, it is neither painful, nor joyous, nor sad; it is outside all particular feeling, as of all finite thought. It is the consciousness of being, and the consciousness of the omni-possibility latent in the depths of this being. It is the sensation of the spiritual infinite. It is the fount of liberty.—What purpose does it serve? To dominate all that is finite, to enable us to perceive our own form, to give us the key of all metamorphoses, to cure us of moral distortions, to make us lords of time and space and let us regain our own totality by shedding everything that is adventitious, artificial, bruised and impaired. This return to the seed is a momentary rejuvenation; more, it is a means of measuring the road that life has travelled, for it leads one back to the point of departure.

*October 22, 1856.*—Life is an apprenticeship that teaches us progressive renunciation, the constant diminution of our claims, our hopes, our possessions, our strength, our freedom. The circle grows more and more contracted; we begin with a wish to learn everything, to see, attain and conquer everything, and in all directions we reach our limit—*Non plus ultra*. Fortune, glory, power, health, happiness, a long life, heart's joy,—all these blessings that others have possessed seem at first to have been promised to us, as they also seem within our reach, and then we are obliged to dispel the dream, accept a smaller and smaller part, make ourselves little and humble, feel that we are limited, weak, dependent, ignorant, mean, impoverished and bereft, and throw ourselves upon God for everything, having no right to anything, wretched as we are; and it is in this nothingness that we recover a measure of life, because the divine spark is in our depths. We resign ourselves. And in the love that believes we capture the true greatness.

*October 27, 1856.*—In all the capital matters of life we are always alone, and our true history is hardly ever deciphered by other people. Most of this drama of ours is a monologue, or rather an inner debate between God, our conscience and ourselves. Tears, griefs, disappointments, vexations, good and evil thoughts, decisions, uncertainties, deliberations,—all these things are our secret, almost all of them incommunicable and intransmissible, even when we wish to utter them, even when we write them. What is most precious in us never reveals itself, never finds an issue even in the closest intimacy. Only a part of it reaches our consciousness, and it reaches the plane of action only in prayer. It is perceived only by God, perhaps, for our past always becomes strange to us.—Our monad may be prodigiously influenced by others, but it remains to them no less impenetrable in its heart and centre, and, when all is said, we ourselves remain outside the mystery of ourselves. Our midmost consciousness is unconscious, as the core of the sun is dark. Everything that we are, desire, do or know is more or less superficial, and the black shades of the unfathomable substance persist beneath the rays, the lightnings, the revelations of our surface.

I did well, therefore, in my theory of the inner man, to place at the bottom of the Self, even when one has disengaged in turn all the seven spheres that it contains, a dark essence, the abyss of the unrevealed, the virtual, the pledge of an infinite future, the obscure self, the pure subjectivity that cannot objectify itself in the mind, in the consciousness, reason, soul, heart, imagination, or the life of the senses, and that makes its attributes and its occasions out of all these forms of itself.

But the obscure only exists that it may cease to exist; it is the cause of every victory, the cause of all progress. Whether one calls it fatality, death, night or matter, it is the pedestal of life, of light, liberty and the spirit, for it represents resistance, that is, the fulcrum of activity, the occasion of its exertion and its triumph.

God wishes to be conquered, in a way, for he desires, on behalf of his creature, dignity, courage, the will to be perfect.

*December 17, 1856.*—This evening, second quartette concert. It stirred me aesthetically much more than the first; the works chosen this time were loftier and stronger and reached into deeper regions of the soul. They were Mozart's Quartette in D-minor and the Beethoven Quartette in C-major, separated by a concerto of Spohr, called a quartette in E.

This latter, as a whole, was brilliant and lively, with fire in the allegro, feeling in the adagio and elegance in the finale, but it reveals nothing more than a fine talent in a mediocre soul. The two others place one in contact with genius and reveal two great souls. Mozart is inner freedom, Beethoven might and rapture. Thus the one liberates us, the other carries us out of ourselves. I do not think I have ever felt more clearly or with more intensity than today the difference between these two masters. Their two moral existences appeared to me with a transparent clarity, and I seemed to read them to the bottom, as at the Last Judgment.

Mozart's work, pervaded with mind and thought, expresses a problem that has been solved, a balance that has been reached between aspiration and strength, between power, duty and will, the sovereignty of a self-controlled grace in which the real and the ideal are no longer separate, a marvellous harmony, a perfect unity.

The quartette tells of the day of one of those Attic souls who taste in advance the serenity of Elysium. The first scene is a pleasant conversation, like that of Socrates on the banks of the Ilissus; its note is an exquisite urbanity, delicate, smiling, playful. The second scene is one of thrilling pathos. A cloud has spread over the azure of this Greek sky. One of those storms that are always arising in life, even among great hearts that esteem and love one another, has come to disturb this harmony. What is its cause? A misunderstanding, some failure of respect, some negligence? Who knows?—but the storm breaks. The andante is a scene of reproach and complaint, but only as these might be among the immortals. What elevation in this complaint! What controlled emotion in the reproach, what sweet nobility! The voice trembles and grows more serious, but it retains its dignified affection.—The cloud has passed, the sun has returned; the explanation has taken place, concord is reëstablished. The third scene paints the joyousness of the reconciliation, which, sure of itself at last, and as if, with a touch of mischief, putting itself to the proof, leads to a little gentle raillery, friendly badinage. The finale brings back the tempered gaiety, the happy serenity, the supreme freedom, the flower of the inner life which is the fundamental theme of the work.

Beethoven's work is the tragic irony that sets the whirlwind of life dancing over the ever-threatening gulf of the infinite. No trace of unity here any longer, no satisfaction, no serenity. We watch the eternal duel between the two great forces, that of the abyss, engulfing all things finite, and life defending itself and affirming itself, dilating in its intoxication. The first measures break the seals and open the caverns of the great gulf. The struggle begins. It is long drawn-out. Life is born; it plays and frolics, careless as a butterfly fluttering over a precipice. Then it extends its conquests and sings its successes. It founds a jurisdiction, builds a nature. But from the yawning gulf arises another tempest; the titans shake the gates of the new kingdom. A gigantic battle is under way. One hears the tumultuous efforts of the powers of chaos like the contortions of some shadowy monster. Life carries the day at last; but the victory is not decisive, and in the intoxication of victory there is a certain undercurrent of terror and bewilderment. Beethoven's was a tormented soul. The passion and the dread of the infinite seem to toss it between heaven and hell; hence his immensity.

Which is the greater, Mozart or Beethoven? Idle question! One is more accomplished, the other more colossal. The first is the peace of perfect art, the immediacy of beauty; the second is the sublime, terror and pity, beauty intrinsic in these. One gives what the other gives the desire for. Mozart has the classic purity of light and the blue ocean, Beethoven the romantic grandeur of the storms of the sky and the seas; and while Mozart's soul seems to dwell on the ethereal peaks of an Olympus, Beethoven's soul tremblingly ascends the storm-swept flanks of a Sinai. All praise to both alike.

Each of them shows us a moment of the ideal life. Each of them does us good. Let us love them both!

*Vandœuvres,*[1] *May 28, 1857.*—Went down to Geneva to hear the *Tannhäuser* of Richard Wagner, performed in the theatre by the German company (from Zürich) that is now playing here.—Wagner is a strong man and he has the high poetic feeling. But his work is more poetic than musical. The suppression of the lyrical element, and consequently of melody, duos, trios, etc., is a *parti pris* in Wagner that is rather systematic than natural; the monologue and the aria disappear together. Nothing remains but declamation, the *arioso,* the recitative and the choruses. To avoid the conventional in singing, he falls into another convention, that of not singing. He subordinates the voice to the articulated word, and, fearing that the muse may take flight, he clips her wings. These works are not really operas but symphonic dramas. The voice is lowered to the rank of an instrument; it is placed on a level with the violins, the kettle-drums and oboes, and treated instrumentally. Man has fallen from his high estate, and the centre of gravity of the work passes into the baton of the conductor. The interest, the meaning, the soul of these productions lies in the poetic idea and in the continual return to the ensemble, somewhat as in the system of the double suns, whose centre of gravity falls in empty space between the various bodies of the system. It is a depersonalized music, a neo-Hegelian, objective, contemplative music, a mass-music, taking the place of individual music. It may thus well be the music of the future, the music of the socialist democracy that is superseding aristocratic art, which is heroic and subjective. In any case, it corresponds as yet only with the Germanic way of feeling; and the other countries of Europe cannot yet abstract themselves to the point of dispensing with visible centralization, the hero and the melody.

I liked the enormous, unnatural overture even less than when I first heard it. In it man has not yet been born; it is the elemental music of the waves, the forests, the animal world where mind is not

[1] A village near Geneva.

incarnate in a soul that can sum up and feel its expression. It corresponds to nature before man was; everything in it is enormous, wild, elemental, like the murmur of forests and the roars of animal populations. It is terrible and obscure because man, the mind, the key of the enigma, personality, the contemplator has no place in it.

The composition has a grand idea, the conflict between pleasure and pure love, between earthly, sensual passion and the divine flame, in a word between the flesh and the spirit, the beast and the angel in man . . . The music is continuously expressive and the choruses very fine, especially in the second act. But as a whole it is tiring and extravagant, too full, too laborious, everywhere too extreme. Intellectually and poetically, it is striking, but one's musical gratification is hesitant, and very often doubtful, and one only recalls the general impression. The orchestration is skilful, conscientious, intricate and varied; but it lacks gaiety, after all, it lacks ease, naturalness, vivacity, it lacks the wings and the smile. With Wagner, as with the Germans generally, thought outweighs art, and the intention outweighs the power. He desires more than he can express. He is still half-choked with his prodigality, with the preëstablished formula, he is obscure and forced. On the other hand, it is pure poetry.

*Vandœuvres, June 17, 1857.*—I have just followed Maine de Biran from his twenty-eighth to his forty-eighth year, through the medium of his private Journal; and a multitude of thoughts, direct, personal, comparative and scientific, have assailed me in turn. Let me disentangle those that concern myself. In this eternal self-observer, I find myself with all my faults: inconstancy, indecision, discouragement, the need for sympathy, the lack of achievement, my pleasure in watching myself pass onward, feeling and living, my growing incapacity for practical action, for the observation of things outside, my psychological aptitude. But I find marked differences that cheer and relieve me: this nature is only one of the men in me; it is one of my provinces, it is not the whole of my territory and inner kingdom. Intellectually, I am more objective and more con-

structive; my historical, geographical, scientific horizon is much
more vast; I have seen more, men, things, works of art, countries
and peoples, books and sciences—I have had a much greater mass
of experiences; I am more capable of production; my philological,
aesthetic, literary, philosophical culture is more complete and more
varied. He has none of my aptitude for teaching, for criticism, for
poetry. In a word, I feel that, in every sphere, I have a great deal
more culture, copiousness, breadth and freedom, in spite of my deficiencies, my limitations and my weaknesses.

Why does Biran make will the whole of man? Because he had too
little will himself. Men always especially esteem what they lack
and magnify whatever they desire. A man who could not think and
meditate would have made self-consciousness the supreme thing.—
Totality alone has an objective value; the moment one isolates a
part from the whole, the moment one chooses, the choice is involuntarily and instinctively dictated by subjective inclinations, which
obey one of the two contrary laws, the attraction of likes and the
affinity of contraries.

*(Noon.)*—The most penetrating intuitions, the most delicate inward apperceptions, the thoughts that are most fugitive and precious
are just those that I never record. Why? First, because I always
postpone the essential; next, because I feel that I shall never forget
them; then because they are parts of an infinite whole and because
scraps and fragments have no value or interest for me and give me
almost a feeling of contempt. Besides, I never think of the public,
of utilizing and exploiting my thought, and I am happy enough to
have shared in a mystery, divined some profundity, touched some
sacred reality; to know is more than enough for me; to express
sometimes seems a profanation; to communicate seems like a sort
of divulging, and, not to debase things, I leave them hidden. This is
a purely feminine instinct, the protection of one's sentiment, the
shrouding of one's individual experiences, the guarding one's best
secrets in silence. It is not the virile point of view of science, broad
daylight, propaganda, publicity. In my aversion to vulgar bragging

I incline to esotericism, a Pythagorean discretion; I belong by instinct to the aristocracy of culture, to the moral and aesthetic caste
of the hierophants. My delicacy, my natural distinction, and also
my timidity of soul and the distrust in my heart disgust me with
the intellectual rabble. If I were stronger, I should conquer spiritual
authority; if I were more loving, I should devote myself to the
masses; it is my faults that keep me a hermit, while my faculties
enliven the solitude of my moral hermitage. This is not enough. I
ought to make up my mind and give myself. Mental epicurism
should give place to an energetic feeling of obligation, a faith that
one can and must be useful to others. To act, to produce, to publish
have appeared to you only in the light of your own self-interest, and
therefore distasteful and optional. You should see a positive duty
in them, a strict obligation, a task that you are commanded to perform; then, as an effort and sacrifice, they will recover their savour
and attractiveness.—*Væ soli!* Alone, one has no object but oneself,
and this object is not worth the trouble of taking a step. We allow
ourselves to drift with the tide when we are not expected anywhere. What is the use of interfering? But courage comes from
love.

*(Five o'clock.).*—The morning has passed like a dream. I have
continued my reading of Biran's Journal up to the end of 1817 (his
fifty-first year). After dinner, joined in the life of the birds, in the
open air, roaming the leafy lanes below Pressy. The sun was brilliant and the air limpid. The midday orchestra was in full chorus;
over the humming ground-notes of countless invisible insects, the
ear caught the outlines of another music, the caprices and improvisations of the nightingales in the ash-trees and the warblers and
finches in their nests. The wild roses swayed in the hedges, the
fragrance of the acacias still perfumed the paths, the light down of
the poplar-balls floated in the air like the soft snow one sees on fine
days. I felt as joyous as a butterfly.

On my return, read the first three books of *Corinne,* that poem
of which I have not reviewed my impressions since I was a boy. I

examined it again in the light of my recollections. The romantic interest seems to have vanished for me, but not its pathos, its poetic and moral interest. I should enjoy studying Mme. de Staël, as a woman, judging her in the light of my present experience.

*June 18, 1857.*—I have just spent three hours in the orchard, in the shade of the hornbeam hedge, mingling with my reading the spectacle of the lovely morning and taking a little turn between the chapters. The sky has covered itself again with a whitish veil, and I have gone back to Biran, whose *Pensées* I have just finished, and *Corinne,* whom I have been following with Oswald in her rambles among the monuments of the Eternal City.

There is nothing sadder or more wearisome than this Journal of Maine de Biran's. It is like the progress of a squirrel in a cage. This unrelieved monotony of reflection, perpetually beginning again, enervates and disheartens one like the endless pirouetting of a dervish. So this is the life of a distinguished man, seen in its last and closest intimacy! It is one long repetition, with one imperceptible change of centre in his way of seeing himself. It took this thinker thirty years to pass from Epicurean quietude to Fenelonian quietism, and speculatively at that, for his practical life remained the same, and his whole anthropological discovery consists in resuming the theory of the three lives (the inferior, the human, the superior) which one finds in Pascal and Aristotle. That is what they call a philosopher in France. Beside the great philosophers, how paltry, meagre, poor this intellectual life seems! It is the journey of an ant, extending to the boundaries of a field, the travels of a mole spending its days digging a poor little burrow. How stifling would a swallow find the circle to which the mole and the ant are confined, the swallow that might traverse the whole ancient world, with a sphere of life that embraces Africa and Europe! I feel a similar asthma and asphyxiation over Biran's book, and as always, also, a paralysis following assimilation and a fascination that springs from sympathy. I am sorry for the man, and I fear my pity; for I feel how close I am to the same distempers and the same faults.

But the case must be taken as a useful example and as a lesson from which to profit. Biran is a sample of the pure psychologist, who ends by becoming a moralist, with little will and still less health, and dependent in every way, except as an enquirer and observer of himself. The lesson to be drawn from his life is: 1., that one should take good care of one's health in the interest of one's mind; 2., that one should create for oneself, early in life, a settled occupation, a stable goal, and not allow oneself to be carried away by all one's intellectual caprices; 3., that one should not shun the world, action, struggle, duty, and all that develops the will; and this should be sought early; 4., that one should come to grips with things, come to conclusions, for irresolution, hesitation, always beginning again, dissipate our forces, wear away our courage, increase our anxiety and incapacity; 5., that one should not separate, in oneself, theory from practice, or the inner man from the outer man; for harmony is moral health.

The survey by Naville is full of interest, noble and dignified in style, grave and sustained in tone, but it breathes sadness almost as much as it suggests maturity. I dislike the exaggeration of Biran's merits. This apotheosis has become a sort of family heritage. For the rest, the slight critical impatience which this volume causes me will be gone tomorrow. Biran is an important link in the French tradition; through him our Swiss writers connect with it, Naville, father and son, Secrétan; from him comes what is good in contemporary psychology, for Stapfer, Royer-Collard, Cousin called him their master, and Ampère, his junior by nine years, was his friend.

*Vandœuvres, July 26, 1857.*—At half-past ten in the evening, under a starry sky, a band of rustics, planting themselves near the M——s' windows, shouted out their disagreeable ditties. Why do these croaks and jeers, notes that are intentionally false, words full of derision, make these people cheerful? Why this brazen parade of ugliness, this grating grimace of the anti-poetic? Why is this their way of expanding and blooming in the great, calm, solitary night?

Why? Because of a secret, unhappy instinct. It is the craving to feel oneself in all one's individual particularity, to assert and possess one's own exclusive self, egoistically, idolatrously, by opposing one's own self to everything else, by setting it up rudely in contrast to nature, the nature that envelops us, to the poetry that carries us out of ourselves, to the harmony that unites us with others, to the adoration that bears us towards God. No, no, no! Just myself, myself the all-sufficient; myself by negation and ugliness, myself by distortion and irony; myself in all my whims and independence, my own irresponsible sovereignty, liberated by laughter like a demon, exulting in my spontaneity, myself as the master of myself, myself for myself, the invincible monad, the self-sufficient being, living at last for once by itself and for the sake of itself! That is what lies at the bottom of all this joy, an echo of Satan, the temptation to make oneself the centre, to be an Elohim, the great rebellion. And it is also a sudden perception of the absolute aspect of the personal soul, the crude exaltation of the subject establishing, by abusing them, the rights of its own subjectivity; it is a caricature of our most precious privilege, a parody of our apotheosis, the degradation of our supreme greatness. Roar away, drunkards! Your ignoble concert in its reeling hubbub reveals unwittingly the majesty of life and the power of the soul; in its repulsive vulgarity, it is not wholly severed from that higher being, which, even in its self-abasement, cannot be entirely perverted, and even though multiplying on its limbs the chains of matter, and the clanking of the links of that chain, still rings out the divine sound of freedom.

*September 15, 1857.*—Finished the *Correspondence* and the *Journal* of Sismondi. Sismondi is essentially the upright man, conscientious, virtuous and respectable. The friend of the public good, and the devoted servant of a great cause, the amelioration of the lot of the majority. Character and heart were dominant in his personality, and warmth of nature was his salient trait. Sismondi is a fine example, too. With middling faculties, little imagination, little taste, little talent, only moderately gifted, without distinction, without finesse, without great elevation or breadth or depth of mind, he yet achieved an almost illustrious career, and left three-score volumes and a fine name. How this latter? His love for men, on the one hand, and on the other his energy for work are the two factors of his glory. In political economy, in literary and political history, in personal action, Sismondi had neither genius nor talent, only solidity, loyalty, good sense, integrity. He was rather lacking in poetic, artistic and philosophical feeling, but he interests and attaches us through his moral feeling. He is the sincere author, the excellent heart, the good citizen, the warm friend, the brave and worthy man in the full meaning of the term, without any splendour or brilliance, but inspiring confidence by his merit, his principles and his virtues. He represents the very best type of the good Genevese liberalism, republican but not democratic, Protestant but not Calvinist, humane but not socialist, progressive without being turbulent, conservative without selfishness or hypocrisy, a patriot without narrowness, the theoretician of experience and observation, the generalizer from facts, the laborious philanthropist for whom the past and the present were only a field of study from which to glean useful lessons, the positive and reasonable man aspiring to the happy mean for all and to the formation of a social science that can assure it for all.

*Aix-les-Bains, September 23, 1857.*—Read forty pages of Lamennais's *Affaires de Rome,* or his whole journey through Italy in 1832; and Chateaubriand's *Atala.*—*Atala* left me rather cold. Except for the descriptive parts, which are very fine, there is something overstudied, affected and precious about the whole thing that reminds me of the false taste of the Empire.—Lamennais proceeds from Chateaubriand, but with a certain reserve of political passion and ruggedness of character, which gives his descriptions a sombre colour that is all his own.

*September 24, 1857.*—Read today. As I reflected on these two episodes of Chateaubriand, the man himself became clear to me. A great artist but not a great man, an immense talent, a pride still more immense, devoured by ambition, yet finding nothing to love and admire in the whole world but himself, a tireless worker, capable of everything, except real devotion, self-negation and faith. Jealous of every success, he always belonged to the opposition so that he could deny the service that anyone rendered and any other glory than his own. A legitimist under the Empire, a parliamentarian under the legitimacy, a republican under the constitutional monarchy, a defender of Christianity when France was philosophical, losing his taste for religion when it became a serious force again,— the secret of such unending contradictions is the need to be alone like the sun, the consuming thirst for apotheosis, the incurable, insatiable vanity that combines with the ferocity of tyranny a supreme distaste for sharing anything.—A magnificent imagination, but an evil character; incontestable power, but an egoism that is antipathetic, a dry heart, unable to endure around it any but worshippers and slaves. A tormented soul and a sad life, all things considered, under its halo of glory and its crown of laurels; sad for want of sincerity and love.

Essentially jealous and choleric, Chateaubriand, from the very beginning, was prompted by defiance, the need to contradict, crush, vanquish, and this remained his motive all his life. Rousseau seems to me his point of departure, the man to whom, in contrast and opposition, all his replies and attacks may be traced. Rousseau is a revolutionary; Chateaubriand writes his *Essai contre les révolutions*. Rousseau is republican and Protestant; Chateaubriand becomes a royalist and a Catholic. Rousseau is bourgeois; Chateaubriand glorifies nothing but nobility, honour, chivalry, knightly prowess, etc. Rousseau conquers nature for French letters, especially the mountains and the lakes of Savoy and Switzerland; he pleads for nature against civilization. Chateaubriand takes possession of a new and colossal nature, that of the ocean and America, but he makes his savages speak the language of Louis XIV, he makes his Atala bow before a Catholic missionary and, with a mass, sanctifies passions born on the banks of the Mississippi. Rousseau makes an apology for revery; Chateaubriand raises a rival monument in *René,* only to shatter it. Rousseau eloquently preaches deism in the *Vicaire savoy-*

*ard;* Chateaubriand surrounds the Roman creed with all the garlands of his poetry in the *Génie du Christianisme.* Rousseau proclaims natural right, and pleads for the future of the peoples; Chateaubriand celebrates only the magnificences of the past, the ashes of history, the noble ruins of empires.—Always the role to play, the shrewd pen, the *parti pris,* always lust for renown, the fanciful theme, faith as a matter of choice, rarely sincerity, loyalty or candour. Always a real indifference simulating a passion for the truth; always an imperious search for glory instead of a devotion to the good; always the ambitious artist, never the citizen, the believer, the man. Chateaubriand posed all his life long as the weary giant, smiling in pity over a world of dwarfs, affecting, in disdain, to wish nothing from it, while if he chose, with his genius, he could take everything from it. He is the type of a baneful race, the father of a very unpleasant line.—But I return to the two episodes.

*René* seems to me greatly superior to *Atala.* The two stories show a talent of the first order, but *Atala* is of a type of beauty that is more transitory. This rendering in the manner of Versailles of the loves of a Natchez and a Seminole, endowing with a Catholic accent the ways of the worshippers of Manitou, was a rather too extreme notion. And yet the work is a *tour de force* of style; and only through the artifices of classicism, achieved in the form, could the romantic substance of sentiment and colour have been introduced into the insipid literature of the Empire. *Atala* is already superannuated, theatrical, outmoded in all the parts that are not descriptive or European, that is, in all its sentimental savagery.

*René* is infinitely more durable. Its theme, the malady of a whole generation (disgust with life, springing from idle revery and the ravages of a vague and measureless ambition), is a true theme. The style is admirable and almost perfect. Unwittingly and unintentionally, Chateaubriand was sincere, for René is himself. This little tale is a masterpiece in every respect, for it is not spoiled artistically, like *Atala,* by any accessory intention or absorbing preconception. Instead of being rapturous over René, later generations will laugh at him; instead of a hero, he will seem a pathological case; but the work, like the phoenix, will endure of itself. A work of art withstands all interpretations; it is adequate to them and it survives them, rich and complex like the idea which it is. A portrait proves anything one wishes. In the very form of the style, characterized by the disdainful generality of the narration, the brevity of the sentences, the series of images and pictures traced with a classic purity and exemplary vigour, there is something monumental. A subject of this century, carved in the antique style, *René* is Chateaubriand's immortal cameo.

*June 14, 1858.*—In my moments of leisure this last week, I have been consumed by a two-fold inner pain: an unsated longing for happiness, anxiety over my sight. The floating motes in my eyes, always increasing, and my heart, which grows emptier and emptier, leave me no peace. Like the cattle in a burning barn, I cling to that which consumes me, to the solitary life that does me so much harm. I do not see my friends any longer, I do not have any conversation, any exchange of thoughts or any chance to open my heart. Like Prometheus, I give my liver over to my vulture. Yesterday, however, I wrestled with this fatal tendency. I went up to Pressy, and the caresses of the M. children did a little toward reëstablishing the equilibrium in my soul . . . After dinner, under the arbour, all three sang a number of little songs and school-hymns. It was charming to hear them. The fairy of spring had scattered flowers over the countryside from a full basket. They put roses in all my buttonholes. In short, it was a little vision of paradise. It is true that the serpent roamed there, too. There was a burglary yesterday close by; sorrow visited another neighbouring place. A sharp word was exchanged in my presence, etc. Death and evil crawl about every Eden and sometimes within its precincts. This is what gives our human destiny its tragic beauty, its mournful poetry. The flowers, the shadows, an admirable view, a setting sun, the freshness of everything, joy, grace, feeling, abundance and serenity, tenderness and songs: there was the beauty of it all. The dangers of the present, the treacherous future: there was the element of pathos. The fashion of this world passeth away. Without the possession of eternity, without the religious view of life, these fugitive days are but a thing of terror. Happiness should be a prayer, unhappiness likewise. Faith in the moral order, in the protecting fatherhood of the Divinity appeared to me in all its grave sweetness,

> *Pense, aime, agis et souffre en Dieu:*
> *C'est la grande science.*

*July 19, 1858.*—I have been stirred to the depths today by the nostalgia for happiness and the appeals of memory. My old self, my dreams in Germany, the transports of the heart, the soul's longings awoke in me again with an unexpected force. Epimenides came forth from the grotto. All the old desires for love, travel, ecstasy, youth, adventure, glory trembled in my breast, passed tumultuously through it. The fear that I had missed my destiny, stifled my true nature, buried myself alive, passed like a shiver also. The thirst for the unknown, the passion for life, a frenzy for the blue vaults of the infinite and the strange worlds of the ineffable, the poignant intoxication of the ideal swept me into a kind of inner whirlpool which I am powerless to convey, a mixture of piercing anguish and mortal delight. Is this a warning? Is it a punishment? Is it a temptation? Is this not one of those storms of passion that assail women, when age comes without love's having come; a secret protestation, the vehement rebellion of the unsated heart, the furious claim of an unsatisfied right, a horrible awakening on the brink of the gulf that is swallowing us up, an agony of happiness, struggling in the grip of implacable fate, the terrors of a hope that is not resigned to dying?

And what has stirred up this tempest? What has struck my desert rock and caused the tears of youth to gush from it? Merely a little reading: the first number of the *Revue germanique,* and, among other things, the little story by Hartmann which is called

*Les cheveux d'or.*—What *Sarah Mortimer* and the *Roman d'un Jeune homme pauvre*, which I read yesterday and today, had not done, this trifle has produced, a strange effect of true poetry.

I had a sudden intuition of my gradual and continuous petrifaction, of my inner death from distaste, detachment, indifference, disillusion, from an immense weariness; of the diminution of my powers from abandoning great ideas and from a discouragement with all things.

The articles by Dollfus, Renan, Littré, Montégut, Taillandier, which carried me back to some of my favourite old subjects, made me forget ten lost years and recalled my life at the university.—I was tempted to tear off my old Geneva gown, to throw up my position and all these chains and set forth, staff in hand, for some unknown land, naked but alive, young, enthusiastic, full of ardour and faith . . .

Dreamed alone after ten in the evening, in the darkness, leaning out of the drawing-room window, while the stars shone forth among the clouds and the neighbours' lights went out one by one in the surrounding houses. Dreamed of what? Of the key of this tragicomedy which we are all playing. Alas! alas! I was as melancholy as Ecclesiastes. A hundred years seemed like an empty vision, a life, a breath, and all a nothingness. What torments of the mind, and all merely to die in a few minutes! What is worth one's interest and to what purpose?

> *Le temps n'est rien pour l'âme; enfant, ta vie est pleine,*
> *Et ce jour vaut cent ans s'il te fait trouver Dieu.*

*July 24, 1858.*—. . . What is the use of living? I asked myself a day or two ago; and I hardly knew what to reply, except that it is the will of God. I have been blowing soap-bubbles half the livelong day. Is not this what I do all my life? And is my life itself anything more than a coloured bubble, floating and empty, a dream, an appearance, the ephemeral glitter of which, the chimerical volume, resolve themselves into a simple tear, into a vain breath?

*July 25, 1858.*—Read over the *Grains de Mil.*[1] How many puerilities! And also how many passages that condemn me!—If I died tomorrow, what would have been the use of my life? Little indeed, truth to tell, either to myself or to others. Is this a good thing? No. And this is the cause of the secret discontent that agitates and consumes me, whenever I am not deadened by inertia. My sin is fear; fear of suffering, fear of being deceived, fear of deceiving myself, fear of destiny, fear of pain, fear of pleasure, fear of life and death. And the cause of this fear? Distrust. And the origin of this distrust? The feeling of my weakness. Unable to conquer, compel, to manage circumstances, I draw back from them, when they are not as I desire them. Lack of courage and will, no moral strength: that is the trouble with me, and it is always the same and always increasing.—To set myself a goal, to hope and struggle, seem to me every day more impossible and more stupendous. I am not even critical or contemplative any longer. I am precisely a cipher, somnolent and flaccid, I mean, listless and indifferent, passive and feeble. "From him that hath not shall be taken away even that which he hath." Thus the cycle completes itself. At twenty, I was all curiosity, elasticity, spiritual ubiquity; at thirty-seven, I have ceased to have either will, or desire, or talent; the fireworks of my youth are only a handful of ashes. Everything used to attract me; nothing attracts me any longer. Everything was open, everything is closed. I have not known how, or been able, or wished to choose, to limit myself and put down roots. I have remained a will-o'-the-wisp, and this is the result—vanity, sterility, anxiety, nonentity, with boredom and sadness to fill the measure. *Alles rächt sich auf Erde,* as Hartmann put it.

*December 13, 1858.*—There is nothing in you but difficulties, bad precedents, repeated evasions. Consider yourself as a stubborn, re-

---

[1] A collection of poems and reflections, published by Amiel in 1854.

fractory pupil, for whom you are responsible in your capacity of mentor and tutor. To sanctify one's sinful nature by gradually, with the aid of God, subjecting it to the angel within, is the whole art of Christian teaching and religious morality. To reclaim, to subdue, to evangelize and angelicize the evil self, reëstablishing harmony with the good self,—that is our work, your work. The way to salvation lies in abandoning the evil self in principle, taking refuge in the other, divine self, accepting with courage and prayer the task of living with one's own demon, making it an ever less rebellious agent of the good. The Abel in us must work to save the Cain. To attempt this is to be already converted, and we must be converted every day, for our natural inclination always leads us back to the old state. And Abel only ransoms and touches Cain by habituating him to good works and exercising him in them. In one of its aspects, to do good is a violence, a punishment, an expiation and a crucifixion, for it is to conquer oneself and make oneself a servant. On the other side, it is the apprenticeship of heaven, of inner sweetness, contentment, peace, joy. The path of holiness is a perpetual martyrdom, but this martyrdom is a glorification. The crown of thorns is the eternal and painful symbol of the life of the saints. The idea of evil and its cure is the best measure of the depth of a religious doctrine.

*July 14, 1859.*—I have just reread *Faust* (translated in verse by the Prince de Polignac). Alas! every year I am impressed anew by this restless life, this sombre character. It is the type of distress towards which I gravitate, and I keep finding more and more passages in this poem that strike straight to my heart. Immortal type, maleficent and accursed! Spectre of my conscience, shade of my torment, symbol of unslaked passion, image of the incessant conflicts of the soul which has not found its nourishment, its peace, its faith, its equilibrium, are you not the figure of a life that eats itself away because it has not found its God, a life which, in its course, wandering through the worlds, carries within itself, like a comet, an inextinguishable fire of longing, a torment of incurable disillusion?—

I too have been reduced to nothingness, and I shudder on the brink of the great abysses that yawn within my being, in the grip of a longing for the unknown, weakened by a thirst for the infinite, humbled before the ineffable. I too feel at times these blind rages against life, these outbursts of desperate yearning for happiness, still oftener utter collapse and speechless despair. From what does all this spring? From the absolute doubt of thought, of oneself, men and life; from the doubt that drains the will and destroys one's strength, that separates a man from his neighbour and makes him forget God, makes him neglect prayer, duty and effort, the restless, corrosive doubt that renders existence impossible and seems to sneer, as it were, at every hope.

*July 17, 1859.*—"Why do you never speak of yourself except in the past tense?" L. H. asks me. "It is as if you were dead."—"Indeed," I replied, "I have neither present nor future."

In fact, it shows my weakness and my moral ruin, this tendency to live, like an old man, only in retrospection and memory, not to have any intentions, to dispense with projects. You are only a sorry elegy, and all this faint-hearted distinterestedness is only a culpable Sybaritism, the cowardice of a resignation which you have no right to entertain. Why all this prattle and talk, these regrets and yawns, and never a single action? Why these hypocritical flagellations, followed by no amendment? Why these empty admonitions, this show of repentance, all these idle gestures in the void if they are not to deceive yourself, to give yourself the illusion that you are moving, the outward propriety of the moral life? You only requite your conscience by making faces, your common sense with appearances, you agitate yourself without advancing, you are always trying to cheat your pain or desires, and to dissipate at almost any price the grave thoughts that haunt you. The truth is, you are afraid of living; to will is a torture for you, to act an agony, and you strive, at all costs, to sleep.

And yet, in accordance with the fatal law, it is precisely will that alone can appease you. Action alone can give you satisfaction.

You have a horror of what you most need, and you execrate what would be your cure. So always and everywhere salvation is a torture, deliverance is a death, peace lies in immolation; one must kiss the burning crucifix in order to receive its grace. In short, life is a series of agonies, a Calvary to be climbed only by bruising one's knees. One seeks distraction, dispersion, stupefaction in order to be dispensed from the ordeal, one averts one's eyes from the *via dolorosa*. And always one has to come back to it. One has to realize that each of us carries his executioner within him, his demon and his hell, even in his sinfulness, and that his sin is his idol, and that this idol, seducing the will of his heart, is his malediction.

To die unto sin! This prodigious phrase of Christianity remains indeed the highest theoretical solution of the inner life. There only lies peace of conscience, and without this peace there is no peace . . . I have just read seven chapters of the Gospel. This reading is an anodyne. To do one's duty through love and obedience, to do good, these are the ideas that rise from it. To live in God and do his works, this is religion, salvation, eternal life. This is the effect, this is the mark of holy love and the Holy Ghost. This is the new man, proclaimed by Jesus, and the new life into which one enters through the second birth. To be born again is to renounce the old self, the natural man and sin, and to take to oneself another principle of life; it is to exist for God with another self, with another will and another love.

*August 9, 1859.*—Nature is forgetful, the world almost more so; just so far as a man indulges it, oblivion, ere long, wraps him as in a shroud. That swift and inexorable expansion of universal life which covers, overflows, engulfs all particular beings, which blots out our existence, cancels even the memory of us, is overwhelmingly sad. To be born, to struggle, to vanish is the whole ephemeral drama of human life. Save in a few hearts, not always even in one heart, our memory passes like an ocean wave, as a breath is lost in the air. If there is nothing immortal in us, what a little thing this life is! Like a dream that trembles and evaporates at the first glimmerings of dawn, all my past, all my present dissolves in me and fades out of my consciousness when it turns back upon itself. I feel, at this moment, as naked and empty as a convalescent who has lost his power of recollection. My travels, my reading, my studies, my plans, my hopes have vanished from my mind. This is a singular state. All my faculties fall away as a cloak drops from one's shoulders, as the shell falls from a larva. I can feel myself casting my skin, or returning, rather, into a more elementary form; I look on at my own divestiture. I forget even more than I am forgotten. I lay myself down in the coffin, meekly, in my living body, like Charles the Fifth; I feel, as it were, the indefinable peace of annihilation and the vague quiet of Nirvana; before me and in me, with the cataleptic calm of the Sleeping Beauty, I feel the swift river of time passing, the impalpable shadows of life slipping by.

I understand the Buddhistic delight of the sufis, the *kief* of the Turks, the ecstasy of the Orientals. And yet I also feel that this voluptuous pleasure is deadly, that it is a lingering suicide, like the use of opium and hashish, that it is inferior, as well, to the joy of energy, the sweetness of love, the beauty of enthusiasm, the sacred zest of a duty that one has accomplished. For this beatitude, soft as wax, is still a self-seeking, a refusal of obedience, a ruse of egoism and indolence, a way of avoiding labour and shrugging our shoulders at our fellow-creatures.

*November 28, 1859.*—This evening heard Ernest Naville speak (the first public lecture for men on the *Eternal Life*[1]). It was admirable in its sureness, integrity, clarity and nobility. He proved that the question of the other life should be put, in spite of everything. Beauty of character, great power of speech, great earnestness of thought shone out in this improvisation, which was as compact as if he had read it and scarcely separable from the citations (Bossuet and Jouffroy) with which it was interspersed. It was firmer and calmer than Pressensé's, less oratorical but possibly stronger, for

[1] *La Vie éternelle,* seven addresses given at Geneva and Lausanne in 1859 and 1860, and published in 1861.

there was not a theatrical touch in it. The great hall of the Casino was packed to the staircase, and one saw not a few white heads.

*December 13, 1859.*—Fifth lecture on the Eternal Life (the proof of the Gospel by the supernatural). Enormous crowd, the same ability, great eloquence; but there was no demonstration, and the audience was won, willy-nilly, by the speaker's feeling. He imagines he is destroying historical criticism, and he does not comprehend its first word; he does not wish to understand that the supernatural must prove itself historically, as indeed it must, if it is to leave the realm of faith and enter that of history and science. He cites Strauss and Renan, and Scherer, but he seizes only the letter, not the spirit. Always the Cartesian dualism, French metaphysics, the absence of the genetic, historical, speculative and critical sense. He remains a stranger to modern science, and his apologetics are obsolete.

The idea of a living evolution has not yet penetrated his consciousness. In a word, with the best intention of being so, he is not at all objective, and he remains, against his will, subjective, oratorical, with no effective power of demonstration for the really critical hearer. That is the irremediable disadvantage of having one's position defined in advance, of polemizing instead of seeking. Morality in Naville dominates over discernment and prevents him from seeing that which he cannot see; in his metaphysics, the will overrides the intelligence, just as, in his personality, the character is superior to the mind. This is all quite logical, but the result is that, while he is enabled to maintain insecure positions that he would otherwise have to yield, he is unable to make conquests. He is a conserver of truths and beliefs, but quite without the faculty of initiative, invention, renovation. He moralizes but does not suggest, he does not awaken or instruct. A popularizer, a vulgarizer in the good sense, an apologist and orator of the greatest merit, he sterilizes knowledge like a scholastic. And, at bottom, he is a scholastic: he argues just as they did in the twelfth century, and defends Protestantism as they defended Catholicism. The best way to show the insufficiency of this point of view is to demonstrate by history how superannuated it is. This chimæra of a simple and absolute truth is altogether Catholic and anti-historical. Naville's mind is purely mathematical, and his object is morality; to mathematicize morals is his business. When it comes to the question of development, metamorphosis, organization, the living and self-renewing, when it comes to the changing world of life, especially of the spiritual life, he is out of the picture. Language for him is a system of established signs; a man, a people, a book are so many fixed geometrical figures, the properties of which are to be discovered. Another application of my old law of the inner contradictions: Naville loves life with his heart and does not understand it theoretically. Scherer understands it with his mind and loves it very little with his heart. Naville steers clear of a science that has no entrails, and his own science is purely formal, also without entrails. Scherer demands a criticism that will give life, and his criticism is deadly.

*December 15, 1859.*—Naville's sixth lecture: this one admirable, because it only attempted to expound the Christian doctrine of the eternal life. An improvisation that was marvellous in its assurance, lucidity, elegance and elevation, in its exact and powerful eloquence. Aside from the first evening, this is the only one that I have liked, for I have no reservations to make here, in the name of criticism, history or philosophy. It was beautiful, loyal, noble and pure. I find, moreover, that Naville has grown in the art of speaking during these last years: he has always had an instructive and dignified beauty, but now he has in addition the communicative cordiality and the moving warmth that complete the orator. He stirs the whole man, beginning with the mind, but ending also with the *pectus*. He has attained now the true virile eloquence, and, granted the form, possesses it almost in its perfection. He has achieved, in its completeness, the virtuosity of his own nature, the adequate, masterly expression of himself. This is the joy and glory of the artist-orator as of any other kind of artist. Naville has become a model in the sphere of an eloquence that is premeditated and self-possessed. There is another kind of eloquence, the kind that seems inspired, that pierces into things and lays them bare, lights them up in sudden flashes, the kind that is born in the presence of the auditors and carries them out of themselves. This is not Naville's kind. Is it better? I do not know; but it makes the heart beat faster . . .

What would I not give to have this power? Or rather (for I have never devoted an hour or a moment's effort to acquiring it, and I distrust myself too much ever to be an orator at all), how I admire those who possess this force! Every sort of mastery is an augmentation of one's freedom.—But I shall never attain this. To deliver such a discourse, one must contain in oneself a whole vast network of ideas, combined oratorically; this means a great effort, and to make it one must have a great love for the public, and I have no love for it at all; one must have an enormous memory and great presence of mind, something that I almost wholly lack; one must be at ease before an audience that looks one straight in the eyes, and I am an embarrassed creature; one must be able to see people's faces, and I can hardly see at all; one must have confidence, conviction, ardour, and I have none of these.—Conclusion: personally, I cannot pretend to eloquence, moving or persuasive. By hard work, I might contrive to be judicious and keen in literature and aesthetics, acute, delicate, perhaps profound in psychological philosophy; but I am and remain disinterested, objective, reflective, I cannot believe in the sympathy of a crowd on my behalf, nor could I make myself its mouthpiece and representative.—Impersonal and sympathetic in the sphere of thought, I feel completely individual and detached in action.—Hence my dialectical contradictoriness. Theoretically, I can easily disengage the general spirit of a book, a life, a nation; practically, I am struck, beyond anything else, by the spiritual differences of individuals, and I never make an instinctive synthesis of a crowd in which I happen to find myself. I give myself to things, to the past, to the future, to objects; but I deny myself to individuals, to the present, to my immediate surroundings. Always through an instinct for liberty. Everything that solicits me directly inspires in me a secret distrust, and I only give my heart unhesitatingly where there is no hope of a return. I have a far-sighted intelligence but I am very slow to enthusiasm; I detest expedience and am only interested in the non-useful. In short, I have a horror of success, just because it would flatter me; I am too proud to will what I desire, or even to acknowledge to myself what I love. Is this a timorous bashfulness? A sullen pride? An utter disillusion? A dumb protestation? An invincible indolence? It is simply an absolute distrust of life and fate, a timidity that has turned to renunciation, a systematic monkishness and total abdication. I do not dare either to hope or live: that is the whole story. An old story but one that has a thousand variations. I do not dare to write, speak, act, risk, attempt, marry, expatriate myself, speculate, begin, conclude, love, hate, affirm, deny or make a career for myself. I ask almost nothing of anyone, and I ask God only to spare me the sufferings of body and soul. This is the source and origin of the objectivity of my intelligence; I consider everything and claim nothing. I always return to the nerveless contemplation which is the form of my egoism and the consequence of my fear. And this is a way of forgetting my duty and silencing my responsibility.

*January 27, 1860.*—Felt, today, a great desire for order; drew up my accounts, brought my note-books up to date; took steps to recover command over my affairs, properly so called. Negligence is an infirmity much like uncleanliness. Disorder depresses me, and yet I am always falling into it from apathy and procrastination. I forget where things are, I waste time looking for them, then I become disgusted and let it all go. Today, for instance, I came across the missing verses of M. Petit-Senn which got me into trouble the other day, and I was unable to find a psychology-note-book (belonging to my two nephews), which would have been invaluable to me, or at least useful.—Oh, order! Material order, intellectual order, moral order! What a comfort and strength, and what an economy! To know where we are going and what we want: that is order. To keep one's word, to do the right thing, and at the right time: more order. To have everything under one's hand, to put one's whole army through its manœuvres, to work with all one's resources: still order. To discipline one's habits and efforts and wishes, to organize one's life and distribute one's time, to measure one's duties and assert one's rights, to put one's capital and resources, one's talents and opportunities to profit: again and always order. Order is light, peace, inner freedom, self-determination: it is power. To conceive order, to return to order, to realize order in oneself, around oneself, by means of oneself, this is aesthetic and moral beauty, it is well-being, it is what ought to be.

*April 17, 1860.*—My blue devils are gone. I feel better. Nothing remains but a sensation as if my back had been roundly cudgelled and left bruised and painful. Up at the usual hour, I took my regular walk on the Treille. All the buds were open, the young shoots turning green on every branch. Strange, the effect on an invalid of the purling of clear water, the blitheness of the birds, the new-born freshness of the plants, the noisy games of childhood; or rather it seemed strange to me to look upon them through the eyes of infirmity and approaching death and enter upon such a form of existence. This way of looking at things is very sad. One feels that one is under the ban of nature, out of communion with her, for she is strength, joy, eternal health. "Make way for the living!" she cries to us. "Do not cloud my azure with your woes. Everyone has his turn; be off with you!"—To take heart, one has to say to oneself: No, suffering and decay are good, for they help one to see the world, they put zest into the joy of the heedless, they are a warning to those who dream. Life has been lent to us, and we owe our travelling companions the spectacle of the use we make of it even to the very end. We must show our brothers how one ought to live and how one ought to die.—These first summonses, moreover, have a divine value. They give us glimpses of life behind the scenes, its fearful realities and inevitable close. They in-

struct us in sympathy. They counsel us to make the most of our
time, while it is yet day. They teach us gratitude for the good
things that remain to us and humility for the gifts that are in us.
These evils are therefore a good, they are a call from on high, they
are a paternal chastisement.

How fragile a thing is health, then, and how thin a casing protects our life against being devoured from without and disorganized
within! A breath, and the skiff splits and founders; a nothing, and
all is imperilled; a cloud, and all is darkness. Life is indeed the
flower of the grass, which a morning fades and a wing-beat reaps;
it is the widow's lamp, extinguished at a puff. To feel keenly the
poetry of a morning's roses, one has to have just escaped from the
claws of this vulture which we call sickness. The background and
the high-light of the human picture is the cemetery. The one thing
certain, in this world of vain agitations and infinite anxieties, is
death, and the foretaste and small change of death, pain.

As long as one averts one's eyes from this implacable reality, the
tragedy of life is hidden; the moment one looks it in the face, the
true proportions of all things are restored, and solemnity takes its
place in existence again. One perceives clearly that one has toyed
with life, sulked, rebelled, forgotten, and that one has done wrong.

We must die and give an account of our life, this, in all its simplicity, is the great teaching of sickness. Do at once what you have
to do, arrange your affairs, set your house in order, reflect on your
duty, prepare for your departure: this is what conscience and reason
cry. Life is brief and great; it has been lent to us for the profit of
God, for the service of the good and the welfare of others. Be
earnest, save your soul, procure for your dying bed the pillow of
a good conscience.

*May 3, 1860.*—Edgar Quinet has tried everything, he has aimed
only at the greatest things, he is rich in ideas, he has splendid
images, he is a serious, enthusiastic, courageous, noble writer. Why
has he not more of a reputation? Why is he not in the Academy?
etc. Because he is too pure. Because he is too uniformly ideal,

prophetic, fanciful, inspired, and all this bores people in France. Because he is too candid, theoretical, speculative, too confident in his language and ideas, he exposes himself too much, he has too little malice and irony, too little trickery and finesse, and all this makes the clever laugh . . . He is too Protestant in his natural bent and too Oriental in his form for the French world. He is a foreigner at bottom, while Proudhon, Michelet, Renan are natives. Naivety kills a man in Voltaire's country. The sublime wearies people in the land of puns. The imaginative spirit discredits a man in the age of hard facts.

*May 5, 1860.*—In the evening, a walk with L. Heard the first nightingales of the year, gathered the first hawthorne, watched from the "End of the World" the rising of the moon. Austere and sadly majestic landscape; then, coming back, gay lights, music and life at Plainpalais. The contrast was striking. In the sky, Venus sparkled against the blue.—She had been ill the last few days and was very weak. The weariness of life pursues her, and she is sometimes utterly exhausted. Poor soul, she suffers from my malady, only more acutely; and I cannot give her pleasure without doing her harm or abstain without distressing her still more. An impasse. Then she is anxious about her mother, anxious about the present and the future, hesitant about an important offer of work. Nothing to give her a moment's peace. A longing for the day, the ordeal and life to end. It is cruel. And I, not knowing what to do, give her what she wishes, try to comfort her from day to day, awaiting, without expecting, some amelioration, some change.

To grow old is more difficult than to die, for it costs less to renounce a good once and for all, and all at once, than to renew the sacrifice every day in some detail. To endure one's decay, to accept the diminution of oneself, is a rarer and more bitter virtue than to brave death. A tragic and premature death is touched with glory; while only a long sadness hangs over increasing decrepitude. But, seen in a better light, a resigned and religious old age seems more moving than the heroic ardour of the youthful years. The maturity of the soul is more precious than the lustre of the faculties and strength in its abundance, and the eternal in us ought to profit from all the ravages that time has made. This thought is consoling.

> *Vouloir ce que Dieu veut est la seule science*
> *Qui nous met en repos.*

*May 22, 1860.*—A certain deep-seated rigidity keeps me from letting my true feelings appear, from saying what might give pleasure or abandoning myself to the present moment, a stupid reserve which I have always noted with chagrin. My heart does not dare to speak seriously, it is ashamed of flattery and afraid that it will not find the proper nuance. I am always dallying with the passing moment, and my emotion is retrospective. It is repugnant to my refractory nature to recognize the solemnity of the present; by an ironical instinct, which springs from my timidity, I always pass lightly over what is at hand, using as a pretext something else or some other time. The fear of being carried away, together with my self-distrust, pursues me even in my tender moments, and a sort of invincible pride keeps me from making up my mind ever to say: Stay! Decide my fate! Be a supreme moment! Stand out from this monotonous eternity and mark a unique point in my life!

*May 27, 1860 (Sunday).*—This morning, heard a discourse by J. C. on the Holy Ghost, fine but inadequate. He showed that life is empty just so long as some great interest does not wholly fill it, and that daily sacrifice alone assuages the thirst of the soul. And the Holy Ghost is the spirit of sacrifice. *Ergo,* let us celebrate its advent in human society.—Why am I not edified? For want of religious feeling in it all. Why was there no religious feeling? Because it is the Christianity of dignity, not of humility; penitence, helpless struggle, austerity all are missing; the Law disappears, sanctity and mysticism evaporate in this rationalistic point of view. It lacks the specifically Christian accent. My feeling remains what it was. Do not deaden faith by dissolving it in mere moral psychology. It gives me a sense of impropriety and actual discomfort to see philosophy in the pulpit. "They have taken away my Lord, and I know not where they have laid him." The simple are justified in saying this, and I repeat it with them.—Orthodoxy is more suitable to preaching, and far more dramatic and affecting. To remove the supernatural is to bring down at one stroke the whole structure of faith and the religious life.—Thus F. C. shocks me with his sacerdotal dogmatism, and J. C. with his rationalistic laicism. It seems to me that good preaching, as with Schleiermacher, ought to unite perfect moral humility with independent energy of mind, a deep sense of sin with a respect for criticism and the passion for truth.

*June 3, 1860.*—Translated (in verse) the page in Goethe, taken from *Faust,* which contains the pantheistic profession of faith. I read it to B. and L.; then retouched it before putting out my lamp. It seems to me not to run so badly. But what a difference between the two tongues in point of distinctness: they are the stub and the burin, one depicting all the effort, the other noting only the result of the action, one bringing out the dream, the vague, the void, the formless, the other determining, fixing, outlining even the indefinite; one representing the cause, the force, the limbo from which things issue, the other the things themselves. German has the obscure depth of the infinite, French the joyous clarity of the finite.

*June 4, 1860.*—When I came in, I set to work filing away like a madman at a few verses of my translation (the page of *Faust*), persistently, obstinately sifting, revising, levelling down a dozen hemistiches. It is absurdly wrong, as a result of my utter self-distrust. I strike out, erase and work it over, unable to believe that my first impulse is not a mistake. My poor little talent is an acid that attacks itself, a self-corrosive. And, as L. said, no critic is as hard on me as I am. This anxiety destroys my naturalness; no zest, no abandon is possible with it, no flow or gaiety. By dint of retouching, repenting, scratching and scraping, I always manage to destroy anything that might seem like inspiration. I always censoriously clip the pin-feathers of genius the moment they begin to sprout. This assiduous, critical self-scrutiny will certainly end in impotence and non-productivity. For there is an element in productivity, a something somnambulistic, unconscious, blind, which reflection cannot suffer. The analysis that turns inward is the *aqua regia* in which I dissolve my life. My instinct is consistent.

*June 14, 1860.*—Books and women—have I had other resources? And, even here, I have had to seek the books, while the affections of women have sought me out. Is there anything like a woman to electrify us, to vivify, console, bless, inspire, counsel and encourage us? Anything to care for us, relieve, support and heal us, soothe the suffering body, the sick heart, calm the troubled mind like the hand, the voice, the breath, the look of a loving woman?—When I think of all we owe to this sex, I am moved; when I think of all the suffering we can cause it, I am troubled; when I think of all that slumbers in it, all that can come to flower under the incitement of a man, I am filled with a sort of rapture, feeling that a new world sleeps hidden in the breast of woman, and that a lovelier humanity, one that is greater and more heroic than ours, waits at the gates of life till man is worthy to engender it. It is woman, the eternal mother and nurse of the generations, who brings forth man's reward and punishment, his affliction and his crown. Happy he who has found woman strong and pure, zealous and courageous, faithful and saintly, the companion of his days and his nights, the support of his youth and his old age, the echo of his conscience, the helper of his labours, the balm of his griefs, his prayer, his counsel, his repose, his nimbus. In her he has nature entire, in her he incarnates his poetry, settles his anxieties, realizes his dream. True marriage is a prayer, it is worship, it is life become religion, for it is at once nature and spirit, contemplation and action, and it participates visibly in the infinite task through toil, fecundity and education, that triple semination of the spirit and life.

*July 4, 1860 (10 a. m.).*—One needs to love and be loved every day; so I felt this morning, reading in my "park". It is not good or auspicious to live alone, even when one is well in body and mind. My heart yearns for affection, not for any particular affection but for affection in general; my happiness is not yet individualized, but it tends to become more personalized. Things no longer satisfy me, people no more than things, nor any woman, but woman still incarnates the secret desire of everything that dreams and longs within me . . . Have I ceased to be worthy of anything but friendship?

*Ai-je passé le temps d'aimer?*

For loving madly, completely, with intoxication? *Dio lo sa.* Do I still deserve it? Am I blind? Am I rebellious? Am I ungrateful? Am I impious, mad? Truly, I hardly know. In things of this order, it is repugnant to me to take common sense as my guide and judge. I am a mystic in love; the infinite alone tempts me. For anything less I have only indulgence, indifference and contempt. In my terror of action I am always eager to clutch at a motive for abstaining, renouncing, abandoning. And these motives are always the limitations, lacks and imperfections of the thing that presents itself as an end to pursue, an object to desire, a plan to carry out. I am willing to yield myself utterly only to the ideal, which leaves in the heart no regret, no restlessness or worry or desire, because it satisfies all aspirations.—But nothing, no one can be the ideal; and thus my instinct has found and always finds a means of detaching itself and losing its taste, liberating itself from any imperious motive, any overmastering influence, any irresistible impulsion, leaving me as free, bereft and empty as a votary of the Grand Lama.

*Car le néant peut seul simuler l'infini.*

Is this not the *schlecht Unendliche* of Hegel? At bottom, this tendency exists in me, with my consent, but against my will. I suffer it but I suffer by it; my consent is not content. It is my nature but also my misfortune. Perhaps this aspiration tends to bring God into life, instead of subjecting life to God, perhaps it tends to the seeking of heaven on earth instead of accepting earth as the abode of imperfection, desire and suffering. You admit trials, grief, sickness, death, but with an immortal beatitude behind them; perhaps this beatitude should change its name, and have a savour of sacrifice instead of perfect harmony. One has to give favours in some quarter, to pardon and excuse, to be able to ask the like in return. If one's conscience approves, then one's self-esteem, one's personal satisfaction, one's pride must learn to endure and be silent. The love that is possible for you would be joyous as much through devotion as through direct delight. This love would be a renunciation, not simple merely but double, a renunciation, at all events, of the solitary life, of oneself, as well as the renunciation of any complete satisfaction with one's new self in the married state. In other words, in sanctified love, charity must be an essential element, a moment that is forever renewed. In general, I should discourage a reflective love like this in which thought has to create the rapture; but for an individual like you, the spontaneity that is lacking in it might be somewhat replaced by such a procedure. You always wish to know before you resolve, and in order to have your own approval. Your evil must supply its remedy, the poison its antidote.

*August 20, 1860 (evening).*—My besetting sin is discouragement; my misfortune is irresolution; my dread is of being duped, and duped by myself; my idol is liberty; to will is my cross; doubt is the chain that binds me; my eternal fault is procrastination. It is my fetish to substitute a sterile contemplation for regeneration. Of my tastes, the most constant is for psychology. My daily error is to miss the right occasion; my passion is the useless; my foible is to be loved and to take advice; my folly is to live without an aim . . .

You have not defined your individuality or discovered your mission; or at least, in this matter, you are always lapsing into uncertainty. Loath to choose, to resign or limit yourself, you have advanced only at one point, the knowledge of yourself and, in general, man. In everything else, you have regressed, you have declined and lost.—You can give advice, you can explain and illumine. Is this nothing? It would be better to set an example by the education of yourself.

*August 21, 1860.*—Might the answer lie there? Is psychology perhaps the thing for you, the thing you can do best, the field in which you can be useful? Here, at least, you have verified, experimented, studied directly; you have exercised your sagacity, disciplined your aptitude; and these 3749 pages represent an apprenticeship that would not be wasted. Here you feel no marked inferiority to the professional men, the pedagogues, moralists, pastors, philosophers. Here you can pass from the rank of amateur to that of a specialist. Here you have less need of memory than in any other field of study, and yet all your special and casual studies can be put to profit. Without throwing anything overboard, you would be able to concentrate here, gird up your loins and assemble your acquisitions. You could reconcile yourself with your past and with Providence. Clarity and peace together would appear in your life. You could have a goal, without denying your nature or scouting your instincts. Your individuality would lie in comprehending individualities, delivering them, like Socrates, by bringing to light the elements of human nature, and multiplying the wealth of psychology.

You who have so long kicked against the pricks, averted your eyes and shunned life, would find here the interest, the gravity, the substance and the charm of which you are in need. You would add your stone to the universal structure, while remaining faithful to yourself. You would serve your country, you would be more of a man, and this central study is the one that best prepares for the future in the present, because it lays hold upon life, the eternal thing. An enormous weight would be lifted from your breast if you were toiling at last at your own task, if you were in your path, if your duty and your pleasure coincided, if your conscience dared to open itself to God and ask for his fatherly blessing on the work of your hands. Perhaps you would also be better able to solve the tormenting problem of marriage, forever pushed aside and forever returning. The woman you need is the one who could best join hands in this sacred work, the deepening of human life by the search for perfection. The moment you had an impersonal motive and measure, you would be able to make up your mind with more maturity and, especially, calm.—Oh, follow this line, preserve this feeling. They must be good, and heaven sends them to you.

*November 14, 1860.*—It appears that my forte, willy-nilly, is to subdue haughty natures, to endow with a taste for slavery souls that shake off the yoke of any obedience; at least, this is the fourth time the thing has happened to me . . . My nature seems to exercise a peculiar magnetism over strong and wilful women, whom I tame without intending it, and who yield to me as the lioness yielded to Androcles, by an irresistible instinct. For, after all, I am the one who always receives the declarations. What is the reason for this odd fact, which has surprised me whenever it has occurred? Is it because I have a touch of the poet, a touch of the diviner, because I am friendly, discreet and a bachelor? Is it because I give the illusion of talent, accompanied by disinterestedness and mildness? Is it because I seem to be a rather balanced, cultivated man, fastidious, qualified for many things and on the road to many of the perfections that people might kindly attribute to me? Is it the reward for my old efforts to distinguish the ideal in man, so that to feminine eyes I erroneously seem closer to the ideal than other men? Intimacy with me appears to be an object of fervent and passionate desire, and my influence produces surprising effects. So there is something in me that satisfies, flatters and appeases some profound need in women: is it not the need to be understood and to receive the spark of fire? To be initiated into the ideal life by loving thought, by intellectual love? To be penetrated in their mystery, that they may open to higher mysteries? To feel themselves transfigured, to develop all the power of life and poetry which they dimly divine in their own breasts? The feminine soul gives itself to him who will fecundate it; it belongs to him who opens the divine world and gives it a glimpse of the life that is possible under the aspect of ideal beauty.

*December 5, 1860.*—I am but an egg without a germ, an empty shell, a skull without a brain, an infertile being, the semblance of a male but in fact a neuter. Men who are clearly marked and determined, who know what they want, who have a faith, a character, an aim, succeed, engender, create; but as for me, I float like an element, I am fluid, negative, indecisive, indeterminable, and as a result I am nothing. What I have known or willed effaces itself in me, as a dissolving view vanishes before one's eyes. My being melts into formless mist; my existence is only an inner phantasmagoria. If I appear to be someone in the eyes of others, to myself I am only a shadow without substance, a dream that cannot be grasped, a mere rumour of life. *(11.15 p. m.)*

*December 18, 1860 (6.30 a. m.).*—For two hours now I have restlessly lain awake. I meditated in bed, anxiously aware all the time that the clock was striking the quarters, halves and hours which sped like a whirlwind of sound. At last I rise; a whip cracks in the street, which is still dark, and I catch a glimpse of the roofs, all white with snow that has fallen during the night. In the house everyone is asleep. At other times, these hours of peace, when the morning lamp illumines the writing-desk, have been filled with a keen sweetness, an intimacy of self-communion. My whole being expanded at these times, I felt I was advancing, joyous, conquering. Today, I might still read with pleasure, but I am tormented with a peevish dissatisfaction, I am unequal to my task, and today's vigil before the dawn is only a taking-up of my cross again. It is the need of arranging and connecting my thoughts that makes improvisation (or composition) a torture for me. I cannot hold a mass of things together in my attention and memory, and my mind, on the other hand, insists that I shall do so. This contradiction between my desire and my power, between what I would and what I can, always paralyzes me, and takes away all my zest and relish.

*January 9, 1861.*—I come back from Victor Cherbuliez's opening lecture dumbfounded with admiration. I am convinced at the same time of my own fundamental incapacity ever to do anything like it, for skill, grace, succinctness, fertility, proportion, solidity and finesse. As a reading, it was exquisite; as a recitation, it was admirable; as an improvisation, it was prodigious, astounding, it left no room for any rival. Against superiority and perfection, as Schiller said, we have but one resource, that is to love them. This is what I did. I was pleased and a little surprised to find that I felt no jealousy and that I put myself at once in my proper place, rendering justice to this young conqueror. . . .

*January 23, 1861 (11 p. m.).*—This evening, read almost the whole of the first volume of *Merlin*. My impression is mixed and rather unfavourable. Merlin is less the legend of the human soul than the legend of the author, the fantastic apotheosis of his inner history, a colossal autobiography. I find in it a strange combination of Faust, Dante, Don Juan, Soumet and Victor Hugo, together with a certain lack of wit, gaiety, good sense, plastic strength; on the other hand, one always hears in it the poet of Ahasuerus, Prometheus, Napoleon, the translator of Herder, a visionary muse, magniloquent, rapturous, wearisome in its everlasting allegory, its strained eloquence and oracular majesty. Quinet is the prophet all the time, there is no truce to his merciless dithyrambs, and the moment he wishes to be simple he falls into the trivial. He is an idealist rioting in colours, a Platonist brandishing the thyrsis of the mænads. At bottom, he has an expatriated mind: useless to banter Germany and curse England, he does not become more French by doing so. He has a Northern intellect united to a Southern imagination, and the marriage is not a success. His malady is a chronic exaltation, an inveterate sublimity; abstractions become for him personified in colossal beings who act and speak in the most inordinate fashion; he is drunk with the infinite. And it is quite plain that his creations are only personal monologues; he cannot escape from subjective lyricism. Ideas, passions, anger, hope, complaints,—it is always himself that one finds on every page. One never has the joy of emerging from his magic circle, seeing the real truth, finding oneself in rapport with the phenomena and beings of whom he speaks, with the reality of things. This imprisonment of the author in his own personality is a sort of infatuation. And yet it is because of his generous heart that his mind is egoistic; it is because Quinet is so sure he is French that he is in fact so little French. This ironical compensation of destiny is very familiar to me; I am always observing it. Man is nothing but contradiction, and the less he knows it the more he is duped. Unable to see things as they are, Quinet's mind is not very just, neither is it well-proportioned. He resembles Victor Hugo in certain respects, with much less artistic power but more of the historic sense. His leading faculty is the symbolic imagination; he seems to me a Franc-comtois Görres,[1] a sort of supernumerary prophet, one whom his country does not know what to do with, since it likes neither enigmas nor ecstasy nor turgid language, and the intoxication of the tripod bores it.—Quinet's real superiority seems to me to lie in his historical works *(Marnix, l'Italie, les Roumains)*, and especially in his studies of nationalities. He was born to understand these souls that are vaster and more sublime than individual souls.

*January 27, 1861 (midnight)*.— . . . The recollection of my pretty blonde last evening (at the play) has also come back to me . . . At the bottom of my sentiment, however, persists a vague melancholy, a regret for things irreparably lost. If the days that know not love count for nothing in life, I have had few days that were not useless. Ardour, enthusiasm, genius, devotion are dried up in my soul . . . Reason in its nobler aspect has all but perished in me, save as a fleeting fancy. My heart is impoverished, my mind sterile, my life insipid, my flame extinguished . . . Isolation has withered me; the gnawing worm is at the root of my tree, and I am blasted on my feet, in all the fullness of my verdure, before I have borne any fruits or flowers.

[1] Joseph Görres (1776–1848), mystical German philosopher, a disciple of Schelling.

*February 4, 1861.*— . . . There is unquestionably a wall between the public and myself, a wall as of glass, cold and almost opaque. We scarcely come into intellectual contact, and my sympathies, striking the barrier, fall back on themselves half frozen. I am quite aware of the reasons for all this. It is my constant desire to hide myself and my wishes have been granted, for I discourage hope and baffle expectation.—Unable to satisfy myself, I am still less able to captivate, cajole, charm, influence an audience. To do this one must be at once the master of one's subject and one's speech, adroit, ambitious, magnetic, and for me all these conditions are totally lacking. A man who is always apprehensive, always on thorns or live coals, can hardly appear gracious. A deep inflexibility prevents all this in me.

*February 25, 1861.*—Sexuality has been my Nemesis, my torment, ever since childhood. My extraordinary timidity, my awkwardness with women, my violent desires and ardent imagination, the mischievous books I read as a young boy, and then the eternal disproportion between my dream-life and my real life, my disastrous propensity to sever myself from the tastes, passions and habits of those of my own age and sex, the fatal attraction I later exercised over delicate, tender hearts . . . all this has sprung from a primitive shame, an idealization of the forbidden fruit, in short, from a false notion of the sexual. This error has poisoned my life . . . It has prevented me from being a man, and, indirectly, it has caused the miscarriage of my career.—One should leave to chance the care of creating in the child's mind the notion of sex, modesty and pleasure!—Let us acquit nature, give it our love and respect, place the notion of decency where it belongs, as a matter of propriety, not a mystery, remove, through simple distaste, the prick from curiosity, and not disguise the plan of Providence, lest we excite the desire to know and the desire to feel, lest we give birth to suspicion, temptation and exaggerated shame in the young hearts that are entrusted to us.

Confusion regarding the sexual functions is, I believe, as a matter of fact, one of the plagues of our generation, which is so nervous and so nerveless. The whole physical life of woman revolves about this centre, and that of man, too, though less conspicuously. What is there so astonishing about it? Is not life the expression of the universe, generation the hearth of life, and sex the key of generation? Here then is the heart of the question of questions. He who can neither reproduce nor produce is no longer living. Will, thought, work, action, speech are engendered in us by the same law as the being that takes shape in the mother. When we have lost all power of communication, all stimulus, the spontaneity that excites, we are no longer males; when we cease to react, to assimilate and attract, when we are purely passive, we are in fact dead . . .

*March 17, 1861.*—This afternoon, a homicidal languor took possession of me again: disgust and weariness with life, a mortal sadness. I wandered off to the cemetery; I hoped to collect myself there and reconcile myself to duty. Delusion! The place of rest itself had become inhospitable. Some workmen were digging up sods and carting them away; the trees were bare, the wind cold, the sky grey; a something arid, prosaic and profane dishonoured the refuge of the dead. I was struck by this great deficiency in our feeling, the respect for the departed, the poetry of the grave, the piety of memory. Our temples are closed too much and our cemeteries are too open. The result is the same. The troubled, tormented soul that would like to find some place, away from the house and everyday cares, where it might pray in peace, pour out its woes to God and meditate in the presence of eternal things, does not know where to go in our world. Our Church ignores these sorrows of the heart, it does not divine them, it has so little compassionate graciousness, so little considerate regard for the finer shades of grief, no sense of the mysteries of tenderness, no religious suavity whatever. Under the pretence of spirituality, we wound legitimate aspirations. We have lost the mystical sense, and what is a religion without mysticism? A rose without perfume.

We are always saying, repentance, sanctification! But adoration and consolation are also two essential religious elements, and we ought to leave more room for them.

*April 28, 1861.*—I was awakened this morning at five o'clock by violent claps of thunder. So the distress last evening was partly that of nature. The electric discharge and the rain that accompanied it have relieved the atmosphere, refreshed the vegetation and brightened the existence of all things living. The Treille is ravishing, the sky is blue again and one carries life with a gay heart. People who are in despair always make a mistake when they hang themselves; the next day often brings the unknown. Several acquaintances, whom I met after breakfast, had passed through the same experiences as mine, yesterday and this morning.—My dejection was therefore partly physical. Just as, according to their nature, dreams transform incidents during sleep, the soul converts into psychic phenomena the ill-defined impressions of the organism. An uncomfortable position becomes a nightmare; a storm-charged atmosphere becomes a moral torment. Not by any mechanical effect or any direct causality; but the imagination and the conscience engender, after their own nature, analogous effects; they translate into their own language, and mould in their form, things that come to them from the outside. So it is that dreams can be of use in medicine and divination. So it is that the weather brings forth from the soul evils that lie confusedly hidden within. Life is but excited from without, and it never produces anything but itself; this is the basis of monadology. Originality consists in producing a clear, quick reaction against this influence from without and giving it our individual formulation. To think is to collect oneself in one's impression, to disengage the impression in oneself and project it in a personal judgment. This also means delivering oneself, liberating and conquering oneself. Everything that comes to us from without is a question to which we owe an answer, a pressure to which we owe a counter-pressure, as long as we are alive and wish to remain free.—The humble docility with which you open your mind to things, without reacting or judging or formulating, is a pure delusion. You permit yourself to be crushed, smothered, cancelled by things and people, who wish nothing better. Whatever allows itself to be devoured is devoured, and nobody thanks one for it. One is simply swallowed alive and becomes a laughing-stock into the bargain.

*August 4, 1861.*— . . . Watched a flock of pretty girls coming out of church; and this delicious sunlight on their fresh dresses stirred amorous feelings in my heart. Climbed up alone to Pressy at the hottest time of the day (two o'clock). Magnificent weather; Mont Blanc looked as if it had just been created. The landscape had a splendid majesty. The mountains and the foliage sported in the blue air, intoxicated with the sky and with joy . . . What gladdened my own heart, after the warm welcome of my relatives, was especially the caresses of the little girls. I was thirsty for tenderness and kisses. And as if Loulou instinctively surmised this, she clambered up on my knees again and again. These childish endearments charm me more than I dare to confess, and when, at my departure, she accompanied me as far as the hedge below, I embraced her almost effusively, though in all innocence.—There is, however, something mysterious in the attraction of the kiss; I know two or three young girls with passionate hearts over whom I have a certain power, and who do not arouse a shadow of desire in me, while a little scrap of a girl like this makes me want to cover her with kisses from head to foot. Philosophers, as they advance in years, always become more sensitive to the charm of grace and always more passionately fond of beauty, that symbolic epitome of all excellence, that intuitive summary of all perfection. At forty, I shall end by feeling as the young lads do, I shall be in love with every woman and the slave of every loving glance. This frightens me a little. In spite of everything, my heart leaps to the encounter of all the tender emotions, as if it were impatient to fulfil its fate and claim its share of youth and happiness.

*September 4, 1861.*—What am I good for nowadays? Nothing. There is only one thing that interests me, affection, women. I do not work any more, I do not study, I have no ambition except for a woman after my heart, and every girl that passes seems like an invitation or a mockery of happiness. I love all women a little, as if they all held in pawn for me a fragment of my ideal, or my ideal itself. I envelop them with my sympathy as the refuge, the sanctuary, the harbour of griefs, joys and affections, as the celestial provision of gentleness and kindness on earth. I never feel really well except when I am with them; and when I obey my nature with a whole heart, they feel that they are so loved and understood that they return all my kindness. I see this clearly in the country, in the mountains, where one leaves behind the mocking eyes and ironical tongues in which the city of Calvin superabounds. It is my nature to be caressing, childlike, attentive, compassionate, sympathetic, to abandon myself to the collective life, to seek to make animals and men happy, to be kind to all creatures, helpful to every living thing, loving to all hearts. But these are the paternal and conjugal qualities, so I am not unworthy to be a husband and father. Then what stands in the way of this vocation? An incurable distrust of destiny, together with the fastidiousness of my ideal. I do not dare to play the last and only card of my happiness, and I have not met or recognized my companion. I have been loved often enough to be very exacting in my affection, and to know in how many ways one can suffer in the married state. Besides, I dread the Nemesis that might cause me to be disdained if I fell in love. And yet I have only one aspiration, only one desire.

*September 12, 1861.*—Grey, cool weather this morning. Coming downstairs felt for the first time in a good while (two years, perhaps) the charm of study, an appetite for intellectual work, an enthusiasm for pure thought. This clearing of my mental air lasted only a moment, but it reopened a vista over my past, as a capricious breeze rends the November fog and allows the traveller to see the valleys that he has left behind him.—How I have changed! But perhaps that old I may not be dead, perhaps it is only dormant! Perhaps I could soar again into the ethereal, sublime regions of the general life!—What would be necessary for this? Heart's ease, contentment. Mme. S. at Villars, as she worked, dug the point of her scissors under her wedding-ring; I saw the blood and exclaimed, "Why, you have hurt yourself!"—"What of it," she replied, "so long as the heart is contented!" How the woman spoke there, the loving woman! She knows only one happiness, only one grief, the full heart or the empty heart. I myself, through sympathy and metamorphosis, have almost reached this point. The only effect of the laborious, studious period of my life has been to postpone for fifteen years the moment of feeling, dreaming, loving and suffering! This immense distraction has come to an end. Sentiment takes its revenge. The great contradiction of my nature is a mind that longs to forget itself in things and a heart that longs to live among others. The common ground in the contrast is the desire to abandon one-self, to will and exist for oneself no longer, to depersonalize one-self, to be volatilized in love and contemplation. What I lack is character, will, individuality. And, as always, the appearance is precisely the opposite of the reality; my ostensible life is the reverse of my fundamental aspiration. I, whose whole being, mind and heart yearn to be absorbed in living reality, in my fellow-men, in nature and God, I, whom solitude consumes and destroys, shut myself up in solitude and appear to be pleased only with myself, appear to be self-sufficient . . . Pride and modesty of soul, timidity of heart have caused me to violate all my instincts and absolutely invert my life. I have always avoided, in fact, whatever has attracted me, fled from that which gave me the most pleasure. No wonder I am impenetrable; the suicidal instinct has become identified in me with the instinct of self-preservation, and I have always turned my back on the path I should secretly have wished to follow. False shame has been the scourge, the curse of my existence. It has not made me false, but it has made a eunuch of me. I have always been afraid of showing what I desired and even of confessing it to myself; I have a horror of seeking my own advantage, a horror of using guile and subterfuge to attain my ends, and I have succeeded at last in having no ends, no clear desire, not even any impulses of the will. False shame, that complex of modesty, pride, distrust, weakness, anxiety, chronic at first, has become a habit, a temperamental thing, my second nature, and now I am only a poor bashful creature who blushes at the thought of making demands, uttering an untruth, lowering himself or even suffering, or struggling to get out of his misery.—Humiliation has become my terror, and dependence is the essence of humiliation. It is quite impossible for me to be dependent on any but those I love. Sympathy is the principle of my life.—And the moment I cease to feel sympathy, the moment I cease to love, I shrivel like a pricked balloon.

To have spent one's life forging a breast-plate for oneself, sheathing oneself in indifference, and all to end up as vulnerable as this! To have made up one's mind in advance that everything is deceptive, vain and irksome, so as to accustom oneself to loving without asking anything in return, and at the end of it all finding out that one cannot petrify one's heart! After staking all on a single card, to feel old age coming, without having lived! . . . Alas!

What is this demon who, just as you are about to reap a joy, always says to you, March on! and, at the moment of acting and going forward, says to you, Stop! False shame all the time. And yet your real joys are childish in their nature, they are quite ingenuous. Underneath your complicated nature the simple human being continues to live, gentle, heedless, frank, the good-hearted fellow, to put it briefly. There is something of the old man in you, something of the woman, and the child as well; all you lack is the manly. You do not develop after a plan of your own, or in accordance with a law of growth that is stronger than circumstances; you are the sport of influences, of your surroundings, of chance, at least in the sense that they cause you to expand through some solicitation from without, for you always recover your freedom when you are self-conscious. Thus you are swept along, and yet you are not dominated. You do not use your will, yet you are not a slave.

You are intelligent, but you are weak, satisfied to understand and observe the currents and cross-currents of your life, without intervening to direct them.

I think the Absolute has rendered you forever incapable of attaching yourself to relative things; it has given you a distaste for individuality, for your individuality at least. You have only lived therefore from a spirit of accommodation, unable as you are to take very seriously a manner of seeing or acting or being that is only one point in the series, one form of the infinite. It is to Hegel that you owe this fundamental indifference, this fatal objectivity as regards practical life, this inability to wish with a whole heart for what you cannot believe to be anything more than half-true, half-good or useful. The craving for the whole has caused you to regard as pitiful the role of a part that is infinitesimal. The sentiment of the ideal, the perfect, the eternal, of the absolute, in a word, has permanently discouraged you.—Duty remains, but the rapturous illusion has vanished.—And devotion without some little return, toil without a touch of illusion are two very heroic things, and to remain constantly heroic one must have an ardent faith and a firm religion, and faith and religion are always wavering in you.— *O du armer!*

*Heidelberg, October 10, 1861 (10.30 p. m.).*—After eleven days of travelling, here I am again, where I was two years ago, under the roof of my friends, the W.'s, in the hospitable house on the bank of the Neckar, with a garden that climbs the flank of the Heiligenberg.

*Heidelberg, October 11, 1861 (10 a. m.).*—Bright sunshine; my room is flooded with light and warmth. Seated on a charming sofa of woolen damask, with a view of the Geisberg at my right, veiled in pale amber, and the town at my feet, I am writing to the murmur of the Neckar, whose green waves, spangled with silver, roll directly below the balcony that encircles the whole floor where my rooms are. A great barge, coming from Heilbronn, passes silently under my eyes, while the wheels of a cart which is out of sight can be heard on the road that winds along the river. The far-away voices of children, roosters, sparrows at play, the clock of the church of the Holy Ghost, striking the hour, measure, without disturbing it, the general tranquillity of all this nature. One feels the hours gently slipping by, and time seems here to hover in its flight rather than to beat its wings. An indefinable peace mounts in my heart. Since I left home, this, to speak strictly, is the first moment of revery and self-collectedness. An impression of morning grace and fresh poetry that is like adolescence and gives one the feeling of German happiness . . . Two barges are ascending the stream, with red flags floating, each with a string of flat-boats, filled with coal, manœuvring to pass through the arch of the great stone bridge; the tow-horses are in water up to their bellies, and a little boat puts off to bring them the end of the cable. I press my face against the window and see a whole procession of boats moving in both directions; the Neckar is as animated as a Corso; and, early as it is, on the slope of the wooded mountain, streaked with wavy lines of smoke from the town, the castle spreads out its shadow like a vast drapery and reveals the outlines of its towers and gables. Higher up, facing me, the Molkenkur unveils its dark profile and on the right the red sandstone quarry cuts its sharp angle in the verdure, with one side lighted by the rays of the sun. Still higher, standing out against the dazzling eastern sky, rise the misty forms of the two belvederes, the Kaiserstuhl and the Trutz-Heinrich, separated by a winding valley.

But let us leave the landscape. What is going on within? . . . Professor W. informs me that his *Handbuch* is already translated into Polish, Dutch, Spanish, Italian and French and has had nine printings of three thousand copies each. Three volumes of his great *Universal History* are already published. And to do all this he has only four hours a day, aside from holidays and vacations. This capacity for work is truly astounding, this tenacity is prodigious! *O deutscher Fleiss!* . . .

This life of a toiling savant and learned compiler troubles me a little. I feel so distracted myself, so divided, so forgetful, that it gives me a feeling of ignorance and incompetence when I compare myself with these fabulous workers who read and make extracts and combinations of all manner of things and never stop. What is the good of all this labour? I ask myself. To popularize knowledge. Has my host the time to think and feel? It does not seem so. His mind is a sort of machine for grinding books and making new books out of the grindings. His principal work, in my opinion, is to have brought up a really fine family by his toil, and rendered good service to the general teaching of history. His merit is the *Gründlichkeit*, his talent for practical arrangement and clarity, his personal charm a cordial honesty. But one cannot glean from the field of his mind the shadow of an original idea. There is the reverse of the medal.

*November 9, 1861.*—Warm weather, good soft rain, air like velvet. Happy enough not to feel my body, the state of perfect health. Is my temperament insensibly changing? Is it possible that I, who used to prefer dry air and a north wind to all other kinds of weather, may end by finding that damp, warm weather and southern breezes best agree with me? I have observed the contrary in my diet. The passion for sweets and milky dishes, unspiced food, has given place to a taste for stronger and more highly seasoned things. My stomach is growing virile and my nerves effeminate. Always compensation, balance, recurrence. Each of our diverse organic systems thus runs through the orbit of our different dispositions and in different ways from one another. A man who has lived sixty years traverses, unawares, the cycle of temperaments and distastes; his general revolution about the centre of life is composed of a multitude of subordinate revolutions and epicycles.—I can remember, too, the series of my acoustic preferences: first the soprano voice, then the bass, then the tenor, then the contralto. At present it is the baritone, or rather the absence of preference and the objectivity that brings it. The conclusion that one draws from this is that the development of our unconscious nature follows the astronomical laws of Ptolemy. Everything is change, cycle, epicycle, metamorphosis, in the microcosm as in the macrocosm.

Everyone thus possesses in himself analogues of everything, the rudiments of everything, of all beings and all the forms of life. Whoever can detect the minute beginnings, the germs and the symptoms, can find in himself the mechanism of the universe, he can divine by intuition the series that he will not himself complete, vegetable and animal existences, the human passions and crises, the maladies of the soul and those of the body. A subtle and powerful mind can pass through all potentialities and draw forth in a flash at every point the monad, the world that it contains. This is to achieve consciousness and possession of the general life and to pass once more into the divine sanctuary of contemplation.

*November 12, 1861.*—Bilac, alias Mustapha, alias Corporal Trim, alias Lollypop, otherwise known as our little striped cat, has just leaped upon my pen, which was writing the date, and has caused me to cover this page with blots. He has paused now and is trying to comprehend this accursed art that Cadmus invented. In his wrath at having wasted all his pains, he begins to scratch again, but ah, woe! he slips on the edge of the desk, carries Fichte's *Anthropology* with him and falls with the philosopher in a general shipwreck. His embarrassment is my deliverance, and off he goes to my sofa to cut enormous capers in the impossible pursuit of his tail. He is a perfect whirlwind.

But I am discontented with myself. Last night, in bed at ten o'clock because my eyes were smarting, I was hoping to be up at six this morning, and I did not waken till half-past seven. I slept like a child, like a dormouse, a top . . . How ill-employed my life is, with all my stupidity, indolence and timidity. I used to read and work all the time, and now I sleep and lounge; what has it all been good for? . . . Bilac is certainly mad with gaiety. He is turning everything topsy-turvy among the books and papers piled on my round table with the red cloth. He has knocked down Michelet's *Amour*, and now, with his four paws in the air, he is juggling a blue envelope.

*Bilac est de ces chats qui, les livres rongeant,*
*Se font savants jusques aux dents.*

The chase continues and begins anew, with a thousand crafty movements, leaps, archings of his back, capers and pirouettes. It is really ludicrous. School-boys could hardly amuse themselves more to their hearts' content, but this school-boy is mute. There is no laughter in his gambollings, no living, joyous, resounding laughter, and, all in all, these silent games seem mad rather than anything else. There is something sinister in muteness.

*November 25, 1861.*—To understand a drama requires the same mental operation as to understand a life, a biography, a man: one has to follow the bird back into the egg, the plant into the seed and reconstruct the whole genetic process of the being in question. Art consists merely in bringing into relief the hidden thought of nature; it is a simplification of the lines and a segregation of the invisible groups. The fire of inspiration brings out the designs that have been traced in sympathetic ink. The mysterious becomes plain, the confused becomes clear, the complicated becomes simple, the fortuitous becomes necessary. In short, art reveals nature by translating its intentions and formulating its wishes (the ideal). Every ideal is the answer to a long enigma. The great artist is a simplifier.

*January 13, 1862.*—This year I have won back two persons who for a long time were at outs with me . . . Forbearance and constant goodwill have ended by dissolving the ice and stone of indifference and prejudice. Happy in disliking or envying no one, I am happier to have conquered this ill will, regained these hearts that have been vindictive and turned so unjustly against me. It is a little like the joy which the lost sheep, found again, gives. Is not everyone the shepherd of the affections that have come to him, or that he himself has won through friendship, kinship, publishing or travel, whether by chance or choice? And is it not the consolation of life to reach the evening of one's days with one's flock multiplied and full? Lay up for yourselves unseen treasures, says the Gospel. After good works, what is it that composes these treasures, if it is not the attachments and the friendships, the tender and grateful relations, in short, the affections that we have been able to create and keep? As for myself, if I have erected no monument to perpetuate my memory, if I have done nothing for the world and posterity, I shall have left perhaps in a certain number of hearts here below the traces of my passage. My only statue will be in the recollection of a few faithful souls; my only funeral oration in the few secret tears of those who have loved me. This is a goodly portion still; and I recall, with sweet and grateful feelings, the precious garland of friendships, deep and even passionate, that already encircle my obscure name and blossom in my memory. In spite of my timidity, reserve, distrust, I have been richly dowered with sympathy, and many different minds and characters have opened themselves to me.—I remember in this connection that persons whom I have scarcely known have sometimes formed the deepest attachments for me . . . so deep that I have ceased to wonder and doubt. They have made an exception to the rules on my behalf and the sanctuary of the secret thoughts of women has been unveiled spontaneously and often for my eyes. This voluntary apocalypse has created for me a confidant's role that is strange but charmingly delicate. I have read private journals and directed several neophytes and even a few young penitents. They feel that I understand, divine, protect them; and as I never betray a confidence, they often confess themselves beyond all reserve, and even embarrass me greatly. How many children, too, of all ages, love me and give their hearts to me! Be sure I shall never forget them in the tale of my affections and my benefactors. Goodness has its promises for the life we live, as for the eternal life. It delivers the soul from the griefs that the evil passions cause; it gives contentment, and, to fill the measure, often wins our neighbour's grateful love. It is so sweet a thing to be good that one can scarcely call it meritorious. Is not goodness the most touching and perhaps the greatest of God's attributes? To live at peace with the good God is the joy of joys, it is the very foundation of happiness, the religion of childhood and old age, the be-all and end-all of the creed and the prayer of the man of thought.

*February 3, 1862.*—Nothing solid accomplished, and my head feels crushed. I think I have become incapable of composing. Re-reading every line a dozen times, I destroy my verve and cannot advance. Aside from my journal and letters, in which my pen runs with a loose rein, I cannot write; anxiety stifles me, and every word sticks like a thorn in my throat. Far from carrying in my mind a whole composition, a chapter, I do not visualize a period; I concentrate on the nib of my pen and the word it is tracing, and see only as far as the end of my nose, and the afflatus vanishes, the wing-beat, the glow, the inspiration, along with gaiety and sincerity. This abominable habit of fettering my mind, through the eyes, to the letters my hand is scrawling puts to rout whatever memory and whatever glow I have left. With every second, I lose anew the speed I have acquired, the warmth that I have mustered, the movement of ideas that has begun, so that I am always empty and bereft and cannot budge an inch. I cannot retain or accumulate anything. This *fluxus perpetuus* is the cause of my sterility. My vitality fatally evaporates, without a sufficient power of concentration to fecundate an idea or an intention. My brain is too feeble to be impregnated with any force; so that it cannot conceive or give birth to a work. It has all the itch of curiosity, but it miscarries when it comes to production.

As I have realized for many years, self-criticism has become the corrosive of all my spontaneity, literary and oratorical. I have failed in my principle of respecting the mysterious, and my chastisement is impotence in procreation. The need for knowledge, turned in upon the self, is punished, like the curiosity of Psyche, by the flight of the loved object. Force must remain mysterious to itself; the moment it penetrates its own mystery, it straightway vanishes. The goose that lays the golden eggs becomes infertile the moment she wishes to know why her eggs are golden.—Consciousness of consciousness is the outermost end of analysis, I said in the *Grains de mil,* but analysis pushed to the limit devours itself, like the Egyptian serpent. One must give it some external matter to grind and dissolve, if one wishes to preserve it against destruction by its action upon itself. We are and we must be obscure to ourselves, said Goethe, turned towards outer things and working on the world that surrounds us. Radiation outward leads to health; an *interiorization* that is too long continued reduces us to a mere point, to nothingness, an unhealthy state inasmuch as it suppresses us, and others profit by it to suppress us. Better to expand one's life, extend it in broadening circles, than obstinately to diminish and restrict it by solitary contraction. Heat tends to expand a point into a globe, cold to reduce a globe to the dimensions of an atom. By analysis, I have annulled myself.

It is high time for me to fashion a body for myself again, a volume, a mass, a real existence, and emerge from the vague, dark, cold world that isolated thought creates for itself. It would be good to reascend the spiral through which I have uncoiled myself to my very centre. It would be well to turn my reflectors, which reflect one another indefinitely, back towards men and things. Hibernating animals, reaching the extremity of leanness, as a result of having done nothing during their long slumber but lick their paws, are obliged to seek for provisions when they reawaken. Dreamer, come forth from your cave, seek your provender likewise. Long enough have you hidden yourself, withdrawn, denied yourself. Think of living.

*Mornex-sous-Salève, April 22, 1862.*—Wakened by the carolling of the birds at a quarter to five, and, opening my shutters, I saw in the sky the orange crescent of the moon looking down on my window, while the east had scarcely begun to brighten. An hour later, I dressed. Delightful walk. Anemones still closed, apple-trees in blossom:

> *Ces beaux pommiers couverts de leurs fleurs étoilées,*
> *Neige odorante du printemps.*

A ravishing sight. Feeling of freshness and joy. Nature festive. Nothing was missing but those bitter-sweet odours (probably of invisible cyclamens) which yesterday, when I was climbing the little Salève, caressed my nostrils more than once. As if for a compensation, a branch of lilacs, placed in a glass of fresh water, perfumes the writing-table which I have leaned against the wall in order to convert it into a slanting desk.—I have breakfasted, read two numbers of the *Presse,* a piece of verse by d'Aubryet (*Au Printemps*), with authentic feeling, in the style of Petronius, and here I am. Peace be with the dead; but it is sweet today to be alive, and thankfulness has its hymns as faith has. It goes without saying that our ladies are still below the horizon, and that I pity them for missing two or three beautiful hours.

(*Eleven o'clock*).—Preludes, scales, études, strummings, fragments on the piano under my feet. Children's voices in the garden. —I have just run through four of this year's numbers of the *Revue des Deux Mondes*. Articles by Saisset (Spinoza and the Jews); Taillandier (Sismondi—Swiss philosophy); Mazade (Women in literature, apropos of Mme. de Sévigné and Mme. Svetchine); Laugel (Chemical analysis of the sun); Rémusat (Theological criticism and the theological crisis in France).—These gentry all put me in mind of Scherer's remark: "I feel here like a one-eyed man in the country of the blind".—What, in my modesty, I have habitually taken for the reticence of superiority, is, among these great leaders of popular thought in France, nothing but a frivolous lack of culture and a positive superficiality. Their moral, psychological, aesthetic, religious, philosophical development has little depth. Their judgment has no great range either forward, or backward, or comparatively. —As a critic, Scherer is superior in culture to Messrs. Taillandier, Montégut, Rémusat, Saisset, etc. His view of things is more just than Taine's. But he has fewer ideas than Renan and less flexibility than Sainte-Beuve. Theology and philology are the great schools of perspicacity.—I can understand why Scherer wishes to launch me in his world. Deep down, he feels he is poorly understood, and we see about eye to eye.—"The essential thing is to have a well-tempered mind," Mme. de Sévigné says. The limitation of the French mind is the inadequacy of its spiritual alphabet, which will not permit it to translate the Greek soul, the Germanic, the Spanish, etc., without denaturing their accent. The hospitality of manners in France is not complemented by real hospitality of thought. The thought of France, like its idiom, is cut off from the living and natural sap and shut up in the conventional world of a much-taught civilization. Versailles is forever being expiated. This detached turn of mind, in which the word, the idea and the feeling of the author and the reader remain on the outside of things, this indelible cartesianism, in which thought never identifies itself with nature, and to which a level gaze would appear a squint, is the other side of the spirit of sociability. One dares not think for oneself; the individual melts into the human mass; and the consequence is that one always feels oneself outside the things that one examines; a dualism of the object and the subject.—I, on the contrary, am an individual in relation to men, objective in the presence of things. I attach myself to the object, and imbue myself with it; I detach myself from subjects, and keep clear of them. I feel my own difference from the multitude and my kinship to nature in its totality. I affirm myself in my sympathetic unity with life, which I love to understand, and in my negation of the tyrannical commonplace of the vulgar. The imitative mob inspires me as much with secret repulsion as the most minute spontaneous and true existence (animal, plant, child) inspires me with attraction. I feel a community of spirit with the Goethes, the Hegels, the Schleiermachers, the Leibnitzes, opposed as they may be among themselves, while the French philosophers, rhetoricians and geometers, in spite of their high qualities, leave me cold, because they do not carry in themselves the sum of the universal life, because they do not dominate the whole of reality, because they suggest nothing, because they do not enlarge existence, because they imprison me, desiccate me or fill me with distrust.—What the French always lack is the sense of the infinite, an intuition of living unity, a perception of the holy, the initiation into the mysteries of being. They are adroit but profane, because they are superficial and calculating.—From the French point of view, all the profound things remain inexplicable, true poetry, true philosophy, true religion; and when pantheism becomes French, it is ridiculous and out of place, and, in consquence, vicious, inasmuch as it has no counterpoise.—What one has a right to expect of the French is the structure of the special sciences, the art of writing books, style, politeness, grace, literary models, exquisite urbanity, the spirit of order, didactic art, discipline, elegance, truth in detail, the *mise en scène,* the desire and the talent for proselytism, vigour in practical conclusions. But to journey through the *Inferno* or the *Paradiso,* one must have other guides; the French remain on earth, in the region of the finite, the changing, the historical, the diverse. The category of mechanism and the metaphysics of dualism are the two summits of their thought. In attempting to go beyond these, they do violence to themselves and awkwardly wield locutions that do not correspond to any real need in their nature.

*Mornex, April 23, 1862.*—Reread with enchantment a great number of pieces from the *Contemplations:* what inexhaustible richness, and what an unending fountain of images and sensations and sentiments are the works of this poet! The author is a perfect Æolian harp, which every breath of nature and passion sets vibrating, singing, throbbing. All the treasures of Golconda are poverty itself beside his heaps of precious stones and his myriads of glittering medallions.

*Mornex, April 24, 1862 (11.30).*—Deep peace, silence of the mountains, in spite of a full house and a village close at hand. No sound is audible save the buzzing of the flies. This calm somehow grips one. It penetrates one to the marrow. Midday is like midnight. Life seems suspended at the moment when it is most intense. It is like the silences in worship; these are the moments when one hears the infinite, when one perceives the ineffable. Gratitude, emotion, desire to share my happiness. Hugo has just sent me travelling through

the worlds again; then his contradictions make me think of L. T.,
in the house next door, the ardent, convinced Christian. The same
sunlight floods both my book and nature, the doubting poet and
the believing preacher, as well as the inconstant dreamer, who, in
the midst of all these existences, allows himself to be rocked by
every breeze and amuses himself, stretched out in the car of his
balloon, by floating and drifting with all the currents of the ether,
and feeling all the harmonies and dissonances of the soul, of sentiment and thought, pass within him.—Sloth and contemplation, the
sleep of the will, the vacation-time of energy, indolence of the being
—how well I know you! Loving, dreaming, feeling, learning, understanding, I can do everything, as long as I am dispensed from using
my will, liberated from the ennui and effort of action. This is my
natural tendency, my instinct, my defect, my sin. I have a sort of
primitive horror of ambition, of struggle, hatred, everything that
disperses the soul by making it depend on external things and pur-
poses. I am more meditative and contemplative than anything else,
and the joy of recovering the consciousness and possession of myself, of savouring my freedom, hearing the rustle of time and the
flowing torrent of the universal life is often enough to make me forget every other desire. This sensitive apathy has ended by extinguishing in me the need to produce and the strength to execute. Intellectual epicurism constantly threatens to engulf me. I can only
combat it with the idea of duty.

> *Ceux qui vivent, ce sont ceux qui luttent; ce sont*
> *Ceux dont un destin ferme emplit l'âme et le front*
> *Ceux qui d'un haut destin gravissent l'âpre cime,*
> *Ceux qui marchent pensifs, épris d'un but sublime,*
> *Ayant devant les yeux sans cesse, nuit et jour,*
> *Ou quelque saint labeur ou quelque grand amour.*[1]

*Mornex, April 25, 1862 (five o'clock).*—Talked a long time this
afternoon with Mme. M. C. I made her remove her blue veil and

[1] Victor Hugo, *Les Châtiments.*

try my smoked glasses for her strained eyes. She felt better already at the end of half an hour. A little familiar cordiality is at last entering into our relations. My aptitude for nursing is awaking again.

Read over a few songs from *Jocelyn*. They brought tears to my eyes (the dog, the death of the mother, the separation from Laurence, the meeting in Paris, the death of Laurence). It is admirable!

> *Ah! malheur à qui voit devant ses yeux passer*
> *Une apparition qui ne peut s'effacer!*
> *Le reste de ses jours est bruni par une ombre;*
> *Après un jour divin, mon père, tout est sombre.*

These pages have carried me back again to Villars, to Glion, and plunged me into nostalgic reveries.

> *Dirai-je mon bonheur, ou mon malheur, hélas?*
> *Fit descendre du ciel un ami sur mes pas . . .*
> *Météore qui donne à l'âme un jour céleste*
> *Et de la vie après décolore le reste.*

And elsewhere:

> *Il se fit de la vie une plus mâle idée:*
> *Sa douleur d'un seul trait ne l'avait pas vidée;*
> *Mais, adorant de Dieu le sévère dessein,*
> *Il sut la porter pleine et pure dans son sein,*
> *Et, ne se hâtant pas de la répandre toute,*
> *Sa résignation l'épancha goutte à goutte,*
> *Selon la circonstance et le besoin d'autrui,*
> *Pour tout vivifier sur terre autour de lui.*[1]

This is true poetry, that which lifts one up towards heaven and pervades one with the feeling of the divine, that sings of love and death, hope and sacrifice, and makes one feel the infinite. *Jocelyn* always stirs me with thrills of tenderness, which it would be odious to me to see profaned by irony. This tragedy of the heart has no

[1] Epilogue to *Jocelyn*.

parallel in French, for purity, except *Paul et Virginie,* and I am not
sure that I do not prefer *Jocelyn.* To be just, one would have to
read them over together.

*Mornex, April 28, 1862 (six o'clock).*—Another night falling. Save
for Mont Blanc, all the mountains are already faded and grey. The
cool of evening succeeds to the heat of the afternoon. The feeling
of the implacable flight of things, of the irresistible rush of the days,
grips me anew—

> *Nature au front changeant, comme vous oubliez!*

and oppresses me. In vain we cry with the poet: O Time, suspend
thy flight! . . . And which days should we wish to hold fast? Not
the days of happiness alone, but the lost days also. The first leave at
least a memory, the others leave a regret, almost a remorse.

*(Eleven o'clock).*—A gust of wind. A few clouds in the firmament. The nightingale is silent. But the river and the cricket are
still singing.

*May 18, 1862 (10 p. m.).*—Home again an hour ago, my heart
light and hilarious, I have been singing a medley of all the tunes in
the world at the top of my voice in my lonely room. Whence this
gaiety? From a wholesome afternoon, passed in merry company,
and a head full of pleasant impressions. I liked everything around me
and my sympathy was returned with affection. Set everything going
at the G.'s', in their new little country-house at Petit-Lancy, the
parents and children and guests; sang, laughed, played football,
quoits, prisoners' base, romped and frolicked. In short, went back to
the childish simplicity, the naive, elementary joy that I so much
love, that does one so much good. I felt the irresistible and conquering influence of goodness. It multiplies life, as the dew multiplies
the flowers.—At supper, the company amused themselves characterizing me. One of them declared that if my writings are serious,
grave, difficult, in other words German *(sic)*, my character is
agreeable and amiable, and all things to all men. The two men even

positively admired me, for the way I have with children, and insisted that I would make a delightful husband . . .

I still feel that I have treasures of candour, of honesty, purity, devotion, if the time were ever to come when married life and fatherhood should claim them. I have no worldly ambition; family life and the life of the mind are the only careers that tempt me. To love and to think are my only urgent and indestructible needs.— With a subtle, cunning, complex mind, the mind of a chameleon, I have a child's heart; I love only perfection and nonsense, the two opposite extremes. The true artists, the true philosophers, the truly religious men only feel at home with the simplicity of little children and the sublimity of masterpieces, that is, with pure nature or the pure ideal. In all my destitution, I feel the same way; I countenance things that lie between, I put up with them decently enough, but my taste is elsewhere.—Half-knowledge, half-talent, half-delicacy, half-elegance, half-merit,—that is the world, and what is to be made of this world if not a school of patience and sweetness? For admiration it offers no place.—Goodness is beyond my criticism, beyond all resistance or reserve; I forgive it everything because it is more important than anything else. I hunger and thirst for simple goodness; for mockery, suspicion, ill-will, jealousy, bitterness, rash judgments and a corrosive malice usurp today an ever-increasing place, creating a war in society between everyone and almost everyone else, and, in private life, the aridity of the desert.

*August 9, 1862.*—They have just observed through the microscope the infusoria of the nux vomica and those of nitrate of silver; thus destruction itself is peopled with living things, poison is animated and that which kills gives life. Why not? The sepulchre teems with life, the ordure of one being is the ambrosia of another, death is fecundity itself. The fable of the salamander immortalizes this view of nature. One tries to imagine a world that would be the inverse of this, and already this world is perceptible in the interstices of ours. Nothingness only is not.

Appetite rises anew in spite of the horrors of nausea, illusion in

spite of disenchantments, sexual attraction in spite of the distasteful secrets of possession, and passion in spite of the illuminations of
abstinence. This is the *vis medicatrix* of nature in operation. The
life that seeks to assert itself in us tends to restore itself without
us; it repairs its own breaches, mends its spider-webs when they
are torn, rebuilds the conditions of our well-being; it weaves the
bandages over our eyes again, restores the hope in our hearts, in-
fuses new health into our organs, regilds the chimæra in our imagi-
nations.—Without all this, experience would fret us away, wear us,
pall us, blight us beyond all remedy, long before our time, and a
young man would be older than a centenarian. The wisest part of
us is the one that knows least about us, the most reasonable part in
man that which does not reason; instinct, nature, divine and impersonal activity cure us of our personal follies; the invisible genius
of our life tirelessly supplies us with the material for the prodigali-
ties of our ego. The essential, maternal base of our conscious life is
the unconscious life, which is no more perceptible to us than the
earth is to the outer hemisphere of the moon to which it is in-
vincibly and eternally bound. It is our ἀντίχθων, to speak with
Pythagoras.

*Paris, October 17, 1862.*—I see how greatly I have changed in the
last ten years and how voluptuous feeling and the curiosity of the
senses has increased its hold upon me. Scruples and repugnances
have taken flight, and the sensuality of the imagination has replaced
my old puritanical prudery. I understand better the cult of pleasure, the religion of Venus and Bacchus, paganism, ingenuous and
joyous. I sympathize more with Tannhäuser and Helios, since I
have felt the sophistical, deceptive power of temptation and have
resisted less Montaigne's *Bonne Nature*. In my own poor little
sphere I sit like Rinaldo in the gardens of Armida. I fly from trouble, strife and heroism, and I spin away effeminately at Omphale's
distaff.—The victory over the flesh, the world, sin, the triumph of
the cross, the martyr's crown, the glorification of suffering, that
watch-word of Christianity, scarcely exist in my consciousness any

longer. I follow my fancy and the instinct of my heart, at will and at random, without firm principle and without conviction, like an indolent sceptic. My punishment is weakness and impotence.—Here I am now back again in the Epicureanism of the days of the Empire, the laxity of decadence. The crisis of the new faith, the passion for death and sainthood, which saved and enraptured the world eighteen centuries ago, must be begun anew in each paganized existence, each existence that has fallen back under the power of nature and the world. Devotion to the immortal, to the invisible, the ideal, the divine, the noble sacrifice of the flesh in behalf of the soul, is the sign of spiritual redemption. Prayer is its means. (*1.15 a. m., on coming back from the Opera.*)

*November 7, 1862.*—How maleficent, contagious and unwholesome is the eternal smile of the indifferent critic, the heartless and corrosive mockery that chaffs and demolishes everything, takes no interest in any personal duty or in any vulnerable affection, and, without caring to act, cares only to understand! To me, this ironical contemplation is immoral, like pharisaism, for it does not preach by example and it imposes upon others the burdens that it rejects for itself. It is insolent, for it feigns knowledge, while it has only doubt. It is deadly, for its Voltairean laugh dispels courage, faith and ardour in those who still possess them,—

*Rire de singe assis sur la destruction,*

as Alfred de Musset says. Criticism that has become a routine, a mere habit and system means the abolition of moral energy, faith and all strength. One of my inclinations leads me to it, but I recoil before the consequences when I encounter types of it that are more pronounced than myself. And at least I do not have to reproach myself for having ever tried to destroy the moral strength of others. My respect for life prevents me from doing this; and my self-distrust has even removed the temptation from me.

This order of mind with us is very dangerous, for it pampers every bad instinct, indiscipline, irreverence, selfish individualism, and it ends in social atomism . . . Only in the great political groups that run along without them and in spite of them are the nay-sayers not injurious. If they multiply with us, they will bring our little countries down to ruin, for small states live only by faith and will. Woe if negation rules, for life is an affirmation; and a society, a country, a nation is a living whole that is subject to death. A people cannot exist without prejudices, for public spirit and tradition are networks of beliefs acquired, accepted, maintained without obvious demonstration and without discussion. In order to act, one must believe; in order to believe, one must decide, determine, cut short, affirm and, in fact, prejudge questions. He who wishes to act only out of the fullness of scientific certitude is unfit for practical life. And we are made for action, inasmuch as we cannot decline duty; and therefore one must not condemn prejudice as long as one has only doubt to set in its place, nor should one laugh at those whom one would be unable to console. This is my point of view.

*January 8, 1863.*—This evening, I have reread the *Cid* and *Rodogune*. My impression is still mixed and confused. There is a good deal of disenchantment in my admiration and a good deal of reserve in my enthusiasm. What I dislike in this dramatic genre is the mechanical abstractness of the characters and the hectoring and scolding tone of the interlocutors. I had a vague impression of giant marionettes, truculently haranguing with a Spanish magniloquence. It is powerful, but one has before one heroic idols rather than human beings. That something artificial, pompous, stiff, strained, which is the plague of French tragedy, is decidedly apparent here; it creaks and grates as if these majestic colossi had all so many pulleys and cords. It is curious to see the faults of decadence (Seneca and Lucan) grafted on a candid and youthful nature.—In a word, the good and the bad are mingled in these masterpieces, and I much prefer, at first sight, Racine and Shakespeare, one for the aesthetic sensation, the other for the psychological sensation. The drama of the South cannot rid itself of the mask. I can put up with comic masks, but in serious heroes the abstract type, the mask makes one impatient. One laughs with tin and cardboard figures; I can only weep with the living and that which resembles them. Abstraction easily turns into caricature; it leads to the effects of the magic lantern, the dancing-Jack, the puppet and the mask. It is psychology in the first degree, as the coloured images of Germany are elementary painting.—And with all this, a refinement that is sometimes sophistical or over-subtle. Savages are by no means simple.—The beautiful side of it is the manly vigour, the intrepid frankness of the ideas, the words and the sentiments. Why was it that so much factitious grandeur had indeed to be mingled with the true grandeur, in this drama of 1640, out of which came the whole theatrical development of monarchical France? The genius is there, but a conventional civilization envelops it, and one cannot wear the wig with impunity; the French ideal is rather a veneering of nature than its final blossoming. The Gallic nature attains the beautiful only at second hand, I would almost say by mimicry. Tragedy is not the expression of the national genius. It is a pedantic importation, an imitation of the antique.—Formalism is the original vice of well-tailored literatures.

*January 10, 1863.*—The most direct and the surest happiness for me lies in the society of women. In their atmosphere I expand at once, like a fish in water, like a bird in the air. It is my natural element, and there is a wonderful reciprocity in our understanding. Is this the reward of my long intimidation by the sex? Is it a kind of electricity by induction? The theory of chivalry always holds true for me, and feminine attraction electrifies and excites all my disinterested faculties. I have not the least desire to conquer and appropriate, but I feel myself dilating and radiating with general love and the purest sympathy, and I am filled with animation. *Das Ewig-weibliche zieht uns hinan.*—What a pity that the occasions are so rare, and that they should ever be lacking for one who is the least blasé in this respect.

*January 13, 1863.*—Read *Polyeucte* and the *Mort de Pompée.*

When all is said, the grandeur of Corneille reconciles us to his mag-niloquent rigidity and his over-ingenious rhetoric. But this dramatic genre is inherently false, and the French oratorical and theatrical taste is apparent as far back as the first masterpieces of its classical period. The majesty here has always a touch of the factitious, the exaggerated and conventional. France pays in literature for its roy-alism. Its heroes are roles rather than men; they play at magnanim-ity, virtue, glory a good deal more than they realize them; they are always on the stage, observed by others or by themselves. With them, *glory,* the solemn life and public opinion, replaces the natural, becomes the natural. They speak only *ore rotundo,* in buskins and sometimes on stilts. And what consummate barristers they are! The French drama is an oratorical tournament, a continual plea for the defence on a day when someone is going to die and all the person-ages make haste to profit by the chance to speak before the fatal hour of silence sounds. Everywhere else, speech serves to make ac-tion understood; in French tragedy, action is only a suitable reason for speaking, a procedure designed to extract the finest discourses from the people who engage in the action, and who perceive it at its various moments and under its diverse aspects. What is really curi-ous and amusing is that the liveliest, gayest and wittiest of peoples should always have understood the grand style in the most formal and pompous fashion. This was inevitable. It springs from the lack of personal dignity, I mean inner dignity; it requires an ostentatious appearance. Manner here has always taken the place of substance, the plated has taken the place of the solid. A sociable nation, the French live in the external and by the external. Their psychology is constructed of movable pieces, as marionettes are, and represents the soul and the nuances of life with scarcely more truth than pup-pets represent the movements of the body.—Love and nature, duty and inclination, and a dozen other moral antitheses are the limbs which the string of the playwright causes to gesticulate and which indicate all the tragic attitudes. A theatre of strings, vaguely recalling those Chinese landscapes manufactured in ready-made sections which the amateur puts together as he wishes.

*April 8, 1863.*—Turned over the three thousand, five hundred pages of *Les Misérables* and sought for the unity of this vast composition . . .

The basic idea of *Les Misérables* is as follows: society engenders sad and frightful evils (prostitution, vagrancy, the class of the homeless, scoundrels, thieves, convicts and war as well, revolutionary clubs, and barricades). It should admit this to itself and not treat as mere monsters those whom the law smites. To humanize law and opinion, to raise up the fallen with the vanquished, to bring about a social redemption,—this is the task. How? By diminishing rebellion and vice through enlightenment, and converting the guilty through forgiveness: this is the way.—Is this not really to Christianize society, by extending charity from the sinner to the condemned, by applying to this life also what the Church applies more readily to the other? To bring men back, by tireless love, to order and the good, instead of crushing them with fierce justice and inflexible prosecution; such is the tendency of the book. It is noble and great. But it is a little optimistic and recalls Rousseau. It seems that the individual is always innocent and society always responsible.—In sum, the ideal is (for the twentieth century) a sort of democratic golden age, a universal republic, in which war, the death-penalty and pauperism will have disappeared: the Religion and the City of Progress, the Utopia of the eighteenth century resumed on a grand scale. Much generosity, but a good deal that is fanciful. The fancifulness consists in an over-external idea of evil. The author does not know or pretends to forget the instinct of perversity, the love of evil for evil's sake, which the human heart contains. That is always the point where the French ear ceases to listen. The Protestant nations fall less often into this illusion.—The great and salutary idea of the work is that legal probity becomes a bloodthirsty hypocrisy when it thinks it can separate society into the elect and the reprobates, and that it confounds the relative with the absolute. The most significant passage is that in which Javert, once off his track, reverses the whole moral system of the rigid Javert, the spy-priest, the arch-correct policeman. In this chapter, social charity transpierces and transillumines strict and iniquitous justice. The suppression of the social hell, the stigmas it inflicts, the endless and irremediable contumely—this idea is truly religious.

And as for the erudition, the talent, the vividness of the execution, the work is astounding, stupefying almost. Its defect is the immensity of the digressions and episodic dissertations, the extravagance of all the devices and the themes, something tense, spasmodic and violent in the style which is very different from natural eloquence and from the real truth. Sensational effect is the pitfall of Victor Hugo, for it is the centre of his aesthetics; hence his exaggeration and bombast, his flair for the theatrical, his tension of will. A powerful artist, but one who cannot make us forget the artist; a dangerous model, for the master grazes all the reefs of the grotesque, and he goes from the sublime to the repulsive more often than he gives a harmonious impression of beauty. And accordingly, he detests Racine.

What power, philological and literary, Victor Hugo has! He is master of all the tongues that our language contains, the speech of the palace and the exchange, the hunt, the navy, war, philosophy, the prison, the speech of the professions and archæology, the book-dealer and the ditch-digger. All the bric-à-brac of history and manners, all the curiosities of the soil and subsoil are known and familiar to him. He seems to have turned his Paris inside out and to know it body and soul as one knows one's pocket. A prodigious memory, a flaming imagination. He is a visionary, the master of his dreams, handling at will the hallucinations of opium and hashish without being their victim; he has made madness one of his domestic animals, and he rides with perfect composure the nightmare, Pegasus, the Hippogriff and the Chimæra. As a psychological phenomenon, he is of the liveliest interest.—Victor Hugo draws in sulphuric acid, he illuminates with the glare of electricity; he stuns, blinds and whirls his reader along more than he charms or persuades him. Strength to this degree is fascinating; without captivating, it imprisons; without enchanting, it bewitches. His ideal is the extraordinary, the gigantic, the stupendous, the incommensurable; his characteristic words are *immense, colossal, enormous, giant, monstrous*. He finds a way of exaggerating even the childish and naive; the one thing that seems inaccessible to him is the natural. In short, his passion is grandeur, his fault is excess, his mark is the titanic, and the strangest discords of puerility are mingled with the magnificence. His weak side is measure, taste, a sense of the ridiculous, wit in the finer meaning of the word.—He is a Frenchified Spaniard, or rather he has all the extremes of the South and the North, the Scandinavian and the African; what he has the least of is the Gallic. And by a caprice of destiny, he is one of the literary geniuses of nineteenth-century France! His resources are inexhaustible, and age seems to have no power over him. What an infinite supply of words, ideas, forms he carries along with him, and what a mountain of works he leaves behind him to mark his passage! His eruptions are like a volcano's, and this fabulous worker continues to upheave, dismember, grind and construct a world of his own creation, a world that is Hindu rather than Hellenic.—I marvel at him; and yet I prefer geniuses who give one a feeling of the true and increase one's inner freedom. In Hugo, one feels the cyclops and the effort; I still prefer the resonant bow of Apollo and the tranquil brow of Olympian Jove. His type is the Satyr of the *Légende des siècles* who stuns Olympus, with the lascivious ugliness of the faun and the thundering sublimity of the great Pan.

*May 23, 1863 (9 a. m.).*—Sluggish, overcast, misty weather; it rained last night, and still the air is oppressive. It is the symbol of gestation, heavy but fecund. Nature is pregnant today and ruminates, contemplating its womb, like the god Ganesa of India, or the omphalopsychists of Athos. This obscure revery is sacred like that of a woman with child, but it torpifies the spectator, and plunges him into a vague listlessness that leads to sleep. Light gives life.

The darkness may cause one to think, but a lowering day, ambiguous luminosity, a leaden sky make one rather

*Soupire, étend les bras, ferme les yeux et bâille.*

These uncertain and chaotic states of nature are ugly like all amorphous things, like muddied colours, like bats at dusk and the viscous
poulps of the sea. Attractiveness begins with character, with distinctness, individualization. Whatever is confused, mixed, indistinct,
without form, sex or accent is anti-aesthetic.—Chaos, the primordial
jumble of things,—like farrago, hash, olla podrida, *ripoquâ,* the
inferior types of stew, mishmash and salmagundi, those unseasonable
later mixtures,—is unpleasant to the eye and the palate. The
mind desires light; light is order; order is first of all the distinction
of parts, then the regular disposition of them.—Reason is the foundation of Beauty. Thus the formless, the colourless and the stammered are the three horrors of art, and even the antipathies of the
clear mind.

*August 7, 1863.*—A walk after supper; sky sparkling with stars;
Milky Way magnificent. Alas, in spite of all, I have a heavy heart,
and I understand the eagerness for life that old men feel who cling
to the days, each day more as the end approaches. The future seems
to me always leagued against me, and there is nothing to hope save
from the past. I therefore advance backwards, without foresight or
prudence; and so it has always been with me. I have never been
able to anticipate the future and take possession of it in imagination
or by the audacity of thought. I have always believed I should die
young, and I have never calculated a year in advance or so much as
three months. Is it not an odd thing? To apply to myself conclusions drawn from another and expect the same chances for myself,
such an idea has never entered my head. All my moral force has
been turned towards abnegation, not towards conquest.—Result:
atrophy of the will, non-operation as a chronic state, heedlessness

regarding my deepest instincts, a narcosis paralysing all my faculties.

*August 9, 1863.*—At the bottom of everything I always find an incurable distrust of myself and life, a distrust that takes the form of indulgence and even benevolence for others but absolute abstinence for myself. All or nothing! This must be my nature, my original substance, my old Adam. And yet as long as I am loved a little, as long as my inward feelings are shared a little, I am happy and ask for almost nothing else. A child's caresses, a friend's talk, the presence of a girl is enough to fill me with joy. Thus I aspire to the infinite, and a very little contents me; everything makes me restless, and a trifle calms me. I have often caught myself wishing to die, and yet my ambition for happiness scarcely exceeds that of a bird, wings! sunshine! a nest! I pass my days and nights in solitude, from taste, it appears. Oh, no, from distaste, from obstinacy, from shame at needing others, the shame of admitting it and the fear of riveting my chains by acknowledging them.—I distrust the malignity of men a little, but disenchantment much more, or rather disappointment.

*September 2, 1863 (8.30 a. m.).*—Blindman's buff in the void, hide-and-seek with malicious destiny, how shall I name the intangible sensation that teased me this morning in the twilight as I woke? It was a charming reminiscence, but vague, without name or outline, like the form of a woman dimly perceived by an invalid through the obscurity of his room and the uncertainty of delirium. I had the distinct feeling that it was a sympathetic figure whom I had somewhere met and who, after stirring me once, had sunk back with time into the catacombs of the forgotten. All the rest was confused, the place, the occasion, the person herself, for I did not see her face or her expression. It was all like a fluttering veil beneath which might have been hidden the enigma of happiness. And I was sufficiently wide awake to be sure that it was not a dream.

Such are the last traces of the things that are engulfed in us, the memories that die: an impalpable will-o'-the-wisp lighting up an uncertain impression, whether a pain or a pleasure one cannot say, a gleam on a sepulchre. How strange it is!—I might almost call these things the revenants of the soul, the longings for happiness, the ghosts of my dead emotions, the roll of the infanticides of my former life. How many of those tears have I not consumed that might perhaps have been fertile? How many of those budding inclinations have I not stifled, how many of those sympathies have I suppressed that asked only to live and grow great in me? If, as might be supposed (and the Talmud seems to affirm it), every outburst of love involuntarily begets an invisible genius that aspires to complete existence, how many of those divine embryos that are born of the exchange of two glances have I not caused to miscarry in my breast? And if these glimmerings that are not yet beings wander in the limbo of our soul, how can we marvel afterwards at those strange apparitions that come to visit at our bedside? I was unable to compel the phantom to tell me its name, or the reminiscence, whatever it was, to come forth from the twilight.

Under how melancholy a cast life can present itself, when one follows the current of these shadowy thoughts! It is like a vast nocturnal shipwreck in which fifty loving voices call for help and the implacable, mounting wave drowns every cry in turn before we have been able to press a hand or give a kiss of farewell in this darkness of death. Viewed in this light, destiny seems harsh, savage, cruel, and the tragedy of life rises like a rock in the midst of the level waters of everyday triviality. Impossible not to be grave in the midst of the indefinable disquiet which this spectacle produces in us. The surface of things may be pleasant or commonplace, but the depths are stern and fearful. The moment one touches the eternal things, the destinies of the soul, truth, duty, the secrets of life and death, one becomes serious, in spite of oneself.

Love that is sublime, single, invincible leads straight to the brink of the great abyss, for it speaks at once of infinity and eternity. It is eminently religious. It may even become religion. When everything around a man reels, wavers, trembles and grows dark in the distant obscurities of the unknown, when the world in nothing but fiction or a fairy-tale and the universe only a chimæra, when one's whole structure of ideas fades away in mist and all the realities are changed into doubt, what fixed point may still remain for a man? The loyal heart of a woman. It is there that one can rest one's head and take heart to live again, recover one's faith in Providence, and, if need be, die in peace, with a benediction on one's lips. Who knows if love and its beatitude, that clear manifestation of a universal harmony in things, is not the best proof of a sovereignly intelligent and paternal God, as it is the shortest road by which to reach him? Love is a faith, and one faith invokes another. This faith is a felicity, a light and a force.—By this road alone one enters the chain of the living, the awakened, the happy, the redeemed, the true men who know what existence is worth and work for the glory of God and the truth. Till then, one only babbles and stammers, wastes one's days and faculties and gifts, without aim, without real joy, like an infirm, worthless, useless being, one who does not count.

It is through love perhaps, that I shall come back to faith, to religion, energy, concentration. It seems to me, at least, that if I found my match, my unique consort, all the rest would be added unto me as if to confound my incredulity and put my despair to shame. Believe in the paternal Providence, then, and dare to love!

*November 25, 1863.*—Prayer is the essential weapon of religion. One who can no longer pray because he doubts if there is a being to whom prayer rises, and who showers benedictions on us, is cruelly solitary and vastly bereft. What is your own belief in this regard? Actually, at the moment, it would be difficult to say. All your positive beliefs are under consideration, ready for any metamorphosis. The truth before all, even when it disturbs and unsettles us! But what I believe is that the highest idea which we can form of the principle of things will be the most true, and that the truest truth will be the one that makes man the most harmoniously good, the wisest, greatest, happiest.

*Dépasse tous les cieux dans ton vol, ô pensée;*
*Grandis sept fois sept fois l'infiniment parfait;*
*Ne crains rien: par l'effet tu seras dépassée.*
*Dieu, la cause, est toujours plus grand que son effet.*
—Penseroso.

In the meantime, my creed, properly speaking, is in process of being recast. I still believe, however, in God and in the immortality of the soul. I believe in holiness, truth, beauty; I believe in the redemption of the soul through faith in forgiveness. I believe in love, devotion, honour. I believe in duty, and in the moral conscience. I even believe in prayer. I believe in the fundamental intuitions of humankind and in the great affirmations of the inspired of all the ages. I believe that our higher nature is our true nature.

Can a theology and theodicy spring from this? Probably, but at this particular moment I do not distinctly see how; for this is a new question for me. It is such a long time since I have examined *my* metaphysics, I have been living so long in the thought of others. I have even reached the point where I ask myself if I am obliged to crystallize my dogmas. The answer is yes, for preaching and for action, less for study, reflection and self-instruction.

*December 4, 1863.*—A singular encounter: a slender brunette, elegant, austere, with a pale complexion, in whom I think I vaguely recognize a certain apparition whom I once glimpsed in church and who vanished ever after from my horizon. Yielding to a youthful curiosity, I retraced my steps and followed her as far as the next street, where I saw her enter a house. Was it her own house? I do not know. Is this incident a hint from Providence? Who knows? Is the lady H. V., of whom people have spoken so much to me? In this case, the coincidence would be thrice curious and might be taken for a positive indication of a kindly destiny. Why has this occurrence almost stirred me, insignificant as it is in itself? Because I am in a restless, poetic state, and my heart is eager to throb, before it goes down to the dust, eager for the romance of its own fancy. I can forgive it for this, and I watch the agitation of its instincts with the indulgent forbearance one has for the first desires of a child or the last whims of a condemned man. Having neither satisfied nor stifled it, how should I refuse this heart the grace that is granted everything about to die? It is a sort of piety that impels me, for it is a slight voluntary expiation for the severities of my earlier days towards every inclination that was born in my breast. Having no illusion that these quests will end in anything, I countenance every innocent battue of the hounds of sentiment. The baffled, defeated longing for a total and perfect attachment takes what it fancies to be a revenge, and one recognizes, at the age of forty, the beating arteries and the secret tremors of one's twentieth year. Everything seems a promise. The romantic instinct avenges itself. In fact, what is so gracious in a literary work, the inner rejuvenations through tenderness and hope, may be even so in reality.

Far from being ashamed to love, one should be rather joyous and grateful for it. What is the merit of being a heap of ashes? I prefer Goethe's way, still adored at sixty, and growing young again himself under the pure homage of enthusiasm. The capacity for loving, in the special sense of the word, is only extinguished with the capacity for admiration and exaltation. Ardent souls and passionate hearts love to the very end, even unto death, and are able to make up for all the repulses of early affection that have ever risen in their path. The intoxication goes, but the effusion remains; and the sympathetic power does not die.

The whole secret of remaining young, in spite of years and even white hairs, lies in defending one's enthusiasm through poetry, contemplation and charity, in other words, more briefly, by maintaining harmony in the soul. When everything is in its place within us, we can remain in equipoise with the work of God. A grave enthusiasm for eternal beauty and the eternal order, a reason that feels, serene goodness, this is perhaps the foundation of wisdom.

Wisdom, what an inexhaustible theme! A sort of peaceful aureole encircles and illumines this idea, which sums up all the treasures of moral experience, and which is the ripest fruit of a well-employed life. Wisdom does not grow old, for it is the expression of order itself, that is, of the eternal. Only the sage extracts from life and every age its full savour, for he feels its beauty, dignity and value. The flowers of youth fade; but the summer, the autumn, even the winter of human existence have their majestic grandeur, which the sage perceives and glorifies. To see all things in God, to make one's own life a voyage through the ideal, to live with composure and gratitude, sweetness and courage: this is the magnificent point of view of Marcus Aurelius. And if one adds the humility that bends the knee and the charity that dedicates itself, it is the wisdom of the children of God, the immortal joy of the true Christians.—But what an evil Christianity is that which slanders wisdom and does without it!—To this I prefer wisdom, which is a justice rendered to God, even in this life. It is the sign of a false religious conception to postpone life and distinguish the holy man from the virtuous man. This is, in some degree, the error of the whole Middle Ages and perhaps of Catholicism in its essence. True Christianity needs to be purged of this fatal error. The eternal life is not the future life, it is life in order, life in God; and time must learn to see itself as a movement of eternity, an undulation in the ocean of being. The being that perceives itself in the category of time can become conscious of the substance of this time, which is eternity. And to live, maintaining one's consciousness *sub specie aeterni,* is to be wise; to live, personifying the eternal, is to be religious.

By what strange windings of reflection has the veil of a young woman brought me to Spinoza?—Bah! everything in the world is linked together and everything invokes everything else, all the radii lead to the centre. Besides, was not the question happiness, and is not true love the brother of wisdom?

*April 2, 1864.*—April showers and caprices, floods of sunshine followed by rays of rain, fits of tears and laughter from the freakish sky, gusts of wind, squalls. The weather is like a mutinous little girl who changes her mind and expression twenty times in the same hour. It is a blessing for the plants, an affluence of life in the veins of spring . . . The circle of mountains about our valley is hung with white to the base, but with a simple muslin that two hours of sunshine would dissipate. Still another caprice, a bit of stage-setting ready to be rolled off when the scene-shifter blows his whistle.

How clearly one feels the infixable mobility of all things! To appear and to vanish, this is the whole comedy of the universe, the life-story of all individual beings, cheese-mites and planets, whatever may be the duration of the cycles of existence they describe. Every individual life is the shadow of a shadow, a gesture in the void, a flash of light that is more or less idle, a hieroglyph traced for a moment on the sand which a breath effaces a moment after, a bubble of air that appears and bursts on the surface of the great river of being, a vanity, a mere nothing. But this nothing is yet the symbol of the universal being, and this ephemeral bubble is an epitome of the history of the world.

The man who has imperceptibly assisted in the work of the world has lived; the man who has become aware of it, at least to a certain extent, has also lived. The simple man serves through his activity, and as machinery; the thinker serves by thought and as a light. The meditative man who raises and consoles and sustains his companions on the way, like him mortal and fugitive, does still more; he combines the utilities of the two others. Action, thought, speech (speech means all communication, expansion, revelation), these are three equal modes of the human life. The artisan, the savant and the man of words are all three labourers of God. To do, to find, to teach, all three are work, all good, all necessary.—Will-o'-the-wisps that we are, we can still leave traces behind us; meteors, we can prolong our perishable inanity in the memory of men or at least in the contexture of later events. Everything disappears, but nothing is lost; and the civilization or the city of man is an immense spiritual pyramid built from the works of everything that has lived in the form of moral being, even as our calcareous mountains are formed by the debris of myriads of billions of nameless beings that have lived in the form of microscopic animals.

*April 5, 1864.*—Read for the second time *Le Prince Vitale,* with an admiration that was almost dazzling. What a wealth of ideas, facts, colours, what erudition, what malice, wit, knowledge and talent, and what irreproachable finish in the style! How clear in its profundity! Save for abandon and warmth of heart, the author combines all the varieties of merit, culture and skill. One could not be more subtle and penetrating or more intellectually free than this ironic and chameleon-like enchanter. Victor Cherbuliez, like the Sphinx, can play on all the lyres, and plays on all, with a Goethean serenity. It seems that passion, grief and error have no hold upon this impassive soul. The key of this thought is Hegel's Phenomenonology of the mind, worked over again in the light of Greece and France. His faith, if he has one, is Strauss's Humanism. But he is completely the master of himself and his language and will be very careful never to preach anything prematurely.

Down at the bottom of this deep spring does a crocodile lurk, perhaps? In any case, he has the cunningest and the most unprejudiced mind that one can imagine, and vast enough to contain all manner of things. One would even say that he knows everything he wishes to know, without having to take the trouble to learn it. He is a calm Mephistopheles, with an accomplished politeness, a smiling grace, an exquisite urbanity. And this Mephisto is a gallant jeweller; and this jeweller is a subtle musician; and this handsome talker, as smooth as silk, is making fun of us. His malice consists in divining everything without permitting himself to be divined, in making one feel that he holds in his hand the secret of the universe and yet that he will not open this hand until his time comes and he chooses to do so. . . . Victor Cherbuliez resembles Proudhon a little, he juggles with antinomies to astonish the bourgeois. Thus it amuses him to banter Luther and the Reformation in favour of the Renaissance. The agonies of the conscience do not seem to be his business. His supreme tribunal is reason. He is certainly Hegelian and intellectualistic to the very core. But he has a magnificent organization. Only, he must be antipathetic to the men of duty who make renunciation, sacrifice and humility the measure of individual worth.

*September 19, 1864.*—Have spent two hours in the company of a beautiful soul, that of Eugénie de Guérin, the pious heroine of fraternal love. How many thoughts, feelings and griefs there are in this *Journal* of six years (1834–1840), which in thirty months has reached its twelfth edition! How it makes one dream, reflect and live! It stirs in me a feeling of nostalgia, a little like certain forgotten melodies, the notes of which, who knows why, move the heart. I saw once more the vistas of my youth, like paths in the distance; I heard confused voices, echoes of my past. Innocence, melancholy, piety, a thousand mementos of an old existence, of a young I, forms as impalpable and fantastic as the fugitive shadows of a dream, on awaking, began to dance before the astonished reader.

*September 20, 1864.*—I have breakfasted alone, with Ali (the cat), of course, who is still planting his claws in my coat in order to ask for bread, a little as children do with their mother, and men with Providence. The good deed seems to bind the benefactor and not the one who is obliged; whoever has given one must give two, and if the munificence stops, the one who complains and feels hurt is he who has received everything and always expects more. We are all like this, and it is good that the animals should remind us of ourselves by their insolent ingratitude.

Similarly, in the State, those who pay nothing find it natural that the peasants should pay double; the oppressors grow indignant when the oppressed make the slightest claims, and when their equals or their superiors grow weary of being forever their donkeys. After the tyranny of weakness, let us note the abusive pretensions of ignorance and incapacity. Children, fools, blackguards make of their inferiority a title for governing the world, as my cat makes of its dependence a right to scratch the hand that feeds it. The despotism of strength is an injustice, but the despotism of impotence is almost an absurdity.

Chivalrous generosity, like all fine things, becomes, if it is immoderate, the cause of an evil, today universal, the neglect of justice. Is it just for the child to treat his father as a comrade? For society to treat the thief better than the pauper? For a rogue to be as good as a decent man, and for the incapable to have, I will not say the same rights, but the same functions as the capable? Equalitarianism, by destroying respect and the feeling for the inequality of acquired merits, tends to a coarsening of society, so that age, sex, experience and virtue no longer win regard or consideration, but, instead, the youngster in the house, the urchin in the street, the merest whippersnapper of a school-boy adopts the cavalier tone with his parents, his master and his pastor, with everybody, and, if need be, with God.

> *Avec quelle irrévérence*
> *Parle des Dieux ce maraud!*

Respect and justice are closely allied. He who respects nothing sets himself above everything, as an absolute monarch sets himself above the laws. All these little equalitarians are thus an ant-hill of petty tyrants. And democracy, so understood, is the prey of vanity and selfishness, which have no measure but arithmetic, and perhaps gunpowder.—To speak more accurately, each regime has its inner menace and its own danger. Democracy, all things considered, is the legitimate heir of monarchy and aristocracy. But its latent malady, its congenital vice, is the abandonment of duty and the substitution for it of envy, pride and independence, in a word, the disappearance of obedience, brought about by a false notion of equality.

If democracy is only the systematic depreciation of legitimate and acquired superiorities, the jealous decapitation of true merits, it becomes identical with demagogy.—But nothing endures save what is just; the democracy, if it grows unjust, will necessarily perish.

The protection of all the weak, the maintenance of all rights, honour for all the deserving, employment for all the capable, these maxims of the just state at once respect *de jure* equality and *de facto* inequality, for what they contemplate is individual activity, spontaneous and free energy, the real man, and not an abstract formula.

The effect of abstract principles (like that of equality) is the reverse of that to which they aspire. Thus fraternity ends in the Terror and the guillotine. The respect of man for man, or equality, ends in the contempt of man for man and universal disrespect.— Improve man, make him more just, more moral, humbler, purer, this is the only reform that has no harmful corollary. Institutions are worth no more than the men who apply them. The name, the party, the costume, the opinion, the system are almost insignificant and frivolous things beside the intrinsic worth of individuals. Orthodox or liberal, conservative or radical, white or black, rich or poor, royalist or republican, I will even say Catholic or Protestant, Christian or Jew, even these are superficial distinctions beside the one I mean.—Tell me what you love and I will tell you what you are, and you are worth only what you are.

*(6 p. m.)*—Reread here and there the volume of Eugénie de Guérin with an increasing sense of its charm. These intimate pages are all heart, inspiration, glow, striking in their sincerity and shining with hidden poetry. A great, strong soul, a clear mind, distinction, elevation, the vivacity of a talent that is unaware of itself, a deep, secret life, nothing is lacking in this Saint Theresa of brother-and-sisterhood, this Sévigné of the fields, who had to hold herself back with all her might not to write in verse, so innate was the gift of expression in her.

*October 16, 1864 (midnight).*—I have just reread a part of Eugénie de Guérin's Journal. It has charmed me a little less than the first time. The soul seems just as beautiful to me, but Eugénie's existence is too empty and the circle of ideas that occupies her is too restricted. What a pity that this rich organization was not brought into contact with a few more books and men of different sorts! A little garden, a handful of poor souls, a shelf of religious books, this was doubtless enough for her salvation,—one can live on a crust of bread and a pitcher of water; but a less severe diet yields a range of sensations that is rather less meagre. A soul is a touchstone, and one would have wished such a choice soul to have been in a position to estimate the greatest possible sum of human things.

It is wonderful and touching to see how small a space suffices for a mind to spread its wings in, but this turning round and round in a cell grows tiresome in the end to minds that are used to embracing more objects in their field of vision. Instead of a garden, the world; instead of a breviary, all the books; in place of three or four persons, a whole people or all history, this is what our virile and philosophic nature demands. We wish for more air, more space, a larger horizon, more positive knowledge; and we end by suffocating in this little cage in which Eugénie moves, even if the breezes of heaven blow and the starlight penetrates there.

*October 27, 1864 (Promenade de la Treille, 8.30 a. m.).*—Aspect of the landscape this morning, a perfect lucidity: one might have distinguished a sentry-box on the Vuache.[1] This clear, glancing sunlight set ablaze the whole jewel-box of autumn colours: amber, saffron, gold, sulphur, ochre, lemon-yellow, orange, russet, copper, aquamarine, amaranth glittered from the last leaves still clinging to the boughs or already fallen at the foot of the trees. It was delicious. The sparkling muskets, the bugle-calls, the martial step of our two gaitered battalions proceeding to the drill-grounds, the sharp distinctness of the house-fronts, still damp with dew, the transparent freshness of all the shadows breathed a healthy and intellectual gaiety.

There are two forms of autumn, the misty, dreamy type and the lively and highly-coloured type; almost the difference between the two sexes. Has not the word for autumn two genders? And indeed

[1] The hill that bounds the horizon of Geneva on the southwest.

is not every season bisexual in its way? Has not each its minor and its major scale, its two sides of light and shade, sweetness and strength? One might so see it. Everything that is complete is double: every face has two profiles, every stick two ends, every medal two sides.—The ruddy autumn is vigorous activity; the ashen autumn is meditative feeling. One pours itself outward, the other retreats into itself. Yesterday one thought of the dead; today they will be gathering grapes.—I myself feel mirthful, hilarious, cheerful as I return from my walk and look at the blue sky through my top-story window.

*November 16, 1864.*—Learned of the death of ——. The will and the intelligence held out until the hemorrhage in the meninges put a stop to everything.

A bubble of air in the blood, a drop of water in the brain, and man is thrown into disorder, his machine collapses, his thought vanishes, the world disappears like a morning's dream. By what a spider's strand is our individual existence suspended! Fragility, appearance, nothingness. Were it not for distraction and our power to forget, the whole fairy-world that bears us along and surrounds us would seem like a solar spectrum in the darkness, an empty vision, a fleeting hallucination. Appeared, disappeared,—this is the whole history of a man, as of a world or a microbe.

Time is the supreme illusion. It is nothing but the inner prism through which we diffract being and life, the mode by which we perceive successively that which is simultaneous in the idea. The eye does not see a sphere all at once, although the sphere exists all at once; it is necessary either for the sphere to revolve before the eye that watches it, or for the eye to encircle the sphere. In the first case, the world revolves or seems to revolve in time; in the second case, our thought successively analyzes and recomposes it. For the supreme intelligence, time is not; what will be, is. Time and space are the breaking up of the infinite for the use of finite beings. God permits these in order not to be alone. This is the mode by which creatures are possible and conceivable. Let us add that it is also by this Jacob's ladder, with its innumerable rungs, that all creation remounts to the Creator, participates in being, tastes life, glimpses the absolute and is able to adore the unfathomable mystery of infinite divinity. There is the other side of the question. Our life is nothing, it is true, but our life is divine. A breath of nature obliterates us, but we surpass nature by penetrating, beyond its prodigious phantasmagoria, even to the immutable and the eternal. To escape the vortex of time through inner ecstasy, to perceive things *sub specie aeterni,* this is the watchword of all the great religions of the superior races; and this psychological possibility is the foundation of all the great hopes. The soul can be immortal because it is qualified to rise to that which is not born and does not die, that which exists in substance, of necessity and with no shadow of change; it can rise to God.

> *Homme, enveloppe ainsi ta vie, ombre qui passe,*
> *Du calme firmament de ton éternité.*
> —Penseroso.

*January 17, 1865.*—It is sweet to feel with nobility, to dwell on a mountain above the bogs and fens of vulgarity. Manufacturing Americanism and Cæsarean demagogy equally conduce to the multiplication of the populace, the crowds that are ruled by appetite, applauding charlatanism, devoted to the cult of Mammon and pleasure and worshipping only force. A shabby pattern of man, this increasing majority! Let us remain faithful to the altars of the ideal.—It is possible that the spiritualists might become the stoics of a new age ruled over by Cæsars. Who knows but that Christianity in Europe may not again dwell in catacombs? Materialistic naturalism has the wind in its sails, and a universal moral decline is on the way. No matter, as long as the salt does not lose its savour and the friends of the higher life guard the fire of Vesta. The wood itself may choke the flame, but, if the flame persists, the pyre will be only more splendid by and by.—The prodigious deluge of democracy will not

do the harm which the Barbarian invasions could not do, it will not
drown at once the effects of high culture; but one must be resigned
to the fact that it will begin by disfiguring and vulgarizing everything, just as the sudden intrusion of the street into the drawing-
room submerges good society and reduces the well-bred to silence.
It is clear that aesthetic delicacy, elegance, distinction, nobility; it
is evident that atticism, urbanity, the suave and the exquisite, the
refined and the subtle, everything that constitutes the charm of a
choice literature and an aristocratic culture vanishes along with the
society that corresponds to it. Not that Bœotia spreads, but the
multitude reigns; and just as the last workman's wife copies
the style of the Empress, so everyone expects to share in all the elegances and almost seriously imagines that the official pronouncement
of equality really equalizes things and people.—If, as I think, Pascal [1] says, the more developed one is the more difference one finds
among men, one cannot say that the democratic instinct develops
the mind very much, since it spreads a belief in the equality of
merits by virtue of the similarity of pretensions.

*January 19, 1865.*—Read the first hundred pages of Eugénie de
Guérin's letters, which have charmed me. A sensitive heart, a beautiful soul, a noble character, a lively mind and a style full of colour,
clear, laconic, abundantly natural, enlivening everything around her,
a charming verve and a very considerable inner life.

*January 21, 1865.*—I have finished Eugénie's correspondence
(1831–1847), a hundred and fifty letters . . . What is the final impression this reading has made upon me? I love and admire the
Sévigné of Le Cayla. But the winged grace of her style, the charming vivacity of her mind and the tenderness of her soul cannot prevent me from regretting a certain too palpable uniformity in this
correspondence. And, comparing this beautiful soul with this book,
one cannot help sighing. Eugénie struggles in vain against a triple influence which, though she does not suspect it, weighs upon her

---

[1] Pascal says: "The more wit one has, the more original men one finds.
Common people do not see the differences among men."

genius: a Catholicism that is fervent and devout to the point of superstition, celibacy, the privation of adequate intellectual resources. If destiny had served her better, she would have presented a personality altogether greater and more remarkable.—The most interesting thing in this sympathetic character is her passion for her brother. The most instructive thing in the volume is the Catholic piety caught, as it were, in the act, and, frankly, the result is not enviable. When one sees what a soul becomes, a beautiful, religious soul, under this discipline, and how little real peace it achieves at the price of the abdication of its conscience into the hands of the priest, the superstitions that it still accepts and the need of tutelage and absolution that continually torments it, one feels one's heart gripped with a genuine pity for these captives of a childish Christianity, and it becomes apparent that the confessional is the citadel of this religion.

How can France be free, as long as the religion of women and that of men cannot be the same and youth is torn between these two hostile cults, papistry, on the one hand, denying modern rights and independent science, and philosophy on the other, denying all the pretenses of a religion that has dissolved in observances and a dogma that interposes a magician between the faithful and God?

*March 20, 1865.*—Heard that the upper class at the Gymnasium has been closed because of insubordination. Our young people are detestable and are becoming more and more unmanageable and insolent. Their motto, in the French style, is, "Our master is our enemy". The baby wishes to have the privileges of the young man, and the young man means to keep those of the ill-behaved little boy. This is a logical consequence of our system of equalitarian democracy. From the moment that difference in quality is officially equal to zero in politics, it is clear that the authority of age, knowledge and function is bound to disappear and that the scapegrace will treat his masters as equals in the academic life.

The only counterpoise to equalitarianism is military discipline. To the officer's stripes and the guardroom, the dungeon and the firing-squad there is no reply. But is it not curious that the regime of individual rights should end simply in a respect for force? Jacobinism brings on Cæsarism, pettifoggery ends in artillery, and the regime of the tongue leads to the regime of the sword. Democracy and liberty are two things. The republic presupposes good behaviour, but there is no behaviour where there is not the custom of respect, and no respect without humility. The presumption that every man has the attributes of the citizen, solely by virtue of the fact that he was born twenty years ago, is equivalent to saying that work, merit, virtue, character, experience are nothing; and to say that one becomes the equal of everyone else mechanically, by mere vegetation, is naturally to destroy humility. This presumption destroys even respect for age: for when the voter of twenty-one is as good as the voter of fifty, the nineteen-year-old individual has no serious reason for thinking himself inferior in any respect to his elder by one or two years. Thus the legal fiction of the political order ends by attaining the opposite of its object. The object is to augment the sum of liberty, and the result is to diminish it for everybody.

The modern State has imitated the philosophy of atomism. The national soul, the public mind, tradition, good behaviour are disappearing like so many empty fictions, and nothing is left to create movement but molecular forces and the action of masses. Whereupon theory identifies liberty with caprice. The collective reason and ancient tradition become mere soap-bubbles that any dunce can disperse with a stroke of his pen. Every man for himself; and every extravagance with a hundred supporters can pass from the Utopian sphere and become a thing decreed.

Am I protesting against democracy? By no means. Fiction for fiction, it is the least evil. But it is a good thing not to confuse its promises with realities. The fiction is this: the democratic government postulates that virtually all the voters are enlightened, free, honest and patriotic. And this is a delusion. The majority is necessarily composed of the most ignorant, the poorest and the least capable; therefore the State is at the mercy of chance and the passions, and it always ends by succumbing at one time or another to the rash conditions that have shaped its existence. One who condemned himself to living upright on a tight-rope would inevitably fall; one does not have to be a prophet to predict this result. Ἀριστόν μὲν ὕδωρ, said Pindar. I stake my faith upon it, the best thing that actually exists is wisdom, and lacking this, science. States, churches, society go astray and fall to pieces. Science alone has nothing to lose, as long as society is not wholly barbarous. Unfortunately, barbarism is not impossible. The triumph of the socialist Utopia or religious warfare may perhaps hold in reserve for us this lamentable ordeal.

*April 3, 1865.*—For power, what doctor is equal to a spark of happiness or one single ray of hope? The great mainspring of life lies in the heart. Joy is the vital air of our soul. Sadness is an asthma with atonic complications. Our dependence on the circumstances about us increases with our debilitation, while our radiation, on the other hand, creates our freedom. Health is the first of the freedoms, and happiness gives the force that is the basis of health. To make anyone happy is thus literally to augment his being, to double the intensity of his life, to reveal him to himself, to magnify him and sometimes transfigure him. Happiness effaces ugliness and even makes the beautiful in beauty. No one can doubt this who has ever seen the roses of love dawning on a young girl's cheeks or the light of the first tender thoughts awaking in a limpid glance. Daybreak itself is less of a marvel than this.

And so in paradise everyone will be beautiful. In fact, as the good soul is naturally beautiful, and the spiritual body is only the visibility of the soul, its imponderable, angelic form, and as happiness makes all that it pervades or even touches beautiful, ugliness will be no more. It will disappear with sorrow, evil and death.

For the materialistic philosophy, the beautiful is only encountered fortuitously, and is, consequently, rare; for the spiritualistic philosophy, the beautiful is the rule, the law, the universal, to which all forms return the moment the fortuitous withdraws.

It is always the question of the ideal. Does it exist? Is it only a fiction? Who is right, Plato or Democritus, the realists or the nominalists? Is the soul a product of the body or does the soul produce the body? Do the type and the idea govern life, are they virtually pre-existent to the development of the individual being, or are they a mirage of the adult and deluded being projected into the past? Is the object of the individual contrived *a posteriori?* Are we the sons of Chance, who engender the object and foolishly imagine that the grandsire is the issue of the grandson? These two great conceptions of the world are in fiercer combat in our day than ever . . .

Why are we ugly? Because we are not in the angelic state, because we are evil, morose, unhappy.

Heroism, ecstasy, prayer, love, enthusiasm trace about the brow an aureole, for they deliver the soul, which makes its sheath transparent and throws light all about it. Beauty is thus a phenomenon of the spiritualization of matter; it is a momentary *imparadising* of the privileged object or being, and as it were a favour fallen from heaven upon earth to recall to us the ideal world. To study it is therefore almost inevitably to Platonize. As a powerful electric current can make metals luminous, and reveals their essence in the colour of their flame, so intense life and supreme joy may beautify an ordinary mortal to the point of splendour. And so man is never more truly man than when he is in the divine state.

The ideal, in short, is truer than the real; for the ideal is the eternal moment of perishable things: it is their type, their cipher, their justification, their formula in the book of the Creator, and consequently their justest and at the same time their most comprehensive expression.

*April 11, 1865.*—Measured, weighed, tried on the pearl-grey plaid with which they wish to replace my highland shawl. The old servant, which has accompanied me on all my excursions for ten years and which brings back to me so many charming reminiscences and even poetic adventures, pleases me better than its brilliant successor, even though this latter is offered me by a friendly hand. Can anything take the place of the past? Have not the witnesses of our life, even though inanimate, a language for us? Glion, Bougy, Villars, Albis-brunnen, the Righi, the Chamossaire, Rochemousse, Pipelune and so many other spots have left something of themselves in the meshes of this fabric . . . a part of my intimate biography.

For the rest, the plaid is the only chivalrous garment of the present-day traveller, the only one that can be useful to others as well as to oneself and can render to ladies the most varied services. How many times has mine served them for a cushion, a scarf, a mantle, a shelter on the damp sward of Alpine pastures, or on hard seats of rock, or against the cold shadow of the fir-trees, at the resting and walking times of the mountain life, the times of reading and talking! How many lovely smiles it has won me! Even to its rents and tears, it is all dear to me, for each wound and its healing is a story in itself; its scars are chevrons.

It was a hazel-tree below Jaman, a strap on the Frohnalp, a bramble at Charnex that made the gashes; every time it was by fairy needles that these little mishaps were repaired.

> *Mon vieux manteau, que je vous remercie,*
> *Car c'est à vous que je dois ces plaisirs!*

And has it not been for me a friend in suffering, a defender in hayricks, a companion in good and evil fortune? It makes me think of that tunic of the centaur, which could not be torn off without carrying away with it the flesh and blood of its master. In piety for my vanished youth and in gratitude to destiny, I shall not willingly sacrifice it. This tattered garment has for its warp impressions of the Alps, and for its woof affections. It sings, too, in its own fashion:

> *Pauvre bouquet, fleurs aujourd'hui fanées!*

And this melancholy song is of those that move the heart, though profane ears neither comprehend nor hear them.

What a dagger-thrust is that phrase, You have been!—when its meaning becomes absolutely clear to us. Thenceforward one feels oneself gradually sinking into the grave. That definite completion sounds the knell of our illusions about ourselves. That which is past is past. Grey hairs will never turn back into black ringlets; the forces, the faculties, the charms of youth are gone with the halcyon days:

*Plus d'amour, partant plus de joie.*

How hard it is to grow old, when one has missed life, when one has had neither the crown of manhood nor the paternal crown! How sad it is to feel one's intelligence ebbing before it has done its work, to feel the body declining before it has seen itself born again in those who should close our eyes and honour our name!—How the tragic solemnity of existence strikes us when, one morning on awaking, we hear these lugubrious words, Too late! The hour-glass has turned, the term is expired. You have not reaped your harvest, so much the worse! You have dreamed, slept, forgotten, so much the worse! Wicked and slothful servant, you have neglected happiness and duty, you have not put your talent to account or the chances that have been granted to you. This faces you. Everyone rewards or punishes himself. To whom and of whom would you complain?—Alas!

*Mornex, April 21, 1865 (7 a. m.).*—Morning intoxicatingly beautiful, fresh as a sixteen-year-old heart, and crowned like a bride with flowers. The poetry of youth, innocence and love has flooded my soul. Even to those light mists that wandered in the distance over the meadows, images of the modesty that veils the virgin's charms and envelops in mystery her sweetest thoughts, everything caressed my eyes and spoke to my imagination. A nuptial and religious day. And the morning bells that rang in some far-away village harmonized wonderfully with the hymn of nature.

Pray, they said, adore, love the paternal and beneficent God! It was the accent of Haydn, childlike gladness, the simple gratitude, the radiant and paradisiacal joy in which evil and pain are not yet perceptible, the holy and ingenuous rapture of Eve on the day of her awakening in the new-born world.—How excellent are emotion and admiration! They are the bread of the angels, the everlasting food of the cherubim and the seraphim. And health and leisure and ease, everything I have been given! . . . O thanks, good Providence! May my heart publish thy praises and not forget any of thy benefactions.

*(Eight o'clock.)*—In the five days, or almost, that I have been here, I have not yet felt the air so pure, so life-giving, so ethereal. It is a blessing merely to breathe. One understands the delights of a bird's existence, the emancipation from gravity, the luminous and empyrean life that floats in the blue space and joins all the horizons with a beat of the wings. One must have a great deal of air beneath one to know this inner liberation, this lightness of being. Every element has its poetry, but the poetry of the air is liberty.—Come, dreamer, to work!

*May 30, 1865.*—One of the advantages that wickedness has over its victims is that it lures them on to its own ground, where the struggle is very unequal.

> *Et gonflé de poisons, il attend les morsures.*

Every serpent fascinates its prey. And pure wickedness inherits this vertiginous power that has been granted to the serpent. It stupefies the candid heart, which sees it but does not comprehend it, touches it without being able to believe in it, and is swallowed up in its quandary like Empedocles in Ætna. *Non possum capere te, cape me,* says the Aristotelian legend. Every one of Beelzebub's diminutives is an abyss. Every diabolical act is a gulf of darkness. Native cruelty, original perfidy and falsity, even in animals, throw, as it were, gleams into the unfathomable pit of the perversity of Satan, which is a moral reality.

And yet a mental reservation tells me that a sophism lies at the bottom of human wickedness, that most monsters like to be justified in their own eyes, and that the first attribute of the Devil is to be the father of falsehood.—Before every crime, there has to be a corruption of the conscience; and every successful evil-doer begins with this. That hatred is deadly is of no avail, the hater must see something wholesome in it. It is to do himself good that he does harm, as a mad dog bites to quench his thirst.

To do harm, even while knowingly harming oneself, is one degree further: it becomes a frenzy, which is intensified until it turns into a cold ferocity. When, impelled by lust, a man follows his bestial or venomous instincts, he must seem to the angels delirious and out of his mind, lighting the fires of his own gehenna in order to consume the world therein, or as much of it as his fiendish desires can reach. Atrocity begins a new spiral that sinks yet further into the depths of abomination, for the windings of hell have this property, that there is no end to them; and progress through the horrible is even more certain than progress through the good.

It seems as if divine perfection were an infinite of the first power, but that diabolical perfection is an infinite of unknown power. But no, for that would make evil the true God, and hell would swallow up creation. In the Persian and Christian faiths, good must conquer evil; perhaps even Satan is to be redeemed and to reënter grace; the divine order is to be everywhere restored. The other point of view would be an irremediable desolation, in comparison with which nothingness would seem to be salvation. The Creator would be universally and invariably accursed, and creation would be only a hideous cancer doomed to consume life increasingly throughout the frightful duration of eternity. This idea makes one's hair stand on end.

Evil therefore, cannot be bottomless; love will prove to be more powerful than hatred. God will save his glory, and his glory lies in his goodness.—But it is very true that gratuitous wickedness troubles the soul, for it shakes the great lines of the moral order in us by suddenly drawing aside the curtain that hides from us the action

of the dark and corrosive forces that are implacably set against the
divine plan. Our vision is obscured by them, and our faith is scandalized.—Another of the disadvantages of solitude: it exaggerates
everything, it delivers us over to the blue devils. *Vae soli!* One must
go forth and fortify oneself with men who feel, men who do their
duty, with the exemplary beings, the beautiful souls.

*June 25, 1865.*—Why did S. weep on my shoulder yesterday? It
was not difficult to guess, but the reason was too delicate, especially
too complicated to be conveyed. A tear may be the poetic summary
of so many simultaneous impressions, the combined quintessences
of so many contrary thoughts! It is like one drop of those precious
Oriental elixirs that contain the qualities of twenty plants, blended
into a single aroma. Sometimes it is even the excess of the soul,
overflowing the cup of revery. What one is not able to say, does not
know how to say or wish to say, what one refuses to confess to
oneself, the confused desires, the hidden sorrows, the smothered
griefs, the secret resistances, the unutterable regrets, the emotions
we are struggling against, the concealed anxieties, the superstitious
fears, the vague sufferings, the disquieting presentiments, the
thwarted fancies, the injuries that have been done to our ideal, the
fatigues that have not been assuaged, the vain hopes, the multitude
of little indiscernible evils that accumulate slowly in some corner
of the heart, like water silently forming into drops on the vault of
a dark cave: all these mysterious agitations of the inner life burst
into sensibility and this sensibility is concentrated in a liquid diamond on the edge of the eyelids. If a tender kiss is a whole discourse
condensed into a single breath, one tear of this sudden tenderness
contains the value of many kisses, and, by virtue of this, its eloquence has a much more penetrating energy. That is why love, when
it is passionate, intense and full of suffering, often has no other
language than kisses, or tears, or sometimes stings.

Tears express, for the rest, joy as well as sorrow. They are a
symbol of the powerlessness of the soul to contain its emotion and
keep its self-control. Speech is a form of analysis; and when we

are overwhelmed by sensation or feeling, analysis ceases, and with
it speech and freedom. Our sole resource, after silence and stupor,
is the language of action, mimicry. The oppression of the mind reduces us to a stage that is anterior to humanity, to the gesture, the
cry, the sob, and finally to faintness and swooning. That is to say
that, incapable as men of supporting the excess of our sensations,
we fall back successively to the stage of the animal being, then of
the vegetable being. Dante was always swooning during his journey
through hell. Nothing better depicts the violence of his feelings and
the ardour of his pity.

And there are few women who do not sometimes suffer from
this excess of the soul. But from modesty, prudence, pride, they
seek in solitude to alleviate their hearts in sighs.—To dare to do
this on the bosom of friendship requires such a confluence of circumstances that it rarely happens. And yet how much swifter is the
consolation, how much more efficacious, how much sweeter, when
one yields to this weakness! S. was entirely changed and happy
after this mute confession. Her heart was unbosomed of its grief,
disburdened of its weight, almost like that of a penitent absolved
by her confessor.

Without being a woman, one may have experienced similar needs
and felt the same desire. This malady is a vague nostalgia for happiness. The cure is the pleasure of confession, a confession relieved
of the burden of speaking.

*Gryon-sur-Bex, August 8, 1865.*—Splendid cloudless moonlight.
The night is grave and majestic. The flock of the colossi sleeps under the watch of the stars. In the vast shadows of the valley a few
roofs gleam here and there, while the eternal organ-note of the torrent swells in the depths of this cathedral of mountains whose
vault is the firmament . . .

A last glance over this blue night, over the immense landscape,
over those familiar peaks and ridges, hung with the silver beams
and the green shadows of the queen of reveries, the moon. Jupiter
has almost set over the spurs of the Dent du Midi, and the voice of

the Avençon fitfully rises, despite the apparent peace of this nocturnal hour. From the starry dome falls a snow of invisible flakes
of dream, inviting one to a chaste slumber. There is nothing voluptuous or enervating in this nature, everything is strong, severe and
pure.—Good night to all creatures, to the unfortunate and to the
happy, to the bridal bed as to the solitary bed. Rest and rejuvenation, renewal and hope.—A day is dead, long live the morrow!—
Midnight strikes. One more step towards the grave.

*January 7, 1866.*—Our life is a mere bubble clinging to a reed;
it is born, expands, arrays itself in the loveliest colours of the rainbow, at moments it even escapes from the law of gravity; but soon
the black speck appears upon it, and the globe of gold and emerald
vanishes in space and is resolved into a mere droplet of impure
liquid. All the poets have made this comparison; it is striking in its
truth. To appear, shine, disappear, to be born, suffer, die: is this not
always the summary of life, for the ephemera, for a nation, for a
celestial body?

Time is only the measure of the difficulty of a conception; pure
thought has almost no need of time, for it perceives the two ends
of an idea almost simultaneously. Nature achieves the thought of a
planet only with great labour, but the supreme intelligence resumes
it in a point. Time is thus the successive dispersion of being, as
speech is the successive analysis of an intuition or a desire. In itself, it is relative and negative, and it vanishes in absolute being.
God is outside of time, because he thinks all thought at once; nature is within time, because it is only speech, the discursive un-
rolling of every thought contained in the infinite thought. But nature exhausts itself in this impossible task, for the analysis of the
infinite is a contradiction. With limitless duration, boundless space
and infinite number, nature does at least what it can do to translate
the richness of the creative formula. In the abysses which it un-
successfully opens to comprehend thought, one can measure the
greatness of the divine spirit. The moment this spirit, emerging
from itself, seeks to explain itself, the discourse heaps universe

upon universe for billions of centuries; and, as it cannot contrive to express its subject properly, the discourse must continue forever.

The Orient prefers immobility as the form of the infinite, the Occident prefers movement. This is because the latter has a passion for detail and the vanity of believing that the individual matters. Like a child who has been given a hundred thousand francs, it fancies it can multiply its fortune by reckoning it up in sous and centimes. Possessing an estate of two square leagues, it fancies it is a greater proprietor because it calculates the surface in inches rather than in yards. Its passion for progress arises in great part from an infatuation, which consists in forgetting the end and becoming absorbed vaingloriously in little steps taken one after another; even under pressure, this child confuses change with amelioration, beginning again with becoming perfect.

At bottom, the modern man has an immense craving for distraction, he has a secret horror for whatever belittles him; that is why the eternal, the infinite, perfection are a bugbear to him. He wishes to have his own approval, to admire himself, to felicitate himself, and, in consequence, he averts his eyes from all the abysses that might remind him of his nothingness. This is what constitutes the real pettiness of so many of our powerful minds, the lack of personal dignity in our giddy civilized folk as compared with the Arabs of the desert, the increasing frivolity of our multitudes, who are always more instructed, it is true, but always more superficial in their notion of happiness.

Here lies the service rendered to us by Christianity, that Oriental element in our culture. It acts as a counterpoise to our leanings towards the finite, towards the transitory and the changing, reassembling the mind by the contemplation of eternal things, by Platonizing our affections a little, constantly turned aside as they are from the ideal world, by leading us back from dispersion to concentration, from worldliness to self-collectedness, by restoring calm, gravity, nobility to these souls of ours, fevered with a thousand paltry desires. Just as sleep is a bath of rejuvenation for our active life, religion is the bath that refreshes our immortal being. The holy has a purifying virtue. Religious emotion encircles the brow with a halo and causes the heart to bloom with ineffable joy.

Thus I think that those who oppose religion in itself are mistaken about the needs of Occidental man, and that the modern world would lose its equilibrium at once if there were any question of its yielding altogether to the unripe doctrine of progress. We always need the infinite, the eternal, the absolute, and, since science is satisfied with the relative, a void remains which it is good to fill by contemplation, worship and adoration. "Religion," said Bacon, "is the aromatic that saves life from corruption", and especially today religion in the Platonic and Oriental sense. Profound self-collectedness is, in fact, the condition of noble activity.

A return to the serious, the divine, the sacred, is becoming more and more difficult, with all the restlessness of criticism that has been introduced into the Church itself, with the worldliness of preaching, the universal agitation, but this return grows more and more necessary. Without it, there can be no inner life. And the inner life is the way to resist one's environment advantageously. If the mariner did not maintain his own temperature in himself, he could not go from the pole to the equator and still remain himself; the man who has no refuge in himself, but lives in his own shop-window, so to speak, in the outward vortex of things, affairs, opinions, is not, properly speaking, a distinct personality, he is not free, original, a cause, in a word, somebody. He is merely an aliquot in a number, a tax-payer, a voter, an anonymous being, he is not a man. He represents the mass, he is reckoned among the consumers and producers in the human form, but he interests only the economist and the statistician, who consider the heap of sand without bothering about the grains, which are uniform and indifferent. These *polloi,* this mob, this rout, this multitude counts only as a massive elementary force. Why? Because the constituent parts are insignificant in isolation, because they are all alike; one adds them like the molecules of water in a river, measuring them by the fathom, not rating them as individuals. These men are therefore estimated and weighed, as bodies are, because they are not, as souls are, individualized by consciousness.

He who drifts with the current, he who does not steer himself in accordance with higher principles, he who has no ideal, no conviction, is nothing but a parcel of earthly furniture, an object that is acted upon and not an acting subject, a puppet, not a reasonable creature, an echo, not a voice. He who has no inner life is the slave of his environment, as the barometer is the obedient servant of the unstirred air, and as the weather-vane is the humble bond-slave of the air in motion.

*January 12, 1866.*—Passed a few hours in the company of Maurice de Guérin; read his *Journal* (three years, from 1832 to 1835), his verses, the articles by George Sand, Sainte-Beuve, Trébutien, Du Breil, and Eugénie de Guérin on this talent carried away in its flower, at the age of twenty-nine, together with the two strange fragments entitled the *Centaure* and *Bacchante*. What is one to think of the writer and the man? I will suspend my judgment until I have read the correspondence. As for the *Journal,* it contains some enchanting passages, but aside from this it gives no precise idea of the culture, the studies, the ideas or the range of the man who wrote it. To speak only in very general terms of the movements of the inner life, it does not suggest a distinct individuality or mark its true proportions, its true nature. I have already had to reproach Lavater's *Journal* in the same way. The journal, understood in this fashion, is an all but impersonal confessional, not characterizing one sinner more than another, without biographical or historical precision, and consequently deceptive, since it does not serve to reconstruct a man in his specific difference from the men of his type. Impossible, for instance, to see in this *Journal* what Maurice did, whom he saw, what were his occupations, etc. One would never be able to guess from it that he was well-read in four or five literatures, one cannot even conjecture how his talent was formed. That is my first objection.—As for talent, properly speaking, when one adds the *Bacchante* to the *Centaure,* the question rises whether a fearful monotony would not have been the end of this originality, and whether the visionary perception of the life of nature, in which Maurice's power as a poet consists, can supply matter for more than one work, without boring the reader, especially the French reader. The interest of this study seems to me psychological rather than artistic. It is curious to find the Hindu and Brahmanical feeling in a young French writer. But to make for it such a pedestal as they have carved for this young man is to exaggerate the value of the novelty. I find that among his three friends, Du Breil, Trébutien and Kertonguy, the last has best preserved his good sense, together with a feeling for proportion and distinctions, although, to express myself a little bluntly, I think they have notably overdone Eugénie's brother.—Having made this reservation, I feel much sympathy for Maurice, an exquisite organization, a literary sensitive-plant, an intuitive and dreamy intelligence, a character that was frightened by real life, timid, irresolute, in short, a personality which I find akin to my own in more ways than one, at least on the weaker sides, such as his uncertainty regarding his proper vocation, the alarming difficulty he found in using his will, his excessively distrustful temperament and that kind of passion, noted by one of his friends, that perpetually urges him to disparage and torture his own faculties by subjecting them to the endless punishment of a sort of moral autopsy. *Me, me, adsum qui feci.*—To be just, I should also confess that if I admire Maurice for his delicacy, and for the multitude of his impressions, poetic, aesthetic and moral impressions that have their value, I suffer, too, from a certain want of ideas, properly so-called, views, truths which, after all, constitute the real wealth of a mind. The author appears to me rather a sensitive man, a dreamer, a musician, than a thinker. What he brings us is a particular mode of the sentiment of nature, an intimacy with the mysterious force of Isis, pantheistic enthusiasm. If, to the day of his death, he was a Christian and a Catholic, and if his family has insisted on saying this and saying it again, his talent had an inspiration that was quite different, and no good judge has been deceived about it.

*January 21, 1866.*—This evening, after supper, I was at a loss where to give my solitude an airing; I was thirsty for conversation, for an exchange of thoughts, for society. It occurred to me to go up and see the R.'s, the model family. They were at supper. Afterwards we went into the drawing-room, and the mother and daughter sat down at the piano and sang a duet by Boïeldieu. The ivory keys of this old grand piano, on which the mother played before her marriage and which, for twenty-five years, has followed and translated into music the destinies of the family, these keys clacked and missed a little; but the poetry of the past sang in this faithful servitor, the confidant of sorrows, the companion of long evenings, the echo of a whole life of duty, affection, piety, virtue. I was more moved than I can say. I seemed to be reading a novel of Dickens. In this aesthetic impulse of tenderness there was scarcely a thought of myself, although these twenty-five years have passed over my head also, and although I was present at A. R.'s wedding. It was a pure tenderness without egoism and without melancholy.

All this seems to me a dream, so far as it concerns myself, and I cannot believe my eyes at this witness of the lustrums that have rolled away. How strange a thing to have lived and to feel so far from a time that is so present to one! One does not know whether one is awake or asleep. Time is only the space between our recollections. The moment we cease to perceive this space, time has disappeared. An old man's whole life may seem to him only an hour long, less indeed. And the moment that time is reduced for us to a point, we have entered eternity. Life is merely the dream of a shadow; I felt this with a new intensity this evening. I perceive myself only as a fugitive appearance, like the impalpable rainbow that for a moment floats over the spray, in the fearful cascade of being that falls incessantly into the abyss of the days. Thus everything seems to me a chimæra, a mist, a phantom, nothingness, my

own individuality included. I find myself in the midst of phenomenology. Strange! strange! . . .

I do not have to repeat to myself that the fashion of this world
passes away; to me everything seems to fly with the wings of the
eagle, and my own existence is only an eddy that is about to be
dispelled.—Is it that I am about to die? Is it that I am old? Is
it that I have become a philosopher? Is it because the gulf of
eternal things always seems near me, so near that the love of temporal and passing things seems to me ridiculous? Of what use is it
to attach oneself to what is about to end? Already I feel the breath
of eternity passing through my hair, and I feel that I behold from
beyond the grave the world of the living. (*Midnight.*)

*January 23, 1866.*—There is always something strange to me
about purely critical organizations who have no feeling of responsibility, who are in no way disturbed by the fate of the human
masses, children, the unfortunate, but instead laugh at everything. If their influence ever dominates, society will dissolve, for
they represent only the negative, corrosive, destructive element in
thought and encourage an aristocratic egoism of the mind. Enthusiasm, charity, country, Church are phenomena of no concern to
them; they are detached and indifferent to everything. Duties are
all someone else's business. The heart, which binds us to others, and
the moral conscience, which binds us to a duty, both seem to be
unknown to this category of men. Their error lies in overestimat-
ing the value of criticism. Being is more important than the consciousness of being; the substance is worth at least as much as its
mould; reality is surely preferable to its image; affirmation is superior to negation; invention, creation, action are more than the
analysis of them, for criticism, left alone, annihilates itself, while
its object subsists without it. There is no escaping the fact that an
aliment is more necessary than the description of this aliment, and
a great man is better than his shadow. Mephistopheles is a shrewd
critic; but without creation and the Creator, what would he be?
Nothing. What is it to demolish, as compared with building?

I conclude. A little criticism liberates us; too much criticism desiccates us. A purely critical being is only half a man, and even so he is not the better half. He does more harm than good, for he promotes every kind of disintegration, moral and social.

*January 29, 1866 (9 a. m.).*—A pretty attack of lumbago nipped me yesterday between the ribs and still has me in its clutches to-day; it is a sort of crick at the waist, of which this is my first experience . . . Another greyish curtain of fog has spread over the city; the weather is dull and gloomy. The bells are ringing in the distance for some festival. Otherwise, it is calm and silent; save for the crackling of my fire, no sound disturbs my solitude, my refuge of reveries and work. Bending over my old black desk, with a woollen scarf about my loins, like an Arab at ease, and dressed in my warm brown frock-coat, I am scribbling these lines between my high window and my little fireplace, with my feet in a furry fox-skin. Over my head slopes the blue wall of my attic. A few dictionaries and other books, spread over two collapsible stools within my reach, over a rustic table and an oldish chest of drawers, are, with a few odd chairs, all the furniture of this modest garret, in which the grown man listlessly continues his student's life, and the sedentary professor his traveller's habits.

What is it that gives its charm to this existence, apparently so empty and bare? Freedom. What to me are all these uglinesses of a semi-poverty, this absence of comfort, this everything else that is lacking in my dwelling-place? These things are indifferent to me. I find under this roof light, tranquillity, shelter. I am near a sister and her children, whom I love. My material life is assured. That is enough for a single man. Besides, a few good souls have visited my garret. Children have played in it. It is filled with memories for me. So it is not uninhabitable, and perhaps I shall leave it with less indifference than I fancy. For am I not a creature of habit who is more attached to known vexations than enamoured of unknown pleasures?—Thus I am free and not uncomfortable. I am well off here, and I should be ungrateful to complain. And indeed I do not complain, and I wish that fate were as kind to ninety-five people in a hundred as it is to my indolent self.—It is only that my heart sighs and longs for something more and better. And the heart is an insatiable glutton, as everyone knows. Besides, who has not longings? That is our destiny here below. The only difference is that some torment themselves to indulge themselves, and do not succeed, while others anticipate the result and resign themselves, economizing efforts that would be sterile and fruitless. Since one cannot be happy, why give oneself so much trouble? One must limit oneself to the strictly necessary, live on a diet, abstain, be content with little, value nothing but peace of conscience, the sense that one has done one's duty.

It is true that this is not a slight ambition, and that one falls into another impossibility. No, the simplest thing is to submit purely and simply to God.

> *Vouloir ce que Dieu veut est la seule science*
> *Qui nous met en repos.*

All else, as the Preacher says, is but vanity and vexation of spirit.

I have known and felt this for a long time now, and this religious renunciation is sweet and familiar to me. It is the outward agitations, the examples of the world and the inevitable allurement of the current of things that make me forget the wisdom I have acquired and the principles I have adopted. This is why living is such a burden. This eternal beginning anew is irksome and distasteful. It would be so good to fall asleep when one has gathered the fruit of experience, when one has ceased to resist the supreme will, when one is detached from one's self, when one is at peace with all men! Whereas one is always having to recommence the circuit of temptations, disputes, vexations, inadvertences, fall back into prose, into the commonplace, into vulgarity! How dismal and how humiliating! It is for this reason that the poets withdraw their heroes from the struggle as quickly as they can and do not drag them, after the victory, along the beaten path of unprofitable days. Those whom the gods love die young, said the ancient proverb.

Yes, but this favour flatters our secret instinct; this is our desire and not the will of God. We must be humbled, drilled, harassed and tempted to the end. The touchstone of our virtue is our patience. To endure life, even without illusions and without hope, to accept this perpetual dust of warfare even though we love only peace, not to withdraw from the world even when it repels us like bad company, like a battle-ground of ugly passions, to keep faith with one's own creed without breaking with the votaries of false gods, not to seek escape from the human hospital, despite the aversion of our nostrils and our horror of the unhealthy multitude, to be patient as Job on his dunghill, this is duty. When life ceases to be a promise, it does not cease to be a task; and indeed its true name is trial.

*(11 a. m.).*—One interruption breaks the spell of thought, and it destroys the charm of an emotion, too. Thus I went downstairs for a few minutes and talked with two or three people, and now I find myself in a totally different region of ideas. It is as if a dream were dissipated, as if a magic captivity had come to an end, as if a cock-crow had dispelled the phantoms with which solitude and twilight had surrounded us. Midday plunges us into reality and wrests us away from contemplation. This is good, too, in its own time. "Work while ye have the light."

*March 5, 1866.*—The whole sky is raining, as far as the view extends from my high observatory. A leaden lid covers the valley, as with a silent sadness. It is grey from the Salève to the Jura, grey from the pavement to the clouds. Eyes, mouth, the whole being sees, tastes, touches nothing but grey. Colour, gaiety, life are dead. Everything shrinks into its shell.—What do the birds do in these circumstances? We who have a table and viands, a fire on the hearth, books around us, pigeon-holes full of engravings in the cabinet, a nestful of dreams in our heart and a tumult of thoughts at the bottom of our inkwell, we find nature ugly and turn away our eyes from it; but you, poor sparrows, what can you do? Be patient, hope, learn. When everything is considered, do we not all do this?

You are patient, or to speak more truly, you postpone, defer, delay—what? The great decision. You hope for—what? Who knows? You are expecting—what? To be younger, more valiant, bolder? Madness!

*Mornex, April 2, 1866.*—The snow is turning to slush again and the whole countryside is wrapped in a damp fog. *Jupiter pluvius* hugs Cybele close; a discreet mantle of clouds, with its folds trailing on the ground, screens their love, for there is no longer any space between them. The asphalt balcony outside the drawing-room is nothing but a quivering sheet of water incessantly pricked by the fast-falling drops from the sky. Only a greyish section of the Arve can be seen winding like a serpent in the depths of the mist. One could touch the horizon with one's hand, and the three cubic leagues of rain that were visible yesterday have become an opaque curtain, or rather a floating cavern, with my look-out at the centre, though the eye cannot pierce either to its vault or its grey walls.

This captivity transports me to the Shetlands, to Spitzbergen, to Norway, to the Ossianic lands of the mist, where man, thrown back upon himself, feels his heart beating all the more, feels his mind meditating, when heart and mind are not frozen by the cold. Fog surely has its poetry, its deep, inward grace, its dreamy charm. It does in the day what the lamp does at night; it impels the mind to composure, it turns the soul back upon itself. Sunshine diffuses us through nature, disperses and dissipates us; the fog reassembles us and concentrates us, and is therefore heartwarming, domestic, moving. The poetry of the sun partakes of the epic, that of the fog partakes of the elegiac hymn and the religious chant. Pantheism is the offspring of light; fog engenders a faith in the protectors that are close at hand. When the universal world is shut away, the house becomes a little universe. In the eternal mists, people love one another better, for then the only reality is the family and, within the family, the heart.—The action of fog is therefore similar to the effects of blindness, and the action of sunlight to the effects of deafness; for the hearing man is more tender and sympathetic, the seeing man is dryer and harder. Why? Because the one lives especially in the human and inner life, the other especially in the natural and outer life. And the greatest thoughts come from the heart, says the moralist.

*Mornex, April 3, 1866 (8 a. m.).*—*Juchhe! Gloria!* The snow and the rainbow of yesterday have kept their promise, and the birds were right. This morning the sun found not a single cloud in the sky, and its beams were flooding my window and a white valley when I opened my eyes.—A morning freshness, limpid air, a sharp, distinct horizon, with the infinite details of a vast landscape clearly marked and coloured and caressed by a delicious light, a sense of the joy of being within us and outside us, such is the compensation for two bad days . . . I multiplied my delight in it all by using opera-glasses. It is a gratification to the eye to perceive distant objects clearly. Only the short-sighted know the prodigious contrast between a confused vision and a distinct vision. People with excellent eyesight have no idea of the happiness that a glass gives to others, or of how one's heart can beat as one descries the details of a vast prospect. It is like a revelation. A second nature, more living, richer, greener, starts up under the first. One is reborn oneself, and one sees with the intoxicated eyes of fifteen.

*April 6, 1866.*—Read the first volume of *John Halifax: Gentleman,* by Miss Mulock, a book that is bolder than it seems, for it takes up, in the English way, the social problem of equality. And the solution is that everyone can become a gentleman, even though he were born in the gutter. In its fashion, this narrative protests against conventional superiorities and demonstrates that real nobility lies in character, in personal merit, in moral distinction, in elevation of sentiment and language, in dignity of living and self-respect. This is better than Jacobinism and is the opposite of brutal equalitarianism. Instead of lowering everybody, the author proclaims the right to rise. One may be born rich or noble, but one is not born a gentleman. This word is the shibboleth of England. It divides the universe into two halves, civilized society into two castes. Among gentlemen, courtesy, equality, harmony; below, disdain, contempt, coldness, indifference. This is the ancient distinction between the *ingenui* and the others, between the ἐλεύθεροι and the βάναυσοι. It is the feudal continuation of the gentlefolk and the commonalty.

What is a gentleman, then? He is a free and well-bred man, who is self-sufficient and knows how to make himself respected. He is something else than the man of good society, the decorous man, even the man of honour: manners, language, civility are not enough. In addition, he must have independence and dignity. By any sort of vassalage or servility, any familiarity even, still more a dishonourable act, a lie, an improbity, one forfeits the title of gentleman.—In short, the gentleman is the English type of the *homme accompli,* and it can be said of the king himself that he is more or less of a gentleman . . . Domestic service in all its forms, suppresses in two ways the sentiment of equality, inasmuch as dependence and vulgarity cannot be confounded with independence and education.—Equality remains a possibility and a right, but inequality is a fact. France insists on the first point, England on the second. A reconciliation lies in saying with Miss Mulock: Let who will become a gentleman. Personal distinction is the flower of virtue, and, like the latter, it is a reward and a conquest.

The gentleman recalls the sage of the Stoics, the type of that which one ought to be. It is better if he has means and is well-born, but this is not absolutely indispensable: it is difficult but not impossible for him to be a merchant or a manufacturer. If he has to earn his living, he must maintain his pride, his reserve, his superiority to fortune and circumstances and present his bills, like an artist or a physician, with a sort of haughty modesty, counting on the delicacy of other people, never confessing his troubles, his needs or anxieties, or anything that would make him inferior to those whose esteem he claims and whose commiseration he rejects. The true gentleman is, or should appear to be, above any constraint; he has no master, and he acts only from condescension or a sense of duty. No man can command him in any way, and, when he obeys, he obeys an impersonal law, or a promise that he has given, or a contract he has accepted; in short, he obeys only himself, only what he recognizes as just and equitable and not any despotism whatever.—"Dieu et mon droit" is his motto. The gentleman is decidedly the free man, the man who is stronger than things and who feels that personality surpasses all the accessory attributes of fortune, health, rank, power, etc., and is the essential fact, the intrinsic and real worth of the individual. Tell me what you are, and I will tell you what you are worth. This ideal happily clashes with the gross ideal, equally English, of capital, the formula of which is: How much is this man worth?—In the land where poverty is an offence, it is a good thing to be able to say that a nabob is not *per se* a gentleman.—The mercantile ideal and the chivalrous ideal counterbalance one another, and if one is the cause of the ugliness of English society, and its brutal aspects, the other serves as a compensation for it.

*April 7, 1866.*—As I awoke, the idea of the gentleman still occupied my mind.—The gentleman is the man who is master of himself, who respects himself and makes himself respected. His essential trait is therefore inner sovereignty. He is a self-possessed character, a force that governs himself, a free agent who affirms himself and manifests and rules himself by the standard of dignity. This ideal is therefore very close to the Roman type of the *Ingenuus consciens et compos sui* and of the *dignitas cum auctoritate*. This ideal is more moral than intellectual. It is suitable to England, whose special trait is will. But from self-respect a thousand things derive, such as the care of one's person, of one's language and manner, vigilance over body and soul, control of one's instincts and one's passions, the desire to be self-sufficient, the pride that neither exacts nor wishes favours, the care not to expose oneself to any humiliation or any mortification, by avoiding the least dependence on human caprice, the constant preservation of one's honour and one's self-esteem: altogether the English type of the sage. This sovereignty, not being easy for any but the man who is well-born, well-bred and rich, was at first identified with birth, rank and especially property. The idea of the gentleman thus derives from feudalism; it is a mollification of seigniory.

In order not to undergo reproach, he will maintain his irreproachability; in order to be treated with consideration, he will always be careful to preserve distances, to distinguish between degrees of respect, to observe all the gradations of conventional politeness, in accordance with the rank, age and circumstances of persons. And in the same way, he will be imperturbably reserved and circumspect in the presence of a stranger, whose name and whose worth he does not know, and to whom he might expose himself were he to show too much or too little courtesy. He ignores and avoids him; if he is accosted, he turns away; if he is addressed, he haughtily cuts the conversation short. His politeness is thus not human and general but entirely individual and adapted to persons. This is why every Englishman is made up of two: the one that is turned towards the world, and the other. The first, the outward man, is a hedgehog, a fortress, a cold and angular wall; the other, the inward man, is a sensitive, affectionate, cordial, loving being. This type has been formed in a moral climate that is full of icicles, where the world is inimical and only the fireside hospitable, where an impenetrable breastplate covers a tender heart, where the leather of the jacket is turned outside and the velvet is within.

By analyzing the national type of the *homme accompli,* we can thus discover the nature and history of a nation, as the tree is revealed to us by the fruit.—The inverse is still more serviceable: with the history and climate given, one constructs the type. But the first investigation is a discovery, while the second is only an observation.—Psychology should use both methods and check the one by the other; beginning now with the seed to learn of the plant, now with the plant to learn of the seed.

*(Later.)*—If philosophy is the art of understanding, it is clear that it must begin by saturating itself with facts and realities, and that the abstract method, attempted too soon, ends by destroying it, as the abuse of fasting at the age of growth destroys the body. Moreover, we can only understand what we find in ourselves. And to understand is to possess first by sympathy, then by the intelligence, the thing understood. Far, then, from at once dismembering and disjointing the object to be conceived, one must grasp it first in its entirety, secondly in its formation and only afterwards in its parts. The procedure is the same for the study of a watch or a plant, a work of art or a character. One must contemplate, respect, interrogate, and not destroy what one wishes to know. One must assimilate oneself to things, give oneself to them, open oneself submissively to their influence, impregnate oneself with their originality and their distinctive form, before violating them by dissecting them.

*April 14, 1866.*—Panic, collapse, general rout at the Bourse in Paris. My poor remaining funds are dropping, dropping! This solidarity of interests, I used to think, counterbalances the tendency to atomism in the affections. In our epoch of individualism and "every man for himself and God for all", the trepidations of the public funds resemble the palpitations of the heart. One feels an obligatory sympathy, somewhat suggesting the patriotism of one's compulsory taxes; one is constrained to keep an eye on the follies of Prussia and America, one feels engaged, compromised in all the world's affairs, and one has to take an interest, in spite of oneself, in the terrible machine whose wheels may at any instant crush us. Credit gives birth to an unstable society, whose trembling base and artificial structure perpetually menace its security. It sometimes forgets that it is dancing on a volcano. But the least rumour of war pitilessly brings this back to mind. Houses built of cards are easily ruined.—This anxiety is unbearable for humble little bondholders like myself, who, renouncing the pursuit of riches, would at least have liked to be able to attend to their modest labours in peace. But no; the world is there, and, like a brutal tyrant, it cries to us: Peace, peace, there is no peace; I mean you to suffer, laugh and skip about with me! And when one reflects that five or six crowned rascals, or merely gold-braided rascals, hold in their hands the tranquillity of the world, and are able to martyr at their caprice the destiny of several millions of their fellows, one feels a little irritated.—To accept humanity as nature, to be resigned before the arbitrary individual as before fate, is not an easy matter. One admits the domination of God, but one execrates the despot, if one cannot shoot him. Nobody likes to be involved in the shipwreck of a vessel upon which he has been forcibly embarked, and which has sailed against his will and judgment.—And yet this is continually the case in life. We all pay for the mistakes of a few. Indeed, according to orthodoxy, a solitary mistake of a single man is expiated by humanity until the end of time. The disproportion between the offence and the punishment has become a part of our habits of thought, although it is revolting to the instinct of justice.

Human solidarity is a more evident and certain fact than personal responsibility or even individual liberty. Our dependence outweighs our independence, for we are independent only in our desire, while we are dependent on our health, on nature, on society, on everything in us and outside us. The circle of our liberty is only a point. This point is that where we protest against all these oppressive and fatal powers, where we say: Crush me, you shall not have my consent! We are able, by will, to take our stand in opposition to necessity and refuse it homage and obedience; this is moral freedom. But save for this, we belong, body and goods, to the world; we are its playthings, as the dust is the plaything of the wind, as the dead leaf is of the stream. God at least respects our dignity; but the world tosses us with scorn and fury on its waves, in order to make it manifest that we are at its mercy.

The theories of the nullity of the individual, the pantheistic and materialistic conceptions are battering now at an open door and felling a man of straw. The moment one ceases to glorify this imperceptible point of consciousness and celebrate its worth, the individual naturally becomes again an atom in the human mass, which is itself only an atom in the planetary mass, which is a nothing in the heavens; the individual is thus only a nothing to the third power, with a capacity for measuring this nothingness. Thought ends in resignation. Doubt of self leads to passiveness, and passiveness leads to servitude.

To escape this requires a voluntary submission, a religious dependence which has one's free consent; that is, an assertion of ourselves as free beings, bowing only to duty. Duty becomes a principle of action, a source of energy, an assurance of our partial independence of the world, a condition of our dignity, a sign of our nobility. The world cannot make me will, nor make me will my duty; here I am my master and my only master, I treat with it as sovereign to sovereign. It holds my body in its claws, but my soul escapes it and defies it. My thought and my love, my faith and my hope are beyond its clutches. My true being, the essence of my personality, my I remains inviolable and inaccessible to its outrages and its wrath. In this, we are greater than the universe, which has mass but not will; we become independent again, even in the face of the human mass, which also can annihilate only our happiness, as the first mass can annihilate only our body. Submission is therefore not a defeat; on the contrary, it is a strength.

*April 28, 1866.*—Read the proceedings of the Conference of Pastors of April 15–16 in Paris. There is discord in the camp of Agramant. The question of the supernatural has split the French Protestant Church in two. The liberals insist on the right of the individual; the orthodox on the idea of the Church. It is true that a Church is an affirmation, and that it subsists by virtue of a positive element, a definite belief; the pure critical element would dissolve it.—Protestantism is a combination of two factors: the authority of the Scriptures and freedom of inquiry. The moment that one of these factors is threatened or disappears, Protestantism disappears, *Troja fuit.*—A new form of Christianity is succeeding it, the form, for example, of the Church of the Brothers of the Holy Ghost, or that of Christian Theism. For myself, I see no harm in this result, but I think that the friends of the Protestant Church are logical in their refusal to abandon the Apostles' Creed, and that the individualists are illogical in supposing that they can preserve Protestantism without authority.

The question of method separates the two camps. I differ fundamentally from both of them. To my mind, Christianity is above everything else religious, and religion is not a method; it is a life, a superior life, supernatural and mystical in its root and practical in its fruits, a communion with God, a deep, calm enthusiasm, a radiant love, a force that acts, an overflowing felicity; in short, religion is a state of the soul. These quarrels about method have their value, but this value is secondary; they cannot console the heart, nor can they edify the conscience. That is why I do not feel interested and stirred by these ecclesiastical wrangles. Whether the one group or the other has the majority and the victory is of no profit essentially, for dogmatics, criticism, the Church are not religion; and religion, the divine sentiment of life, is the important matter. —"Seek ye first the kingdom of God, and his righteousness; and all these things shall be added unto you." What is most holy is most Christian, this is always the least deceptive criterion: "By this shall all men know that ye are my disciples, if ye have love one to another."

As much as the individual is worth, so much is his religion worth. The popular instinct and philosophic reason coincide in this criterion. If religion is essentially a state of the soul, and if the subjective, inward, mystical fact is the end, the *raison d'être* of everything else in religion, one can say to an individual: show me what you are, and I shall know the value of your belief, or rather what value I should attach to your formulas and dogmas. The method is something, but the object is something else; and if one has to choose, the object should be chosen and warranted first. Be pious and good, heroic and patient, faithful and devoted, humble and charitable: the catechism that has taught you this does not have to pass any further test. Salvation is something higher than the means of salvation, as the work that is accomplished surpasses the project. Through religion one lives in God, while in all these quarrels one lives only with men and their black gowns. There is thus no equivalence between them.

Perfection as the goal, an example for support, the divine proved simply by its excellence: is not all Christianity summed up in this? God as all in all—is not this its consummation?

*September 20, 1866.*—My friends, the old guard, are, I fear, dissatisfied with me. They think I am doing nothing, that I am cheating their expectations and hopes . . . And I am dissatisfied myself. . . . What would make me inwardly proud seems to me inaccessible and impossible, and I fall back upon trifles, nonsense and distractions. I always have a certain amount of hope, energy, faith and determination. But I oscillate between desolate melancholy and an easy-going quietism. Still, I read, talk, teach, write. No matter, it is all a kind of somnambulism. The Buddhistic tendency dulls the faculty of free self-disposition, dissolves the power of action; self-distrust kills desire, and I always come back to an inner scepticism. I love only the serious, and I cannot take seriously either my circumstances or myself; I disparage and jeer at my personality, my aptitudes and my aspirations. I hold myself perpetually in contempt in the name of what is beautiful and admirable. In a word, I carry within myself a perpetual detractor of myself; this is what takes away all my ardour.—Spent the evening with Charles Heim, who, in his sincerity, has never paid me a literary compliment. As I love and respect him, I forgive him for this. I have no vanity in these things, and yet it would be sweet to me to be well regarded by an incorruptible friend. It is painful to feel oneself silently disapproved of . . . I mean to try and satisfy him and to think of a book that would give pleasure both to him and to Scherer.

*October 6, 1866.*—Picked up on the staircase a little yellowish kitten, very ugly and doleful. Now, curled up beside me on a chair, he seems entirely happy and asks for nothing more. Far from being wild, he has been unwilling to amuse himself away ·from my presence and has followed me from room to room as I came and went. I have nothing whatever to eat in the house, but what I have I give him, namely, a glance and a few caresses, and this is enough for him, for the moment at least. Little animals, little children, young lives are all one in their need for protection and kindness.— P. tells me that all weak creatures feel at home with me. This comes from my nurse's instincts. P. is right, for I have had a thousand proofs of this particular influence, a sort of calming and beneficent magnetism.—Animals are glad to come and sleep on my lap; a little more and the birds would nest in my beard as they do on the head-dresses of the saints on the cathedral.

This is the natural state and the true relation between man and the lower creatures. If man were truly good and conformed to his type, he would be whole-heartedly adored by the animals, to which he is only a capricious and bloody tyrant. The legend of St. Francis of Assisi is not as legendary as people think, and it is by no means certain that the wild animals attacked man first.—But not to exaggerate, let us except the beasts of prey, the carnivorous, rapacious animals. How many other kinds there are, thousands and tens of thousands, that ask for nothing but peace and on which we insist upon making brutal war! Our race is by far the most destructive, the most maleficent, the most formidable of all the species on the planet; it has even invented for its use the right of the strongest, a divine right that sets its conscience at rest in regard to the vanquished and the crushed; it has placed all that lives, save itself, outside this right. A revolting and manifest abuse, a signal and shameful violation of justice, an act of bad faith and hypocrisy that every triumphant usurper repeats on a small scale. People always make God their accomplice, to legalize their own iniquities. Every successful butchery is consecrated with a *Te Deum*, and the clergy have a blessing for every victorious outrage. This applies between peoples and between man and man because it began between man and beast.

There is an expiation for all this, one that is not observed but very just. Every transgression is paid for; and the sufferings brutally imposed by man on the other living creatures are repeated among men by slavery. The theory bears its fruits.—Man's rights over the beast seem to me to cease where the need ceases, the imperative need of defence and subsistence. Thus unnecessary murder and torture is cowardly and even criminal. A service of utility imposed on the animal imposes on man a debt of protection and kindness. In a word, the animal has rights over man, and man has duties towards the animal.—No doubt Buddhism exaggerates this truth, but the Occidentals disregard it. And a day will come when human virtue will be more exacting than it is today. *Homo homini lupus,* said Hobbes. Some day man will be human to the wolf, *homo lupo homo.*

*November 11, 1866.*—What an odd note-book this is! I have just been reading it over again. I had forgotten what was in it. Whereas my friend J. H., who has a confident and compact nature, always has himself well in hand, I, a diffluent, wavering, scattered being, have infinite trouble assembling my molecules, I am continually escaping from myself, in spite of my daily meditations and this journal of mine. The cohesive force of individuality is the will, and especially continuity in willing; as I am never continuous myself, it is clear that I am several and not one. My name is Legion, Proteus, Anarchy. What I lack is a force that is determined and constant, a character. Living from day to day, counting on nothing, aiming at nothing, I flutter like a feather in the wind and quiver with every changing breath of the atmosphere. My readings and labours, my projects and my tastes have no consistency or compass, because I put no passion into them, no persistent interest. I only exist provisionally, for I am not in earnest with myself. Disillusion with oneself and disenchantment with life cut the Achilles tendon

in man. . Ambition null, indolence complete. One loves only peace
and revery now, garlanded with affection.

> *Quand le bonheur n'est plus rien qu'un mensonge,*
> *On veut dormir la vie, et prolonger le songe.*

A benevolent apathy, an old man's detachment, seems then the
point of view of wisdom. It is so sweet to withdraw from the turbulent bustle of vulgar existence and to regard the follies of illusion
from the height of one's peaceful tower. This serene and indulgent
irony is, as Cicero says, the reward of old age. It is the state of
mind that is granted to the dwellers in the Elysian Fields and pursued by the religious anchorites, the yogis, the sufis of all epochs
and nations.—The grave disadvantage of this peace is that it is a
luxury and a temptation. Has one the right to recompense without
effort, to the victor's crown without having fought the fight? Can
one thus withdraw from one's kind? Will not one's heart, conscience, pity straightway drive one back to the human crowd, to
the anxious and the suffering, even when one's soul craves and all
but possesses the repose of the blest?—In your good fortune at
present, two things must be distinguished, one of them excellent,
your detachment from false goods and deceptive desires, the other
less good, your exaggerated distrust of life and women.—One must
set the best example possible. Well! for this you have two duties
to fulfil: as a man, you should make more people happy, as a particular man, you should turn your talent to better account.—You
approve neither of celibacy nor unproductiveness; then you should
not resign yourself to them so easily. Your enemy is timidity,
which breeds indolence. What you need is courage, faith, perseverance, action. One should be able to force one's nature when it
makes the mistake of being too mild.—Burn your ships, compel
yourself to be energetic, take the plunge, bind yourself; for this is
indeed that great advance which you have yet to achieve. To place
oneself in dependence is to condescend to be a man, it is to hum-

ble oneself voluntarily, to make a sacrifice, to ennoble. oneself; for heroism alone ennobles, and it is heroic to sacrifice freely one's rest, comfort, security and tastes to the idea of a duty.

Reason says, Be prudent; conscience says, Be rash!—Reason is a good sermonizer, but conscience does not accept defeat. It has a leaning towards all the beautiful follies, the impossible is its secret craving.

*December 13, 1866.*—Supped at J. H.'s, with two Frenchmen and four Genevans, two of them professors and two members of the governing board, besides two women, the wife and sister of the host. I am forgetting an Englishman, M. H., whom I took home under my umbrella, just a moment ago, and whose Anglican ears must have suffered this evening, for everyone there was as rationalistic and anti-Christian as possible . . . The conversation was very lively and very well sustained. I have an impression, however, that the excessive sharpening of people's minds may become a sort of tyranny, and that this way of understanding liberty has the fatal effect of sapping it. I thought of the Renaissance, of the Ptolemies, of the reign of Louis XV, when a joyous anarchy of mind had as a correlative a despotism of power, and, inversely, of England, Holland, the United States, where political liberty is bought at the inevitable price of preconceived views and prejudices.

For society not to crumble away, a cohesive principle is necessary, consequently a common belief, principles accepted without discussion, a series of practical axioms and institutions that cannot be overthrown by every momentary caprice of opinion. Where everything is brought into question, everything is compromised. Doubt is the accomplice of tyranny. "If a people is unwilling to believe, it has to serve," said Tocqueville. Every liberty implies a dependence and has its conditions. This is what the fault-finders, the negative critics, forget. They imagine they are snuffing out religion; they do not know that one cannot destroy religion and that the only question is which religion one is to have. Voltaire creates the strength of Loyola, and *vice versa*. Between them there is no peace; nor can there be any peace for a society that has fallen into this dilemma. The solution lies in a free religion, a religion of free choice and free adherence.

*January 11, 1867.—*

> *Eheu fugaces, Postume, Postume,*
> *Labuntur anni. . . .*

I distinctly hear the drops of my life falling into the devouring gulf of eternity. I feel my days flying to meet death. The weeks, months or years that remain for me to drink the light of the sun seem to me, all together, scarcely a night, a summer's night that does not count, it is to end so soon. There is a poetry in this point of view, but it should turn to laborious energy, not to barren melancholy.

> *Avant d'aller dormir sous l'herbe,*
> *Fais ton monument ou ta gerbe.*

Death! Silence! The abyss!—Frightful mysteries for the being who aspires to immortality, happiness, perfection! Where, O my God, shall I be tomorrow, in a little time, when I have ceased to breathe? When a stranger's hand shall write under my last line—

> End of the journal of H.F.A.
> died ————
> at ————,

where will be those whom I love? Where are we going? What are we? The eternal questions forever rise before us, in their implacable solemnity. Mysteries on every hand! Faith is one's only star in this darkness of incertitude, through which resounds lugubriously the *que sais-je?* of the dead!

No matter! It is not necessary that *we* should live, provided that the world is the work of the Good and the consciousness of duty has not deceived us.—In any case, even though God should disappear, we owe ourselves to something other than ourselves; we can consecrate ourselves to our race and sacrifice ourselves for our fellows. To give happiness and to do good, this is our law, the anchor of our salvation, our reason for existence, our beacon. All the religions may crumble away; as long as this subsists, we still have an ideal and it is worth the pain of living.

The religion of love, disinterestedness, devotion will dignify man as long as its altars are not deserted, and nothing can destroy them for you as long as you feel that you are able to love.

*April 11, 1867.*— . . . Awake, thou that sleepest, and arise from the dead!

What you must continually refresh and renew is your store of courage. Your natural tendency leads you to a distaste of life to despair, to pessimism. "The happy man, the favourite of the age", according to Mme. ——, is, on the contrary the *Weltmüde*,[1] who cuts a good figure only before the world and distracts himself as best he may from his secret thoughts, thoughts that are sad unto death, thoughts of the irreparable. His peace is only a desolation which he carries well; his gaiety is only the carelessness of a disillusioned heart, the indefinite, disenchanted postponement of happiness. His wisdom is to be used to renunciation; his gentleness is a patience with privation, not resignation to it. In a word, he submits to a joyless existence, and he cannot conceal from himself that all the advantages with which it is strewn do not fill his soul to the depths. The thirst for the infinite is not slaked. God is absent. There is a void beneath the riches of the surface.

To experience true peace, one must feel oneself guided, pardoned, sustained by the supreme power, one must feel that one is in one's path, in the order of things, at the point where God wishes us to be. This faith gives strength and calm. You do not possess it. That which is appears to you arbitrary, fortuitous, able to be or not to be. Nothing in your circumstances seems providential to you; everything seems to be left to your own responsibility, and it is this very

[1] The world-weary.

idea that disgusts you with the management of your life. You
needed to give yourself to some great love, to some noble aim; you
would have wished to live and die for the ideal, for some sacred
cause worthy of your devotion; and this employment of yourself
you have failed to achieve. After this impossibility once became
plain, you never again seriously took heart for anything, and you
have done nothing but play with a destiny of which you had ceased
to be the dupe, *nada!* The riddle of the sphinx, once we have deciphered it, drains our courage,

> *Le long effeuillement de nos illusions . . .*

What irony!

Sybarite, dreamer, idler, will you go on thus to the very end,
tossed between duty and happiness, without resolutely making up
your mind? Is not life a trial of our moral strength, and are not all
these inner vacillations the temptations of the soul? One may have
missed one's opportunity, but to what purpose are groans and regrets? One must play with the cards in one's pack. Everything that
is given is providential, everything that is irreparable, imposed,
fated, your age, for instance, your sex, your name, your antecedents,
your present post, your current obligations. The question is simply
this: in your circumstances, what is the best thing for you to do?
To throw up the sponge is forbidden, to desert or abdicate. Therefore you must resign yourself first to the human condition and then
to your individual condition.

*April 15, 1867 (7 a. m.).*—A squall of rain last night. My old
housekeeper says the gusts of wind were like the reports of a cannon. April caprices!—It is grey and dismal out of the window, and
the roofs are glossy with water.—*Gleba putris* and a sluggish brain.
Spring does its work, and implacable age drives us towards our
grave. After all, everyone has his day.

> *Allez, allez, ô jeunes filles,*
> *Cueillir des bleuets dans les blés!*

Melancholy. Languor. Lassitude.—A yearning for the great sleep comes over me, though it is combatted by the need for a sustained sacrifice, an appetite for the heroic. Are not these the two ways of escaping from oneself? To sleep or to give oneself, in order to die to the self: this is the longing of the heart.—Poor heart!

*Weissenstein,*[1] *September 6, 1867 (10 a. m.).*—Marvellous view, blindingly beautiful! Over a sea of milk, drenched in morning light, whose rolling waves beat at the foot of the wooded ramparts of the Weissenstein, the infinite circle of the Alps soars to sublime heights. The eastern horizon is drowned in a splendour of rising mists, but beginning at the Tödi the whole chain floats, pure and clear, between the snowy plain and the pale blue sky. The assembly of giants holds council above the valleys and lakes, which are submerged in vapour. The Clarides, the Spannörter, the Titlis, the Sustenhorn, then the Bernese colossi, from the Wetterhörner to the Diablerets (the steep Schreckhörner, the sharp Finsteraarhorn, the trio of the Eiger, the Mönch and the Jungfrau, the sparkling Bietschhorn and the roof-like Blümlisalp, the Doldenhorn, the pyramidal pair of the Balmhorn and the Altels, followed by the Wildstrubel and the Wildhorn), then the Vaudois peaks (the grand Muveran, Mosseron, Chamossaire, Tour d'Aï, Naye), the Valaisian Dent du Midi, the Fribourg mountains (the Moléson), the Chablaisian Cornettes, and beyond these high ranges the two kings of the Italian chain: Mont Blanc, softly rose, and even the bluish peak of Monte Rosa, shooting up through a notch in the Doldenhorn: such is the composition of the assembly seated in the amphitheatre. The outline of the horizon assumes every kind of shape: needles, pinnacles, crenels, pyramids, obelisks, teeth, hooks, pincers, horns, cupolas; the indentation bends, rears, twists, forms a thousand sharp points, in the angular style of sierras. Only the inferior and secondary massifs present rounded tops, tapering and curving lines. The Alps are more than an upheaval, they are a laceration of the earth's surface. Far from caress-

[1] Summit of the Jura, above Soleure.

ing the sky, the granite rends it. The Jura, on the other hand, rises like a cat's back under the blue dome.

(*11. a. m.*).—The ocean of mist has risen to the assault of the mountains, which have been towering above it like haughty reefs. For a long time it foamed in vain against the flanks of the Alps, but, turning back on itself, it has succeeded better with the Jura. And now we are enveloped in its roving waves. The milky sea has become a vast cloud, swallowing up the plain and the mountains, the observatory and the observer. Through this cloud the bells of the flocks tinkle and the rays of the sun are circulating. It is a fantastic spectacle.

The *Musikdirector* has left. A family from Colmar has left, who only arrived last night (four people). The young girl and her brother, with figures like poplars. Very pretty, the girl, delicate in type, smartly elegant, touching nothing except with her finger-tips or with the tips of her teeth, a gazelle, an ermine, interested in nothing, unable to admire, and thinking more of herself than of anything else. This is rather the disadvantage of a beauty and stature that attract everyone's attention. Besides, she is urban to the marrow and out of her element in the open country, which one might easily find ill-bred. Accordingly, she does not put herself out for it, but parades on the mountain with her little toque and her imperceptible parasol, as if it were a boulevard. This is one of the tourist-types that Tœpffer has so ludicrously sketched. Character, an inexperienced infatuation. Country, France. Criterion, fashion. Intelligence, but lacking a feeling for things, an understanding of nature, a sense of the outer diversity of the world and the right that life has to be what it is, in its own way, not in ours.

These absurdities spring from the same national prejudice that gives France the sovereignty of the fashionable world and causes the French to neglect geography and languages. The ordinary French city-dweller is exquisitely fatuous, in spite of his natural wit, for he comprehends nothing but himself. Like certain monks of Athos, he lives in the contemplation of his navel. His pole, his axis, his centre, his all is Paris; less than this, the Parisian tone, the taste of the day, the mode. Thanks to this well-organized fetishism, there are millions of copies of one original pattern and a whole people manœuvring like the bobbins in a single mill, or the legs in the same army corps. It is wonderful and it is wearisome, wonderful as material power, wearisome to the psychologist. A hundred thousand sheep are no more instructive than one sheep, but they provide a hundred thousand times as much wool, meat and manure. This is all the shepherd needs, i.e., the master. Yes, but from this one can only make farms and monarchies. A republic requires men and demands individuality.

*(Noon.)*—Ravishing sight. A great herd of cows is crossing the pasture at a run, under my window, which is lighted up with a furtive ray of sunshine. The tableau is as fresh as an apparition; it makes a gap in the mists that are closing in around it, like the circle thrown by a magic-lantern. What a pity that I must leave when everything is so pleasant around me and life has such an Elysian airiness!

*January 10, 1868 (11 p. m.).*—Philosophic evening at Edouard Claparède's.[1] The question for discussion: the nature of sensation. Claparède concludes in the absolute subjectiveness of all empirical findings, in other words in pure idealism. This is amusing in a naturalist. Only the self exists, and the universe is only a projection of the self, a phantasmagoria which we create without suspecting it, fancying that we are contemplators. It is our noumenon that objectifies itself in phenomena. The self is an irradiating force which, modified, unaware of the modifier, conceives that the effect takes place by virtue of the principle of causality, in other words gives birth to the great illusion of the objective world in order to explain itself to itself. Waking is only a better concatenated dream. The self is thus an unknown quantity that engenders an infinity of unknowns by a fatality of its nature. Knowledge is summed up in the

---

[1] A Genevese zoölogist, born in 1832, died in 1871.

consciousness that there is nothing but consciousness. In other words, the intelligent emerges from the unintelligible only to return to it, or rather the self explains itself to itself by the hypothesis of the non-self, though at bottom it is only a dream that dreams itself. With Scarron, one can say of it:

> *Et je vis l'ombre d'un esprit,*
> *Qui traçait l'ombre d'un système*
> *Avec l'ombre de l'ombre même.*

This abolition of nature by naturalism is consistent, and it is Schelling's point of departure. From the point of view of physiology, nature is only a compulsory illusion, a constitutional hallucination. One only escapes from this bewitchery by the moral activity of the self, which feels itself a cause, a free cause, and which by responsibility breaks the spell and steps out of the enchanted circle of Maya.[1]

Maya! Might this be the true goddess? Hindu wisdom has already made the world the dream of Brahma. Should one, with Fichte, make it the solitary dream of every self? The merest fool would then be a cosmogonic poet, lighting the rockets of the universe under the dome of the infinite.—Then why do we take such gratuitous pains to learn the little we know? In our dreams, when they are not nightmares, at least, we bestow upon ourselves ubiquity, omniscience, complete freedom. Why should we be less ingenious awake than asleep?

*January 16, 1868 (6 p. m.).*—Blessed be the childhood that leaves a little room for heaven among the harsh realities of earth, that sometimes serves to bring souls together on a neutral ground! Somewhere I have said that births are the moral rejuvenation of mankind, as well as the means of its survival. The good feelings that rise around the cradle and childhood are one of the secrets of Providence, ever present; were it not for this refreshing dew, the mad

[1] Maya, in Brahmanism, is diversity as opposed to unity, appearance and illusion as opposed to reality, to being.

scramble of selfish passions would scorch human society like fire. Grown people inevitably cloy one another and would end by fraying one another's nerves, like ship-passengers on a long voyage, if death did not renew the *vis-à-vis*, and especially if new passengers, frail, innocent creatures, against whom no one has any personal grievance, did not relax the situation by bringing tenderness back where arid hostility reigns, and disinterestedness in the place of deadlocked egoisms.

Blessed be childhood for the good it does and for the good it occasions, without knowing or intending it, making itself beloved, letting itself be loved! What little of paradise we can still find on earth is due to its presence. Without fatherhood, without motherhood, I think that love itself would not suffice to prevent men from endlessly devouring one another, men, be it understood, as our passions have made them. The angels do not need birth and death to make life endurable because their life is celestial. Our life, on the contrary, is a perpetual warfare, and the dearest concern of man, after his concern for his personal interests, is too often the art of creating vexations for his fellow-beings. "It isn't so much that it amuses me, but it vexes my neighbour; and that's how it is with everything!" is the formula of this gracious tendency.

Let us be careful not to form an aversion to our surroundings and our kind, for where can we go to escape from our difficulties? What is even worse is to form an aversion to oneself, for how can one jump out of one's own shadow? Inasmuch as one cannot change things, it is simplest to change one's way of looking at things. Overturning the world is troublesome and useless; it is better to renew ourselves and cast off our asperity. Discontent poisons life; acceptance gives it back its poetry and a kind of severe beauty. The religious idea of a trial and a mission, a task and a duty, is necessary to overcome these morbid irritations of sentiment that hold our reason in check. All roads lead to Rome and to folly. There are very few that lead to the good, perhaps only one; and we only find the beginning of this road by going out of ourselves.

*January 25, 1868.*—My mouth is in a pitiful state. My tongue, my gums and my teeth are all aching at once. Since the dentist set to work, two molars that had never failed me have become sensitive, and the whole thing is a mess. These innovations that menace one's peace of mind! Here I am in the ranks of the Dysodonta, those poor wretches who, because of their jaws, are at the mercy of every intemperance, and the dentist-gentry as well. I had forgotten this dismal dependence, which certainly adds to one's distaste for life, reminding one at every pause of the Trappist's phrase, Brother, we must die! Brother, you are going to pieces, you are gradually going back to the dust, you are bending gradually towards the grave. There is nothing very gay in this crabbed warning.

Mere rags and tatters, if you will, my tatters are dear to me. This is the capital point in the belief in the immortality of one's being, and in thinking with the apostle that, if the outer man is destroyed, the inner man is renewed from day to day.—But for those who doubt this, those who do not hope for it? What remains of their career is only the forced dismemberment of their little empire, the successive dismantling of their being by inexorable destiny. It is hard to watch this long death with its lugubrious stages and its inevitable end. One can understand why Stoicism maintained the right of suicide.—What is your own faith at the present moment? Has not the universal, or at least the very general, doubt of science invaded you in your turn? You have defended before the sceptics the cause of the immortality of the soul, and yet, when you have reduced them to silence, you are not sure that at bottom you are not of their mind. You would like to dispense with hope, and it is possible that you have now hardly the strength for this, and that, like others, you need to be sustained and consoled by a belief, and by the belief in forgiveness and immortality, which means religious belief in the Christian form. Reason and thought grow weary like muscles and nerves. They must have sleep. And this sleep is the relapse into the tradition of our childhood, into the common hope. It is so fatiguing to maintain an exceptional point of view that one falls back into prejudice merely by giving way, as a man who is standing always ends by letting himself sink to the ground and by reassuming the horizontal. We stand at our full height only at moments. Our surroundings fetter us and drag us down to the general level, the moment our vigour diminishes and the fire of our years dies down in us.—It is thanks to this law that Catholicism recaptures on their death-bed most of the flock that have broken away during their best days. Thence comes the proverb: The devil becomes a monk when he is old.

What are we to become when everything leaves us, health, joy, affections, the freshness of the senses, memory, the capacity for work, when it seems to us that the sun is growing cold and that life is being stripped of all its charms? What is one to become, if one has no hope? Must one try to forget and turn to stone?—The answer is always the same: cleave to your duty.

> *Vis pour autrui, sois juste et bon,*
> *Fais ton monument ou ta gerbe,*
> *Et du ciel obtiens le pardon*
> *Avant d'aller dormir sous l'herbe.*

The future is immaterial, if one possesses a peaceful conscience, if one feels reconciled and in order. Be what you ought to be, the rest is God's affair. It is for him to know what is best, to attend to his glory, to bring happiness to whatever depends upon him, whether through survival or annihilation. And even if there were no good and holy God, nothing but the great, universal being, the law of all, the ideal without hypostasis or reality, duty would still be the key of the enigma and the polar star of humanity on its way.

*February 16, 1868.*—I have finished About's *Mainfroy* (the first of the *Mariages de province*). What wit, verve, assurance and finesse! About is a true grandson of Voltaire, he is incisive, malicious, he has a rapid, glancing style, a cavalier ease over a background of subtle irony, and an inner freedom that permits him to play with everything, to make fun of others and himself, while he is simply amusing himself with his ideas and even with his fictions. This has certainly the authentic mark, the signature of wit.

An irrepressible malice, an unweariable elasticity, a luminous mockery, a joy in the perpetual discharge of numberless arrows from an inexhaustible quiver, the inextinguishable laugh of an imp of nature, a never-failing gaiety, a radiant gift of epigram: the real wits have something of all these things. *Stulti sunt innumerabiles,* said Erasmus, the Latin master of these fine mockers. The stupid, the vain, the foppish, the silly, the stiff, the vulgar pedant, the scribbling pedant, the pedants of every colour, of every rank and form, everyone who poses or stands on stilts, shows off, puts on airs, prinks himself, makes up, struts, pampers or obtrudes himself,— all these are game for the satirist; so many targets provided for his darts, so many victims waiting for his blows. And we know how greedy for wit the world is. It is a true benediction! A Cockaigne-feast is served in perpetuity to the sarcastic mind; the spectacle of society offers it an endless Camacho's wedding. And how whole-heartedly it forages through its domains! What slaughter and carnage around this great hunter! The universal havoc means health for it. Its bullets are enchanted and it cannot be wounded itself. Its hand is infallible, like its glance, and it braves retorts and re-prisals, because it is both lightning and space itself, because it is bodiless, because it is an elf and a sprite.

Men of wit recognize and tolerate nothing but wit; authority of any kind only makes them laugh, superstition of every kind amuses them, everything conventional excites them to contradiction. They spare only strength, and tolerate only perfect naturalness. Yet ten men of wit are not worth one man of talent, nor are ten men of talent worth one man of genius. And in the individual the heart is more than wit, reason is as important as the heart and conscience outweighs reason. So if the man of wit cannot be mocked, he can at least not be loved, or regarded, or esteemed. He can make himself feared, it is true, and he can make his independence respected; but this negative advantage, the result of a negative superiority,

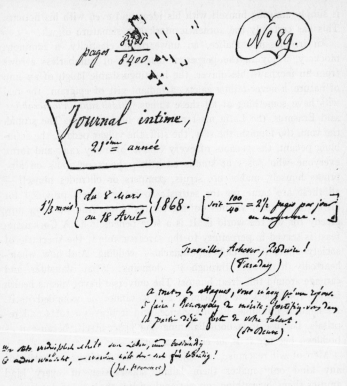

FACSIMILE OF THE COVER OF ONE OF AMIEL'S NOTE-BOOKS

does not yield happiness. Wit, therefore, is not enough either to make him who possesses it happy or to make those around him happy.

> *L'esprit sert bien à tout, mais ne remplace rien.*
> *Soyez donc gens d'esprit, mais surtout gens de bien.*

236

*March 8, 1868.*—Madame —— kept me for tea with three young friends of hers, three sisters, I think. The two younger were extremely pretty, the dark one as pretty as the fair. Placed between these two charming girls, I let my eyes dwell on their fresh faces, joyous with youth in its flower. How good for a man of letters this aesthetic electrification is! It positively restores him, by a sort of inductive current. Sensitive, impressionable, receptive as I am, the presence of health, beauty, wit, virtue exerts a powerful influence over all my being, and, reciprocally, I am affected and infected as easily in the presence of troubled lives and sick souls.—Miss C—— H—— said of me to someone that I must be "superlatively feminine" in my perceptions. This sympathetic sensitiveness is the reason. Had I at all wished it, I might have had the magic clairvoyance of a somnambulist, I might have been able to repeat in my own person many strange phenomena. I know this, but I have kept away from it, either from indifference or by intention. When I think of the intuitions of every kind, and kinds that have nothing in common, which I have had since my adolescence, it seems to me that I have lived many dozens and almost hundreds of lives. Every person who has marked traits leaves in me the mould of his ideal, or rather for a moment forms me in his image, and I have only to watch myself living, when it happens, to comprehend this new way in which human nature exists. Thus I have been a mother, a child, a young girl, a mathematician, a musician, a scholar, a monk, etc. In these states of universal sympathy, I have even been an animal and a plant, a particular animal, a specific tree. This faculty of metamorphosis, rising and descending, this faculty of disentangling and re-entangling oneself has sometimes astonished my friends, even the most subtle (Edmond Scherer). It undoubtedly springs from my extreme facility in impersonal objectification, which in its turn occasions the difficulty I find in individualizing myself on my own account, in being only a particular man, with his own number and label. To return to my own skin has always seemed odd to me, something arbitrary and conventional. I have always seemed to myself a magician's box, a point of vision and perception, a subject without a determined individuality, a pure determinability and formability; and consequently I have resigned only with effort to playing the quite arbitrary role of a specific person registered as a citizen in a certain city, of a certain country. In action I feel cabined; my true element is contemplation. Any ambition, chase or pursuit is a bore to me, a diminution of myself, a concession I meekly make to usage. I only breathe freely when I have put off this borrowed role and become again ready for metamorphosis. Pure virtuality, perfect equilibrium is the refuge of my predilection. There I feel free, disinterested, sovereign. Is this a call? Is it a temptation?

It is the oscillation between the two geniuses, Greek and Roman, Oriental and Occidental, the ancient and the Christian. It is the struggle between two ideals, that of freedom and that of holiness. Freedom makes us gods, holiness humbles us. Action limits us, contemplation expands us. The will localizes us, thought universalizes us. My soul wavers between two, four, six general and contradictory conceptions, for it obeys all the great instincts of human nature, and aspires to the absolute, which can only be realized by a succession of contraries. It has taken me a long time to comprehend myself, and sometimes I find myself beginning again the study of this problem which has already been solved, so hard it is for us to maintain in ourselves a constant position. I love everything, and I detest one thing only, the irremediable imprisonment of my being in an arbitrary form, even one chosen by myself. Thus inner freedom must be my persistent passion and perhaps my only passion. Is this passion permitted? I have thought so now and again, but I am not perfectly sure of it.

*March 17, 1868.*—Woman wishes to be loved without a reason, without a why or wherefore, not because she is pretty, or good, or well brought-up, or gracious, or clever, but because she is. Any sort of analysis seems to her a diminution and a subordination of her personality to something that dominates and measures her. Therefore she resists it, and her instinct is right. The moment one is able to say *because,* one is no longer under the spell, one is judging and weighing, one is free, at least in principle. And love must remain a witchcraft, a fascination, a sorcery for the empire of woman to maintain its existence. Once the mystery has disappeared, the power vanishes with it. Love must appear indivisible, insoluble, superior to all analysis, to preserve that appearance of the infinite, the super-natural, the miraculous, which makes the beauty of it. Most people scorn what they understand and bow only before the inexplicable. The feminine triumph is to catch in the very fact of its obscurity the manly intelligence that pretends to light. And when women inspire love, they feel the proud joy of this triumph.—I admit that this vanity is well-founded. And yet love in its profundity seems to me a light and a calm, a religion and a revelation, which in its turn scorns these inferior victories of vanity.—Great souls desire only the great. Every sort of artifice seems shamefully puerile to one who is buoyed in the infinite.

*March 19, 1868 (9 a. m.).*—North wind and cold; nevertheless, my head is still sluggish, and I feel twinges in my brain. I have no vigour to spare. Why? I cannot guess, unless it means that I am imperceptibly wasting away, unless there is some escape of nervous force that has given no sign of its passage. It is queer and un-pleasant.

To make a person wait for a slight service is ruder than politely to refuse a large one. There may be serious reasons for the refusal; for the delay there seems to be nothing but a want of good will. Alacrity is all the more fitting in trifles in that it dispenses one from making concessions in important things. This is what a woman especially should never forget. But negligence causes a thousand stupidities, which it does not permit to be repaired any more than it has been able to prevent them. We should be attentive to others and alertly maintain our presence of mind. This is an irksome but necessary duty.—What we call the little things are the causes of the great, for they are the beginnings, the ovule, the embryo; and the point of departure of all things usually decides their whole future. A black speck is the beginning of gangrene, or of a hurricane or a revolution, a speck and nothing more. From some imperceptible misunderstanding hatred and divorce may spring in the end. Which was that Carlovingian empress who lost the throne over a dispute that began in a hair-cut? An enormous avalanche begins with the breaking loose of a single atom, the burning of a city with the fall of a match. Almost everything, it seems, comes from almost nothing. The first hundred francs of a fortune are more difficult to earn than millions, sometimes, later. Mohammed took more pains winning the first six believers for his religion than his successors took conquering six kingdoms. Only the first crystallization is the work of genius; the subsequent aggregation is the work of mass, of attraction, momentum, mechanical acceleration. History, like nature, shows us the application of the law of inertia and agglomeration, which is facetiously formulated as "Nothing succeeds like success." Find the right way, strike squarely, begin well: that is the whole thing. Or, more simply, have luck; for chance plays an immense part in human affairs. Those who have best succeeded in this world all acknowledge it; calculation is not useless, but chance makes brazen sport of calculation (Napoleon, Bismarck, Machiavelli), and the result of a scheme is in no way proportional to its merit. From the supernatural point of view one says: this so-called chance is the act of Providence; man flounders, God shows him the way (Fénelon). The unfortunate thing is that, by the supposed intervention, zeal, virtue and devotion miscarry, and crime, folly and selfishness succeed as often as the reverse, indeed more often. A rude trial for faith, which extricates itself with the word, Mystery! This means that it recognizes too late that its explanation does not explain and is therefore only a well-meaning phrase, a pious logomachy.—It is in the origins of things that the principal secret of destiny lies, although this does not prevent the tumultuous sequence of events from reserving surprises for us also. Thus, at first sight, history is nothing but disorder and chance; at the second glance, it all seems logical and necessary; at the third glance, it appears a mixture of necessity and liberty; and when one examines it the fourth time, one does not know what to make of it; for, if might is the origin of right, and chance is the origin of might, we come back to the first explanation, only in a rather less cheerful spirit.

Was Democritus right? Was chance the foundation of everything, all the laws being only figments of our reason, which, born of chance, has this property of deluding itself and proclaiming laws it believes to be real and objective, much as a man dreaming of a meal thinks that he is eating, while actually there is neither a table nor food, neither guest nor nourishment. Everything happens as if there were order, reason, logic in the world, whereas everything is actually fortuitous, accidental, apparent. The universe is only the kaleidoscope revolving in the mind of the being who is said to be thinking, who is himself a causeless curiosity, a fortuity conscious of the great fortuity, and amusing himself with it as long as the phenomenon of his vision lasts. Science is a lucid madness that finds an explanation for these compulsory hallucinations. The philosopher laughs, for he is the dupe of nothing, while the illusion of the others persists. He is like a malicious spectator at a ball who has adroitly removed all the strings from the violins and yet sees the musicians and dancers moving as if there were really music. The experience would rejoice him by demonstrating that the universal St. Vitus's dance is an aberration of self-consciousness, and that a sage is right as against the credulity of everyone else. Does one have to do more than stop one's ears in a ball-room to convince oneself that one is in a madhouse?

For one who has destroyed the religious idea in himself, the cults that exist on earth must all produce a similar effect. But it is dangerous to place oneself outside the law of the human species and to be right against all the world.

*Vieux soldats de plomb que nous sommes,*
*Au cordeau nous alignant tous,*
*Si des rangs sortent quelques hommes,*
*Nous crions tous: A bas les fous!*

Laughers seldom devote themselves. Why should they? Devotion is serious, and to stop laughing would be to give up their role. To be devoted, one must love; to love, one must believe in the reality of that which one loves; one must be able to suffer, forget oneself, give oneself, in a word become serious. Eternal laughter means absolute isolation, it is the proclamation of perfect egoism. To do good to men, one must pity and not despise them; one must say of them not that they are fools, but that they are unfortunate. The deriders tire one's patience because their minds have destroyed their hearts and because they have lost interest in humanity. A pessimistic and nihilistic sceptic seems less glacial than a jeering atheist. But what does the sombre Ahasuerus say?

*Vous qui manquez de charité,*
*Tremblez à mon supplice étrange:*
*Ce n'est point sa divinité,*
*C'est l'humanité, que Dieu venge.*

It is better to be lost than to be saved alone, and it is doing a wrong to one's kind to wish to be right without sharing one's rightness. It is an illusion, moreover, to imagine the possibility of such a privilege, when everything proves the solidarity of all individuals and when nobody can think except in terms of the common thought that has been matured by centuries of culture and experience. Absolute individualism is puerile nonsense. One may be isolated in one's own special, temporary environment, but every one of our thoughts and every one of our feelings finds, has found, and will find its echo in humanity. In the case of certain representative men whom great portions of humanity adopt as guides, revealers, reformers, the echo is immense and resounding, but it is not a nullity in anyone's case.

Every sincere expression of the soul, every testimony rendered to a personal conviction serves someone and something, even though one may not know it, even though a hand is placed over one's mouth and there is a noose about one's neck. One word spoken to anyone has its indestructible effect, as an impulse may pass through a hundred changes without being obliterated.—It is reason enough for not laughing, for not holding one's tongue, but rather for affirming oneself and for acting, that we are all members one of another and that no effect is altogether lost.

Conclusion: one must have faith in truth and make it a duty to show this faith in action. One must seek truth and spread it. One must love men and serve them, without any hope of gratitude.— Instead of ἀπέχου καὶ ἐπέχου, one should rather say, Open your heart and give yourself.

*Mornex-sous-Salève, April 8, 1868 (5 p. m.).*—Gave a lecture this morning on the school of the Stoics, with a lively distaste for most of my audience. Took leave of my usual little world, made the necessary arrangements and preparations, left town in the midst of a great windstorm that raised all the dust in the outskirts, and two hours later here I am, established at the Hotel Bellevue, in the room I had last year. The weather has grown stormy. Under a sky veiled with heavy clouds, the south wind blows in squalls and fills the vast expanse with a grey fog. The distant semicircle of mountains that lies unrolled before my window is only vaguely discernible through the vaporous atmosphere. The landscape is dull, almost threatening, and yet I feel already a certain well-being, and I can congratulate myself for having left the city. My breathing is freer, my head is lighter; I am writing near my open window, and already it all seems just as it should be. The sensation of strangeness, or rather of being a stranger, which always causes one a certain discomfort, disappeared the moment I opened my journal, and has given way to the feeling of being at home.

I plan to spend my week here and have made my arrangements accordingly. As always, at the last minute, all the obstacles seemed to conspire together, and it really was as if my friends had stationed themselves along my road to stop me and make me miss my chance. To keep to one's programme firmly, even in small matters, is difficult and meritorious. . . . Brr! a flash of lightning! Thunder, the howling of the gale, immense spasmodic downpours, a rent in the veil of clouds over by Mont Blanc, which shines forth in a sort of pallid glory. My dwelling, like a tower, rends the air and from my room at the top, as from an observatory, I have the sensation of a lookout-man perched in the rigging of a ship! . . . Three thunderclaps, from the Mole to the Voirons; everything is drowned in the whirling mists; my shutters grate, and the wind, rushing into the room, obliges me to shut everything up . . . The light appears again, a strange light, like the glimmering at the end of an eclipse. The trees frantically bend and twist in all directions . . . I begin my journal again. The landscape has gained greatly in colouring. It is a composition in tender green, deep brown and a very soft grey. The drenched rocks and patches of earth have warm tones that soothe the eye. Another paroxysm of the elements, furious gusts of wind, shivering waves of rain in a cubic space of sixteen leagues, a bluish-leaden water-spout swept along with the speed of an arrow. To see this strange spectacle almost from top to bottom, to be in the midst of this grand phenomenon without being touched by it, is a lively pleasure. Ethereal sweetness of contemplation. This is the way the wise man looks at life and the great poet dominates the passions of his characters . . . A moment of respite. Then new furies. The rages of nature, like those of men, are intermittent. Its fits follow one another, but in rhythm. Let me profit by the magic lantern that is offered to my curious eye. It is months since I have had any communication with nature. This is a good opportunity to return to my old familiar relations with her.

*April 9, 1868.*—Spent three hours with Lotze's bulky volume, *(Geschichte der Aesthetik in Deutschland [1]).* The attraction I felt

---

[1] Hermann Lotze (1817–1881), author of a great many philosophical works.

at the outset has worn away and ended in boredom. Why? Because the grinding of the mill puts one to sleep and because these un-paragraphed pages, these interminable chapters and this incessant dialectical droning produce the effect of a mill of words. I end by yawning like any simple mortal over these dense, ponderous com-positions from Germany. Erudition and even thought are not every-thing. A little wit, keenness, vivacity, imagination, grace do not go amiss. Can one recall a single image, or a formula, or a striking or new fact on setting down one of these pedantic books? No, one is only fatigued and befuddled. The terrible phrase, "Sausage-eaters, idealists" (Taine), comes back to one with a vengeance. Oh, clarity, perspicuity, brevity! Diderot, Voltaire, even Galiani! One little article by Sainte-Beuve, by Scherer, Renan, Victor Cherbuliez can inspire more enjoyment, revery and reflection than a thousand of these German pages, crammed to the margin, in which one sees the labour but not the results. The Germans heap up the faggots for the pyre, the French apply the torch. Spare me the lucubrations; give me the facts or the ideas. Keep your grape-skins, your vats and your must; I want the finished wine, sparkling in the glass, stimu-lating and not oppressing my spirits.

*Mornex, April 11, 1868.*—Another great cloud has just shaken down snow on us. The flakes have been falling in bright sunshine. The struggle of winter and summer. I watch it from my open win-dow, wrapped in my shawl. The sounds of life, the far-away barking of a dog, the dim blows of a hammer, the voices of women at the fountain, the songs of birds in the lower orchards melt together in a vague harmony. Wisps of vapour rise from the distant clouds, but there is not a trace of fog; the soil has not softened enough, the sun is not warm enough. Spring is playing the prelude of its kind-nesses, but it is still severe. It had gone too far last week and has now assumed a less affable attitude. The green carpet of the plain is spotted and damasked with shifting and fleeting shadows, which the clouds trail over it. I am besieged with sensations.

*Mornex, April 12, 1868 (Easter, 8 a. m.).*—Solemn and religious impression. The valley is full of the sound of bells. The very fields seem to be breathing a hymn.—Mankind must have its worship; is not the Christian cult, taken all in all, the best of all those that have existed on a grand scale? The religion of sin, repentance and reconciliation, the religion of rebirth and eternal life is not a religion to be ashamed of. In spite of all the aberrations of narrow fanaticism, all the superstitions of a stupid formalism, all the additional uglinesses of hypocrisy, all the fantastic puerilities of theology, the Gospel has consoled the earth and changed mankind. Christian humanity is not much better than pagan humanity, but it would be worse without a religion, without its own religion. Every religion sets up an ideal and a model; but the Christian ideal is sublime and the model is divinely beautiful. One may detest all the churches and yet bow down before Jesus. One may hold all the priesthoods in suspicion and taboo the catechisms, and yet love the Holy and the Just who came to save and not to curse. Jesus will always be there when Christianity is criticized; and when Christianity is dead, the religion of Jesus will survive. After the Jesus-God will reappear the faith of the God of Jesus.

*(5 p. m.).*—A long walk *à deux* through Cézargues, Eseri and the Yves woods, returning by the Pont du Loup. Raw, grey weather . . . A great popular merry-making, with blue blouses, fifes and drums, has been going on for an hour under my window. This throng, all men, has been singing all sorts of things, drinking-songs, refrains, ballads, all in a very heavy and ugly way. The Muse has not touched our countrypeople, and when they are gay they are not more graceful for being so. They are like bears on a spree. What passes for poetry with them has a sad vulgarity, a frightful banality. Thanks to art, we are above the ignoble, but we remain trivial. Why? First, because, despite our democratic pretentions, the classes that are bowed to the earth in toil are aesthetically inferior to the others, and then because rustic poetry, the poetry of the peasants, is dead; and when the peasant takes part in the music and poetry of the cultivated classes, he caricatures rather than copies them. Democ-

racy, acknowledging only one rank among men, has thus transgressed against all that is not first-class. Since one can no longer, without giving offence, judge men as they really are, one compares them only with the most accomplished, and they seem more mediocre than before, uglier, more rudimentary. If equalitarianism potentially raises the average, it actually degrades nineteen people out of twenty below their previous situation. Juridical progress, aesthetic retrogression. And the artists see their *bête noire* multiplying: the bourgeois, the Philistine, the ape of the man of taste, the presumptuous ignoramus, the knowing vulgarian, the blockhead who imagines that he is the equal of the intelligent man.

"Vulgarity will prevail", as de Candolle said of the gramineous plants. The equalitarian era represents the triumph of mediocrity. It is annoying, but inevitable; it is a retribution for the past. Humanity, after having been organized on a basis of individual dissimilarities, is now in process of organization on a basis of resemblances; and this exclusive principle is as true as the other. Art will lose by it, but justice will gain. Is not universal levelling the law of nature, and when all is at the same level is not all at an end? The world tends thus with all its strength to the destruction of what it has brought forth. Life is the blind pursuit of its own negation. As it has been said of the wicked only, life also does a work that deceives it, labours at what it detests, spins its own shroud and heaps up the stones for its own tomb. It is quite natural that God should pardon us, for "we know not what we do".

Just as the sum of force is always the same in the material universe, showing neither a diminution nor an augmentation, but metamorphoses only, it is not impossible that the sum of good may in reality be always the same and therefore that any progress in one direction is compensated inversely in another direction. If this is true, one can never say that a given time and people absolutely surpass another time or another people; one can say only that there is a superiority in some particular respect.—The gross difference between man and man consists in the art of extracting from oneself the greatest intellectual power available for the higher life, in other words, transforming one's vitality into spirituality and one's latent powers into useful energy. This same difference exists between people and people. The extraction of the maximum of humanity from the same fund of animality forms the object of the simultaneous or successive rivalries of history. Orthobiotics, education, ethics and politics are only variations of the same art, the art of living. And this art, the application of cosmetic chemistry and alembication to the things of the soul, is only the art of disengaging the pure form and the most subtle essence of our individual being.

*April 26, 1868 (Sunday at noon).*—Dismal morning. Bad night; weakness. Received a cheerless letter from Berlin. Wasted my time in trifles. Languor, discontent, even a kind of boredom; emptiness, despondency.—Melancholy prospects on all sides. Felt the sands running out in the hour-glass of my life, and my forces slipping away without effect or profit. Disgust with myself.

*(10 p. m.)*—Calls . . . Spent the evening alone. It has been raining for several hours. Things have been giving me a series of lessons in wisdom. I have seen the thorn-bushes bursting into blossom and the whole valley coming to life under the breath of spring. I have observed instances of misbehaviour in various old men who are unwilling to be old and rebel in their hearts against the law of nature. I have seen the results of some frivolous marriages and heard various babbling exhortations. I have witnessed vain sorrows and pitiful examples of loneliness. I have listened to jocular conversations about the foolishness of other people, listened as well to the merry songs of the birds. And it has all had but one message for me: Place yourself again in harmony with the law of the universe, accept the will of God, use your life religiously, work while you have the light, be at once serious and joyful. Be able to repeat with the apostle: "I have learned in whatsoever state I am, therewith to be content".

*May 17, 1868 (11 a. m.).*—Why does my poor heart feel a kind of shudder? Why do the tears mount to my eyes? What is it that so moves and oppresses me? Ah, I well know and feel what it is, but I cannot say it and I cannot write it.—It seems to me, too, that my fate is being decided, and this decision is a crisis, an anguish, an inner death . . . Is it really possible? I have wept, I have shed many tears. My vision and my soul are troubled. What am I to do, O God? Uncertainty, confusion, chaos. I dare not look life in the face; I no longer know what my duty is, what wisdom prescribes, what reason counsels. Ballast and compass, anchor and sails— everything seems to fail me at once. Agitation, perplexity, obscurity, struggle. Melting, suffocating. I wish and I do not wish. Thoughts of the wildest recklessness tempt me and frighten me. Storm, hurricane, tempest.

How happy the finches, the children seem to me, as I hear them singing through my open window! They do not have to pronounce on their destiny, they do not have to take these fatal and irrevocable resolutions that irremediably bind the future and that one may regret to the grave and beyond it. They do not run the risk of mortally wounding anyone. They are in harmony with themselves.

You are as weak at heart as a woman; you should do something rash to preserve your self-respect, and yet you are afraid of any elation because you fear the anti-heroic reactions in yourself. You have impulses but no confidence in your impulses. You cannot endure the idea of causing unhappiness to one who loves you, nor yet the thought of a humiliation, nor the prospect of regret, remorse, repentance. You lack the courage to will, for your conscience, your reason and your heart do not wish to yield either way, and you spurn any arbitrary determination. The divided man draws down upon himself thunderbolts and woes, and, as he foresees this, he shuns adventures and is loath to quit the port.

*(3 p. m.).*—My eyes are dazzled. I am overcome with tender feelings. Horror of the desert. Everything seems to me vain, empty, useless, except love. And on the other hand, love without peace of conscience is only a stupefaction or a gnawing of the mind. One must feel that one is in order, in one's proper form, in the path of duty, to be able to die or even to be able to live. Unhappy soul,

you have no energy left, no will, no heroism. You seek for nothing but that which pampers your over-feminine instincts of sympathy and affection. The malaria of indifference has sterilized your intelligence and whatever talent you have. And for this there is no remedy, for you cherish your infirmity, and you do not believe there is any cure. All manly ambition is extinguished in you. The enjoyment of struggle, the illusion of success, the passion for victory, the craving for power and influence, the thirst for riches, the desire for reputation, the curiosity of the mind are reagents that have ceased to be capable of biting into your indolence. Inner peace is your one and only longing. To make those who are around you happy and reduce your existence as much as possible is your sole instinctive aspiration. You no longer have the stuff in you for anything but a poor little paterfamilias, and, even there, the life of a husband and father seems to you too complicated and difficult at your age and with your habits of mind. To avoid destitution or humiliation you would renounce everything in advance and with a good grace. Incredulity, timidity, sloth, discouragement.—This is all wrong. We must give pleasure to those who love us, those who respect us and have faith in us. This is reason enough, and this stimulant has not lost its efficacy.

*May 21, 1868.*—After supper, a pilgrimage to La Prairie. Violent storm. Enormous downpours, frightful lightning, furious thunderclaps . . . Why, I ask myself, does love always make one think of death? Because it is itself a death, death to ourselves, the annihilation of the sombre despot of whom the Persian poet speaks, the extinction of egoism, of the personal, solitary life. And this death is a new life; but this life is indeed a death.—Why is it that woman, nervous, feeble, timid as she is, feels that danger has ceased to exist when she is with the one she loves? Because to die on the heart of her beloved is her secret dream. Paradise for her is to be *together;* whether in suffering, joy, pleasure or death is a secondary matter. To cease to be two, to make a single one, at all costs, everywhere, always: that is her aspiration, her soul, her cry, her instinct.

Woman has only one religion, love; love has only one concern, ecstatic identification, the combustion of isolated beings and their union in a single flame. And there are people who deny and scoff at mysticism, when half of our species has no other cult, no other faith, no other ideal, when the supreme state glimpsed by the tender feelings, by lofty piety and great poetry bears witness to this moral reality! Mysticism, which disturbs the reason, is the natural home-land of the soul. Its more summary method ends in the same result as speculation; it brings one back to Unity and the Absolute. It breaks down the temporary and fictitious barriers of individuality. It gives vent in the finite breast to the overflowing sentiment of the infinite. It is an emancipation, a metamorphosis, a transfiguration of our poor little Self.

*August 26, 1868 (7.30 a. m.).*—Fine weather, clear and fresh. Awaking is decidedly more favorable to reason than to feeling, to work than to revery, and consequently to personal independence than to voluntary subjection. Perfect clearness is not as propitious as agitation for the tender feelings. When one sees through the medium of one's emotion, one does not perhaps see quite truly . . .

*(9 a. m.).*—Littré has led me to the *Roman de la Rose,* and the prolonged allegorical blackguardism of the last canto has made me quite wretched.—Thus the imagination is always more vulnerable than the senses, and the dream more dangerous than the reality. That is why seminarists are exposed to satyriasis, and the cloisters to nymphomania. The erotic poets cause more disaster than the women of the street. It is the mystery that excites the feelings, the unknown is the poison. Marriage is the grave of physical love, and this is a great blessing. It frees one from the obsession of carnal illusions and redeems one's freedom of mind. The generative stimulus is a powerful but disturbing impulsion; it is like a cloud charged with electricity, a storm that has the power of fecundation. But above the cloud there is the blue sky, open space, the ether; above desire is thought; above the illusions there is truth; above passion and its storms is spiritual serenity.—After all these tempests

of the heart, these agitations of the organic life that have so par-
ticularized, localized, imprisoned me in my individual existence,
shall I at last be able to reascend to my old empyrean, the region
of pure intelligence, the disinterested and impersonal life, the Olympian indifference to the miseries of subjectivity, the purely scientific
and contemplative state of mind? Shall I at last be able to forget
all the needs that bind me to the earth and humanity? Can I become a pure spirit again?—Alas, I cannot believe it for a single
moment. I see too plainly my next infirmities before me, I feel
that I cannot exist without affection, I know that I have no ambition and that my faculties are declining. I remember that I am
forty-six, that my teeth and hair are dropping out, that my eyesight
and my memory are impaired and that the whole retinue of my
youthful hopes has taken wing and vanished. Therefore I cannot
be deceived in regard to the lot that awaits me; increasing isolation,
inner mortification, long regrets, an inconsolable sadness that cannot
be confessed, a gloomy old age, a slow agony, death in the desert.

> *Ce qu'on rêva toute sa vie*
> *Rarement on peut l'accomplir . . .*
> *Lutte inutile, il faut mourir.*

A terrible impasse! For what is still possible to me I have no
relish, and everything I might have desired escapes me and will
escape me always. The end of every flight is eternally fatigue and
disappointment. Discouragement, dejection, depression, apathy, low
spirits; this is the series that must be recommenced, without respite,
as long as one rolls the rock of Sisyphus. Does it not seem shorter
and simpler to plunge head foremost into the gulf?

To die, to sleep . . . perchance to dream, said Hamlet. Suicide
settles nothing if the soul is immortal. No, there is only one solution,
to return to the order of things, to accept, submit, resign oneself
and do as best one can while one has the light. What must be sacrificed is one's own will, one's aspirations, one's dream. To renounce

happiness once and for all, that is the only thing. The immolation of one's ego, death to self, this is the only suicide that is useful and permitted. In your present indifference there is a secret spite, a wounded pride, an abdication out of perversity, a measure of bitterness, an egoism, in short, that leads you to seek for rest before you have earned it. Indifference is absolute only in the perfect humility that grinds up the self to the profit of God,

> *De quelque grand labeur, de quelque saint amour.*

You have no strength left, you desire nothing, but that is not the point. One must desire what God desires, one must pass from detachment to sacrifice, and from sacrifice to devotion. An abnegation that takes no active form is like faith without works; it is the salt without the savour.

The cup that you wish to see pass from you is responsibility, and the chastisement of life; it is the shame of existing and suffering as a common mortal who has missed his calling; it is the bitter and increasing humiliation of one's own diminution, of growing old without one's own approval, grieving one's friends and eating out one's heart. To dwell increasingly on the irreparable, to grow besotted in one's stupefaction seem to you simply two kinds of hell. How much sweeter would nothingness be than this holocaust of the self. —"Wilt thou be made whole?" was the text of the sermon on Sunday.

"Come unto me, all ye that labour and are heavy laden, and I will give you rest" . . .

"For if our heart condemn us, God is greater than our heart" . . .

*(3.30 p. m.).*—Took up the *Penseroso,*[1] so many of the maxims of which I have violated, while I have forgotten so many of its lessons. But this book is indeed the child of my soul, and its muse is indeed the inner life. When I wish to resume the connection between tradition and myself, it does me good to reread this collection of

---

[1] *Il Penseroso,* maxims in verse, by H. F. Amiel, Geneva, 1858.

gnomic verses to which so little justice has been done and which I would gladly quote if it were another's (though who, aside from Émile de Girardin, can warrant his own authority?). It pleases me that I can always subscribe to all the thoughts in it and that I can feel in it the relative truth that we call self-consistency, the agreement of appearance with reality, the harmony of word and sentiment, sincerity, in short, candour, inwardness. It is personal experience in the strictest sense of the term.

. . . A longing has reawakened in me, the wish to take up my talent again, to get back to my better self, my veritable being, the poetry of my past. I have the feeling that I have strayed into an enervating sentimentality and shammed in my official career. My true nature has been thwarted, deflected, atrophied by unfavourable circumstances and surroundings. I have allowed the results of my vast labours, my patient meditations, my varied studies all to go for nothing. This is the form of suicide that I have adopted, through a sort of discouraged stoicism. That I might live for others and spend myself for a sympathetic country and society was the vague hope with which I returned to Geneva. But very soon I felt my heart tighten, and all hope vanished; I realized that life had mismated me and that in espousing Geneva I had espoused death, the death of my talent and my joy in living. All the compensations in detail that have been granted to me have not changed the underlying fact, the fact that after a scrutiny of the situation I gave myself up for lost. I saw that I could never meet my family or our society on common ground, that their gods were not mine, that we were not of the same clay and did not share the same heaven; from that time forward a hopeless discouragement took possession of me and all ambition withered away in my breast. To conquer, to command the esteem of this mole-hill? This seemed to me too paltry to be desired; the game was not worth the candle. Go away? I only wished to work for the love of it, and abroad I should have had to make a career. In short, I remained . . . I responded to the advances of affection that came my way, but I was unable to marry, for I wished to reconcile prudence, honour and tenderness. And now here I am, tired, failing, growing old, with a battered desk for company and for all my wealth a heart full of dreams and stricken with grief. I do not know what course to follow or in what way to profit by my books, my friends, my position, my age, by what remains of my strength and the hoard of my recollections. I am a little like the melancholy keeper of a graveyard, or like that good old soul who tells the story of *Paul et Virginie*.

What I lack, and this lack has always existed, is will, the hard will that settles things for itself, without love and without weakness, that wills because it wills and to which the evidence of its own utility and the certitude of duty are manifest. At bottom, I have wished for only one thing, to act through a great love and for a great cause. I needed a life that was secretly sublime, and I have never been able to resign myself to the parody of my dream. The ideal has brought me inner desolation by making still uglier for me the ugliness of the real and the poverty of the possible. The voiceless desolation of isolation! I have never confessed the depths of my grief except to my journal. And the world about me sometimes takes me for a merry soul who has reached a philosophical indifference and has so ordered himself as not to take part in the oscillation of human destinies, sometimes for a fool who has stupidly lost all his opportunities to acquire the good things that everyone covets, some-times for an eccentric who is incomprehensible and unsociable and likes to do everything differently from other people, sometimes for a besotted egoist, sometimes for a carping, morose hermit, sometimes for a lazy devil who, in his sheer indolence, pretends to be dead. The world has never looked me in the eyes or looked into my heart. It prefers to imagine that I amuse myself by playing with the peace of mind of young girls or by making rhymes in idle moments. It shall not have my secret, I do not respect it or love it enough for that; and it is even more indifferent to me than I am to it. Save for a few choice souls and minds, this greedy little world in which I live does not exist for me; it is certainly further removed from me than the population of Newfoundland or Formosa. Our true individual world is composed only of the beings who rely upon us or to whom we are able to do good. The rest are merely a mass, an atmosphere, an element through which we have to steer our course without doing harm to them, but without entering into relations with them, aside from the juridical relations.—O misery! While the heart sings, *Seid umschlungen Millionen!* the world rebuffs all true warmth of heart and we are driven back upon ourselves.

*(6 p. m.)*.—Back to the torture, tireless and futile babbler! You have said yourself:

> *Se guérir c'est se vaincre et non pas discourir.*

What do you expect?

*(10 p. m.)*—Magnificent evening. A walk along the quays, as far as the beacon in the roadstead, with my friend H. Thoughts of the sea. Moonlight.

*September 1, 1868.*—Passion is a marvel worthy of worship. I feel in the presence of its mystery a sort of religious communion. Yes, love is holy, and its sacred folly is nobler than all the wisdoms. I listen on my knees to the dithyramb of its tenderness and the hymns of its exaltation; and as I recall my memories of yesterday, I am gripped and dazzled in my inmost being. To live in the heart of a woman, to share in some sort her secret devotion, to hear as it were in hiding the rapturous litanies of her worship, to breathe the intoxicating incense of that altar on which burns the flame of ecstasy, is a rare and terrible privilege. It is as if Isis had lifted her veil and one were about to be struck by thunder. It is more than moving to bend over the depths of this abyss; one runs the risk of vertigo.—Passion is one of the forms of prayer. There is something sublime about anything that transports us out of ourselves. And the sublime consoles us for the uglinesses of everyday life, above which our natures command us to soar.

*Villars*,[1] *September 12, 1868*.—Oh, the family! If the pious, traditional superstition with which we envelop this institution would let us tell the truth about the matter, what a reckoning it would have to settle! What numberless martyrdoms it has required, dissemblingly, inexorably! How many hearts have been stifled by it, lacerated and broken! How many oubliettes there have been in its annals, how many *in paces*, dungeons, abominable tortures, more sombre than those of the Spanish Inquisition! One could fill all the wells of the earth with the tears that it has caused to be shed in secret; one could people a planet with the beings to whom it has brought unhappiness, one could double the average of human life with the years of those whose days the family has shortened. The suspicions, the jealousies, the slanders, the rancours, the hatreds of the family: who has measured their depth? And the venomous words, the insults for which there is no consolation, the invisible dagger-thrusts, the infernal *arrière-pensées*, or only the irreparable wounds of speech, the deadly blabbing and babbling, what a legion of sufferings have they not engendered? The family arrogates to itself impunity for everything mean and base, the right to utter insults, irresponsibility for affronts. It punishes us for defending ourselves from it and it punishes us for putting our trust in it. One is never betrayed except by one's own people, a famous proverb says. The family may be all that is best in this world, but too often it is all that is worst. Kinship is a torture-chamber that will survive all the Middle Ages, and no philanthropy will abolish it. One might also liken it to the baneful field that yields its tares to the hundred-fold and chokes all one's wheat. It punishes a wrong to the fourth generation, and six hundred good deeds done to it are carefully buried under the stone of oblivion. By whom is one slighted, rebuffed, envied, vilified more than by one's family? Where, if not in the family, can one undergo the hard apprenticeship of mockery

[1] A station in the Alps facing a splendid amphitheatre of mountains, above Bex and the Rhone valley. The author more than once spent his university vacations there.

and ingratitude? There is a sort of tacit conspiracy to present only the good sides of the family and leave the rest to be taken for granted, an official lie that paternal preachers and sentimental poetry swing like a censer. In the same way, by mentioning only quaternaries and quinaries, the credit of the lottery is upheld and simple souls are ruined. The serious moralist, like the sincere novelist, lovers of justice both, must tear the mask from this idol, atrocious sometimes in its hypocrisy.

The truth is that the family relation exists only to put us to the proof and that it gives us infinitely more suffering than happiness. It must be accepted as Socrates accepted Xanthippe, as the providential exercise of our patience and as a constant occasion for obscure heroism.

*Villars, September 14, 1868 (8 a. m.).*—Awakened at six o'clock by the rustling of the rain on the gravel of the terrace. I open my shutters. We are enveloped in a cloud; the fog spreads its hood over the house, and the rain drips upon us without falling, since we are a part of the sponge in which it is formed. This weather agrees with my state of mind and gives me a feeling of balance and strength.

Felt the fascination of routine, the attraction of habit, the sweetness of oblivion, the narcotism of the beaten path. Thus, in three months, the cycle is complete. The thirst for change ends in the quietude of continuation. All those tempests have resulted only in a fraying of the will and a weariness of anything new. Incessant warfare satiates one even more than torpor.—I long to live now only for thought, for work. I fared so ill from my descent from the mountain of contemplation into the valley of human sentiments that I almost regret my failure to steel my heart. But illusion is no longer possible; I know that I cannot live without love, the love of home, family, friends and country; and I know that family and country will never give me happiness or understand me. I am condemned, therefore, to a gradual suffocation, unless I marry and the marriage gives me absolute independence of my surroundings and inner joy as well. Pure disinterestedness, detachment, renunciation drain away all one's energy and lead one only to a resigned stillness. The wish to die is not what gives us the means of living well and being useful. But all these storms of the heart, these tempests of the feelings obscure the clear vision of our duty, the calm notions of good sense. There seems to be an opening in your clouds, thanks to a week in the mountains and a day of captivity. Make the most of it. A moment of silence falls on the house and falls on your soul. Employ this truce that fate has granted you . . . Not to change things as they are is scarcely a solution, for this is to pass shamefully through the Caudine Forks of gloom. Review, pen in hand, all the possibilities, and choose, by the method of elimination, among the evils, that which is least.

*(11 a. m.).*—Musing over the heroine of the *Histoire hollandaise.* Thus through tears themselves one's eyes are dried at last; sorrow spends itself while spending us. No one can suffer beyond a certain limit; having reached this, one is saved by death or apathy. This is one of the mercies of nature. The suffering of someone else renews and revives our own; but if the other person falls asleep, one is likely to end by drowsing too, like a child after its sobs. This must be the therapeutics of passion. I seem to note in myself, with a sort of vague contempt, this incapacity for any suffering that is excessive or too prolonged, this discreditable deadening of pain. But in this, perhaps, in my usual way, I reproach myself too soon and disparage myself too strongly. I ascribe to myself as real a calm that is only apparent. Actually, one only knows oneself when one is put to the proof, and I have already so astonished myself in things I have done, that I dare not make any conjectures about new situations. I no longer venture to have either a good or a bad opinion of myself, for fear that I shall see it belied in the event. I no longer know what my heart is equal to, or whether it is equal to anything. Is it serious or frivolous, forgetful or constant, fickle or faithful? One might take any wager, and I do not know myself which would be right. I should say that I am fickle in my emotions and tenacious in my affections; but is this certain, has it been demonstrated? I hardly

think so . . . It would be more just then to say that I have exaggerated the metamorphoses and phenomena of my emotional life rather than belittled them. By doubting my heart I slander it; and all the feebler souls who have put their trust in me protest against this doubt. It is true, however, that your pride, which makes you ashamed of an over-feminine weakness and causes you to regret advances that you have made and that were disregarded, has often thrown you back into a false impassiveness . . .

To sum it all up, you may be reassured about your heart. It is better than your world thinks it is; and in spite of the fearful education in the art of self-defence which this detestable world has imposed upon it, it is still more sensitive and sweeter, tenderer, more benign than it needs to be to give happiness to those who do not oblige it to bristle like a hedgehog in spite of itself but are content simply to be loved.

*Villars, September 19, 1868.*—Does one ever know what lies beneath the story of a man?

\*

\*     \*

To initiate the young man into his sexual rights and duties, doing it at the useful moment and in a sane and suitable way, is an essential part of education. I myself had, to an eminent degree, every delicate instinct and elevated aspiration, every sort of virtuous inclination, and yet I have missed life because I had no direction, no counsel or encouragement or initiation in matters of sexual decency. I morbidly exaggerated every scruple and, instead of living like a man, I burned like a monk. At thirty-nine I was still as chaste as a virgin, and even now I am still harassed by Lilith, like a seminarist. Is it not absurd? And what contempt a physician would have for me! To whom and for what have I made this long, vain sacrifice? To an idea, a prejudice, the dutifulness of an anchorite. And who punishes me and calumniates me now for persisting in my ridiculous chastity? Precisely the object of my respect, the women, the virgins. Celibacy is honoured of the gods and accursed of women. It is abominated in life as we know it, and the monasteries alone promise it, as a compensation, the palms of the life to come.—In short, I can only regard with bitter irony this folly to which I have sacrificed my health, my strength and my existence, this folly of continence, taken for a virtue. I feel what unmarried women of forty feel, a secret fury against the myths of public opinion to which they have offered up as a holocaust the deepest instincts of their nature. They feel that they have deified a fiction and taken the voice of a prejudice for the voice of conscience. To die for an error, a duty that may be only a sham, this is always noble; but to die disillusioned is a great affliction.

This is an outburst of rebellious nature. The protest goes too far. Purity, reserve, chastity are certainly virtues, and one need not regret having believed in them and suffered for them.

*Villars, September 21, 1868.*—A pleasant autumnal effect. Everything was overcast this morning, and the grey muslin of the rain spread all over the circle of our mountains. Now the strip of blue that appeared first behind the distant peaks has grown larger and steadily mounts towards the zenith, and the dome of the sky, almost cleared of clouds, sheds down upon us the pallid golden beams of a sun that is still convalescent. The day promises to be benign and tender. All's well that ends well.

Thus, after the season of tears, the sweetness of joy comes back. Tell yourself that you have entered the autumn of your life, that the graces of spring and the splendours of summer have passed beyond recall, but that the autumn also has its beauties. Rain, clouds, mists often overshadow the fall of the year, but the air is still mild, the light still caresses the eyes and the yellowing leaves; it is the time of fruits, the harvest and the vintage, the time to lay in provisions for the winter.—The herds of cows have reached the level of the châlet, and next week they will be below us. This living barometer tells us that the time has come to leave the mountains. There is nothing to gain and everything to lose by neglecting the example of nature and making arbitrary rules for one's own existence. Our liberty, wisely understood, is only a voluntary obedience to the universal laws of life.—Your life has reached its month of September. Know how to recognize this and order yourself accordingly.

*November 13, 1868.*—I have glanced through and partly read two works of Secrétan (*Recherches sur la méthode,* 1857; *Précis élémentaire de philosophie,* 1868). Secrétan's philosophy is the philosophy of Christianity considered as the absolute religion. The subordination of nature to intelligence, of the intelligence to the will and of the will to positive faith: such is its general structure. Unhappily, it is deficient in the critical, comparative, historical point of view; and this kind of apologetics, in which irony is allied with the apotheosis of love, leaves one with the impression of a *parti pris.* The philosophy of religion without the comparative science of religions, without a disinterested, general philosophy of history, remains more or less arbitrary and factitious. The rights and the role of science are insufficiently guarded and established in this reduction of human life to three spheres, namely, those of industry, law and religion. The author seems to me to have a vigorous and profound mind rather than an open mind. He is not only dogmatic, but he dogmatizes in behalf of a positive religion that dominates and subjects him. In addition, Christianity being an X which each Church defines in its own way, the author, taking the same liberty, defines the X in his own fashion, in such a way that he is at once too free and too little free with regard to Christianity as a particular religion. He does not avoid the arbitrary and he is not sufficiently independent. He does not satisfy the believing Anglican, Lutheran, Reformist or Catholic; he does not satisfy the free thinker. This Schellingian speculation, which consists in deducing necessarily a particular religion, in other words making philosophy a handmaiden of Christian theology, is a heritage of the Middle Ages.

For, after one has believed, the question of judging arises. A believer is not a judge. A fish lives in the ocean, but as it cannot envelop the ocean with its eye, as it cannot dominate the ocean, it is consequently unable to judge the ocean. To understand Christianity, one must put it in its historical place, in its setting, make it a part of the religious development of humanity, judge it not from the Christian point of view, but from the human point of view, *sine ira et studio*. But of all the objects of study there is none in which confusions are more common, easier, more obstinate, more stubborn than the religious questions. An infinite measure of nonsense is the curse attached to this class of problems, and this is what arouses the disgust of people whose intelligence is exact and whose minds are open. What is the use of stirring up the wakeful and furious fanaticism that is bound to rise up from every defeat and even be reborn from its own ashes? Science finds its advantage in ignoring theology and building its structure of knowledge on nature and history, quite regardless of this dethroned queen, who has been able to rouse so many passions and raise so many storms. Free science does not replace religion; but it obliges the positive religions to become more spiritual, purer and more true in their teachings about the world and about man. It constrains them, as Diderot said, to "enlarge their God".

*December 16, 1868.*—I am in distress for my poor gentle friend Charles Heim. Copied a few German poems (Rückert, Salis, Tanner, Geibel) which I am sending him. They should sweeten the last hours, by speaking of hope and immortality. Besides, they are in the language that he loves, the tongue that his father spoke. Since November 30th, I have not seen the handwriting of my dear sick friend, who on that day gave me his last farewell. How long these two weeks have seemed to me! How I have understood that ardent longing to have the last words, the last glance of those whom one has loved! These last communications are a sort of testament; they have a solemn and sacred character that is certainly not an effect of our imagination. One who is about to die shares in some measure in eternity. It seems as if a dying man spoke to us from beyond the grave; what he says seems to us a judgment, an oracle, an injunction. He is almost a prophet for us. And certain it is that for one who feels his life slipping away and who sees the coffin opening, the hour has struck to speak serious words. The depths of his nature are sure to appear, and whatever divinity there is within him has passed the time for concealment through modesty, fear or prudence.

*Au lit de mort, l'ange s'est dévoilé.*

Oh, let us not wait, to be just, compassionate, demonstrative towards those we love, till they or we are struck down by illness or threatened by death. Life is short, and there will never be too much time to rejoice the hearts of those who are making the dark voyage with us. Let us make haste to be good.

*December 26, 1868.*—My dear and sweet friend Charles Heim died this morning at Hyères. A beautiful soul is going back to heaven. Was he able to read my letter of the day before yesterday? I do not know, but perhaps he saw it and smiled; and this thought, this smile of a dying man, does the heart good. So his sufferings are over! Is he happy now?

*January 22, 1869 (11.30 p. m.).*—I am shivering in my top-story room, while the north-wind rattles my shutters and draws off all the warmth from my fireplace . . .

*January 23, 1869.*—Of what use to me are the bright sun and the blue sky? A heavy coating of dull frost covers my window-panes and makes a prison of my chamber. I am in a sad plight, life has made a fool of me. Down, down, my heart! as Corneille would have said. You must get command of yourself again, subdue the prancing charger in your soul. None of these little vexations could get the best of a manly will. One burst of ill-humour is one too many.—As you make your bed, so you must lie, and most of these annoyances have come from your carelessness. You hate to bother about these domestic trifles, and they take their revenge by conspiring against your comfort just when they can be most disagreeable to you. You have no memory to spare for such paltry things as a wardrobe, a store-room or a linen-closet. Whose fault is that? You would like to forget these vulgar cares, escape from this humiliating net of insignificant necessities; and this entire Lilliputian world chastises you for your contempt.—In your disdain, you lack all foresight and order in household matters, you ignore them and refuse to be interested in them; and then what happens? They make you repent this proud indifference.

This is really the same fault that you commit with men, by neglecting to flatter their self-esteem, which means to manipulate the infinitesimals. All the little obstacles become big ones the moment one fails to allow for them; the frogs puff themselves up to the size of oxen when, by paying no attention to them, one puts them on their mettle.

I know all this; but I feel an insurmountable repugnance to busying myself with certain details. And being unwilling to fret and fume, as a matter of self-respect, or to subject myself to precautions that seem to me humiliating, I always end by simply detaching myself from the thing that slips my mind. I cultivate a protective and medicative indifference. To govern things or to free oneself from them are the two proper attitudes. To permit oneself to be troubled or dominated by them, in a word, to depend on them, is what I cannot abide. A variation of the *all or nothing.* The precious thing is inner liberty, that of Epictetus. When one no longer cleaves either to comfort or health, to life or the opinion of others, one is all but inviolable.

*January 27, 1869.*—What, then, is the service that Christianity has rendered to the world? The preaching of good tidings. What are these good tidings? The forgiveness of sins. The God of holiness loving the world and reconciling it with himself through Jesus, to the end of establishing the kingdom of God, the city of souls, the life of heaven on earth. This is all, but this is a whole revolution. "Love one another, as I have loved you." "As thou, Father, art in me, and I in thee, that they also may be one in us," such is the eternal life; this is perfection, salvation, felicity. Faith in the paternal love of God, who chastises and pardons for our good, and who desires not the death of the sinner, but his conversion and his life: this is the motive force of the redeemed.

What is called Christianity is an ocean into which flow a multitude of spiritual currents of different origins: for instance, several religions of Asia and Europe, and especially the great ideas of Greek wisdom, Platonism in particular. Neither its doctrine nor its morality, as they have been established by history, is new or the work of a single projection. The essential and original element is the factual demonstration that the divine nature and human nature are able to co-exist, to be fused in a single, sublime flame, that holiness and pity, justice and mercy can be one thing in man and consequently in God. What is specific in Christianity is Jesus, the religious consciousness of Jesus. The sacred sense of his union with God through the submission of the will and the rapture of love, that deep, calm, invincible faith, has become religion. The faith of Jesus has become the faith of millions and billions of men. This torch has produced an immense conflagration. This revealer and this revelation have appeared so luminous, so effulgent that the dazzled world has forgotten justice ever since and attributed to a single benefactor all the benefactions inherited from the past. Religious criticism is impossible for all but a few men. The moment religious questions come up, the judgment is obscured by prejudices, confused by terror and ill-feeling, agitated by the passions, and one sees persons of the utmost distinction losing their capacity for method, losing their composure and impartiality. The open minds (by no means the hostile minds) can be counted on one's fingers. Let any question of faith arise, and logic, reason, the moral sense cease to function normally; the absurd is no longer absurd, contradiction is no longer contradictory, immorality is no longer immoral. One who does not lose his head is merely a profane unbeliever.

The conversion of ecclesiastical and confessional Christianity into historical Christianity has been the work of biblical science. The attempt to convert historical Christianity into philosophical Christianity is in part illusory, since faith cannot be wholly dissolved in science. But the displacement of Christianity from the historical sphere to the psychological sphere is the endeavour of our epoch. This involves the detaching of the eternal Gospel; and for this to take place, history and the comparative philosophy of religions will be obliged to put Christianity in its true place and judge it. Then people must distinguish between the religion that Jesus professed and the religion that has taken Jesus for its object. And when one has put one's finger on the state of consciousness which is the original cellule, the principle of the eternal Gospel, this is the thing to which one must cleave. It is the *punctum saliens* of pure religion.—*Ama et fac quod vis.*

Perhaps the supernatural will then give place to the extraordinary, and the great geniuses will be regarded as the messengers of the God of history, the providential revealers through whom the spirit of God stirs the human mass. What will pass away will not be the wonderful but the arbitrary, the accidental, the miraculous. The local, paltry, doubtful miracles will be extinguished like the poor little flares of a village festival or the flickering tapers of a street-procession, before the great marvel of the sun, before the law of the world of spirits, the incomparable pageant of human history guided by the all-powerful dramatist whom one calls God.— The future philosophy of History must be to that of Bossuet what his is to the sermonizings of the Loriquets of the sacristy. *Utinam!*

*February 3, 1869.*—"How can those who look at history with their hearts manage not to die for the sadness of it?" asked a Parisian reviewer yesterday, apropos of the work of the American, Draper (*History of the Intellectual Development of Europe*). To reply to this question let us ask, What is it that diminishes from age to age? Not so much the evil, which is only displaced and changes its form, but rather the ignorance of one part and the

267

privilege of the other. What increases is knowledge and equality. Humanity is always gaining in its knowledge of the world and itself; it is always placing more and more within the reach of all, for the use of all, the fruits of the labour of all. This is the best that can be said. But perhaps this is enough to justify history.—Suppose this evolution were to reach its limit, suppose that the absolute equality in rights and advantages of all human beings were realized; if history did not stop there, what would happen? The reconstitution of the spiritual hierarchy, everyone being valued at precisely what he is worth, and doing what he was made for. And there we have the Republic of Plato. In twenty or thirty more centuries, provided we had no geological cataclysms, humanity would reach this phase. But what would be the use if the sum of evil, that is to say of suffering and sin, had not sensibly diminished? The ideal still to be realized would be analogous to the Millennium, the sanctification of all, the good made manifest in all, heaven on earth, with death, sickness and separation thrown in.—But, again, what would be the use if complete happiness still floated before the eyes of this third humanity, panting on a terrestrial globe that had been subdued and domesticated? It would still aspire to something better. The eternal life would be its dream. And one might as well grasp this at the outset. The eternal Gospel will be the solution that is asked for. In order to accept history, one must therefore have a faith. For the sceptic, the spectacle of human destiny is bitter beyond all remedy and fathomlessly sad: always assuming that the sceptic has a heart, that he is not merely curious but a man.

Positivism, by proscribing the notion of an end, destroys activity; for activity without an end, without hope, without direction is only a form of madness.

What happens as a matter of fact? What happens is that a society changes only the object of its faith; for example, when it no longer believes in the other life, it wishes to amuse itself in this, and, when it has dethroned the God-spirit, it substitutes the worship of the Golden Calf. Atheism serves as a pillow only for a few.

An atheistic society, for all the ages and for both the sexes, is difficult to imagine, as long as the instinct for happiness and perhaps the need for absolute justice continue to exist in the human soul.

The higher and general faith of a society consists in its religion. For the present epoch, this religion has ceased to be that of the dominant churches. The religion of Progress, perhaps that of Nature, or rather of Science and the abstract laws, is in process of replacing, in the cultivated classes, the religion of the personal God revealing himself and intervening by supernatural action. The miraculous has been summoned to dissolve. Hero-worship, the cult of the extraordinary souls who have become the beacons of humanity, is preparing the way for the worship of the Spirit who fashions the universe and brings to birth the suns, the flowers and the heights of thought. The universal theism will strongly resemble the *panentheism* of Krause, and the reign of the Holy Ghost of the Christian mystics. Chrysippus, Aristotle and Plato proclaimed nothing else. The world is made for the good; the moral idea is the light of all nature, and the pursuit of the perfect good is the motive of the universe. The Epicurean conception and the Stoic conception, the world of chance, matter and force, on one hand, the world, on the other, of order, thought and spirit, these are the two antagonistic philosophies. Positivism, with nothing to propound, is not a philosophy but the anticipation of a philosophy. It represents only an abstention, an exclusion, a negation, an endurance. "Let us be content to observe phenomena and to discover their laws; causes, ends, principles are inaccessible to us. Let us ascertain without understanding. Let us treat appearances seriously, and, shadows ourselves, let us work with shadows. Everything is superficies." This wisdom is a compulsory fast that resembles science only through an imperfect analysis of the faculty of knowing. Plato demonstrated long ago that if we know only appearance we know nothing, and that the science of appearances is a science only on condition that it is not an appearance any longer.

*March 1, 1869.*—Impartiality and objectivity are as rare as justice, of which they are only two particular forms. Self-interest is an inexhaustible source of flattering illusions. The number of persons who wish to see truly is extraordinarily small. What dominates men is a fear of the truth, unless the truth happens to be useful to them, which comes back to saying that self-interest is the principle of the philosophy of the common man, or that the truth is made for us but not we for the truth.—As this is a humiliating fact, most people naturally prefer neither to ascertain nor to recognize it. And thus a prejudice of self-esteem protects all the prejudices of the understanding, which are born of a stratagem of egoism.—Humanity has always put to death or persecuted those who have disturbed its self-interested peace of mind. It never grows any better except in its own despite. The only advancement it desires is an increase of enjoyments. All advances in justice, in morals, in sanctity have been imposed upon it or wrested from it by some noble violence. Sacrifice, the delight of great souls, has never been the law of societies. It is too often by employing one vice against another, vanity, for instance, against cupidity, vainglory against positive inclination, lust against sloth, that the great agitators have overcome inertia.— In a word, the human world is almost entirely directed by the law of nature, and the law of the spirit (justice, beauty, morality, goodness), the simple yeast in this coarse dough, has had small effect as a generous leaven.

From the point of view of the ideal, the human world is sad and ugly; but, comparing it with its probable origins, mankind has not altogether wasted its time. Thus there are three ways of regarding history: pessimism, when one starts from the ideal, optimism, the retrospective view, heroism, when one reflects that every advance costs oceans of blood and tears, and that the better, like the Mexican divinity, demands hecatombs of smoking hearts.

The hypocrisy of Europe veils its face before the voluntary immolations of those fanatics of India who cast themselves under the wheels of the triumphal car of their great goddess. Yet these immolations are only the symbol of that which happens in Europe as everywhere else, the offering that all the martyrs of all the great causes make of their lives. The sanguinary and ferocious goddess is indeed humanity itself, which advances only by remorse and only repents through the excess of its crimes.—These fanatics who devote themselves are the continuous protest against the universal selfishness. We have overturned only the manifest idols, and still the perpetual sacrifice goes on; everywhere, and on every hand, the choicest souls of every generation suffer for the salvation of the multitudes. This is the austere law, the bitter, mysterious law of solidarity. Mutual redemption and perdition are the destiny of our species. And selfishness is the motive of individuals, and selfishness is blind. The human race thus does a work that deceives it; it is less free than it thinks and toils like the coral-insects of the sea to build a structure of which it is unaware. The conclusion of all this revery, which has flowed of itself without my will, is submission to the universal order. No revolt against one's time or against things. Enter into the concert of historical forces and actions, pay one's debt and one's ransom, and leave the rest to God. Not to despise one's kind, but to remain the champion of the good, without illusion and without bitterness. A kind and serene goodness is better than irritation, and more manly than despair! Do what you ought to do, come what may.

*March 18, 1869.*—Coming back from a walk outside the city, I am horrified at the cell I live in. It is a dark dungeon, cluttered and hideous as the hovel of Faust. Outside, the sunlight, the birds, the spring, beauty, life; here ugliness, old papers, sadness, death.— And yet my walk was very melancholy. I wandered along the Rhone and the Arve, and all the memories of the past, all the disappointments of the present, and all the anxieties of the future besieged my heart, like evil things in robes of sorrow. I counted up my dead, and all my faults arrayed themselves in battle against me. The vulture of my regrets tore at my liver. My secret thoughts grew in me like the acrid taste of the choke-pear. The feeling of the irreparable caught at my throat like an iron collar. It seemed

to me that I had missed life and that life was escaping me now.——
Ah, how terrible spring is to the solitary. All the sleeping desires
reawake, all the vanished griefs are born again; the old man, beaten
and gagged, rises once more and begins to groan. Scars become
bleeding wounds again, and these wounds vie with one another in
lamentation. One had forgotten them all, one had managed to
deaden oneself in work or distraction, and of a sudden the heart,
that prisoner in solitary confinement, moans in its dungeon, and
this moan shakes the whole palace in the depths of which it has
been walled away.

*Maudit printemps, reviendras-tu toujours!*

Secure as one may be against all the other fatalities, there is one
that brings us back under the yoke, the fatality of time. You have
succeeded in freeing yourself from all the servitudes, but you have
reckoned without the last, that of the years. Age comes, and its
weight is as the weight of all the other oppressions put together.
Mortal man is only a kind of ephemera. When I considered the steep
banks of the Rhone, which have seen the river flowing for ten or
twenty thousand years, or merely the trees in the avenue of the
cemetery, which, for two centuries, have seen so many processions
filing past; when I came to the walls of the town again, the dikes,
the paths that saw me playing when I was a child; as I watched
other children, running over the sward of this meadow of Plainpalais, which supported my first steps, I had the sharpest sensation of the inanity of life and the flight of all things. I felt floating over me the shadow of the manchineel. I perceived the great,
implacable abyss wherein are swallowed up all these illusions that
are called beings. I saw that the living are only phantoms, fluttering for an instant on the earth, formed of the ashes of the dead,
and soon reverting to the eternal night, as marsh-fires return to the
ground. The nothingness of our joys, the emptiness of existence,
the futility of our ambitions filled me with a quiet distaste.——From

regret, through disenchantment, I have drifted into Buddhism, a weariness of all things.—The hope of a blissful immortality would be better . . .

With what different eyes does one see life at ten, at twenty, thirty, sixty! Those who live solitary lives are conscious of this psychological metamorphosis.—There is another thing that surprises them: the universal conspiracy to conceal the sadness of this world, to make one forget suffering, sickness, death, to hide the laments and sobs that rise from every house, to gloss the hideous mask of reality. Is it from a generous motive towards childhood and youth, is it from fear that we thus veil the sinister truth? Is it from a feeling of equity, and does life hold as many good things as evils, or even possibly more?—However this may be, we are nourished by illusion rather than truth. Every man unwinds the thread of his delusive hopes, and, when he has exhausted it, he sits down to die, and leaves his sons and his nephews to begin anew the same experience. Everyone pursues happiness, and happiness eludes the pursuit of everyone.

The only useful viaticum in making the voyage of life is a great duty and a few serious affections. And even the affections perish, or at least their objects are mortal: a friend, a wife, a child, a country, a church may precede us to the grave; duty only is as enduring as we.

> *Vis pour autrui, sois juste et bon;*
> *Fais ton monument ou ta gerbe,*
> *Et du Ciel obtiens le pardon*
> *Avant d'aller dormir sous l'herbe.*

This maxim exorcises the spirit of revolt, anger, discouragement, vengeance, indignation, ambition, which by turns agitate and tempt the heart, swelling with the sap of the springtime.—O all you holy ones of the East, of antiquity, of Christianity, phalanx of heroes, you have known the languors and the agonies of the soul, and you have triumphed over them. Risen from the lists in victory, shade us with your palms, and may your example revive our hearts!

For the rest, the sun is sinking, nature is less beautiful. The inner storm has passed.

*April 3, 1869.*—I have finished Renan's magnificent volume (*Les Apôtres*). How many things it stirs up, what questions and ideas! It is dazzling. And yet I constantly feel a disproportion between the cause and the effect, between the role and the actor. If the apostles and their hallucinations are only that, why is their work so important? If fraud, illusion and trickery are indispensable to religion, why not revolt against religion? The aesthetic point of view, with Renan, dominates everything and explains this apparent contradiction.

*Mornex, April 6, 1869 (8 a. m.).*—Magnificent weather. The Alps are dazzling in their gauze of silver. Sensations of every kind have flooded me: the soft pleasure of a good bed, the delights of a walk at sunrise, the charms of a wonderful view, the enjoyment of an excellent breakfast, a longing for travel, as I glanced over pictures of Spain (by Vivian) and Scottish pasture-lands (by Cooper), a thirst for joy, a hunger for work, emotions and life, dreams of happiness, musings of love; the need for being, an ardour still to feel and launch myself into life stirred in the depths of my heart. A sudden reawakening of youth, a welling up of poetry, a springtide of the soul, a sprouting forth again of the wings of desire. Yearnings to conquer, wander, adventure. A forgetting of age, ties, duties, cares; outbursts of youth, as if life were beginning anew. It is as if the fire had reached the powder, as if our soul were blown to the four winds. One longs to devour the world, to try everything, see everything. The ambition of Faust; lust for the universe; the horror of one's cell; one throws off the cowl, and one longs to press all nature in one's arms and against one's heart. O passions, one beam of the sun is enough to kindle all of you together! The cold, black mountain becomes a volcano again and its crown of snow evaporates under a single blast of its burning breath. The

spring brings on these sudden, impossible resurrections. By making
the vital juices thrill and bubble, it produces impetuous longings,
terrible inclinations, frenzies of life that are unforeseen and inextinguishable. It bursts the rigid bark of the trees and the iron mask
of all the austerities. It makes the monk tremble in the shadow of
his monastery, the virgin behind the curtains of her chamber, the
child on his bench at school, the old man in the toils of his rheu-
matism.

> *O Hymen, Hymenæe!*
> *Notusque calor per membra cucurrit.*

All these stirrings are only the infinite variations of the great instinct of nature; they sing the same thing in every tongue; they
are the hymn to Venus, the yearning for the infinite. They witness
the exaltation of the being who longs to die to the individual life
and absorb the universe into himself or be dissolved in it.

Love that is conscious of itself is a pontificate; it feels that it
represents the great mystery, and it communes with itself religiously in silence in order to be worthy of this divine worship.

*Mornex, April 8, 1869, last day (5 p. m.).*—A great, calm, luminous view. Swallows are crossing the expanse. Facing me, towards
Bonneville, I can see the ruins of the château which has given its
name to the whole province (Faucigny), ruins which for me too
preserve so many memories. This vast landscape seems to look on
me with friendly eyes. But in spite of myself, in the presence of
Mont Blanc the eternal, and all these snow-crowned peaks, I feel
sad thoughts coming over me.

> *Car l'éternelle harmonie*
> *Pèse comme une ironie*
> *Sur tout le tumulte humain.*

The shadows are beginning to fill the plain. On! on! Wandering
Jew. The day falls, the temperature drops, one must go back to
work, care, duty. The city calls you. Your holidays are over. Take

up the yoke again, chain the ball to your ankle. Surrender the mountains, the wide air, revery, liberty. Galley-slave of teaching, released on parole, be present at the muster. Hail, sweet country-side, dear amphitheatre of green hillsides and white mountains, cradle of my youth, refuge of my riper years, I have no more confidences to give you, but you behold a dreamer who leaves you only with a pang, for he knows not what his life will be in three months, or tomorrow.

*April 24, 1869.*—Might Nemesis be more real than Providence? The jealous God truer than the good God? Sorrow surer than joy? Darkness more certain to conquer than light? Is it pessimism or optimism that is right? Is it Leibnitz or is it Schopenhauer who has understood the universe best? The healthy man or the suffering who sees better into the depths of things? Which of the two is deceived?

Alas, the problem of suffering and evil is always the greatest enigma of being, after the existence of being itself. The faith of mankind has generally postulated the victory of good over evil; but if the good is not the result of a victory, but a victory in itself, it implies an incessant, infinite battle; it is an interminable conflict, and its success is eternally menaced.—And if this is life, was not Buddha right in regarding it as itself evil, since it is agitation without respite and war without mercy? Rest can then be found only in nothingness. The art of self-annihilation, of escaping from the torture of rebirths and from the wheel of misery, the art of attaining Nirvana would be the supreme art, the method of deliverance. The Christian says to God: Deliver us from evil. The Buddhist adds: And to this end deliver us from finite existence, return us to nothingness! The first considers that, once freed from the body, he can enter into eternal happiness; the second believes that individuality is the obstruction of all quietude, and he aspires to the dissolution of his soul itself. The dread of the first is the paradise of the second . . .

My own feeling is that suffering, sin and loneliness are an evil, but that existence is good, even individual existence. If the individual, who represents a will, felt completely at one with the universal will, he would have destroyed sin. If he felt at one with all other men, he would have destroyed his loneliness. And if he had a purely spiritual organism, he would have done away with suffering. Saintly souls, gathered in fellowship about God and glorifying him: this, in effect, is the Christian paradise. But this conception rests on many hypotheses: that there are souls, that individual life is possible without limitations and without a body, that friendly souls reunite and recognize one another, that mothers can be happy when their children are not, that they can love less, in other words, on entering the kingdom of love, that progressive beings can become perfect, when perfection and progress are mutually exclusive, etc.—Alas, how many doubtful things and yet all necessary to faith!

One thing only is needful: abandonment to God. Be in the order of things yourself, and leave to God the care of unravelling the skein of the world and destiny. What matters nothingness or immortality? What must be will be. What will be will be good. Faith in the good; perhaps the individual needs no more in order to pass through life. But one must have taken the side of Socrates, Plato, Aristotle, Zeno, against materialism, the religion of chance and pessimism.—Perhaps one must even decide against Buddhistic nihilism, for the systems of conduct are diametrically opposed if one works to augment one's life or to annul it, if the question is to cultivate one's faculties or methodically atrophy them.

To employ one's individual effort for the increase of good in the world, this modest ideal suffices. To aid in the victory of the good is the common aim of the saints and the sages. *Socii Dei sumus*, Seneca repeated after Cleanthes.

And the fabulist gave this familiar variation of it, which has become proverbial:

> *Que chacun fasse son métier,*
> *Les vaches seront bien gardées.*

Whoever does his individual work fulfils the Law and the Prophets, he is in the order of things, he toils at the great Work, he rejoices mankind and the angels. *Age quod agis.* Be calm, laborious, resigned, and do your little task conscientiously. Heaven and earth ask no more of you.

*April 30, 1869.*—Finished the work of Vacherot,[1] which has filled me with reflections. I have the feeling that his notion of religion is not rigorously exact and that therefore the inferences need a little retouching. If religion is a psychological stage anterior to that of reason, it is clear that it must disappear in man, like the organs— saving man's grace—of the tadpole when the frog is formed; but if it is a mode of the inner life, it can and must endure as long as the need endures to feel, side by side with the need to think. The question is this: theism or non-theism? If God is only the category of the ideal, religion rightly vanishes like the illusions of adolescence. If the Being can be felt and loved as well as thought, the philosopher can speak in religion, as he speaks in art, in oratory and in citizenship. He can unite with a religious cult without any condescension. And I incline to this solution. What I call religion is life in the presence of God and in God.

And if we define God as the universal life, provided it is positive and not negative, our soul, pervaded with the feeling of the infinite, is in the religious state. Religion differs from philosophy as the naive self differs from the reflecting self, as synthetic intuition differs from intellectual analysis. One enters into religion through the feeling of voluntary dependence and joyous submission to the principle of order and the good. It is in religious emotion that man collects himself; he finds his place again in the infinite unity, and this feeling is sacred.

But, in spite of this reservation, I offer my acknowledgments to this work, which is a fine book, very mature and very serious. The author, too, is a noble character.

[1] *La Religion,* 1869.

*May 13, 1869.*—Great slashes in the clouds. Through the blue gaps a lively sun darts its roguish beams. Storms, smiles, whims, rages and tears: in May nature is a woman. She pleases the fancy, moves the heart and wearies the reason with her incessant caprices, and the unexpected vehemence of her extravagances.

This recalls to me the 213th verse of the second book of the Laws of Manu: "It is in the nature of the feminine sex to seek to corrupt man here below; and it is for this reason that the wise never abandon themselves to the seductions of women." Yet the same legislation has said: "Wherever women are honoured, the divinities are satisfied"; and elsewhere: "In every family in which the husband is pleased with his wife and the wife with her husband, happiness is assured"; and again: "A mother is more to be revered than a thousand fathers". But knowing how much is irrational and tempestuous in this frail and charming being, Manu concludes: "At no age should a woman be ruled according to her liking".

Even to this day, in several contemporary and neighbouring codes, woman is a minor all her life. Why? Because of her dependence on nature and her subjection to the passions, which are diminutives of madness, in other words because the soul of woman has something obscure and mysterious in it that lends itself to every superstition and enervates the virile forces. To man belongs law, justice, science, philosophy, all that is disinterested, universal, rational; woman, on the contrary, everywhere introduces favour, exception, personal prepossession. The moment a man, a people, a literature, an epoch becomes effeminate, it declines and diminishes. The moment woman quits the state of subordination in which she possesses all her merits, her natural defects increase visibly and rapidly. Complete equality with man makes her quarrelsome; domination makes her tyrannical. Honouring her and governing her will for a long time be the best solution. When education has formed strong, noble and serious women in whom conscience and reason dominate the effervescences of fancy and sentimentality, then we shall have to say: Honour woman and win her! She will be truly an equal, a fellow, a companion.

For the moment, she is this only in theory. The moderns are toiling at the problem and have not solved it.

*June 15, 1869.*—The deficiency of liberal Christianity lies in its too facile idea of sanctity, or, what comes to the same thing, a too superficial idea of sin.[1] The weakness of the half-liberals is repeated in the liberals, namely, a half-seriousness, a too expansive conscience, a salvation that is too accommodating, a religion without a real crucifixion, a redemption that comes too cheap, a too shallow psychology of the will, and especially of the perverse will: in a word, a sort of theological worldliness. On souls that are deeply pious they produce the impression of rather profane talkers who grate upon the deeper feelings by vocalizing on sacred themes. They shock the proprieties of the heart, they disquiet the reserves of the conscience by their indiscreet familiarities with the great mysteries of the inner life. They are like inveiglers of the spirit, instruments of the Prince of this world disguised as angels of light, religious rhetoricians after the fashion of the Greek Sophists, rather than guides on the *via dolorosa* that leads to salvation.—It is not to the men of wit, or even of science, that the empire over souls belongs, but to those who give the impression of having overcome nature by grace, of having passed by the burning bush and of speaking not the language of human wisdom but that of the divine will. In short, in the realm of religion, it is sanctity that makes authority, and love or the power of devotion and sacrifice that goes to the heart, persuades and touches.

What religious, poetic, tender, pure souls are least able to forgive is that their ideal should be reduced or diminished. That is why to touch Jesus seems to them a sacrilege and why it seems to them a transgression to open too wide the gates of paradise.—It never does to set an ideal against oneself; one must present another ideal, purer, higher, more spiritual; if possible, one must erect, behind

[1] At this time, in Geneva and all Protestant Switzerland, the debates between Orthodoxy and "liberal Christianity" had reached their liveliest pitch.

the loftiest peak, a peak that is loftier still. Thus one despoils no one, one strengthens everything by making people reflect, one gives a glimpse of a new aim to him who desires to change his aim. One only destroys that which one replaces, and one only replaces an ideal by satisfying all the conditions of the old one, together with certain advantages over and above.—When the liberal Protestants present Christian virtue with an inwardness, an intensity, a sanctity greater than those of old, and this in their own persons and in their influence, they will have passed the test required by the Master: the tree shall be known by its fruits.

*June 22, 1869 (9 a. m.).*—Drowsy weather. Out of doors everything is ugly, grey, lowering. A fly has died of the cold on my *Revue moderne,* in the midst of summer! What is life? I asked myself, as I looked at the lifeless insect. It is something lent to us, like motion. The universal life is a total sum that displays its units here and there, everywhere, as an electric wheel throws off sparks at its surface. Life passes through us; we do not possess it. Hirn [1] admits three irreducible principles: the atom, energy, the soul; the energy that acts upon the atoms, the soul that acts upon the energies. Probably he distinguishes between anonymous souls and personal souls. My fly would be an anonymous soul.

*(Same day).*—Now the national churches are contending against the Christianity that is styled liberal; Berne and Zürich have fired the first shots. Today, Geneva enters the lists. The Consistory, at the moment I am writing, is deliberating on two petitions, one for the omission of the creed in the liturgy, the other to permit Fontanès to preach. They will soon be doing the egg-dance.—It is becoming apparent that historical Protestantism is going to risk taking the final plunge, and that it has no longer a *raison d'être* between pure liberty and pure authority. It is, in fact, a provisional stage, founded on Biblicism, that is on the idea of a written revelation and a book divinely inspired and consequently authoritative. The moment this

[1] G. A. Hirn, Alsatian physicist (1815–1890).

thesis enters the class of fiction, Protestantism collapses. It will be obliged to fall back upon natural religion, or the religion of the moral consciousness. Messrs. Réville, Coquerel, Fontanès, Cougnard, Buisson accept the consequences. They are the vanguard of Protestantism and the laggards of free thought (Vacherot).

Their illusion lies in not seeing that every institution rests on a legal fiction and that every living thing admits of a possible logical misconstruction. To postulate a Church based upon free inquiry, absolute sincerity, is to be a logician; but to realize it is another matter. The Church lives by something positive, and the positive limits inquiry. They confound the right of the individual, which is to be free, with the duty of the institution, which is to be something. They take the principle of science for the principle of the Church, and this is a mistake. They do not perceive that religion is different from philosophy, and that the one attempts to unite people through faith whereas the other maintains the solitary independence of thought.

For bread to be good, it must have leaven, but the leaven is not the bread. That liberty should be the method for attaining an enlightened faith is all well and good, but people who could agree only by this criterion and this method could never found a Church, for they might differ entirely in regard to the result. Imagine a newspaper whose editors were of all possible parties; the paper would no doubt be curious, but it would have no opinion, faith or creed. A drawing-room filled with good company and polite conversation is not a Church, and a discussion, however courteous, is not a mode of worship. There is a confusion of kinds here.

*July 14, 1869.*—Lamennais! Heine! Tormented souls, one from having mistaken his vocation, the other from a desire to astound and mystify. The first lacked good sense and cheerfulness; the second lacked seriousness. The Frenchman was a violent and absolute dictator, the German a jeering Mephistopheles with a horror of philistinism. The Breton was all passion and melancholy, the Hamburger all caprice and malice. Neither of the two was a free being or had a normal life. Both, because of an early mistake, launched themselves into an endless quarrel with the world. Both were rebels. They did not fight for the good cause, for impersonal truth; both were the champions of their own pride. Both suffered much and died alone, rejected and accursed. Magnificent talents, devoid of wisdom, doing to themselves and others much more harm than good! The more intellectual power one has, the more dangerous it is to misconceive life and to begin it badly. It is just as with firearms: the greater the range of a rifle or a cannon, the greater the error that a simple deviation in the aim produces in the shot. How lamentable are those lives that are spent in maintaining an original defiance, or even a blunder, a slip!

These foolish wars, which invariably end in catastrophe, inspire in me a profound pity.—We think we are free, when we are usually the slaves of a fatality, and of the worst of fatalities, that of trifles! A mere nothing weighs upon our entire life, and we have the stupidity to be proud:

> *Marionettes du destin*
> *Ou pantins de la Providence,*
> *Chaque soir et chaque matin*
> *Se raillent de notre prudence.*

*July 20, 1869.*—Read five or six scattered chapters of Renan's *Saint Paul.* The author is often annoying with his ambiguous ways and his contradictory alternatives, intended to please every taste. In the last analysis, he is a free thinker, but one whose flexible imagination grants itself the delicate epicurism of religious emotion. He considers a person coarse if he will not lend himself to these gracious myths and narrow if he takes them seriously. He amuses himself with the variations of the conscience, as with the play of a kaleidoscope, but he is too refined to make fun of them. The true critic has neither conclusions nor exclusions; he likes to understand without believing, and to benefit from works of enthusiasm while retaining the freedom of a mind that is not encumbered with illusion. This manner of approach seems like a sort of juggling; it is nothing but the smiling irony of a very cultivated spirit, who wishes not to be a stranger to anything or the dupe of anything. It is the perfect dilettantism of the Renaissance.—With all this, countless perceptions and the joy of science! To see clearly, in all ways at once, is really something delightful.

*August 14, 1869.*— . . . In the name of heaven, who are you? What do you wish, inconstant, infixable being? What is your future, your duty, your desire? You long to find love, peace, the thing that will fill your heart, an idea you can defend, a work to which you can devote what remains of your strength, an affection that will quench your inward thirst, a cause for which you can die with joy. But will you ever find them? You feel a need for everything that is not to be found: the true religion, serious sympathy, the ideal life; you feel the need of paradise, eternal life, sanctity, faith, inspiration, who knows what? You would have to die and be reborn, reborn to a transformed self in a different world. You can neither stifle your aspirations nor be deceived by them. You seem to be condemned to roll unceasingly the rock of Sisyphus, to feel the waste of spirit of a being whose vocation and destiny are in perpetual discord. "Christian heart and pagan head", like Jacobi; tenderness and arrogance; breadth of mind and weakness of will; the two men of St. Paul, an ever-seething chaos of contrasts, antinomies, contradictions; humility and pride; a childlike candour and unlimited distrust; analysis and intuition; patience and irritability; kindness and dryness of heart; heedlessness and anxiety; vivacity and inertia; indifference and passion; all in all, incomprehensible and insupportable to myself and to others.

Left to myself, I return to the fluid, vague, indeterminate state of mind, as if every form were a violation and a disfiguration. All ideas and maxims, habits and acquirements are obliterated in me, like ripples on a wave, like the folds of a cloud; my personality has the minimum of individuality. I am to most men what the circle is to the rectilinear; I am at home everywhere, for I have no particu-

lar substance that bears a name.—All things considered, this imperfection has something good in it. Being less a man, I am possibly
closer to man in general, possibly a little more man. Being less an
individual, I am more the species. My nature, extraordinarily unfit
for practical life, is rather well adapted for psychological study. By
preventing me from adopting a course of my own, it permits me to
comprehend all courses . . .

It is not sloth alone that keeps me from coming to conclusions;
it is a sort of secret aversion for intellectual negative prescriptions. I feel that it takes all kinds to make a world, that all citizens
have rights in the State, and that if every opinon is equally insignificant in itself, all opinions are share-holders in the truth. Live and
let live, think and let think, are maxims that are equally dear to me.
My tendency is always towards the whole, the totality, balance. To
exclude, to condemn, to say no is difficult for me, except when things
themselves are exclusive. I always fight for the absent, for the lost
cause, for the neglected truth or portion of truth; which means that
I seek to complete every discussion, see every problem from all
sides, see everything in every possible aspect. Is this scepticism?
Yes, as a result; no, as an aim. It is the feeling for the absolute and
the infinite, reducing to their right value and putting in their place
the finite and the relative.

But here again your aspiration is greater than your talent; your
philosophic perception is superior to your speculative power; you
lack energy for your own views; your range is beyond your initiative. In your timidity you have allowed the critical intelligence to
consume the creative genius in you.—Is this really from timidity?

Alas, a little more ambition or good fortune might have made of
you a man such as you have never been but such as your youth gave
glimpses of.

*Villars, August 16, 1869.*—I am struck and almost alarmed to
find how well I reflect Schopenhauer's man: "That happiness is a
shadow and suffering a reality, that the negation of will and desire
is the path of deliverance, that individual life is a woe from which

impersonal contemplation can alone set one free", etc. But the principle that life is an evil and that nothingness is a good lies at the base of the system, and I have not dared to pronounce this axiom in a general way, admitting it as I do for this or that individual.— What I relish in the Frankfort misanthrope is his aversion to current prejudices, to all the hackneyed European thoughts, the hypocrisies of the Occidentals, the success of the moment. Schopenhauer is a great disillusioned spirit, professing Buddhism before all Germany and absolute detachment in the midst of the orgy of the nineteenth century. His chief defect is his utter aridity, his total and arrogant egoism, his adoration of genius and indifference to everything else, precisely when he is teaching resignation, abnegation, etc. What he lacks is sympathy, humanity, love. And here I recognize the dissimilarity between us. By pure intellection and solitary work, I could easily reach his point of view; but the moment the heart is aroused, I feel that contemplation is untenable. Pity, kindness, charity, devotion reassert their rights and even claim the first place.

*La grandeur la plus grande est encor la bonté.*

If anything is, God is; if God is, whatever is is of him; thenceforth life cannot be an evil; it must be, on the contrary, the diminution of evil and the growth of the good. The amplification of being thus becomes the universal law. The conversion of being into consciousness, increasing spiritualization and moralization are the reason of nature. God does not increase; but love multiplies itself by multiplying the instances of loving and being loved; and the world is the infinite laboratory of life, producing the infinite multitude of spirits, which in their turn produce the true form of the divine existence, namely, the infinite raised to the infinite power through the imperishable fecundity of intelligence and love.—Thus I protest against the desolate pessimism of Schopenhauer. The reduction of things to nothingness is a last resort.—The question is theism or non-theism.

*Charnex-sur-Clarens, August 29, 1869.*—A pleasant morning . . .
Spent some happy hours among the trees a hundred feet or so above
the village, meditated with Schopenhauer, soared high above the
blue waters, forgot my own sorry story and my pitiful self, as I
have done so often and as the Frankfort philosopher would have
one do. Gnats, ants and other little creatures of the woods devoured
me there, but my mind was free . . . Schopenhauer vaunts impersonality, objectivity, pure contemplation, the non-will, calm and disinterestedness, the aesthetic study of the world, detachment from
life, the abdication of all desire, solitary meditation, disdain of the
multitude, indifference to all the goods coveted by the vulgar. He
approves of all my defects, my childishness, my aversion to practical life, my antipathy for the utilitarians, my distrust of every desire. In a word, he flatters my natural inclinations, caresses them
and justifies them.

> *Redoutable flatteurs! présent le plus funeste*
> *Que puisse faire aux rois la colère céleste.*

This preëstablished harmony between Schopenhauer's theory and
my natural man causes me a pleasure that is mixed with terror.
I might indulge myself, but I am afraid to strew flowers on my conscience. Besides, I feel that goodness cannot admit this contemplative indifference and that virtue consists in overcoming oneself.

*Charnex, August 30, 1869.*—A few more chapters of Schopenhauer . . .—Schopenhauer believes in the immutability of the original elements of an individual and in the invariability of his nature.
He doubts the new man and the genuineness of the process of perfection, of any positive improvement in a being. The appearances alone
grow more refined. The bottom remains the same.—Is it possible
that he confuses nature, character and individuality? I am inclined
to think that individuality is fated and radical, that the nature,
however deep-rooted, is alterable, that character is a later development and susceptible of involuntary or voluntary modifications. In-

dividuality is a psychological thing, nature an aesthetic thing, and character alone is a moral thing. Liberty and the use of it have no share in the first two; character is the historical fruit and result of the life-development.—For Schopenhauer, character is identical with nature, as will is with passion. In a word, he simplifies too much and regards man from the more elementary point of view that is sufficient with the animal. He can call the vital and even chemical spontaneity by the name of will. But analogy is not equation; comparison is not reason; similitude and parable are not exact language. —Many of Schopenhauer's originalities evaporate when they are translated into a more exacting and more precise terminology.

*(Later.)*—Only half-opening the *Lichtstrahlen* [1] of Herder, one feels the difference from Schopenhauer. The latter abounds in strokes and perceptions that leap from the page and stand out in bold images. Herder is much less the writer; his ideas melt into their context and do not condense in any brilliant way, in crystals and gems. Where the latter advances by stretches and currents of thought that have no defined and sharply bounded contours, the other sows islets, salient, picturesque, original, that are impressed upon the memory. There is the same difference between Nicole and Pascal, Bayle and Saint-Simon.

What is the faculty that gives relief, lustre, keenness to thought? It is imagination. Through this, expression becomes concentrated and takes on colour and character. Individualizing what it touches, it vivifies and preserves it. The writer of genius turns sand into glass and glass into crystal, ore into iron and iron into steel; he marks with his talons every idea that he seizes. He borrows much from the common patrimony and returns nothing, but his very thefts are gladly granted him as private property. He has a sort of letter of credit, and the public allows him to take what he will.

*Charnex, August 31, 1869.*—Wandered over the wooded slopes.

---

[1] Collection of thoughts and fragments drawn from the writings of this author.

Read under the walnut-tree by the red house . . . Heavy, misty, congested weather.

| CONTRASTS | | ALTERNATION |
|-----------|---|-------------|
| | HARMONY | |
| EQUILIBRIUM | | TOTALITY |

Felt all the opposed systems clashing in my consciousness: stoicism, quietism, Buddhism, Christianity. It is in vain for Schopenhauer to preach to me abdication, resignation, immobility in order to attain peace; something within me objects and protests. The death of the will and desire, absolute disenchantment with life, this is easy for me, and for this very reason I suspect it. Is life only a trap, an illusion, a snare, an evil? I cannot believe this yet. Is love a superstition? A contemplation? An immolation? Is happiness only a tacitly accepted lie? Shall I never then be in accord with myself, shall I never be able either to practise my maxims or to make maxims of my practices? If impersonality is a good, why should I not persist in it; if it is a temptation, why should I return to it after having judged it and overcome it? In order to answer these questions, you would have to know, once and for all, what you most love, what you believe to be truest, what seems to you the most exact and the best.——The fundamental reason for my distrust is that the last wherefore of life seems to me a snare. The individual is eternally a dupe who never obtains what he seeks and is always cheated by what he hopes. My instinct concurs with the pessimism of Buddha and Schopenhauer. This incredulity persists at the very bottom of my religious impulses. Nature for me is indeed a Maya. And therefore I look upon it only with an artist's eyes. My intelligence remains sceptical. In what respect have I faith then? I do not know. And what do I hope for? It would be hard for me to say.——A mistake! You believe in goodness and you hope that the good will prevail. In your ironical, disillusioned nature a child still lives, a simple creature, a sorrowful but open-hearted spirit that believes in the ideal, in love, in sanctity, in all the angelic superstitions. A whole millennium of idylls sleeps in your heart. You are a mock sceptic, a mock neutral, a mock mocker.

> *Borné par sa nature, infini dans ses vœux,*
> *L'homme est un dieu tombé qui se souvient des cieux.*

*Charnex,*[1] *September 8, 1869 (9 a. m.).*—Magnificent weather. An hour of mute contemplation at my window. Watched the coming and going of the butterflies, the boarders, the cats, the swallows, the wisps of smoke over this vast and splendid landscape in which grace is blended with severity. Every creature seemed to delight in the joy of living, in this balmy air, under the caressing beams of this autumn sun. There is something blissful in this morning, as it were a breath from heaven graciously bathing the mountains and the shores; one somehow feels that one is under a benediction. No vulgar, no unseasonable sound breaks in upon this religious peace. It might all be one immense temple in which all the beauties of nature and all beings have their place. I do not dare to stir or breathe, I am so oppressed by emotion and so afraid of dispelling the dream, a dream filled with the wings of angels, a moment of holy ecstasy and intense adoration.

> *Comme autrefois j'entends, dans l'éther infini,*
> *La musique du temps et l'hosanna des mondes.*

[1] *Entre le clair miroir du lac aux vagues bleues*
*Et le sombre manteau du Cubly bocager,*
*Dévale, ondule et rit, à travers maint verger,*
*Sous les noyers pleins d'ombre, un gazon de deux lieues.*

*C'est ici, c'est Charnex, mon nid dans les halliers,*
*L'asile aimable et doux où mon loisir s'arrête:*
*Les Pléiades, le Caux, l'Arvel sont sur ma tête;*
*Chillon, Vevey, Clarens, Montreux sont à mes pieds.*
                                        —Amiel, *Jour à Jour.*

Like the goodwife of Fénelon, I am speechless and can say nothing but *Oh!* But this bare exclamation is a prayer, a transport of gratitude, wonder and tenderness. In these seraphic moments, one feels the cry of Pauline rise to one's lips: "I feel, I believe, I see!" All the woes, all the cares, all the griefs of life are forgotten, one is united with the joy of the universe, one enters into the divine order and the beatitude of the Lord. Labour and tears, sin, pain and death do not exist any more. Merely to be is to bless, and life is happiness. In this sublime pause, all the dissonances have disappeared. It is as if creation were nothing but a gigantic symphony, unfolding, at the feet of the God of goodness, its inexhaustible treasures of praise and harmony. One doubts no longer that this is so, one could not tell if it were otherwise. One has become oneself a note in this concert, and one emerges from the silence of rapture only to vibrate in unison with the eternal ecstasy.

*October 14, 1869.*—Yesterday, Wednesday, death of Sainte-Beuve. A great loss.

*October 16, 1869.*—*Laboremus!* seems to have been the motto of Sainte-Beuve as it was of Septimius Severus. He died on his feet, and the pen did not fall from his hand until the eve of the last day. He surmounted the sufferings of the body by the energy of his mind. Today, at this very hour, he is being laid in the breast of his foster-mother. He stood fast and refused the sacraments of the Church; he did not connect himself with any confession. He belonged to the *great diocese*, that of the independent seekers; he allowed himself no final hypocrisy. Like Voltaire and like Lamennais, he wished to deal with God quite alone, or perhaps with the mysterious Isis. Unmarried as he was, he died in the arms of his secretary. He was sixty-five years old. His power of work and memory was immense and unimpaired.

Who were his table-companions on Fridays? Scherer, Nefftzer, Weiss, Prévost-Paradol, Taine and a few others. What does Scherer think of this life and this death?

*October 19, 1869.*—A fine article by Edmond Scherer on Sainte-

Beuve, whom the *Temps* makes the prince of French critics and the last representative of the epoch of literary taste, the future being given over to the quacks and braggarts, to violence and mediocrity. The article breathes a certain virile melancholy, which is fitting in the obituary of a master of the things of the mind.

The fact is that Sainte-Beuve leaves a greater void than Béranger or Lamartine; these latter were already historical and far-away greatnesses, while he was still helping us to think. The true critic is a *point d'appui* for everybody. He is judgment itself, the public reason, the touchstone, the balance, the cupel that measures the value of everybody and the merit of every work. Infallibility of judgment is perhaps the rarest of all things, for it requires so many qualities in equilibrium, qualities both natural and acquired, qualities of mind and heart. How many years and labours, studies and comparisons are needful to bring the critical judgment to maturity! Like Plato's wise man, only at fifty does he reach the level of his literary priesthood, or, to be less pompous, his social function. Only then can he have made the rounds of all the ways of being, only then can he possess all the nuances of appreciation.—And to this infinitely refined culture Sainte-Beuve added a prodigious memory and an unbelievable multitude of facts and anecdotes stored up for the service of his thought.

*December 8, 1869 (8 a. m.).*—Lowering sky, grey atmosphere, cheerless weather. This landscape corresponds with the state of a downcast soul and a hopeless heart. My little pattering housekeeper, who puts up with everything, has just left, after bringing me the day's letters. I have breakfasted, and here I am at my desk, meditating before my work. Conscientious and solid labour, is not this still the thing that deceives us least?

I do not yet feel really established in my new lodging. I cannot place my hand instantly on every object, book, paper, garment or engraving. Nor do I know how to make the best use of my principal room, on which I counted the most. All sorts of things lie about or hang loose or get in the way. In short, the Bohemian in spite of himself is not yet settled. And a little comfort would be rather pleasant.—But, as my housekeeper said this morning, "The good God doesn't want us to be happy". This profound idea, which sums up the whole of Christian philosophy—for it is the pious glorification of suffering—has sunk into the consciousness of the humblest and least important. Unhappiness is what the good God wishes, therefore suffering is good. This prodigious paradox has become quite simple and even popular. It means that this life is only a trial of our patience, and that the true life is coming later. Christianity is a snare if the soul is not immortal, for it postpones justice and happiness until we reach heaven and only gives a foretaste of moral equilibrium through faith in the promises of the future. The religion of suffering is that of hope. "Blessed are they that mourn: for they shall be comforted."

From this I conclude that there is no means equal to religion for popularizing the great moral ideas. And I infer that as the need for authority on one point grows in proportion to one's emancipation in every other respect, the democracy of the future will always dispense less with religion and will even perhaps regress to Catholicism, in order to escape from moral atomism. The unbelieving epochs are always the cradles of new superstitions. "If a people is unwilling to believe, it has to serve."—One always has a religion, and a faith, just as one speaks prose, unawares, like Monsieur Jourdain. So the choice is not between faith and science, but between one faith and another, between a crude religion and a better one. It is possible that the religion of goodness, without hope of reward or immortality, in other words stoicism, may become some day the faith of humanity. Hitherto, however, this religion has only sufficed for the noblest souls, and paradise has been a necessity for Christians and for Moslems. If paradise were only an imperfect symbol of the Eternal Life, and consequently an illusion, its fortifying virtue would none the less have been a fact. The error of narrow minds lies in their not doing justice to illusion, in other words to relative truth, purely psychological and subjective. Vulgar intelligences always lack critical delicacy, and form the most naive idea of religious truth and even truth itself, because they do not comprehend the nature and the laws of the human mind. Phenomenology is a closed book for these pachydermatous beings who live on the surface of their souls. They are the dull, the dense, the obtuse, who see clearly only in arithmetic and mechanics and are incompetents in the moral world. Geometry is their domain; the *fieri*, the becoming, life, and consequently the last and deepest reality is not in their province or their game-bag.

But of what was I speaking? The necessity of a faith of some sort, to be able to act and live. Scepticism rigorously concludes in quietism. In doubt one abstains. Infinite uncertainty imposes absolute immobility. Therefore, if action is obligatory, one needs a hope, a persuasion, a faith to determine one's free will. Interest and duty are motives; but no motive has value except through a faith that is implied, faith in the good, for example, or faith in pleasure. It is true that such faith is an experience; but to believe in one's experience is already an act of faith, which a true sceptic might forbid himself. The basis of my certitude is therefore my inner experience, but its principle is the act of sovereignty by which I decide *motu proprio* and without reason that my experience is valuable, that it is true, that I believe in it. The passage from illusion to truth is thus a spontaneous act of will. The basis of certitude is our will. Without the will, we remain in scepticism. Without it, consciousness exists, but there is no knowledge and no reality.—But if the individual is at bottom nothing but a will, the universe, too, is nothing but a will. And if will is extinguished, everything vanishes like a dream. Will and imagination, in these consist all man and all nature. Reality is only the infinite phantasmagoria of the primordial Will. Maya is the dream of Brahma.—This is one of the great possible *Weltvorstellungen*. Schopenhauer has constructed his system from it.

*(Later)*.—This morning everything congealed me, the cold of the season, my own physical inertia, and especially the *Philosophy of*

*the Unconscious.*[1] This book establishes the desolate thesis that the creation is a mistake, that being, as it is, is worse than nothingness, and death is better than life.

I felt again the gloomy impression that *Obermann* caused me in my boyhood. The black dreariness of Buddhism enveloped me in its shades.—If, in reality, illusion alone·masks from us the horror of existence and gives us power to endure life, existence is a snare and life an evil. Like Annakeris, the Πεισιδάνατος, we must counsel suicide, or rather, with Buddha and Schopenhauer, work for the radical extirpation of hope and desire, which are the cause of life and resurrection. Not to be born again, that is the point, and that is the difficulty. Death is but a recommencement, and annihilation is the thing that matters. Since individuation is the root of all our sufferings, the problem is to avoid the infernal temptation and abominable possibility of it.—How impious this is! And yet it is all logical; it is the final consequence of the philosophy of happiness. Epicureanism ends in despair. The philosophy of duty is less disheartening.—And salvation lies in the reconciling of duty with happiness, in the union of the individual will with the divine will, in the faith that this supreme will is guided by love. If we are not to curse creation, we must believe, in spite of appearances and experience, that it is a work of love, and that the universal principle is at once wisdom, sanctity and goodness. If not, let it be anathema! And let us invoke nothingness.

*February 23, 1870.*—Recognized with terror the causes of my obsession of yesterday. They lay in the instinct of perversity; the instinct of bravado,—and the instinct of suicide. Whatever we may say, evil tempts because it is evil; Satan does not always need to disguise himself as an angel of light to make us listen to him and follow him; he piques our curiosity, and that is enough. People talk about the fear of danger, but danger also exerts a powerful and ver-

---

[1] Hartmann, *Philosophy of the Unconscious,* 1869.

tiginous attraction; one wishes to measure oneself with it and rejoice in one's strength.

We dwell upon the instinct of self-preservation, but the contrary instinct is also real. What is fatal to us excites an unhealthy relish in us, which is not blind but depraved.

So, too, that which hurts our conscience and self-interest may still be able to tempt us. Why? By flattering our instinct for revolt, which fears neither God nor devil, which does not admit the superior and rebels against all counsel and every injunction.—There is in us then the satanic element, there is an enemy of all law, a rebel who accepts no yoke, not even that of reason, duty or wisdom. This element is the root of all sin: *das radicale Böse* of Kant. Independence, the condition of individuality, is at the same time the eternal temptation of the individual. That which makes us what we are is also that which makes us sinners.

Sin is thus indeed in our very marrow, it runs in us like the blood in our veins, it is mingled with all our substance. Or rather I am putting it badly: temptation is our natural state, but sin is not necessary. Sin consists in a wilful confusion of the good with the bad independence; its cause is the semi-indulgence one grants to a first sophism. We close our eyes to the beginnings of evil because they are small, and in this weakness lies the germ of our overthrow.— *Principiis obsta.* This maxim, well followed, would preserve us from almost all our catastrophes.

We wish no other master than our caprice; which is as much as to say that our evil self does not desire God, that the bottom of our nature is seditious, impious, insolent, refractory, contradictory, and contemptuous of everything that presumes to dominate it, and consequently contrary to order, ungovernable and negative. It is this bottom that Christianity calls the natural man. But the savage that is in us and constitutes our primitive substance must be disciplined, policed, civilized in order to produce a man. And the man must be patiently cultivated to become a wise man. And the wise man must be tried to become a just man. And the just man must have replaced his will with the will of God to become a holy man. And this new man, this regenerate man, is the spiritual, the heavenly man, of whom the Vedas, like the Gospel, speak, the Magi like the neo-Platonists.

*March 17, 1870 (11 a. m.).*—A fine brass band has just played a few pieces in the street, in the rain. It was most comforting for the inner man. O Pythagoras, if music thus transports us to heaven, it is because music is harmony, and harmony is perfection, and perfection is our dream, and our dream is heaven.—This world of strife, bitterness, selfishness, ugliness, misery makes us sigh involuntarily for the eternal peace, for boundless adoration and bottomless love. It is not so much the infinite that we thirst for as it is beauty. It is not being and the limitations of being that weigh upon us; it is evil, within us and outside us. It is not necessary to be great, provided one is in order. Perfection in the relative perfectly suffices our need for the absolute. Moral ambition is without pride; it desires only to be in its place, to sing its note well in the universal concert of the God of love. The sanctity of the servitor, without power, without knowledge, without dignity is all the felicity it wishes. To be only a worm, but in the way of God, was the desire of Cleanthes and of Thomas à Kempis . . .

I do not know whether it is Dixon's chapter on the *Shakers*,[1] or the fact of convalescence, or that of the music, but I feel a great need of religious meekness: "As much as lieth in you, live peaceably with all men." Seclusion, labour, meditation, prayer, in the manner of the Essenes, smile upon me as a life to choose. A loving, pious inwardness, calm and cultivated, is almost the only thing that tempts me.—The contemplative and mystical instinct reawakens in me. But I remember that I am wavering and many-minded: *Homo sum, nihil humani* . . . Let us do our task.

*March 30, 1870.*—Nature is indeed iniquitous, shameless, without probity or faith. She will admit only gratuitous favour and insensate

---

[1] W. H. Dixon, *New America*, 1867.

aversion, and has no thought of compensating one injustice save by another. The happiness of the few is therefore expiated by the unhappiness of the many . . . Useless to cavil with a blind force.

The human conscience revolts against this law, and, in order to satisfy its instinct for justice, it has conceived two hypotheses out of which it has constructed a religion: the first, the idea of an individual providence, the second that of another life. If our incomprehensible accidents and misfortunes are the paternal dispensations of a God whose will it is to try us, our revolt at once yields to the spirit of filial submission. If the astonishing iniquities of this world are to be made good later, in a better existence, where there will be joy for all the afflicted and where justice dwells, the trials at once become endurable. Thus from faith in a divine protection and the hope of a reparative immortality humanity draws its courage, and this is the vivifying method by which it is reconciled to the harshness of destiny.

It is indeed a protest against Nature, declaredly immoral and scandalizing. Man believes in goodness, and, to exalt the just alone, he affirms that the injustice he encounters is but an appearance, a mystery, a deception, and that justice will be done.

*Fiat justitia, pereat mundus!*

It is a great act of faith. And since humanity did not create itself, this protestation has some chance of expressing a truth. If there is a conflict between the natural world and the moral world, between reality and conscience, conscience must be right.

It is by no means necessary that the universe should be, but it is necessary that justice should be done, and atheism is obliged to explain the absolute stubbornness of the conscience on this point. Nature is not just, and we are the products of nature; then why do we demand and prophesy justice? Why does the effect assert itself against its cause? This is a singular phenomenon. Does this demand spring from a puerile blindness of human vanity? No, it is the profoundest cry of our being, and it is for the honour of God that this cry is uttered. Heaven and earth may pass away; but the good must be and injustice must not be. This is the credo of the human species. And it is right. Therefore, the Spirit will overcome nature, and the Eternal will have the best of time.

*April 1, 1870.*—It is natural enough that for woman, following the intention of nature and often indeed after every kind of lay or ecclesiastical instruction, religion should be love, and that love should consequently be the supreme authority, that which judges the rest and decides what is good. For man love is subordinate to the good; it is a grand passion, but it is not the source of order, the synonym of reason, the criterion of excellence. It seems then that woman has for an ideal the perfection of love, and man the perfection of justice.—It is in this sense that St. Paul was able to say that the woman is the glory of the man and the man the glory of God.— Thus the woman who is absorbed in the object of her tenderness, who makes an idol of her hero, is, so to speak, in the line of nature, she is truly woman, she is queen in the art of loving, she does not demean herself, she is radiant, she realizes her fundamental type. On the other hand, a man who confined his life to conjugal adoration, and imagined he had lived enough in making himself the priest of a beloved woman, would be only a half-man; such men are despised by the world and perhaps even secretly scorned by women themselves. The really loving woman wishes to lose herself in the effulgence of the man of her choice; it is her longing that her love should render the man greater, stronger, manlier, more active. Here each of the sexes is playing its proper role: woman is rather destined for man, and man is destined for society, and each of them finds his peace, his satisfaction and happiness only when he has discovered this law and accepted this equilibrium.—What would be idolatrous for the one is thus not so for the other. The aim of a being determines that which constitutes its form of beauty. And thus the same thing may be good in woman and bad in man, valour in the former, weakness in the latter.

There is, therefore, a feminine morality and a masculine morality, preparatory chapters, as it were, of human morality; beneath the angelic and sexless virtue, there is a *sexualized* virtue. And this latter is the occasion of a reciprocal instruction, each of the two incarnations of life applying itself to converting the other, the first preaching love to justice, the second justice to love. From this results an oscillation and a mean that represent a social state, an epoch, at times an entire civilization. Such, at least, is our European idea of the harmony of the sexes in the hierarchy of functions.

*April 15, 1870 (8 a. m.).*—It humiliates me to begin anew the series of winter afflictions: catarrh, colds, fatigue in the eyelids, the brain, the back. Does it mean that health wishes to smile on me only at intervals? Must I always feel that my carcass is damaged at one point or another? Is the sun going to injure me now, as the shadow did before? Am I irremediably out of order? . . . What I find unbearable in my situation is my wearing away more than is reasonable, being destroyed quietly, by inches, uselessly and needlessly, from simple ignorance of what is expedient for me or because it is a nuisance to take care of myself.—All gratuitous destruction of life, every avoidable demolition of a masterpiece, seems to me ferocity and vandalism. In this I come back to my antipathy to stupid suffering, unhappiness where one has an option, devotion that is unintelligent. To die for a good cause is all very well, but to die for a folly is repugnant to me . . . When one has loved useless action so much, one must harden oneself to the idea of accidental decrepitude and premature death, for this is only so much more of the useless . . . Nature and men conspire equally to demolish us and to return us to the dust, before we go back to our native ashes. To live is to defend oneself, to conquer, to impose oneself without respite or relaxation; it is continually to maintain oneself by a renewed cohesion, to affirm oneself through will, to dilate through production; it is to execute a continuous *tour de force* of unwearying equilibration. The moment the game fatigues us and the struggle tires us, we are lost. It is just as it is with a man travelling in the tropics: the moment he ceases to kill, he is devoured. To live is incessantly to fight death, night, nothingness; it is to feed, like a Guebre, the flame of one's personality, to be the protector of that phantasmal individuality, the griffin of that imaginary treasure, the conscientious warder of that soul whose pain alone attests its existence to us and which has no more consistency than a tenacious dream or a chronic nightmare . . .

Crucifixion!—That is indeed the word to ponder on this day. Is it not Good Friday?

> *L'art de la vie, ami, tu voudrais le connaître,*
> *Il est tout dans un mot: employer la douleur.*

Are you going to reprove suffering now as vain, as useless, ferocious, tyrannical, when once you were able to draw a lesson and a good from it? To curse it is easier than to bless it, but this is to fall back into the point of view of the earthly, the carnal and natural man. Through what has Christianity overcome the world, if not through its divination of suffering, through that marvellous transfiguration of punishment into triumph, of the crown of thorns into a crown of glory, and of a gallows into the symbol of salvation? What signifies the apotheosis of the cross, if not the death of death, the defeat of sin, the beatification of martyrdom, the *imparadising* of voluntary sacrifice, the defiance of pain?

"O death, where is thy sting? O grave, where is thy victory?" By force of working on the theme of the agony of the Just, peace in agony, and radiance in peace, humanity has realized that a new religion has been born, that is, a new way of explaining life and understanding suffering.

Suffering was a curse from which men fled: it becomes a purification of the soul, a sacred trial sent by eternal love, a divine dispensation intended to sanctify us, a succour that faith will accept, a strange initiation into happiness. O power of faith! Everything remaining the same, everything is yet changed. A new certitude denies the appearance; it transpierces the mystery, it places an invisible father behind visible nature, it causes joy to shine from the depths of tears and makes of pain the first incarnation of felicity.

And lo, for those who have believed, the grave becomes heaven; on the pyre of life, they sing the hosanna of immortality; a holy madness has renewed all things for them, and when they wish to express what they feel, their rapture makes them incomprehensible; they speak in *tongues*. The ecstatic frenzy of devotion, the scorn of death, the thirst for eternity, the delirious desire for crucifixion, all this the incorruptible mildness of the Crucified has been able to arouse. By pardoning his executioners, and by feeling himself, in spite of all, indissolubly united with his God, Jesus, from the height of his cross, kindled an inextinguishable fire and revolutionized the world. He proclaimed and realized salvation through faith in the infinite mercy and in the forgiveness granted only to repentance. By saying: "Joy shall be in heaven over one sinner that repenteth, more than over ninety and nine just persons, which need no repentance", he made humility the gate of entry into paradise.

Crucify the ungovernable self, mortify yourself completely, give all to God, and the peace that is not of this world will descend upon you. For eighteen centuries no greater word has been uttered; and although mankind seeks an application of justice that is always more exact and more complete, it secretly has no faith save in forgiveness, the forgiveness that alone reconciles the inviolable perfection of purity with infinite pity for weakness, that safeguards, in other words, alone the idea of sanctity, while at the same time permitting the free flight of love. The Gospel is the tidings of the unutterable consolation, that which appeases all the sorrows of earth, and even the terrors of the King of Terrors, the tidings of irrevocable forgiveness, which means the eternal life. The cross is the warrant of the Gospel. It has been its standard.

Humanity has believed Jesus, it has believed him in his word and in his example; it has even believed in him and made him its God. If the true God is he who consoles, who sanctifies and strengthens, then has not Jesus on these grounds won his divinity? Who can doubt that the passionate gratitude of the heart imposes certain illusions on the mind? But what is harmful in this? It is through its affections and adorations that the human soul rises, and not only the soul of every individual but the soul of humanity also.

*May 7, 1870.*—The faith that clings to its idols and resists all innovation acts as a retarding and conservative force; but it is the property of every religion to serve as a check on our unlimited emancipation and stabilize our restless disquiet. Curiosity is the impulsive, expansive, radiating force which, dilating us beyond all bounds, would volatilize us *ad infinitum;* belief represents the gravitation, the cohesion, the concretion that makes bodies of us, particular individuals. A society lives by its faith and is developed by its science. Its base is thus mystery, the unknown, the foreshadowed, the intangible, religion; its ferment is the need to know. Its permanent substance is the uncomprehended or the divine; its changing form is the result of its intellectual labour.—The unconscious adherence, the vague intuition, the obscure presentiment that determines the first faith is therefore paramount in the history of peoples. All history moves between religion, which is the genial, instinctive and fundamental philosophy of a race, and philosophy, which is the ultimate religion, that is, the clear perception of the principles that have engendered the whole spiritual development of humanity.

It is the same thing that is, that was and that will be, but this thing manifests with more or less transparency and depth the law of its life and its metamorphoses. This thing is the absolute. So far as it is fixed, it is called God; so far as it is changing, the world or Nature. God is present in nature, but nature is not God; there is a nature in God, but it is not God himself.—I am neither for immanence nor for transcendence, exclusively. I hold that, in the absolute, the eternal is as true as the changing, mind as true as nature, the ideal as the real, noumenon as phenomenon, and that the whole phantasmagoria of being is only being under the category of unfolding without in any way increasing the sum of being. Just as all chemical metamorphoses are indifferent in the scales, and as the formation or dissolution of a solar system does not by one atom change the quantity of cosmic matter, so there is change of state but neither increase nor diminution of being in being. If humanity perished, a great efflorescence would be lost, but what would this matter in eternity? The absolute as subject is thought, and as object is nature. Supposing that the absolute were for an instant to cease its inner activity, and fall back into the sleep of Brahma, the universe would vanish, but only to begin again with the reawakening of the absolute.—It is the greatness of man that he can dream the dream of God and in his monad reconstruct the architecture of the infinite. But the work is always beginning anew, because each life is only a flash and each mind only a soap-bubble that is made iridescent by this flash.

*May 9, 1870.*—Disraeli, in his new novel (*Lothair*), shows that the two great forces at present are revolution and Catholicism, and that the free nations are lost if either of these two forces triumphs. This is exactly my idea. Only, while in France, in Belgium, in Italy and in Catholic societies, it is only through a deadlock between these two forces that the State and civilization can be maintained, in Protestant States things are better: there is a third force, a mediating faith between the two other idolatries, which makes liberty here not a neutralization of two contraries, but a moral reality, subsisting of itself, having in itself its centre of gravity and its motive principle. In the Catholic world, religion and liberty reciprocally deny each other, in the Protestant world they accept each other: thus much less force is wasted in the second case. Catholic Christendom is therefore in an inferior situation; it has fallen from the first rank. The Anglo-Saxon race is in the ascendant historically at the present time.

Liberty is the laic and philosophic principle, the juridical and social aspiration of our species. But as there is no society without a rule, without a check, without a limitation of individual liberty, especially without a moral limitation, it is fitting that the freest people legally should have for ballast its religious consciousness; this is the way it is in the United States. In mixed States, Catholic or atheist, the limitation, being penal only, incessantly incites men to contravene it. This is the spectacle that France presents whenever it returns to the Republic.

The puerility of the free thinkers consists in their believing that a free society can stand and preserve its cohesion without a common faith, without some kind of religious prejudice. Wherein consists the will of God? Does the common reason express it, or is a clergy, a Church, the depository of it? As long as the answer is ambiguous, doubtful and oblique in the eyes of half or more than half of the conscious population (and this is the case in all States where the population is Catholic), public peace is impossible and public law is unstable. If there is a God, one must have him for oneself; and if there were none, it would be necessary first to win everybody over to one identical idea of what is right or useful, that is, to construct a lay religion, before one could build solidly in politics.

Liberalism feeds on abstraction when it thinks that freedom is possible without free individuals, and when it overlooks the fact that freedom in the individual is the fruit of a previous education, a moral education that presupposes a liberating religion. To preach liberalism to a population that has been Jesuitized by its education is like recommending marriage to a eunuch or dancing to a one-legged man. How could a child walk if its swaddling clothes had never been unfastened? How could an abdication of one's conscience conduce to a government by one's conscience? To be free is to be one's own director, it is to have come of age, to be emancipated, master of one's acts, judge of the good; and ultramontane Catholicism never emancipates its flocks, who are obliged to accept, believe, obey, because they are always minors and because the clergy alone possess the law of the good, the secret of the just, the norm of the true.—That is where the idea of external revelation leads, skilfully exploited by a patient priesthood.

But what surprises me is the short-sightedness of the statesmen of the South, who do not see that the capital question is the religious question, and who, even now, do not yet perceive that the liberal State is unrealizable with an anti-liberal religion, and almost unrealizable in the absence of religion. They confound accidental conquests and precarious advances with definitive results.

I believe that in France, on the contrary, everything is possible, and that everything can be lost anew, in the matter of liberty. France will be socialistic and communistic before it will be able to realize the liberal republic, because equality is infinitely easier to establish than liberty, and felling a hundred trees is a shorter business than making one grow. Socialism is a confession of impotence. And there is a certain likelihood that the uproar which is going on professedly in behalf of liberty may end in the abolition of liberty: I can see that the International, the irreconcilables and the ultramontanes aim equally at absolutism and dictatorial omnipotence. Happily, they are many, and they can be set by the ears.

If liberty is to be saved, it will not be by the doubters, the phenomenalists, the materialists, it will be by religious convictions, it will be through the faith of individuals who believe that God wishes man to be free but pure, it will be through those who aspire to sainthood, through those antiquated devotees who speak of immortality, the eternal life, who prefer the soul to the whole world, those who have escaped from the secular faith of mankind.

In the conflict of light with darkness, I believe then that a purified religion, primitive Christianity, will be a force for equity. This is what will disillusion people in regard to false progress and false liberty, by maintaining the ideal of a human life that is saintly, truly noble, worthy of heaven.

*June 5, 1870.*—The efficacious in religion lies precisely in what is not rational, philosophical or eternal; the efficacious lies in the unforeseen, in the miraculous, in the extraordinary, in the anecdotal. Religion is loved the more, the more it demands faith, that is, the less credible it is for the profane. The philosopher wishes to explain mysteries and resolve them into light. And it is mystery itself that the religious instinct demands and pursues, mystery that makes the essence of worship and the power of proselytism. When the cross has become the madness of the cross, it has transported the multitudes. And even in our time, those who wish to dissipate the supernatural, to clarify religion and husband faith, are as little encouraged as poets would be who spoke against poetry or women who disparaged love. The spell of religion lies in faith; faith is the adoption of the incomprehensible, and even the pursuit of the incomprehensible; and faith becomes intoxicated with its own offerings and with its multiplied exaltations. Like a loving woman, it finds its delight in sacrifice, and the more one demands devotion of it the happier it is.

It is the ignoring of this psychological law that makes the liberals so obtuse; it is the understanding of it that gives its strength to Catholicism . . .

It seems as if no positive religion could survive the supernatural which is its *raison d'être*. Natural religion appears to be the tomb of all the historic cults. All concrete religions perish in the pure air of philosophy. As long, therefore, as the life of the peoples needs the religious principle as a motive force, as the sanction of morality and the nourishment of faith, hope and love, so long will the multitudes turn from pure reason and naked truth, so long will they adore the mystery, so long and rightly will they rest in faith, the one realm in which the ideal can appear for them in the form of a compelling charm.

*June 9, 1870 (8 a. m.).*—I awoke an hour too late for the first train for Lausanne and gave up the meeting of the Historical Society, not without a secret self-dissatisfaction, for it would have been better to meet these colleagues and consult the general opinion a little than to moulder away here in my alchemist's cell. But it is always the same thing. I like to be left out, by chance or by impossibility. The *too late* is in league with my apathy, and only in appearance do I dread the sight of a steamer, a carriage, an occasion or a joy setting off without me.

> *Là-bas, là-bas!*
> *Est le bonheur, dit l'espérance.*

But, as my tendency is not towards hope, I say to myself:

> *Là-bas, là-bas!*
> *Est l'ennui, la déception.*

And I remain in my retreat. Truly, with more or less of that one element, hope, in the soul, everything changes. All a man's activity, all his efforts, all his undertakings presuppose in him the hope of attaining an end; once this hope vanishes, movement is meaningless, it is only spasmodic and convulsive, like that of a person falling from a steeple. There is something childish in striving in the face of the inevitable. To entreat the law of gravity to suspend its action would surely be a grotesque prayer. Well, when one loses faith in the efficacy of one's efforts, when one says to oneself: You will be no better this way than that; you are incapable of realizing your ideal; happiness is a phantom, progress is an illusion, perfection is a snare; even if all your ambitions were satisfied, you would find in them only emptiness, satiety and bitterness of heart,—

> *Ixion, Sisyphe et Tantale,*
> *Les suppliciés de l'espoir,*
> *Démontrent à qui veut le voir*
> *Que toute espérance est fatale;*

it dawns upon one that a little blindness is necessary for living, and that illusion is the universal motor. Complete disillusion would mean absolute immobility. He who has deciphered the secret of the finite life, and who has read its riddle, escapes from the Great Wheel of existence; he has come forth from the world of the living, he is no longer a dupe, he is indeed dead. Is this perhaps the meaning of the

ancient belief that to raise the veil of Isis or to behold God face to
face annihilates the rash mortal? Egypt and Judea had verified the
fact, Buddha alone gave the key to it: that individual life is a nonentity which is unaware of itself, and that the moment this nonentity
becomes aware of itself individual life is abolished in principle. The
moment the illusion vanishes, nonentity resumes its eternal reign,
the suffering of life is ended, error has disappeared, time and form
have ceased to be for this enfranchised individuality; the coloured
bubble has burst in infinite space and the misery of thought is dissolved in the immutable repose of the unlimited Nothing. The absolute, if it were spirit, would still be activity; and it is activity, the
child of desire, that is incompatible with the absolute. The will is
a restless thing. The absolute must be the zero of all determination,
and the only manner of being that befits it is Non-existence.

*June 15, 1870 (5.30 p. m.)*.—Overwhelming heat, clouded sky,
light like that of an eclipse, gloomy aspect of all things. It seems
to me as if we were crossing the tail of a comet and as if all living
creatures were about to be extinguished in the aridity of this thick
air. The torpifying influence overcomes my brain and beclouds my
understanding. I do not react alertly to the outer world, and I have
no clear perception of my freedom. How frightful is nature and
how desolate life when one regards them through the yellowish
glass of such an impression as this: it is as if the ball of the eye
were injected with soapy water. I feel as if I were drowning in
ugliness. Never have my shabby shutters, my yellowed curtains, my
faded carpets, my shelves, with all the books topsy-turvy, appeared
so disagreeable to my eyes. Never has my face looked so unpleasant
and aged. O light, O youth, O freshness, O beauty, I feel vague
temptations to adore you; you absent ones, you whom my heart
calls and regrets; you, blessings vanished and lost; you, enchantment of the senses and the imagination! I am seized with a dislike
for everything that limps, halts, whines and grimaces, everything
that has lost its freshness, that is nicked and worn, and I feel, as
a little girl of fifteen might feel, an instinctive aversion to every-

thing unpleasant, everything that is old, my *Wenigkeit* included.

Under the spell of this aversion, one would gladly proclaim the divine right of the beautiful and the obliteration of ugliness in all its forms. And yet, such is my apathy that, even while repudiating the ugliness in everything that surrounds me and depends upon me, furniture, rooms, clothes, etc., I do not feel in the least the courage to create elegance and grace about me or to mould things to the taste of my ideal. These architectonics are the business of woman; it is she who should arrange, ornament, decorate life. I should feel a kind of shame in fitting up my interior as a clever woman would do it, spending money without hesitation for my personal comfort. A ready-made paradise enchants me; but to build a nest for myself alone is repugnant to me.

Alas, in this, as in all else, I am only too certain to die without having seen my dream realized. I have, so to speak, renounced *en bloc* the hope of ever being satisfied in anything I do; and this gives me, if not contentment, at least calm. The sighs one has told off do not prevent a fundamental resignation. It is easier to stifle than to satisfy one's desires: this is the course I have ordinarily taken, even with things that might have been within my reach.

*June 16, 1870.*—Reading: reread the *Cid*, with all the supplementary documents, notices and dedications; and the biography of Corneille by Louandre.

Corneille is an excellent example of the want of harmony and balance, so frequent among the moderns, which would have revolted the aesthetic sense of the ancients: a feeling for the sublime, a childish ignorance of the world, grandeur and clumsiness, heroism and lack of wit, pride and servility, loftiness of invention, stupid, heavy, tedious dialogue, the talent for writing verses, an inability to read them tolerably; a great man but a great clown. Is it not odd that all this should exist together, and that a noble soul should be cloaked in the semblance of a numskull and a boor?—Whence does this arise? From our ridiculous education, especially that of the seventeenth century, from our social division, which subverts the man in the interest of classes, and ranges individuals, especially under a monarchy, like the genera, species and families of insects or crustaceans in the show-cases of our museums. The civilization that is called Christian has, in eighteen centuries, been unable to fashion complete, free, noble men, such as the age of Pericles created. The outside and the inside do not correspond among the moderns. This is because it is easier to create prodigies and monsters than genuine men; every excess is more realizable than beauty. We are so far from being able to organize the individual and the social life after the aesthetic ideal that we do not even have this hope in the Utopian state. With us it goes without saying that harmony and the beautiful are rare flashes of lightning in our cloudy world. Therefore the most salient characteristic of our historical world is contradiction, or, in other words, discord, dissonance, ugliness, sham. —And to top it all, we try to extract vanity from this grotesque lack, as a toad might establish by conclusive reasons that warts are an element of distinction because his own back is covered with these foul rugosities.

Our infatuation with ourselves, while true men are so rare, is a sorry buffoonery.

*July 3, 1870.*—Reading: Gérusez (*Calvin*; *Anne Dubourg*; *Rabelais*). The French point of view, in regard to Protestantism, is always absurdly contradictory. The national chauvinism seems incurable in its fatuity, and brings to mind that of the song of *La Palice*. For it, there are two things that go without saying: that the national genius is sacrosanct, and that the age-old preceptors, Romanism and monarchy, although they may be suspected of abuse, are none the less above discussion, except from the revolutionary point of view. Protestantism, accordingly, which, on the one hand, is not very Catholic and has small respect for monarchical absolutism, and, on the other hand, would have forestalled the Revolution, is repudiated, in advance, as having risked changing the history of France. That naive optimism which consists in saying, There is nobody like us and we are perfectly content with what we are, is truly farcical. It suggests a hunchback who would like to become a handsome man without losing his hunch. The French, like all amiable sinners, cling to their sins as they cling to their salvation, and will concede in detail everything one wishes provided they can take back *en bloc* everything they have conceded.—Is it not silly to criticize the consequences of an institution and stop short at the institution itself, or to grow indignant over the burning of Anne Dubourg while one is casting stones at Calvin? Writers like Gérusez wear out one's patience with their puerility. They understand only a mocking, sterile opposition, never the heroic remedy. They accept Rabelais, the Fronde, Menippean satire, Voltaire, but they are afraid of men of a serious cast of mind. They wish the effect without the causes and the fruit without the tree, which is high treason against good sense. "The triumph of Calvin would have changed the nature of France!" Gérusez takes this for an argument; it is clear that if one puts on boots, one is no longer in slippers. The only real question is whether, for crossing the muddy spots of history, one kind of footwear is not better than another. Does the history of France, say, since Louis XI, show us a model people, moral, prosperous, free, happy, enviable? Say yes, and let us speak no more of it. If you say no, your optimism ceases to buttress French society, whose secret vices and deep superstitions can then be laid bare. One of its vices is the frivolity that substitutes public proprieties for truth and absolutely disregards personal dignity and the majesty of conscience. The people of appearances is ignorant of the ABC of individual liberty and persists in a wholly Catholic intolerance towards ideas that do not win the universal mind, that is, the majority of beliefs. The nation regards itself as a flock making up mass, number and force, but not as an assemblage of free men in which individuals derive their worth from themselves. An eminent Frenchman derives his worth from others; if he has the stripes of office, the cross, the sash, the sword, the cassock, in a word, the function and the decoration, he is considered to be something and he feels himself to be somebody. It is the insignia that declares his merit, it is the public that raises him out of nonentity, as the Sultan creates his viziers. These sheep-like, disciplined, sociable races have an antipathy to individual independence; with them everything must derive from military, civil or religious authority, and God himself does not exist so long as he has not been decreed. Their instinctive dogma is thus social omnipotence, which treats as usurpation and sacrilege the pretension of truth to being true without an official stamp, and that of the individual to possessing a solitary conviction and a personal worth.—Everyone must do as everybody does,—this formula, characteristically French, contains in itself the justification of every tyranny, every vulgarity, every persecution and every platitude.

*Bellalpe,*[1] *July 20, 1870 (3 p. m.).*—The panorama is one of grandeur and majesty. It is the symphony of the mountains, a cantata of the Alps to the sun.

I am dazzled and overwhelmed by it. And what dominates is the joy of being able to admire, that is, of having become a contemplator again through physical well-being, able to escape from myself and give myself to things, which is my normal state when I am well. Gratitude is mingled with enthusiasm. I am coming back to myself. What a blessing!

*(8 p. m.).*—Spent two hours, at the foot of the Sparrenhorn, in a continuous rapture.—Drowned in sensations. Looked, felt, dreamed, thought.

*Bellalpe, July 21, 1870 (4 p. m.).*—Climbed the Sparrenhorn (9050 feet) after breakfast. This peak on which we are perched demands of the tourist a walk of two and a quarter hours (I came down in one hour and a quarter). The summit is not very easy to reach, because of the loose rocks and the steepness of the path, which skirts two chasms. But how one is rewarded!

It was perfectly beautiful weather. The view embraces the whole chain of the Valaisian Alps, from the Furka to the Combin, and

[1] Bellalpe, an Alpine station above Brigue, is situated on the southern watershed of the northern range of the Valais, facing the Simplon pass. "Villars was a nest, but Bellalpe is an eyrie", the author said once.

even a few hoary Ticinese peaks beyond the Furka; and if one turns around, one sees behind one a whole polar world of snow-banks and glaciers forming the southern back of the enormous Bernese massif of the Finsteraarhorn, the Mönch and the Jungfrau. This massif is repeated in the Aletschhorn, about which pivot the ribbons of the various Aletsch glaciers, twisting in front of the peak from which I was contemplating them. The five superimposed zones, fields, woods, grass, bare rocks, snow, and the four kinds of moun-tains, varying with their height (wooded, grassy, rocky, snowy mountains).—Among the mountains of the first magnitude, the principal types: the table, Monte Leone; the cupola, the Fletscher-horn; the dome, Monte Rosa; the pagoda, the Mischabel, with its four ridges like flying buttresses and its group of nine peaks in a sheaf; the pyramid, the Weisshorn; the obelisk, the Cervin (pick, tooth, horn, needle).

About me fluttered butterflies in pairs, curious flies and insects with spidery legs; but no plants grew, save a few lichens. Flurried evolution of a big white cloud over my head.—The empty bottle, with the names of tourists who have been up since July 4, names written on bits of paper.—The great, void, dead spectacle of the upper Aletsch glacier, a glacial Pompeii.—Blue gentians, pansies, marguerites, buttercups, forget-me-nots, anemones. No eyebrights. Thick, resilient grass. A few saxifrages. Stayed an hour at the top.

The backs of the rocks are levelled with the sun; the circular depressions like grass-covered cupolas, the transition between the rocky zone and the grassy zone.

*Bellalpe, July 22, 1870 (4.30 p. m.).*—The sky, misty and streaked this morning, has become perfectly blue again, and the giants of the Valais are bathed in the tranquil light.

Whence comes this solemn melancholy, besieging and oppressing me? I have just been reading a series of scientific works (Bronn, *Laws of Paleontology;* Karl Ritter, *Laws of Geographical Forms,* etc.) and a good many other articles from the *Revue germanique* of 1859. Is this perhaps the cause of my inner sadness? Is it the majesty of this immense landscape, the splendour of this sinking sun that almost makes me weep?

"Creature of a day, of an hour's agitation," I know what it is that seems to suffocate you, the sense of your nonentity. These names of great men (Humboldt, Ritter, Schiller, Goethe), which have just passed under your eyes, remind you that you have been able to do nothing with your gifts; this Revue of 1859 is a secret reproach for the paltry employment of your last eleven years; and this great, impassive nature tells you that tomorrow you will disappear, an ephemera, without having done your work, without having lived. Is it even perhaps the breath of eternal things that makes you shudder as Job shuddered? What is man, that grass which a sunbeam withers and which is cast into the furnace? What is our life in the infinite gulf? I feel a sort of sacred terror, and no longer only for myself, but for my species, for everything that is mortal. Like Buddha, I feel the Great Wheel turning, the wheel of the universal illusion, and in this mute stupor there is a veritable anguish. Isis lifts the corner of her veil, and the vertiginousness of the spectacle confounds him who beholds the great mystery. I do not dare to breathe or stir; I seem to be suspended by a thread over the unfathomable abyss of destiny. Is this a communion with the infinite, an intuition of the great death?

> *Créature d'un jour qui t'agites une heure,*
> *Ton âme est immortelle et tes pleurs vont finir.*

End?—when the gulf of ineffable desire opens in the heart, as vast, yawning as widely as the gulf of the immensity that opens round us. Genius, devotion, love, all the thirsts awaken to torture me at once. Like a shipwrecked man about to sink beneath the waves, like a condemned man whose head is about to roll under the axe, I feel the maddest ardour binding me to life; a desperate repentance grips me and makes me cry out for mercy. And then all this invisible agony subsides into dejection. "Resign yourself to the inevitable! Hang with weeds of mourning the mirages of your youth! Live and die in the shadow! Utter your evening prayer, like the cricket. Let yourself be extinguished without a murmur when the Master of life breathes on your imperceptible flame. It is with myriads of unknown lives that each clod of earth is built up. Infusoria only count when there are thousands of billions of them. Do not revolt against your nothingness." Amen!

But there is peace only in order. Are you in order? Alas, no! Will your infixable, restless nature torment you then to the end? You will never see precisely what you ought to do. The love of the best will have forbidden you the good. Anxiety for the ideal will have caused you to lose all the realities. Vague aspiration and undetermined desire will have rendered your talents useless and neutralized your forces. An unproductive nature who thinks he is called to produce, you will have caused yourself, through an error, a superfluous remorse, like a woman who, from ignorance of her sex, might be inconsolable for having never been a father.

The words of . . . come back to me:

> *Chacun use, soit peu soit prou,*
> *Au moins une cape de fou.*

And also those of Scherer: One must accept oneself as one is.

*Zürich, September 8, 1870.*—All the exiles are returning to Paris: Edgar Quinet, Dufraisse, Louis Blanc, Hugo, etc. Uniting their experiences, will they succeed in making the Republic last for a while? This is a thing much to be desired. But I would not risk my little finger on the chance. Whereas the Republic is a fruit, in France they make it a sowing. Elsewhere it presupposes free men, in France it is, and must be, a tutor and instructor, which means that it is artificial and contradictory. It commits sovereignty to universal suffrage, as if this were already enlightened, judicious, reasonable; and it is obliged to school that which, through a fiction, is the master. The past makes every kind of doubt legitimate; it rests upon France to give proofs of amendment and wisdom. A conversion is not likely, but it is not impossible. Let us wait, with sympathy, but with circumspection . . . France is ambitious for self-government, but this is only a hankering. The question is to show its capacity for it. For eighty years France has confused revolution with liberty. One has the right to wait upon events.

*Basel, September 11, 1870.—Die Wacht am Rhein!* It is late and I am keeping watch, and the old Rhine sounds under my window and breaks against the arches of the bridge . . .

*Basel, September 12, 1870.*—As ten years ago, as twenty years ago, the great grey-green river rolls its mighty waves, the horses trample over the planks of the twelve-arched bridge, the red cathedral darts its two spires up at the sky; the ivy along the terraces that skirt the left bank of the Rhine hangs on the walls like a green mantle; the indefatigable ferry goes back and forth, as it always did; in a word, things seem eternal, while one sees one's hair turning white and feels one's heart growing old. I passed through here as a Zofingian,[1] then as a student from Germany, then as a professor; I am returning in the decline of age, and nothing in the landscape has changed except myself. *Eheu fugaces, Postume, Postume* . . .

No matter if this mournfulness of memory is banal and childish; it is true and there is no end to it, and the poets of all the ages have been unable to escape its attacks . . .

What, really, is individual life? A variation of the eternal theme: to be born, to live, to feel, to hope, to love, to suffer, to weep, to die. A few add, to grow rich, to think, to multiply, to conquer, etc.; but, in fact, talk wildly as one may, throw out one's chest or tear one's hair, one can only make the line of one's destiny waver a little more or less. If one renders a little more salient for others or more distinct for oneself the series of fundamental phenomena, what does it matter? Taken as a whole, it is always the fluttering

---

[1] Member of the patriotic society of Swiss students named after Zofingue, the little town in Aargau where it was founded, in 1819.

of the infinitely little and the meaningless repetition of the un-changeable theme. Truly, whether one is or whether one is not, the difference is so entirely imperceptible in the totality of things that all complaint and all desire are ridiculous. Humanity as a whole is only a flash of lightning in the duration of the planet; and if the planet turned back into gas the sun would not feel it even a second. The individual is thus an infinitesimal part of nothingness. He is interesting only to himself and in the measure of his obtuseness.

What is Nature? It is Maya, that is an unceasing phenomenism, fugitive and indifferent, the apparition of all the possibles, the in-exhaustible play of all the combinations.

Well, does Maya amuse someone, a spectator, Brahma? And does Brahma work towards some serious end, which is not egoistical? From the theistic point of view, does God wish to create souls and increase the sum of wisdom and the good by multiplying himself in free beings, facets that reflect upon him his holiness and his beauty? It must be admitted that this conception is much more alluring to our hearts. But is it truer? The moral conscience affirms it. If man can conceive the good, the general principle of things, which cannot be inferior to man, must be serious. The philosophy of work, duty, effort seems superior to that of phenomenism, play and indifference.

Maya, the capricious, would be subordinate to Brahma, eternal thought, and Brahma would in turn be subordinate to the holy God.

*October 25, 1870.*—Each function to the worthiest, each place to the most capable, to each man according to his merit: this maxim dominates all the constitutions and serves as a criterion by which to judge them. There is nothing to prevent democracy from apply-ing it, but democracy applies it rarely, because its presumption is, for example, that the worthiest is he who pleases it, while he who pleases it is rarely the worthiest. Democracy is like a nervous woman who gives her support according to her whim, her whim of the moment, and has little resemblance to the wise man who appreciates the intrinsic merit of things and people, disregarding their accidental circumstances. More briefly, the democratic system presupposes that reason guides the masses of the people, whereas in fact they more commonly obey passion. And every fiction is expiated, for truth takes its revenge.

This is why democracy, so fine in theory, can, in practice, end in notorious uglinesses.

Alas, whatever one says or thinks, wisdom, justice, reason, health will never be anything but exceptional and the portion of a few chosen souls. Moral and intellectual harmony, excellence in all its forms, will always be a pearl of great price, an isolated masterpiece.

All that one can expect of the most perfected institutions is that they should permit individual excellence to be produced, not that they should produce the excellent individual. Virtue and genius, grace and beauty will always be a nobility that no regime can fabricate. Useless, therefore, to be infatuated with or enraged against revolutions, which have an importance only of the second order,— an importance I do not wish to undervalue or misapprehend, but one that is rather negative, after all.

Whether my coach or my carriage jolts me a little more or less, if I am well conducted I arrive; and this is the essential thing. Political life robs us of much too much time, for it is only the means of the true life. Whatever may be the inconveniences of a habitable lodging, they could not outweigh those of perpetual moving. Under the pretext of perfecting and finishing, we make life very uncomfortable for ourselves; for, after all, if I spend my day and my night and my morrow making over my bed, and this to begin again the day after tomorrow, I sacrifice the end to the means, and sleep, which is the necessary, to the bed, which is only a trifle. If I bake my bread, when am I to eat it? If, to walk better, I stitch, unstitch, restitch and endlessly perfect my boots, when am I to do my walking? Is it not better to sleep on a hard bed, eat what is at hand and walk barefoot than to make oneself the slave of such a tyrannical hobby?

Measure! That divine word of Greece, how we forget it! We

spoil and poison the best things, for want of proportion, moderation and good sense. The natural man, the vulgar man is only an intemperate animal. Measure is the sign of inner maturity; equilibrium is the mark of wisdom. *Rara avis*.

*October 26, 1870.*—Sirocco. Bluish sky. The crown of the trees has fallen to their feet. The finger of winter has touched them.— My poor little housekeeper spends whole nights trotting from her sick sister to her equally sick husband, and she works all day long. Her eyes are red and swollen as a result. Poor little woman, what an existence! Resigned, indefatigable, she will go on forever without a complaint until she drops.

Such lives as this prove something: that the true ignorance is moral ignorance, that work and suffering are the lot of all men, and that to classify men as more or less stupid is not as sound as to classify them by their more or less of virtue. The kingdom of God is not to the most enlightened, but to the best, and the best is he who is most devoted. Humble, constant, willing sacrifice thus constitutes true human dignity. This is why it is written that the last shall be first. Society rests upon conscience and not upon knowledge. Civilization is first of all a moral thing. Without probity, without respect for the right, without the worship of duty, without love for one's neighbour, in a word, without virtue, everything would be threatened and everything would crumble; and not letters, or the arts, or luxury, or industry, or rhetoric, or the police, or spies, or customs officers could hold erect an edifice that was faulty at the foundation.

A State founded on interest alone and held together by fear would be an ignoble and precarious structure. The substratum of every civilization is the average morality of the masses and the sufficient practice of the good. Duty is what supports everything. Those who, in obscurity, fulfil it and set a good example are the salvation and support of the brilliant world that ignores them. Ten righteous men would have saved Sodom, and it takes thousands and thousands of worthy men and women to preserve a people from corruption and collapse.

If ignorance and passion jeopardize the popular morality, it must be said that moral indifference is the malady of the very cultivated. This schism between enlightenment and virtue, between thought and conscience, between the intellectual aristocracy and the honest but crude multitude, is the greatest danger that threatens liberty. The refined, the ironical, the sceptical, the witty, in their multiplication, point to the chemical disorganization of society. They are the subtle ammoniac floating on the drains. Examples: the age of Augustus and that of Louis XV. The disgusted and the derisive are egoists who have no interest in the general duty, and who, exempting themselves from all effort, never take a step against an evil. Their refinement consists in their ceasing to have a heart. They remove themselves in this way from true humanity and approach the diabolic. What was it that Mephistopheles lacked? Not wit, surely, but goodness . . .

And so when I see limited creatures, I worship wit. And when I see men of wit, I incline towards men of heart. Equilibrium alone contents me. The choice is a hardship, but, if it is obligatory, I take the indispensable, and I prefer what tires my patience to what I contemn.

*October 28, 1870.*—A curious thing is the absolute neglect of justice to which these conflicts of nations lead. Almost the whole observing public judges solely through the medium of its subjective tastes, its angers, fears, desires, interests or passions, which means that its judgment is a nullity. To judge is to see the true, to be preoccupied with the just, and, in consequence, to be impartial; more than this, to be disinterested; more than this to be impersonal. How many unexceptionable judges are there in the present conflict? Not ten, perhaps not three. People make it a point of honour to be patriotic, that is to say, not to be just; they are joyfully, frantically unjust, and, what is curious, they glory in it. So much easier is it to hate or love passionately than to rise to true humanity, to the sincerely religious point of view. This horror of equity, this antipathy to justice, this rage against a merciful neutrality is the eruption of the animal passion in man, of the blind, ferocious passion that is absurd enough to take itself for a reason, while it is only a force.

I thank God that I belong to a country and am in a situation that permit me to divest my soul of these vulgar transports and prejudices, and to seek only justice, as a man calm, *sine ira nec studio*.

*December 6, 1870.—Dauer im Wechsel,* "persistence in mobility", this title of a poem of Goethe's is the motto of nature. Everything changes, but with such different degrees of rapidity that one existence seems eternal to another. Thus a geological age, compared to the duration of a being, or the planet compared to a geological age, appears an eternity, as our life appears compared to the thousand impressions that pass through our minds in an hour. On whatever side one looks, one feels besieged by the infinity of infinites. A serious look at the universe is terrifying. Everything seems so relative that one does not know what has a real value.

Where is the fixed point in this boundless and bottomless gulf? Is it not that which perceives relations, in other words, thought, infinite thought? To perceive ourselves in the infinite thought, to feel ourselves in God, to accept ourselves in him, to will ourselves in his will, in one word, religion, that is the immutable. Whether this thought is fatal or free, the good lies in identifying oneself with it. Stoic and Christian alike abandon themselves to the Being of beings, which the one calls sovereign wisdom, and the other sovereign goodness. Saint John says, God is light, God is love. The Brahman says, God is an endless poem. Let us say, God is perfection. And man? Man, in his imperceptible littleness and his inexpressible frailty, can discern the notion of perfection, can aid in the supreme will and die with a hosanna on his lips.

*December 31, 1870 (10 p. m.).—* . . . But the year is about to end. This is the moment to compose oneself and cast a glance backwards.

What have I made of this year and what do I remember of it? My family has become still more scattered, and my isolation has increased. At the Academy, foresaw and prepared for my retirement, even tried one semester's leave. I have only worked, however, at public duties. The *Société intercantonale des Études supérieures,* the *Société genevoise pour le progrès des études,* the *Section de littérature de l'Institut genevois,* the *Société de chant du Conservatoire* know something of this. The Disdier and Hentsch competitions, Blanvalet's works, Fournel's manuscripts, the orthographic question, the university question have taken quite a little time. I have also given aid to two new unusual minds . . . I have seen several parts of Switzerland that were unknown to me, seen Heidelberg again, watched the struggle between Germany and France, and spent much time with men. Scientifically, I seem to have made little gain; but I have made some moral experiments and various observations. I have written a good many letters, verses enough, several reports, and I have printed one that was quite substantial in its brevity.[1]

Even so, it seems to me that I have day-dreamed, idled, trifled with my time a good deal, and that I might have done better. It is the provisional that sterilizes me, through dispersion, uncertainty and distaste. Besides, little physical troubles and worries about health have hindered me, and a growing disillusion about men, about the present, about the future has not contributed to set me up.

What still leaves upon me the sweetest impression are the proofs of attachment and gratitude, evidences of esteem and sympathy. In fact, I think I no longer care about anything else. And this cordial has not been refused me. If several of my relations have cooled, I

---

[1] The Disdier and Hentsch competitions are foundations of the Faculty of Letters; Amiel was working at the publication of the posthumous works of the Genevan poet, Henri Blanvalet (1811–1870), a friend of his, and those of the Frenchman, Charles Fournel (1817–1869), whom he had known at Berlin; the "substantial report" to which he alludes is entitled: *Les intérêts de la Suisse romande en matière d'instruction publique,* Geneva, 1870.

have come to know a few new souls, and I have been able to sound a few noble hearts.

What I have completely neglected is my literary reputation and my credit with the family. My inertia in these two matters has been complete, from carelessness in one case and pride in the other. You do not like to dispute what is refused, because you wish to be independent of outside things and people.

Altogether the year has been passable, and it is rather you who have disappointed fortune than fortune that has disappointed you. Your defect has been always the same one: indolence and apathy of will. And the cause? Inner doubt, lack of evidence.

What is done is done, said Faithful Jacob. We shall do better another time. For the moment, let us give thanks.

Midnight approaches. St. Sylvester's eve is about to expire. It would be more agreeable to be with sympathetic souls; but it is much better to be alone than with indifferent ones.

Do I hate anyone? No. Then I can thank God and go to sleep in peace.

*Vernex-sur-Montreux, January 3, 1871.*—It is clear to me that the nocturnal side of consciousness, the occult part of psychology, the mystical life of the soul is as certainly real as the other aspect of human existence. It is here one finds the origins and keys. Everything springs from darkness, from the unknown, from mystery. But the difficulty lies in penetrating this divine darkness with the lamp of science and not with the will-o'-the-wisps of the imagination. To bring method into this quasi-madness, that is the point. To trace the geography of the bottom of the oceans is a good deal easier. The world of germs, larvæ, phantoms, mothers,[1] secrets, is, or seems to be, the inaccessible and the inexpressible. A sacred horror guards

[1] The *mothers, die Mütter,* an allusion to a strange, enigmatic but very effective conception in Goethe's *Faust* (Part II, Act I, Scene V). The *mothers* are the prototypes, the abstract forms, the generative ideas of things. *Sie sehn dich nicht, denn Schemen sehn sie nur.* Goethe had borrowed the expression from a passage of Plutarch, but the ideas he connected with it were half Plato's and half the creations of fable.

its approaches, like those of dark Avernus. The Greeks, lovers of light, even believed that the Olympians recoiled in dread before the infernal mysteries, before the monsters of the Plutonian night. We moderns, aflame for the origins of things, have no fear of anything subterranean. The daring race of Japhet wishes to weigh all the mysteries in the scales; and as, for the ancients, the gods all sank into the Fatum, their cradle and common gulf, so for us all super-stitions are consumed on the altar of Isis which has now become Science.

*January 19, 1871 (10.30 a. m.).—* . . . The griefs that are deep and personal must be silent, for in becoming the object of art they are healed. The exercise of a talent is consoling.—And when a father who has lost his daughter can say to himself, How well I have ex-pressed paternal grief, how pitifully I have wept, he is wanting in respect for her whom he laments, he is introducing self-love into grief, he is flattering his ego under a pretence of reverence for the dead. The poetry of subjective grief is pure and touching only when it is an inner monologue, or at most a dialogue between the soul and God. The moment it admits or calls upon the public, it becomes vain and in consequence profane.

Advice to whom it may concern. Be on your guard with yourself. The shade of distinction is delicate, and the boundary easy to pass. Even in the most individual lyricism, the poet must have a general value; he expresses a state of mind which may be his own, but which must also be that of many others. All intimate poetry must be representative; that is, it must render and translate the human soul and not the self of the poet. The poet must be the spokesman of his readers, and not do the honours of his own person. In academic terms, he must objectify his subjectivity and generalize the accidents of his life. Poetry is thus anti-egoistic; and the father who weeps as a poet must weep for all the fathers who are unable to sing as he sings, but are capable of feeling much as he feels. It is fitting that he personally should be forgotten and that each reader should think only of himself. He, the lyrist, must be impersonal by virtue of being psychologically true; it is for the reader to be confined within the narrow precinct of his own feeling. The poet thus belongs to everybody; he suffers, weeps and sings with others and for others. If the self-love of the artist were reduced in him to nothing, and he were no longer a man but man, he would be the perfect poet.

Poetic objectivity is health. Just as we are conscious of our vital organs only when they are unwell, so the true poet must be impersonal, and his sufferings purely sympathetic, or his poetry becomes mean and sickly. He observes the suffering that he undergoes, but he envelops it as the calm sky surrounds the storm. Poetry is a deliverance because it is freedom. Far from being an emotion, it is the mirror of an emotion; it is outside and above, tranquil and serene. In order to sing an affliction, one must be already, if not healed of the affliction, at least convalescent. Song is a sign of equilibrium, it is a victory over agitation, it is the return of strength. The poet is for his own life, in miniature, what God is for the world. He enters it by sensibility, but he dominates it essentially. His nature is contemplative, and activity is only his inferior mode. Song is an intermediary between thought and action. Art is a weak symbol of the work of the great poet, Creation.

*(5.30 p. m.).*— . . . The life, the sap, the ardour are in those who are supplanting us. We have only to bear ourselves well . . .

> *Sans trêve convertir la minute en pensée,*
> *Le jour en œuvre utile et la vie en bonté,*
> *C'est suivre la sagesse et d'une main sensée,*
> *Tirer de la sagesse une félicité.*

It is in this art that Goethe, Schleiermacher, Humboldt were masters. So long as we renew ourselves, we are alive. A continual metamorphosis through curiosity, sympathy and production is the only defence that holds back, not death, but mummification. The weariness that secludes itself, the ill-humour that sulks, the irritation that draws back, the spite that refuses itself are faults that precipitate the effects of age and swiftly run the spirit aground.—

In the colossal caravan that bears and sweeps us all along, he who loses his footing is jostled, trampled, buried and forgotten in less than no time by the crowds, which, numberless as locusts, are renewed like the waves.

Always more and more, the men of renown will increase on the surface and endure for a briefer and briefer time. To work for posterity will be a chimerical incentive. But renown is a poor aim. One must be a man from self-respect and artistic zeal, from pure conscience . . .

To maintain one's life, one must be constantly rejuvenated by an inner moulting and by love in the Platonic manner. The soul must unrelaxingly create itself, and try itself in all its modes, and resound in all its fibres and arouse new interests in itself.

*(11.30 p. m.).*—What I have read today of Goethe *(Epistles, Epigrams, The Four Seasons)* does not make him lovable. Why? Because he has little soul. His way of understanding love, religion, duty, patriotism has something mean and shocking in it . . . It all lacks ardent generosity. An inner dryness, an ill-dissimulated egoism strikes through this talent, which is so flexible and so rich. One hails the poet but one is on one's guard with the man, who seems hardly capable of devotion and sacrifice and who has scant compassion for the unimportant and the disinherited here below. Let the world perish, if only the poet can calmly stroke his lyre and cultivate his personal inclinations! But moral indifferentism is avenged. All the little Goethians run the risk of offering sorry counterfeits of this cool indifference and being simply worthless bohemians.—Good night!

*January 20, 1871 (10 a. m.).*—No letters. Peace and silence.

In this Goethian egoism there is at least one excellent thing; he respects everyone's freedom and rejoices in every originality. Only he aids no one at his own expense, he never troubles himself over anyone, he charges himself with no man's burden; in a word, he suppresses charity, the great Christian virtue. Perfection, for Goethe, lies in personal nobility, not in love. His centre is aesthetics,

not the moral. He does not know sanctity and has never been willing to reflect on the terrible problem of evil. Spinozistic to the
marrow, he believes in individual chance, not in freedom, nor in
responsibility. He is a Greek of the great age whom the anterior
crisis of the religious consciousness has not touched at all. He thus
represents a state of mind anterior or posterior to Christianity, that
which the prudent critics of our epoch call the modern spirit; and,
further, the modern spirit envisaged in one of its tendencies only,
namely, the cult of Nature, for Goethe is a stranger to the social
and political aspirations of the masses, he is in no way interested
in the disinherited, the weak, the oppressed, any more than nature
herself, an uncaring and ferocious mother who is deaf to all the
unfortunate.

Our epoch is really very strange: it rejects the law of Malthus
and applauds the law of Darwin, without seeing that they are the
same thing. Vogt,[1] for example, is a materialist and a liberal, without seeing that materialism or the deification of force is the proclamation of the right of the strongest, which justifies every tyranny.
—The abolition of all superstition and all religion would still leave
standing the two conceptions of the world, the moral conception,
the fatalistic conception. Those who believe in duty and those who
believe only in interest can never be put in the same boat. If Christianity were eliminated, the antinomy would still remain, Epicureanism and Stoicism; and this cannot be resolved. The metaphysical and religious question always returns in one way or another.
Has the universe a goal, does it tend towards an object, yes or no?
Has man a duty, yes or no? Natural science says no, the conscience
says yes; how decide? . . .

For Goethe and his school, none of these embarrassments exist.
This is easily explained: there are no dissonances for the deaf. One
who does not hear the voice of conscience, the voice of regret and

[1] Carl Vogt (1817–1895), one of the principal champions of Darwinian materialism, at that time professor of zoölogy in the University
of Geneva.

remorse, does not even divine the anguish of those who have two masters, two laws, and belong to two worlds, that of Nature and that of Liberty. They have already made their choice. But humanity cannot exclude. All needs cry out together in its suffering. It hears the naturalists, but it also listens to religion. It desires an easy happiness, but it does not wish to renounce exalted happiness. Enjoyment attracts it, but devotion moves it. It scarcely knows any longer whether it hates or adores the crucifix. What still pleases it the best is an awkward compromise that combines everything: enjoying itself and letting itself be redeemed by another's sacrifice; that is, Epicureanism and orthodoxy. These two Churches are the most popular, and they will end perhaps by being confused with one another. Pure Christianity, with its austere simplicity, regeneration and death to self, converted into ardent charity, will never be the practice of vulgar souls; but it will all the more be their theory. Fine principles are the best pillow for hypocrisy; the tent covers the merchandise; and when one cannot pay in deeds, that is the very time to pay in sounding words.

At bottom, what have the Christians, taken all in all, which the pagans have not? An anguish. They are scarcely better, but they reproach themselves more. They do almost as much wrong, but they do it with a bad conscience. What has been gained, then, is a little more delicacy and scrupulousness. The ideal has become higher. There were just and wise men of old time. Now humanity says that there is only one who is Just, one who is Good, one who is Wise, that is God; we are all sinners, but we must become perfect as the heavenly Father is perfect. Greatness of aspiration, this is our only greatness. The ancient world attained equilibrium, unity, beauty. All this has been lost, but there is a compensation.

> *Borné dans sa nature, infini dans ses vœux,*
> *L'homme est un dieu tombé qui se souvient des cieux.*

This, too, is ancient, for Christian poetry has pillaged Plato. But the Christian world has Platonized more than Plato himself, and a divine nostalgia has become its mark and seal.

Will the religion of the future dispense with hope and immortality? Will it be able to dispense with faith? Yes, if it succeeds in setting up heaven on earth and realizing justice for all here below. Or else if it persuades humanity to universal suicide. Is there a chance that Optimism or Pessimism will replace Christianity? As the latter is a combination of the two, since it wishes to extract evil from good, to save that which was lost and shape blessed souls by the cruel ordeal of earthly life, Christianity has more chance of vanquishing than of being vanquished in this struggle of moral ideas. The religion of salvation, in purifying itself, will appear as the religion of deliverance. Its mythological, anthropomorphic part may fall away; it will remain the victory over Sin, Suffering and Death, the marriage of Heaven and Earth, God and Mankind, through love, and the glorification of love through holiness. Be perfect and you will be happy; be one in will with the divine will and you shall be perfect; love God and you will wish as he wishes. This is the alpha and omega of theology.

*(9 p. m.).*—You have come to a cross-roads in your life. Various paths lie open before you, but you do not know which to take; you would even like not to take any, but to remain in your retreat. And this is the only alternative that is prohibited. Is it because you are eccentric, or that life is bizarre? You have a horror of the lottery, and you have to play. What is the cause of this outlandish arrangement, this ridiculous law? You have an antipathy to action, which almost always does the opposite of what it intends to do; and necessity forces you to act. How preposterous this is!

Those, for example, who think that one is here to amuse oneself will be put to it to explain this teasing and baffling passion of destiny, which strives so to place fish in a guitar and poets in a wasp's nest.

I can well understand why delicate souls like you are particularly afraid of what would be good for them and incline towards whatever does them harm; so that constraint is rather good for them, as for the newly married. But it is not the less hard to be thus left without lights for the guidance of one's efforts and without some secret impulsion towards one's social end.

*(Midnight.)*—Read fifteen sonnets and nine mixed poems by Goethe. The impression left by this part of the *Gedichte* is much more favourable than that which the *Elegies* and the *Epigrams* give; so, too, the *Spirits of the Waters, My Goddess, The Harz Journey, The Divine* have great nobility of feeling. One must never be in a hurry in judging these multiple natures. Without reaching the sentiment of obligation and sin, Goethe attains high seriousness by the path of dignity. Greek statuary has been his catechism of virtue . . .

*February 4, 1871.*—Eternal effort is the character of modern morality, and even of the majority of Christians. This painful becoming has taken the place of harmony, equilibrium, joy, that is to say, being. We are all fauns, satyrs, Silenuses who aspire to become angels, we are ugly and we toil for our beautification, unlovely chrysalises giving birth laboriously each to his own butterfly. The ideal is no longer serene beauty of soul; it is the anguish of Laocoön, struggling with the hydra of evil. The die has been cast. Today there are only candidates for heaven, galley-slaves on earth.

> *Nous ramons notre vie en attendant le port;*
> *Nous souffrons dans tout le passage,*
> *Et ce n'est qu'au jour de la mort*
> *Que la sérénité brille en notre visage.*

Molière said that reasoning banishes reason. It is possible, too, that the struggle for perfection of which we are so proud is only a pretentious imperfection. Becoming still seems more negative than positive; it is the diminishing of evil, but it is not good; it is a generous discontent, but it is not felicity; it is the unceasing pursuit of an inaccessible goal, that is, a noble folly but not reason; it is a nostalgia for the unrealizable, a pathetic malady which is nevertheless not wisdom.

This tendency depreciates the individual life, which becomes only a means towards an external result, to which it must be sacrificed. The living generation makes of itself a fertilizer for its successor, which will do as much for the third, and so on. And will there spring from this long series of torments a generation at least more satisfied and more harmonious? By no means, for discontent is proportional to the increase of one's resources, and it is among the favoured of this world that one finds the most insanity and suicide. Indefinite perfectibility is thus a self-contradictory doctrine. Progress, vulgarly understood, is the idlest nonsense. It believes it is building up the happiness of men, but it proves this neither in the present nor in the future.

Each being can attain to harmony: when he does so, he is in order, and he represents the divine thought at least as clearly as a flower or a solar system.—The vulgar system of progress makes people ashamed of the present and scornful of the past; it causes the unwarranted belief that only at the end of the ages will living be worth the pains. A dangerous and absurd heresy! Perfecting does not take the place of perfection. Perfection does not become, it is. Perfection is inner harmony. Harmony seeks for nothing outside itself. It is what it should be; it expresses the good, order, law, and that just as well in the present as two thousand years from now. Harmony expresses a truth, it is superior to time and represents the eternal.

*February 8, 1871.*—Goethe and Schleiermacher, present harmony and the pursuit of the ideal; these are the two poles between which I oscillate. "What are you becoming?" I once asked Victor Cherbuliez. "I?" he replied, "I am not becoming, I am content to be!" My conscience and my taste are still in conflict. Is there a way to reconcile them? Perhaps. By communicating harmony to others, one seems to unite duty and happiness, the good and the beautiful, the καλοκάγαθον of Socrates. To humanize men, to electrify them by induction, to help them to live the higher life and to light their lamp without extinguishing or over-fanning the flame of science, would perhaps be the solution. I would thus go a little farther than Rückert and Goethe, who ask the rose only to be a rose. I would ask the lamp to communicate its flame, to share its light and even to spread it freely in the dark places, first maintaining itself and living its own life. No one exists for himself alone, though no one exists only for others. To give happiness, one must have happiness. To preach harmony, one must first be harmonious.

*February 9, 1871.*—I am rereading the *Chansons du Soir* of Juste Olivier,[1] with a heavy heart. All the poet's melancholy is passing through my veins. But I have suffered in a literary way, sympathetically, not by reflecting on myself, on my destiny. A whole existence has risen before me, a whole world of mournful revery.

How characteristic are *Musette,* the *Chanson de l'alouette,* the *Chant du retour, la Gaîté!* How fresh are *Lina, A ma fille!* Better pieces still are *Au delà, Homunculus, la Trompeuse,* and especially *Frère Jacques,* the author's masterpiece, with *les Marionettes* and the song *Helvétie.*[2]—The most serious symbolism under a childlike playfulness, the furtive tear in the mischievous smile, a resigned and pensive wisdom in some popular roundelay, the sublime incognito, the everything in nothing, this is the triumph of the Vaudois poet. He is always surprising and touching the reader. And this author has a kind of rustic artfulness which finds amusement in slipping what look like nuts to its favoured ones, nuts that have diamonds inside them. Like the fairies, Juste Olivier adores these delicate mystifications. He dissembles his little gifts. This is his good-heartedness. He promises nothing and gives a great deal. He is a surly prodigal, whose forthrightness is extremely subtle and whose

---

[1] Juste Olivier (1801–1876), a poet of his race, candid and thoughtful, whose name is dear to French Switzerland and whom Sainte-Beuve loved as a person, while relishing his genius. It is he whom the author of the *Pensées d'Août* addresses in the sonnet:

> *Pardon, cher Olivier, si votre alpestre audace*
> *Jusqu'aux hardis sommets ne me décide pas.*

[2] These last two pieces are to be found in the *Chansons lointaines.*

malice is pure tenderness, the fine flower of *vaudoiserie* at its dreamiest and most affectionate.

*February 10, 1871.*—Reading: a few lusty, hoarse chapters of Taine *(Histoire de la littérature anglaise)*. I feel a painful sensation with this writer, as of the odour of a laboratory, a grating of pulleys, a clicking of machinery. This style suggests chemistry and technology. The science in it seems inexorable. Moreover, one feels in it only clearsightedness, no delicacy, no sympathy. It is rigorous and dry, penetrating and hard, strong and rough; but it is altogether lacking in humanity, nobility, grace. This sensation as of verdigris, painful to tooth, ear, eye and heart, that is, wounding one's taste in every way, probably springs from two things, the moral philosophy of the author and his literary principles. The profound contempt for humanity that characterizes the physiological school, and the intrusion of technology into literature, undertaken by Balzac and Stendhal, explain the inner aridity that makes itself felt in these pages and that catches at one's throat like the unhealthy exhalations of a factory of mineral products. This reading is instructive in a very high degree, but it is anti-vivifying; it is withering, corrosive, saddening. It is no more inspiring than the sight of a pharmacy, an osteological museum or a herbarium; it only adds to one's knowledge. I imagine that this will be the literature of the future, in the American style, a profound contrast to the art of the Greeks: algebra instead of life, the formula instead of the image, the effluvia of the alembic instead of the intoxication of Apollo, cold vision instead of the joys of thought, in short, the death of poetry, flayed and anatomatized by science.

This criticism savours of the anatomical chart, of chlorine and reagents, and one is hardly grateful to it for the glimpses it opens up, because it drains away at the same time the source of our illusions and creations. It stupefies one like an anæsthetic, it is as cheerful as a morgue. What it lacks is not depth, perspicacity, information, but love and the power to inspire love.

*February 15, 1871.*—The nations, without intending to do so, mutually educate one another by simply pursuing their selfish interests. It is France that has made the present Germany by aiming for ten generations at the opposite result; Germany that will regenerate contemporary France by seeking only to break her. Revolutionary France will have taught equality to the Germans, who are naturally hierarchical; serious Germany will teach the French that rhetoric is not as good as science and appearance is not as good as reality. The worship of prestige, that is, lies, the passion for vainglory, which means for sound and fury, this is what must die, to the advantage of all. It is a false religion that is being destroyed. May its adorers be disillusioned, and live. History does not wish the death of the sinner, but his conversion . . . I sincerely hope that from this war a new equilibrium will arise, better than the old one, a new Europe in which the Germanic element will have the supremacy, that is, in which the government of the individual by himself will be the cardinal principle of society, the Latin principle being to make the individual the means, the thing, the instrument of the Church or the State.

The order and harmony resulting from free adherence and voluntary submission to the same ideal, this is another moral world; it is the lay equivalent of the universal priesthood. The symbol of the model society is a great, free musical society, in which everything is organized, subordinated, disciplined for love of art and to execute masterpieces. No one is constrained, no one is exploited, no one hypocritically plays an interested role. Everyone brings his talent or his mite and contributes consciously and joyously to the common work, to the higher goal shining before the eyes of all. Self-love itself is obliged to concur in the collective action, under pain of being wounded in the fact of attracting attention to itself.

*February 16, 1871 (midnight)*.—One understands women as one understands the language of the birds, either by intuition or not at all. Trouble, study, effort count for nothing here: it is a gift and a grace. To understand these living enigmas one must love them, though this is not enough, for one can adore them without seeing them more clearly. One must have had the good fairy at one's cradle. Two drops of poetry in our first drink and a sprig of sweet marjoram under our first pillow endow us with this magic clairvoyance. Those who possess it exercise at the same time an indefinable attraction over women, who divine this power and feel its charm, as the sap hears the call of spring, as the moth flies through the night towards the distant curtain through which sifts the vague light of a lamp. He who is dowered with sympathetic lucidity seems a sorcerer. He is in reality a liberator, and women know it well. He receives their confidences, because he can understand and console. He receives their passionate gratitude, for he has the key to hearts and he guards secrets faithfully. Happy are the fairy's godchildren, for they give happiness. He who knows the language of the birds is initiated into many other mysteries. He is a Rosicrucian by birth and grand-master in the freemasonry of love.

*February 18, 1871.*—It is in the novel that the average vulgarity of German society and its inferiority to the societies of France and England is plainly perceptible. The notion of the "shocking" is absent from the aesthetics of the Germans. Their unrestraint is illbred; their elegance is without grace; they do not divine the enormous difference between *ladylike* distinction and stiff *Vornehmlichkeit*. Their imagination lacks style, good usage, education, *monde;* it has a touch of the plebeian even in its Sunday clothes. The race is poetic and intelligent, but it is unmannerly and common. Suppleness, gracefulness, manners, wit, *brio,* taste, dignity, charm are for others.

Is it possible that the inner freedom of the soul, the deep harmony of the faculties which I have so often observed in superior individuals among this people, will not reach the surface? Will not the conquerors of today civilize their forms? By the novel of the future we shall judge. When they have novels that are altogether in good taste, they will be their own masters. Until then they will lack the finish, the polish, the maturity of social culture; they have the humanity of the feelings, but they have not yet the *comme il faut* or the *je ne sais quoi*. They possess probity; they are destitute of *savoir vivre*.

The repugnance of many of my friends for the Germans is therefore not a foolish prejudice; but it is unjust because it accentuates the defects of this people to the point of forgetting their qualities. To speak of English stiffness, French frivolity, German ponderousness is not to speak falsely, but it is to take the wart for the face. As for myself, I feel no ethnological antipathy, and I detest the faults, not the races, the sin and not the sinner.

*February 22, 1871.*—Evening at the M——s'. Solid elegance. Thirty persons of the best society; a happy proportion in sexes and ages. White heads, young girls, lovely shoulders, intelligent faces. The whole framed in Aubusson tapestries that provided the various groups in evening dress with a soft perspective and a charming background . . .

In society, one must have an air of living on ambrosia and having only noble preoccupations. Care, want, passion do not exist. All realism, being brutal, is suppressed. It is taken for granted that these goddesses have come down from Olympus and are not subject to any of the earthy infirmities. They have no vital organs, no weight; they retain, of their human nature, only that which is needed for grace and pleasure. In a word, what is called the great world grants itself for the moment a flattering illusion, that of being in the ethereal state and breathing the life of mythology. For this reason, any vehemence, any cry of nature, any real suffering, any unreflecting familiarity, any frank token of passion shocks and reverberates in this delicate atmosphere; any crudity at once destroys the collective work, the palace of clouds, the magic architecture that has been erected by the common consent. It is rather like the harsh cock-crow that dissolves all the enchantments and puts the fairies to flight. Gatherings of the *élite* unconsciously try to produce a sort of concert of the eyes and ears, an extempore work of art. This instinctive collaboration has a real charm, for it is a festival of wit and taste and transports the actors into the sphere of the imagination; it is a form of poetry and the way in which cultivated society recomposes, by reflection, the vanished idyll and the engulfed world of Astrea. Paradox or not, I believe that these fugitive attempts at the reconstruction of a dream that pursues beauty as its sole end are vague recollections of the golden age that haunt the human soul, or rather aspirations towards the harmony of things which everyday reality refuses us and of which art alone gives us glimpses.

*April 23, 1871 (10 a. m.).*—Felt last evening a confused cerebral impression, as of some congestion that is approaching. These anticipations of storms in the blood are the presentiments of the flesh. They say to you very plainly: There is your limit, you are not going any further, have no illusions about it. This dry little warning is almost as effective as the still voice in the vision of Job; one feels the abyss, and one's skin begins to shrivel. Thus in all directions I touch my bounds: the heart, the bronchial tubes, the kidneys, sight, hearing, the bones, the stomach, the brain have successively threatened to stop work and shown me the limits of their obligingness. I am a little like a general whose army finds fault with him, argues and resists before breaking into mutiny, or like a government that sees the relaxing of all the bonds of respect and obedience before its taxes are refused and barricades rise against it. I have reached the vanguard of my destroyers. For a psychologist, it is indeed very interesting to have an immediate consciousness of the complication of one's organism and the play of one's machinery. It is as if my joints were loosening and parting just enough for me to have a glimpse of the way I am put together and a distinct feeling of my fragility. This makes personal existence an astonishment and a curiosity. Instead of seeing only the surrounding world, one analyzes oneself. Instead of being a single block, one becomes legion, multitude, vortex, one is a *cosmos*. Instead of living on the surface, one takes possession of one's inwardness. One perceives oneself, if not in one's cells and atoms, at least in one's organic systems and almost in one's tissues. In other words, the central monad isolates itself from all the subordinate monads that it may contemplate them, and resumes its harmony in itself when it sees the plural and intermonadic harmony in turmoil. It is thus that a king, after his abdication, withdraws into private life.

Health is thus an equilibrium of our organism with its component parts and with the outer world; its chief service is to acquaint us with the world. Organic disorder obliges us to achieve another, more inward equilibrium, to retire into our soul; and thenceforward our body itself becomes our object, it is no longer we, though it is still ours; it is only the vessel in which we make the voyage of life; we study the damages it has incurred and its structure without identifying it with our individuality.

Where does our final Self reside? In thought, or rather in consciousness. But beneath consciousness lies its germ, the *punctum saliens* of spontaneity, for consciousness is not primitive, it becomes. The question is to know whether the thinking monad can fall back into its enveloping substance, that is, into pure spontaneity, or even into the dark gulf of potentiality. I hope not. The kingdom goes, the king subsists. Or would it perhaps be only the royalty that subsisted, namely, the idea, the person being in his turn only the transient garment of this durable idea? Is Leibnitz right, or Hegel? Is the individual immortal in the form of a spiritual body? Is he eternal in the form of an individual idea? Who saw the more justly, St. Paul or Plato? The theory of Leibnitz is the most pleasing to me, because it opens the infinite in duration, in multitude and in evolution. One monad being potentially the universe, infinite time is not too long for developing the infinite that is in it. Only it would be necessary to admit that outer actions and influences cause fluctuations in the evolution of the monad; its independence would have to be a mobile and growing quantity between zero and infinity, without being ever complete or ever nothing, as the monad can be neither absolutely passive nor entirely free.

*June 12, 1871.*— ... My mind keeps coming back to the anxiety of the day, to the affairs of France. Thiers, with his hand on the valve, is delaying the explosion of the boiler, but that is all. Civil war is in prospect. Besides, the universal bugbear, the international socialism of the workers, crushed with so much difficulty in Paris, is celebrating its approaching victory. No fatherland exists for it, no memories exist, no property, no religion; it knows nothing and no one but itself. Its dogma is equalitarianism, its prophet is Mably, and Babeuf is its God. "Enjoyment is everything, wealth is the way to it, labour is the source of wealth; we are labour and we are equal. Let the world perish, then, if it will not order itself after our idea, the absolute levelling of goods and enjoyments! Existing society as a whole, with its religion, its usages, its capital, its capitals, its functions and its hierarchy, is detestable to us; it is unjust, since we are not the masters. And we will destroy it. Your civilization is nauseous to us as long as it is not our prey. The barbarians submitted to the prestige of Rome; we are not so foolish. We hate what you love, and we are irreconcilable."

What is the answer to this? That the International is quite in the logic of the revolutionary spirit and represents the annihilation of every acquired right, absolute contempt for the right of others; that it is the catholicism of vengeance; that the spectacle of the unbridled luxury of the great capitals teaches contempt for wealth, which appear to be not the result of labour but its gnawing canker; —that French society, unable to combat this new barbarianism except by repression, clericalism or the hypocritical indignation of the more favoured classes, cannot hope to cure the evil. Perhaps indeed this evil, which is smouldering everywhere, and which is nothing else than the terrible war of the poor against the rich, will end by setting Europe in flames.

How resolve the conflict, since there is no longer a single principle in common between the partisans and the adversaries of our existing society, between liberalism and equalitarianism? Their notions of man, duty, happiness, that is, of life and its purpose, are altogether different. I even suspect that international communalism is only the harbinger of Russian nihilism, which will be the common grave of the old races and the servile races, the Latins and the Slavs; in this case, the brutal individualism of the Americans will be the salvation of humanity. But I think the peoples are heading rather towards their punishment than towards wisdom. Wisdom, being an equilibrium, is encountered only in individuals. Democracy, by placing the masses in power, gives the preponderance to instinct, nature, the passions, that is, to blind impulse, elementary gravitation, generic fatality. Perpetual vacillation between opposites becomes its sole mode of progression, because it is the childish, stupid and simple way of the small mind, which, in its infatuation, renounces, adores and curses, always with the same precipitation. The succession of contrary stupidities gives it the impression of change, which it identifies with improvement, as if Enceladus were better off on the left side than on the right, as long as the weight of the volcano remains the same.—The stupidity of Demos has no equal except in its presumption. It is an adolescent that has strength and cannot attain to reason.

How right Luther was in comparing humanity to a drunken peasant, who is always falling off one side of his horse or the other!

It is not that I deny the rights of democracy; but I have no illusions as to the use it will make of its rights as long as wisdom is rare and pride abundant. Number makes law, but the good has nothing to do with figures. For every fiction there is an expiation, and democracy rests on this legal fiction, that the majority has not only strength but reason, that it possesses wisdom at the same time as right. A dangerous fiction because it is flattering. The demagogues have always pampered the consciousness of the masses, as one strokes a cat one wishes to cajole. The masses will always be below the average. Moreover, the age of majority will be lowered, the barrier of sex will fall, and democracy will become absurd by referring the decision of the greatest matters to the most incapable. This will be the punishment for its abstract principle of equality, which dispenses the ignorant from instructing themselves, the weak from judging themselves, the child from becoming a man, and the scoun-

drel from mending his ways.—The public right that is based on po-
tential equality will be shattered by its consequences. It disregards
the inequality of worth, merit, experience, in other words, of individual work; it will end in the triumph of the dregs and platitude.
The worship of appearances is always paid for. The regime of the
Paris Commune has been a sample of what comes to power in this
time of furious bombast and universal suspicion. A madman lasts
three days and immediately finds one who is madder still to declare
him a traitor. The steeple-chase of frenzy becomes confused with
the service of the revolutionary idea. It is only a question of being
sufficiently frantic and able to maintain a crescendo. Delirium is
taken for Delphic inspiration.

> *Voilà donc quels vengeurs s'arment pour ta querelle!*
> *De quels impurs bourreaux tu te fais maquerelle*
> > *O Révolution!*
> *Va, fais du monde entier sauter la Sainte-Barbe,*
> *Stupide et folle, vois Satan rire en sa barbe*
> > *De ton illusion.*

But then, humanity is very tough and survives all catastrophes.
Only it is annoying that it should always take the longest road, that
it must exhaust every possible mistake before it achieves a definite
step towards the better. These innumerable arbitrary follies are the
cause of my bad humour. If it surprises anyone, let me ask him if
he would stand unruffled before an interlocutor who tried every
word before he found the right one and stammered all the letters
of the alphabet before he pronounced this unhappy word properly?
The history of politics and religion is as insupportable as the history
of science is majestic; the progress of the moral world seems an
abuse of the patience of God.

Stop! There is nothing refreshing in misanthropy and pessimism.
If our species is tiresome, let us be modest in the presence of its
woes. We are all shut up in the same boat, and we must go down
with it. Let us pay our debt and leave the rest to God. Bound up as

we are with the sufferings of our race, let us set a good example: this is all that is asked of us. Let us do what good we can, speak what truth we know or believe, and, in addition, let us be submissive, patient and resigned. God does his work, let us do ours.

*August 15, 1871.*—Read for the second time Renan's *Vie de Jésus*, sixteenth popular edition. The characteristic thing in this analysis of Christianity is that sin plays no part in it. And if anything explains the success of the Good Tidings among men, it is that they brought deliverance from sin and, in a single word, salvation. It would be fitting to explain a religion religiously, and not avoid the centre of one's subject. This "Christ in white marble" is not he who gave the martyrs their strength and wiped so many tears away. The conqueror of Sin and Death is something more than a delightful moralist and the initiator of a priestless religion. The author has not really come to grips with his subject, and, if he destroys a host of harmful prejudices, he lacks moral seriousness and confounds nobility with sanctity. He speaks as a sensitive artist of a touching subject, but his conscience seems uninterested in the question. Religious dilettantism is one of the forms of indifference; real and sincere piety is not deceived by it. How confound the epicurism of the imagination, granting itself the delights of an aesthetic spectacle, with the agonies of a soul passionately seeking truth? Our amateurs of religious studies amuse themselves with the naive credulities of the past, and indulge themselves with the sensation, just as, reading Homer, one becomes a Greek, inconsequentially. This saccharine irony of a devotion that is purely artistic wears out the patience of positive natures, who feel they are being mystified. Better, they think, an open enemy than a prestidigitator in white gloves who makes a mummy out of a religion by covering it with wrappings. There is in Renan a residue of seminarist trickery; he strangles with sacred cords and cuts throats with a honeyed air. Leave these disdainful refinements to a more or less sophistical clergy. To sincere souls one owes a more respectful sincerity. The everlasting coquetry of the critic who laughs up his sleeve at his audience has something inhuman and glacial in it. I admit the use of irony against the presumption of dunces, against charlatanism and convention; but I do not approve of it as a universal method, for it shows a lack of courage, loyalty and goodness. Banter the pharisaical, but speak straight to honest men. Transcendent disdain is a good defensive for egoism, but it is not an act of charity and fraternity.

*Charnex, September 22, 1871 (4 p. m.).*—A rift in the rainy vault lets through a white beam that breaks in my room like a sardonic laugh and passes more quickly than it came.

After dinner, a walk as far as Chailly, between two showers . . . The landscape grey but vast, a handful of sunbeams falling on the lake, far vistas, mountains bedimmed with mist, and, in spite of everything, the beauty of the country. One cannot weary of this picturesque and soothing view. I find a charm in rainy prospects; the dull colours are more velvety, the flat tones grow more tender. The landscape is like a face that has been weeping; it is less beautiful, certainly, but more expressive.

Behind the superficial beauty, joyous, shining, palpable, the aesthetic sense discovers a whole order of beauty that is hidden, veiled, secret, mysterious, akin to moral beauty. This latter beauty reveals itself only to the initiate, and it is all the sweeter for this. It is a little like the refined joy of sacrifice, like the madness of faith, like the pleasure of tears; it is not within the reach of everyone. Its attraction is a curious thing and gives one the impression of a strange perfume or a bizarre melody. Once one has acquired the taste for it, one delights in it, one becomes enamoured of it, for one finds in it

*Son bien premièrement, puis le dédain d'autrui,*

and it is so agreeable not to be of the same mind as the fools. And that is not possible with the obvious things and the incontestable beauties. Charm is the name of this esoteric and paradoxical beauty that escapes the vulgar and sets one adream. This is why the ugly, when it has charm, does not charm us half-way. A sphinx that pleases enchants its lover, for it has two philtres instead of one.

Beside charm, simple beauty seems dull, poor and almost stupid. What figure does a little schoolgirl, with regular features and rosy cheeks, but insignificant, cut beside a woman whose face is lined but tingling with spirit and passion?

Women of transparent ugliness, whom the soul transfigures on occasion, play a large part in the world and can record flattering successes (Pauline Viardot, Jenny Lind, Mme. de Staël). It is pleasant to have a mask when one can put it on for those who are worth the trouble. Classic beauty belongs, so to speak, to the eyes of all, it does not belong to itself; esoteric beauty is a second modesty, unveiling only for eyes that are opened, and favouring only love.

That is why my friend S., who places herself at once in rapport with the soul, does not see the ugliness of people when she has become interested in them, as a mother does not see the ugliness of her new-born child. She likes or she does not like; and those whom she likes are beautiful, those whom she does not like are ugly. It is no more complicated than that. The aesthetic is dissolved for her in moral sympathy; she looks only with her heart; she passes over the chapter of beauty and passes on to the chapter of charm.—I can do the same thing; only it is by reflection and second thought. My friend does it involuntarily and immediately; she lacks the artistic fibre; the prosaic, the useful, the good suffices for her. The need for a perfect correspondence between the inside and the outside of things, between the substance and the form, is not in her nature. Ugliness does not make her suffer; she hardly notices it. As for me, I can only forget what shocks me, I cannot help being shocked. All bodily defects set me on edge, and lack of fairness in the fair sex, something that should not be, shocks me like a rent, like a solecism, like a dissonance, like an inkspot, in a word, something out of place. Conversely, beauty delights me, restores me, fortifies me like a miraculous aliment, like the Olympian ambrosia.

> *Que le bon soit toujours camarade du beau,*
> *Dès demain, je chercherai femme,*
> *Mais comme le divorce entre eux n'est pas nouveau,*
> *Et que peu de beaux corps, hôtes d'une belle âme,*
> *Assemblent l'un et l'autre point . . .*

I do not complete the quotation, for one must be resigned. A beautiful soul in a healthy body is in itself a rare blessing, and if one finds heart and sense as well, thought and courage, one can do without that ravishing delicacy which is called beauty, and almost that delicious seasoning which bears the name of grace. One lets it go with a sigh, as a superfluity, happy enough to possess the necessary.

> *J'ai vu beaucoup d'hymen, aucun d'eux ne me tentent:*
> *Cependant des humains presque les quatre parts*
> *S'exposent hardiment au plus grand des hasards;*
> *Les quatre parts aussi des humains se repentent . . .*

And those who do not marry, still more.—Certainly the married life is a delicate problem; but the solitary life is monstrous. Man does not go without woman, according to the Lord and according to nature. Only the Latin races, with their shabby opinion of woman, have made marriage a sort of domestic duel between two wills.—True marriage is a normal state, salutary, fortifying, sanctifying, but it should be maintained in the religious point of view.

*December 29, 1871.*—Read Bahnsen (*Critique of the Hegel-Hartmann Evolutionism, in the Name of the Principles of Schopenhauer*). An execrable writer! Like the cuttlefish in the water, he produces, in his toiling and moiling, a cloud of ink that cloaks his thought in darkness; his language seems to have been conceived for the purpose of hiding his meaning, and the more he explains himself the less one comprehends him.—And what a doctrine! A rabid pessimism that finds the world absurd, "absolutely idiotic", and reproaches Hartmann for allowing a little logic to subsist in the evolution of the universe, whereas this evolution is eminently contradictory (dialectic) and has not a shadow of reason (logic), except in the poor brain of the reasoner.—Of all possible worlds that which exists is the worst. Its only excuse is that it tends to its own destruction, that is to suicide. The philosopher's hope is that reasonable beings will cut short its agony and hasten the return of everything into non-existence. This is the philosophy of a desperate Satanism, which cannot even offer the resigned perspectives of Buddhism to the soul that is disabused of every illusion. God is only the *Welt-Krokodil,* who enjoys the torments of all beings that are struggling under the impossibility of happiness. The individual can only protest and curse.—This frantic Sivaism derives from the conception of the world as arising out of blind will, the universal principle. It professes that the world is an infamous monstrosity, the work of an omnipotence in delirium.

*Nur werth, dass es zu Grunde gehe.*

Evolutionism, fatalism, pessimism, nihilism: is it not curious to see the spread of this terrible and desolate doctrine, at the very time when the German nation is celebrating its greatness and its triumphs? The contrast is so glaring that it makes one wonder.

This orgy of philosophic thought identifying error with existence itself and developing the axiom of Proudhon, God is evil, will lead the crowd back to the Christian theodicy, which is neither optimistic nor pessimistic and which declares that the felicity it calls the eternal life is attainable.

The blasphemous bitterness of the doctrine leads to epithets in bad taste, such as "the lackey of Jehovah", the "Satan-God", etc., which prevent one from believing that it is a simple assumption of a paradoxical theorist. We have to do indeed with a theophobe, one who foams with rage at any faith in the good and stamps with scorn on the joy of the innocent. To hasten the deliverance of the world, he crushes in the egg everything that consoles, every hope and illusion, and he replaces the love of humanity that inspired Sakyamuni

347

with the Mephistophelian hatred that sullies and withers and cor-
rodes all things. Ugh!

*January 21, 1872.*— . . . There are souls that live by love and
religion, that seek only the good and the beautiful, that expand in
sacrifice. They are more than disinterested, they are devoted. They
are the little church, the *élite* of the noble souls. There is the good
example, there is the true *point d'appui.*

*January 25, 1872.*—At Berne, the revision proceeds in a rather
violent way, according to the Bernese idea of a self-interested centralization.[1] The brutal exploitation of the frontier cantons, injured
in all their economic interests, is being pursued without restraint.
Peoples have no more power than men to stop within the bounds of
wisdom. They exaggerate their principles and march straight into
the face of Nemesis. Democracy is no more temperate than an element and runs out the cycle of its destinies like a typhoon or a
tide-rip. Its basis of right is the will of the numerical majority, and
its fiction is that this will is, moreover, enlightened, judicious and
prescient.—But it is a ridiculous psychology that sets up the will as
a guide and a mentor to the intelligence, and causes the father
to be led by the child, the officer by his soldiers, the ruler by the
masses, the informed by the ignorant, reason by passion, the head
by the tail. It is fundamentally stupid to confuse right with competence and insight. The majority has the right to make the law;
does it follow that it will make it well? The grown son of a family
has the right to ruin himself by his follies and errors; but is it not
a pity? In professing that the people are always *right* in their numerical majority, our democracy confounds the rightness of the
strongest with the rightness of the most clear-sighted. This fiction
rests in turn on the assumed equality of the voters, an equality of
right which becomes an equality of social, civic or personal worth,

[1] The federal assembly (National Council and Council of States, meeting jointly in Berne) was deliberating at this time on a project for the
revision of the federal Constitution, which, however, was rejected by
the Swiss people.

a primary fiction the sophism of which is veiled for reasons of State . . .

The principle of the equality of rights, waiving as incongruous the fact of the inequality of merits, or fancying that the crowd always chooses the most deserving and not the most pleasing, this principle flatters the vanity of the citizens and is the undoing of the common-wealth. In addition to this, consider Socrates and his dialogues with the democrats of his time. When the army, the taxes, the finances, public instruction and diplomacy are in the hands of demagogues, the State does not last long.—Personally, I believe that everyone should stick to his own last, and I prefer the government of the really superior. Even if an officer is harsh, I accept him, if he is a good officer. I even think that a first-rate shepherd is better for a flock of sheep than the government of a dozen sheep, which are stupid, however zealous.

In other words, fictions vex me because they dazzle the foolish; I like things to go well, even if they ruffle the vanity of fools; for me, the forms of government are a means and not an end, and I judge democracy by its results. When it sets cooks to clock-making, and the incapable to governing, on the presumption that they have the right and that they are never wrong, I laugh in its face. The nature of things makes fun of these grotesque fictions. Without an engineer, the locomotive will jump the tracks; without statesmen, the republic will go adrift or founder.

The great fault of democracy is that of all despots: weakness for its flatterers and courtiers, favouritism towards the pleasantly in-capable, in other words aversion to the independent experts. With us, superior men sometimes still slip through the meshes of the electoral system, but the majority of those who are elected already belong to the coarse mob and even to the lowest of the lot. When one observes who it is that proposes the great laws (Capital Punish-ment, Separation of Church and State, Compulsory Insurance, Pub-lic Instruction, etc.), one is dumbfounded: it is always presumption

taking itself for competence, will that thinks it is thought, the tail
lording it over the head . . .

The most irksome thing in this world is that the ignorant lead
those who know and that the illusioned carry along with them in
their follies those who no longer share their illusions. Always and
everywhere the will overrides the intelligence in practical matters,
which means that force makes game of reason and that the inevitable direction of the movement of history is contrary to good sense.
So Democritus laughs and Heraclitus weeps at the spectacle of
human things.—There is nothing entirely consoling but the progress
of science, for science escapes this ridiculous hurly-burly of civil
and religious politics and constantly enlarges its capital of truths
that are acquired and proved.

The State and the Church weary me almost equally. I have no
respect for the public, no admiration for my time. I delight in
knowledge that is sure, and I love fine souls. This is what remains
to me from my travels through the world and things.

*Que produit l'idéal? le désabusement.*

The human world is interesting only in detail; taken as a whole,
it is disheartening and wearisome. The more one knows it, the more
it freezes one's enthusiasm. Only the chosen souls, the geniuses, the
noble characters reconcile one with this nauseous rabble and this
lamentable history.

*January 28, 1872.*—To live is to be healed and renewed every
day; it is also to rediscover and reconquer oneself. A journal is
the confidant, the consoler, the doctor of the solitary man. This
daily monologue is a form of prayer, a conversation between the
soul and its principle, a dialogue with God. It is this that restores
our integrity, brings us back from confusion into clarity, from agitation to calm, from distraction to self-possession, from the accidental to the permanent, and from specialization to harmony. Like
the magnetic bars, it restores our equilibrium. It is a kind of con-

scious sleep, in which, ceasing to act, to will, to strain, we return to the universal order and seek our peace. Thus we escape the finite. Self-communion is like a bath of the soul in contemplation, and the Journal is only self-communion, pen in hand.

> *Le monde fait silence et l'âme entend son Dieu.*

This reminds me of a thought I had as I awoke. I said to myself this morning: at your age, it would be best to let the details go and reserve your effort and your desire for the totalities, for the great things. Replace your rambling discursiveness with the habit of summaries, syntheses, general recapitulations, balance-sheets. It is certain that study is boundless and knowledge without end. But the individual is mortal, and before he dies he ought to draw the moral of his existence and extract from his individual experiences whatever they contain that is best for others and most useful for his successors.

The three great motives of the writer have all been lacking in you, self-esteem, material necessity, the sympathetic appeal of an encouraging public. But you retain two that are not exhausted, the sweetness of giving pleasure to those who still love you and the religious sense of human duty.

Neither God nor your friends coerce you, but they excite your zeal by respecting your liberty, by saying, Give us your heart,

> *Rends gloire ou témoignage à temps, avec amour,*
> *Ton âme de la vie a bientôt fait le tour,*
> *Qu'au jugement elle soit prête.*

The world has no right to your love, it has a right only to your justice. And since it is not just itself, you have the right to be on the defensive against it, the right of reserve and silence; you are not bound to give yourself up to wild beasts, any more than to those who mock, to the malevolent, the suspicious, the indifferent.—But free goodness, voluntary generosity, bondage through charity are better things than justice. One must love men, not because they deserve it, but because love is beautiful, because God is love. One must overcome one's instinct of modesty and one's instinct of justice by the devotion that offers itself without any expectations, that gives its reciprocity, acts unwearyingly and superabounds without counting the cost.

*February 7, 1872.*—How far from easy it is to place the faith of the simple in contact with the results of historical and critical science without appearing impious and scandalizing the poor believer! Perhaps, at least, a grave and pious tone on the part of the initiator must somewhat reassure the person whose world he is turning upside down. The conscience of this latter must feel that it is in the presence of another conscience, not of an indifferent or scornful science. Sacred errors have a tougher life than any truth; one must use a respectful knife in cutting their throats. What the priest has blessed is embalmed for centuries, even an obscurity, even a crime. It is the property of faith to assure an asylum to whatever it takes under its wing, an asylum that is inviolable even to truth. Thus religious faith defends itself even against God, if God does not give the password and show his credentials at the door he wishes to open. Faith is therefore a terrible thing, since it can be blind through piety and can curse what it thinks it adores, failing to recognize it when it is not in a certain livery. Like that historic sentry, ineptly sublime, it can present a bayonet to its emperor and cry, "Little corporal, stand back." Without faith, nothing can be done, yet faith can muzzle all science.

What is this Proteus, then? Does it come from God or from the devil?

Faith is certitude without proofs. Being a certitude, it is an energetic principle of action. Being without proof, it is the opposite of science. Hence its two aspects and its two effects. Is its point of departure in the intelligence? No. Thought can shake or strengthen faith but not engender it. Is its origin in the will? No. Goodwill can favour it, ill will can impede it, but one does not believe from will, and faith is not a duty. Faith is a feeling, for it is a hope; it is an instinct, for it precedes all outward feelng. Faith is the heritage of the individual at birth, that which binds him to the totality of being; it is, so to speak, the umbilical cord of his soul. Only with pain does the individual detach himself from the maternal womb; only with effort is he isolated from the nature that surrounds him, the love that envelops him, the ideas that bathe him, the cradle that contains him. He is born in union with humanity, with the world and with God. The trace of this original union is faith. Faith is the recollection of that vague Eden from which our individuality has emerged, but which it inhabited in the somnambulistic state previous to its individual life.

Our individual life consists in separating ourselves from our surroundings, in reacting to them in such a way as to become conscious of them and constitute ourselves spiritual persons, that is, intelligent and free. Our primitive faith is only the neutral matter which is worked over by our experience of life and things and which, in consequence of our studies, studies of every kind, may perish completely in its form. We may ourselves die before being able to recover the harmony of a personal faith that can satisfy our mind and our conscience, at the same time as our heart. But the need of faith never leaves us. It is the postulate of a higher truth that will bring everything into accord. It stimulates our searching, it gives the prospect of reward, it shows the goal. This is true, at least, of the finer faith.—That which is only a childish prejudice, which has never known doubt, which is unacquainted with knowledge, which does not respect or comprehend or tolerate different convictions, is a stupidity and hatred, the mother of all the fanaticisms. One may thus repeat in regard to faith what Æsop affirmed of the tongue:

*Quid melius lingua, lingua quid peius eadem.*

Faith is too often the opposite of good faith, and in this case the man of faith resembles, to the point of being mistaken for him, the man without faith. In order to disarm our faith of its poisoned fangs, we must subordinate it to the love of truth. The supreme adoration of truth is the way to purge all the religions, all the confessions, all the sects. Faith must take second place, for it has a judge. When it makes itself the judge of everything, the world is enslaved; Christianity from the third to the sixteenth century affords the proof of this. The evil of contemporary Catholicism lies in false authority, which corrupts the conscience and reprobates scientific truth. Science, to overcome papistry, must revolutionize not only Romanism but Christianity itself. Truth, which is of God, will have to shatter theology, which is of man, and the hierarchy, which is of the Evil One. Fraud engrafted on superstition has fabricated this jungle that chokes all life, in which the greater part of Christendom is spiritually wasting away. Fire and sword will be necessary, the fire of science and the sword of criticism. Once purged, will it overcome crude faith? Let us hope so. Let us have faith in a better future.

And yet there is a difficulty here. Narrow faith is much more energetic than enlightened faith; the world belongs much more to will than to wisdom, and it is therefore far from certain that liberty will triumph over fanaticism. The unfortunate thing is that the thick-skinned have the character, and that independence of thought will never have the violence of a prejudice.

The solution lies in dividing the task. After those who have disengaged the ideal of a pure, free faith, will come the men of violence who will carry it into the sphere of acquired things, prejudices and institutions. Is not this what has already happened with Christianity? After the mild Jesus, the impetuous St. Paul and the stormy councils.—Just this, it is true, has corrupted the Gospels. But, all in all, Christianity has done still more good than harm to humanity. Thus the world moves on, by the successive putrefaction of ideas that are continually better. Thus the director of history reduces the measure of evil by a steady inoculation of the good. Error yields gradually to truth. Typhon sees Osiris perpetually reborn, to his confusion and his overthrow.

*June 19, 1872.*—The hubbub continues at the Paris Synod.[1] The supernatural is the stumbling-block. In regard to the idea of the divine they might reach an agreement; but no, it is not a question of this, the chaff must be separated from the good grain.—The supernatural is miraculous. And the miraculous is an objective phenomenon, outside all antecedent causality. Well, the miraculous, so conceived, cannot be established experimentally; besides, the subjective phenomena, immeasurably more important than the others, have ceased to come under the definition. They do not see that the miraculous is a perception of the soul, the vision of the divine behind nature, a psychic crisis analogous to that of Æneas on the last day of Troy, bringing to view the celestial powers that give an impulse to the actions of men. There are no miraculous facts for the indifferent; only religious souls are able to recognize the finger of God, that is, the supernatural in certain facts touching which the scales fall from their eyes.

Minds that have attained to immanence remain incomprehensible to the fanatics of the transcendental. Never will these latter guess that Krause's *panentheism* is ten times more pious than their dogma of the supernatural. Their passion for objective, isolated, past facts prevents them from seeing the eternal and spiritual facts. They can worship only that which comes to them from without. The moment their dramaturgy is interpreted symbolically, everything seems to them lost, just as in the case of any mythology. Their faith is connected with the imagination, not with reason. Their conscience is overwhelmed the moment analysis attacks the notion of the miraculous. They must have miracles that are local, that have vanished and are uncontrollable, because for them the divine is in these only.

Now, in an epoch of universal suffrage, this faith cannot fail to flourish, especially among the races that are dedicated to the Cartesian dualism, races that find the incomprehensible clear and that ab-

[1] A Synod of the French reformed churches was trying to determine the constitutive conditions of Protestant belief.

hor the profound. All women find the local miracle more plausible than the universal miracle, and the visible and objective intervention of God more plausible than his action psychologically and inwardly. The Latin world, by its mental form, is condemned to petrify its abstractions and never to penetrate into the inmost sanctuary of life, the central hearth where ideas themselves are not yet divided, determined and fashioned. The Latin mind objectifies everything, because it keeps outside of things and outside of itself. It is like the eye, which perceives only the external and only sees itself artificially and at a distance, in the reflecting surface of a mirror. The Germanic mind dwells in itself and is self-conscious to its centre. For the latter, immanence is a manner of feeling and thinking; for the Latin mind, it is a monstrosity or a gamble.

*August 30, 1872.*—Reading: Ch. Secrétan (analytic résumé of the *Philosophie de la liberté*, 1849); O. H. Jäger (*Die Freiheitslehre als System der Philosophie*, 1859), *rudis indigestaque moles,* unreadable.

These lucubrations *a priori* bore me at present as much as anything that exists. All scholasticisms are nauseous to me. They make me doubt what they demonstrate, because, instead of searching, they affirm the end from the beginning. Their object is to construct retrenchments around a prejudice and not to discover the truth. They are obstructions, not aids. They gather clouds, not beams of light. They all hold to the Catholic method, which excludes comparison, information, preliminary examination. The question for them is to produce adherence by legerdemain, to provide arguments for faith, to suppress inquiry. To persuade me, one must have no *parti pris,* but set out with critical sincerity. I must know where I stand, I must be shown what the questions are, their origin, their difficulties, the various solutions that have been attempted and their degree of probability. My reason, my conscience and my freedom must be respected. Scholasticism is always *ad captandum;* authority has the air of explaining itself, but it has only the air, and its deference is only illusory. The dice are loaded, and the premises are preconceived. It is presupposed that the unknown is known, and all the rest is deduced from this. One begins with a thesis in regard to God and concludes that an omelette is criminal on Friday, lawful on Sunday.

The speculative constructions of the mass or the benediction are more or less ingenious curiosities, but they have nothing to do with the truth, since the Brahman and Arab theologies have done the same thing for quite different dogmas and quite different rites. Do not theologians and rhetoricians demonstrate whatever they wish, and, if they are the only ones to speak, are they not always right?

Philosophy is complete freedom of mind, and consequently independence of every religious, political and social prejudice. At the outset, it is neither Christian nor pagan, monarchistic nor democratic, socialistic nor individualistic. It is critical and impartial; it loves only one thing, truth. So much the worse if this disturbs the ready-made opinions of the Church, the State or the historical environment in which the philosopher is born. *Est ut est aut non est.*

Philosophy is doubt, first of all, and then the consciousness of knowledge, the consciousness of uncertainty and ignorance, the consciousness of limits, distinctions, degrees, possibilities.—The common man doubts nothing and surmises nothing. The philosopher is more circumspect. He is even unfitted for action, because, seeing the end less indistinctly than others, he is yet too well aware of his weakness and has no illusions about his chances.

The philosopher is a man who fasts amidst universal drunkenness; he perceives the illusion of which created beings are the docile playthings; he is less than others the dupe of his own nature. He judges more sanely the substance of things. His freedom consists in this, to see clearly, to be sober, to reckon the worth of things. The basis of philosophy is critical clearness. Its summit would be the intuition of universal law, of the first principle and the last end of the universe. Not to be deceived is its first desire, to comprehend is its second. Emancipation from error is the condition of real understanding. A philosopher is a sceptic in search of a plausible hypothesis to explain the sum of his experiences. Imagining that he has found this key, he proposes it to others, but he does not impose it.

*Gryon-sur-Bex, September 19, 1872.*—I have just read J. J. Rousseau's *Lettre à l'archevêque de Beaumont,* with a little less admiration than . . . ten or twelve years ago, I do not know just when. This tirelessly meticulous precision is wearisome in the long run. This intense style gives one the impression of a book of mathematics. One feels the need to relax, with something easy, natural and gay. Rousseau's language is prodigiously studied and gives one an appetite for a little recreation.

But how many writers and works derive from our Rousseau! As I have gone along, I have found points of connection in Chateaubriand, Lamennais, George Sand and Proudhon. The last, for instance, copied the plan of his great work, *De la Justice dans l'Eglise et dans la Révolution,* from Rousseau's letter to Beaumont; his three volumes are a chaplet of letters to an archbishop, and their eloquence, audacity and erudition dwindle into a sort of fundamental persiflage.

How many men in one man, how many styles in one great writer! Rousseau, for example, created many genres. Alpine painting, political eloquence, lay religious unction, impassioned dialectics, the lapidary legislative style, refutation point by point, apologetic egoism . . . who knows how many more? Imagination transforms him, and he is equal to the most varied roles, even to that of a pure logician. But as imagination is his intellectual axis, his master faculty, every one of his works is half sincere and half a gamble. One feels that his talent has made with itself the wager of Carneades, that of not losing any cause, even a bad cause, once it has become a point of honour. But this is the temptation of every talent, to subordinate things to itself and not itself to things, to conquer for the sake of conquering, substituting self-esteem for conscience.

Talent asks nothing better than to triumph in a good cause; but it readily becomes a *condottiere* and is quite content to carry victory wherever it carries its flag. I am not even sure that success when the cause is weak and bad is not infinitely more flattering to talent, which in this case shares its success with no one.

Paradox is the choicest morsel of men of wit and the joy of men of talent. It is so agreeable to be right against the whole world and to dumbfound banal good sense and vulgar platitude! Talent and the love of truth therefore do not coincide; their propensities differ and often their paths as well. To oblige talent to serve, when its instinct is to command, one must have a very vigilant moral sense and a vigorous character. The Greeks, artists in words, were artificial even in the time of Ulysses, sophists in the age of Pericles, rhetoricians, courtiers and tricksters up to the end of the Lower Empire. Their talent produced their defects. Napoleon, a virtuoso of battles, could not check himself before his ruin: his talent was the cause of his downfall.

As for Rousseau, he himself explains his literary career. "A wretched question set by the Academy, exciting my mind in spite of myself, threw me into a field for which I was not created; an unexpected success revealed to me attractions that seduced me. Throngs of adversaries attacked me without comprehending me, with a giddiness that afforded me amusement and with a pride that may have inspired some in me. I defended myself, and, what with one dispute after another, I felt myself engaged in the career almost without having thought of it . . ." (Beginning of the *Lettre à l'archevêque de Beaumont*.)

To open fire with polemics, as Rousseau did, is to condemn oneself to exaggeration and perpetual warfare. One expiates celebrity by a double mortification, that of being never entirely truthful and of an inability to resume the free disposition of oneself. To quarrel with the world is attractive, but dangerous.

*October 9, 1872.*—Took tea with the M——s. These households in the English manner are very pleasing. They are the reward and the result of a long civilization and an ideal followed with perseverance. What ideal? That of moral order founded on a respect for oneself and for others, on respect for duty, in a word on dignity.

The masters of the house show consideration for their guests, the children are deferential to their parents, everyone and everything is in its place. People know how to command and how to obey. This little world is governed and seems to go along by itself; duty is the *genius loci,* but duty with that shade of reserve and self-mastery which is the British colouring. The children give the measure of this domestic system: they are happy, smiling, trustful and yet discreet. One feels that they know they are loved, but that they also know they are subordinate. Our children behave as if they were masters themselves; and when a definite order comes limiting their overflowing importunity, they see in it an abuse of power, an arbitrary act. Why? Because in principle they believe that everything revolves around them. Our children can thus be gentle and affectionate, but they are not grateful and they do not put themselves out for anyone.

How do the English mothers obtain this result? By an impersonal, unvarying, firm rule, in other words by law, which forms the mind in a free way, whereas giving orders only incites it to revolt and discontent. This method has the immense advantage of creating characters that are intractable to the arbitrary but submissive to justice, knowing where their duty lies and what is due to them, vigilant in conscience and trained in self-control. In every English child one feels the national motto, *Dieu et mon droit.* In every English home one also feels that the home is a citadel or, better, a ship. And so family life, in this world, is worth what it costs. It has its sweetness for those who bear the weight of it.

*October 13, 1872.*—At bottom, what do I deserve? Have I worked so hard, suffered so much? Can I complain of the severities, the injustices of destiny? Indeed, no. I have certainly been one of the fortunate souls, I have been relatively privileged. Only I find this good fortune itself a little flat, and life rather poor.—Have you drawn out all its possible savour? By no means. You have lacked *savoir faire,* will, energy.—Of whom do you complain? Of no one. Of what do you complain? Of not having realized one of the dreams of your youth. What is to blame for this? The disharmony between yourself and circumstances, more briefly your failure to adapt yourself. You have not been able to create an environment in your own image, and you have only been able to resign yourself to your life without taking pleasure in it. Might you have had better luck? Perhaps. Might you have had more courage? Certainly. But is not this premature disgust, this antipathy to a useless struggle, this feeling of the impossible the first of your fatalities? A bird obliged to live in a cage, a fish obliged to live in the air could not be happy. The eternal constraint of our best inclinations and our liveliest tastes ends by breaking in us the great mainspring of existence, desire. The perpetual experience of our weakness and our relapses takes from us the last illusion that fortifies us, hope. An interminable series of disappointments and disillusionments, of losses and bereavements, exhausts in us the strength that consoles, faith. Stripped in this way, what is our life? A wearisome state of defence against a despoiling that is greater still, a parley disguised as a serenade, the simulacrum of a great review for the purpose of masking a rout, a show of celebration to cover our bankruptcy, in other words a bluff that our pride maintains, a comedy played for decorum's sake but with death in our hearts. Sad.

*October 14, 1872.*—For a terribly long time I have exacted nothing of myself but lived along like the vegetables. The one genuine interest of my life lies in a few affections. The rest is only pretence. I still believe in that romantic old rubbish called love, as the charm, the motive, the reason, the hearth-fire of existence. If I were not sure of a few serious sympathies, if no one clung to me, I should not have the least taste for living. I scarcely know any happiness now except that of cheering those who are attached to me. And I feel that charity alone survives faith and hope. I feel that the act of charity has replaced for me aesthetic and scientific action, and I am no longer good for anything except being good.—This meekness of age, this premature mildness, is the compensation of impotence, the result of a lack of ambition, of desuetude and indolence. I have at least the secret joy of feeling no envy and of lavishing on young talents the encouragements and counsels which I never had myself. Personal ambition wearies me, but I can be ambitious, inventive, tireless for others. This is a harmless peculiarity, and one in which rivalry is not to be feared.

With me, the personality has spent in curiosity about itself the force that others use to expand it and set it in relief. Some people wish to dominate matter or men, make themselves rich, influential, powerful, famous; I have sought only to know myself, or rather to experiment with myself. I have tried to dispense with everything except the necessary, and for me the necessary is a little material independence and an attachment. A more complete deprivation seems to me beyond my strength. If I were shorn of affection and reduced to want, I think I should die very quickly, for even with my advantages, I hold to life only by a thread. No one is less tied to his body than I, and the fatigue of existing has already often troubled me. I believe that my memory has no more cohesion than my molecules and that disintegration has at last set in while I am still alive. The contemplative man observes his life rather than guides it, he is more spectator than actor, he tries rather to understand than to do. —Is this an illegitimate, immoral way to live? Is action required of us? Is this detachment something to respect, or is it a sin to combat? I have always wavered on this point, and I have wasted years in ineffectual reproaches and useless impulses. My Occidental conscience, pervaded with Christian morality, has always persecuted my Oriental quietism and my Buddhistic tendency. I have not dared to approve of myself, I have not been able to amend myself. In this, as in everything else, I have remained hesitant, divided, confused, perplexed, uncertain, and I have vacillated between opposites, which is a way of safeguarding one's equilibrium but which prevents any crystallization.

Having early had a glimpse of the absolute, I have not had the rash effrontery to be individual. By what right should I make a title of a defect? I could never see the necessity of imposing myself on

others and being successful. I have had no evidence of anything but
my own deficiencies and the superiority of others. Not in this way
does one cut a path for oneself. With various aptitudes and moderate intelligence, I had no dominant impulsion or imperious talent,
with the result that, being capable, I felt free, and, being free, I did
not discover what was the best. Equilibrium has produced indecision, and chronic indecision has sterilized all my faculties.

*November 9, 1872 (9 a. m.).*—Overcast sky. I do not feel very
wide-awake. My head was too low, and I went to bed after midnight. It is the opposite of waking up fresh, with bounding elasticity. Perhaps it would be better to break this habit, to leave my
shutters half open and rise with the day. It would be better for my
eyes and my brain; but it will never happen.

> *Vouloir est un ennui, changer est un effort,*
> *La vie est après tout un tissu d'habitudes;*
> *D'ailleurs nouveaux projets, nouvelles attitudes*
> *Valent-ils bien la peine? on est si vite mort! . . .*

As Louisa [1] says: "The unnerved heart yields to fatality".

> *Quand vient l'amour avec le bonheur pour amorce,*
> *Nous le regardons fuir d'un œil désenchanté,*
> *Nous demeurons passifs, nous n'avons pas la force,*
> *Le cœur énervé cède à la fatalité.*

Poor Louisa! We play the Stoic, but always in our side we have
the poisoned dart, *lethalis arundo*. Like all passionate souls, what do
you wish, Louisa? The opposites at once, glory and happiness. What
do you adore? Reform and Revolution, France and the opposite of
France. And your talent also has the two opposed qualities, intimacy
and brilliance, lyricism and the sounding bugles. And you break the
rhythm of your verses while you take pains to make them rhyme.
And you waver between Valmore and Baudelaire, between Leconte

[1] Louisa Siefert, author of the *Stoïques,* 1870.

de Lisle and Sainte-Beuve, which means that your tastes also unite the extremes. You have said so yourself:

> *Toujours extrême en mes plaisirs,*
> *Jadis, enfant joyeuse et folle,*
> *Souvent une seule parole*
> *Bouleversait tous mes plaisirs.*

But what a fine keyboard you possess, what a strong soul and what wealth of imagination!

*November 11, 1872.*—Sometimes, in fun, I have talked of the advantages of being a foreigner in Geneva. The citizen has all the financial and other burdens that are heavy to bear, and his reward is the vote, which is always onerous. Thus he pays dearly for the rods with which he is beaten. The foreigner, for a simple *permis de séjour,* costing a few sous, profits from all the benefits, including free education, and escapes all the taxes and oaths to which we submit in his place. Conclusion: Why should we not apply for the position of a foreigner?—What keeps one from desiring this is patriotism. And yet what remains of the fatherland, when all the elements that compose it have disappeared? When people no longer have in common religion, public spirit, desires, hopes, political faith, convictions, when one has ceased to feel at home in the ideas, the wishes, the tastes of those around one, when one no longer has ancestors or descendants and is, in brief, without roots and without ties in one's country? The fatherland becomes a myth; and yet, willy-nilly, it remains an affection.

I feel very isolated from the real Geneva; but the ideal phantom of Geneva still means something to me. Superstition? So be it. A faith without a motive? Agreed. But the heart needs an object and even an illusion. One loves things and people not for the happiness they give one or promise one, but stupidly, without knowing why, or nobly, without hope of recompense.

*November 18, 1872.*—A morning of revery. Asked two people by letter if they knew what was individual in me; if their judgment

should coincide, they would probably be right. As for me, I have
lost the key to myself and no longer know the essential thing, my
particular gift, the thing for which I was made, and consequently
my strength, my mission, my charge.

> *Edle Seelen vorzufühlen*
> *Ist der wertheste Beruf.*

"To think today what will be accepted and popular in thirty
years."—There are two answers, that of Goethe and that of Schopenhauer. As for me, I have rather said to myself: To comprehend
all the modes of human nature and to do well whatever one does.
This last motto seems to indicate little originality, little creative or
inventive force, little will, a sort of indifference to action. To act
correctly, to think and feel justly is not the ideal of an artist, an
ambitious man, an orator, but merely that of an attentive critic and
a good man. I am not fitted to dominate people and overturn
things. To contemplate, divine, love, console has always been more
attractive to me. My talent is for disinterested neutrality and impersonality of mind; my taste is for the life of the affections. I have
objective intelligence and a tender heart. What is antipathetic to me
is the vulgar life that is woven of prejudices, passions, interests that
are at once selfish and heated, narrow and resolute. What I find un-
endurable is to act on my own account and for myself. I cannot
take an interest in my personal welfare, my career, my plans, my
future. All this seems coarse, ignoble and base. And as the world is
the arena in which all the appetites struggle for satisfaction, I do
not feel a part of the world, which is given over to the covetous,
the strong and the clever.

Between the relative, which overwhelms me, and the absolute,
which I despair of attaining, I float listlessly and act only at the
last extremity, all action being a lottery except when it is a positive
duty. When in doubt, abstain, says the proverb: well, in every action that offers a choice I doubt, and in every speculative decision I

hesitate.—I lack that which creates determination, I mean that power of illusion which corroborates one's will and makes one believe it is good because it is one's own. I always have a doubt in the back of my mind whether the contrary of what I am about to say or do is not perhaps equally true or equally good. I lack self-infatuation, or that obstinacy of will which takes the place of infatuation. I am never sufficiently of my opinion or my party to work energetically with it. I have not the least idea what is expedient for me or what it is expedient for me to do. My sagacity, my tact, my resolution, my zeal can serve only others.

A singular organization, really Buddhistic and monastic. I was made for devotion, on condition that some other devotedly tender person assumed the guidance of my personal interests. And destiny has had the irony to condemn me to self-government from my childhood, to isolation and celibacy in my riper years. In what way has my independence served me? It has simply caused me to abstain. I have been unable to build an existence to my liking; I have only drawn my paws into my shell to withstand the inclemencies of the outer world. And yet I have not dared to be a Stoic or a Buddhist altogether, with an intrepid logic. I have been neither Oriental nor Occidental, neither man nor woman entirely; I have remained amorphous, atonic, agamous, neuter, lukewarm and divided. Pah!

*November 23, 1872.*—Quarrels, disputes, dissension everywhere; how tiresome the world is! The pride of our race has converted the impossibility of peace into a sign of greatness, very much as hunchbacks, if they were in the majority, might decree that their hunch was an ornament of mankind. An oscillation between contrary blunders seems the law of our species; wisdom, that is, the reconciling of contrasts, is the lot only of a few privileged persons. The human world is given over to parties, and parties are partialities which, though ignorant of one another, tear at one another's throats. What does all this prove? That Heraclitus is right: the majority of wingless bipeds are ungifted creatures, ruled by folly and malignity.

The more a man is really a man, the more isolated he is; in proportion as he grows in vision and goodness, the fewer fellows he has; if he were perfect, he would be unique. So his excellence creates a void around him and separates him from his surroundings, from the vulgar, from the multitude. Happily, charity enables him to bridge the abyss. The less men deserve his deference and love, the more he devotes himself to them. The less to his taste they are, the more he tries to be useful to them. The more he finds them unintelligent and bad, the more his pity suppresses his repugnance. From his superiority he draws a motive, not to disdain men, but to be their apostle.

Religious and political quarrels are too much for you; the everlasting childishness of excited crowds, which are the masters of everything in a democracy, perpetually cloys and nauseates you. The necessity of wrangling over everything, the truceless redemonstrating of elementary truths, the wearisomeness of current prejudices, the daily banalities, the familiar tricks dishearten and sicken you. The certainty that the best idea will always be the last in the preference of the masses discourages you.—Therefore, you lack energy and love for your fellow-man. Disillusion makes you cold.

It is certain that changing the world seems to you chimerical, and that you find it difficult enough to reform yourself. Learning to see more clearly and to act better satisfies your ambition. To this, add help for everyone who asks it and whose hopes are in you; this is as far as your sacrifices go. You have no distinct notion of any more general charge of souls, any public mission, any duty towards those who make no appeal to you and do not offer you the floor. You have no hankering for proselytism, propaganda or even publicity. The feeling of universal self-sufficiency, produced by the regime of democracy, has taken from you even the desire for discussion.

*November 28, 1872.*—Anniversary of the death of S.[1] the birth of M., and the marriage of H.; the three great occasions of life for three of my friends fall on the same date or rather on the same day

[1] S. designates an old friend whom the Journal had baptized Sibylle.

of the year. To be born, to double one's existence, to die, these are the three great juridical and religious moments. How many years is it since S. entered into rest? Since M. arrived on earth? Since H. was married? I no longer know. Time is an indifferent affair to me and leaves no mark on my memory. Dates relative to outside things interest me and still have a value for my mind. But my own life knows nothing of chronological categories; I do not see myself *sub specie temporis*. These divisions of weeks, months, years, decades are not linked to anything in my soul, and they remain foreign to it. Why? Because action is not my form of existence, and because action alone involves us with the outside world recorded by the calendar. The inner life, like the dream, has nothing in common with these artificial stripes and notches of duration. If I lost these note-books that make up my journal, my autobiography, like the history of India, could never be reconstructed. I perceive in myself neither a course nor progress, no growth, no events. I feel that I *am* with more or less intensity, sorrow or joy, health or lucidity, but nothing happens in my life and I am pursuing no career, moving away from no fixed point and approaching no desired end. My ambition (if the word is not absurdly unsuitable) is to experience life, to become conscious of the modes of human existence, not to will but to feel and think, in other words contemplation. For contemplation, time is consumed in eternity. And that is why I do not see time passing and years running out save through external observation, as, for instance, when I see one of my comrades become a grandfather, but not through personal and direct perception.

My baptismal certificate proves that I have passed the half-century; but I might attain to twice this without becoming habituated to the world or even to my own body. The roll of time seems strange to me and repels me still, as much as, even more than twenty-five years ago. I watch the show of my own magic-lantern, but the I that looks on does not identify itself with the spectacle. I am to myself the motionless space in which my sun and stars revolve. My mind is the place of my phenomena; it has time in it and is consequently outside of time. It is to itself what God is to the world, eternal by opposition to that which appears and disappears, begins and ends, with that which is in continual metamorphosis.

*December 1, 1872 (9.45 a. m.).*—What an odd dream! I was to suffer capital punishment in two days. It appears that I had deserved it, for I did not feel the least indignation. But the curious thing is that I had no recollection of the crime, that my conscience was perfectly clear and I had no dread whatever of death. In a word, I was at once guilty and innocent, I had no fault to find with either life or death.—Was this dream perhaps the result of the combination of an aphorism of November 27th (Life and death are indifferent) with my lecture of the 29th (on capital punishment)? Perhaps there should even be added, as a third element, Determinism (with which my head was crammed by the Disdier competition), which does away with the guilt of the criminal.—Or was it possibly the phrase of Othello about himself, "Honourable murderer", on which my imagination may have been working?

What secretly pleased me as I awoke was the feeling that even in a dream I could not identify myself with a scoundrel, and that if, in fact, I had committed some homicide, it was unawares, as a sleep-walker falling from a roof might crush a passer-by.

Another explanation that occurs to me for my dream is the exercise in the reading of tragedy during this last fortnight, an exercise in which the reader lends his voice and person to alien terrors or ferocities, to such an extent that he is not what he is, since he does not really experience what he obligingly represents. Dreaming in the same way, I was a criminal without a crime, and I was about to be executed without fear. While seriously believing myself lost, I felt the security of one who perceives the fiction.

I had the illusion and did not have it. I played the comedy to myself, deceiving my imagination without being able to deceive my consciousness. This power of dreams to melt together things that are incommensurable, to unite things that are mutually exclusive, to identify the yes with the no, is what makes them marvellous and symbolic. In dreams, our individuality is not closed; it envelops, so to speak, its surroundings, it is the landscape and all it contains, ourselves included. But if our imagination is not ours, if it is impersonal, the personality is only a particular case, reduced from its general functions. This is still more true in the case of thought. Thought might exist without possessing individuality, without assuming concrete form in an ego. In other words, dreams lead to the notion of an imagination that is freed from the limits of personality, and even of a thought that is no longer conscious. A person dreaming is in process of dissolution into the universal fantasy of Maya. Dreams are an excursion into limbo, a half-deliverance from the human prison. The dreamer is no longer anything but the theatre of various phenomena of which he is the involuntary spectator; he is passive and impersonal, he is the plaything of unknown vibrations and invisible goblins.

A man who never emerged from the state of dreaming would not attain to humanity, properly speaking, but a man who had never dreamed would know the mind only as ready-made and would be incapable of comprehending the genesis of personality; he would be like a crystal, unable to imagine crystallization. Thus waking emerges from dream as dream emanates from nervous life, and as this latter is the flower of organic life. Thought is the summit of a series of ascending metamorphoses which are called nature. Personality thenceforward recovers in internal depth what it loses in extent, and recompenses the riches of receptive passivity with the vast privilege of self-direction which is called liberty. Dreams, jumbling and abolishing all limits, render us well aware of the severity of the conditions attached to a higher existence; but conscious and voluntary thought alone enables us to know and permits us to act, is alone capable of science and perfection. Let us, therefore, be glad to dream from psychological curiosity and for our relaxation; but let us not disparage thought, which gives us our strength and our dignity. Let us begin as Oriental and end as Occidental man: these are the two halves of wisdom.

*December 9, 1872.*—What truth is there of the moral order that is not debased in being vulgarized and does not become false in becoming popular? It is thus with liberty, equality, sanctity, piety, faith, freedom of thought, progress and so many others. Every truth is relative, limited, shaded, conditional. But the populace rushes upon it as a bull rushes on a red rag, sees nothing but the thing alone, isolates it, exaggerates it, takes it for an absolute and turns a truth into an error. Man has a kind of itching for truth, but he reaches truth only after exhausting all the possible combinations; in other words, the crowd has a natural affinity for error and invariably proceeds towards the goal which it sets for itself by the longest and most tortuous of zig-zags. It suggests the stupidity of bees in a cage, bumping against all the walls before they find the way out. The masses lack foresight, almost by definition, and experiment with all the blunders that reason has clearly proved, because they see nothing but what they touch. Intelligence consists in anticipating experience and economizing the errors into which stupidity falls. In this sense, the masses have no intelligence; they know nothing but attraction, passion, prejudice; they resemble animals, stripped of their instinct.

Universal suffrage, convenient for settling questions of legality, vitiates, on the other hand, by its very nature, all questions of truth. Scientific, moral, religious, artistic truth has always advanced through minorities, through scattered individuals, and always has against it the crowds, chaffing, scoffing, persecuting, martyrizing the excellent wherever it shows itself, but never acknowledging it. When this appears not to be so, it means that enough public modesty remains for the voices of good judges to be heard, and that the mob has been ashamed to judge for itself. But when the mob takes itself seriously, when, having the strength and the right, it aspires in addition to decide concerning what is true, or beautiful, or holy, the level of everything drops, drops even to grossness. *Ne sutor ultra crepidam.*

The thing that everyone is most willing to practise, and performs worst, is judgment, criticism.

The easiest and most commonplace of things is to judge; the most difficult and the rarest thing is to judge well.—Why? Because, for judging, thoughtlessness and folly are sufficient, while to judge well requires much reflection and wisdom.

A madman who judged himself mad would be cured in principle, since his madness would be subordinated to his reason. A fool who could gauge his folly would be a man of intellect who had had an accident. But crowds are mad and foolish without knowing it, and this is what renders their case incurable, or at least desperate.

(*10 p. m.*).—An ant that trifled with the wrath or the interests or the vanities of its ant-hill would not be a patriotic ant. A man who plays with that which impassions those who surround him ceases to be considered a serious man. The mind that laughs at itself is the antipode of seriousness; conversely, the serious seems comic to a mind that is not deceived by its illusion. Seriousness is therefore a faith, a credulity, a *parti pris;* a purely critical critic is more likely to be merry (I might cite living proofs, *nisi odiosa essent exempla*). A person's serious side is the sensitive and vulnerable part of him, the thing to which he holds, whether this thing is his purse, his honour, his conviction, the object of his veneration, his country, his mother, his title makes little difference. The moment this thing is menaced, he ceases to laugh and places himself on the defensive. This is the part of his being that is engaged and not free. Our neighbour divines that his hold upon us can only be on our serious side, and that if we laugh at everything we escape all bondage, all association, every tie. He is right. The serious is our umbilical cord, which attaches us to humanity.

Are you not a serious man? Little enough in one sense, for you have remained much freer of mind than most men of your age, and you can trifle with many interests that are indifferent to you but to which they attach great importance. As you are neither married, nor ambitious, nor a magistrate, nor a party man, nor a man of means, nor the head of a house, the surface of your serious side is much more reduced. It is at its minimum. A few affections, the material conditions of independence and health, the moral law, this is all or almost all of it.

Inspiring neither fear nor hope, unable to be either classified or exploited, how should I be taken seriously? Besides this, I avoid any sort of posture, I seek the shadow, I efface myself, I play dead, I wish to be asked and not to offer myself. This procedure reduces me to zero. Who would reckon with me?

Happily, independence pleases me better than power or celebrity or wealth, and I almost have independence.

*December 11, 1872.*—Slept my seven and a half unbroken hours like a little Saint John; a blue and dreamless sleep. Again the grey, low, rainy sky which we have had so long for company. It is mild, sad weather. I dare say my rather dingy windows contribute to this sullen aspect of the outer world. The rain and the smoke have besmeared their surface.

> *Et remplacé la transparence*
> *Par la diaphanéité.*

Between us and things, how many screens there are! Our mood, our health, all the tissues of the eye, the window-panes of our cell, fog, smoke, rain or dust, and even light itself, and all this infinitely variable! Heraclitus said that one never bathes twice in the same river. I will say that one never sees the same landscape twice, for a window is one kaleidoscope and the observer is another.

> *Que le monde est bizarre et que l'homme est étrange!*
> *Le spectateur changeant d'un spectacle qui change*
> *Croit qu'il reste le même et qu'il tient le réel. . . .*

What is madness? It is illusion to the second power. Good sense establishes regular relations, a *modus vivendi* among things, men and itself, and it has the illusion that it is in touch with stable truth, with the eternal fact. Unreason does not even see what good sense sees, and it has the illusion that it sees better. Good sense identifies the fact of experience with the inevitable fact, and takes in good faith that which is for the measure of that which might be; madness does not see the difference between that which is and that which it fancies; it confounds its dream with reality.

The real is true and necessary: simple illusion. The real is real: illusion to the second power, or squared. Might there be such a thing as a cubed illusion? Would not this be the case if the consciousness of a madman were conscious of its madness, but *in petto* took it for wisdom?

Wisdom consists in judging good sense and madness, and in lending oneself to the universal illusion without being deceived by it. To enter into the game of Maya, to take one's part with a good grace in the fantastic tragi-comedy that is called the Universe is the most fitting thing for a man of taste, who knows how to play with the playful and be serious with the serious. It seems to me that intellectualism ends there. The mind, in so far as it is thought, reaches the intuition that all reality is only the dream of a dream.—What makes us emerge from the palace of dreams is suffering, personal suffering; also the feeling of obligation, or that which unites the two, the suffering of sin; love also does it; in a word, the moral order. It is conscience that wrests us from the enchantments of Maya. Conscience dissipates the fumes of kief, the hallucinations of opium and the placidity of contemplative indifference. It thrusts us into the terrible mesh of human suffering and human responsibility. It is the spoil-sport, the alarm-clock, the cock-crow that drives away the phantoms, the archangel armed with a sword who drives man from his artificial paradise. Intellectualism is like an intoxication that delights in its own taste; moralism is a fast, it is a hunger and thirst that will not sleep.—Alas! Alas!

*January 6, 1873.*—Read the seven tragedies of Æschylus. The *Prometheus* and the *Eumenides* are still the great among the great; they have the sublimity of the prophets. Both depict a religious revolution, a profound crisis in the life of humanity. *Prometheus* is the wresting of civilization from the jealousy of the gods; the *Eumenides* is the transformation of justice and the substitution of expiation and pardon for implacable retaliation. *Prometheus* shows the martyrdom of all the saviours; the *Eumenides* is the glorification of Athens and the Areopagus, that is, of a really human civilization. How magnificent this poetry is, and how paltry all passionate individual adventures seem beside this colossal tragedy of the fates!

*January 20, 1873.*—Passed the morning with Cantu, History of the Italian Republics, the Crusades, the Middle Ages in general, the Hanseatic League.

What is universal history? The exhaustion of all the possible combinations and mistakes. Does it tend to justice? Yes, in the form of a distributive levelling or the participation of all in everything; it leads to equality of conditions, then to equality of goods. It aspires to the best and never finds the good; if it were to find the good, it would destroy it at once. The good is an equilibrium, and equilibrium would be the death of history. History is thus eternal agitation in the pursuit of the unrealizable. Individuals can realize wisdom in themselves. Nations can realize only the appearance of it, namely, equality in freedom.

Supposing that mankind were to perish of old age, supposing it had reached the end of its geological period, what object would it have served? That of converting into an idea the whole sum of the planetary life which is incarnate in it; and more than this, it would have translated the poem of the *cosmos* into the special language of Cybele. Our humanity would be one chord and measure in the colossal symphony played by the worlds that are subject to our sun. It represents a world compounded to the fiftieth power; but relatively to the human races of our coördinated planets, it is only a unit in a number.

To become spirit is to enter into eternal life. Is it to make one's

individuality eternal? Is it to resume one's place in the circle of the
invisible? To what does death lead? A return to God. Whether the
result is a reabsorption into universal being or worship through a
persisting personality, that which will be will be good, for it will be
the divine order. If God is love, to be loved must be fitting for
him. But without limits, without form and life, what can the individual be? Of this we know nothing. It does not follow, because
one believes in God, that the soul is immortal. One can believe in
the good without believing in God.—The Stoic acceptation of order
and destiny is superior to all religious revolutions and all the crises
of theology.—If vigorous hopes, powerful affections, profound aspirations were arguments, survival would be plausible. But what of
the wicked who dread another life, and the half of mankind who
long for annihilation? One could imagine an optional immortality,
granted to ardent faith, as long as this faith itself did not ask to
sleep the eternal sleep. One might win immortality as one wins
liberty, by an effort that God respects and rewards. Certain it is
that the spiritual life, beyond error and sin, can become alluring; the
life of contemplation and love would attract me; but paradisiacal
dreams are one and all moulded of inner contradictions, which rather
attest the play of the imagination than the perception of clear
thought. The ultimate things are a matter of faith and conjecture.
Nothing is *known* of them. Generally, one believes in regard to them
what some predecessor, some fine religious soul has believed, a
Pythagoras, a Plato, a Buddha, a Jesus. Beliefs and cults are only
the prolongation of an original emotion and intuition, and the confession of them ten billion times repeated cannot increase the value
of their content and their certainty. Man is content to go where
that which he loves goes, whether to life or to death, whether to
immortality or annihilation. But it must be acknowledged that, in
view of human frailty, faith in immortality gives an inner courage,
hope and serenity that prepare men better for the battle of life. If
it is an illusion, it does good. If it is a chimæra, it fortifies.

*March 31, 1873 (4 p. m.).*

> *En quel songe*
> *Se plonge*
> *Mon cœur, et que veut-il?*

For an hour I have been feeling an indefinable restlessness: I recognize my old enemy

> *Agnosco veteris vestigia flammæ.*

It is the nostalgia for the unknown, a fever without a name, the thirst for happiness, the stirring of old ashes, the rebirth of youthful desires, the itching of the wings, the rising of the sap of spring. It is an emptiness and an anguish, a lack of something. What? Love, peace, God perhaps. It is an emptiness certainly, and not a hope; it is an anguish, too, for neither the ill nor the remedy can be determined. It is a thirst for tenderness, a longing for caresses, for sympathy, for the married life, and also for travel, for the joy of the eyes. It is the languor of voluptuous pleasure.

> *Le renouveau me trouble: ô nature cruelle! . . .*
> *O printemps sans pitié, dans l'âme endolorie,*
> *Avec tes chants d'oiseaux, tes brises, ton azur,*
> *Tu creuses sourdement, conspirateur obscur,*
> *Le gouffre des langueurs et de la rêverie.*

*(7 p. m.)*—Carried to the twenty-first verse this complaint against the malignities of the springtime. Of all the hours of the day, when the weather is superb, it is the afternoon, around three o'clock, that I find particularly formidable. Never more than then do I feel the "fearful emptiness of life", the inner unrest, the painful thirst for happiness. This torture of the light is a strange phenomenon. Does the sun, as it brings out the spots on a garment, the wrinkles of the face and the fading of the hair, light up with inexorable clarity the rents and scars of the heart? Does it make one

ashamed of existing? In any case, the shining hours can flood the soul with sadness, give one the desire for death, for suicide or annihilation, or for their diminutive, a stupefaction in the voluptuous. This is the hour when a man is afraid of himself and longs to escape from his misery and solitude,

> *Le cœur trempé sept fois dans le néant divin.*
> —Leconte de Lisle.

People speak of the temptations of the dark hours of crime. To these must be added the mute desolations of the resplendent hours of the day. At one time, as at the other, God has disappeared; but at the first, a man follows his eyes and the cry of his passion; at the second, he is lost and feels that he is abandoned by everything.

> *En nous sont deux instincts qui bravent la raison:*
> *Le goût du suicide et la soif du poison.*
> *Cœur solitaire, à toi prends garde!*

*April 2, 1873 (4 p. m.)*—A torrent of indeterminable and contradictory impressions, reading a mass of newspapers and talking with De——, Do—— and H—— in the Place de la Taconnerie. Scarcely had I reached home when I felt a nostalgia for the indefinable, a thirst for pleasure, a restless longing for love, a weariness of myself and my solitude, the deadly sloth of the cloister. The reading of a few of Goethe's songs only sharpened this desire for life and this disgust with Puritan asceticism. All the monastic renunciations seem at such times a pious dupery, an enormous fiction, even, to put it more bluntly, a stupidity. The temptation to fling one's cap at the moon and dance the *cachucha* with Minerva and the Grand Duchess of Gérolstein, the itch of madness, the hankering for extravagance and pleasure, unsettle the professors as well as the monks. One feels that one would like to parody wisdom and box the ears of dignity, as ridiculous conventions and professional humbug. This is the "crisis" so prettily described by Feuillet, it is the weariness with virtue, the doubt about principles, the reawakening of nature which has been tyrannized over, the revenge of Caliban, who has been subjugated too long by the magic formulas of Prospero, the higher spirit; it is the carmagnole of the flesh, bored with its pedagogue and its tyrant, decorum; it is the desire for novelty, for the unknown, for intoxication, the carnival spirit throwing into confusion all the habits of the regular life; it is the malice of Beelzebub, breaking the reins of morality and bent on his feast of asses, his witches' sabbath, his black mass, his hour of saturnalia. This broad, Anacreontic gust of wind, this orgiastic titillation that reappears for a moment in the spring, even in grave and well-ordered lives, once held a very different place in the religious institutions of mankind. There were entire cults that gave an outlet to this craving for a frantic intoxication, this rage for life that is so akin to mutilation and suicide . . . This divine fury has a very simple and natural outlet, that which the *Pervigilium Veneris* sings . . . but, lacking this solution, it foams up in poetry, in transports and storms, as impeded electricity turns into crashing thunder and lightning.

Here, too, virginity and continence bring on tempests, magnificent, doubtless, but morbid, from which the married are free. The imagination is a fulminate, the most explosive of all, which the confused desire for generation has the property of setting off. In this colossal uproar one would say that heaven and earth were involved, when it all comes down to a single point: will Jacquot carry the day with Jacqueline? What a racket for one kiss more or less! A little rain lays a great deal of dust. A voluptuous shepherd girl quells Attila. A baker's maid extinguishes Raphael. Delilah, with her tresses, does more than a whole people to reduce Samson . . .

In short, the sexual function is the most terrible of the tributes that nature has imposed upon us. And of all the ways of escaping this bondage, the surest, the only good one, is obedience to its law. Calm comes from using it, not from privation or mutilation.

Woman cures us of the curiosity, the desire and the madness of sex. She cures us of the ill that she causes. She tempts, but she satiates; she excites, but she allays. And reciprocally. Each sex thus attains a balanced humanity only through the other sex. Sexuality is an imperfection in the individual which can be corrected only by pairing . . . Only those who have passed the natural initiation, and looked into the eyes of Isis, can be enlightened judges of life, history, literature, law, society. Without the possession *par excellence,* one cannot possess a correct idea of the nature of things; one is a stranger to the universal experience. With possession, one is no great scholar, but one has passed the preliminary examination and taken one's first step in the matriculation of general life. This initiation is an immense disillusion, but it is a salutary disillusion. One learns from it that pleasure is nothing or almost nothing, that it is only a false promise and the symbol of something excellent, namely, love. Love itself is only the exalted and fugitive form of something better, which is tenderness; and tenderness is only an application of charity or divine pity. To commiserate life, to help it, befriend it, console it, to brood over it, so to speak, is the point of view of the great of heart, who have become maternal, whatever their sex may be. For them pleasure, intoxication, sensuality, selfishness have ceased to exist. Their joy is to give joy, their happiness is to make others happy and to combat suffering and, consequently, sin, which is a false hope, that of finding gladness outside the good. Charity understands everything, bears with everything, excuses everything because it has the compassion of a mother and the forbearance of goodness. It knows that unhappy souls exist, it is not interested to know whether some of these souls may be guilty.

*April 3, 1873.*—Visit with my —— friends. Their niece came in with two of her children, and the talk was about Père Hyacinthe's lecture.

Enthusiastic women are curious when they speak of orators and extemporizers. They imagine that the crowd is inspiring and that inspiration suffices for everything. How innocent and childlike, as an explanation for a real address in which nothing has been left to chance, neither the plan, nor the arguments, neither the ideas, the images or even the length, in which everything is prepared with the greatest care! Women, with their love of marvels and miracles, prefer to ignore all this. The meditation, the toil, the calculation of the effects, the art, in a word, detracts for them from the value of the thing, which they like to think has dropped from heaven and has been sent from on high. What they wish is the bread; they cannot bear the idea of the baker. The sex is superstitious and hates to understand what it wishes to admire. It would be vexed if it had to humble its prejudices in regard to sentiment and give a larger place to thought. It wishes to believe that imagination takes the place of reason, and that the heart takes the place of knowledge, and it never wonders why women, so rich in heart and imagination, cannot perform a work of oratory, that is, combine into a unity a multitude of facts, ideas and impulses. These women do not even divine the difference between the heat of a popular harangue, which is only an outburst of passion, and the deploying of a didactic apparatus that is intended to establish something and to convince the auditors. So, for them, study, reflection, technique are nothing; the extemporizer mounts to the platform and Pallas springs fully armed from his lips to wrest applause from the dazzled assembly. It follows that orators are divided for them into two groups, the toilers who burn the midnight oil to piece their laborious discourses together and the inspired ones who only take the trouble to be born. They will never comprehend Quintilian's phrase, *Fit orator, nascitur poeta.*

Productive enthusiasm is a light, perhaps, but receptive enthusiasm seems very much like blindness. The latter confuses values, confounds distinctions, obscures all intelligent criticism and muddles the judgment. The "eternal feminine" favours exaltation, mysticism, sentiment, lyricism, the fantastic, it is the enemy of clearness, a calm and rational view of things. It is the antipode of criticism and science. The preponderant influence of women is all to the advantage of the religions and the priests, and subsidiarily the poets, to the detriment of truth and liberty. This influence is an intoxication analogous to the intoxication of love.—So Athene prefers the males, and Proudhon has shown that the accession of women destroyed ancient society, because, as a reciprocal effect, it made the men effeminate.

I have had only too much sympathy and weakness for the feminine nature; its infirmity becomes plainer to me through the very excess of my early deference to it. Justice and science, right and reason are virile things; and imagination, sentiment, revery, fancy must come afterwards. When one thinks that Romanism is sustained by women, one feels how necessary it is not to give the reins to the eternal feminine, the charm of which at bottom is dangerous and deceptive.

*Good Friday, April 11, 1873 (11 a. m.).*—I have just read over the whole story of the last week of Jesus, and a number of articles on the Resurrection, on religious unity, on Faith and Science. Stirred up many ideas and doubts. Felt the weight of solitude. A flood of indecisions. A cloud of question-marks. I am forgetting all the conclusions I had reached. I am chilled and sad. Everything is uncertain, and faith proves nothing as to the intrinsic and objective truth of things; faith is only the measure of a soul, through its aspirations.

In what, at this moment, do I believe? The beauty of the soul of Jesus, the nobility of certain individualities. For example, I believe in the admirable character of S.; but I believe in it because I see it, because I experience it. Like Dante, I would willingly contemplate heaven in the eyes of an inspired woman. Faith is a voluntary self-deception that is born of love; it is the sharing of an illusion, a dream, a hope, an ideal. The only reality of faith is a moral reality. It is the communion of souls who recognize one another in their desire; this reality is psychological. Religious faith is the longing to escape from one's isolation and form bonds with other souls. Religion is not a proof of God, it is the proof only of an attribute of man, the need of putting oneself into harmony with the totality of things, and of feeling at one with the infinite. It springs from a feeling, the restless and profound feeling of mystery;

it satisfies this by an instinct, faith, which is a provisional formulation of the mystery, and by an act, prayer or worship, which is a testimony of submission to the divine principle.—Union with one's fellows and union with the eternal Unknown, according to the procedure or the ritual of this or that great soul, clothed in a sacred character: that is what makes the Israelite, the Buddhist, the Musselman or the Christian. To love, to glorify, to will what he has loved, glorified and willed whom one takes for a guide, for an initiator and a model, this is what the religious faculty has done and caused men to do. Religion is transmitted, like magnetism, through a medium; it is acquired, spread, inoculated like a moral virus, through the confused, unconscious region in us, that through which we can love without knowing it, through the mimetic and receptive faculty of the soul. Faith is a magnetization to which one abandons oneself and in which one finds a certitude without proofs, a tranquillity that dispenses with motives, an indefinable well-being.

*April 20, 1873.*—Last evening, took my sister to the concert of the Société de Chant sacré. Heard Handel's *Messiah,* with a feeling of sadness. Why? Because of so many happier memories; then from thinking of Berlin, of my golden years, of Professor Gervinus. Felt, too, the poetry of the orthodox belief and the severe beauty of this music. But, in spite of all, an impression as of ruins filled my mind, the ruins of my life, the archæology of beliefs and works of art, the transiency and frailty of all forms, the inevitable engulfment of all that has lived. Gulf and abyss. Everything is a dream. God alone abides.

> O gouffre, je te sens; je te vois, morne abîme!
> Tout ce que nous croyons grand, noble, glorieux,
> Siècles et nations, les mondes et les dieux,
> Que sont-ils? moins que rien; un soupir de l'infime
> Qui traverse un instant l'éternité des cieux . . .
> O stupeur formidable et vision sublime!
>
> Rien n'existe, sinon l'inexorable loi.
> L'être n'est que chimère, apparence, vaine ombre.

*La triple immensité de l'espace, du nombre,*
*Du temps, vaste sépulcre, engloutit tout en soi,*
*Dans l'océan sans fond de l'infini tout sombre;*
*L'homme croit vivre, et vit seulement par la foi.*

*April 21, 1873.*—Enough of this beating about the bush, this wandering, idling, postponing, shilly-shallying. The important thing is to suppress the useless, to pursue the indispensable, to simplify one's desires, to concentrate, epitomize oneself. You were thinking this three years ago, you proposed several revolutions at once. Then, as you were unable to carry out the principal one, you let them all go, as your habit is. You fell back into your day-by-day existence; negligence has become your wisdom. You have tucked your head, like the ostrich, under your wing, in order not to see the danger or the enemy. You have had, as aids to your life, three friendships with women, especially one that has become intimate and serious and that has enabled you to know a very beautiful soul. But the sweetness of the present has caused you to avert your eyes from the menace of the future. Living in better lodgings, in better company and with better health, you have been pleased to forget the sorrows that lie before you and the provisional nature of all these things. Your repugnance to looking ahead has had its own way . . .

O carelessness that is full of care! What you detest is to will, to make up your mind, because you always doubt your insight and because you do not know what is best . . . Your second instinct always brings you back to this, the instinctive feeling of weakness that cannot bear humiliation or even the idea of it. Your first instinct is for activity through love and through the aesthetic impulse also. What you lack, in fact, is a virile ruggedness of will and the audacity of your true interest. Your misfortune is to have the feminine nature without being a woman. You wish to be summoned and not to impose yourself. You lack the necessary infusion of ambition and combativeness. Boldness, hope, courage are missing in you. You have never been able to toughen your style, treat fortune bluntly, steel your sensibility.—A pity.

*April 29, 1873.*—Before we are fifty, the world is the frame in which we work at our portrait; after fifty, when our personality saddens us and fades, we must forget ourselves in something that is better and greater than we, our country, science, art, humanity. This is the way, if not to grow young again, at least to escape premature death, to conquer melancholy by quitting a skiff that is sinking for a vessel that spreads its sails. Beware of the discontent that brings into scorn and dislike not only the shipwrecked man, but the only means of rescue. Your instinct is to leave behind what leaves you behind, but this pride surrounds one with isolation. Better to set oneself aside, one's preferences, one's pretentions, rights and tastes, and ask for neither consideration nor justice, neither for sympathy nor kindness, and to dream only of the good and the welfare of something great and durable, like an institution or a community. Is that not, in other words, to place oneself at the service of God?

*May 23, 1873.*—The fundamental error of France lies in her psychology. She has always believed that a thing said is a thing done, as if rhetoric outweighed propensities, habits, character, the real being, as if words took the place of will, conscience, education, regeneration. France always proceeds by blasts of eloquence, guns or decrees. She thinks that in this way she can change the nature of things; but only ruins and catchwords result. She has never understood the first line of Montesquieu: "Laws are the necessary relations that derive from the nature of things."—She is unwilling to see that her incapacity to organize liberty comes from her very nature, from the notions she has of the individual, society, religion, law, duty, from the way she brings up her children. Her way is to plant the trees upside down, and she is amazed at the result! Universal suffrage, with a bad religion and a bad popular education, means a perpetual see-saw between anarchy and dictatorship, between the red and the black, between Danton and Loyola. Being obstinate in her illusion, she is always chasing her own tail. How many scape-goats will she butcher before she beats her breast? . . .

*July 15, 1873 (7 a. m.).*—Melancholy. Bad cough, many more

grey hairs, a feeling of the impossible and the irreparable, a sense of folly and stupidity, weariness of life, boredom with myself, humiliation, regret. Observation of my own decay. A clear perception of what will always be refused me. I forget, but I can neither resign myself nor use my will. I stifle my desires, being unable either to suppress them or satisfy them. Too proud to complain of my lot, too discouraged to struggle against it, too clear-sighted to count on myself or on the world, I do not know what figure to cut before fate. I am neither happy nor unhappy. I am a shipwrecked man who will not accept his condition. I am a thwarted aspiration and a life that has miscarried. Doubt has destroyed in me even the faculty of hoping; I scarcely believe in what I have, so present to me is the fragility of everything that is good. I feel that everything, everything slips away; if I pressed the hand of a loyal woman, saying, Will you belong to me? I should feel underneath that death would almost instantly freeze this hand in mine. Life is so treacherous and so cruel that in order to escape from its tyranny I ask nothing of it. I profit by what it sends my way, but without any more counting on anything than one counts upon good weather.

. . . A knock at the door. It is the maid bringing me a letter. One might think it a trick of the theatre or a response from Providence. The letter comes from Céligny; it is from a very dear friend, she who asked me to think of her in my dark hours. There is really a touching coincidence in this, one that might set a man thinking.

*July 17, 1873 (10.30 p. m.).*—Sky clear and swarming with stars. Feeling of emptiness. Is it not against nature to be thus absolutely alone? In any case, it is against my nature. I am sociable, loving, even tender; who would suspect it? I am stifled in my forlorn state, but I pretend a stoical indifference. Concert, fireworks this evening; but what would have been the use of going alone? I went out and took a turn in the Plaine and then came home and spent the evening eating out my heart.

*July 23, 1873.*—Three things chill me very quickly, being suspected, not being understood and finding that the other person

wishes to be independent of me. The first offends me, the second
discourages me, the third makes me indifferent. I open my door to
anyone who wishes to go out, I withdraw from anyone who wishes
to think less of me, I am silent with anyone who ceases to understand. So my companion is always the master of the relations that
hold us together.

*Selon qu'il a semé chacun récolte en moi.*

I cannot change this in any way, nor do I wish to do so. Those
who can do without me, I am obliged myself to do without. Their
freedom and my dignity demand it. Whether it is painful or easy,
this sacrifice must be made. The preparatory cooling makes it easier.
If the love of others makes a slave of me, their injustice or their
disdain releases me. To break with anyone is almost impossible for
me, but to accept a break is not too hard for me. In other words,
I have a soft heart and a stiff pride. The moment anyone separates
from me, I am separated. As long as I think there is a misunderstanding, I can make endless overtures and explanations. But to dispute a heart that is bargaining to withdraw, this is not within my
scale. That terrible self-abasement of love (which is never of any
use, since love is not a matter of gratitude and, far from repenting,
hardens in its offences), that vain and senseless prostration has
been spared me, thank heaven. I am well aware that the formidable
ordeal of frantic passion has also been spared me, and that I have
never felt that all my happiness, all my future, all my hope depended on a single card, on a single being, on a single wish of that
being or one caprice of that card. This absolute servitude excuses
many things. Similarly, the furies that treachery brings to its victims
are personally unknown to me. I have never been betrayed, although people have more than once been treacherous towards me.
    Therefore, although my secret life has not been without its tor-
ments, I have not undergone the worst tortures, those of slighted
love, love betrayed, the passion that turns to madness, the bereave-

ment of a beloved wife or child. I have been comparatively privileged. The trials of destitution, prolonged humiliation, cruel physical infirmity have not come near me. I owe many thanks to God for my destiny, which has been rather contemplative than active, but which has reaped more goods than it has suffered ills.

Conclusion: let us bear one another's burdens, and consequently let us think less of personal defence than of charity. If we can be useful to someone, let us be so, even if it is without much expectation or attraction. Let us sow without counting the grain.

*July 25, 1873.*—There is no comfort in your renunciation, you are not in harmony with circumstances, you suffer without admitting it, you have no peace, because you no longer have hope, or a goal, or faith . . .

These are the moments of chaos of which Othello speaks. Night comes over my soul. Everything is turbid and confused. I can no longer see any sense in my life, nothing acquired, no results. I have ceased to be conscious of any talent, any habit of mind or rule of living. I see only my nothingness and the desire not to be. Oh, the black vortex!—And yet I see dancing like the stars in the sky the bluish specks in the sunbeam that filters through my shutters; and this Jacob's ladder leads my mind away among the magnificences of the universe. The swallows are twittering in space; I hear the voices of the children at play on the balconies. We are in July, and many of the houses in the fifty square leagues that surround me would welcome a visit from me. Books, mountains, travel, the human spectacle are open to me and call me. Is not this mute desolation a fit of hypochondria, a folly, an ingratitude? Is it, then, having nothing not to have everything? Is not this despondency repressed ambition? Is not this detachment sulkiness, which means spite, insubordination, almost revolt? To adjust oneself to the real, to its imperfections and its limits, to convert one's sighs into active and beneficent energy, to accept one's fate and one's lot, to reconcile oneself with one's fellows and with circumstances as they are, to make one's experiences godlike and discover a paternal intention in the joys and sorrows of which our days are woven is the way to recover strength and peace.

*Scheveningen, August 18, 1873.*—A few notes on the *corso* of yesterday.—Tonic air. Landscape clear, bright and distinct, a gay sea of a rather ashen, whitish blue, in no way suggesting the azure and indigo of the Ionian Sea. Pretty effects of beach, ocean and distances; the outline of the steeples of the capital stood out as though cut in cardboard. Lovely tracks of gold on the waves, when the sun dropped below the bands of vapour in mid-sky before entering the mists of the sea's horizon. A fair-sized crowd. All Scheveningen and The Hague, the village and the capital flooded the terrace with its thousand tables and submerged the strangers and the bathers.

The mothers, nurses, the children, the young girls of the place with their red-lined kerchiefs, their white or black aprons and their scarves fastened at the belt, paraded with their hunched and oval figures, effacing the differences in age. A few officers (marine or cavalry). Jewesses faded to blonde, but with curved noses and sensual lips. A variety of toilettes, French styles. Little hats of every kind, shaped like wafers or like water-spouts, or escarpments a foot high, with floating ribbons and light fluttering veils, all the harmonies of colour, grey and rose, grey and blue, rose and black, blue and white, rose and russet, white and red. Pretty girls not too rare; elegant, supple, undulating figures, easy and distinguished postures less frequent.

The orchestra played some Wagner (*Lohengrin*), some Auber and a few waltzes. What were all these people doing? They were enjoying life, the half that were in motion strolling among the half that were seated.

A thousand thoughts wandered through my head: the right and the value of European fashion; leisure; Sunday; the aesthetics of colours; the symbolism of dress; how much history was necessary to make possible what I saw (Sunday, music, dress, leisure, social classes, the state of Holland, cosmopolitanism, etc., etc.). Judea,

Egypt, Greece, Germany, Gaul and all the centuries from Moses to
Napoleon, all the zones from Batavia to Guiana had collaborated in
this assemblage. The industry, science, art, geography, commerce,
religion of the whole human race is discernible in every human
combination; and that which is here under our eyes, at one point, is
inexplicable without everything that has been. The interlacing of the
ten thousand threads that necessity weaves to produce a single phenomenon is enough to stupefy one. One feels oneself in the presence
of the Law, one seems to catch a glimpse of the mysterious work-
shop of Isis. The ephemera perceives the eternal.

> *Donc ne fléchissons point, la crainte est insensée;*
> *Si notre Père occupe et le temps et le lieu,*
> *Toujours, ravissante pensée,*
> *Partout, nous habitons en Dieu.*

What matters the briefness of our days, since generations, centuries and worlds themselves unendingly reproduce the hymn of
life, in the hundred thousand modes and variations that compose
the universal symphony? The theme is always the same; the monad
has but one law; all truths are only diversifications of a single truth.

The universe is the joy of Brahma and the will of the Eternal.
It represents the infinite wealth of the Spirit trying in vain to exhaust all possibilties, and the goodness of the Creator whose will
it is that everything should participate in being which is dormant
in the limbo of omnipotence.

To contemplate and adore, to receive and render, to have uttered
one's note and moved one's grain of sand is all that is required of
the ephemera. This is enough to give meaning to its fugitive appearance in existence.

. . . A lady-bug with transparent wing-shells has tumbled on my
paper and is drinking the ink of these lines. It, too, finds what it
needs, and it is my pen that quenches its thirst. Was it foreseen in
the book of fate that on August 18th, 1873, at eleven o'clock in the
morning, a Genevan would give this insect this pleasure? I do not

think so. But it is written, He who seeks shall find, and it is provided that all creatures shall find their equilibrium. Only, Nature knows scarcely anything but combat; while man knows benevolence as well, even charity.

> *Edel sey der Mensch,*
> *Hülfreich und gut,*

as Goethe says. Let him accept for himself the law of effort, the necessity for struggle, the day of toil, but let him be helpful, brotherly, generous, attentive to his fellow-man.

*(Same day)*.—Last evening, after the concert, the brick esplanade behind the hotels and the two roads leading to The Hague were swarming with movement. I thought I was on one of the great Paris boulevards, when the theatres are out, so many coaches, omnibuses and cabs were moving along. The stream lasted for nearly an hour. Then, when the human tumult had disappeared, the peace of the starry firmament shone down and there was no response to the dreamy glimmer of the Milky Way but the far-away murmur of the ocean.

Theatre here tomorrow. *Cabbage-soup* is on the bill of fare: Thus my friend Marc [1] salutes me at the extremity of the continent. Benvenuto! What is he doing now, he the tireless athlete, the inexhaustible man of letters? The *Journal des Débats*, the *Bibliothéque universelle*, the *Revue des Deux Mondes* constantly see his prose, and the whole edition of his volume on Genevan literature must have been sold out, just as his new house is about to receive its first tenants. He, for one, is not wasting his life; he knows how to exploit his time and the trend of things. He is right. He has done everything at the right moment and I have done nothing, that is the difference between us. So he is cheerful and well-known, while I am solitary, sterile, in the shadow. It is quite just.

What is it, then, that has been interposed between real life and

[1] Marc Monnier.

you? What screen of glass has as it were cut you off from enjoyment, possession, contact with things, allowing you only a glimpse of them? It is false shame. You have been ashamed to desire; you have made disinterestedness a useless point of honour; you have condemned yourself to a superfluous renunciation and a gratuitous detachment. With the best intentions, you have treated yourself as the doctor of Barataria treated Sancho; you have reduced yourself to abstinence and privation without the necessity for it. The fatal effect of a timidity that has been aggravated by an illusion. This resignation in advance of all the natural ambitions, this systematic setting aside of all the lusts and all the desires, may have been a mistaken idea; it seems like a senseless mutilation, a fanatical or cowardly eunuchism. This mistaken idea is also a fear.

> *La peur de ce que j'aime est ma fatalité.*

And I even think that this fear of all passion springs from a need of independence combined with a feeling of secret weakness. One does not brave danger when one has not the impulsiveness of temerity or some presentiment of victory.

I discovered very early that it was simpler to renounce an aspiration than to satisfy it,

> *Car le néant peut seul bien cacher l'infini,*

and, being unable to obtain everything that my nature would have wished for, I renounced it *en bloc,* without even taking the trouble to determine in detail what would have attracted me. What would have been the use, after all, to stir up one's miseries and picture to oneself treasures that one could not reach? Thus in my mind I have anticipated all the disillusionments, after the method of the Stoics. Only, with a defective logic, I have sometimes allowed regrets to linger, and I have looked with vulgar eyes on a conduct that was based on exceptional principles. One has to be a thorough-going ascetic, contenting oneself with contemplation, especially at a time of life when the hair is turning grey. All very well. But I am a man, not a theorem. A system is impassive and I suffer. Logic requires only consequences, and life has a thousand needs; the body desires health, the imagination invokes the beautiful, the heart demands love, pride asks for consideration, the soul longs for peace, the conscience weeps for sanctity, our whole being thirsts for happiness and perfection; and, incomplete, staggering, mutilated, we cannot feign a philosophic insensibility, we stretch out our arms to life and whisper to it, Why have you cheated my expectation? Was I not wrong in following a solitary road? Was not this renunciation a mistake? Where is wisdom? It does not lie in contradiction, neither does it lie in arid sorrow.

*Es irrt der Mensch, so lang er strebt.*

*Scheveningen, August 19, 1873 (8 a. m.).*—Feeling well. Uninterrupted sleep, thanks to a cautiously attempted ventilation of my room. Morning walk. It rained last night; the sand is spotted on the surface as if by smallpox. Big clouds. The sea, veined with green and buff, has resumed the serious air of work. It is about its business, not threatening but not sluggish. It is manufacturing its mists, piling up the sand, visiting and bathing its shores with foam, rising for its flood-tide, carrying the ships and nourishing the universal life. Found an expanse of fine sand, wrinkled by the water like the pink roof of a kitten's mouth, also like a sky dappled with clouds. All things repeat themselves by analogy, and every little canton of the earth reproduces in a reduced and individual form all the phenomena of the planet.—Farther on, I found a bank of shells in process of crumbling away, and it flashed upon me that the sand of the sea might well be the detritus of the organic life of former ages, the archmillenary pyramid of the innumerable generations of molluscs that have laboured at the architecture of the shores like good workmen of God. If the dunes and the mountains are the dust of the living that have gone before us, how can we doubt that our death will be as useful as our life and that nothing is lost that has been lent? Mutual borrowing and temporary service seem the law of existence. And yet the strong exploit and devour the weak, and the concrete inequality of fortune in the abstract equality of destiny is disturbing to our sense of justice.

*(Same day.)*—A letter from my nephew ——. The heat in Paris is intolerable, he tells me. These letters of a few lines are characteristic. A person is born a merchant, and thenceforth it does not even occur to him that the pen can picture things or communicate thoughts and impressions. To exchange facts and figures is not correspondence, it is commerce. His brother —— has more of the literary instinct. There are touches and images in his words: he observes and he knows how to render what he sees. But he has no desire to communicate with me, since he cannot hope to dazzle me. At his age, self-esteem guides the pen. Besides, this generation is utilitarian; and since I cannot help it to obtain what it is seeking, prosperity and success, we have nothing to say to one another. It is quite simple, and I am neither offended nor surprised. What must be is.

In other respects, too, and beside the thinking men of from twenty-five to thirty, I feel that I have entered the *landwehr*. A new spirit governs and inspires the generation that is following me. It is a singular thing to feel the grass growing under one's feet, and to feel uprooted intellectually. One must talk with men of one's own age; younger men will not listen to one. One is considered an old fogey, a withered leaf, *ad acta*. Thought is treated like love, and grey hairs are not wanted in it. "Science itself loves the young, as Fortune used to do." Contemporary civilization has no use for old age; in proportion as it deifies natural experimentation, it disdains moral experience. From this it can be seen that Darwinism is triumphing. It is a state of war, and war demands youth in the soldier. It permits age in its leaders only if they have the strength and temper of bronzed veterans.

Nowadays, one must be strong or disappear, one must be constantly renewed or perish. Anything that is infirm is trampled under foot and abandoned. It is as if humanity in our generation had, like the migratory birds, an immense voyage to make across space; it cannot bear up the weak any longer, it cannot carry the stragglers. The great assault of the future renders it hard and pitiless for all who weaken on the road. Its motto is: *Arrive qui peut. Væ victis!*

The cult of force has always had its altars, but it seems as if, in the measure that people speak of justice and humanity, the other god sees his empire increasing. This results probably from the growing domination of the physio-biological sciences. Nature is built on the type of force, and the modern God is Nature.

*Scheveningen, August 21, 1873.*—Bricks and vowels have the same name in Dutch, *Klinkers* (the sounding). Everything is brick here, the houses, the palaces, the roads, the canals; baked sand is used to combat shifting sand, water, wind and wave, *similia similibus curantur.*—Language would be mute without vowels, and the Netherlanders have an affection for double vowels. A Holland without brick could not be imagined. As a matter of fact, the white cement that is used with these brown bricks (made of pulverized shells) is as hard as marble, and thirty years of rain on these cottages leaves them intact and as tidy as so many glass bottles.

There is an immense difference between the air inside and outside the dunes, even between the two sides of the same house, if it is on the dunes; not only a different temperature, but a different physiological effect. The sea-air is bracing, tonic, full of oxygen; the air inside is limp, sluggish, tepid, flat. The air of my little room is mild and relaxing. Twenty feet away from it one finds the salt breeze. Just as the foam is phosphorescent, this breeze has something electric in it. It is invigorating, while the sheltered atmosphere palls upon one.—Just so there are two Hollands in every Hollander: the man of the polder, pale, heavy, sallow, phlegmatic, slow, patient and impatient; and the man of the dunes, the harbour, the beach, the sea, who is tenacious, well-tempered, persevering, tanned, enterprising. The synthesis of the two is found in a calculating prudence and a methodical obstinacy in effort.

*Scheveningen, August 22, 1873 (8.30 a. m.).*—Why do physicians so often give bad advice? Because they never sufficiently individualize their diagnostics and their treatment. They classify the patient in some conventional pigeon-hole of their nosology, while in fact every patient is a *hapax*.[1] How can a judicious therapeutics permit a classification that is so crude and superficial?

. . . The doctors hope to catch water in their nets, they think they can imprison the subtle and volatile in their approximative categories; they have the courage or rather the audacity to apply their elementary procedures to cases of a more highly complicated order. They are blacksmiths who have the effrontery to manipulate a microscopic watch; they are varnishers who think they are fit to restore a canvas by Raphael; they are schoolboys who, because they can tear wings from flies, think they are able to make them grow again. The true physician sees general divisions dissolving into particular cases. Every sickness is a simple or complex factor multiplied by a second factor that is always complex, namely, the individual who is suffering from it; so that the result is a special problem, always demanding a special solution, and particularly so the further one is from childhood, and from country life, out-door life or military life. Women, men of letters, artists, after forty-five or fifty, are excessively complicated and delicate pieces of machinery, to be touched only with qualms and trembling. A newcomer, unless he has a transcendent intuition, botches and bungles everything with them, when he does no worse. The phrase of Tiberius is always true; but I know not what unreflecting heedlessness and what vague hope are always causing us to begin over again with the same mistake. "Down there, down there is health, down there, down there!" . . . and we snap at the bait all the more merrily. Alas, with or without hope, one goes from Charybdis to Scylla.

[1] A special case, a unique example.

Be strong, this is everything; and, if you are not this, be prudent and resigned, this is all that remains for those who have to sit at the second table, to speak with La Fontaine.

*(Later.)*—Rainy weather. Generally greyish effect. Hours favourable to composure and meditation. Friday and Monday are the days of relaxation here. I like these days when one resumes the old conversation with oneself and re-enters the inner life. They have an air of peacefulness; the notes they sound are flats and they sing in the minor keys. The earth seems carpeted with velvet, and the hours glide over it in silken slippers, without making the least sound as they pass. At such times one turns one's fur inside and the soul curls up, at home with itself. One is nothing but thought, but one feels oneself existing to the very centre. Sensations themselves are transformed into reveries. It is a strange state of mind; it is like the silences in worship, which are not the empty moments of devotion, but the full moments, full because, instead of being polarized, dispersed, localized in particular impressions, the soul is then in its totality and is aware of it. It tastes its own substance. It is no longer tinctured, coloured, jarred, affected; it is in equilibrium. At these times it can open and give itself, contemplate and adore. It glimpses the immutable and the eternal enveloping all the phenomena of time. It is in the religious state, in union with the order of things, at least in intellectual union; for sanctity requires more, it requires the union of the will, the perfection of devotion, the death of the self, absolute submission.

I feel very distinctly that my present peace is only of the first kind; that it rests on the absence of pain and opposition; that it is a favour and, so to speak, a luxury. Consequently, it is fragile and dependent. It is at the mercy of the first sign of physical suffering, the first grief that man or woman, nature or the world can bring me. It is an interim, a respite. I am grateful for it as for a calm in the storm; but I cannot delude myself about its duration.

Psychological peace, the harmony that is perfect but virtual, is only a zero, the potentiality of all numbers; it is not moral peace, victorious over all ills, tried, real, positive and able to brave new tempests. The peace of fact is not the peace of principle.—There are indeed two happinesses, the natural and the conquered, two equilibriums, that of Greece and that of Nazareth, two kingdoms, that of the natural man and that of the regenerate man.

Why, then, having known and often tasted the more substantial of these beatitudes, does one insensibly return to the other? Why descend again from the spirit to nature, from the divine point of view to the human point of view? No doubt from the weakness of the flesh, but also no doubt because of the contemporary crises in religion. Without a firm and tenacious faith, how is it possible not to waver over one's own principles and one's personal religion? Besides, I am forever being remoulded, and I am continually going astray. My indeterminable fluidity is a property, perhaps an infirmity of my nature; this facility in progressive or regressive metamorphoses deprives me of the privileges of men of strong conviction and well-tempered character. When one can understand everything, it is difficult to permit oneself to harden in a conventional form. When one does not feel one's individuality, and when one has neither vanity nor respect for it, one finds it almost impossible to be compact, homogeneous, consistent in one's way of feeling and acting. One is not a rock in the midst of the waves, but rather a buoy; fixed, it is true, by its anchor, but floating with the tides and the winds around its mooring, and only sustaining itself by yielding.

*Scheveningen, August 30, 1873.*— . . . The roar of the ocean was the only sound breaking the silence at one o'clock this morning. It seemed as if it were going to take back its domain and overwhelm the hotels and the dune, as, on the last day, the apocalypse overwhelms the expanse of the stars.—This morning I found it bristling with five ridges of foam, and of a tempestuous colour, which showed the sullen humour of this formidable lion. But the murmurs of life, the sound of work, the rattling of the carriages on the clinkers, the puffing of the steam-engine near my windows submerge now the great voice of the waves, or rather banish it to the distance. Enor-

mous clouds, grey over a white body, fly with the speed of arrows
towards the north. The furze shivers on the dunes like the scattered
wheat in a fallow field; and the trailing scarves of fine sand dance
before the breeze like the puffs of smoke from a volcano or the will
o'-the-wisps over a marsh. In spite of a few pale rays, snapping here
and there like whip-strokes of light, the landscape, surrounded by a
horizon that is grey, dull and low, has a Northern melancholy. Happily, everything changes quickly here, and uniformly sullen days,
like yesterday, are not common at this season.

. . . Already the sky is sensibly brightening. Its veils are fading
out. The bandages of Isis are falling one after another. Her smile
reappears, like a promise from the menacing depths. But we must
still wait for the clear blue. Let us hope.

*Amsterdam, September 11, 1873.*—Doctor —— has just left. He
finds that I have a fever and does not think I can prudently leave
for three days . . . I feel here, however, as at Scheveningen, as always, that doctors, giving me drugs in accordance with their general
pigeon-holes, invariably do me harm. That damp neck-cloth, which
filled me with secret apprehension, has in fact made my voice hoarse
and left my chest with a slight feeling of constraint. When I am
manipulated like an average being, I am very quickly crushed.

Were it not that I dread the responsibility, and that I distrust
myself too much, I should never carry out a prescription that is not
approved by my instinct, I should rely only on my own experience.
Unhappily, the moment I am ill I throw up the sponge and fall
back into the forgetful candour of faith, faith in other people. And
yet this faith has always been deceived. I can hardly recall one
counsel that was altogether good or one doctor who has been for me
a sure and penetrating friend.

This contradictory two-fold fact, that of an ingenuous hope reborn after every disappointment, and that of an almost invariably
unfavourable experience, is to be explained, like all illusions, by a
desire in our nature either to be really deceived or to act as if we
were so. Is it not the same case, for instance, with the promise of

sexual pleasure, that perpetual lure of all living creatures? The imagination beclouds the memory, and charm, twenty times convicted of emptiness, succeeds in fascinating the eye and inflaming one's desire.

Scepticism is wiser, but, in suppressing error, it paralyzes life. Maturity of mind consists in entering upon the game we are obliged to play with an air of knowing that we are dupes. This good-natured compliance, tempered with a smile, is always the part of intelligence. One lends oneself to an optical illusion, and this voluntary concession is not unlike pride. Once we are imprisoned in existence, we must submit to its laws with a good grace. To resist it only leads to a vain rage, granting that suicide is prohibited.

Submissive humility, or the religious point of view, an undeceived indulgence touched with irony, or the point of view of worldly wisdom: these two attitudes are possible. The second is sufficient for disappointments and vexations; the other is perhaps necessary for the great sorrows of life. The pessimism of Schopenhauer takes for granted at least enough health and intellect to sustain oneself against everything else. But one must have a Stoic or Christian optimism to bear the tortures of the flesh, the soul and the heart. One must believe that the very least is good, and that suffering is a paternal grace, a purifying ordeal, in order to escape from the bonds of despair.

It is certain that the idea of a blissful immortality, serving for a port in the tempests of this mortal existence, and rewarding the fidelity, the patience, the submission, the courage of the voyagers, it is certain that this idea, the strength of so many generations and the faith of the Church, gives an inexpressible consolation to those who are tried, burdened, tormented with anxieties and suffering. To feel that one is personally under the watchful protection of God gives life a particular dignity and beauty. Monotheism makes the struggle for existence easier. But does a study of nature leave any foothold for monotheism, especially the local revelations that are called Judaism, Christianity, Islam? Can these religions, based on a childish *cosmos* and a fanciful history of mankind, face contemporary astronomy and geology? Is individual immortality likely? And without this immortality, what becomes of the whole eschatological system of the religious consolations and hopes of monotheism? The evasion of the present moment which consists in distinguishing science from faith, the science that says no to all the old beliefs, and the faith that takes it upon itself to affirm the ultramundane and unverifiable things, this evasion cannot hold out forever. Every conception of the *cosmos* requires a religion that corresponds to it. Our age of transition does not know which way to turn between its two incompatible methods, the scientific method and the religious method, between its two contradictory certitudes.

The reconciliation must be sought, it would seem, in the line adopted by Sécrétan and Naville, in the moral fact, which is also a fact, and which, on one point after another, demands for its explanation a different *cosmos* from the *cosmos* of necessity. Who knows whether necessity is not a particular case of liberty, and its condition? Who knows whether nature is not a laboratory for the fabrication of thinking beings, who become free creatures? Biology raises a hue and cry; and, in fact, the supposed existence of souls outside of time, space and matter is a fiction of faith, less logical than the Platonic dogma. But the question remains an open one. The notion of an end, even if one rules it out of nature, being a paramount notion of the higher existence of our planet, is a fact, and this fact postulates a direction in the history of the universe.

The sails of my own bark are flapping in the wind and I stray from the course. Why? Because I have no creed. All my studies end in question-marks; and, in order not to conclude prematurely and arbitrarily, I have come to no conclusions at all.

Critical, doubtful, contemplative, in a word sceptical from humility, from indecision and open-mindedness, such is my present situation. For me to emerge from it, what would be necessary? I should have to write a book. What I lack is concentration and continuity.

And everything conspires to disperse me, the want of health, the lack of a home, the absence of a dominating interest, of a group of men who desire or seek or delve at the same questions. I have no feeling of a coterie, or a party, or a school, or a church or a flag to which I belong.

*Barbarus hic ego sum, quia non intelligor illis!*

Hence this restless emptiness of an unstable life, which has not found its centre, its support, its joy, its work, which has not even discovered its talent or determined its goal. Alas, it was my desire to act only through love, and, when I was obliged to think of defending myself and calculating my interest, all this disgusted me and all that I ever reached was inertia, or at least a minimum of action.

*Clarens, September 24, 1873.*—Here I am at Clarens, with a great feeling of well-being. My little room pleases me. It faces the east. It is a prodigiously starry night. Never have I seen the firmament sparkle so, as if it were full of twinkling eyes. I dimly see in the darkness the vague profile of the beloved mountains, and on my right the scattered lights of the street-lamps of Vernex and Montreux. There is something indescribably peaceful and happy in these shores of the lake that greets me and caresses me. Gratitude and almost hope return in the depths in my heart, a stone's throw from the spot where I have chosen my last dwelling-place. Is it possible that the grave gives us a fatherland, and that one lives nowhere better than where one has wished to die? A group of friends one loves, a work on the loom and, for a setting, the beauty of nature: it seems to me that this would be enough. The things of the world, ambition, politics, vainglory are nothing to me. A little would suffice for my desires; but that little is too much, and I shall never have it.

*Clarens, September 26, 1873.*—I have just spent two meditative hours in the graveyard which I see from my window . . . My wish to rest here has grown with this visit . . . What is the idea that all these departed have in common, the idea that floats over their graves? Faith in the Resurrection, the assurance of salvation through

Jesus Christ. Is it possible that the millions and billions of creatures who have gone to their rest in this hope have been the dupes of an illusion? This would be horrible to think, considering the immense sacrifices that have been made to this illusion; it would be horrible to think that people have thrown away their lives for a chimerical future. No, this hope consoles one and helps one to live better. It is therefore not a snare . . .

*(Later.)*—One can do nothing without faith; and I have no faith in the unknown; I detest lotteries, and I do not feel myself borne up or sustained or inspired by a Providence. So I am yes and no, wavering and divided in all my ways, free but with no taste for responsibility, obliged to choose at random and not consenting to my choice; in a word, persisting as I am, for want of something better and from a distrust of all action.

So my life is dull, grey, ambiguous, as the sky is today. All the peaks are overspread by a horizontal mist, and a pale light envelops only the slopes and the shores.

*October 4, 1873.*—Mused for a long time in the moonlight that is drenching my room with its beams filled with vague mystery. The state of mind in which one is plunged by this fantastic light is itself so crepuscular that analysis gropes and stammers in it. It is the indefinite, the intangible, not unlike the sound of waves, formed of a thousand tones mingling and melting. It is the reverberation of all the unsatisfied desires of the soul, all the dull aches of the heart, uniting in a vague sonority that dies away in vaporous murmurings. All these imperceptible complaints that do not reach the consciousness, added together, yield one result. They convey a feeling of emptiness and aspiration, an echo of melancholy. In youth, these Æolian vibrations are resonant with hope, a proof that these thousand indiscernible actions compose indeed the fundamental note of our being and give the pitch of our total situation.—Tell me what you feel in your room, alone, when the full moon pours in, and your lamp is out, and I will tell you how old you are, and I shall know if you are happy.

This moonbeam is like a luminous plummet that is dropped into the well of our inner life and gives us a glimpse of its unimagined depths. It shows us to ourselves, and makes us feel not so much our uglinesses, our wrongs and our faults, as our sorrows.—For others, perhaps, what it reveals is the state of the conscience. This no doubt depends on conduct and circumstances. The lover, the thinker, the ambitious man, the guilty man, the sick man are not affected in the same way.

As for myself, at the present moment, what does this nocturnal beam teach me? That I am not in order and that I do not possess true peace, that my soul is only a restless gulf, at once dark and consuming, and that I have not squared my accounts either with life or with death.

*October 7, 1873 (9 p. m.).*—Another thunderbolt worse than the last: the death of —— at forty-five, on Sunday the 5th of this month. I was dining at his table on September 22, as on the 29th at Burier. It is as if the reaper were on my trail, striking down my hosts before attacking me. Two sudden deaths in four days. This is terrifying . . .

Rain by fits and starts since the moon rose; sky overcast and blackish. Indefinable feeling of emptiness and anxiety. These sudden deaths, the darkness of the future and the gaps in the present, the fragility of men's lives, the instability of all things, the insubstantiality of my life and the unsatisfied aspiration of my heart, all this passes and repasses before me like an uncertain vision, throws my imagination into a turmoil and fills my mind with anxious care.

"This night thy soul shall be required of thee." The biblical threat resounds in my ears. Am I ready? I do not dare to say yes. I might have done more and better than I have done; but nothing and no one needs me and, aside from three or four persons who would certainly miss me a little, the world will be indifferent to my disappearance and will not call it a loss. I can therefore be removed without causing too many tears or disturbing too many things. My name will not outlive me, but what does that matter? If God forgives me for having had too little ambition, for having been too sensitive and too quickly discouraged, I am entirely consoled for my charity and my nothingness. I shall go to sleep at Clarens, at peace with men and resigned to the will of God . . .

Life frightens me more than death, because it creates and multiplies responsibilities, while death liberates, dispenses and dismisses us.—My creed has melted away, but I believe in God, in the moral order and in salvation. Religion for me is to live and die in God, in perfect abandonment to the holy will, which is a fact of nature and destiny. I believe even in the Gospel, namely, in the return of the sinner into grace with God, through faith in the love of the forgiving Father.

*October 15, 1873*— . . . Well, here I am, like Montaigne, making it my task to look myself up and down and disabuse myself beyond any necessity for it. Is the pleasure of scourging oneself a refinement of self-love, to be occupied with oneself even in meting out justice to oneself or to prove to oneself that one is not the dupe of one's instincts? Is this a residue of the conscience, which prefers condemning oneself to conquering oneself and disarms blame by forestalling it? No, all things considered, this way of acting is not so Machiavellian, it is only the old habit of psychological analysis and a desuetude of moral effort. Contemplation attracts me and interests me, struggle tires me, defeat disgusts me. It is no more mischievous than that. The odd thing is that, being sterile, I sympathize with the productive, that, lacking moral energy, I am loved by strong souls, that, having no longer an effective religion, I am sought out by religious natures. The probability is that I am judged more to my advantage by others than by myself and that my friends do not measure the extent of my weakness and my distress.

*October 18, 1873.*—Supper and evening with the R——s. In high spirits with the children. Tried to set the guest of honour going, a doctor of philosophy from Saxony, . . . I know not what comic humour drove me to romp with these drowsy gravities. It was the temptation that lively women feel to make fun of men who are playing chess. Trifling seems a wonderful freedom of mind beside the grotesquely solemn; the dragon-flies love to pester the great, stupid quadrupeds. The contrast intensifies the freedom. Be careful, just the same. A greybeard and a professor of philosophy cannot be facetious, cannot even be gay with impunity. One too easily loses all dignity and bearing. You must no longer overstep a shade of playfulness, on pain of having an air of forgetting the proprieties and being looked upon as one whose waggishness is quite unseasonable. Except in the case of really lively people, one must not at your age drop the decorum that is expected of your profession. It is very dangerous to be amusing; the only reward one gets from those who have laughed is to be found fault with afterwards. Even graceful trifling is advisable only with intimates, that is, with those who know us in our serious aspect. Other people may see vanity, bad taste or persiflage in it, and make a grievance of it against us. With people of this stamp, one must hide one's wings and appear armoured in Roman majesty. In this garb, they would not recognize Minerva herself. Worldly people do not believe in the merit of a person who makes fun of appearances, which are the essential things with them.

In your aversion to stiff pedantry and stupid heaviness, beware of appearing frolicsome. Carry your head, on the contrary, like a monstrance, and smile only with an air that is self-contained and mysterious, an air like so-and-so's. Tell yourself remorsefully that pleasantries displease, and that it is better to pass for a conscientious blockhead than for an eloquent clown. For all that the gravity of your neighbour seems to you diverting and ludicrous, let this not be seen, for he is neither tolerant nor good-natured. Be diligent to assume the tone of the company in which you are talking, if you do not wish to be misunderstood and misjudged.

The half-hour rings from Saint Pierre. Sunday has begun. End of vacation. On Monday, the winter semester opens and the first year of the *University* [1] of Geneva. The time for laughing and idling is past. Here you are again, caught up in your position, your duty, work. Sheathe your wings and clothe yourself in the solemn cloak of a doctor in office. Ugh!!

*January 22, 1874.*—The tiresome thing in this world is that error reproduces itself all by itself and everywhere, while a million obstinate repetitions of truth are not enough to shake the credit of error.

> *L'homme est de glace aux vérités,*
> *Il est de feu pour le mensonge.*

Man defends himself as much as he can against truth, as a child does against a medicine, as the man of the Platonic cave does against the light. He does not willingly follow his path, he has to be dragged along backwards. This natural liking for the false has several causes: the inheritance of prejudices, which produces an unconscious habit, a slavery; the predominance of the imagination over the reason, which affects the understanding; the predominance of the passions over the conscience, which depraves the heart; the predominance of the will over the intelligence, which vitiates the character. A lively, disinterested, persistent liking for truth is extraordinarily rare. Action and faith enslave thought, both of them in order not to be troubled or inconvenienced by reflection, criticism and doubt. Humanity in the mass is as practical as the animals, as incapable of detaching itself from the useful and the agreeable. The *theoria*, the life of thought, as Aristotle said, belongs to the privileged few. But it is these rare individuals who make humanity progressive and, after all, superior to the other species.

*January 29, 1874.*—The criminologists who construct the theory of Punishment without reference to justice are like cooks making up a meal without reference to the appetite and stomachs of the guests. If punishing is not the work of justice, punishing is not just, and the whole theory rests on nothing; it is the penal system that

[1] The act of 1873, concerning Public Instruction, by creating a Faculty of Medicine at the old Academy, had just transformed it into a University.

is wrong and that must be extirpated. Only yesterday, I was talking with one of our judges, and it convinced me of the wretched principles that govern our most important institutions. Always a quarter of the truth taken for the whole, points on the surface taken for the centre of the subject, accessories taken for the essential. And it is with these confusions that the laws are made which direct the tribunals, the assemblies, the councils, the multitudes. The husks are taken for the fruit itself; three errors are equivalent to one truth. The mass of men, on every subject that has several sides, seem to be incapable of seeing more than one at a time and especially of seeing them all in their true relation. The rarest of all things is a just, objective and impartial mind. It is true that nobody cares for this, and that everybody prefers his passion, his prejudice, his interest to intellectual justice.—That is why there is a dynamics of history; the multitudes in their action present only the resultants of forces that are unknown to themselves, and hence blind and irresistible. The multitudes wish to be free and do not even divine what freedom is; when their instincts meet with no constraint, they think themselves free; breaking one yoke, they think they are liberated from all the others. Freedom is an ideal; only the sage approaches it. All the others are serfs without knowing it, almost as much as the animals.

*February 4, 1874.*—Among the very social peoples, the individual fears ridicule above everything else, and the ridiculous is to be thought original. No one wishes to stand apart, everybody wishes to do what everyone else does. This "Everybody" is the high and mighty, it is the sovereign, and it calls itself *One*. One dresses, one dines, one takes a walk, one sends presents, one goes out, one comes in this way and not that way. This One is always right, whatever it does. It might be the Padishah, or even the infallible Pope. The subjects of *One* are more prostrate than the slaves of the Orient before their sultan. The pleasure of the sovereign decides beyond appeal; his caprice is the law and the prophets.

*One* has three faces and consequently three mouths. The first mouth declares what *One* says or does and is called usage; the second declares what *One* thinks and is called opinion; the third declares what *One* considers good or beautiful and is called fashion. When the three mouths have spoken, everyone knows all that it is necessary to know. Among the prosperous classes, *One* is the brain, the conscience, the judgment, the taste and the reason of all; everyone, therefore, finds everything decided without his troubling himself about it; he is dispensed from the toil of discovering anything whatever. Provided he imitates, copies and repeats the models supplied by *One,* he has nothing more to fear. His salvation is settled in this world and the next.

The natural inclination of these peoples, fortified by social discipline, by historical education, by the protracted solicitude of Church and State, has produced this fine result, the complete levelling of all individualities, the supplanting of the personal soul by the popular soul, universal sheephood.

One speaks of the language of *si,* the language of *yes,* the language of *ja,* the language of *oïl.* I think one might in the same way speak of the people of *One,* and add that the peoples of *One* will always be the opposite of the peoples of conscience. They will represent collective power, social force, perhaps grace, vivacity, wit, but they will never know individual freedom or deep originality.

*(Midnight.)*—Continued with Havet (*Origines du christianisme*). The work pleases me and displeases me. It pleases me for its independence and courage; it displeases me for the inadequacy of its fundamental ideas and for the imperfection of its categories.

Thus the author has no clear idea of religion; his philosophy of history is superficial. He is a pure Jacobin. "Republic and free thought", he does not go beyond that. It is the same point of view as Barni's: honest rationalism, dry and thin, which is content with a small outlay and repeats itself to satiety: *Ecrasons l'infâme, prenez mon ours!* This narrow and abrupt way of thinking is the refuge of proud minds that are scandalized by the colossal fraud of ultramontanism; but it consists rather of cursing history than understanding it. It is the criticism of the eighteenth century, entirely negative as a whole. And Voltairism is only one half of the philosophic spirit. Hegel liberates the mind in quite a different way.

Havet commits still another error. He identifies Christianity with Roman Catholicism, and this with the Church. I am quite aware that the Roman Church does the same thing, and that it considers this equation perfectly fair play; but scientifically it is inexact. One should not even identify Christianity with the Gospel, nor the Gospel with religion in general. Critical precision is obliged to dissipate these perpetual confusions that abound in practice, preaching, etc. To unravel ideas, to distinguish them, to limit them, to place them is the first duty of science when it seizes upon chaotic and complex things like customs, idioms and beliefs. A muddled disorder is the condition of life; order and clarity are the sign of serious and victorious thought.

Formerly it was the ideas of nature that were a tissue of errors and incoherent suppositions; now it is psychological and moral ideas that are a nest of baroque superstitions and antiquated views. The Augean stables of the present epoch are to be found in the realm of religious, historical, pedagogical and anthropological notions. The best way out of this babel would be to establish or sketch a science of man that would be scientific.

*February 15, 1874.*—What always astonishes me is the kind of impetuous enthusiasm with which women side against the accused. A prisoner is in their eyes a culprit. Far from distrusting their own passion, they glory in it; they have an antipathy to impartiality, to calm, to the spirit of justice. Great God, what would become of the tribunals if women sat there under the ermine? Not one of us, not one of them would wish to be weighed in this balance and have no other security for our honour than this blind and violent verdict of beings who are incapable of perfect equity. Suspected and condemned, arraigned and convicted, judged and executed is all one thing with the ladies. Twenty errors on their part, consecutive and proved, gives them neither greater modesty in their accusations nor

more reserve in their procedure, nor more charity in their judgments. *Cosi fan tutte*. They know only love and hatred and do not
conceive even the fringe of justice. These gentle creatures are truly
ferocious the moment they cease to be partial. Beware then of theological women, political women, socialistic women, beware of the
women with the knitting-needles, the women who pour petroleum
on the flames, those that light the pyres. Having a horror of reason,
they are the prey of every extravagance and they can go to
every extreme. The moment the feminine element dominates, over-
excitement and orgies are imminent; religions, art, poetry, customs,
states are impaired and fall into decadence.—I have believed too
much in woman, I must lower my estimate. Her role must be subordinate in order to be salutary. Her preponderance would be disastrous.

It seems to me that we already have an exaggeration of the feminine element. Proudhon, the robust misogynist, is not altogether
wrong in his anti-feminist crusade (see his book *La Justice*). Science, reason, justice, all that is best in the patrimony of our race, is
threatened by the advent of woman, who is all feeling, imagination,
caprice, passion, credulity, favour, without respect for general interests.

"Woman is the wise man's affliction", the moment she becomes
proud of her infirmity and obstinate in her weaknesses. It is necessary therefore that she should obey. But this is a sorry expedient,
for she must still be persuaded, won over, complied with in her unbelievable contentions . . .

What attaches me to S. is that she has the fine manly attributes,
strict rectitude, the love of the truth, the instinct of justice and the
practice of charity, in short, that she is a noble creature who reacts
against the vexatious instincts of her sex, without neglecting its virtues.

*February 16, 1874.*—Ran through the work of James Fazy [1]

[1] James Fazy, instigator of the revolution of 1846, at Geneva, and
head of the radical government for a score of years.

(*Cours de législation constitutionnelle,* 1873). It is the apology and
the apotheosis of radicalism, considered as a method and as an expression of the collective intelligence of societies. I am astounded at
the extraordinary weakness of this theory . . .

One thing interests me, however, in this old champion, that he is
now working to arouse a scientific struggle between the two schools,
the doctrinaire and the socialist.—Why did he not do this before he
began his revolutionary career? His work would have been less
mixed with errors, fraud and difficulties. But this tardy bravery
must be duly acknowledged, although one may doubt its sincerity.
This powerful demagogue, our Cleon, has always possessed the convenient faculty of not hearing objections and of seeing only what it
pleases him to see. Thus the "self-consciousness of the masses" has
become the "collective intelligence of societies", while the blind and
blinding role of the passions has never been perceived, or rather
recognized, by the theoretician whom this fact would have embarrassed.

To the multitudes, who are already force, and even, in the republican notion, right, Cleon has always cried that they were light as
well, wisdom, thought, reason. This is a trick of all political charla-
tans, enabling them to whisper next to the so-called god what he
must will and decree. The adulation of the crowd, to the end of
making an instrument of the crowd, is the game of all these jug-
glers and prestidigitators of universal suffrage. Like all rascally
priests, they prostrate themselves before the idol they exploit; they
assume an air of adoring the puppet of which they hold the strings.

The theory of radicalism is a hocus-pocus, for it takes for granted
a premise which it knows is false; it manufactures the oracle whose
revelations it pretends to revere; it dictates the law which it professes to receive; it proclaims that the crowd creates a brain of itself, while some clever fellow is the brain who thinks for the crowd
and hypnotically suggests to it what it is supposed to have discovered itself.

To flatter in order to rule is the practice of the eunuchs of all the sultans, the courtiers of all the absolutisms, the minions of all the tyrants. It is ancient and banal enough; it is none the less odious for that. To crawl before an autocrat seems to me less vile and less shameful than to crawl before the multitudes, because in the first case there is the excuse of historic majesty and the possibility of sincere illusion, while

*La grande populace et la sainte canaille*

cannot conjure up any such sorcery. Thus Bossuet does not seem as degraded as Anitus, and Haman before Ahasuerus is less ignoble than the shallow rogues of the Paris Commune. Valet for valet and lackey for lackey, the tool of a Richelieu or a Napoleon seems to me almost less base than those who tickle the mob and inflame the revolutionary clubs. The idolatry of a man, dreadful as it is, is on the whole better than the idolatry of a polyp or a hydra; and the multitude is

*La bête aux milles têtes,*

as Heraclitus says and La Fontaine repeats.

Tyrant for tyrant, the most dangerous is not the one who has only a single life and a single stomach, but the one that is indestructible and insatiable, the populace abandoned to its appetites and its rages. Its courtiers, by telling it that it is a god, take the risk of turning it into a wild beast.

Upright politics should revere only justice and reason, and preach them to the crowds, who represent on the average the age of childhood and not that of maturity. One corrupts childhood by telling it that it cannot be mistaken and that it has more insight than those who have preceded it in life. One corrupts the crowds by telling them that they are wise and clear-sighted and possessors of the gift of infallibility.

Montesquieu shrewdly observed that the more wise heads one puts together, the less wisdom one obtains (in criticism of deliberative assemblies that are too large). Radicalism asserts that the more illiterates one brings together, the more passionate, unreflecting people, young people especially, the more light one will see emanating from them. This is indeed the converse of the other thesis, but it is a sorry joke. It is true that in algebra — A multiplied by — A gives + A$^2$, but darkness multiplied by itself has never produced a glimmer of light.

What emanates from a crowd is an instinct or a passion; the instinct may be good, but the passion may be bad. And instinct does not yield a clear idea, nor does passion lead to a just resolution.

The crowd is a material force; the multitude gives to a proposition the force of law. But wise, mature thought, which takes everything into account, and which consequently has truth in it, is never engendered by the impetuosity of the masses. The masses are the substance of democracy, but the form, which means the laws that express reason, justice and general utility, is the product of wisdom, which is by no means the property of everyone.

The fundamental paralogism of radical theory is in the confusing of the right to do good with the good itself, and universal suffrage with universal wisdom. Its legal fiction is that of the real equality in insight and merit of those whom it proclaims voters. Actually, voters may very well not desire the public good, and, even when they desire it, may be grossly deceived in regard to the way of realizing it. Universal suffrage is not a dogma, it is an instrument; depending on the population to which it is entrusted, the instrument kills its possessor or does him great service.

*February 24, 1874.*—Lecture by V. at the Temple Neuf, on liberal Christianity. Skilful, well considered, interesting. Text: "I am the way, and the truth, and the life". The first part, on the two paths (paganism and Judaism), weak and inexact. The second part, on the essence of Christianity, much superior to the other. Dogmatism a secondary matter, the moral life the primary thing. To live in the spirit of Jesus, this is Christianity . . .

The vulnerable point in this way of understanding religion, noble and pure as it is, is this: its conception of sanctity is a little earthy, and one does not find in it the need for salvation by a complete renewal, by a baptism of fire, by a second birth. The psychology of the conscience is not tragic or profound enough.—But it was by this that Christianity took possession of the world: We are lost, we can be saved. God so loved the world that he gave his son to the world, that whosoever should believe in him might not perish, but might have eternal life. Dead through our sins, brought back to life for our justification. Historically, here lies the power of attraction, the spiritual fascination and exaltation which Christianity possesses. It is the supernatural, the superhuman that has transported men. It is through faith that religion saves, redeems, justifies, gives assurance and strength, zeal and security. Will the Christianity of redemption be replaced by the Christianity of emulation and gratitude? This is doubtful. The multitudes see God only in the Mysterious and the Supernatural; everything that is comprehensible is natural; but that which is natural is not divine. Such is their instinctive reasoning. A clear and easy religion loses its charm over souls. A belief without bitterness, without salt, without the marvellous has no forceful hold on the heart and the will. Faith does not wish to know; the twilight is its strength. As the strength in us is inversely proportional to the light, the religion that is the most impenetrable to reason will give us the most energy. Faith is unmixed only in blind fanaticism. The more enlightened it is, the less impetuous. When it is entirely transformed into knowledge, it is no longer active and it no longer impels to action. One must choose, then, it would seem. If action is the essential thing, faith is necessary, and mystery is necessary to faith. If one places the truth above everything, the criticism of faith is good, but this criticism dissolves faith, that is, every positive religion.

The philosophy of Religion is the explanation of this curious psychological fact, the antinomy between Will and Thought, between centrifugal energy and centripetal energy. It is an application of the metamorphosis of forces. Religion is a force precisely because it is not light. Philosophy is light, and in so far as it is light it ceases to be force.

It might be supposed that equilibrium between faith and reason is the desirable state for the individual, the state that represents the most intense sum of life; but one cannot say that the essence of faith is to seek light, or that the essence of reason is to abdicate before faith.—The most convenient categories to express the relation between the two terms of our antinomy are those of Aristotle and Leibnitz: faith is the substance or the virtuality of reason, reason is the form or the actuality of faith. In other words, to remain efficacious, religion must not be resolved into philosophy; its very efficacy depends on its being a latent truth, implicit, virtual, obscure. There is no serious religion without darkness, as there is no ardent faith without fanaticism.

*February 27, 1874.*—What is a revolution? It is an uprising that has contrived to secure power in the name of a certain principle blazoned on its flag. To succeed, it must have a well-chosen watchword to allure the multitudes and a ringleader to guide the movement. Generally, a revolution gives precisely the opposite of what it promises, since the flag was meant for the foolish and the leaders have had in view more personal ends. The ambitious know how to exploit pretensions, enlist wrath, infatuate the ingenuous and make a team for their carriage out of the valour of others. Clever revolutionists are like the priests of all times; they make the faith of others lay eggs for them. A revolution may be necessary, but it is none the less, in practice, a partial or total deception for those who have honestly put their shoulders to its wheel. In politics, one only escapes deception by knavery or irony, and never proceeds from an evil to a good, but from one bad condition to another. One can be happy when the last is less bad than the one that preceded it; this is what is called progress. The malady of the political animal is incurable, but there are narcotics and emollients for its aches and pains, and likewise there are doctors who are gentler and more agreeable than certain others of their *confrères*. The invalid has some feeling for those who relieve him, but most of all for those who (even through simple charlatanism) promise him a cure.

It is the thinkers and philanthropists who discover the formulas for amelioration, and the decent people who apply them; it is the tricksters who profit by them. God invented the hive; the honey is made by the bees; but it is the drones that eat the best part of it.

The exploitation of the simple by the clever is as old as the world and only changes its mask. The leaders of the International or the demagogy are the direct heirs of the Brahmans, and their hypocrisy is almost more shameful; for if a priest speaks in the name of God, he ends by being sincere; while the charlatan of the revolutionary clubs is aware to the very end that he is creating the popular passion before which he kneels in sham devotion. He directs the monster with the air of obeying it. *Omnia serviliter pro dominatione.* He pulls the strings of the puppet, the sacred idol, to whose oracles he is supposed to be listening with filial admiration. Juggler for juggler, I like the other better. The priestly fiction is less base in kind than the ventriloquism of the Jacobins. Authority for authority, it is less degrading to be led by the brains of society than by its feet or its entrails.

But if the future offers us the choice of two tyrannies (clerical socialism and atheistic socialism), the present gives us at least the possibility of individual liberty; and since this good comes to us from 1789, in spite of all the frauds and charlatanisms of the years between, let us accept revolutions on the basis of non-liability, admitting the principles and repudiating the mountebanks who have brought them to fruit for their own profit.

Men, crowds sully every idea they touch, but this is the condition of history. One must be resigned to it. The idea of God and the idea of justice have been the occasion of a thousand horrible things, the pretext for a thousand abominations; but without them, things would be still worse in the world. Progress through the centuries consists only in the surplus of the useful, in the slight advantage gained by the forces of good over the forces of evil. Therefore indignation is childish.

The sharpers are in turn taken in by Providence; for the wicked man performs a work which cheats him and, pursuing only his own interest, works in spite of himself and unconsciously at a more general interest. But only the generous, noble, devoted man collaborates directly in the great work; selfishness contributes to it unwillingly. In the end, one has glory and the other shame. Providence extracts the good from the evil. This does not mean that the wicked are not wicked; it means that the Master of history is still cleverer than they.

*April 29, 1874.*—Strange reminiscence! At the end of the Promenade de la Treille, on the east side, as I stood looking at the slope, there reappeared in my imagination a little path that existed in my childhood, through the bushes, which were thicker then. That impression had vanished at least forty years before. The *reviviscence* of that dead and forgotten image set me dreaming. Our consciousness is thus like a book of which the leaves, turned by life, successively cover and hide one another, in spite of their semitransparency; but although the book is open at the page of the present, the wind can bring back, for a few seconds, even the first pages to one's eyes. At the rate of one page a day, my life would be at its nineteen-thousandth page, or at its nine thousand, five-hundredth leaf. I have by chance just caught a glimpse of the eighteen-hundredth leaf, an image of my ninth year.

May it be that at death, for instance, the leaves cease to cover one another, and we see our whole past at once? Might this be the passage from the successive to the simultaneous, that is, from time to eternity? Would we understand then, in its unity, the poem or the mysterious episode of our existence, hitherto spelled out phrase by phrase? Might this be the cause of that glory which so often circles the faces and brows of those who have just died? It would be in this case like the arrival of the tourist at the summit of a high mountain, whence he sees spreading out before him the whole configuration of a country that he has seen before only in glimpses and fragments. To hover above one's own history, to perceive its meaning in the universal concert and the divine plan is the beginning of felicity. Till then, one has sacrificed oneself to the order of things, then one savours the beauty of the order. One has toiled under the leader of the orchestra, one becomes the surprised and enchanted listener. One has seen only one's little path in the fog; a wondrous panorama, immense perspectives suddenly unroll before the dazzled eye.

Why not?

To know as we have been known, to suffer no more, to live no more, to be, to be without sin, to be without shadow, to be without effort, this is the Christian hope, this is paradise, this is heaven. It would be hard to renounce this refuge which faith desires. This gradual promotion, as the reward for trial, is the support, the stimulant, the consolation of a multitude of souls. The heart revolts at the idea of an unrequited sacrifice. Is it not the other life, the immortality of the soul, that saves from despair all those who are the victims of this existence, the afflicted, the slandered, the disinherited, the persecuted, the outcasts and the unfortunate of every kind? And yet a desire is not a proof. It is hard to renounce this faith; but if God has wished it so, if there is no survival or immortality, and this faith is only a pedagogical and protective illusion, we must still make the best of it and accommodate ourselves to this scheme of things.

Why should the individual be indestructible, when the human race is not imperishable, when its appearance is only an episode in the history of a planet that is by no means eternal? Existence outside space, existence outside time, are unknown to us save through intuitions of the mind. Their possibility is a conjecture; their reality is doubtful. Do you even know what mind is? And supposing mind (that is, God) eternal, does the immortality of the human individual follow? By no means. It may be, if it has seemed fit to the immutable being that it should be so. It is *if* it is. But is it in fact? The proof is lacking.

Thus it is only a matter of faith, though Socrates, Plato and Kant have rendered it admissible and plausible to the reason. As for me, I incline to an optional immortality; an ardent longing for annihilation should have an equal hearing. To every man according to his desires. Thus the divinity would allow each to decide his own fate, to be punished or rewarded by his actual choice. Life is in fact neither an ill nor a good, it is a vehicle for pain and joy. The eternity of the wicked seems frightful, the annihilation of the good seems a mistake. But God is just, and, if he grants survival, he does not give felicity to those who do not deserve it, though he may grant, to those who curse being, dispensation from being. By such an arrangement as this, the liberty of the soul would be respected, the divine justice would be intact, and the longings of the creature for happiness could be satisfied. Hell would be closed and a final paradise would be possible.—*Utinam!*

*May 31, 1874.*—Philosophic poems of Mme. Ackermann. Here in beautiful verses is rendered the bleak desolation into which I have often been led by the philosophy of Schopenhauer, Hartmann, Comte and Darwin. What a tragic and terrible gift! What a subject, that of the abolition of faith and the death of all the gods!

> *En es-tu plus heureux? es-tu du moins content?*
> *—Plus triste que jamais.—Qui donc es-tu?—Satan,*

Vigny says. This woman has the great audacities and attacks the greatest subjects.

Science is implacable. Will it put an end to all the religions? To all those, no doubt, that conceive nature falsely. But if this conception of nature cannot give man equilibrium, what will happen? Despair is a situation that cannot last. A moral city will have to be built without God, without the immortality of the soul, without hope. Buddhism and Stoicism come to the fore.

But supposing that finality is alien to the cosmos, it is certain that man has ends; the end is therefore a real phenomenon, however circumscribed. Perhaps physical science is limited by moral science and *vice versa*. But if the two conceptions of the world make an antinomy, which must yield?

I always incline to believe that nature is the virtuality of mind, that the soul is the fruit of life and liberty the flower of necessity, that everything persists and that nothing is replaced. Our contemporary philosophy has gone back to the point of view of the Ionians, the φυσικοί of the naturalistic thinkers. It will pass again through Plato and Aristotle, through the philosophy of the good and the goal, through the science of the mind.

*July 3, 1874 (7 a. m.).*—Wakened at two o'clock by the heat. Opened my shutters; an orange moon, a beautiful, still night.—At the moment, the wearisome necessity of making a plan, choosing a course, using my freedom besets me.

Strange fellow! I have an aversion to governing my life, to the trouble of using my will. To act is my torment. I like neither dependence nor freedom; I can neither hope nor make up my mind; I should like to be dispensed from being, I should like to be myself no longer, for I do not feel that I am in the order of things, I do not believe in happiness, I expect nothing from the future, I have no compass, beacon, port or goal. I know neither what I am, nor what I should be, nor what I still can be. To love and to think would be the desire of my nature, and I must act, which I detest.

*(8 a. m.).*—Revolting against good sense is a childishness of which I am only too capable, but this excess of puerility does not last long. I recognize presently the advantages and the benefits of my situation. I take a calmer view of myself. It undoubtedly displeases me to see what is irremediably lost, what is inaccessible to me, what will always be refused and forbidden me; but I weigh my privileges also, I appreciate my particular opportunities, I reckon what I have and not only what I lack. So I escape that dreadful dilemma of the *all or nothing* which casts me into the second alter-

native. Then it seems to me that one can, without shame, content oneself with being something and somebody—

*Ni si haut, ni si bas . . .*

This abrupt return to the formless, to the indeterminate, is the price of my critical faculty. All my previous habits suddenly liquefy; it seems to me that I am beginning to be, and that consequently all my acquired capital has disappeared at a stroke. I am a perpetually newly-born creature, never able to harden in a definite mould; I am a mind that has not married a body, a country, a prejudice, a vocation, a sex, a type. Am I even sure that I am a man, a European, a tellurian? It seems to me so easy to be something else that the choice appears arbitrary to me. I could not take seriously a structure that was quite fortuitous, having a purely relative value. From the moment that one has tasted the absolute, everything that might be otherwise than it is seems *adiaphoron.* All these ants pursuing particular ends make one smile. One looks down on one's cottage from the moon; one gazes on the earth from the height of the sun; one regards one's life from the point of view of the Hindu thinking of the days of Brahma; one contemplates the finite from the angle of the infinite, and thenceforth the insignificance of all these things that are considered important renders effort laughable, passion ludicrous and prejudice merely comic.

*Clarens, August 7, 1874.*—A perfectly beautiful day, luminous, limpid, shining.

Spent the morning in the "Oasis" [1], with the August number of the *Bibliothèque universelle* on my knees. Innumerable sensations, sweet and grave, solemn and peaceful. Society of the dead. Splendour of the surrounding country. Mysteries of the foliage. Blowing

[1] Name given by Amiel to the graveyard in Clarens, in the piece in *Jour à jour* which begins thus:

*Calme Eden, parvis discret,*
*Qui fleurit toute l'année . . .*

roses, butterflies, murmurings of birds. Mournful note (the black-
birds, the creeping cat). Two ladies tending the plants growing on a
grave. Biography of Michelet and Gleyre,[1] two of *our* men who
have lately passed away. The feeling for nature among the Israelites
(Furrer).—Felt sure that the Oasis of Clarens is indeed the place
where I should like to sleep.

*Clarens, September 1, 1874.*—On awaking, looked into the future
with frightened eyes. Is it really I who am involved in this?[2]
Shocking to be so demolished. Face seamed and hideous, jaw in tatters, throat that might have been beaten black and blue; incapacity
for energetic work; weakness, dependence all along the line. Endless
and growing humiliations! My bondage is becoming heavier and my
paddock smaller. The operation will sequester me for a month,[3] and
after it I shall be in no better health than before. What is abominable in my situation is that deliverance will never come, and that
one trouble treads on the heels of another so as to leave me no
respite, not even in prospect, not even in hope. All possibilities are
successively closed to me; it is hard for the natural man to escape
dumb rage at a punishment that is inevitable.

*(Noon.)*—Indifferent nature? Satanic power? God, good and
holy? Three points of view. The second is unlikely and horrible.
The first calls for Stoicism. My organic structure has never been
anything but mediocre. It has lasted as well as it could. Every man
has his day; one must be resigned. To go all at once is a privilege;
you will die piecemeal. Submit. Rage would be senseless and useless.
You are still among the luckier half, and your lot is better than the
average.

---

[1] M. C. G. Gleyre (1806–1874), painter of the *Illusions perdues,* a
Vaudois who lived and died in Paris.—Konrad Furrer, a Zürich minister, had published in 1865 his *Wanderungen durch Palästina.*

[2] This concerned a medical opinion that gave Amiel sad prospects for
the future.

[3] The removal, not serious in itself, of a little growth on the cheek.
It left a scar that often vexed Amiel, who was troubled about his face,
which, as a matter of fact, was handsome to the last.

But the third point of view can alone give joy. Only is it tenable? Is there a particular providence directing all the circumstances of our life, and consequently imposing our woes upon us to the end of educating us? Is this heroic faith compatible with our present knowledge of the laws of nature? Hardly. But one can subjectify what this faith makes objective. A moral being can moralize his sufferings by making use of the natural fact for his inner education. What he cannot change, he calls the will of God, and to will what God wills brings him peace. Nature cares nothing about our persistence, nor about our morality. God, on the contrary, if God is, desires our sanctification; and if suffering purges us, we can be consoled for suffering. This is what gives the Christian belief its immense advantage: it is the triumph over pain, victory over death. One thing only is needful, death to sin, the immolation of one's self-will, the filial sacrifice of one's desires. Evil is to will for oneself, that is, to will one's vanity, one's pride, one's sensuality, even one's health. Good is to will one's fate, to accept and embrace one's destiny, to will what God commands, to renounce what he forbids us, to consent to his depriving and refusing us.

In your particular case, what has been taken away from you is health, that is, the thing that you would most like to have, the surest foundation of all independence; but there remains to you material ease and friendship. You do not yet suffer either from the slavery of want or from the hell of absolute isolation.

The lack of health means that travel, marriage, study and work are curtailed and compromised. It means that life is reduced by five-sixths in charm and usefulness.

*Thy will be done!*

*Charnex, September 14, 1874 (noon).*—Two hours' talk with S., intimate talk, with a splendid view before us. We had followed a path up the mountains. We sat on the ground, our feet braced against the trunk of a young walnut-tree, and spoke with open hearts, our eyes wandering over the blue immensity and the outlines of these smiling shores. Everything was soothing, azure, friendly. I always marvel as I read in this deep, pure soul. It is like taking a walk in paradise. "For fifteen years", she said to me, "I have been studying you, and I think I know you. You should have constant protection, for you are too confiding and not distrustful enough. The source of your happiness lies in yourself, and, since to make others happy is enough for you, one has only to let oneself be loved by you, without pretending to be necessary to you or even to give you anything."

*Charnex, September 21, 1874.*—Magnificent dawn. Then a long battle of mists. At last the sun is victorious. The grey is absorbed in the blue again; a splendid autumn day has come to caress "the land that God loves."

A short walk with S., who has had nightmares for three nights. She is out of breath after a hundred steps, her voice fails her almost every day; in a word, she is frail, broken, debilitated, and she has lost in a week a good part of what she had gained here. I can think only with regret and anxiety, almost with terror, that she is going to take up again so soon the burden of her duties and her work, which will be greater and heavier than ever. It is all but impossible that she will not sink under it. And, for another thing, this debilitation puts an end to other plans, too. So tragedy spreads beneath the eclogue, the serpent glides beneath the flowers. And if I think of myself, there are other anxieties that equally grip me. The future is troubled, and nothing in it is arranged to my liking. The ghosts that have been dispelled for two or three weeks are waiting for me behind the door, as the Eumenides watched for Orestes. My operation, bronchitis, my income, my professorship, the literary engagements that I have broken, everything bothers and worries me.

> *On ne croit plus à son étoile,*
> *On sent que derrière la toile*
> *Sont le deuil, les maux et la mort.*

I cannot think any more of setting up a household, or making any of the three happy who would be willing to share my destiny.

Impasse on every side. Irresolution, apathy, despair, into the bargain. I dare not look the impossible in the face or accept or choose anything at all.

I have been happy for a fortnight, and I feel that this happiness is going.

No birds left, but there are still butterflies, white and blue. The flowers are becoming scarce. A few daisies in the meadows, meadow-saffrons and blue or yellow chickory, a few wild geraniums along old fragments of the walls, brown privet berries, this was all that we encountered. They are pulling up the potatoes, shaking down the nuts, beginning to gather in the apples. But the leaves are growing sparse and changing hue; they are turning red on the pear-trees, grey on the plums, yellow on the walnuts, and staining with tints of russet the ground on which they are strewn. The turning of the fine days has come, and the colouring of autumn. One does not avoid the sun any longer. Everything is becoming more sober, more moderate, more transient and more temperate. Strength has gone, youth has passed, prodigality is at an end, the summer is over. The year is in its decline and slants towards winter; it is catching up with my age, for on Sunday it will mark my birthday. All these things coming together form a melancholy harmony. An old village woman said to S. the other day, "It has done you good to be here. You look better. *You will get through the winter*". These words, which S. gaily repeated to us, sent shivers up and down my back. Are they prophetic perhaps? I . . .

*September 26, 1874.*—Love contains in itself the principle of its dissolution. The moment one resumes possession of one's unity, one's self, one's liberty, even if only for a day, one feels that the life of lovers is only provisional, episodic, transient, and that love will end. This is the melancholy side of love. Friendship presents nothing like it, for friendship has no illusion at the outset and has never dreamed of an identification of wills and destinies.

On the other hand, this is true only of passionate love, the love that is shared, rapturous love. It is clear that maternal love, sacred love, the love that gives without illusion, without the need of reciprocity, is freed from this law of death. And Samaritan charity is the joy of the soul; it is compatible with all the renunciations and all the disenchantments of the heart. It is as rich in forgiveness and indulgence as the heart is susceptible and absolute. Only it is not love.

One enters into religion only when the hope of the heart is disappointed or lost. When one cannot touch with one's hand perfection on earth, one asks it of heaven. The cloister is the refuge of the shipwrecked.

*October 29, 1874.*—Finished the biography of Pestalozzi; a very sad story. Saviours are thus inevitably martyrs. Sorrow alone fecundates new ideas. Terrible and revolting law! It is evident that we suffer because of one another and for one another. The punishment, if not the fault, is reversible.

Pestalozzi is an example of genius without talent. All the talents were lacking in him: he did not know how to speak, or write, or administrate, or govern, or calculate. With a great mind and a great heart, he was never able to clarify his method and was never equal to the practical conditions of any of his innumerable undertakings. He made every imaginable blunder and had every imaginable disappointment. He was horribly unhappy. And yet he is the father of modern pedagogy and popular education.

*December 12, 1874.*—To will, that is, to plunge into the mesh of obstacles and resisting forces, to run the risk of defeat, to take the measure of one's weakness, to open the gulf of insatiable desire has for a long time frightened me. My constant initiation has been a renunciation and a detachment, that is, the extirpation of desire. But the desire for good brings suffering like every other desire, because it is never satisfied. I have therefore been a quietist and Buddhist spontaneously. That is not the Christian point of view.

The existence of God and the immortality of the soul, those two premises of religious morality, have in fact become for you uncertain and debatable; and not to suffer, or to suffer as little as possible, has remained the sole end of an existence which is thus destitute.

S. asks me what I believe. Alas, at the moment I should be embarrassed to make it out, for it is long years since I have questioned myself on the matter. I do not know very much and I do not know what I believe. As belief is subjective, it appears to me without intrinsic value, and I can amuse myself contemplating mine, if I still have one, as one contemplates a dream, not confusing it with truth. —Buddhist, Stoic, dreamer, critic: neutrality has replaced every prepossession. Perhaps I am only a psychologist.

*Hyères, December 22, 1874.*[1]—Gioberti says that the French mind assumes only the form of truth and, by isolating this, exaggerates it, in such a way that it dissolves the realities with which it is concerned. I express the same thing by the word speciousness. It takes the shadow for the object, the word for the thing, the appearance for the reality and the abstract formula for the truth. It does not go beyond intellectual assignats. Its gold is pinch-beck, its diamond paste; the artificial and the conventional suffice for it. When one talks with a Frenchman about art, language, religion, the State, duty, the family, one feels from his way of talking that his thought remains outside the subject, that it does not enter its substance, its marrow. He does not seek to understand it in its inwardness, but only to say something specious about it. This spirit is superficial and yet not comprehensive; it pricks the surface of things shrewdly enough, and yet it does not penetrate. It wishes to enjoy itself in relation to things; but it has not the respect, the disinterestedness, the patience and the self-forgetfulness that are necessary for contemplating things as they really are. Far from being the philosophic spirit, it is an abortive counterfeit of it, for it does not help to resolve any problem and it remains powerless to grasp that which is living, complex and concrete. Abstraction is its original vice, presumption its incurable eccentricity and speciousness its fatal limit.

[1] The author had been obliged to suspend his course and ask for a leave of absence to spend the winter in the south of France.

The French language can express nothing that is budding or germinating; it depicts only effects, results, the *caput mortuum*, and not the cause, the movement, the force, the becoming of any sort of phenomenon. It is analytical and descriptive, but it does not make one understand anything, for it does not make one see the beginnings or the formation of anything. With it, accordingly, crystallization is not the mysterious act of passing from the fluid to the solid state, it is the finished product of the act. It can represent the totality of the movements of a soul only by a crude architectural image (the moral *disposition*), as if the musical state of the heart were a mosaic of fragments in juxtaposition, etc., etc.—Far from being psychological, philosophical, poetic, it is mechanical and geometrical. It is external and formal; that is, it analyzes the details of the object which it wishes to make known but does not reach its soul.

The thirst for truth is not a French passion. In everything, what appears is more relished than what is, the outside than the inside, the style than the stuff, the glittering than the useful, opinion than conscience. That is, the centre of gravity of a Frenchman is always outside him, in others, in the gallery. His supreme judge is *one*. *One* says, *one* does, *one* thinks so-and-so, *one* dresses in this way, *one* judges in that fashion. Individuals are ciphers; the unity that makes a number of them comes from outside; it is the sovereign, the writer of the day, the favourite newspaper, in a word, the momentary ruler of fashion.

The French in isolation are nothing, and the moment there are fifty of them together half of them become the slaves of some *one* or other, and the other half set up a tyranny. The compensation of their servility towards opinion is their intolerance towards the ill-advised who wish to remain free. The independence of one individual seems a personal affront to the whole phalanx of the *servum pecus*.—All this may perhaps derive from an exaggerated sociability which kills in the soul the courage to resist, the capacity for examination and personal conviction, the direct cult of the ideal . . .

*Hyères, January 2, 1875.*—Grey weather. In spite of my sleeping-draught, it has been a bad night. Indeed, for one moment I thought I was strangling, being unable to breathe either out or in, with my face congested and my mouth open. I had sat down abruptly on my bed. This is probably the way that people die of catarrh. If I had not been in a perspiration, I should immediately have leaped for my pen and written a word or two of instructions for my funeral, for I wish always to rest at Clarens, and there is a risk that sudden death may thwart this desire . . .

I hear the arterial pulsation throbbing in my ears. Will a stroke or strangulation finish me off? In any event, I feel that my life hangs by a thread. Perhaps I shall burst a blood-vessel in my effort to breathe, in fighting for my breath with the rusty valves that choke it.

Am I not fragile, sensitive, vulnerable enough? It is vain for S. to imagine that I am still capable of a career. I feel that the earth is slipping from under me and that to defend my health is already a hopeless endeavour. At bottom, I live only out of complaisance and without the shadow of an illusion. I know that not one of my desires will be realized, and for a long time I have desired nothing. I merely accept what comes to me, like the visit of a bird to my window. I give it a smile, but I am well aware that the visitor has wings and will not stay long. Renunciation from despair has a melancholy sweetness. It looks on life as one sees it from the deathbed, when one judges it without bitterness and without vain regrets.

I do not hope any longer to be well again, or to be useful, or to be happy. I hope that those who have loved me will love me to the end. It has been my wish to do them good and leave them a kindly memory. I should like to be extinguished without revolt and without weakness. That is about all. Is this residue of hope and desire still too much? Let it be as God wills. I give myself back into his hands.

*Hyères, January 27, 1875.*—Wonderful weather. It is Arcady still. Fair sea, blue dome, velvety plain. Air serenely luminous and limpid. Distinct, pure lines and contours. The Isles swim like swans in

a golden fluid. Mythological impressions. Alacrity within. Renewal
of youth. Gratitude and bliss. Bath of poetry, emotion. I watch the
sweet hours pass without daring to move, for fear that I shall
frighten them away. I wish I could tame happiness, the wild, strange
bird. I should particularly like to share it with others, and I think
of my poor sensitive-plant, bent with toil and shivering in the icy
mists of the Geneva winter.[1] Why is she not here? I have just sent
her two letters in three days with a few blades of fragrant grass.—
And would not my literary god-daughter, who has such a good eye,
enjoy the delicious light and the beauties of this lovely country? . . .
I should like to give them some of this elemental joy that enters
my veins with the sea-breeze and the morning rays.

Surveyed for a long time through my glasses the plain, the sea
and the horizon. The smoke rising from the roofs; the old women
with parasols strolling among the plots of their kitchen-gardens,
a few palms and eucalyptus-trees lifting their foreign plumes above
the Provençal verdure; the tugs in the distance drawing barges, and,
in the pale yellow space over the waves, the sea-birds hovering. The
sound of spades and cart-wheels, the bay sparkling far away, smooth
as a lake, the quiet hermitage at the summit of its hill. Peace, am-
plitude and splendour.

These happy mornings give me an indefinable impression. They
intoxicate one and force one outwards. One feels lifted out of oneself and dissolved in sunshine, in the breezes, in the fragrance, in
flights of joy. At the same time one feels a nostalgia for I know
not what unattainable Eden. If one had a beloved woman at one's
side, one would have to kneel and pray with her and then die in a
kiss.

Lamartine, in the *Préludes*, has admirably rendered the oppres-

---

[1] "More delicate than a sensitive-plant, she lives only by thought and
the heart. She is only a breath, but a divine breath." (*Journal intime,*
July 27, 1873.) This is the friend whom the Journal most often calls
*Seriosa.* See the Introduction, and also the fragments written in Charnex,
in September, 1874.—The "literary god-daughter" was Mlle. Berthe
Vadier (1836–1921), see p. 454.

siveness of this felicity for a fragile being. I suspect that the cause of this oppressiveness is the invasion of the finite creature by the infinite. There is a vertigo in it, crying for the abyss. The too intense sensation of life aspires to death. For man, to die is to become a god. Touching illusion. Initiation into the great mystery.

*(10 p. m.).*—From one end to the other, the day has been adorable.—From three to five o'clock, a walk to Beauvallon with R. This walk was for me a continual enchantment. This Southern nature delights me by its contrasts with our own. I never weary of studying its secret harmonies of colour, shape, formation and line. The only harsh notes in this concert of the eyes are the oaks of the North, with their dry, shivering leaves: they are like louts in a drawing-room, or ghosts of the dead in a joyous company. And what precocity! Periwinkles in abundance, buttercups, red anemones, heliotropes, jasmins, chrysanthemums. And, in the verdure, what a scale of all the tones! And what a variety of scenes, contours, aspects produced by a few rocks, a few clumps of trees, two or three hillsides, thickets and plots of land rising tier upon tier in terraces. Every minute renews the combinations. I had a kaleidoscopic sensation, and a sort of sure intuition regarding the analogies between this landscape and that of Greece. Here was a rustic, leafy nook where a nymph would have been in place, there a live-oak with a rock at its foot, suggesting an ode of Horace or a sketch of the Tibur. And what completes the resemblance is the sea, which one feels nearby, though one does not see it, and which one suddenly finds at the end of the vista, at a turn of the valley.—We happened upon a certain cottage, with a dog, cats, a yellow two-wheeled cart and a leafy garden, and a proprietor who might have been taken for a rustic out of the Odyssey. He could scarcely speak French, but was not without a certain grave assurance. I translated for him the Latin inscription on his sun-dial, *Hora est benefaciendi,* which is beautiful and gave him great pleasure. It would be an inspiring place in which to compose a novel. Only I do not know that one could

find a tolerable room in the little hamlet, and one would have to live on eggs, milk and figs, like Philemon.

*Hyères, February 15, 1875.*—Fine weather. Tumult of birds. I am rereading the two academic discourses of Alexandre Dumas and the Comte d'Haussonville, relishing every word and weighing each idea. This style is a delicacy for the mental palate, for it consists in the art of "expressing truth with all possible finesse and courtesy", the art of being perfectly at ease without falling from the best tone, of being sincere with grace and giving pleasure even while criticizing. A heritage of the monarchical tradition, this particular eloquence is that of the best-bred men of the world, the gentlemen of letters. Democracy would never have invented it, and, in this dainty style, France is more than a match for all rival peoples, for it is the flower of a sociability that is refined without being insipid, engendered by the court and the salon, literature and good society, by a mutual education that has been continued for centuries. This complicated product is as original in its kind as the Athenian eloquence, but it is less wholesome and less durable. If France ever becomes Americanized, this style will perish for ever.

*Hyères, April 16, 1875.*—Have already gone through all the emotions of leaving. Settled my little accounts in town, strolled slowly through the streets and over the hill where the château stands, absorbing memories and the forms of things, went through my belongings, brushed off my clothes and my trunks. Tasted drop by drop the bitterness of being torn away. But why is my heart heavy? Because it seems to me that I have not loved enough and that I have not done here what I should have done. I have not reopened the *Méandres*,[1] have not written the two promised articles; I am not well yet. The conscience groans as much as the heart. Besides, I have just been greeted by a thousand impressions of spring. They are making hay under my window, the gardens are full of roses,

---

[1] Collection of verses which Amiel, during the last few months, had been composing and thought of publishing, but did not publish, at least under this title.

irises, wall-flowers, etc.; all the colours are breaking out at once on the hillside; between the stones of the walls, the fresh verdure is spreading and enriching the old green beneath it as children enliven a population of grown-ups and mature people, and flowers of every kind carpet the edges of the fields and roads . . . Traced out again with my eye the bay, the Isles, the furry outlines of the Maures and the Esterel, the Marshes, the Pasquins, the Hermitage. Tried to carry away, on my retina, the landscape with all its lines, its light, the ensemble and the details.

*June 10, 1875.*—The pessimism of the present day sickens me to the marrow. It makes a system of desolation; it seems to stake everything on despair. And what breaks one's heart is the force of its arguments. A thinker who belongs to no party suffers from all the woes of all the systems. His life is a self-inoculation with all the spiritual maladies of mankind.

*June 11, 1875 (8 a. m.).*—Sky streaked with cirrous clouds, delightful temperature. Little by little the blue is consuming the clouds, good overcoming evil: a blow to pessimism, but one detail is lost in the whole.—Is life as a whole good? That is the question. Would it be better if the world were not? That is the problem.

*June 17, 1875 (7 p. m.).*—This morning, at a quarter to nine, I went down to my neighbour R.'s. I sang my new song to him, he noted it for me on the stave, and I came back with the thing in my pocket. S. thought it good and my god-daughter very good.

The latter is showing me the elements of musical notation, keys, tempo, pitch, measure, notes, rests, scales. It is very amusing, after having composed an air which one is told is correct and pleasant, to see all that one has done, quite unknowingly, turned into flats, sharps, cadences, etc. So it was in F, in 4-4 time, and in twenty-two measures that I dictated this morning to my friend R. I am very glad to learn it. It was just in this way that Jourdain marvelled at everything in an A or a B, and Vestris at what a minuet contained.

Knowledge has indeed one disadvantage: it alarms the ingenuousness of productivity. Who would dare to dance if he had first to calculate the very intricate functioning of the nerves, muscles and bones necessary for that exercise? The humblest peasant, if he is gifted, can contrive the air for a song and the song itself. But our refined and civilized city-people find the thing so difficult that they leave the problem to the professionals.

As a rule, we wear ourselves out in preparations and anxieties. *Das Beste geschieht ohne so viele Umstände.* A little naivety and confidence carry one much further than all this perplexity and ceremony. Circumspection comes from the evil one. It stops our inventive flight, as awakening cuts short the strange feats of a somnambulist. It is often good to have done a thing before one asks oneself how one will do it, if one will do it, if it is possible.—This little, insignificant example enables me to put my finger on a mistake which I have constantly made during my life, that of not daring, of reflecting too long, of doubting too much my powers, my talent, the knowledge I have acquired, circumstances, etc. Marc Monnier's procedure (like Goethe's before him) is to throw himself into the midst of a literary undertaking, a new work, and so break the dangerous spell of fear and postponement. Once one has fallen into the water, one has to thrash about and discover how to swim. The whole thing is to begin bravely; if one waits to learn the best way to begin, one never begins at all, for the study of method is itself endless.

*August 16, 1875.*—Life is only a daily oscillation between revolt and submission, between the instinct of the self to expand, to delight in its calm inviolability, if not in its triumphant royalty, and the instinct of the soul to obey the universal order, to accept the will of God.

What makes abnegation more difficult for you is that, nine times out of ten, necessity seems to you tyrannical and brutal, oppressive and blind, not divine, i.e., not good, paternal, holy and merciful. And before force, even when it is irresistible, your conscience does not bend . . .

The cold renunciation of disillusioned reason is not peace. Peace lies only in reconciliation with destiny, when destiny appears religiously good, that is, when man feels himself directly in the presence of God. Then only does the will acquiesce. It does not even acquiesce entirely except when it adores. It is the inner evidence that causes it to make the *salto mortale*. Therefore, without the love of God, there is no perfect resignation, no serious abolition of the self, no genuine acceptance, no cordial, sincere submission, no real abnegation, because there is no contentment. Thus the soul submits to the hardships of fate only when it finds a magnificent compensation, the tenderness of the Almighty. If it loses the visible, it is indemnified by the invisible. It cannot, that is, put up with poverty and dearth, it has a horror of emptiness and must have the happiness of hope or faith when it sees itself losing such positive goods as the joys of the present life. It is quite able to change its object, but an object it must have. It will renounce its former idols, but it demands another cult. The soul hungers and thirsts for felicity, and, although everything leaves it, it never accepts its abandoned state...

Your great woe is this eternal beginning again, the impossibility of fixing your mind on a great thought, your heart on a supreme affection, your will on a permanent plan . . .

*August 28, 1875 (6.30 a. m.).*—I am struck by a word of Sainte-Beuve's in connection with Benjamin Constant, the word *consideration*. To have or not to have consideration seemed to Mme. de Staël a capital matter, to have lost it an irreparable misfortune, to win it an urgent necessity. And what is this blessing? It is the esteem of the public. What procures it? An honourable character and life, in conjunction with a certain sum of services one has rendered and successes one has achieved. It is not a good conscience, but it resembles this a little, as the testimony from without if not from within. Consideration is not reputation, still less celebrity, illustriousness or glory; it does not attach to *savoir faire*, and it does not always follow talent or genius. It is the reward that is granted to constancy in duty, probity in conduct. It is the homage rendered to a life that is held to be irreproachable. It is a little more than esteem and a good deal less than admiration. A well-considered man is not an important man, but important men do not always succeed in keeping consideration. Public consideration is a pleasure and a strength. To be deprived of it is a misfortune and a daily punishment.

Here I am at fifty-three, without ever having given this thought the least place in my life. Is not this odd? To seek consideration has been for me so little of a motive that I have never thought of it, and I dare say one might look for the word in vain in the thirteen thousand pages of this Journal. To what is this phenomenon due? To the fact that the people about me, the gallery, the public has never had for me any but a negative importance. I have never asked or expected anything of it, not even justice, and to place myself in dependence upon it, to seek its good graces or its approval, has seemed to me an act of toadyism and vassalage, which my pride has instinctively rejected. My *entourage* has seemed to me quite capable of doing harm, of grieving and tormenting, and I have tried to escape its tyrannical intermeddling, as one defends oneself from wasps, gnats and other outward inconveniences. But that is all. To work for a fine funeral is a preoccupation that has always remained alien to me. I have not even tried to win a coterie, a newspaper, a mere electoral vote. And yet it would have been a joy to me to have been acclaimed, loved, encouraged, welcomed and to have obtained what I myself have offered in abundance, favour and good will. But to pursue consideration and fame, to force the esteem of others, fie, for shame! It has seemed to me unworthy of me, a violation of my modesty, almost a degradation. I have not even dreamed of it.

Have I brought upon myself discredit by emancipating myself from consideration? It is probable that I have deceived the expectations of the public by withdrawing, from inner vexation, into my tent. I know that the world, intent upon shutting a man up when he speaks, is irritated by his silence when it has taken away from him the desire to speak. It is like the ferocious public of the theatre which, having taken a dislike to an actor, hisses him at its own good pleasure and yet expects him not to stop or withdraw.

It is true that to hold one's peace with perfect security of conscience one should not occupy any public post. *In petto,* I say to myself indeed at the moment that a professor is morally bound to justify his title by publications, that this is the wise course with regard to students, the authorities and the audience, that it is necessary if he is to be held in consideration, necessary perhaps to his situation. But this point of view is one to which I am not accustomed. I have tried to conduct my courses conscientiously, and I have faced as best I could all the subsidiary tasks. But I have not been able to stoop to struggle against disfavour, having disillusion and sadness in my soul, knowing and feeling that people have systematically "created a void around me", and that they have adopted, in regard to me, a tactics of pin-pricks, ingeniously combined with that of silence; being, in a word, disgusted with our public and our journalism and asking only to have no more to do with them.

Thus it has come about that I have awkwardly combined the ways of both sexes. I have a feminine fear of lacking consideration, and I have not been equal to a manly quest for public attention and fame. My fear and my indifference have been equally harmful to me. O philtre of sympathy!

I needed more combativeness, ambition, ruggedness, energy, brutality than I have had. I yielded to a premature despair, a profound discouragement. Nature of a loving woman whose heart has been deceived and broken. Unable to take an interest in my talents for my own sake, I allowed them all to perish when I lost the hope of being loved for them and through them. The coldness of those about me has frozen me. I have withdrawn, like the tortoise, head and paws, into my shell. Nor, a hermit in spite of myself, have I found peace in solitude, for my innermost consciousness has been no more satisfied than my heart.

Is not all this a melancholy destiny, a despoiled and abortive life? What have I profited from my gifts, from my particular circum-

stances, from my half-century of existence? What have I made my
acres yield? Are all my mouldy papers put together, my infinite
correspondence, my thirteen thousand private pages, my lectures,
my articles, my rhymes, my various notes anything but so many
dry leaves? To whom and to what shall I have been useful? Will
my name live a day longer than I or signify anything to anybody?
—A blank life. Much ado, coming and going and scribbling all for
nothing. The sum of it all, *Nada!* And as a final misery, it is not a
life spent in behalf of some adored being, or sacrificed to a future
hope. Its immolation will have been vain, its renunciation useless,
its abnegation thankless and its aridity without compensation . . .
I am mistaken. It will have had its secret richness, its sweetness, its
recompense; it will have inspired a few most precious affections, it
will have given joy to a few souls; its buried life will have had a
certain value. Besides, if it has been nothing, it has understood
much. If it has not been in order, it will have loved order. If it has
failed in happiness and duty, it has at least felt its nothingness and
asked to be forgiven.

> *Il eut quelques talents, de l'âme et de l'esprit,*
> *Mais de cœur faible et tendre, il se tut et souffrit.*

*(Same day, 9.30 a. m.).*—An affinity in me with the Hindu
genius, imaginative, immense, loving, dreaming, speculative, but
deprived of the brutal element of the virile, without ambitious personality, the egoism that dominates and absorbs, will, in a word.
Pantheistic disinterestedness, the effacement of self in the great
whole, effeminate mildness, the horror of brutal injury, the antipathy for action are also to be found in my being, at least as it has
become with the years and circumstances. I have been too much
condemned to my cell, and I have lived too much with women not
to have become a Brahman. Yet there has also been an Occidental
in me.—What has been difficult for me is to preserve the prejudice
of any form, any nationality or any individuality whatsoever and

not to feel the rightness of the opposite. Hence my indifference to my personal self, my usefulness, my interest, my opinion of the moment. What do they all matter? *Omnis determinatio est negatio.* Suffering localizes us, love particularizes us, but thought in its freedom *depersonalizes* us and makes us live in the great Whole, vaster even than God, since God, as a spirit, is opposed to matter, and, as eternal, is opposed to the world. To be one man is paltry; to be a man is good; to be man, this alone is attractive.

Yes, but in this Brahmanic aspiration, what becomes of the subordination of the individual to duty? The pleasant thing would be not to be an individual, but duty lies in doing one's microscopic task. The problem would be to accomplish one's daily work under the dome of contemplation, to act in the presence of God, to exist religiously in one's little role, and so to do two things at once.

> *Homme, enveloppe ainsi tes jours, rêve qui passe,*
> *Du calme firmament de ton éternité.*

Thus one gives to the detail, to the passing, to the temporary, to the insignificant a beauty and a nobility. One dignifies, one sanctifies the meanest of occupations. Thus one has the feeling that one is paying one's tribute to the universal work, to the eternal will. One is reconciled with life and ceases to fear death. One is in order and at peace.

*September 1, 1875 (8 a. m.).*—Thinking of the anxiety that throttles me whenever I write to produce an effect; every word troubles me and my pen falters at every line, because of my struggle to find the right word and the multitude of possibilities that open at every phrase. To compose is a torture, because I can make only a rough plan in advance and I have to find every detail as I go along. A deplorable habit, which I cannot call a method.

*(11 p. m.).*—Worked several hours at my article, and have scarcely been able to make even a rough draught of a few pages, so strongly do the gaps make themselves felt the moment I take

up the pen.[1]—Discovered some new sources. Reading: took up Mme. Necker again, Chateaubriand *(Mémoires d'outre-tombe,* Vol. VIII) . . . Headache, both at dinner and supper. Evidently this kind of static contention with a botchery that makes no headway and trips at every phrase is very tiring to the brain. I lack the plan, I lack the details, I have neither the flow nor the vein, and the effort, fruitlessly prolonged, strains me like a fixed idea.

Composition demands a concentration, a decision and a fluidity which I no longer possess. I cannot weld my materials and my ideas together, and an imperious domination of the thing is indispensable if one wishes to give it a form. One must bully one's subject and not tremble for fear of mistreating it. One must transmute it into one's own substance. This kind of confident effrontery is lacking in me. My whole nature tends to an impersonality that respects the object and subordinates itself to it; in my love of the truth, I fear to conclude, to cut short.—Then I constantly retrace my steps; instead of going forward, I turn in a circle; I am afraid of having forgotten a point, forced a shade of meaning, put a word in the wrong place, while all the time the necessary thing is to aim at the essential and frame it on a broad scale. I do not know how to sacrifice or abandon anything at all. Noxious timidity, bothersome conscience, fatal splitting of hairs!

The trouble is that I have never reflected on the art of making an article, a study, a book, or seriously and methodically followed the apprenticeship of an author. This would have been useful to me, and I have been afraid of the useful. One must have gone through the graduated exercises with the profession in prospect. The discipline and routine would have given me ease, assurance, good humour, wanting which the verve dies out. With me it was just the other way. I acquired two opposed habits of mind, the scientific analysis that exhausts its material and the immediate nota-

[1] This was the article on Mme. de Staël, which appeared in 1876 in Volume II of the *Galerie suisse,* published at Lausanne by M. Eugène Secrétan.

tion of shifting impressions. The art of composition lies between the two: it requires the living unity of the thing and the sustained gestation of thought. Have I then become incapable of composing? Does one begin anew at fifty-three? Does one refashion one's nature and one's education?

You have hoped to learn to swim without jumping into the water, to grow strong without descending into the arena, to escape from trouble by postponing it, to find your measure without risking defeat. You have been indolent, fearful, proud, improvident. Whose fault is that? You have missed all the coaches. Travel on foot, then, or go back to your chair.

*September 2, 1875 (8 a. m.).*—To compose is not so terrible. You make mountains and phantoms of everything. All one needs is a little gradation and a tolerable amount of practice. In this art, as in everything, you have contented yourself with laborious preparations, you have exhausted yourself in the trifles of beginning and in preliminary acquisitions, you have tried to understand but not to master. You have not advanced beyond the preludes, from false modesty and a silly self-denial, from excessive distrust of yourself and terror at the thought of perfection.—Nature of a bashful lover, who is afraid of being too happy and dreads good fortune, because he fears that his strength will fail him. Glory has never been a stimulus for me, but I have always had a fear of shame and a horror of humiliation.

Remaining in one's own room, as Pascal advises, one never knows what one is able to do; and, having no measure of one's social value, one ceases to risk oneself among men.

To compose is to lead an army, an army of thoughts and images, to an end appointed in advance. The possession of a subject is only one of the conditions requisite for this literary campaign. One must know how to manœuvre, and, above all, one must clearly determine one's purpose. This purpose is to reach the public or a portion of the public, to enlighten, convince or amuse it.

I see that what is holding me back at present is the obscurity of the end, indecision as to what can be realized in the given conditions. I am forever studying and not properly engaged in the task of working things out. I fluctuate, hesitate, waver, I shift and shuffle in the execution, because I have not resolutely chosen a point of view, an audience, an objective, or made the appropriate arrangements.—Like Martha, I am busy with too many things, when only one is necessary.

To proceed with courage, one must know where one is going, why one is going. One must feel that one has legs and a desire, one must have an itinerary and money in one's pocket, one must be cheerful and determined.

To compose is therefore to show character. To compose would be a moral hygiene for you, an intellectual discipline, a sort of penitential exercise that might be profitable, for it would be a victory won over yourself; it would be to make your indolence accept commands, your pusillanimity, your indecision; it would be to constrain your weakness to undertake an act of strength, to exact from your sterile dispersiveness a moment of fecundity . . .

*October 25, 1875.*—Heard Taine's [1] first lecture (on the *Ancien Régime*). Extremely substantial work, clear, instructive, compact, solid. Monotonous reading, unflattering and even inelegant voice. His art is to simplify in the French way in great, striking masses; his defect is strain, angularity, abruptness. The excellence is historical objectivity, the desire to see truly. For the rest, an immense openness of mind, freedom of thought and precision of language.

*October 26, 1875.*—Always limitations and growing obstacles and multiplied privations . . . This is the opposite of expansion . . .

To whom and to what can this pitiless constriction be useful? Renunciation is a defensive measure, but it has no more real value than a tooth the less or an amputated leg. Moral education is a compensation for those who have hopes of an after-life. But for one who, like myself, is without this hope, the sacrifice is of no use

[1] Taine was then reading, in the great amphitheatre (Aula) of the University, selected passages from his *Ancien Régime*.

either. This at least remains: envy and revolt are ugly, and therefore it is good to forbid oneself to share them. And to do good
without recompense is the maxim of noble hearts. So I shall change
nothing in my conduct. But melancholy is the reverse of a spring
of action, while happiness gives one wings.

If I believed at least in an individual Providence! But I have
none of these props that are so convenient and fortifying. My one
support is the affection that people feel for me. My existence has
this joy and this comfort, and this only. It is thus suspended by
a thread.

How imprudent not to have any more reasons for living, any more
ties than this! An illness, and less than an illness, one of those
hazards that create misunderstandings and turn hearts away from
us, can reduce me to penury and distress. I am at the mercy of
fortune. Impossible to deceive myself as to the fatal fragility of
my present state. All I can do is to forget it and divert my thoughts.
—It is certain that an accident may take away from me what remains of my health and the two friendships that make my life
endurable. But what is to be done about it? Can I shelter these
treasures from the risk of destruction? No. Should I commend
them to the goodness of Providence? This is a vain measure, consoling to faith, but it does not change the event by one iota. All
that remains is to resign oneself to this absolute dependence and
draw from it the moral good it holds, as if it had behind it a
paternal intention and a protective direction. The God whom the
religions place in heaven and outside ourselves exists perhaps only
in our own depths. This God is the voice of the good, the secret
admiration of virtue. It is true that what exists in the effect should
virtually exist in the cause. If God is in us, he is in the origin of
things. If the good is our end, it is also our principle. Thus there
should be at least a general Providence, the restoring and healing
force that maintains the universal life in spite of unceasing per-
turbation and death. That which desires life to be for the good, and
the good for the better, that primordial and indefectible power, is

what we call God. *In Deo movemur, vivimus et sumus.* This persuasion is the philosophic religion that can outlive all the superstitious, imaginative and legendary cults, all the beliefs that have turned into allegories. The essential thing is that man has always had a presentiment of a higher order, of which he was the organ and the agent, the contemplator and the neophyte, of which he was meant to be the herald and the hero.

What does it matter, after this, if the individual is more or less happy, if he plays a role, comes to flower or not? The universal work is none the less accomplished . . .

There are always a good many wasted powers and useless victims, because error plays an immense role in the history of human opinion and action. It is doubtless a pity to be one of those who are crushed and ignored; but there is a silent service that each can always render, to be good, just, courageous, patient. What makes the great social machine go is rather the sum of the works that win no glory, the humble virtues, the anonymous merits than the display of the headmen, the officers and directors. An immortal name is a luxury reserved for the chosen of fortune; one can do without this privilege, and there is more stoicism in depriving oneself of it than in pursuing it. Contentment in mediocrity and neglect has a certain beauty, when one has the stuff of something greater than greatness. Abauzit could have done without the resounding praises of Rousseau,[1] but Rousseau could not have done without glory. The latter was the great man, but the former was the sage.

*(Later.)*—All the origins of things are secret; the principle of all life, individual or collective, is a mystery, that is, something irrational, inexplicable, indefinable. Let us carry this to the end: every individuality is an insoluble enigma, and no beginning can be explained. Everything that has become can be explained retrospectively, but there is no beginning that has become. The beginning represents always the *fiat lux*, the initial marvel, creation, for it is the issue of nothing else, it simply appears among the anterior

[1] Firmin Abauzit (1679–1767). See *La Nouvelle Héloïse*, Vol. I.

things that provide it with a setting, an occasion, an environment and are present at its appearance without comprehending whence it has come.

It may indeed be that there are no true individuals, and in this case no beginning, save one, the primordial fillip, the first movement. All men would be only man in his two sexes; man would in turn be absorbed into the animal, the animal into the plant, and the sole individual would be living nature, reduced to living matter, to the hylozoism of Thales. Yet even on this hypothesis, in which there would be but a single beginning in the absolute sense, there would still remain relative beginnings, multiple symbols of the other. Every life, called individual by courtesy and by extension, would represent in miniature the history of the world, and for the eye of the philosopher it would be like a microscopic abridgement of it.

*January 3, 1876.*—National self-esteem, a curious subject of study. This is one more force that resists the truth. This self-esteem, like that of the individual, is a *Noli me tangere*. It is a variant of self-justification, that is, of deliberate blindness, self-interested illusion. This stupid vanity sings a *Te Deum* for deformities which it pretends are beauties. I seem to hear a chorus of hunchbacks magnifying humps and gibbosity. To feel the utter absurdity of this chant, one must have an open mind.

I feel as if I were no longer infatuated with any nationality or any church. From year to year, critical impartiality grows in me, and it is the type of the successful man, complete, harmonious, superior, genuine, that serves me in judging all the various caricatures who arrogate to themselves the privilege of the type. I do not feel that I am either French, or English, or Russian, or Swiss, or Genevese, or European, or Calvinist, or Protestant, or anything in particular. I feel that I am a man and sympathetic to everything that is human; but I am in vassalage only to the ideal. The prejudices of religion, language, nationality, political regime, social class, party, coterie do not imprison me; I judge them, they are inferior and indifferent to me. I have an antipathy to fraud, guile, untruth, and consequently to the institutions that live by them; but if Romanism has not my esteem, it is not as a Protestant or even a Christian that I am repelled by it, but as a man. Sacerdotalism, so understood, seems to me as baleful in Tibet as in Madrid. The insolent usurpation of the priest seems to me shocking in the name of truth, in the name of morality, in the name of human dignity. Denominations no longer exercise any spell over me, and if a man calls himself my co-religionist, my fellow-citizen, my kinsman, my *confrère,* my colleague, my co-heir, my pastor, my policeman, it means nothing to me; the title is worthless in my eyes, for it proves absolutely nothing, and a presumption, a hundred times belied, is without significance. Tell me what you are, what you are worth, you personally, that is something like; your scraps of paper, cockades, signatures, liveries mean no more than the speeches at a fair or the advertisements in the newspapers. I believe in certain individuals; I believe because they are proved. As for the rest, I abide in philosophic doubt. I no longer believe in man, woman, church or country in general; I insist upon choosing and discriminating.—Life begins in confidence and unlimited credit extended to all; it ends in a universal reserve, save for deserving exceptions. When the bitterness of disappointment has passed, prudence at least remains, and this does not forbid either good will or piety. One does not have to be self-deceived in order to be good. Not to expect righteousness, integrity, gratitude, faithfulness, discretion, reciprocity, rightness, justice, good will does not prevent one from giving, and giving oneself, with a calm resignation.

*January 30, 1876.*—Went out after dinner. Stepped over to Marc Monnier's, to hear *Le Luthier de Crémone,* a comedy in one act, in verse, by Coppée, read by the author. An aesthetic feast, the choicest literary fare. The little piece is a pearl. It is in rehearsal at the Théâtre Français. It is pure poetry, and each verse is a caress to the taste.

Happy those who are masters of their art, and who enable us to feel the delights of liberty. Moreover, to watch verse blossom is a delightful sensation, especially when it blossoms better than one can make it oneself. One sees the champagne bubbling and tastes it at the same time.—And what a hand this young maestro has! One feels in him the gifted man, a luminous facility, an involuntary order that finds the shape, the form, elegance, distinctiveness as it plays. This man is talented to his finger-tips. Slender, swarthy, nervous, with a Portuguese complexion and eyes without lustre, he suggests the violin of which he speaks, fragile and vibrant, sensitive and passionate. But he has the Parisian quickness and grace, the delicacy and keenness that are necessary to make simple, naive, hearty, daring things acceptable to a refined people.

By force of art to return to nature; a pretty problem for arch-composite literatures like ours. Rousseau similarly attacked letters with all the resources of the art of writing and vaunted the delights of savagery with all the address of the most artful of the civilized. It is indeed this marriage of opposites that gives pleasure: pungent sweetness, knowing innocence, calculated simplicity, the yes and the no, mad wisdom. It is this supreme irony that flatters the taste of advanced epochs, epochs that are high as game is high and that wish two sensations at once, as the smile of the Gioconda combines two contrary meanings. Satisfaction is thus conveyed also by the ambiguous smile that says, I feel the charm but I am not deluded, I am both within and outside the illusion. I yield to you, but I see through you. I am willing, but I am proud. I feel the sensations, but I am free. You have talent, I have wit; we are quits and we understand one another. *Musa ales*. What a prodigious contrast between a brain like that of my friend K. and that of Coppée, between the Teutonic philosopher and the Parisian artist! Solidity, constancy, weight, uniformity, abstraction, on the one hand, and, on the other, malice, vivacity, lightness, colour, music. The cyclops and the warbler are not more different. Each of them incapable of entering into the role of the other, reciprocally antipathetic. It is the property of criticism to have a more complete psychology and to reproduce these two contrary types (as well as all the others) with the same fidelity.

*February 1, 1876.*—Evening at the Passerine,[1] all four together. Discussed the infinitely great and the infinitely small. S. cannot yet understand that a cubic millimeter is as vast relatively to the mathematical point as the globe is to a cheese-mite. The untrained mind always takes the limit of its sense-perceptions for the limit of things. The great seems clearer to it than the small because the great is a multiple of itself, while it is unable to analyze that which has to be measured differently. The thought in its own brain seems explicable to it, but in a brain a thousand times smaller it seems a mystery.

Women, encountering everywhere the incomprehensible, very quickly accommodate themselves to it, and form the habit of converting everything into questions of faith and opinion. The difference between the knowable and the unknowable is never clear to them. Scientific criticism is not their business; they shine only in the analysis of the feelings.

To place oneself at all points of view, to make one's soul live in all the modes, this is within the power of thinking beings; but it must be confessed that very few profit by the privilege. Men, as a rule, are imprisoned and bound in their circumstances much as animals are. They scarcely suspect this, because they do not judge themselves. To place oneself within all one's states of mind and perceive from the inside one's life and one's being is the business of the critic and the philosopher.

*February 25, 1876.*—To preach is a vain thing; to set an example is twice as good, for this is more persuasive and does not sacrifice the preacher.

The same remark holds for the professor's life. Much better to

[1] "L'Ile d'Azur" and "la Passerine" were the names given by Amiel to the salon of his friend Seriosa, who lived with her mother and her sister.

write books; the students find you more to their liking and you win more honour by it.

Devotion and abnegation may therefore be a folly. The world prefers intelligent egoism, and society finds more advantages in it. A strange application of the proverb, Charity begins at home.

The heart longs for a realm in which everyone would think first of others, a realm of brotherly love and radiant sympathy, in which the common good would result from universal self-forgetfulness. But the world is constructed on another plan. It rests on personal interest and self-esteem. That everybody should work energetically at his own business, his trade, his fortune, his reputation, his credit, that he should contrive to outdo his equals, to eclipse his rivals, to procure for his family, his town, his country, procuring it first for himself, wealth, glory, superiority, is all that is asked of him. The world has always scouted or crushed the enthusiasts, the dreamers, those who are generous and self-forgetful. It exploits them and does not revere them, except in theory and centuries after their death, and then only to create the belief that it is magnanimous itself. In practice it is oblique, and its teaching is only a ruse. Morality is for appearances; reality has its own maxims. The Gospel is quoted at the door, but within the shop Mercury is God.

The unconscious sophism, self-interested contradictoriness are to be found everywhere among the people who are called Christian, as in the clergy themselves. The law of irony: the more ethereal the maxims, the crasser the substance. The base in practice has the most prudish airs and the smoothest words.

He who does not inspire a little fear will never inspire much love. He who does not defend himself will always be vilified, and, far from admiring, people will scorn his gentleness. The world respects only force and recognizes only the force that imposes itself upon it. *Mundus vult decipi*, said Erasmus. The world, to be sure, wishes to be deluded, but it wishes also to be constrained, it wishes to be forced. It is by nature carping, cross-grained, anarchic, sterile; and it instinctively absolves those who bully, whip, drive and quell it.

Only it wishes to be flattered. This is what the demagogues do. The public as a whole is a herd of fools, but one must permit it to believe that it represents sagacity, taste, justice, reason; this is what the journalists and critics do. One dictates to the geese their opinions, while ostensibly prostrating oneself before them. This is the method of the ambitious courtier with all the despots. The many-headed beast is the sultan at present, and they garland it like its one-headed predecessors.

*February 26, 1876.*—This evening, an anonymous letter, in a forged hand and using the familiar pronoun, attacks me as a professor, asserts that my students are deserting my course and consider me a babbler of generalities, and that secret steps have already been taken to demand my replacement, that, in short, a storm threatens me . . . I suppose the cowardly pleasure of causing pain and anxiety is the motive of the anonymous author of this note. I am not unaware that hatred is constantly watching over us and me. Just the same, these underhanded plots do me harm. I can no longer fail to recognize that my course does not satisfy me, that I am becoming unfit for teaching, for want of memory and ease of mind, which prevents me from improvising. The advantages of my course, exactitude, precision, order, method, proportion are not those that impress students, either at the time or even later, when they review the stages through which they have passed. One thing only catches their attention, that my nose is in my notes and that my little papers look disordered. Appearances are against me. On the other hand, I cannot begin life over again, my work or my ways, for my principal interest lies elsewhere now and I am not mad enough to sacrifice my last years to a barren and useless effort.

If, then, my defects outweigh my qualities and cause these to be overlooked, the best thing would be a complete break. Either they must take me as I am, either they must ask me for what I have, or they must let me go, I mean retire.

Much as one may despise anonymous letters, one must profit by them to examine one's conscience. Well, I am perfectly aware of my deficiencies, my weaknesses, my impotence and my offences. What I rather need is encouraging testimonials; for as I am always doubting my usefulness and my adequacy, it is easy to persuade me that I am good for nothing.

Another lesson. In order to lighten my subject, I have discarded the bibliography; and perhaps my students have drawn the conclusion that I have ceased to keep up to date. I have shunned the vanity of erudition, the ostentatious display of my resources, and I am being punished for it.

Forgetful of my interest, which is to appear as an authority, I efface myself before the thing, I think only of the course itself; and the upshot is that to listeners who are not captivated by the thing I appear a cipher. These are two ways that cannot understand each other; I am impersonal, and our people never emerge from personal matters.

Again, there is nothing on which I pride myself; I am altogether detached from my gown and my labours. All this is indifferent to me, alien, inferior. I do not know how, I do not wish, I am not able to push myself, to throw myself into relief, to impose myself, win people over or carry them away.

Thus it always comes back to a breach between my nature and my surroundings. No adaptation. People do not enjoy me, they do not understand me, they do not accept me for the best that is in me. They are forever wishing me to be something other than I am.

The same old mortifications coming to life again. I had forgotten them, but they do not forget me. How well this falls in with the literary projects for these next three or four months, which required health, calm of mind, cheerfulness, enthusiasm!

Damnation! . . . To whom? God help us, to nobody, or at most to the cruelty of chance. I regret these wretched circumstances because they take away happiness and strength, and beget only sorrow and sterility. As for myself, I do my utmost not to offend, vex, put out or hush up anyone. But deep as I dig the solitude about me, and although between my life and the world I place a vast zone of renunciation, the poisoned arrows cross this space and strike me, none the less.—O melancholy!

*March 19, 1876.*—The well-tempered minds are an imperceptible minority among the throngs, the masses and the millions that form the public; but they are the *élite,* and they alone count for quality. The masses have numbers on their side, might and even right; but they have neither reason nor taste, neither excellence nor distinction. Their natural inclination is for a spurious grandeur, a false magnificence, a brutal mediocrity; and when democracy has brought people to believe in cultural equality and the equivalence of opinions, they cease to trouble themselves about their preferences and their applause.

Moral. In order to diminish the chances of posthumous caricature, one must simplify in one's lifetime the lines of one's appearance in the eyes of the public. One must choose oneself what is to endure in the memory of others, throw into relief one's own best and strongest, give, if not a definition, at least a signature of one's being; one must concentrate oneself, sum oneself up in a work that will serve as a medal. This medal is a monument and autobiographical document.

If you were to die tomorrow, what would remain of you? Various knick-knacks, a few verses, a few reports, some old professorial papers. What would people say of you? He had various talents, but he used in concealing them all the patience that others employ in exhibiting them. He might have made a name for himself, he preferred to remain incognito. *Amen!* We shall say no more about him.

You have a place in a few anthologies (Staaf's,[1] among others), you are mentioned in Daguet's *Revue des écrivains suisses,* in Marc Monnier's *Genève et ses poètes.* At the Institute, at the University, in Geneva, you would be forgotten in a few months. Perhaps the *Roulez tambours!* and your *Escalade* will linger a few years more

[1] Staaf, *La Littérature française,* Paris, 1871, Vol. III, p. 584.

in the popular memory.[1] That is all. Not quite all. My god-daughter will try to erect a graceful mausoleum for me in one of her novels.[2] But, taken all in all, is this result worth a half-century of study, experience, meditation and action? *Pulvis et umbra sumus.*

*April 15, 1876 (Easter Eve)*.—This moral oscillation between despair and love, between Zeno and Jesus, between my old man and my better self, reappears in my soul periodically. The experience of my life leads me inevitably back to pessimism; then the ideal protests and takes the upper hand again. I alternate between the cold and desolate view of reality and the religious view of our destinies. The heart and the conscience take their revenge on reason. Is this to be contradictory, illogical, divided? Are not these two instincts, these two tendencies, these two principles equally human? Is not melancholy a natural thing in relation to all that is mortal and perishable, our life included? Is not the return to that which triumphs over death, evil and sorrow legitimate and healthy?

Happy, beyond doubt, the souls that can maintain in themselves unceasingly the superior tendency, the feeling of the divine and the indestructible, the sacred flame. For myself, I can only return to it after long wanderings in the desert, and kindle the flame anew after long periods of darkness.

What is divine in us is the power of sacrifice, the faculty of devotion, holy love, charity, willing immolation for the welfare of others and for the glory of the Good; this is the dignity of the race, its flower and its crown. This does not create individual immortality, but this is the immortal thing, the supernatural, super-

[1] Amiel here refers to the Literary Section of the National Institute of Geneva, of which he was for a long time the president. The *Escalade de 1602*, a historical ballad, 1875. The *Roulez tambours!*, the words and music of which Amiel had composed in January, 1857, in the dark days when the Swiss Confederation was preparing to repulse the invasion of a Prussian army, has become a patriotic song that is popular throughout the whole of Switzerland.

[2] It was she, "my literary god-daughter", who was to write a biography of Amiel: *Henri-Frédéric Amiel, a Biographical Study,* by Berthe Vadier, Paris, 1886.

human thing that is nevertheless human. It is because this flame burned in the heart of Jesus that the world has made Jesus the man-God. It is because humanity does not deserve the sacrifice that the sacrifice is so great and the martyr so noble. Man has no right to expect from us anything but reciprocity and justice; but to love without cause, to superabound in forgiveness, kindness, pity, generosity, goodness is to be the child of heaven, it is to be as we imagine that God himself is, it is to imitate the Nazarene.

*April 16, 1876 (Easter)*.—What I lack is consistency, tenacity, stability, resistance, that egoistic vigour of the being who appropriates everything he can to himself and who retains about himself, his interest and his will, the things, the people, the impressions, the ideas that confirm and expand his personality. As for myself, I am too immaterial, too disinterested and purified for that; my subtlety throws off all weight of substance as a sort of gross encumbrance of its meshes. I am a critical and contemplative nature, approaching pure spirit, form without matter. The sum of my impedimenta and acquisitions is limited to an aptitude and a method and amounts to a simple virtuality. I have nothing any more, but I am someone. I have no extension any longer, but extension is in me, in the state of potentiality. This ethereal subtlety is the cause of my apparent passivity; I am only something possible, reabsorbed, implicit, like a force that has returned to its latent condition. I am simply an indeterminate capacity, not a talent that is established and proved, in exercise and function . . .

There is certainly something intangible in me, something incoercible, indefinable, unfettered and subtle, which is spirit; and the resources, the metamorphoses and the caprices of this defy calculation and mock the classifiers. Beside this airy flame, everything seems heavy, mummified, crystallized, thick, uniform, opaque, pedantic. The spirit is a will-o'-the-wisp that leaves the fools, the pedants, the philistines, the creatures of routine, the ruminants and crustaceans floundering in the mud and has not even a fleeting wish to prove to them that it has wings. It laughs at their stupidity and

amuses itself with their blunders. All those who are captive, limited,
gagged think themselves free, and treat the free as extravagant.
This is a pleasure that must be left to them.

Stop! This absolute freedom of the spirit has two disadvantages.
It tends to make one inhuman towards inferiors who are mad
enough to think they are superior; it tends to make man forget his
dependence on God and sin.—The free man must contain his joy
in goodness and humility. Every advantage creates a duty and
produces a responsibility. The spirit does not dispense one from
setting a good example; it must reassure, if possible, the extreme
susceptibility of the mediocre and the many! It must cause itself
to be forgiven by the envious and the jealous, by the deformed and
feeble-minded, on the score of its indulgence, good nature and
modesty. Otherwise, it has all the world against it and it can render
no service. In other words, it misses its vocation.

*April 19, 1876 (noon).*—The rain has stopped. The sparrows are
chirping rather cheerlessly. The morning has flown away while I
looked over the three note-books, 137, 138 and 139, which precede
this, to gather up the thread of my life again. The Journal depersonalizes me to such an extent that for myself I am someone else,
and I have to renew my acquaintance with this other, biographically
and morally. This power of objectification makes one forgetful.
My earlier states, my configurations and metamorphoses, escape me
like transitory accidents. They have become foreign to me, objects
of curiosity, contemplation and study; they do not affect my inner
substance; I do not feel that they are mine or in me, that they are
myself. I am not then a will that continues itself, an activity that
accumulates, a consciousness that grows richer. I am a flexibility
that becomes more flexible, a moulting creature always more rapidly
moulting, a negation of negation and a reflection that is reflected
like two mirrors facing each other. The slight frame of each of these
is the only measure of the quantity of reciprocal images which one
indefinitely encloses in the other. My identity may be found to
exist between the I and the you, but how fluid it is!

This is omphalopsychics.—The evaporation of my being will be greatly facilitated by it, for I see myself as resembling the phantoms of dawn, already diaphanous, insubstantial, vaporous, illusory. My sense of myself when I awake is like the dream of a dream. I have no weight, or solidity, or fixity, and I do not have that opaque presumption which weighs on the eyes of men, the presumption of existence. Impersonality has done its work of subtilization even to the source of thought, even to the I.

It would be impossible to convey this Buddhistic state to any of those imprisoned ones who cannot emerge from their individuality and who think that they are positively real because they have hands with which to take hold of their feet, together with a consciousness of willing.

That which binds men to existence seems to me to be pain. He who suffers cannot imagine that he is not suffering; he is brought back to one particular point, he becomes subjective again. Suffering is therefore the limit of objectivity. Through thought, we should become gods, we should be dissolved into spirits; it is pain that brings us down again to our humanity.

*April 20, 1876.*—Spent the evening with S., to whom, as she wished me to do so, I read a few dozen pages, taken from the last two books of this journal . . . Observed, while doing so, a bad habit of my natural style, the superabundance of synonymous nuances. I grope into every nook of the idea, and I have a desire for completeness. Is this bad, is it good? I do not know. Instead of the single, central stroke, I send forth a volley of blows, probably because I am meditating, that is, searching. When one knows what one wishes to say, one can proceed by simple formulation; when one thinks pen in hand, one tacks and veers about one's subject.— This results in two wholly different styles.

*April 30, 1876.*—The professor is made for the students, and not *vice versa,* as the doctor is made for the sick and the sabbath for man. You must therefore speak to them in their own tongue, win them in their own way, adjust yourself to their pace, since they absolutely will not and cannot accommodate themselves to yours. Intrinsically, the course will be less good, less perfect, less complete; but the professor must think more of the people than of the thing. His task is pedagogical. If he has permitted his students to become inattentive, if he lets them desert him, the goodness of the course itself means nothing: the object is lost. The state pays him to interest his auditors and to entice them to study. How? That is his affair. But this is the very thing that is antipathetic to me in the profession, the need for cunning, oratorical calculation, rhetorical coaxing, the trick of putting oneself forward, condiments, allusions, in short, the cuisine and the artifices of teaching *à la française* . . .

I cannot endure eloquence when the question is one of pure instruction. There is something inveigling and fraudulent about it which seems to me an infidelity to the thing in hand, something base in one who employs it, a contempt for those upon whom it is exercised.—But this loyal austerity is treated as if it were impotence by the vulgar, who wish to be cajoled, *mundus vult decipi;* this respect is called coldness; ideas seem only vacuities to these lazy, lumpish, positive understandings. The people run after the golden calf, after superstitions and abuses, and oblige their leaders to give them what they like, heady wine, humbug of the grossest kind. Give us back our idols, treat us like brutes, and we shall be satisfied; but tell us that we are gods and makers of gods.—It is certain that to address the lower instincts, the tendencies of custom, inveterate habits is the way to be successful. The old dodges are always the best.

But the question is this: do you wish to harden yourself in your personal method or make concessions to the raw material of your audience? Better to make concessions, try to please. But are you able to do so? To isolate a few special subjects and develop these further, to improvise more freely would perhaps be a way to bring back the pupils who are getting out of hand. But this would be a good deal of trouble for nothing. Opinions once formed, repugnances that have once been acquired, obstruct any perception of subsequent changes. Unpopularity is not to be conjured away, for it is a verdict that is never revoked and never revised. What is done is done, what is said is said. One is classed among the professors to be avoided; and this academic interdict persists, whatever one does to meet it. It is really childish, therefore, to protest against this blind, deaf sentence. One is merely running one's head against a wall.

Two other solutions, to drop a career that is sterile and thankless or simply to let the stream flow, to regard the position as a retiring pension and work away, meanwhile, at literary publications. This is the attitude of many old professors, the compensation for the good years that have been spent in a very unremunerative service. I have been engaged in it for twenty-six years, and I have sacrificed to this sorry career the most precious things, marriage, reputation, a life that would have been more to my taste. Even if at present more were paid for these services than they are worth, the claims of equity would not be met. My pride would merely be wounded.— The first solution tempts me more . . . But I should like to leave by the front door, with the honours of war, and not like a runaway.

I see nothing ahead but inextricable difficulties and humiliations. This does not put one in a good humour. That is why I have a horror of thinking of the future. I advance towards it backwards and with my eyes shut, to safeguard the present at least from worry, bitterness and despair. Work is only a protective shield. One is forever screening the abyss, cheating one's unsatisfied hunger, repressing the griefs of the heart, putting a good face on a lost game. When everything is sinking beneath the waves, health, friends, memory, illusions, faiths, one falls back successively for refuge on the parts of one's being that are not yet submerged. That is why I make rhymes, as the circumstances arise, and play chess on occasion. If one's eyes were always on one's yawning deficiencies, one would go mad.

*May 13, 1876 (9 p. m.).*—A good day. Wound up the *Etrangères,*[1] at least the sixty-one translations, for the appendix and the notes

---

[1] *Les Etrangères, poésies traduites de diverses littératures,* by H. F. Amiel, 1876.—This was an experiment in various rhythmic innovations.

remain to be corrected.—Have I any feeling of relief, joy, pride, hope? Not too much. I feel nothing at all, or at least the sensation is so vague that I cannot analyze it. I should rather be tempted to say to myself, What a lot of work for such small results! "Much ado about nothing!" The new rhythms leave me cold.—And yet the work is successful. But what is translation in verse! I am already losing interest in it. My mind demands something else, my active self also . . .

What is Edmond Scherer going to say about this volume? That will interest me, for his criticism is pitiless.

*May 15, 1876.*—This morning, corrected the final proofs of the *Etrangères*. One job off my hands. I am pleased with the prose speculation that ends the volume; I like it better than the second part (New Rhythms). The work as a whole represents the solution of a problem, the problem of translation into French verse, considered as a special art. It is science applied to poetry. The result is of a nature not to discredit a philosopher, for it is only applied psychology.

*May 21, 1876.*—What have I done since last September? A study of Mme. de Staël; *Les Etrangères*, about 2000 lines; *L'Escalade de 1602*, 450 lines; *Charles le Téméraire*, 1200 lines.

I have presided at a few meetings, conducted a literary competition, corrected proofs, reread La Fontaine, written a good many letters. But that is all. I must have wasted a prodigious amount of time wool-gathering, day-dreaming, stumbling and bungling. Oh! I forget: I have studied the fifteenth century, with the chroniclers and *Volkslieder,* and the historians J. de Müller, Barante, Vuillemin, de Gingins, Daguet, Laurent, Zellweger, Comines, Delamarche, Cantu, Lavallée, Michelet. Ran through a good many poems in various languages before adopting my sixty-one specimen pieces for the *Etrangères.*—Reread Victor Hugo, Coppée, Sully-Prudhomme; read the fourth year of the *Critique philosophique.*

Then why do I seem to have been asleep? Because everything is much the same as nothing, and nine months vanished are, to my consciousness, only so much thin air. Impossible to take myself seriously. Everything I do seems to me a mere nothing, a trifle, a way of deceiving the menacing void which I feel within me. I have neither resignation, serenity nor hope.

*May 31, 1876.*—The whole movement of the universe is merely matter for thought. Therefore the mind seeks isolation from it, in order to subject it to itself. Meditation is a withdrawal into the self; it constructs an invisible cell, to serve as an observatory and laboratory in which the whirling phenomena may be sifted, selected, analyzed, converted into general laws, into ideas, into modes of the mind. It presupposes two things, communication with the world and the faculty of abstracting oneself from it.

We do not need to seek the world, for it comes to us of itself; the defensive operation is the difficult one. Dissipation is the natural thing, while useful concentration implies a great deal of art and discipline, many precautions and arrangements. We have to imitate the optic apparatus, through which, given the light-rays, direct or reflected, that swarm and quiver in space, the individual becomes aware of forms, bodies, colours and distances. We have to manufacture for ourselves the analogue of the pupil, the crystalline lens, the retina. Our mind has to discover the best apparatus for its proper functioning, the eye-shade, the lenses, the compasses, the prisms that · permit it to grasp its object, truth.

*July 12, 1876.*—Misery upon misery . . . On awaking, dullness of the senses, a fit of coughing, eyelids in a wretched state, incapacity, dejection. Dressing, breakfast, a rubbing down and the fresh air have restored me a little, and my nervous collapse is less complete. But I am still in a state of prostration. Oh, health! To be fit, light-hearted, gay, with a good appetite, in cheerful spirits, in possession of one's faculties, what a blessing! Nowadays, alas, I have no longer any teeth to eat with, and everything is difficult for me, sleeping, digesting, working, travelling. I cannot endure the daylight, per-spiration, down pillows, a warm bed or a cold bed, etc. In short, I am horribly sensitive and effeminate, or, I should say, vulnerable and delicate. Everything hurts me, and I can scarcely adapt myself to anything any longer. Things cannot go on this way. I shall have to grow stronger or vanish. Nervous invalids are wretched creatures. Only laboriously and by artificial means can they recover their equilibrium and get the upper hand. They know they are going under, and they experience the sensation in every detail.

Another proof that my nerves are generally worn out is that I am going to pieces. Everything is leaving me, hair, teeth, memory and will. I watch my hoops and staves giving way; my poor old barrel is bursting at the seams and cannot hold anything inside it any longer. Discouragement and indifference are hastening the ruin, for I detach myself from everything that detaches itself from me. In short, all my native appurtenances and appendages and all my acquired riches are leaving me, one after another. Unseasonable spoliation, painful ordeal.

*Après tant de malheurs, que vous reste-t-il? Moi.*

This I is the central consciousness, the axis of all the branches that have been cut away, the thing that endures all the mutilations. I shall soon have nothing more than that, naked thought. Death reduces us to the mathematical point; the destruction that precedes it drives us back in narrower and narrower concentric circles towards this last impregnable retreat. I am having a foretaste of this zero, in which all forms and all modes expire. I see how one goes back into the night, and I find, conversely, how one emerges from it. Life is only a meteor, and I embrace its brief duration. To be born, to live and to die assume a new meaning at each phase of our existence. To see oneself as a rocket, to observe the fleeting phenomenon of one's own being is practical psychology. I greatly prefer to observe the world, a much vaster and richer firework; but when illness narrows my horizon and throws me back upon my misery, my misery is still a spectacle for my curiosity. What interests me in myself, in spite of my distaste, is that I find here an authentic example of human nature, and consequently a specimen of general value. My meal has only one dish now, but it is still a meal. The sample enables me to understand great numbers of analogous situations and a multitude of my fellow-beings.

Supposing that this I persists after the dissolution of its present organism, it would find it curious to compare with this another manner of consciousness and thought, that, say, of the beings of Mars, Jupiter and other planets of our system, or the inhabitants of Sirius or other solar systems.

To become conscious of all the possible modes of being would be an occupation to fill ages and ages, at least for finite minds, dependent on time. It is true that this progressive felicity might act upon such minds as a poison, owing to their ambition for the absolute and for the all at once. But it might be replied that aspirations are necessarily prophetic, since they can come to life only under the action of the same cause that will permit them to reach their end. The soul can only dream of the absolute because the absolute exists. The consciousness of possible perfection is the guarantee that perfection will exist.

Thought is eternal. It is the consciousness of thought which, through ages, races, humanities, gradually grows. This is Hegel's doctrine. The history of the mind would be an approximation of the absolute, and at the two ends of this history the absolute differs. It *was* at the beginning, it *knows itself* at the end, or rather it advances in the possession of itself with the unfolding of creation. So likewise thought Aristotle.

If the history of the mind and consciousness is the very marrow and essence of being, then to be brought to a stand in personal psychology is not to go wide of the mark. It is to be at the heart of the matter, at the centre of the universal drama. This idea is consoling. Everything may be taken away from us; if we still have thought, we still cling by a magic thread to the axis of the world. But we may lose thought and speech. In this case there remains simple feeling, the feeling of the presence of God and of death in

God; this is a last vestige of the human privilege, that of participation in the whole, communication with the absolute.

> *Ta vie est un éclair qui meurt dans son nuage,*
> *Mais l'éclair t'a sauvé s'il t'a fait voir le ciel.*

*July 14, 1876.*—Received *Echos poétiques* (fol-de-rols for the Federal Shooting-match at Lausanne) . . . Third-class beer-foam; wish-wash of incorrect rhymes and stale banalities, which the populace takes for poetry; rude copper buttons which it confuses with jewels.

O patriotism of the canteen, you were created to disgust us with everything you handle in your crude fashion. After you, one would not dare to sing of country, liberty, the rifle: just as one revolts at drinking from the cup which the unwashed stableman has just brushed with his lips. But why this disgust?

> *Nous sommes de ce monde où les plus belles choses*
> *Ont le pire destin.*

All the great ideas are destined to vulgarization. The noblest words must be trailed through cabarets, as the supreme name of God ends by forming a part of every oath. The holiest, the greatest, the most ethereal, the most mysterious is condemned to this inevitable degradation. The mantle even of goddess or Madonna, falling lower and lower, ends on the dungheap. The sewer is the universal heir of all the magnificences of history.

And why not? It is the right of the gross and the many to fuddle their wits, in turn, on all that has enraptured the thinkers, the heroes and the saints. The idiots lie down in the bed of the geniuses. This gives them an illusion of self-esteem.

Delicate things must inure themselves to this prospect, that of being grasped some day by heavy black hands. But yet I should rather wish this fate for them than that they should be exploited by sharpers, hypocrites, impostors. And we must choose between these two evils. To hope that truths may find a refuge in souls that are worthy to understand and honour them is a delusion. The multitudes debase them, the clever make use of them as means to fraud and power. The true human *élite*, which is everything from the point of view of quality, is a mere nothing in quantity.

Let us be resigned. It must needs be that hoarse and drunken voices should bawl out Progress, bellow Liberty, vociferate Fraternity. The masterpieces of plastic art reach the market-place in the form of grotesque reflections. What does it matter! If the uglification of the copy encounters eyes that are more and more boorish, there is a mutual propriety in this. The print that charms the child and the savage makes the artist wince, but it has found its public.— Heine did not wish to share atheism with his shoemaker. What would he have been gaining? In vain men repeat the same creed; each of them understands it only according to his stature, his culture and his range.

All sophisticated people have the same superstition as the women of England, that of distinction. They are anti-plebeian, anti-equalitarian; they recognize as equals only those who resemble them. They cannot be prevailed upon to ignore as nothing differences of culture, education, native nobility, clearsightedness and taste and to treat clowns, clodhoppers and boors as hail fellows well met. For them, glass beads, tinware and slops cannot be confused with diamonds, steel and fine wine. In other words, in spite of everything, they perceive differences and degrees. The democratic spirit, on the other hand, wishes only to see resemblances. True criticism consists in seeing both things at once. The popular writer is he who disengages whatever there is in common in all the social strata and addresses that average of prejudices, sentiments and passions to which the particular diversities do not attain.

To be popular, to be national would be possible for you if you encountered a little more sympathy, recognition and justice, although personally your affinities with your environment, and with your double fatherland, Genevese and Swiss, are not very marked.

But impersonality is so easy for you.—Only when people refuse to recognize you, the need for defensive operations chills you and you exaggerate the contrasts lest they be overlooked. Good nature lets its rights sleep if they are not contested; an insolent denial obliges it to assert them. To disavow the best in oneself is cowardly. To bow before the errors of mediocrity or the arrogances of inferiority is base. Of this I think I am incapable.

Disdain is better than anger, pity is better than disdain, indulgence is better than pity, and kindness is better than indulgence.

*July 16, 1876.*—If five hundred of the fourteen thousand pages of my Journal are preserved, this would be a good deal, enough, perhaps. One urn is enough to hold our ashes and to preserve our name for a few more generations, if we are among those who have the possibility of a name. Of the thousand billions of men who have lived, how many have left a trace of glory? One in a hundred millions. All the others go to form the anonymous humus of history which the ages accumulate. Few of us escape the common pit of oblivion. The Book of Memory has few places in it and grants these only to the privileged. It is difficult enough to leave a lasting memory in more than two or three loving hearts.

*July 22, 1876.*—Reading: fifty pages of Töpffer (*Bibliothèque de mon oncle*). Sadly disappointed. Spell broken. My earlier impressions placed him too high. A mass of imperfections become apparent to me in what I thought was a masterpiece (incoherences, tricks, artificiality, mannerism, lack of moral unity). Very mixed value. Rather laboured originality. These critical revisions ten or twenty years afterwards often make large displacements in relative values. The *distinguo* comes forward and abounds. The perfect resists, but whatever is fissured, swollen, artificial takes a lower place. The surprising thing in Töpffer is the lack of homogeneity in the thought, the tone, the style. The pages do not hang together and do not seem to be of the same period or from the same hand. Improprieties of diction, errors in French are not uncommon. A vein of rather vulgar bantering runs through this talent, the strength of which lies in the picturesque and the charm in the sallies of sensibility and good sense, alternating with malice.

*July 23, 1876 (10 p. m.)*.—We finish the *Bibliothèque de mon oncle*, first part, and are beginning the *Voyage autour de ma chambre*.

This latter is more elegantly written and more homogeneous than the other, but one feels too much the element of bluff and badinage. The Genevan work has more sap, more heart, more picturesqueness, more serious feeling; it grips one more and in better passages. But I have only reread the first two love-affairs of Jules, with Héloïse and Miss Lucy. The Jewess is greatly superior, if my recollections do not deceive me.

A little more naivety and verisimilitude would greatly heighten the quality of this delightful tale, the defect of which is the disparity of the pages and the tones. It is possible to see at once with the eyes of fifteen and fifty, provided that the same character is telling his own story and judging himself; but the intervention of the author, a third personage, with his own private spites and tricks, spoils for us the reality of the story.

In what does the charm of humour reside? In the fact that it makes us live in many ways at once. We are sad and merry at the same time, illusioned and disillusioned, young and old, tender and mocking.—But the art of the humorous novelist consists in maintaining, in spite of this, the unity of character, and in remaining within the premises of his own fiction. The moment he infringes this rule, the spell vanishes and he bursts the iridescent bubble which we were so happy to be blowing with him; this inadvertence vexes us and pains us; the dream flies away; the enchanter awakens us from our enchantment by the mistake that he makes, and we hold this against him.

The secret of happy fiction, then, also has its logic, a logic of fancy, illusion, sentiment which is logical none the less, that is, a concatenation of the parts, a convergence of effects, a unity of impressions. This is equally the secret of style and the secret of the theatre. It is the concentration of a thousand delicate proprieties, the harmonizing of the contrasts themselves, the simulation of life, which is continually resolving this problem.

What one tells must have the air of having happened, and he who tells it must be the first to believe in it; otherwise, we are no longer in the realm of poetry, we are in the realm of prose. Irony chills us, and the improbable leaves us indifferent. Therefore the poet must be a sincere magician who mocks neither himself nor his audience, nor yet his art. Mockery is necessarily sterile and unfruitful; it destroys everything and creates nothing. Therefore the novelist must be ingenuous, at least when his pen is in his hand.

*Pour me tirer des pleurs il faut que vous pleuriez.*

Madness itself thus has its method, fantasy has a kind of reason, the appearance of life, like life, has its mystery. This means that all production has the same profound law; to produce is to engender; the spark of existence is communicated only in love, and in love there is always illusion, for it always contains the ideal.

*July 24, 1876 (8 a. m.).*—Disadvantage of a private journal: it puts up too readily with our lamentations; it replaces the action that heals us with the description of our ills; it usually drifts towards apology; it is a kind of epicurism rather than a discipline, at least when one passes from morality to psychology and substitutes contemplation for sanctification, Montaigne for Pascal.

To journalize is to dream, in a way, and consequently to loaf away one's time. It is a kind of busy idleness, a recreation that simulates work. There is no work without a useful purpose, without effort and the sense of consequences. But I write here without any purpose whatever, without continuity of ideas or intentional direction. —In what way is this interminable soliloquy of use to me? In thinking and in writing, or rather in preserving from utter torpor my faculties of reflection and expression. This is something. But, at the same time, this all too convenient practice keeps me from writing a book or constructing a theory. Indolence is not conducive to strength. Letting things go their own way does not sharpen or augment any aptitude. By eternally knocking the billiard-balls about, one does not win games.

*A préluder sans fin l'œuvre ne vient jamais.*

A monologue that runs unchecked, without bounds and without intentions, may preserve one from annihilation, but it is weakening, none the less. It leads by repetition to inertia, as, by vain discharges, it leads to exhaustion. It is a dripping away of the sap, a fistula that wastes one's forces, it is an open drain . . . A folly that dissolves, undermines, devours and consumes life without profit to anybody. It is a holocaust to the sterile goddess, Inutility.

You will therefore have spent your whole life brooding on eggs of stone, first by dutifully devoting yourself to fruitless works and ungrateful beings, then by endlessly protracting on your own account the preludes of expectation and the sighs of discouragement; finally by refusing in your pride to turn to account what is still left of you (as if this could give your measure, the measure of your original capacities and ambitions) and by taking refuge in trifles. Inadaptation to your environment, rupture with circumstances, disgust with your lot, a wounded heart, stiffening yourself and abstaining, distracting and scattering yourself . . . A melancholy tale! It suggests a life that has miscarried.

Yes, but whose fault is it? Are you to be blamed or pitied? The moral climate in which you have lived has withered your soul, your talent, your character. You would have liked to be accepted, but you would have had to impose yourself by force. This necessity filled you with disgust. The animosity, the hatred, the suspicion, the perfidy, or simply the incurable misunderstanding, the lack of intelligence in those about you have dumbfounded you. And a calm despair removed from you even the temptation to struggle. This is a Darwinian world, and you are not of this world. The disharmony is fundamental.

*July 26, 1876.*—Read over note-book 141,[1] before sewing up its successor. A journal is a pillow for indolence; it dispenses one from going around subjects, it puts up with all one's repetitions, it bears with all the whims and meanderings of the inner life and sets no goal for itself. This journal represents the stuff of forty-six volumes of three hundred pages each. What a prodigious squandering of time, thought and strength! It will be useful to nobody, and even for me it will have served as an aid rather to avoid life than to live it. A journal takes the place of a confidant, a friend and a wife; it takes the place of production, it takes the place of a country and a public. It is a pain-killer, a counter-irritant, a subterfuge. But this factotum, taking the place of everything, really performs almost no part at all. It reminds me of that article of which Töpffer speaks, at once an umbrella, a cane and a seat, which was inadequate however it was used. A journal is a makeshift, certainly. But when we are travelling we simplify our impedimenta, and my provisional life never emerges from the state of a traveller . . .

*(11 p. m.).*—What is it that constitutes the history of a soul? It is the stratification of its progress, the summary of its acquisitions and the march of its destiny.—If your history is to instruct anybody, if it is to interest yourself, it must be disengaged from its materials, simplified, distilled. These fourteen thousand pages are only the heap of leaves and peelings lying around the tree, the essence of which must be extracted. The value of a forest of cinchonas is only a hogshead of quinine. A whole rose-garden in Smyrna is condensed in a vial of perfume.

This twenty-nine years of chatter may come to nothing at all, for people are really interested only in their own stories and their own personal lives.—You may never have the leisure to reread it yourself. And so . . . so what? You will have lived, and life consists in repeating the human type and the human *ritornello,* as for ages and

[1] Note-book 141 of the Journal, which, among other remarks jotted down on its cover, bears the following: "June 20–July 25, 1876, a hundred pages in one month; this figure greatly exceeds the average."

ages legions of your fellows have repeated, repeat, and will repeat them. To become conscious of this *ritornello,* of this type, is something, and we can hardly do anything more. The realization of the type is more successful and the *ritornello* is more joyous if circumstances are clement and propitious, but whether the marionettes have acted this way or that way . . .

*Trois p'tits tours, elles s'en vont!*—

all this drops into the same abyss, all comes to much the same thing.

To resist fate, to struggle to escape from the inevitable issue, is almost puerile. When the life-period of a centenarian and that of an ephemera virtually amount to the same thing,—and geology and astronomy permit us to regard these life-periods from this point of view,—what signify our imperceptible tumults, our efforts, our angers, our ambitions, our hopes? For the dream of a dream it is ridiculous to raise these sham tempests. Do the forty million atoms that make up a cubic inch of chalk count very much for us? Do the forty million men who make up France count more for an inhabitant of the moon or Jupiter?

To be a conscious monad, a nothing who knows that it is a microscopic phantom of the universe; this is all that we are able to be.

*July 28, 1876 (11 p. m.).*—Reading: Töpffer (*Le Presbytère,* first part). The scenery is a little mild, and the tale has various improbabilities. But how delicately done is the picture of a young man's reveries! The ducks, the dog, Pernette are charming. Prévère and Reybaz, Charles and Louise are full of life and reality.—It is clear that the extraordinary is not indispensable to art. Everyday things and people serve well enough as subjects, but one must be able to render and reproduce them truly, in relief and gracefully, preserving their character and colour, and, first of all, seeing them. To see the picturesque and the poetic in everything that surrounds us and concerns us, this is what constitutes original talent, a very different thing from derivative talent, which sees only through the literary forms that have been created by others and receives its magnetism only from another magnet. He who draws directly from nature keeps the privilege of novelty. He may be incorrect, he is at least inventive, and, in this respect, there is something durable in him. The style that springs from imitation, the rebound from repercussion, is to the original style as the second bow is to the first in a double rainbow, as the reflection is to the shining object.

The world and man are everywhere; wherever we are everything exists that is necessary for art. It is therefore not the material that is wanting, it is the workman, the ingenious observer and the industrious stylist. How to make the most of this tree, this wall, this anecdote, this impression, this particular confluence of radii and circumstances? That is the question. Men of genius make trifles important and create the value of things. Thousands of spots and villas surpass Rousseau's Les Charmettes, but they have had no Rousseau. The subjects abound, it is the vanquishing mind that is scarce. The great mind makes everything great; the inventor makes something of nothing; he who thinks evokes more treasures from a grain of sand than the unreflecting from a whole island.

The supreme art is therefore the art of making all subjects fruitful, the method that creates and innovates, wresting from everything the hidden spark, the gleam of the diamond, the expressive note, the characteristic trait, the accent or the lesson.

*Tout ce qu'il a touché se convertit en or.*

*August 8, 1876.*—Woman is loving but passive, receiving the idea and the spark, but without the gift of self-electrification. Virility alone originates things spontaneously and is an origin, a *punctum saliens.* Thus the feminine principle is subordinate, it comes afterwards and in the second place. Man is by nature the master in art, legislation, science, industry; woman is the pupil, disciple, servant, imitator. Chivalrous courtesy dissembles this in vain, for there is no equality between the sexes. They are indispensable one to another, but one is the leader and the other led. The ram is the master of the ewe; the reverse would be an aberration and monstrosity. The pride of the American women will bring about a reaction; for whatever these ladies are they owe to man. If the latter wearies of his generosity and leaves them to their own merits, the expiatory plunge will oblige them to measure the immensity of their ingratitude.

Nature has willed the subordination of woman. Civilized man dignifies his companion, submits willingly to grace, sweetness, frailty, creates for her the right to protection, gives her a privileged place. But the condition is such that, if she denies the benefaction and claims to have earned what has been given to her and to be indebted to no one, her benefactor may bring this course to an abrupt end.

The illusion consists in this: superiority constitutes a moral duty on the part of the superior towards the inferior, but inferiority does not constitute any legal right on the part of the inferior over the superior. Generosity is beautiful and noble, but it is optional; the cripple who demands that he should be carried dispels one's desire to aid him. Man enjoys protecting woman, but when woman imperatively summons him to serve and protect her, he whom an entreaty would have softened loses his inclination at once.

By substituting the legal sphere for the moral sphere, the emancipation of women will desiccate society, as legal charity destroys real charity, as love by command would sterilize the marriage-bed. —In asking more than civil equality and economic equality, women are playing a dangerous game. Equality in services will be demanded of them, and this will serve them right.

*August 14, 1876.*—A trustful ingenuousness, that is to say, abandon, is the distinctive trait of the good-natured German. With it, one has more security than with any other type because it has more candour, more probity, more simplicity. In this type man is closer to man, hand touches hand, heart speaks to heart, with fewer veils

and bandages, dodges and precautions. *Die Treue* is still the reigning virtue. Hence also its susceptibility to the mockers, its awkwardness with the adroit, its antipathy for the crafty, its naive
admiration of elegance and its stiff exaggeration of the manners of
the well-bred. When the German is driven out of his good-natured-
ness, he does not know what figure to assume.—The absence of the
noble shocks me, but I have a weakness for this affectionate candour, this loyalty of the *Gemüth,* which feels at ease only in reciprocal good will. It is not purchasing at too high a price immediacy in
human relations if one pays for it with a familiarity that is a little
vulgar. Frank sincerity also has its grace.

But beware of quarrels in this atmosphere; their crudity soon
degenerates into grossness. When one does not wear gloves, one's
nails appear very quickly. One realizes then the value of politeness,
dignity, reserve. Similarly, the German burlesque is intolerably low.
The German nature being already of the earth earthy, it is evident
that, descending a step or two, one reaches the trivial, brutal and
ignoble.

Thus there is compensation in everything. And this is why one
cannot set one nation above another. But with individuals it is not
the same thing; they are able to combine the good qualities of several nations and attenuate the corresponding faults. And so, without
liking the defects of the Germans, French or Italians, the English
or the Genevese, for instance, I find distinguished people everywhere whom I can like and esteem. It has often been thought here
that I have an enthusiasm for Germany, which is a complete mistake; but I know what Germany is worth. People at Lausanne consider me very Genevese, but God knows how much the Genevan
spirit is to my taste.

*August 21, 1876.*—It is the growing tendency of contemporary
thinkers to reject freedom, immortality, theism. The doctrine of
Evolution tends to replace the others. Everything that contradicts
it, dualism, revelation, moral freedom, is energetically attacked.
There are several misapprehensions at the bottom of this. Faith

rests on mystery, which it does not explain but which it accepts. Science wishes to ascertain, check, verify, explain; and it accepts nothing without warrant.—If faith could and would agree that it knows nothing of what it believes, science would recognize more readily that the unknown is immense and that the unknowable is vaster than the unknown.

Faith is an imaginary anticipation of knowledge, a provisional and hypothetical explanation, which feeling discovers and welcomes, but which it confounds with proved and demonstrated truth. Sometimes faith is a stimulus to research and consequently a means of discovery; sometimes it is a barrier and obstacle to any pursuit and any innovation. In the first case, it is the philosophic faith in truth; in the second case, it is the ecclesiastical faith in a dogma, a formula, a system. The one believes in a hidden but real truth; the other in an apparent and received truth. It is the faith in the paradoxical that causes the orthodox faith to be attacked. Faith in science contends with religious faith. Or rather two religions are at grips. Tradition and Revolution, the old and the new, the conservative spirit and the spirit of innovation are joining in the *mêlée*.

*August 29, 1876.*—My life is not healthy and normal, for it is given over to every sort of inner whirlwind and does not fulfil any plan. I do not merely live from day to day, but I pass through all the ways of seeing and feeling, without any fixed rule, without any settled purpose, without unity of character or conduct. I will nothing; I let myself float on all the winds of the air and all the currents of the sea, like a dead leaf with the property of feeling its own existence. I am only a psychological consciousness, a medium in which phenomena occur, phenomena which I do not direct but am content to observe. I watch myself live, as one follows a dream, by a forced curiosity. This is to be a thought, and even less than that, an inner perception, a registering sphygmometer; it is not to be a man. A man makes a work of his life, and he leaves a work; his activity has a goal and becomes an employment; his tendencies are sorted and selected; he becomes a character, an individual, somebody. As for yourself, you remain indeterminate, in a state of virtuality; you represent only a promise, a hope, a prospect . . . Like the clouds, you wait for the wind to move you, for the sun to gild you, for the heat to lift you.

You have passed from morality to psychology, from voluntary and responsible activity to meditative passivity, from virile living to a vegetable existence, from the valiant life to revery. Society being only an arena, you are no longer of this world; you no longer speak its language, nor does it understand you . . .

Christians, Jews, Moslems, materialists, Stoics, Epicureans can make nothing of you; the economists can do no better. There would be no place for your Buddhistic quietism even in the last of our monasteries. The evolutionists, too, would find you an aerolite, an odd, abnormal specimen, a droll monstrosity. The danger of this singularity is absolute isolation. One must not break with one's time, for that is quite indifferent to it. It does not give two thoughts to creatures that are enigmatic; it tosses them disdainfully among the worthless. In order to be of this world, one must be useful in some way, one must have form, figure, weight, colour, constant properties, a suitable energy, and become a cog in the wheel of the passions, the prejudices, interests, institutions, services that constitute society. What would be done with an inhabitant of the moon or Saturn who happened to fall among the human throng? He would not be able either to walk, speak, or understand, and there would be nothing for him to do but to die without delay.

I see very plainly that my acquired culture is not of one substance with myself, that I am inside of it and ready to detach myself from it, as a butterfly from its chrysalis. The fact of being a male, a Genevan, a European, a person of the nineteenth century who has learned this or that, is only a superficial accident. All this particularization is fortuitous, and it seems to me an envelope that might easily drop away. I do not feel between myself and any conceivable form of sentient being any distance that cannot be crossed. I could wake up a Japanese, a woman, a madman, a child, a camel, an inhabitant of Jupiter or the moon without exclaiming that it was impossible. Time and space do not exist in any solid sense for me, and consequently every metamorphosis is easy. As early as 1846, thirty years ago, I felt for two weeks that my body was outside my real self; I regarded it with curiosity, as an alien thing, and the sound of my steps on the floor made me turn and look. There is therefore no vigorous adhesion between my appearance and my reality, between my form and my substance. My central monad tolerates this or that aggregation as its provisional expression, but it has no illusions about the fragility of this configuration. Its essence is polymorphic, and, in consequence, it is completely indeterminable, however momentarily determined . . .

My individuality consists in having no individuality, and in containing all potentially, in feeling this and being conscious of it. To define me, one must reverse the method of definition, and, instead of classifying me by specifying me, one must specify me by making me a class, genus, type. It is my nature to be not a person, such as Ulysses, but a non-individual personality, a general personality. I am anonymous, because no name would characterize me. I am amorphous, because any conclusive form would be a sort of lie. I am nothing (in particular) because I can be anything (I do not say everything). Beware of the disadvantages, unlucky moon-man.

Protean spirit, you must consent to remain in the state of the caterpillar, to be and to act some role. That which is necessity for others you must concede; you must condescend to it, accept it. The eternal must become historical, the spirit must be made flesh, the possible must be confined to one of its algebraic cases if there is to be reality in it. No doubt this incarnation is an abasement, it represents a lapse as compared to the divine state. But this metaphysical lapse is a moral nobility, because it is a sacrifice in which one acquiesces. It is vexatious, perhaps, that the world exists; but, granted that there is a humanity, its gradual redemption depends on this secular labour of spirits that resign themselves to their captivity and toil away at the point where their predecessors have left the collective task . . .

From the moral point of view, you would accept this incarnation, this abasement, determination, solidarity, participation in the collective work, infinitesimal though your part might be. You would labour in humility and religion; you would do as everybody does, at least as the better souls do.

Is not this to pass from Hellenism to the Gospel, from Olympus to Gethsemane? From the worship of joy to the religion of sorrow? The pursuit of beauty is transformed into charity. The son of God becomes the servitor, the just man dedicates himself to the cross in order to save those that are lost, the happy man submits to suffering in order to console all who suffer. The beautiful seemed higher than the sublime; now the sublime seems more beautiful than the beautiful. Sin is disclosed as the sickness of the world; and to bring others to health by first purifying oneself seems the duty of all. And indolence, negligence, apathy, discouragement, carelessness are the opposite of the struggle against sin. One perceives that indulgence with oneself is a complicity with evil, and one says to oneself that abdication is not permitted, that to be a good example is a duty. If despair is not revolt, it is a fault, none the less, for it does good to no one and it increases the sum of evil. We are all condemned to suffering, mutilation and death. Those who have received more and have more to lose owe also the example of magnanimity.

*September 8, 1876 (8 a. m.).*—Grey, cold, lowering weather. A fit of coughing makes me feel as if my eyes were full of vinegar. Melancholy.

The imagination anticipates ills and feels and depicts them in advance; this lessens the surprise when they occur; the surprise, yes, but not the pain. Oddly enough, one even feels that they are cruel when they come to despatch their wounded; that is, we think we are quits with them for the pains we have suffered and imagined in advance. There is something of the ruminant in our imagination:

it digests its sufferings twice. It takes a preliminary sip of the cup, then it tastes the dregs. It grieves for what it is going to lose, then for what it has lost.

But all this, with me, does not lead to defensive effort, to action, to revolt. It is only the ambiguous dream of my expectant passivity. The idea of escaping my fate, of making my fate never even enters my head. I feel as the Orientals feel. I see, I hear the rolling of the car of fatality. Is it coming for me? Perhaps. But the thought of stopping its wheels or avoiding them seems to me childish. Effort presupposes hope, and I cannot hope any longer. The minimum of will that remains to me is expended in acceptance and resignation.

I look on, motionless, at my dismemberment. This Buddhistic inertia is the proof of intellectualism, the conversion of all the forces of the being into simple, reflective consciousness. The meditation of zero on itself, the vanishing of all phenomena into the substance of the self, and of the self into the void, this is indeed psychological Nirvana. A nothingness that is aware of itself is pure thought.

*September 12, 1876.*—It is fitting that, in regard to every question, the critic should have the spirit of the thing, together with a measure of competence and modesty. It is true that these qualities are an inconvenience and that, in order to be trenchant, it is better to do without them. But the intelligent man who does not feel his limitations is lacking in intelligence; the critic who cannot criticize himself is no true critic. To understand is four times more difficult than to judge. To understand is to enter objectively into the conditions of that which exists, while to judge is simply to utter an individual opinion.

This makes me think again of Edmond Scherer, who does not always perceive the difference between his personal taste and an impartial verdict. In poetry and aesthetics, he has various preconceived opinions and various unreflecting habits, the subjectivity of which he does not feel. His confidence in himself, a trait of character, diminishes his critical superiority. A trenchant scepticism is a curious oddity. I explain it, like so many other things, by the law of irony. When one doubts everything else, one does not doubt one's own sagacity. Similarly, when the Holy Brotherhood condemned in the name of the God of mercy, it knew no scruples in its ruthlessness. And when men take the vow of poverty for themselves they are rapacious for their order. It is useless to pique oneself on any virtue, for there is always somewhere a comic compensation, of which we are unaware. We always lend ourselves to laughter. What is your own absurdity? Abounding in maxims, heaven knows, not one of which you follow; wearing yourself to the bone learning wisdom, which you never practise; always getting ready for nothing, living without living. The contemplation that does not dare to be contemplative purely, the renunciation that does not wholly renounce, chronic contradictoriness, this is your case. Inconsistent scepticism, irresolution incorrigible though unconvinced, the weakness that will not accept itself but cannot convert itself into strength, this is your misfortune. Its comic aspect is that the capacity to guide others turns into an incapacity to guide oneself, that the dream of the infinitely great is stopped by the infinitely little, that gifts appear utterly useless. To arrive at immobility through excess of motion, at powerlessness through the excess of attempts, at zero through the plethora of numbers is strangely ridiculous and sadly droll; and the pettiest-minded gossip can laugh at it.

Extremely subjective in feeling and objective in thought, the nature of your individuality is to be impersonal, as it is the plague of your life to have to be individual. Your deficiency lies in the will, the principle of your abstention lies in doubt, and doubt arises from the impossibility of seeing everything, in combination with the probity that rejects assumption and arbitrary decision. In other words, you are ill adapted to the human condition, and you will die without having really shown your mettle, because your surroundings have not suited you and have not been suited with you.

Your self condemned to be itself only, while its profound instinct is to be the non-self, this is the punishment from which you cannot escape. You would have to limit yourself, and this may be impossible to you, either because your soul does not consent to it, or because your mind does not know what should be chosen. Irresolution in despair, this is the state in which your central being persists and which always remains in your consciousness beneath your particular distractions, enterprises, diversions.

My soul is a gulf and nothing has ever satisfied its desire, and the extirpation of desire has not yet pacified it. It longs to be able to give itself completely, in love, faith, enthusiasm; and there has been no object to absorb it or even to give it an illusion. This vast, vague aspiration is a thirst which is never extinguished. Does one ask in what respect it differs from the suffering of the reprobate? The latter is eternal remorse; the former has a dim hope, either of happiness or of non-existence.

Thus I neither rebel nor submit, another ambiguity. My state is the unquiet, unstable state, indefinable, anxious. Enigma that knows itself for enigma, chaos that perceives its chaos, disorder that feels its condition but does not clear itself up, this is my situation. In fact, alas, even when intuition has crossed and illumined the abyss with its mighty flash, the vision melts away and is soon forgotten and the effort must be taken up anew. The individual mind cannot contrive to grasp itself in its essence, perhaps because its essence is not to be individual.

*September 19, 1876.*—Reading: Doudan (*Mélanges*, two hundred and fifty pages of volume I). It is delightful! Wit, grace, delicacy, imagination, thought, everything is to be found in these letters. How I regret not having known this man, the Frenchman in his most refined form, a fastidious soul who was born sublime (Sainte-Beuve's phrase), who shunned the public from a too ardent love of perfection, but who, in his lifetime and his circle, was regarded as the equal of the best. Almost the only thing he lacked was an interfusion of the material, the blending of brutality and ambition that was necessary to give him his place in the sun. But as he was appreciated in the best society of Paris (the world of the de Broglies), he sought nothing further. He reminds me of Joubert.

*September 20, 1876 (8 a. m.).*—Continued Doudan as far as the hundred and twenty-ninth letter. He was forty-two, with one foot in the grave already, suffering from perpetual headaches, living a confined life, apprehensive to the last degree. Yet he lived thirty years more. Is this what my future is going to be? I do not think so. For this one must have a solid chest and the vegetative functions in good order. And it is in the respiratory tracts that I am giving out. I have a crab in my bronchial tubes. This does not spare its man like the nervous disorders.

A pale sun slashes with its morning rays the Palais de Justice, across from me. These rays are neither warm nor luminous; they are like the smile of an old man. This is not the "gigantic smile" which Doudan attributes to Vinet, it is the smile of sad resignation, a transient flash that leaves nothing behind it.

*(Later.)*—Wit consists in satisfying the wit of others, by giving it two pleasures at once, that of hearing one thing and that of divining another, in other words, by making a double stroke. Thus Doudan scarcely ever speaks his thought directly; he disguises it and insinuates it by images, allusions, hyperbole, litotes, light irony, feigned anger, mock humility, amiable malice. The more the thing to be divined differs from that which is said, the more of an agreeable surprise there is for the interlocutor or the correspondent. This subtle and charming way of expressing oneself permits one to teach anything without pedantry and to dare anything without offence. There is something aerial and Attic about it, mingling the serious and the trifling, fiction and truth, with a light grace that La Fontaine or Alcibiades would not have disclaimed. This Socratic playfulness presupposes a freedom of mind that is able to dominate illness and low spirits. This delicate badinage belongs only to the rarest natures, whose superiority conceals itself in finesse, and reveals itself in taste. What a balance of faculties and culture it proclaims! What distinction it testifies! Only a valetudinarian, perhaps, is capable of this delicacy of touch, in which virile thought is united with feminine refractoriness. The excess, if there is an excess,

lies in a certain effeminacy of feeling. Doudan has ceased to be able to endure anything but the perfect, the perfectly harmonious, and everything that is rude, harsh, powerful, unexpected, brutal, throws him into convulsions. Boldness of every kind sets him on edge. This Athenian of the Roman epoch is an epicure of the ear, eye and mind. The wrinkling of a rose-leaf is enough to make him tremble. He recalls the princess of the fairy-tales who felt through twelve mattresses the hardness of a pea that had slipped into her bed.

*Une ombre, un souffle, un rien, tout lui donnait la fièvre.*

What this exquisite creature lacks is strength, creative force as well as muscular force. His circle is not as large as I assumed. The classic world and the Renaissance, the horizon of La Fontaine, is his horizon. He is quite out of his element in the Germanic and Slavic literatures. He has never caught a glimpse of Asia. Humanity for him is not much larger than France. Nature is not a Bible for him. In music and in painting he is quite exclusive. In philosophy he stops at Kant. (It is true that the volume of his correspondence takes him only as far as 1843.) To sum it all up, he is a man of excessively refined and ingenious taste, but he is not a complete critic, still less a poet, philosopher or artist. He was an admirable talker, a delightful letter-writer, who might have become an author by concentrating himself. Let us wait for the second volume, return to this provisional impression and rectify it. (He detests Port-Royal and finds nothing in Vinet but wit: this places him.)

*(Noon.)*—Ran through the whole volume again, relished all this atticism, reconsidered this original and distinguished mind. Doudan was a penetrating and curious psychologist, an investigator of talents, an educator of intellects, a man of infinite taste, wit, discernment and delicacy, but he was deficient in persevering energy of thought, in patience, in execution. He was an obstetrician rather than a procreative mind. He was content all his life to squander the fruitful germs without brooding on them and maturing them. Timid-

ity, insufficient interest, indolence, indifference confined him to the role of a literary counsellor and judge-at-arms, when he might have entered the lists. Am I the one to blame him? Good heavens, no. In the first place, it would be to fire on my allies; and then perhaps he chose the better part.

Did not Goethe make the general observation that, in the circle of all famous men, one finds individuals who have not become famous, and whom the former regard as their equals or their superiors? Descartes, I think, says the same thing. Renown does not run after those who are afraid of it. It laughs at the timorous and respectful lovers who deserve its favours but who do not snatch them. Renown is a virago who must be solicited and even forced,

*Et veut dans son amant un bras qui la fouaille,*

The public gives itself only to the bold and imperious talents, the enterprising and the clever. It does not believe in modesty and sees in it only a pretence on the part of impotence. Conclusion: the Golden Book contains only a part of the real geniuses; it mentions only those who have deliberately broken their way into glory. The Gospel itself, in another sense, says that only the bold enter heaven and that it is the violent who will prevail.

*November 15, 1876.*—Read Laveleye's brochure,[1] with which I am in agreement, as with everything I have read of this writer, whom I find sympathetic. His thesis is that the pure Gospel can provide the religion of the future and that the abolition of all religious principles, which present-day socialism demands, would be as baneful as Catholic superstition; this is the conclusion of Laurent (*Religion de l'avenir*). The Protestant method is the way to this transformation of sacerdotal Christianity into the simple Gospel.—Laveleye believes that civilization cannot continue without the belief in God and the other life. He seems to forget that Japan and China prove the contrary. But it is enough to prove that general

[1] Emile de Laveleye, *L'avenir religieux des peuples civilisés,* 1876.

atheism would produce a moral decline in the average man to make us feel that we should dissuade men from it. This, however, is only religion in the utilitarian sense. A belief is not true because it is useful. And it is truth alone, scientific, established, proved, rational truth, that satisfies today the disillusioned of all classes.—One may say, perhaps, that faith rules the world, but the faith of the present day is no longer in revelation or the priesthood; it is in reason and in science. Is there a science of happiness and the good? That is the question. Do justice and goodness depend on a particular, determinate religion? How to form free, honest, just and good men? There is the point. The art of purifying religion is subordinate to this higher interest.

Caught, while reading, various new applications of my law of irony. Every age has two contradictory aspirations, which are mutually repellent logically and actually in league with each other. Thus in the last century philosophic materialism was the partisan of liberty. Now, the Darwinians are equalitarian, while Darwinism proves the right of the strongest. The absurd is the very nature of life; real beings are contraries in action, living and walking paralogisms. Harmony with oneself would be peace, rest, perhaps immobility. Almost universally, human beings conceive of activity and practise it only in the form of warfare, the inner warfare of vital rivalries, the external and bloody warfare of nations, warfare, finally, with oneself. Thus life is an eternal combat, wishing what it does not wish, and not wishing what it wishes. This gives rise to what I call the law of irony, that is, unconscious dupery, the refutation of the self by the self, the concrete realization of the absurd.

Is this consequence necessary? I do not think so. Combat is the caricature of harmony, and harmony, the association of contraries, is also a principle of motion. War is a brutal and ferocious pacification, the quelling of resistance by the destruction or enslavement of the vanquished. Mutual respect would be better. Conflict is born of the egoism that recognizes no limit but an alien force. The laws of animality prevail through almost all history. Human history is essentially zoölogical; it is only humanized after the event, and then only in the fine souls who are enamoured of justice, goodness, enthusiasm and devotion. The angel peeps forth in the higher animal rarely and with difficulty. The divine aureole appears only in fugitive gleams about the brows of the race that dominates over the earth.

The Christian nations manifest in its fullness the law of irony. Their profession is the citizenship of heaven, the exclusive worship of the eternal goods, and never has the eager pursuit of perishable goods, attachment to the earth, the thirst for conquest been more ardent than among these nations. Their official motto is precisely the opposite of their practical aspiration. Under a false flag they carry on their smuggling and privateering with a ludicrous security of conscience. Is this hypocritical fraud? No, it is an application of the law of irony. Deceit is so much a matter of course that the delinquent ceases to be aware of it. And all the nations belie themselves as part of the day's work, and nobody feels how ridiculous it is. One must be a Japanese in order to see the preposterous contradictions of Christian civilization. One must be a man of the moon to comprehend the depths of man's absurdity, and the constant illusion in which he lives.

The philosopher, too, falls under the law of irony, for after having mentally ridded himself of all his prejudices, impersonalized himself from top to bottom, he is obliged to come back to his body and his rags again, eat and drink, be hungry, thirsty, cold, and do as all the other mortals do, after having for the moment done as no one does. It is here that the comic poets lie in wait for him; the animal needs take their revenge on this excursion into the empyrean and mockingly cry to him, You are clay, you are nothing, you are a man!

*November 26, 1876.*—Reading: second part of *Mademoiselle de Saint-Maur*.[1] What talent, wit, learning, style! It is the work of a

[1] Victor Cherbuliez, *Le fiancé de Mademoiselle de Saint-Maur,* 1876.

jeweller setting precious stones that sparkle with a thousand fires.
And yet the heart is not satisfied. The Mephistophelian romance
leaves sadness behind it. This over-ripe society, these artificial
women are an echo of the Lower Empire. This refined world is
singularly close to corruption. Not a single character that has not
wit and to spare, nor one who has not transmuted his conscience
into wit. These elegances are only the mask of immorality. These
stories of the heart where there is no heart left make an impression
that is strange and painful.

Not being able to move us, Victor has turned to casting spells.
His women are nixies, female demons, who entice man to his ruin.
Their enchantments are baleful. In short, this literature is unhealthy. The reader, even though dazzled, feels that everything is
false around him, but he drinks the potion of Circe. He scents the
fraud, the magic, and yields nevertheless, but he retains a feeling of
uneasiness and shame. Thus the pleasure which this reading gives is
like a guilty pleasure. The imagination and the senses have stunned
the soul. An evil success; for it is like Imperia's. Victor is a magician, but he misuses his wand and tried too exclusively to please the
roués.

*December 4, 1876.*—Thinking and musing a good deal about Victor Cherbuliez, who fills the *Revue des Deux Mondes,* not only as a
novelist, but as a publicist and art-critic. He is a consummate
writer, the best we have had since Rousseau. The novel is perhaps
the most debatable part of his work, for there he lacks naivety,
feeling and illusion. But what learning, style, finesse and wit, how
many ideas everywhere and what mastery of the idiomatic! He
astounds me, and I marvel at him. What I like least in him is his
shrewd obsequiousness in regard to French chauvinism. This is
Cherbuliez's only prejudice, and it is a useful prejudice. I prefer a
generous recklessness, a disinterested boldness. He is a superior
man, but he is not a great soul; he lacks warmth of heart and depth
of conscience. Not goodness but thought is his category. His mind
is extensive, subtle, cunning, full of resources; he is a refined Alex-

andrian, extraordinarily cultivated in every sense, but with no devotion to anything and replacing with the irony that leaves one free the *pectus* that makes one earnest. As Pascal would say, he has not risen from the order of thought to the order of charity.—Let us not be ungrateful; a Lucian is not the equal of a St. Augustine, but he is Lucian. Those who liberate men's minds render a service as well as those who persuade men's souls. The liberators have a part to play after the leaders; the negative minds and the critics have their function side by side with the men of conviction, the inspired and the affirmative. The positive thing in Cherbuliez is not the good, the moral or religious life, but it is the beautiful. His seriousness lies in the aesthetic realm; what he respects is language. He is therefore following his vocation, for he is a writer, an exquisite, supersubtle, exemplary writer. He does not inspire love, but one must pay him the tribute he deserves.

*January 5, 1877.*—One stroke of bad luck after another. I had to catch cold yesterday, and I have slightly dislocated a knee by some twisted position in my sleep. So I am quite wretched this morning, half suffocated with mucus and glair, crippled for walking, with my right temple aching and my brain taut (the thing I fear the most, for it is with meditation that I defend myself against the other troubles). Active deterioration of my forces, invisible wasting away of the higher organs, cerebral decay: what a merciless ordeal, though unsuspected by anyone! Others pity you when your hair turns white, when you lose your teeth and your face grows wrinkled, when you grow old outwardly. What is all that? Nothing, when one feels that one's faculties are intact. This boon has been granted to so many studious men that I had rather hoped for it. Alas, is this sacrifice also asked of me? Sacrifice is almost easy when one believes it is imposed, asked, rather, by a paternal God and a particular Providence. But I cannot have this religious joy. This mutilation of myself diminishes me without profiting anybody. If I were to go blind, who would gain by it? Only one motive remains to me, manly resignation to the inevitable, and an example for others; the pure Stoic morality.

Is this moral education of the individual soul going to be lost? When our planet has completed the spiral of its destinies, to whom and to what, in heaven's name, will all this have been of any use? It will have added a note to the symphony of creation. We become conscious of totality and the immutable, and then we disappear, we, the individual atoms, the perceptive monads. Is not this enough? No, it is not enough, for if all is lost again there is no progress, no increase, no profit, there is nothing but a play of chemical forces, an equivalence of all the combinations. Brahma engulfs us after having created us. If we are a laboratory of the mind, at least may the mind grow greater through us. If we realize the supreme will, may God have the joy of it. If a trustful humility of the soul rejoices him more than greatness of thought, let us enter into his plan and his intentions. That is to live for the glory of God, to use theological language. Religion consists in the filial acceptance of the divine will, whatever it may be, provided one sees it distinctly. Well, is there any doubt that decay, sickness and death are all in the programme of our existence? Is not what is inevitable fate? And is not fate the nameless designation of that which or whom the religions call God? To descend without murmuring the river of one's destinies, to undergo wtihout rebelliousness the initiation of successive spoliations, diminutions that have no limit but zero, this is the thing that must be. Involution is as natural as evolution. One returns gradually into the darkness, as one has emerged gradually from its womb. Our equipment of faculties and organs, the splendid apparatus of life is replaced piece by piece in the box. One begins with instinct, one must learn how to end through perception, one must see oneself waste away and expire. The musical theme, once exhausted, must come to rest and take refuge in silence.

*January 19, 1877 (10 a. m.).*—Magnificent weather, blue and silver. Discussion with my students (on capital punishment). Walk afterwards. The trees on the Bastions and the Treille, covered with

hoar-frost, were bathed in a joyous light. The elastic, healthy air
made one feel like dancing. This is winter in its aesthetic and beneficent form. I felt as if I were encountering the manly beauties of
justice after the weaknesses of sentimentality. A touch of severity
has its charm. The clear-cut style is restful after the softness of the
dreamy and vague. Good education and normal society cannot do
without an element of fear. It is good to be nipped a little by the
cold, kept in respect by censure, spurred by frankness. Beware of
softness! All these thoughts occurred to me in the train of those
sickening arguments against capital punishment, pleas in which
sophistry and sentimentality join forces to enervate the feeling for
the true and the just. Good God, what a mess these reasonings make
of things, half-baked analyses, worthless axioms, quarter-truths
drowned in three quarters of error! One-eyed, halting, hunch-backed,
bandy-legged theories, taking themselves for Antinouses! And these
are the fooleries that become popular. Their simplicity agrees with
the crowd, which does not reflect and never sees more than one side
of subjects that have many sides. The art of capturing public opinion is the opposite of the search for the true, it is the art of ma-
nipulating false appearances. Sentimentality and imagination help
every fraud. The campaign against capital punishment (since Victor
Hugo) amply proves this.

*January 21, 1877 (11 a. m.).*—Blue sky, bright sun. Is it that I
prefer aristocracy, monarchy, despotism? Not by any means. Would
I destroy democracy if it depended on me? Not in the least. Systems of government in themselves are neither good nor bad, and
the democratic system has the virtue, that, theoretically, it stands
for man. It is human stupidity that irritates me. But in order that
the stupid may leave me in peace, I grant them the right to exist
and to throw out their chests and strut as they wish. My ill-humour
is only a matter of self-preservation. If people do not wish to profit
by my gifts and have no use for them, that is their affair. I ask only
for what I give them, freedom.

In point of fact, I am always becoming more *unbrauchbar;* for I cannot howl with the wolves, and even my good nature makes me less and less sociable. How many people are there with whom I feel in harmony, in spiritual consonance, with whom any sort of exchange is easy, pleasant, sure and does me good? How many men? Are there ten, seven, three, two? I do not dare to count. We agree on one point, we differ on four.—Better to count those whom one esteems, without agreeing with them; then there would be more of them. So I do not admit my incompatibilities. Moreover, by shunning clubs, coteries, official societies, I give them no occasion to arise.

I need harmony, agreement, understanding, abandon; and it is in order to remain kindly and gentle that I keep or increase my distance. I prefer not to see the chasms that I cannot fill. I prefer not to know people rather than to fight and quarrel with them. Polemics seem to me sterile and vain.

*Et pour avoir la paix, je garde le silence.*

If, by chance, I feel bitter, four, five, ten or twenty penfuls of ink and my journal are enough to clear it up. It all flows off in soliloquy, and this harms nobody and gives me back my inner balance.

*February 3, 1877.*—I set out with a fleet, as Schiller says, and I have come back to port with only one plank. What slaughter of hopes, what carnage of illusions! Everything was open and possible to me; now I shrink into my corner, disputing my health with nature and my peace of mind with men. I have led the life of a dreamer, and I shall have left no trace of my mind. I shall have lived; this was a good deal at the time of the Terror, but it is not very remarkable now. My career will have been all but nothing, something less than modest, without display or adventures, without effect, without a visible sign.

*February 6, 1877.*—Evening at the Passerine, discussing the anarchy of ideas, the general lack of culture, what keeps the world on its feet, the assured advance of science in the midst of the universal superstitions and passions, etc.

One of the rarest of things is intellectual exactness, order, method, criticism, proportion, the mind that sees distinctions. The common state of mind is confusion, disorder, incoherence, presumption; the common state of hearts is the passionate state, the state that cannot be equitable, impartial, accessible, open. The will always outstrips the intelligence, the desires outstrip the will, and chance gives birth to desires, so that people only express fortuitous opinions, which are not worth the trouble of being taken seriously, and which have no reasons to give but this puerile argument, I am because I am. The art of achieving the true is very little practised, it is not even known, because there is no personal humility or even love of the true. We desire, as a matter of course, the kind of knowledge that strengthens our hand or tongue and serves our vanity or our desire for power; but the criticism of ourselves, of our prejudices and inclinations, is antipathetic to us.

Man, a covetous and headstrong creature, projects himself outward, using his thought to satisfy his inclinations; but he does not serve truth, he is repelled by personal discipline, he detests disinterested contemplation and action with regard to himself. Wisdom irritates him, because it throws him into confusion and because he does not wish to see himself as he really is.

Most men are only tangled skeins, incomplete keyboards, torpid or violent fragments of chaos, absurd specimens of the true species, shocking caricatures of the ideal. And what makes their situation almost irremediable is that they revel in it. One cannot cure an invalid who believes he is in perfect health.

*February 7, 1877.*—Everything should be treated after its own nature, and I find more and more that objectivity and impersonality are the wish and the gift of my being. The readiness to place oneself at the point of view of every subject, to divine the proper conditions of any science, any art, work or existence whatever, and thus to discuss law like a jurisconsult, theology like a theologian, a practical question like a practical man, pedagogy like a pedagogue, this flexibility is rare. Everyone is imprisoned; everyone has his tic, his limitation, his mental deformity; his vision is good in the things of his own province, but his competence is narrow. Omnicompetence could only belong to the perfectly just mind, harmoniously cultivated in every way. To confuse nothing, to do violence to nothing, to slight nothing, to allow things their proper place and significance; to discern their value, their measure, their originality, their rank; to class them, to weigh them, this is the task of the critic and the philosophical critic. To be able to make them over is the property of the talent that has penetrated to their essence and identified itself with the cause of which these things are the effects. To understand and to reproduce are functions that reciprocally control each other. The two activities are the two proofs of the power of objectification which the mind possesses. I suppose it is my philosophic culture that has imbued me with this need and habit of tending to the centre of the real by the uniting of contrasts, of exhausting all the ways of being, all the combinations, all the forms of thought that are relative to each particular thing, in a word, this taste for spherical totality which is characteristic of me.

Anything that is partial, in either sense, shocks me as much as that which is false, out of its proper place or disproportioned. That which presupposes something else, anything that might be something else, has no authority over my mind. The feeling of the absolute, the perfect, the ideal, the complete follows me everywhere, even when I am unaware of it. Thus what people call considerable, important, capital, seems to me on a level with the trifling; and conversely, for me, there is no such thing as a trifle. The earth is only a grain of sand, and a grain of sand is a little world: everything depends on the point of view.

I am thus emancipated from the superstition of bigness, greatness, etc., enfranchised from space and time, liberated from history; I am not confined in any of the national, local, professional compartments. This is the privilege of impersonality.

This inner freedom is a secret delight, undreamed of by those captives who boast of their chains, reptiles of a sort that are proud because they have not wings. They do not even know what a mind is, or what mind is. They postpone this knowledge to what they call heaven, the other life, eternity. And yet it is not forbidden to thought, provided one is disinterested. I realize, however, that many other indispensable conditions are wanting to most men, that the animal needs, the passions, ignorance, care, grief, illness exile men from the higher world.

Regard yourself as a privileged being. Be humble, thankful, generous. Seek to spread abroad what you have received, and, in your way, make known the method of freedom.

*February 11, 1877 (11 p. m.).*—Several games of chess and draughts.

I find a double interest in games of calculation, first the geometrical exercise and then the psychological experimentation. To cultivate one's own faculty of calculation, to study the character and mental operations of one's partners, is highly pleasurable and even profitable. Indeed, there is something to be said for playing with the weakest opponents, giving them the greatest possible advantage; one's hand forgets its cunning a little in such contests but one develops tact, for one has to divine the kind of error the adversary is going to make and the extent of the imprudences which one can risk with impunity with a given person. This means a constant and delicate calculation of probabilities, which is more fruitful and requires more skill than the simple calculation of correct playing. The first is vitally useful, the second is only a mathematical problem. In ordinary play, all the data are on the chessboard; in unequal play, the great unknown lies elsewhere, it is in the mind of the opponent; one must divine his unconscious method, his probable illusion, the degree of his penetration, the nature of the snares that will catch him; one must dominate him by clairvoyance, conjecture even his caprices, foresee what he desires to do, his anxieties, his impulses, his feints; in short, envelop him and comprehend him. I remember that at nineteen I felt in the palm of my gloved hand the whole organization of the girl with whom I was waltzing, a sort of intimation by magnetism, intuition through contact. It is something analogous to this that I feel in the unequal game of which I am speaking; here, too, there is an intellectual palpation, here, too, a mental measuring, psychological intuition, human study, the approximation of an individuality, the deciphering of a hieroglyphic, the penetration of the invisible. One's perspicacity is sharpened and refined, quickened and increased by this subtle analysis.

Psychological divination is indeed one of my gifts, perhaps the most evident of all. People reproduce themselves, just as they are, in my soul, and, in order to know them, I have only to wind them on the reel within myself. Through sympathy, they affect, oppress and permeate me; they astonish and they disturb me; then I recover myself, through reflection and analysis, and when they are understood I am free, restored to indifference and elasticity. The medium of this divination is a double one: the impressionability of an electroscope and the habit of interpreting shades of distinction. Its preliminary condition is inner equilibrium, together with a general good will that is neither impulsive nor exclusive, *sine ira et studio,* in one word, disinterestedness.

*April 5, 1877.*—Thinking over the graciousness of our evening yesterday, in which the joys of friendship, the charms of mutual understanding, the delights of aesthetic admiration, and the pleasure of comfort were so well interwoven and united. There was not a wrinkle in the rose-leaf. Why?—Because "whatsoever things are true; whatsoever things are honourable, whatsoever things are just, whatsoever things are pure, whatsoever things are lovely, whatsoever things are of good report" were all brought together, in unison. "The incorruptibility of the mild and peaceful mind", the innocent laugh, fidelity to duty, fine taste, a hospitable imagination create an atmosphere that is attractive, restful, salutary. *In petto* I blessed

my azure isle, and I felt that this vacation retreat of the Trifolium [1]
was a holiday for others as well as for myself.

*Rendre heureux est encor le plus sûr des bonheurs.*

Where one brings joy, one is almost certain to find it,

*Le mérite est petit, la récompense est grande.*

To illumine for a moment a soul like that of Seriosa seems to
me an act of piety, a good work, a virtuous deed. To do good to a
daughter of heaven, who bears sympathetically the burdens of so
many afflicted hearts and so many suffering lives, is a blessing and
a privilege, and I feel its value. There is a sort of religious felicity
in fortifying the strength and courage of noble characters. One is
surprised to find that one possesses this power, of which one is not
worthy, but one wishes at least to exercise it with composure.

I feel intensely that man, in everything he does or is able to do
that is beautiful, great, good, is only the organ and vehicle of something or someone higher than himself. This feeling is religion. Religion is disappropriation. The religious man observes with a thrill of
sacred joy these phenomena of which he is the intermediary, without being the origin of them, the theatre without being the author,
or rather the poet. He lends them his voice, his hand, his will, his co-
operation, but with a respectful anxiety to efface himself in order to
impair as little as possible the higher work of the genius that is
momentarily making use of him. He *impersonalizes* himself, he
obliterates himself in his feeling of wonder. His self must disappear
when the Holy Spirit is speaking, when it is God who is acting, when
that which is taking place is an incomprehensible marvel. Thus the
prophet hears the call, thus the young mother feels her fruit stirring, thus the preacher sees the tears on the faces of his congrega-

[1] This "Trifolium" designates Miss Fanny and Miss Pauline Mercier
and their mother.

tion. As long as we feel our self, we are thwarted, limited, egoistic, imprisoned; when we are in accord with the universal order, when we vibrate in unison with God, our self disappears. Thus in a choir that is perfectly symphonic we must be out of tune ourselves if we are to hear ourselves sing. The religious state is one of tranquil ecstasy, composed enthusiasm, moved contemplation, calm adoration.—But how rare this state is for the poor creature who is harassed by necessity, by the world's wickedness, by sin, sickness, duty! It is the state of inward happiness; but the substance of existence, the general tissue of our days, is struggle, action, effort, dissonance. Battles forever renewed, truces brief and always threatened, this is the picture of the human condition.

Let us hail then, as an echo from heaven, as the foretaste of a preferable state of things, these swift moments of perfect accord, these pauses between two storms. Peace is not in itself an illusion or an impossibility; but, on this earth, it is an unstable equilibrium, in other words an accident.—"Blessed are the peace-makers: for they shall be called the children of God."

*April 26, 1877.*—Ran through Victor Hugo's *Paris* (1867). In the last ten years, the prophet has been belied again and again, but the confidence of the prophet in his fantasies has not dwindled for that. Pooh! Humility and good sense are only for Lilliputians. Gulliver never recants and never retracts. Victor Hugo never sees anything that gets in his way, he haughtily ignores everything that he has not foreseen. He does not know that pride is a limitation of the mind and that limitless pride is smallness of soul. If he knew his place, his own place among other men and the place of France among other nations, he would see more justly and would not fall into his senseless exaggerations and his extravagant oracles. But clarity of perception, proportion, accuracy will never be among his notes. He is devoted to the titanic, the inordinate and the illusory. His gold is always mixed with lead, his intuitions with puerilities, his reason with folly. He cannot be simple, natural, limpid, luminous; he can only throw light, like a conflagration, by blinding us at the same time.

In a word, he astonishes but he irritates, he stirs us but he pains us. He is always half or two-thirds wrong, and this is the secret of the uneasiness which he is perpetually causing us. The great poet cannot disburden himself of the charlatan within him. He is always raising his voice, posing, throwing out his chest; he does not know the joy of being true, of being in conformity with the true. A few good pricks of Voltairian irony would have deflated this balloonlike genius and would have made him stronger by bringing him to his senses . . . It is almost a public misfortune that the most powerful poet of the nation should not have understood his role better, and that in the opposite fashion to that of the Hebrew prophets, who chastised the people out of love, he, in his pride, systematically burns incense to them. France is the world, Paris is France, Hugo is Paris. I am Alpha and Omega, Sinai and Tabor. Peoples, down on your noses!

*May 2, 1877.*—News of the great world. England declares herself neutral in the Russo-Turkish war, but the first thing she has done has been to lay hands on Egypt, holding the customs, the navy, the railroads, the finances, the canal as a preliminary to encamping her army of occupation, twenty-five thousand Sepoys awaiting at Bombay the order to embark.—England has always identified what is useful to her with her right and has always found that her interest was a sufficient and legitimate reason. The effrontery of egoism becomes, with her, candour. The world must bow before whatever is convenient to Albion. *Primo mihi* is the eternal maxim of the insular.

> *Sa justice,*
> *C'est son utilité, son besoin, son caprice.*

I am always astounded by the cynicism of this policy, the basis of which is quite simply an appeal to force, in other words brutality, which means barbarity. And to be the strongest, amply to satisfy her appetites and leave to others what remains, this is the English theory and practice. The Christian virtues are an individual embroidery that serves to dissimulate the national tendency. This tendency is anti-Christian, even anti-human; it is the Darwinian and animal tendency, the crushing of the weak by the strong, the survival of the most vigorous. England is an appetite. Regarded from the outside, this nation is, in respect to others, what the predatory and carnivorous animals are; it thinks of nothing but its own affairs and its own advantage. Industry, commerce, conquest, any means are good that will maintain it as the richest, the strongest, the most independent, the most robust among its congeners. There are individuals in it who are generous and noble, disinterested, in a word; but the national ideal is gross, the role of the nation with respect to other peoples is revolting. Covetous pride and boundless selfishness inspire neither attraction nor respect. England's reverses would never grieve anyone, for her profit is never the profit of humankind. Her triumph is even a bad example from the historical point of view. One does not like to see anything triumph but justice, and the least of England's cares is to be just to anything that is not English. The only sacrifice that she has made to a disinterested cause is the abolition of the slave-trade, and even this abolition may have been for her a means of augmenting her naval strength and justifying the right of search.—The service she renders unintentionally to civilized humanity is in exploiting the virgin countries, peopling the uninhabited lands, stimulating production everywhere by competition and by a working example of political liberty. But an Englishman is man diminished in all the parts that make him splendid, in his human nature, he is man *trained* like a racehorse or an athlete, in view of an aim determined in advance. He always gives an impression of the *voulu*, the partial, the strained, and what characterizes him is the exaltation of a primitive force. Scratch his skin, and you will find the Scandinavian, the untamed berserker. But he guards himself in this way against the musical effemination of Italy, against the indolence of the Orient, against the gallant and libertine preoccupation of France, etc. If he outrages the Christian and delicate feeling, at least he offers an example of healthy and energetic life;

he is a barbarian polished by culture, who only deludes himself about his real god, which is Thor and not the Crucified.

Which nation, in point of fact, is the best? There is not one of them in which the evil does not counterbalance the good. Each is a caricature of man. A proof that none of them is worthy of suppressing the others and that all have something to receive from all. I am struck, in turn, by the qualities and the defects of each, and perhaps this is fortunate for the critic. I feel no preference myself for the faults of the North or the South, the Occident or the Orient, and I should be embarrassed if I had to say what my own predilections are. But, in fact, they are quite indifferent to me, for the question is one not of approving or blaming, but of understanding. My point of view is philosophical, that is, impartial and impersonal. The only type that pleases me is perfection, man, simply man, the ideal man. As for the national man, I tolerate him and study him. I do not admire him. I can admire only the fine examples of the species, the great men, the geniuses, the sublime characters, the noble souls, and these examples are to be found in all the ethnographical compartments. The "fatherland of my choice" (to speak with Mme. de Staël) is that of the choice individuals. I have no special weakness for the French, the Germans, the Swiss, the English, the Poles, the Italians, any more than for the Brazilians or the Chinese. The patriotic, chauvinistic, family, professional illusions do not exist for me. I am inclined to feel, on the contrary, all the more keenly, the deficiencies, the uglinesses and imperfections of the group to which I belong. My critical impartiality begins by disencumbering me personally of these superstitious prejudices and these deceptive presumptions. I am not even of my own sex. Far from dictating my manner of seeing, my interest causes me to lean in the opposite direction. My inclination is to see things as they are, abstracting my own individuality, correcting all that springs from desire and will. Imprisonment in a particular self is repugnant to me. Objectivity is a need with me. I am antipathetic therefore not to this or that, but to error, the *parti pris*, prejudices, stupidity, exclusiveness, exaggeration. I love only justice and probity. Impressions, impulses, petulant sallies of indignation, quarrelsome outbursts are only superficial with me; the fundamental tendency of my nature is impartiality and detachment. Inner freedom and the aspiration to dwell in the true, this is my taste and my pleasure.

*May 22, 1877.*—Nobody doubts me without finding an accomplice in myself. In fact, I see myself in the comic aspect more readily and more easily than in the serious. The importance that I have attached to my Essay [1] is a conventional attitude, to arouse my own interest and give some sort of pleasure to my god-daughter. Deep down, at the back of my mind, all this is indifferent to me; it seems to me Lilliputian. When I compare myself with others, I feel a kind of relative satisfaction, but I consider these trifles useless in themselves, and this success or failure insignificant. One has to play at something, and, when one plays, one has to play correctly, as a matter of honour. I like to win my bets, but this desire is purely Platonic.

To take anything seriously is to place oneself in dependence on the public, and I could not endure to tremble before this master or stand in need of its suffrages to live. I throw it whatever amuses myself, as one tosses a straw into a brook. But whether the straw sinks or floats, whether it strikes a snag or reaches the bank is only a diversion or a spectacle for me. My imagination alone is engaged, not my heart.

I do not believe in the public, I do not believe in my work, I have no ambition, properly speaking; and I blow soap-bubbles just for the sake of doing something.

*May 30, 1877 (noon).*—Lecture on the Hebrews and the Jewish genius.—Unable to be sympathetic, I try to be just to the subject. This accidental, priviliged, chosen people was repellent in all its in-

---

[1] Amiel here designates the *Appendix* which, with the sub-title, *Concerning a few new expedients for translation into verse and perhaps for our poetry*, concludes the collection of *Etrangères, Poems Translated from Various Literatures* (Paris, Sandoz et Fischbacher, 1876).

stincts, lascivious, cruel, rapacious, treacherous, wanting in honour and pride. But Jesus was a Jew, and this redeems everything.— The philosophers who have loved the human race have had little taste for the Jews (Voltaire, Hegel, Renan). They are shocked at the nimbus of prestige with which our education invests this little people, immeasurably overrated and so unlovable, neither creative, inventive, generous nor spiritual.

The Judaic manner of understanding religion is enough to disgust one with religion itself. To imagine that God is a Jew, what a sorry joke! Every nation has had a similiar notion, but the other peoples have ended in conciliation and tolerance, in an Olympus and a Pantheon. The right of others has counted for something with them. The Jews, obstinate and egoistical, have said, Let humanity perish sooner than my belief! Faith with them has always come before reason and triumphed over justice. Fanatical obstinacy is second nature with them. But the Jewish faith is the greatest known example of faith, for it has continued to hope for the Messiah ever since the return from Babylon, that is, for twenty-four centuries of disappointment.—Faith, so conceived, is a petrifaction, it is a mummification, or at least a long tetanic spasm of the soul, which cannot react any more. It is a psychological curiosity, which deserves attention, but scarcely admiration, for admiration should be reserved for sublime greatness, not for maniacal obstinacy.—For all this, Judaism has ended by impressing its mould on a part of humanity, for the religious spirit dominant in the Christian Church is still faith in the accidental, the exceptional, in the local, supernatural, arbitrary intervention of God, in election and privilege, miracles and grace. This is the childish conception, in short. The Semite cannot rise above this point of view. His God is a partial and vigilant pedagogue, who proceeds only by particular cases and not by universal rules. The Semite has no conception either of natural law or of moral law, he is anti-philosophical by instinct; there is no law, there are only personal commandments, issuing from God's initiative. The Semite is purely authoritarian; the true has for him no direct evidence; the only question for him is obedience or acceptance with regard to this or that man who has been sent by God. Once the credentials have been verified, one must believe, one must submit, cost what it may. The inner persuasion of the reason that understands or of the conscience that approves is merely a superfluity. This is the religion of children, of spiritual slaves. In it, man is always credulous, always in tutelage, always in the power of his leader, whether this leader is the priest of today or the prophet of former times. Religion, so conceived, confiscates in principle the liberty of man; it tends to maintain him in perpetuity in the state of nonage.

*June 3, 1877.*—Intimacy with women, the Platonic and sacred intimacy which has so often been granted me, has always been, in spite of everything, a source of suffering for one of the two parties, or more exactly for both. But what is one to do? That which brings death was at first that which brought life. The gall comes out of the honey. Nature is never more than half-way generous, and only in appearance. We find our torment in our joy, our punishment in our privilege. To marry, I should have had to find my match, my complement, the woman who would have satisfied my whole being. And I have never met one with whom the idea of passing the whole of life and all eternity did not frighten me a little. I have always seen the dark side, the limitation, the insufficiency, the obstacle, the ominous speck, and I have never been capable of the illusion that is necessary for faith. This critical perception does not in any way prevent friendship, the affection that pardons, encourages, uplifts, supports, amelioriates, but it dispels the magic, it prevents the dazzled admiration that makes one see a woman as womankind, as the desired, the unique, the sufficient, in a word, the wife.

*June 4, 1877.*—Grand concert at the Salle de la Réformation: *Roméo et Juliette,* by Hector Berlioz. The work is called a dramatic symphony for orchestra with choruses. The execution was very good, and, as the work has not undergone any philological transplanting, it can be judged directly and as it is. Berlioz has a mania for originality and the science of orchestration. What has he produced? His work is interesting, piquant, finished, curious, but as a whole it leaves one cold.—If I reason out my impression, I can explain it to myself. To subordinate man to things, to annex the voices as a supplement to the orchestra is a false idea. To convert a dramatic theme into a simple narration is wantonly to detract from it. This means that the *genre* is false. A *Roméo et Juliette* with Juliet and Romeo left out is a queer business. To condemn souls that have speech to express themselves only by gestures, to reproduce a painting merely in pencil, to put the inferior, the obscure, the vague in place of the superior and the clear is to fly in the face of good sense. One violates the natural hierarchy of things, and one does not violate this with impunity. The musician invents a series of symphonic pictures, without any inner connection, a perfect rosary of riddles, requiring a text in prose to give the key and constitute the sequence. This is a decorative art, an art of veneering that deludes itself. The usurpation of instrumental music on vocal music ends in the absurd. The one intelligible voice that appears in the work is that of Friar Laurence; since his admonition could not be dissolved in chords, it is sung distinctly. But the moral of the drama is not the drama, and the drama has been juggled away in recitative.

What twistings and turnings, poor composer, to mask an actual impotence, that of rendering passion in its natural language! The pursuit of the aura of genius is only an artifice which is meant to deceive the public. Unable to achieve the beautiful, one racks one's brains to produce the new. False orginality, false grandeur, false genius. Thus the music-mongers flood us with their *Caprices,* formless dabs of pulp that are expected to delude us in regard to their vacuity of substance and ideas. Thus fashion throws dust in our eyes to hide its fundamental sterility. This bedaubed, twisted, ambitious, flashy art is antipathetic to me. The skill that simulates genius is only a variant of charlatanism.

As a critic, Berlioz sparkles with wit. He is a scholarly musician, ingenious and inventive, but he lacks the elementary virtues of his profession, he believes he can do the greater when he cannot do the less. He is an eccentric without the generative faculty. Thirty years ago, in Berlin, I had the same impression after hearing the *Enfance du Christ,* executed under his own direction. I do not find in him a healthy and fertile art or solid and true beauty.

Liszt must be of his line.

*June 9, 1877.*—I am not happy, that goes without saying. I am not resigned. I have not found peace. I alternate between indolence and anxiety. The centre of my calm is despair. That which wounds me I have not accepted; what would break my heart I do not wish to see. I hide from others, and even try to ignore the fox that is tearing at my vitals. I assume the attitude of Stoicism, but I have neither the pride nor the vigour for it. An incurable sadness lies at the bottom of my apparent serenity. I am meek before destruction, but there is death in my soul because I feel that this life has miscarried and I expect no compensation for it. Nothing, nothing, nothing! *Nada.*

*June 11, 1877.*—To resign oneself is not an act of cowardice, and, if one carries it off with a certain air of liveliness, it is not even a humiliation. Infirmities, needs, constraints are our lot; it is better to yield to them cheerfully than to kick against the pricks as if they were offences against our majesty. To forget the irreparable, to accept the irremediable, to go to meet the inevitable is much wiser than to waste one's strength or be embittered in a vain struggle.

*July 2, 1877.*—What a rare thing health is among men of letters! Yet what can be done without it? To be literary is almost synonymous with being unwell, valetudinarian, damaged, ailing, sickly. Worse luck for literature! The delicate, the half-well, the indisposed, the infirm, the cacochymic are weak, and the weak no more than the enervated represent the normal man, who is the healthy man, or nature, which is invulnerable. Moral development can go with an ill-conditioned state of body or mind, which is a long trial of the soul; but artistic development demands health, which is a beauty, a strength, a harmony, a joy. Education through suffering makes good men, it awakens poetry, but healthy works have to be fathered by health. The melancholy, the hypochondriac, the ascetic, the afflicted, the tried engender only productions that lack vitality. There is something good in suffering if it comes adventitiously, but it is baleful when it forms the very foundation of life. One must have felt it and passed through it in order to be human, but one must be outside it in order to produce. Things are in a bad way when the doctor is an invalid; one must be in sound health to judge and attack illness properly. The artist, the writer must be in possession of all their power, all their verve and exuberance, in order to do good work; and that is the opposite of the depression, the dejection, the weakness, the debility that result from too much sadness.

*July 3, 1877.*—The soul proceeds only by zigzags and oscillations. The inner life is only the resultant of infinite contradictions. Feeling is as unstable as the waves and the clouds. The impersonal contemplator who wishes to do or undo nothing, but only to perceive and understand, is condemned to see repetitions endlessly and ceaselessly, for the soul passes through all the states, all the modes and vibrations, and is always beginning anew its restless metamorphoses, always returning to its deficiencies, its inveterate tics, as to its natural abode.

Your own defect is a whirling revery, seeking nothing and leading to nothing. You are content to take note of whatever stirs within you, you collect yourself with no other end than self-collectedness, forgetting the past and the future, shunning action, dreading everything that might involve, engage or shackle you; in short, you make an opium of meditation, a means of forgetting, a method of escaping obligation, an unconscious stratagem for eluding the censures of conscience. This revery, pen in hand, seems to be a seeking for yourself, while it is actually a flight from yourself. You pretend to think that it strengthens you, while all the time it softens you. It is an Epicureanism that plays at asceticism, a vague day-dreaming that simulates thought. It is an abuse of your true being, it cheats your hunger, but it helps you to cross the great desert of life. He who has no home, no child, no wife, no strong interest, no illusion of glory, no career or ambition, he whom nothing encourages, summons or sustains, who feels all but useless to his country, to science, to the Church, to humanity; how could he not wish to forget himself? He can only keep a remnant of good humour by shutting his eyes to what he lacks or amusing himself with the description of his woes.

*July 4, 1877.*—But this "whirling revery" has a more serious disadvantage than those I noted yesterday. It has destroyed my power of consecutive thought, of rational construction and philosophical speculation. I have ceased to be able to dominate the whole of a subject; to limit, one by another, all the particular ideas it includes, to build up a course of lectures or a book, even an article or a single lecture. A vagrant, gypsy habit of mind has taken the place of methodical exploitation; the scattered plaints of the Æolian harp have almost destroyed my capacity to compose a symphony. In a word, this journal has injured me artistically and scientifically. It is only a kind of busy idleness, a phantom of intellectual activity. Without being itself a work, it stands in the way of other works, of which it appears to take the place . . . But what am I to do? Can we make of ourselves something we are not? I have never treated myself as the means or the instrument of something else. I have never seen in myself a machine for earning money, making laws, writing books. To become conscious of human nature has been my oldest and most active taste. Why curse and vilify it now? This taste is rare and certainly not illegitimate.

*July 15, 1877.*—A curious impression. Everything leaves me free, unoccupied, disengaged. I can follow any direction I choose, and I feel no impulse that compels me. I exist in the neutral state of equilibrium and indifference, like a sphere suspended at the end of a thread or floating in motionless air. Shall I go or stay, travel north or south, work or amuse myself? All courses seem to be open to me . . . But I forget that I have to move, that I must find some treatment for my throat, and that I have plenty of other definite obligations, beyond the convenient and the useful, to keep in sight. The absolutely indeterminate state is thus only a momentary appearance, depending on my forgetful unconcern, and also on the fact that nothing arouses or disturbs me in my cell, that I have no calls to make, no letters to write, no lectures to give, that I am expecting nothing and no one, and that I can dream away at will without being called back to order. This pure and complete leisure is so rare in other peoples' lives that I should testify to its presence and sweetness. It represents the minimum of annoyance and encumbrance that one could wish to enjoy, and the maximum of quiet and freedom from care that one can experience and possess. It is delightful to be one's own master, to be at nobody's orders, to taste the full flavour of one's freedom and calm. Surely, this felicity is too brief to be really harmful, however Epicurean it may be.

*(7 p. m.)*—Brilliant sunset, effects of light as in Holland, limpid air, strong shadows, colouring of the leaves very vivid, damp and almost melancholy splendour. The days already seem to be growing shorter. Something warns one that time is short and that summer is on the wing.

Feel also the need of renewing myself, changing the circular routine of my everyday habits, the need of seeing and doing something new. I seem absurd to myself, encrusted, half-buried, unnecessarily so and from pure stupidity. One must demummify oneself, give one's eyes and imagination fresh fields and pastures, find out what other men are doing, make use of one's freedom. When one has wings, it is a sin not to put them to some employment; when one has money one ought to spend it; when one is not a galley-slave, one ought to quit the bench, drop the oar for the alpenstock, drop one's books for nature, leave one's studious cave for "vanity fair". Go and turn over the leaves of the good God's landscapes, foreign things and living humanity. You need to look about you, you need to talk and travel and shake the sloth out of your muscles.

Refresh yourself, divert yourself. Renovation is rejuvenation. Your life demands a moulting and a revolution, a different current of ideas, a freshening of your nerves. All sorts of things need to be changed to put you back into the normal state.

The mind can thus have a sudden pang of hunger for change, and in this mood the customary things, the familiar faces weary it. The mind seems to be surfeited, and, to recover its appetite, it calls for a different diet and a new cuisine.

Even one who dreads the unknown needs it therefore in a certain measure, and the absolute *status quo* is therefore against nature. Immobile conservatism and the monastic life are mistakes. Fixity is wholesome on condition that it is complemented by its opposite. The art of life consists in uniting continuity with innovation, persistence with progress, identity with change. We should imitate time, which transforms our faces, but gradually, in such a way that they are the same and yet become different. A well-regulated existence ought to combine in its tissue one or two constants with three or four variables.—The momentary satiety that you feel proves that you have violated the law of hygiene and that the element of uniformity has had more than its share. Reëstablish the balance; a change of air, change of occupation, atmosphere, horizon. You will come back with much more pleasure to your ordinary interests, to your usual surroundings, your habitual regimen.

A strange thing. Your life is one of the most monotonous that anyone could imagine; all the months, all the weeks, all the days of the week are alike. Mechanical habit governs it. And so it seems as if eternal repetition and daily uniformity are just the things that would not frighten you, and yet the one anxiety which the idea of marriage gives you is the fear of satiety and the possibility of revolt. One who, for months together, does not set foot out of doors trembles at the thought of being condemned, for a few weeks, to prison or to custody. Theoretically, we wish to be free, to be able to renounce our servitude, if it wearies us or displeases us. It is therefore the irreparable that disturbs us; to be a prisoner, even in paradise, would be disagreeable to us; the perpetualness of the chain, were it a chain of gold or a chain of flowers, this is what we fear; to bind ourselves in advance, to alienate our will for all time when we know it is inconstant, intractable, changeable, seems to us a temerity, almost a folly. It is the vow that frightens us, because it affirms what we do not know, because it promises that which does not depend upon us, the indestructibility of love, immutable attachment, invariable affection. We can swear to die for a flag, to remain faithful to honour, to bear our cross, because by wishing to do so we are able to do these things; but we cannot swear to love forever, because we do not love at will, and because our feeling laughs at our commands. Even today, when I am past fifty, I do not know myself well enough to conjecture what I shall be in ten or twenty years, at least in regard to particular cases. I know that I shall always love perfection, the good, the healthy, beauty, justice, harmony, truth, virtue. It seems to me that I could swear to this. But will my present idea about this or that, my present feeling about a given person, remain unchanged? I cannot possibly say.

How do other people meet this question? They deceive themselves in good faith; they dispose of eternity without a thought and leave to the future the burden of clearing their minds in regard to the validity of their promises and the constancy of their nature. Moved, touched, they engage themselves for life; they are sincere; but things take their own course and vows prevent nothing, coldness or regrets, revolts, hatreds, mistakes or moral separations. The vow merely aggravates the guilt. What is the use of ignoring the nature of things? A surreptitious or unreasonable stipulation is a flaw in essence. One can declare on oath that one loves, but not that one will love. To make one promise and swear honesty, kindness, patience, fidelity, protection, support is all well and good; but to make one promise and swear perpetual love is to count one's chickens before they are hatched, it is to assume control of the future. It deceives both parties, it is a snare.

We should only bind ourselves in matters that depend upon us, and only where it is just. As for gratuitous love, forgiveness, generosity, heroism, no one has the right to demand them of us. That rests with us inalienably.

*July 17, 1877.*—Glanced at my La Fontaine yesterday. Observed what he has left out. He does not include the butterfly, the rose, the nightingale. He does not make use of the crane, the quail, the dromedary or the lizard. He has no mementos of chivalry. The history of France for him dates from Louis XIV. His real geography covers only a few square leagues and does not reach to the Rhine or the Loire, the mountains or the sea. He invented none of the subjects of his fables but lazily takes ready-made themes. Etc., etc. But in spite of all this, what an adorable writer, what a painter and observer, what a comedian and satirist, what a story-teller! I never weary of rereading him, though I know half his fables by heart. He is the only one of our authors whose work can take the place of all the rest and furnish a quotation, an *à propos* for every public and private circumstance, an epigraph for all the monthly reviews. In the matter of vocabulary, turns of phrase, tones, idioms, his language is perhaps the richest of the great epoch, for it skilfully combines the archaic and the classic, the Gaulois and the French. Variety, finesse, malice, sensibility, rapidity, concision, suavity, grace, gaiety; at need, nobility, gravity, grandeur. One finds everything in the fabulist. And the felicity of the epithets, the piquant adage, the inspired outline, the unexpected audacity, the stroke that remains in one's mind, one scarcely knows what his deficiencies are, among these multifarious aptitudes.

If one compares his "Woodcutter and Death" with that of Boileau (written later), one can measure the prodigious difference between the artist and the critic who thought he could show him how to do it. La Fontaine makes one see the poor peasant under the monarchy, Boileau only shows one a sweating labourer. The first is a historic witness, the second is only a scholarly rhymster. The one is picturesque, concrete, living, touching; the other is cold, meagre, bare and correct.—Accordingly, through La Fontaine one can reconstruct the whole society of his epoch, and the goodman of Champagne with his animals turns out to be France's only Homer. He gives as many human portraits as La Bruyère, and Molière himself is not more comic.

On what side is he vulnerable? Perhaps in an Epicureanism that is very far from ideal; and it is because of this no doubt that La Fontaine is antipathetic to Lamartine. The religious string is foreign to his lyre; he does not seem to have known Christianity or the sublime tragedies of the soul. Horace is his prophet, and Ninon his Egeria. Good Mother Nature is his goddess, and Montaigne his Gospel. In other words, his horizon is that of the Renaissance; and he has never heard of Bossuet and Fénelon, the Pope and the Gallican church. This pagan isle in the midst of a Catholic society is a very singular thing. The paganism is perfectly naive. As a matter of fact, Rabelais, Molière and Saint-Evremond are much more pagan than Voltaire; it seems as if for the French who are entirely French Christianity is only a conventional veneer, a costume that scarcely touches the skin, and *a fortiori* has no connection with the heart, with the central man, the depths of the nature. This two-fold essence is visible in Chateaubriand; it is common in Italy. It is the effect of the political religions, in which the priest is separate from the layman, the believer from the man and worship from sincerity. The fabrication of artificial consciences is one of the consequences of Romanism, as d'Azeglio has pointed out.—In this case, the artist does well to ignore a religion which is only a domino and to remain in natural religion. Pious humbug is the reverse of poetry, as it is of beauty. There is nothing uglier than a Capuchin, nothing so repulsive as a Tartuffe, nothing so disagreeable as a hypocritical fiction. A frank and honest paganism is much better. I incline to think that traditional pretence, the half-voluntary duplicity of conscience, is the plague of Christendom, one that endures and can endure for hundreds and thousands of years. In it the natural man wears the cockade of the Crucifixion and crucifies only good faith. One affects and professes a religion, but one lives by another principle. The real God is quite different from the official God. High politics are full of fraud, and fraud fills the private conduct of the faithful. The universal worship is that of appearances.—I prefer La Fontaine, even if hypocrisy is "an homage that vice renders to virtue". This eternal fiction has degraded the Occidental. Nine times out of ten, the Christians are rascals if one compares them with the Mohammedans, rascals in their piety, comedians of religion.

*(11 p. m.)*—Reading: Mme. de Souza (*Adèle de Sénange*) . . . In *Adèle de Sénange,* encountered a certain character with a mechanical habit of using synonyms. Have a care, I said to myself, that is a danger of yours, *hic tua res agitur.*—In trying to find the right shade for your thought, you exhaust the whole keyboard of synonyms, and very often your pen proceeds by triads. Watch out! Avoid all mechanical habits, all inflexibilities and mental ruts: they are weaknesses. One must use indifferently stroke 1, 2, 3, 4, or 5, according to the subject and the occasion. To proceed by the single word gives the expression vigour; doubling the word gives clarity, by naming the two extremities of the series; trebling the word gives completeness, by supplying the beginning, the middle and the end of the idea; quadrupling and quintupling the word gives the expression richness, by the enumeration.

Your chief defect being that you feel your way rather vaguely, you have recourse to a redundancy of locutions, successive retouches and approximations. You resort to them at least in this extempore journal. When you compose, 2 tends to become your category. It would be a good thing to exercise yourself in the single word, that is in the stroke that your hand naturally makes, without any correction. To do this, you would have to overcome your hesitation. You see too many ways of saying a thing; a mind with more decision hits upon the right note at once. The single expression is an intrepidity that implies self-confidence and clear perception. Somnambulists and animals do not waver; instinct is all but infallible. To be capable of the single stroke that is exactly right, one must have no doubts, and you are always doubting.

*Quiconque est loup agisse en loup;*
*C'est le plus certain de beaucoup.*

I wonder if, were I to assume some other character than my own, I should gain anything by it. My undulating style arises from my scrupulousness, or at least from the two merits of being exhaustive and sincere. Were it to become succinct, affirmative, resolute, would it not be a borrowed style?—Answer: no subjective and uniform style is any affair of yours. Your nature is supple, assume the *style of the subject*. Only vary the subjects so that you will have to vary the tones, the turns, the cut, the rhythms and the pace of your style.

As the journal is only a dreamy meditation, a soliloquy, not embarrassed by time, it beats all the bushes at random without following any definite scent. Talking to oneself about oneself is an illumination of the mind that comes about gradually. Hence the synonymies, the recurrences, the repetitions, the undulations. He who affirms is brief, he who seeks is long, he who confesses winds his way, and the path of the dreamer is anything but regular.

I feel indeed that there is only one exact expression, but in order to find it I wish to choose among all the expressions that resemble it; and consequently my instinct runs over all the verbal scales to find the nuance that will translate the idea most precisely. Indeed, it is my idea itself that I turn and turn again in every direction, in order to know it better and become conscious of it. I literally think pen in hand, I unravel and unwind myself out of pure curiosity. It is clear that the form of style corresponding to this pastime cannot have the qualities of a thought already in possession of itself and having the simple desire to communicate itself to others, distinctly, with authority, rapidly. A journal observes, dissects, analyzes, contemplates, searches and gropes; an article is intended to excite reflection; a book must demonstrate.

Conclusion. The journal is not a preparation for teaching or for the art of composition. It does not tell one how to speak or write, or how to think connectedly and methodically. It is a psychological relaxation, a recreation, an epicurism, an indolent activity, a kind of mock-labour.—It might be a moral account-book, but this disciplinary point of view ceased to be mine many years ago. I try to understand myself, but I no longer seriously govern or chide myself. I no longer know what asceticism is, the work of daily sanctification, the zealous pursuit of a goal, any goal whatever. I let myself live, feel, study, think, and I look into my soul as if it were a magician's box, without disturbing anything by the brutal and pedantic intervention of my will. Discouragement has produced my detachment, detachment has fallen back upon contemplation. I can still work for the happiness and perfection of others; but as for myself, I seem to revolve on myself, without desire, without progress, without object. I no longer become, I am. My only wish is to be, thinking and loving, and that I may not suffer.—I have been as it were erased from the list of efficient and final causes, subtracted from human society, expunged from the roll of individual existences, which count only through their needs, their efforts, their effects, their action on things and persons, in one word, through their will.

Have I become pure spirit, inaccessible to the tyrannies of nature and humanity, above suffering and pleasure, tears and laughter? Alas, no. Man would be a god if he could be self-sufficient. I never had any thought of being a god, any more than of being consistent, insensible, holy or celebrated. I never set out to be anything at all. I have allowed myself to breathe, grow, live and dream. Odd fish . . . "incomprehensible monster"!

*July 21, 1877 (11 p. m.).*—Superb night. Starry firmament, Jupiter and the moon gossiping opposite my windows. Grand effects of shadow and moonbeams in my Calvinist close: Mantegna, Rembrandt, Gustave Doré would have feasted their eyes upon it. A sonata rose from the black gulf, like a prayer of repentance escaping from the place of punishment. The picturesque melted into poetry, and admiration into emotion.

*July 30, 1877.*—Concerning Renan, A. S.[1] makes a rather acute observation, apropos of the volume, *Les Evangiles*. He brings out the contradiction between the artist's literary taste, which is fine, personal and sure, and the opinions of the critic, which are borrowed, out of date and vacillating. This wavering between the beautiful and the true, between poetry and prose, between art and erudition, is in fact characteristic. Renan has a lively taste for science, but he is still more a writer, and, if necessary, he will sacrifice saying a thing exactly to saying it well. Science is his material rather than his aim; his aim is style. A fine page, to him, has ten times the value of the discovery of a fact or the rectification of a date. And on this point I feel as he does, for a fine page is fine through a sort of truth that is truer than the registering of authentic materials. Rousseau shared this opinion. A chronicler can scratch out Tacitus, but Tacitus survives all the chroniclers. I am quite aware that the aesthetic temptation is the French temptation, and I have often bewailed it. Still, if I desired anything, it would be to be a writer, a great writer. To leave a monument *ære perennius,* an indestructible work that would evoke thought, feeling, dreams through generation after generation, this is the only glory that I would long for, if I had not been weaned even from this longing. Such a book would be my ambition, if ambition were not a vanity, a vanity of vanities.

*(Later.)*—In spite of all the ages that have passed, the mind alone in Germany has worked itself free; the statue has not emerged from its sheath of stone, and of the head itself only the brow is modelled. The German is a barbarian from the cheek-bones to the soles of his feet. Up to the ears he is a faun and nothing else.—One has only to look at the features of the great Germans of today, Bismarck, Moltke, Emperor William, to see of what clay they are made, and how crudely modelled, a race that is strong but crass, rude though calculating. Aesthetically, they are distressing, and the women are as imperfect as the men in appearance, bearing, form, in

[1] Article by Auguste Sabatier, in the *Journal de Genève,* July 29, 1877, on Ernest Renan, *Les Evangiles et la second génération chrétienne.*

all that meets the eye. Both sexes are equally lacking in grace, distinction, nobility, dignity, beauty. German vulgarity is vulgar ten times over, German corruption and blackguardry are ten times uglier than elsewhere. The Germans are condemned to being honest, solid, serious under pain of being nothing else, in this resembling women, who lose everything when they lose their modesty.

In my younger years, the uglier aspects of Germany escaped me. I mantled them with my sympathy and submerged them in my good will. I cannot say as much nowadays. I like many Germans and many things in Germany; but I have no bandages over my eyes, and their defects are as disagreeable to me as to anyone.

*Ems, August 9, 1877 (evening)*.—Justice consists in recognizing the rights of others, the reciprocal, mutual, equivalent rights of other nations, peoples and societies, the rights of humanity. Might not the little peoples be the ones who could best work out the ideas of international justice? All the great peoples have more violent appetites and more passionate interests. They are like the great carnivores. Justice presupposes nobility of soul and disinterestedness. —A federation of the little free peoples, who wish for nothing but independence, seems the natural fatherland of the more humane historic ideas, the soil for purified theories of civilization. An Englishman, a German, a Frenchman, a Russian, an American always has some mental reservation regarding the supremacy, the hegemony of his own nation. Unconsciously, he desires the glory of his people and believes in its superiority. A Netherlander, a Dane, a Swiss escapes this temptation and this illusion. It is not these who would like to Americanize, Frenchify, Germanize, Russianize Europe. They feel in advance the advantage and the rights of diversity. They are freer from the prejudices of nationality, race, creed, language. And the Swiss has perhaps the most privileged position of all, for his country speaks four languages, has three religions and twenty-five political communities. He therefore knows best on what conditions people become united and live in common, without too much treading on one another's toes.

It is true that the spreading triumph of Darwinism, that is, materialism, or force in philosophy, threatens the idea of justice. But this last will have its turn. The higher human law cannot be borrowed from the animals, and justice is the right to the maximum of individual independence compatible with the same liberty for others: in other words, it is respect for man, the minor, the adult, the weak, the small, for human collectivities, associations, States, nationalities; it is the guarantee accorded to all the groups, spontaneous or deliberate, that can increase the sum of good and satisfy the desire of personal beings. The exploitation of some by others is an offence to justice. The right of the strongest is therefore not a right; it is a simple fact that has the right only as long as there is no protest or resistance. It is like cold, night, weight, which make themselves felt only until one has found fuel, illumination, machinery. All human industry is an emancipation from brute nature; the progress of justice is similarly a series of retreats on the part of the tyranny of the strongest. Medicine consists in overcoming sickness, and the good consists in conquering the blind ferocities and lawless appetites of the beast in man. Thus I always see the same law; the increasing liberation of the individual, the ascent of being towards life, towards happiness, towards justice, towards wisdom. Ravenous greed is the starting-point, intelligent generosity the destination. The caterpillar must turn into a butterfly, and the baby into a wise and just man.

*Ems, August 11, 1877.*—All the guests in the salon sang the *Lorelei* in chorus, and various other popular melodies. That which, in our countries, is only done for worship, is done in Germany for poetry and for music also. People's voices mingle, without undue familiarity. Art shares the privilege of religion. It is not so in France, or in England, or even, I think, in Italy. This spirit of artistic devotion, anonymous collaboration, disinterested communion in harmony, is Germanic; it counterbalances certain prosaic dullnesses of the race, which is full of feeling, but sensual as well.

*Ems, August 13, 1877.*—I think it is Schopenhauer and Hartmann who have most bluntly unveiled the legerdemain of nature, and all the wiles with which sexuality entwines human beings. Pessimism escapes from the fraudulent tyranny of the erotic tendency. Who is deceived here? . . .

In love there is a suicidal instinct, for it drives one to caresses, and the supreme caress kills it; and, if this is refused, it kills the lover. It is therefore a flame that is obliged to burn, that is, to destroy the thing that feeds it, that is, to annul itself.—Wisdom consists in changing the ephemeral conflagration into a light, an enduring hearth, that is, in husbanding love; for the frozen heart and the blazing heart destroy man equally . . .

*Ems, August 14, 1877.*—What is a well-bred man? One who knows and practises all the little duties of courtesy. He has the air of the world, *savoir vivre,* good form, manners, the behaviour of a gentleman; he knows how to vary his attentions, because he always feels what is fitting. He enters, he leaves, he accosts, he asks, he replies, he pays, he entreats, he offers differently from the common and vulgar man. His attitudes, his silence, his way of sitting or eating indicate that he is used to good society. The principle of these countless and diverse effects is respect for himself and others, manifested in every possible nuance, according to circumstances and persons.

What is a cultivated mind? It is one that has passed through a great many apprenticeships of thought and is able to look at things from a great many points of view. Culture is proportional to the number of categories which an intellect has at its disposal. The more possible ways of being that one has in oneself, the more modes and moulds one has acquired, the more forms, methods, and resources, the more cultivated one is. The cultivated man understands a great many things, but he is not necessarily inventive, ingenious or clever. He is merely practised, receptive, open-minded. His original gifts may have been mediocre, but he has turned them to account by effort.—Half-cultivation may spoil one's naturalness (and this is the case with all the bourgeois, the philistines, the *parvenus,* the vulgarians and pedants of the universe); but a happy nature completely cultivated gives the true dilettante, the judicious amateur, the enlightened connoisseur, the public that every artist and every writer desires for himself.—A purely scientific cultivation is not enough to make a cultivated mind. One must have in addition the knowledge of men, which means that one must know more than one language, one must have travelled and read. Letters are still the chief means of cultivation; *litteræ humaniores*.

An educated man has not only trained his faculties and rendered them supple, but stored up positive knowledge. The cultivated man can learn anything; the educated man has already accumulated the provisions.

A well-bred, cultivated, educated man is much more agreeable than a scholar, who may be a blockhead, or a learned specialist, with whom, outside his specialty, one is at a loss what to do.

*Clarens, September 23, 1877.*—Beautiful, bluish morning, poetically misty. Wandered a long hour on the Belmont road, a gracious belvedere reproducing on a small scale the terrace-road to Charnex . . . With eyes, ears and lungs I breathed in the pure air, the sensations of every kind that arise from this sweet morning countryside. Slanting sheets of sunlight, the Dent du Midi, sheer white, emerging from a vast collar of mists; wooded, rolling slopes, the lake glittering and full of motion, mountains of emerald and amethyst, lacy effect of walnut-trees, trailing shadows, ripening vines, red apples, butterflies, a few couples on their way to church, a few sails on the water, trains creeping shyly along with their plumes of smoke, the Oasis with its roses, its cypresses and weeping willows, all in that magic circle bounded by the Pléiades, the Cubly, the Caux, the Sonchoz, the Arvel, the Dent du Midi and the Grammont. The whole country seemed to me like a censer, and the morning was a prayer. It is good to meditate here, to live, dream and die.

A light breeze stirs the fringe of the striped cloth awning that shelters my balcony. The songs of a few birds, the pounding of wheels, a few women's voices rise to my open chamber. But one feels the Sabbath repose of some vaster silence, enveloping these little nearby sounds. There is no gainsaying it, this composure has its beauty, and eternal activity has a savour of bondage. The soul, too, would like to retire into itself, hearken to the voices of the immutable, live in its eternal part, escape from motion, experience peace; it has its dominical need. This is the hour of worship, this is the office of religion, this is the place of the divine.

*October 31, 1877.*—Is it a symptom of maturity or decline? I feel a great moral weariness over the obligation to maintain a foothold in the torrent of philosophical publications, and keep my head above the water; it even bores me to do so. My curiosity about new facts is not exhausted; but the eternal erasing and recommencing of ideas about things satiates and oppresses me.

At bottom, I have, like Schopenhauer, little taste for teaching philosophy, as for inculcating poetry or teaching religion. My vocation is no longer to my taste, and my self-distrust, my doubts in regard to results, my indifference, indolence and scepticism perhaps make me unfit for it. The critical spirit has consumed everything. Besides, three months of vacation have estranged me from this whole mode of existence. I have grown literary, Epicurean, valetudinarian and lazy. My old self is I no longer; I scarcely recognize myself. Detachment has stripped it of the acquisitions of its whole life; it has thrown off the robe of its former being as my jaw-bones are widowed of their teeth. This state of inner penury, of want and emptiness, uncertainty and indifference is a strange ordeal. I seem to be emerging from a long illness or even from the grave; and I ask my present being: Who are you? What can you do? What do you know? I do not feel any will in myself, and I simply float like a derelict. Should I be frightened by this abnormal situation? Is it a morbid state? It seems to me that it is, for in this way one cannot be useful either to oneself or to others. The virile career has come to an end; one is used up and finished as a man; honour murmurs, pride blushes, conscience cries out.—Everyone has his particular duty, beyond the general duty of doing something. You should be a serious professor; you should apply yourself to some important work; you should economize the remainder of your forces, instead of throwing up the sponge. And as for that which depends on your choice, you should choose what nobody will do better than yourself or can do in your stead, or would do in as short a time. You must play your own game and not somebody else's game, play with your cards and not with the cards you lack, play without delay and not vaguely propose to yourself to play.

Resume the government of your life, administer and improve your days, become responsible for yourself again, retrieve your activity and your will. Regulate your affairs, your time, your occupations, your relaxation, your work. Put a resolute end to vacations and sloth. Awake, thou that sleepest, and arise from the dead. You are not exempt yet: mere fancies, listlessness, the divided mind must be shown the door.

*November 6, 1877 (8.30 a. m.).*—I have caught my instinct in the act. The four verses above [1] have practically no connection with the occasion which is supposed to have produced them. It was the *word* "délaissement" that started my pen off, then one line led to three others, and an imperceptible vexation set me thinking of much greater ones, and a personal impression became enlarged and generalized. The *Méandres* [2] were done in this way. They do not so much transcribe as utilize my individual circumstances. Passing impressions become simply texts for higher or more enduring observations. Poetry changes everything it touches and even what it reflects; of a nothing it makes something, since from the accidental it ascends to the law, from a particular case to the type, from the fact

[1] The quatrain to which Amiel alludes ends some gloomy reflections of the previous evening:

> *Pourquoi de ses ennuis recommencer la gamme?*
> *Ruminer ses chagrins, c'est deux fois en souffrir.*
> *A tous délaissements accoutumons notre âme,*
> *Sans révolte sachons renoncer et mourir.*

The third line had been written first. Later, Amiel changed the order of the quatrain.

[2] The title that Amiel long thought of giving to the collection of poems that appeared in 1879, under the title *Jour à jour*, Fischbacher, Paris.

to the idea, from the real to the ideal. And this tendency is as plainly manifest in a single verse as in a whole poem and in the expression of a purely subjective feeling as in that of a contemplative survey, the recounting of an action or a descriptive picture. Language itself necessarily generalizes, poetry incarnates the generalizations, vivifies the thoughts, gives birth, in other words, to selected realities, a world that is nobler and choicer than the matter-of-fact world. It renders to things the service that religious faith, for the faithful, expects of the resurrection; it reproduces them in a more beautiful form, purer, grander, surrounded with an aureole of immortality. The poet is thus the prophet of another mode of existence, the visionary of a transfigured nature and humanity, while prose is the language of this world. The poet is an inhabitant of Olympus, travelling through the lower existence, he is Apollo at the house of Admetus, and it is almost literally correct to call poetry the language of the gods.

Apprehension by assimilation almost always anticipates intimate and personal experience. Thus we speak of love many years before we know it, and we think we know it because we name it, or because we repeat what people say of it and what books tell us about it. There are thus many degrees of ignorance, and there are degrees of knowledge that are quite illusory. In fact, the perpetual tiresomeness of society arises from this tournament of impetuous, inexhaustible verbosities, which have an air of knowing things because they talk about them, an air of believing, thinking, loving, searching, while really it is all just so much empty sound, mere appearance, vanity and babble. The worst of it is that, as self-esteem lies behind the babble, these clouds of ignorance are usually ferociously assertive, these cacklings are taken for opinions, these prejudices pose as principles. The parrots look on themselves as thinking beings, the imitations give themselves out as originals, the shadows of ideas expect to be treated as substances, and politeness demands that one should enter into the convention. It is very irksome.

Language is the vehicle of this confusion, the instrument of this unconscious fraud.—The evils of Babelry and parrotry are prodigiously augmented by universal education, the periodical press and all the processes of popularization that are current nowadays. Sheaves of paper money pass through everybody's hands, and very few ever touch gold. People live on tokens, and even on tokens of tokens, and they have never possessed the things, verified them, felt them, experienced them. They judge everything, but they know nothing.

How few original, individual, genuine people there are, worth the trouble of listening to them! Their real self is swallowed up in a borrowed atmosphere. It comes out only in their will: there alone they are sincere, through this alone one comes in contact with their real nature. Everybody, considered as force, as character, deserves our observation. But how few are anything beyond their inclinations, anything but varnished animals simulating, with their language and their posture as bipeds, a nature that is higher! The presence of a conscience in them, protesting against their manner of being, together with a reason that often perceives the vacuity, the inanity of their verbiage, is all that places them a little above animality.

In fact, the immense majority of our species are only candidates for humanity; nothing more than this. Virtually we are men, we could and should be men; but not only are we far from being angels, we do not succeed even in realizing the type of our own race. Semblances of men, copies, caricatures, counterfeits of men fill the inhabitable earth, people the islands and the continents, the cities and the countryside. When one wishes to respect men, one must forget what they are and think of the ideal that they belie, and yet carry hidden within them; one must think of the just, noble, great, intelligent, good, inventive, inspired, creative, true, loyal, faithful, steadfast man, the superior man, in a word, the divine pattern that we call a soul. The only men who deserve the name of men are the heroes, the geniuses, the saints, the harmonious, powerful and complete beings. Is an unstrung, broken lyre still a lyre?

Is a sword without hilt or blade still a sword? Is a singer with a false voice a singer? Is a three-footed horse a horse? We are thus only discarded samples, cheap wares, cast-off garments, waste-paper, potsherds, dross, sketches, often scarcely blocked in, mere fractions of men.

Few persons deserve to be listened to; all deserve to be looked upon with compassionate curiosity and humble perception. Are we not all shipwrecked, mutilated, sick, mad, condemned to death? If every one toiled to perfect himself and found fault with none but himself, things would go a little better with everybody. However impatient our neighbours make us, however much indignation our race arouses, we are all bound together, and the companions of a chain-gang have everything to lose by mutual insults, reproaches and recriminations. Let us hold our peace, let us aid and tolerate, let us even love one another. If we lack enthusiasm, let us have pity. Lay aside the whip of satire, the red sword of anger; the oil and wine of the helpful Samaritan are much more precious. One can extract scorn from the ideal; it is a lovelier thing to draw kindness from it.

*(11 a. m.)*.—The solitary man is a very poor judge of the relative value of the gifts he possesses; it is in the market that he learns this. For him, in his hermitage, his diamonds are only pebbles. It is entirely possible that what he considers bagatelles and trifles have value for the people outside. Thus, in your case, these 14,000 pages of Journal seem to you *ritornelli* and repetitions because the inner life turns in a circle. Who knows if others might not find in it a more serious attraction, instruction, even edification? The author of *Africa* thought lightly of his little love-sonnets, and it was these little sonnets that brought him his glory. Most famous men are famous perhaps for something quite other than what seems to them the best of their portion. The world has its own measure, not necessarily the best, but historically the only one that serves.—You have never consented to look at yourself through the eyes of opinion and the public and to subordinate yourself to this exterior judgment,

because that is what the clever people, the utilitarians, do. You have not wished to exploit yourself, like a mine, like a factory, like a forest, like an ox, by trying to find out what the vogue is, what sells, what succeeds in the literary or the social market. This is a permissible pride, but you have pushed it rather far. Self-respect is all very well, but utter disdain for current preferences, for the taste of the public, for fashion is imprudent. One ceases to know one's own value, one grows more and more timid. One is distanced by all the Bœotians, who have tenacity and a nose for things; and this is a pity, after all . . .

*November 19, 1877.*—Discovered today that the written text, with its erasures and variations, dulls the imagination and paralyzes one's energy. When I had cast about for a long time, writing, pencil in hand, I rose and, after taking three turns around my room, the thing came freely of itself. Poetry should be sung or dictated; the laborious effort of a man bent over his desk frightens it and puts it to flight. When the eye is fascinated by the written characters, the mind ceases to soar and merely crawls. One must speak one's thoughts and sing one's dreams; improvisation and dictation are liberators of talent. I perceive this rather late in the day.

*December 9, 1877.*—This evening, read part of Banville's *Cariatides*. I strive in vain to like this manner of conceiving poetry. The Parnassians sculpture urns of agate and onyx, but what do these urns contain? Ashes. What is lacking here is real feeling, the soul, the moral life, the serious, the moving, the elevated life, sincerity. The talent is magical, but everything is hollow underneath. The imagination tries to take the place of everything else. One finds metaphors, rhymes, music, colour; what one does not find is man. This superficial, factitious poetry may enchant one at twenty, but what can one make of it at fifty? Banville makes me think of Pergamos, Alexandria, the epochs of decadence, when beauty of form conceals poverty of thought and a spent heart.—I feel intensely the repugnance which this school of poetry inspires in good, simple people. One would say that its only concern is to please the libertines, the blasé, the over-refined, the corrupt, and that it is unaware of the healthy life, regular habits, pure affections, steady work, honesty and duty. This elegant Bohemia is no better than the sodden Bohemia. It is the art of harlotry. It is the fanfaronade of vice. It is an affectation, and, because it is an affectation, the school is smitten with sterility. The reader desires in the poet something better than a rhyming-quack and a mere trickster in verse; he wishes to find in him a painter of life, a contemplative man, a friend, a fellow-creature, a being who thinks and loves and has a conscience, passion and remorse, not a merry-andrew juggling with the voluptuous. The school whose banner is "art for art's sake" is judged by its fruits. It disgusts the reader with its gods and its worship, because underneath these grand words its utter frivolity appears. This pseudo-paganism is only a posture. It does not take hold of the real man. It is only gold-dust sprinkled on a corpse.

*December 19, 1877.*—The world and you look at one another with the eyes of strangers. It does not understand you, you have ceased to understand it. You will soon have nothing in common. This is the way centenarians must feel, when everything they have loved has gone down to the grave. This is the sere and yellow leaf, the sinking in the sands, the petrifaction against which Gudule [1] wishes to strive. She sees in it the invasion of death. And certainly it is the opposite of life. And yet I do not really feel empty, languid, bored. If this is decay, it is not very painful; the rebellions of the flesh appear no more. One might rather call it a peaceful consumption of the will, a slow emaciation of the soul.—I feel as if I were emerging from a long swoon. Epimenides coming forth from his cave must have had a similar impression.

Two intensities of contemplation: in the first degree, it is the world that is volatilized and becomes a pure dream; in the second degree, it is our self which, in turn, becomes a mere shadow, the dream of a dream. Brahmanic phantasmagoria.

[1] One of the names used in the Journal to designate Fanny Mercier.

*March 24, 1878.*—A sex that prefers favour to justice, superstition to wisdom, opinion to knowledge, error to truth, must be kept out of the great historic questions and decisions. It has only a lieutenant's faculties, not a general's. It is invalid, and would be dreadful as judge, as legislator, as revolutionary, as institutor, as inventor. It is proper that the sex should be employed in everything, but it should not be given the supreme direction in anything. To grant it complete equality with the other sex in functions and in rights would be to check the advance of humanity and civilization. The manifest exceptions prove nothing. A few extraordinary women do not prevent the average from being the sentimental, passionate, retarding element of society, passive and committed to routine. Progress does not come from them, but in spite of them. Progress is essentially progress in truth, and it is man who invents, finds, discovers, innovates, undertakes, attempts, man who creates and conquers. *Cuique suum.* The male has many weaknesses and makes many mistakes; but everything would be worse if he ceased to be the master. The age of gynæcocracy must have been a sad age, and a return of it is not to be desired. The effemination of a race alone means that the race is decadent . . .

It will be a singular thing if the democratic era ends in the complete emancipation of women, which will put an end to democratic customs. All women have the aristocratic weakness, they detest vulgarity and equality; their taste is for distinction, for arbitrary favour, for the inequality of merits. Their first care will be to arrange a good tyranny after their own heart, the dictatorship of the priest and the artist. The reaction will be amusing.

Liberalism in politics and religion is the last thing that women will like or practise. Respect for science is the opposite pole from their inclination.

*March 25, 1878.*—The feminine tendency is to a swift and usurping assimilation. Things that they remember they convert at once into personal finds. They think things have happened for the first time . . . The critical need to indicate one's sources, to acknowledge one's borrowings, to cite those from whom one has borrowed, to give others their rights is not properly feminine. The echo pretends to originality. The small additional element of recombination poses as the equal of the mother-wit that creates. The talent of the pupil considers itself the equivalent of the master's genius. And this illusion has its good faith, or at least it guards itself against any examination of conscience that might disturb it. Women do not wish to distinguish between giving birth and procreating, between exploiting and originating, between the power of imitation and that of innovation. The moon, which reflects, imagines also that it is a light by itself, and secretly thinks itself a little sun. Eagerness to receive, facility in reproducing are, however, only secondary qualities of the intelligence. The male alone labours over things and creates something new. The feminine mind pumps ideas out of man and imagines it has drawn them from nature itself. This perpetual unconfessed larceny is the comedy of cultivated epochs. Women are a good deal like those stewards who contrive to collect in their money-boxes the gold that has been produced by the unceasing toil of other men, and who think they are superior to those who produce it because they have carried it off.—The drones of the intellectual hive mock the bees who make the honey and think themselves better than their collaborators.

The *imaginative faculty* is not the same thing as the imagination. Woman does not produce the fruitful ideas, but she discovers the details, she dresses, polishes, finishes, perfects, she observes the overlooked, she embellishes the exterior. She represents adroitness and taste, finesse and care. In a word, to be done well a work should be created, hewn by man, finished by woman. To one the architecture belongs, to the other the dressing and trimming. Masterpieces, in fact, demand both genius and talent, one providing the stuff and the proportions, the other eliminating the seams and the defects. And humbler works demand no less the concert of two forces, both of which indeed exist in the artist, but one of which as a rule predominates in one of the sexes.—I have therefore been very fortunate and highly favoured in having been able to review *à deux* everything I have done during the last few years. This auxiliary and this check is very useful to me, not to mention my great advantage in having, instead of a simple copyist, an intelligent, sympathetic and zealous secretary.[1]

*March 27, 1878 (midnight)*.—Continued Rousseau [2] (*Correspondance; Origine de l'inégalité*, and controversies relating to this). How difficult it is to form a final judgment about a man who has provoked and warranted every antipathy, and whose life belies his principles, whose standard and talent are mutually contradictory! Etc., etc. Every day I pass through opposite impressions, and I feel alternately disesteem and admiration for him. The disparity between

[1] In February, 1879, Amiel, for several years a familiar visitor at the house of the Benoît ladies, became their regular guest, a boarder at 13, rue Verdaine. Mlle. Valentine Benoît, already well-known in Latin Switzerland for her stories and comedies for children, published under the pseudonym Berthe Vadier, had found in Amiel a literary guide and censor and a master in poetry. This precious friendship, gracious and enjoyable, the fruit of a mutual interest and admiration for poetry and art, eased the anxieties and the increasing infirmities of the author of the *Journal intime*, who indicated the real nature of this relationship by calling Berthe Vadier "my god-daughter".—"She is my neophyte, my pupil, my initiate" (September 9, 1880).—"Long talks about every page we read together, biblical, scientific and literary reading. My god-daughter is reaping what so many others have passionately desired, but then she has had the courage to make this possible by providing me with a nest and a shelter for health and for sickness, work and recreation. Beyond this, all she seeks is to understand and humour me . . . Her mother, in turn, is quite maternal. In short, this is not just a comfortable pension; it is a family that extends to me the care with which it surrounded the brother and the father who are now dead. That is why to be ill here is a pleasure instead of a terror" (September 11, 1880). And the last words written in his Journal by Amiel's hand were a testimony of gratitude to this domestic and literary friendship, which was so intelligent and so devoted.

[2] In rereading, during the first months of 1878, most of the works of J. J. Rousseau, Amiel was preparing to write the lecture that he was to deliver on the occasion of the centenary celebrations of the Citizen of Geneva, in July of that year. The lecture was published in the collection: *J. J. Rousseau, jugé par les Genevois d'aujourd'hui* (Sandoz, Geneva and Paris, 1879).

talent and character, between conduct and thought, between the
man and the author causes one painful sensations. There is something that hurts one in observing an enigmatical, discordant being.
—A conscience that was far from delicate and an immense pride,
a fiery talent and a taste for posing, disharmony in everything and
at every point. Governed by impressions and imagination; thought
in the service of passion. Perhaps the victim of an ambiguity, which
is at the bottom of his life and his books: Nature. Does human nature consist of inclination, appetite, instinct?—Paradoxical, intractable to every assumption, refractory, explosive, the enemy of all
constraint, holding a wager all his life. A specimen to support Schopenhauer's theory, with an intelligence unwittingly the slave of the
unconscious will, the blind and unreflecting impulse. An Epicurean
acting the Stoic, a voluptuary playing at the austere: the imagination is the centre of his being. It is always the others (society, if need
be) that are wrong. He, he is the only one who is right, the only
one who is good, the only one who is just, and if the trumpet of the
last judgment sounded . . . we know the rest. The antipode of
Christian psychology. Neither humility nor repentance, conversion
nor sanctification. The natural man apotheosizes the natural man;
the sinner draws from his sin the proof that he is the best of
men. Just the opposite way from the publican, he does his penance
on the backs of others. When he confesses a mistake, it is his neighbour or circumstances that are the original cause of it; therefore he
is the victim and not the culprit. A false notion of evil and sin, a
notion resulting from the resistance of the ego to any humiliation,
is thus the axis of his life, the origin of all his errors. His ego was
never able to renounce itself, mortify or crucify itself. The phenomenon of the new birth remained unknown to him. He loved, in-
dulged and approved of himself to the end. He repulsed at first
with indignation the unjust accusations of his contemporaries, then
the just reproaches of his conscience. He wished to get the better
of his conscience itself, and even the divine severity, by the magic
of his plea for the defense.—He is not a wise man searching for the

truth, he is a powerful advocate anxious to win his case. He has only the air of a philosopher; actually, he is an orator, who works himself into a rapture for his thesis, and one who, putting sophism at the service of his passion, is for the moment no longer a sophist, because he deceives himself. This is the dangerous miracle wrought by the imagination. It contrives to delude itself in good faith.

*April 14, 1878.*—Perhaps the need to think for oneself and to ascend to principles is wholly characteristic only of the Germanic mind. The Slavs and the Latins are willingly dominated by the collective wisdom, by tradition, usage, custom, prejudice, fashion; or else they break this like slaves in revolt, without perceiving themselves the law inherent in things, the true rule, unwritten, not arbitrary, not imposed. The German wishes to come into contact with nature; the Frenchman, the Spaniard, the Russian halt in the conventional. It is always the old quarrel of the Greek philosophers, Θέσει ἢ φύσει? The root of the problem lies in the question of the relation between God and the world. Immanence or transcendence, this determines the significance of all the other things, one after another. If the mind is outside things, it does not have to conform to them. If the mind is destitute of truth, it must receive it through revelation. This is the characteristic of the mind that scorns nature and submits to the Church; this is the Latin world.

*April 22, 1878.*—A letter from Cousin Julie . . . These good old relatives are difficult for busy men to satisfy. Complaints if one does not write. Complaints if one writes briefly. Complaints if one describes one's occupations and preoccupations and wishes to let them know what one is thinking and doing. Instead of rejoicing because one is at work and entering into one's circumstances, complaints and almost reproaches. They are unable and even unwilling to understand a man's life, especially the life of a student. These hermits of revery are frightened by the world, out of their element in action. These ingenuous fowls always look with terrified stupefaction on the creatures whom they knew in the egg, and raise an outcry when they see some of them attempting the spaces of the

air, others sailing away over the great levels of the water. Unhappy
eagles! Unhappy swans! Unhappy ducks! Unhappy canaries! How
dare you leave home and quit the poultry-yard, foolhardy creatures!
—These lamentations are a little tiresome, and these remonstrances
are a little absurd. But, after all, people do not change at seventy,
and a good, old pious village soul, who is half blind, cannot be expected to broaden her point of view or imagine what lives are like
that have no relation to her own.

At what point are these souls, enveloped by the minutiæ of daily
life, attached to the ideal? Through their religious aspirations. Faith
is their raft of salvation. They know the higher life, their soul
thirsts for heaven. They are ignorant of the hundred thousand geographical particulars of Europe, but they are not ignorant of Europe. All their opinions are imperfect, but their moral experience is
great. Their minds are full of darkness, but their souls are full of
light. One cannot talk to them about the things of the earth, but
they are ripe for the things of the heart. If they cannot understand
us, it is for us to meet them, to speak their language, to enter their
sphere of ideas, their way of feeling. They must be approached on
the side where they are strong; and to show them all the more respect, one must encourage them to open the casket of their most
cherished thoughts. When the vineleaves are shrivelled and dried,
the grape is sweeter and ruddier. There is always some nugget of
gold at the bottom of every honourable old age. We should try to
bring it to light and provide the occasion for it to reveal itself to
affectionate eyes. This we can do.

*May 19, 1878.*—Is criticism a science? Yes, in a sense, inasmuch
as one can draw up the catalogue of its preliminary conditions and
prefatory exercises; but it is above all a gift, a touch, a scent, an
intuition, an instinct, and, in this sense, it cannot be taught and cannot be demonstrated, it is an art. The critical genius is the aptitude
for discerning the true beneath appearances and amid the imbro-
glios that conceal it; for discovering it in spite of the errors of witnesses, the frauds of tradition, the dust of time, the loss or cor-

ruption of texts. It is the sagacity of the hunter, which nothing deceives for long and which no stratagem can throw off the track. It is the talent of the examining magistrate, who knows how to investigate circumstances and bring to light a secret that is lost in the prison of a thousand lies. The true critic can understand everything, and he never consents to be duped by anything; never to any convention does he sacrifice his duty, which is to find and speak the truth.—When he is concerned with the living, with existing institutions, with anything that is vindictive, armed, menacing, irritable, he may be forced into deference and discretion, into attentions and reserves that vex him; but his desire is to see clearly, even if he cannot or dare not make others see clearly. Affectation, pose, mummery, charlatanism, humbug, fraud are things that hold him in aversion. Towards the false he must be like the dreaded and legendary voice that made the reeds whisper:

*Midas, le roi Midas a des oreilles d'âne.*

Oh, where is the open-minded and indulgent, but incorruptible and infallible critic, the Æacus of letters, without weakness or ill-humour? How many of his kind exist? Who has taken the motto of Jean Jacques, *Vitam impendere vero?* Alas!

*May 20, 1878.*—A sufficiency of learning, general culture, absolute probity, an eagle eye, human sympathy, technical capacity, how many things are indispensable to the critic, without speaking of grace, delicacy, good-breeding, touch:

*L'esprit bien rarement arrive à la justesse.*

The perfect critic does not exist. Let us be content with the passable critic, the critic who is honest and enlightened.

*June 20, 1878 (9 a. m.).*—With what a frightful rapidity do my work and thought become strange and unknown to me! I have just had a proof of it. I was obliged to make up a list of questions for an examination, and I had great difficulty in recalling the courses themselves, and the subjects that were treated; it was only thanks to my detailed surveys that I was able to save the day. I should lose my legs and my head, if they were not tacked on pretty firmly. If my notes were stolen or mixed up, the twenty-nine years of my professorship would have to be started all over again. This utter want of cohesion and the faculty of appropriation is a great plague; every day I return to my original destitution and privation. I have only the reversionary interest of my knowledge, an imaginary investiture; I am poor and empty. The moment I finish my study of Rousseau, the twenty thousand pages I have read in preparation for it will be blotted from my memory; I feel as if my mind were like the glaciers, which reject from their bosom the earth, the stones and the logs; it exudes everything that comes to it from without; it continues in its formal purity. What it desires is flexibility, and it repudiates wealth, materials, facts. The least illness, a shock, a fall would leave the book of my intelligence blank. It is likely that the tendency to externalize myself from myself, to detach myself from myself by constant criticism, has brought about this weakness of my mind in the matter of retaining images, signs and things, all those rubbish-heaps that constitute learning. The famous equation of Fichte, $I = I$, has almost become my formula. My mind is the Nirvana of all particular knowledge. Indifference to the provisional, the accessory, the accidental, the relative has ended by producing a semi-impotence to keep any stock whatsoever. Just in this way light consumes the colours . . . Stop! There are evils that one increases merely by looking at them. This is one of them. Philosophy has evaporated my faculty of memory, making me omnimodel and neuter. It has placed me as it were beyond the grave, where the world is only a vague memory for the soul and all phenomena melt into their law.

*July 15, 1878.*—Consolation. The moment I begin to meditate, pen in hand, I am carried away from moral suffering; I forget the horrors of practical life; I enter the contemplative state once more. Thought is almost impersonal; it opens the realm of calm. The very monsters are nothing but curiosities and images for him who thinks about them; he is no longer under their dominion.

*July 20, 1878 (7.30 a. m.).*—Advantage of the noble style: it conceals the mediocrity of perceptions and comparisons. *"Une chaleur de chien"* is slang; "the burning dog-days" becomes epical. The dog-days are the month when the dog is ascendant, the dog being Sirius; it is the month (July 24 to August 24), when Sirius rises and sets at the same time as the sun, and as this month is the hottest of the summer, the dog appeared to be the cause of it: *cum hoc, ergo propter hoc.* A dog with its tongue hanging expresses thirst; the dog in the heavens causes thirst. This is the way the popular imagination goes, and astronomy ennobles it all. Thanks to Egypt, *"une chaleur de chien"* becomes good style.—The general rule is that the familiar becomes sublime by being associated, in the imagination, with some reminiscence of an exalted order, historic or natural. For example, terms of hunting and the stable, even to the dung of animals, are in the grand style in French, by reason of the chivalry and nobility that have employed them; scientific terms are considered pedantic, and the terms of trade are accounted low, because gentlemen have not used them. These traditional repugnances are preserved in democracy, surviving the social regime that engendered them. What is called taste consists in arousing only the ideas that are consonant with the effect to be obtained, ideas that do not derange the impression produced and that even, if possible, augment it. Taste, therefore, carefully selects colours, sounds, words, images, in order to avoid incongruities and all unpleasant encounters; it multiplies the harmonics on the fundamental note and all the engaging allusions about the theme which it is developing. Taste is literary tact . . . The orator, the poet, the composer follows the procedure of the florist. It is a matter of creating the most expressive and the most charming bouquet. Every gracious work of art is a flower-writing, and every flower-writing is meant to persuade. Taste is the instinctive method of pleasing.

*(Evening.)*—Dr. Z. has frankly acknowledged that the end of my

illness may be death from suffocation, and even from three causes
of suffocation: emphysema, the swelling of the thyroid cartilage and
laryngeal viscosity. Three mutes of the seraglio hold the bow-string
to strangle me. I shall be hard put to it to escape from all three.

*July 26, 1878.*—I awake every morning with the same feeling
that I am used up and finished, that I am struggling in vain against
the rising tide that is going to engulf me. I must die by suffocation,
and the three stranglers are at their work, and their progress incites
them to continue. One of them fills up from below the aerial cavity,
another strangles the respiratory vent, the third is trying to bottle
up the orifice. The last, moreover, by the spasmodic efforts which it
imposes on me, hopes to cause the bursting of one of the inner
canals. There is something odious to the individual in feeling the
agents of Siva thus at work at his destruction; devoured from
within, he witnesses this homicide and does the honours of it. It is
against nature. It is like a torture of the Inquisition.

One cannot bore others with one's groans, useless enough, in any
case. One cannot undertake anything, when every day brings some
fresh nuisance. One cannot even make up one's mind in a confused,
uncertain situation in which one foresees the worst, but in which
everything is doubtful. Has one a few years before one, or only a
few months? Is death going to be slow, or will there be a swift catastrophe? And what am I to do if I must stay in my room or my
bed? If I submit to this, who is going to care for me? Where shall I
find shelter for my end? How shall I bear the days, and how shall I
fill them? How end with calm and dignity? I do not know. I do
everything badly when I do it for the first time, and here everything
is new; nothing is prepared, rehearsed, there has been no experi-
menting; one ends as chance will have it. What a mortification for
one who has too dearly cherished independence! He depends on a
thousand things all unforeseen. He does not know what he will do,
what he will become; he can predict nothing. He would like to talk
of these things with some friend who is sensible and well-advised.
But, lo, there is none to be found. He does not wish to alarm the

two whose affection for him is most devoted, and he is almost certain that others would only strain their wits to distract him and would not enter into the truth of the position.

And, while one waits (awaiting what? health? certainty?), the weeks flow away like water, one's strength is consumed like a flaring taper. One's clarity of vision keeps pace with the advances of the malady, which it makes no attempt to remedy; it has the fatalistic indolence of the Moslem and the pure irresolution of the sincere sceptic. How can one decide, when all courses are evil and one believes too little either in this or in that? To be content with the least evil is certainly very wise; but this does not go far as a motive.

Is one free to give way to death without offering any resistance? Is self-preservation a duty? Do we owe it to those who love us to prolong this despairing struggle as far as we can? It seems to me that we do, and this is a further constraint. One must thus feign a hope that one does not possess, conceal the utter discouragement that one feels. Why not? It is generous in those who succumb not to diminish the ardour of those who are struggling or rejoicing. We are all, from the greatest to the least, condemned to death.

> *Un peu plus tôt, un peu plus tard,*
> *Ce n'est pas grande différence.*

(*Later.*)—Thus two parallel paths lead me to the same result: meditation paralyzes me, physiology condemns me. My soul is dying, my body is dying. Whichever way I turn I meet a wall. Left to myself, I am consumed with sadness; and medicine also says to me, You have no further to go. These two verdicts seem to point to the same thing, that I have a future no longer and that I must pack my bags. This seems absurd to my incredulity, which would like to regard it as a bad dream. It is useless for the mind to say, This is so. The inner assent refuses to come. Another contradiction. I have not the strength to hope, and I have not the strength to resign myself. I believe no longer, and I still believe. I feel that I am finished, and I cannot conceive that I am finished. Is this madness already? No, it is human nature caught in the act; it is life that is a real contradiction, since it is an incessant death and a daily resurrection, since it affirms and denies, destroys and reconstructs, assembles and disperses, humbles and exalts at once. To live is to die partially and to be partially reborn; it is to persevere in this vortex with its two contrary aspects, it is to be an enigma.

If the invisible type traced by this double current, flowing in and out, if this form that presides at your metamorphoses has itself a general and original value, what does it matter whether it continues its play for a few moons or a few suns longer? It has done what it had to do, it has represented a certain unique combination, a particular expression of the species.

These types are shadows, manes. The ages appear to be occupied in fabricating them. Glory is an evidence that one type has seemed to the other types newer, more rare and beautiful than the rest. Commonplace men have souls, too; but they are interesting only to the Creator and to a very small number of people.

It is well to feel one's frailty, but to be indifferent to it is a loftier view. To measure one's wretchedness is useful, but to perceive one's reason for being is more useful still. To mourn over oneself is just one more vanity; one should regret only that which has value, and to regret oneself is to show unwittingly that one attaches importance to oneself. And, at the same time, it is to misconceive one's real value. To live is not urgent; the important thing is not to disfigure one's type, to remain faithful to one's ideal, to protect one's monad against deterioration and degradation. If this is not possible, Nirvana becomes desirable. But is this impossible?

You have not been able to realize your dream. This is not the question, for our dream comprises our surroundings, our environment, human society, many things that do not depend upon us. But can you not defend your type, realize your originality? This depends more on you. You are probably a psychological experimenter.

In this case, these 14,800 pages of Journal are a fulfillment of your vocation. You have conversed with yourself as an apple-tree bears apples. This does not enlarge the patrimony of science. But it proves something, perhaps: that the inner life should be only a last resort? That this variation of the cloister is no better than the cloister? That the desuetude of the will serves no great purpose in a world constructed on the plan of universal war? That the feminine virtues are almost harmful in a man? That timidity and false shame can render the finest gifts useless? That irresolution increases with the years, and that a prolonged cessation from willing becomes an impotence of the will? This would be a terribly meagre result.

What is your genuine originality? It is probably the psychological flexibility that permits you to comprehend and reproduce the most varied states of the soul and consciousness. To unravel difficult skeins, to disengage unforeseen laws; to this perhaps you should limit yourself henceforward, after a long dispersion in your investigations. Concentrate yourself then in the role of Œdipus; you have little time left for doing it.—Do not broach or attack any more problems that are not worth the trouble or that require more than a minimum of erudition and memory. Perhaps, too, you had better let synthetic construction, composition, alone; it only upsets and puzzles you. Make the most of your inclination for analysis. Do what pleases you the most and what you are most successful with: this will be doubly profitable. You have worn yourself out doing what was fitting; now use your sense of things only to understand your circumstances, and think only of saving whatever is most interesting in the bazaar of your intuitions and personal experiences. One survives only through that which cannot be replaced . . .

My wish would have been not to suffer but to maintain myself in the impersonality of thought; this was my second position, once I had lost the first, an affectionate, reciprocal harmony with a sympathetic environment.—But the second position has been lost as well: the death of desire does not give one rest. As Vinet says:

*Vide affreux d'un cœur sans désir,*
*Peut on le sentir et survivre?*
*Peut-on respirer sans poursuivre*
*Un but, un rêve, un avenir?*   ·

Will a third position be more tenable? That of a submissive humility, resigned to diminution, consoling itself for all its shipwrecks, content to cultivate a patch of garden on a little isle, with or without a helpmate, with whatever time it pleases the Master of life to bestow? The happiness of plenitude, the immobility of non-existence, would be more pleasing to my pride; in both these cases, the Self would have remained unconquered. The hardest thing is to accept mutilation, abasement, the return to the dust and the commonplace. Wholesale renunciation has something majestic about it, but to be dismembered is insulting. To have his mane torn out hair by hair is more than a lion can endure. To be meek in the presence of death requires less self-command than to remain meek under the endless affronts of spoliation. The law of irony. It is a quarter of a century since renunciation was last preached to me, and I do not believe that I had then renounced myself, although I had renounced many things. It is always the story of the Sibyl; one wants the same price for the last book as for all the others before they were burned.

*August 11, 1878.*—Reflected on the difficulties of the devil's work, I mean composition and style. Its demands are numberless, and they go in contradictory pairs. With me, almost all of the living force is absorbed by various kinds of friction, by reflections, prepossessions, anxieties, scruples that run athwart my impulse and paralyze my energy. All the parts of my being hold one another in check, and, aiming at harmony, arrive at immobility. To compose is to resolve this strange problem of acting like a somnambulist with all the circumspection of a man who is wide-awake, the problem of doubting without doubting, of being assured, joyous, bold, in one's speech, while all the time one is divided, uneasy, anxious in one's heart. It is to be in bed, yet standing upright, to be carried away in cold blood; it is to realize the absurd, to astound good sense.

Obviously, the thing that embarrasses me is that my inner critical sense comes too quickly into play,

*Car se regarder voir peut empêcher de voir.*

All one's scruples are in order when one is deliberating, but in action one must know one's mind and strike with headlong impetuosity. One who is forever analyzing himself, wrangling and debating with himself, destroys his power of impulse. Hesitation over the phrase, the word, the idea, the substance and the form kills one's energy. Fear drives away joy, and the extinction of joy freezes talent . . .

Conscience, timidity, hesitation, the lack of memory render composition almost impossible. Procreation requires more warmth and assurance. That is why your style smells of the lamp. It is made and not born. It has no wings, no grace, no gaiety, no felicity or naturalness. Sustained practice in the art of writing would have increased your flexibility; you have never followed the proper method, the one that speaks its discourse before writing it and thus proceeds from one living thing to another, from the sketched form to the final form. Your professorial and didactic habits have led you to proceed in a different way. You analyze your subject for itself, without permitting yourself the personal entertainment that would amuse yourself or the dialogue with the reader that would amuse him. You are too detached, too sober, too strained, too pontifical. Your gratuitous discomfort procures you nothing but the ill-humour of others. The more effort you make, the less you succeed; that is the law . . .

With you, God knows, it is the same thing in composition as in everything else. You cannot pluck and gather, you cannot finish anything. You do not dare; self-distrust stifles you.

*(Later.)*—What I find most difficult in composition is the rigorous combining of the parts, when one is anxious to forget nothing, repeat nothing, put nothing out of its place. Convergence of effect represents, in the academic style, what unity of action represents in the drama. Everything that retards or deflects, everything in the wrong tone, everything that obscures is bad.

*August 12, 1878.*—Lessons to be drawn from this last experience:[1] 1, You have made the task horribly difficult for yourself, by wishing to read and examine everything; 2, by not venturing to conclude, to cut short, to decide more quickly; 3, by approaching your subject from too lofty and distant a point of view; 4, by demanding too much of your discourse, your style and yourself.

These encyclopædic monographs, summarizing eighty volumes in thirty pages in a lapidary and sententious style, are a brain-twisting business. What they cost nobody ever repays, and the only words that are ever uttered about them are the not very flattering words "close and minute". You fancy, in your conscientiousness, that you are the Tribunal of the Dead, and that you are weighing the destinies of a soul . . .

I have not used good sense. I have spent ten thousand francs to grow a bunch of asparagus. The asparagus may be superb, but it is infinitely too expensive. I have been an unmitigated fool. The piece may well be called passable but it is none the less a simple specimen of criticism, which will do Rousseau no good, and will do me no more. It will leave my fellow-citizens indifferent and will make no friends for me anywhere else. For twenty persons who will thank me for it, I shall have consumed months of time. One would be hard put to it to be more stupidly prodigal of one's pains.

[1] The composing of his *Caractéristique générale de J. J. Rousseau.* A few weeks later, the Journal says: "It is the only one of my works that is certain to be read in 1978 . . . I have judged as. I should wish to be judged, were I Jean-Jacques instead of being only Henri-Frédéric. It seems to me that I have presented the work of our compatriot in all its greatness, while criticizing the man, his theories and his talent. It seems to me it would be hard to say more things in forty pages."

After this, it must be acknowledged that without the pressure of circumstances I should not have done this work; that the work is better than nothing; that it is my nature to take subjects in their largest aspect; that to have sought justice is never a cause of regret; that to have written thirty pages in good style is never a thing to be ashamed of. Come, forgive yourself. Only, do not accept any more official commissions, renounce all public discourses. You lack the voice now, you have neither the sympathy nor the favour of the public, you have no affinity with the public; you have not even the desire to please it. Be content with writing, on subjects, moreover, if it gives you pleasure, to your own taste and of your own choosing; take your own time, without haste or obligation. Besides, to write is not to publish. Compose for your own satisfaction, bring out only whatever has a chance of being useful or of being welcomed.—For all Rousseau's glory, you would not like to have a quarter of his misfortunes. You are not ambitious. Therefore do not drive yourself from foolish motives or from too much candour.

*(11 a. m.)*—The true use to be drawn from a work is to be led into beginning another, profiting at once from the numberless perceptions which the practice of the art brings into play. Thus one profits from one's blunders, one capitalizes one's experience and increases one's virtuosity.—When I consider that I have always postponed the serious study of the art of writing, from fear and trembling before it and a secret love for its beauty, I am furious at my stupidity and my awe. I have had a sort of scruple against surprising the secret of the masters, dismembering masterpieces for my own use. And when I have been forced to write, I have done so at random, groping my way like a timorous amateur, a respectful schoolboy. I lack the professional attitude, as teacher, philosopher, poet, just as I lack it as a writer. I am a novice in all fields, with no authority and no assurance. The reason for this insufficiency is less incapacity than indecision. Timid people do not dare to appropriate a realm and say, This is mine. None of my aptitudes has attained to mastery, to inner security. I have not even discovered my special

gift, my individuality, my originality; and my only principle has been to catch the spirit of things and do the best I could with whatever was to be done.—I have thus improved my talent no better than my fortune. I have let everything be lost from a chivalrous negligence, an aversion to cunning. What a fool you have been, you poor fellow! . . . And as for the things of the heart, it has been just the same. You have not turned to account one of the favours of destiny.

*August 27, 1878.*—The organism is a scaffolding as hazardous as credit; it is nothing but gas and ashes momentarily woven together by the caprice of life. This mountain of cells is harassed by the tendency to return to its elements. Individual existence is only a meteor, an effervescence, a phosphorescence, which appears and disappears. The shadow of a shadow, a vain form, a phantom that perceives its state. That which constitutes its reality is a transitory resistance to destruction, a reaction against external influences. To live is to act, above all to radiate. Passivity is the state of inertia. It is not worth the trouble of being alive if one anticipates death by apathy . . . To sleep, to dream, to think, to act are the four degrees of being. This is to be plant, animal, contemplative being, man . . .

Is the preceding hierarchy certainly correct? Aristotle held contemplation more divine than action. Action, like all generative creation, is in great measure blind and impetuous. Is it better to see clearly? Voluntary and conscious production, if it were possible, would combine two privileges. We assume that the pure spirit, God, knows what he is doing while he is doing it; but our inspired men, our inventors, our geniuses do what they do not know, they are swept along, carried, urged on by a secret force of which they are the agents rather than the masters, the vehicles rather than the directors.

In any case, there also exists a fecundity of ideas; and cerebral power consists in combining and constructing something. Everything that is unconnected, scattered, confused is only material and not a production, merely stuff, not a work. Works are intellectual actions.

The thinker in his cell thus also acts, provided he sets himself a goal, elucidates an idea, aids in the labour of the species. Only mere bungling is time thrown away; floundering in the futile is the thing to be condemned.

Will these pages, for instance, these fourteen thousand, nine hundred and six pages be useful to anyone or anything? Will they clear up any question? Will they provide any science with materials? I doubt it. They have helped me to live, but what has my life helped? —A poor little professor, an apprentice at writing, the fourth part of a savant, the eighth part of a poet: this comes to nothing, this can leave no trace behind it.

*August 30, 1878.*—Importance of a word in philosophy. Schopenhauer says, All life is action, all action effort, all effort pain, therefore life is an evil. Pessimism.—But it is not true that every action is an effort; action is often impulsive, that is, a joy, a feeling of power; the bird that soars aloft does not suffer as he flies, nor does it cause suffering for a walker to walk. The simple fact that a word is missing causes a confusion here between the employment of force and effort, between expansion and will, action and fatigue. We must distinguish between two kinds of conscious activity, spontaneous activity and willed activity. The first is almost as easy as unconscious activity. Everything that is done with pleasure, with love, with enthusiasm is done easily.

*August 31, 1878.*—The hour is propitious. Light, temperature, sounds are agreeable. Nothing to disturb one. Let me take advantage of it. Let me enjoy, instead of ruminating over my troubles and my wounds. We tolerate others, why not tolerate ourselves? It is a sin to disparage oneself forever and regard oneself in one's worst light. The portrait-painter strives to discover the attitude, the pose that best brings out all the lines of his model. Why persist in doing the opposite with yourself, relentlessly noting your faults, your flaws, your shortcomings, your weaknesses, your losses? Can you not look upon yourself with a little more satisfaction and charity, do yourself the honours of your person? You are certainly no longer young, you are not handsome, or elegant, or strong, your capacity for work is slight; it is by no means certain that you have a mind any longer; but, after all, you are not a cipher in Geneva. You have a measure of education, a certain talent, a little taste; you have rendered a few services; you occupy a place, not brilliant perhaps, but at least respected, among the Genevan thinkers and men of letters. In the literary history of this country, your name is almost certain to have a line. This *aurea mediocritas* has its value.

*September 23, 1878.*—Feeling cannot promise anything, for it does not know what it will become and does not depend on the will. The oaths of passion are not recorded by Jove. Then what is the value of conjugal vows? One can promise fidelity and obedience; but can one promise that love will endure? The vow, even if it is sincere, is mad; accordingly it is rarely kept, exactly as if it had not been made. Man hopes to diminish his weakness by denying it. He plays the gallant in order to hide his fear. He tries to bind his inconstancy by his signature. Poor stratagems! Better to promise only what depends upon us, probity and integrity. The heart will not let itself be bound by any juridical procedure; but the conscience escapes the sophisms of the heart. The duty of the married remains, when the charm and the attraction of the common life have disappeared. One loves as long as one is able, and one honestly aids when one no longer loves.

Just the same, this is a vicious circle. The husband who demands love when it is his business to inspire it has the law on his side, and yet he is ridiculous nevertheless. Is there a better proof that the vow is only a legal fiction here, a measure of decorum?—And, on the other hand, to obtain by constraint that which has value only when it is given with joyous consent is discouraging, not to say nauseous.

I conclude that a marriage is not to be advised unless it is irresistible. Only the indispensable being should be taken for a life-companion. In this case, whatever the outcome may be, one can say to oneself, It was written, it was my destiny, God willed it, let us be resigned. As a work of art is worthless without inspiration, so an irreparable decision is worthless without a preternatural impulse. We must have the illusion that God has had a hand in it, that we are obeying a suggestion of Providence. There is an incommensurability between our approximate calculations and an irremediable resolution. Perpetual vows are a treason to human weakness, which can indeed presumptuously bind itself, but which ought not to be held by its own words, for it has the right to repent, and its liberty cannot be alienated forever by a single act.

*October 25, 1878.*—Exercises in intuitive ingenuity: metagrams, logogriphs, words in stars, words in which the syllables are represented by single characters, problems in dots, alphabetical problems, poetry made on given rhymes and the reverse (verses to be completed). The *Journal de la Jeunesse* (Hachette, 1878) contains a rich assortment of them. What is the use of these exercises? They sharpen one's sagacity, they train the mind in many ways, render it more attentive, quicker, more flexible, keener. Charades, anagrams, enigmas, even rebuses are not without use. The object is always the same, to cultivate the faculty of divination, the cryptological instinct. There is no harm in developing the Œdipus which is dormant in us. One should be able to face about, discover trails, contrive attacks, invent methods, change one's procedure, exhaust the possible. One who knows how to interrogate things and find out their secret is prepared for study as well as for practice. After all, this comes back to my principle, to catch the spirit of things, to turn one's mind to everything. Intelligence is the universal tool; it includes all the moulds and all the modes. A psychologist disdains nothing, and games are a mine which he takes care not to overlook.

*November 4, 1878 (10 a. m.).*—Rather a miserable night. Awakened three or four times by my bronchitis; bowels out of order. Low spirits, anxiety. It is possible that I may choke to death one of these winter nights. It is right and fitting, I see, to hold myself in readiness, and to add the last touches to the few productions which I have kept in manuscript. Then there are steps to be taken about Clarens, my will, my affairs, my correspondence, which must be arranged. Put everything in order, so as not to leave behind one difficulties, embarrassments, bothers, or anything to cause reproaches, anything, at least, to merit them. Do what you can to leave regrets and a kindly memory.

To begin with, pass the sponge over your grievances and bitternesses. Pardon everyone, judge no one, not even those who slight you and ill-treat you. See only misunderstanding in malevolence and animosity. "As much as lieth in us, let us live peaceably with all men."—On the bed of death, the mind should see only the eternal things. All the petty things of time disappear. The fight is over. It is one's privilege then only to remember the benefits one has received and to adore the ways of God. It is natural to centre oneself in the Christian feeling of humility and mercy. "Father, forgive us our trespasses, as we forgive those who trespass against us."

Prepare yourself as if the coming Easter were to be your last Easter, for your days henceforth will be brief and evil, and the omens are unfavourable.

*November 7, 1878.*—Talked with my god-daughter today about the visual illusion in still-life painting, and in this connection about the poetic and artistic illusion, which must not be confused with actual reality. The visual illusion in painting is meant to impose on sensation, while true art wishes only to charm the imagination without deceiving the eye. When we see a good portrait, we say it is *alive,* in other words, we impute to it life in addition. When we see a wax figure, we feel a sort of consternation; this immovable life gives us an impression of death, and we say, This is a phantom, this is a ghost. In this case, we see what is lacking and we demand it; in the other, we see what is given us and we give in response. Thus art addresses itself to the imagination; everything that addresses itself only to sensation is beneath art, almost outside art. A work of art must set the poetic faculty working in us, it must induce us to imagine, to complete the perception. And we only do this in imitation of the artist and at his instigation. Copy-painting, realistic reproduction, pure imitation leaves us cold because the author of it is a machine, a mirror, an iodized plate and not a soul.

Art lives only in appearances, but these appearances are visions of the mind, dreams arrested and fixed. Poetry represents for us a nature that has become consubstantial with the soul, for it is only an aroused recollection, a vibrant image, a form without weight, in short, a mode of the soul. The most objective productions are only the expressions of a soul that objectifies itself better than others, forgets itself more completely in the presence of things, but they always express a soul; and from this comes what one calls style. Style may be only collective, hieratic, national, when the artist is still the interpreter of the community; it tends to become personal in proportion as society comes to terms with individuality and wishes to see it flower.

Originality is individuality in style, as style is the psychological mould of the objects that are presented, or rather the involuntary trace of the moulder.

*December 6, 1878 (11 p. m.).*—Reading: von Loeper *(Goethe's Faust)*.

Goethe is treated here like an ancient, or like Dante. Apotheosis of the man and the work. Introduction, commentaries, bibliography. Variants. And yet nothing suggests less than *Faust* a creation that is all of a piece, in which everything holds together in a single mass. It is a cathedral, rather, built over sixty years and without an original plan, without strict unity. It is not a tragedy, but a mystery-play. And this mystery, which is supposed to represent human life, and the struggle of the finite being with the infinite, leaves an impression of something lacking. Faust is not the central man, for he has little heart and little conscience. His enthusiasm is of the head, he is a powerful intelligence, he is not a great soul, a beautiful character, a hero or a martyr. This thinking organization is permeated with dryness and egoism.—His reception into the Christian Paradise does violence to logic, it is an arbitrary conclusion, a *deus ex machina*.—He is saved by the intercession of women; but he has not deserved it. Faust is an Abelard, a Paracelsus, a Bruno, an enchanter and a seeker, but he knows nothing of humility, sacrifice, charity, holiness. He is outside the religious sphere and even the moral life, for he is indifferent to duty and to his own duty. This is the glacial side of this work of genius. One can be interested in Faust, because he has suffered; but one cannot love him, for his ideal is neither pure nor beneficent.

*December 24, 1878 (noon)*.—Fine weather, brilliant and hard. Last lecture on Spinoza, clear, compact and, I think, convincing. Students never guess how many things are needed to produce such a simple thing as the complete exposition of a philosophical subject in three quarters of an hour, with an appreciation of it, together with its subsequent history and the reason for its influence. Everything seems natural, easy, insignificant to the inexperienced, and it no more occurs to them to be grateful for the simple, concise clarity of a lecture than for the light of day. To be just, one has to compare, one must have some conception of the labour of exegesis, reduction, construction, mensuration, information which the task implies. And how much of this occurs to them? They are ingenuously ungrateful, as all schoolboys are, and as we all are, as children to our parents, as men to society, as worshippers to our Church, as mortals to our God. We are conscious only of our merits and our claims, not at all of the things that are freely granted to us. Those who are spoiled never perceive it until the favour ceases and privation begins.

*December 28, 1878*.—Attempted yesterday a little *impetus philosophicus*, to speak with Bacon. This is a glimpse into the Infinite in mathematics by means of the variations of a triangle. By this, one easily reaches infinity to the fourth power. These little experiments should not be useless to the mind, for they habituate it to precision, complete analysis, the exhaustive exploitation of a subject.

If the most elementary of finite forms opens upon the infinite twenty-three doors at the outset, and afterwards many more, one may say:

> *L'infini nous entoure: il est si près de nous,*
> *Qu'un enfant même peut l'entendre.*

To become aware of the meaning of limits is to emerge from the common grossness, which sees only the wholesale and the more or less and lowers everything to its own stature.

In reality, the poetic, the immense, the sublime are on all sides, but people rarely know how to see them. Thus the Jews knew only two or three sacred numbers (7, 12, 40), but Pythagoras saw that number, that is, all numbers, had a divine meaning, a symbolic value, and contained a sacred mystery. Thus Leibnitz saw a monad in the meanest particle of matter, and this monad is the key of theology itself. It is our dullness that makes life dull . . .

*January 5, 1879.*—Try to look at yourself from the outside, and even from a distance, and answer this question: Why have so many women's hands been held out to you? Why has so much sympathy been felt, on so many sides, for you?—What is surprising about it? First, you understand and like women; and, in the second place, you need them. You do them good, and they return it. There is nothing marvellous in mutual attraction when there is mutual benefit. Affinity is only the translation of a harmony. Still, your inclination is naturally aesthetic, disinterested, cordial, while masculine love, as a rule, is a form of appropriation; it wishes to possess, to subject, to enchain, to monopolize what it loves. It is the roughness of the usual thing that makes your way seem singular. Platonic love, spiritual love is indeed a possibility, I should rather say a reality; but it appears to be very rare. Sexual love alone is understood between the two sexes, and people think they dignify this love by making it jealous and exclusive. They reserve for the future life the holy love, the angelic attraction, which is founded on admiration. Why this postponement? Is it not a divine law that attachment is proportional to perfection? Is a divine law not eternal? Is there any reason why an eternal law should not be applied without delay?

*January 10, 1879.*—I am depersonalized so easily that I confuse myself momentarily with other people; my own way of being is lost in a crowd, and I cease to be aware of my individual existence, because my individuality interests me no more than its analogues and congeners. I like to be conscious of all life, and if my own life attracts my curiosity in a measure it is simply because it is more at my disposal and more accessible for me to study. In my own eyes I am only a laboratory of phenomena, a psychological sample of mankind. It pleases me to have myself at hand as a subject for experiment and observation, but the almost universal craving to set one's little Self up over things and people, to enlarge its sphere of domination and property, to make a great career for it, to make it important, powerful, famous, this instinct is almost foreign to me; I know it only under the negative form, a repugnance to the violation of my nature or my independence, the dislike of injustice, trickery and oppression.—That ardour of the Self to invade and conquer, which is thought to be characteristic of all mankind, is only a more or less general fact, like gluttony and lewdness. It is not in the essence of the species, nor in its ideal. The thirst for death exists also; and the need to give oneself to something greater than oneself is not so extremely rare; truly religious natures know this well and prove it.

*January 13, 1879.*—Wasted a good deal of time looking for a newspaper and arranging my books and papers in order on my tables. Sad thoughts. I am all the time meeting with obstructions, things neglected or forgotten, errors resulting from my indolence, the weakness of my memory, my ineffectual whims; I am ashamed and grieved. Impossible even to recall what notes I wrote yesterday. A single night opens an abyss between the I of yesterday and that of today. The continuity created by the will and effort when they act together is a thing I do not know. Perseverance, constancy, pertinacity are no longer known to me except by name. My life is desultory, without any unity of action, because my actions them-selves escape me . . . Probably my mental force, employed in possessing itself in the form of consciousness, lets go of everything that usually peoples the understanding, as the glacier rejects all the stones and logs that have fallen into its crevices, in order to remain pure crystal. The philosophic mind is loath to encumber itself with material facts, with insignificant recollections. Thought clings only to thought, that is, only to itself, to psychological movement. To enrich its experience is its sole ambition. The inner study of the play of its faculties becomes its pleasure and even its aptitude and habit. Reflection becomes only the apparatus for registering the impressions, emotions, ideas that pass through the mind. It sheds things so energetically that the mind is not only divested, but even stripped of itself, and, so to speak, desubstantialized. The wheel turns so rapidly that it melts around the mathematical axis; and this alone remains cold because it is impalpable and without density.

This is all very well, but it is most dangerous.

So long as one is numbered among the living, so long as one is involved in the world of bodies, interests, conflicts, vanities, passions, and duties as well, one must renounce this rarefied state; one must consent to be a definite individual, with a name, a position, an age, an organism, a particular sphere of activity. Tempting as impersonality may be, one must come back to being a creature imprisoned in certain conditions of space and duration, an individual who has congeners, associates, friends, enemies, a profession, a country, who must be fed and lodged, must inspect his linen, pay his taxes and his tradespeople, keep an eye on his affairs, in a word, act like the first animal or the first person he passes in the street. There are days when all these details seem to me a dream, when I am astonished at the desk under my hand, at my body itself; when I ask myself if there is a street in front of my house and if all this geographical and topographical phantasmagoria is indeed real. On days like this, extension and time become simple points again. I witness the existence of pure mind, I see myself *sub specie æternitatis.*

Is it not possible to think of mind as the capacity for dissolving finite reality into the infinity of possibility? Or, in other words, is not mind universal virtuality? Or the latent universe? Considered thus, its zero would be the germ of infinity, expressed in mathematics by the double zero joined ($\infty$).

Consequence: the mind, in itself, can experience infinity; in the human individual at times arises the divine spark which permits him a glimpse of the existence of the source-being, the basis-being, the principle-being, in which all rests as a series in its generative formula. The universe is only an irradiation of mind; the irradiations of the divine Mind are more than appearances for us, they have a reality parallel with ours. The irradiations of our mind are imperfect mirrorings of the fireworks set off by Brahma; and yet our science has this control, that it can predict phenomena (astronomy); that it can engender new phenomena (chemistry), and, by explaining the past, reconstruct it (linguistics, philosophy of history).—Our errors, our dreams, our delusions are ours alone. They also engender something, the subjective world of superstitions and monsters.—Great art is great only because it has points of conformity with the divine order, with that which is (music, plastic art, poetry).

The ideal is the mind's anticipation of order. The mind is capable of the ideal because it is mind, that is to say because it perceives the eternal. The real, on the contrary, is fragmentary, it is transitory. Law alone is eternal. The ideal is therefore the indestructible hope of the better, the involuntary protest against the present, the ferment of the future. It is the supernatural in us, or rather the super-animal, the ground of human perfectibility. One who has no ideal is content with what is; he does not dispute the existing fact, which becomes for him identical with the just, with the good, with the beautiful.

But why is the divine irradiation not complete? Because it is still going on. Our planet, for instance, is in the midst of its experiences. Flora and fauna continue. The evolution of humanity is closer to its origin than to its conclusion. Well, the complete spiritualization of animality seems singularly difficult, and this is the work of our species. It is impeded by error, sin, sickness, selfishness, death, and, besides these, terrestrial catastrophes. The structure of the good life, of science, morality and justice for all has been sketched, but it is only a sketch. A thousand retarding and disturbing factors interrupt this gigantic work, in which the nations, the races, the continents all play their part. At the present time, humanity is not yet established as a physical unity, and its education as a common whole has not yet begun. All the attempts at order have been local crystallizations, the rudiments of a momentary organization. In our own time the possibilities are drawing closer together (the postal and telegraph unions, universal expositions, voyages round the world, international congresses, etc.). Science and interests bind together the great fractions of humanity which languages and religions hold apart. A year in which a network of African railways is projected, running from the coasts to the centre, joining, by land, the Atlantic, the Mediterranean and the Indian Ocean, suffices to mark a new era. The fantastic has become the conceivable; the possible tends to become the real. The planet is becoming the garden of man. Man's chief problem is to make cohabitation possible among the individuals of his species, that is, to find the balance, the right, the order of the new times. The division of labour enables him to seek for everything at once; industry, science, art, law, education, morality, religion, politics, economic relations, everything is in process of being born.

Thus everything can be reduced to zero by the mind, but this zero is a fecund zero; it contains the universe, and, in particular, mankind. It is not more fatiguing to the mind to follow the real in the innumerable than to become aware of possibilities. $\infty$ can emerge from $0$ or return to it.

*January 14, 1879.*—Bad headache. Everything vies with everything else to rub me the wrong way and set me on edge: the letters I receive, a lecture to give (which is not ready), the wood, which does not burn, the prospect of a disagreeable meeting over which I have to preside this week, an accident to my unmentionables, and, worse than anything else, a feeling of embarrassment, or rather humiliation, an irreparable mortification. Reflecting on it, I recall that, except for M. de Banville, not one of the Parisians to whom I have written or sent something during the last two years has even acknowledged the receipt of my letter; and even my acquaintances, Edmond Scherer, for instance, Victor Cherbuliez, Coppée, Taine, Pelletan, have taken the same attitude. Even Rambert, even Tallichet [1] no longer pay any attention to me. Is not this sinking rather low? It appears that I have become an idiot, that I am nothing, at least in the unanimous opinion of all these people. The discovery is certainly not very pleasant, and a little revolt is permissible, since one is allowed twenty-four hours for cursing one's judges.—But this will not last.

I perceive with a certain curiosity how one's temper can grow peevish. This is the indirect way in which mortified self-esteem takes its revenge. The self is not content to remain depressed, and it treats itself to a little fit of sullen overbearingness. It has suffered, it wants to cause suffering. It has been hurt, it hurts. And all this instinctively, by a sort of reflex action. How triumph over a bad temper? First, by humility: when one knows one's weakness, why be irritated when others point it out? It is not very kind of them, of course, but they have the truth on their side. Then by reflection: in the end, one remains what one is, and if one has thought too highly of oneself, this is merely an opinion to be modified. The incivility of our fellow-beings leaves us just as we were.—Especially by forgiveness: there is only one way not to detest those who hurt and wrong us, and that is to do them good. One surmounts one's anger by kindness. One does not change them by this victory over one's own feelings, but one subdues oneself. It is vulgar to be indignant in one's own behalf; one should feel indignation only for great causes. One only removes the poisoned dart from one's wound

[1] Eugène Rambert (1830–1886), painter of the Vaudois Alps, critic and literary historian, professor at Zürich.—E. Tallichet (1828–1911), director of the *Bibliothèque universelle* at Lausanne.

with the balm of silent and watchful charity. Why allow ourselves
to be embittered by human malignity? Why permit ingratitude,
jealousy or even perfidy to irritate us? There is no help in recriminations, complaints and punishments. The simplest thing is to wipe
them out. Grievances, rancours, anger becloud the soul. Man is an
administrator of justice; but there is one evil which he is not bound
to punish, that of which he is the victim. For these evils one must
have a method of healing. Fire purifies everything.

> *Mon âme est comme un feu qui dévore et parfume*
> *Ce qu'on jette pour le ternir.*

*January 19, 1879.*—For all of us the world is only an occasion
for asserting ourselves, and in this sense all minds are subjective;
but the difference is that some have many more free notes in their
keyboard and can reproduce melodies outside themselves, denaturing them less, while the rest resound like a bell or a drum or a
tuning-fork, that is, with the same sound, more or less intense, but
monophonous. Polyphony and polychromy are the signs of the critical
vocation. The compact, massive, unisonorous, unicoloured minds
may be original and may have value in themselves, but they are
made to be classified and not to classify, to be deceived, not to
understand.

A cat may look at a king: this is the excuse of all the dull wits
when they try to judge a fluid mind. Have I not heard absurdities
enough about Victor Cherbuliez? But is the Bœotian mind ever
aware of itself? Is it ever modest enough to admit its own incompetence, does it ever possess the instinct to hold its peace? No. Were
it otherwise, it would already be on the borders of Attica; it would
be breathing the air of Cithæron. To suspect one's own stupidity
is to have half escaped it. To condemn oneself is to be ready for
conversion. To be ashamed is to be oneself no longer. Does a goose
ever blush for being a goose?

It is kindness that voluntarily limits a too exacting eye. The intellect left to itself would be pitiless, for the great mass of minds are like a menagerie or a book of natural history. Everything is plebeian to the subtle mind. To the Olympian mind, everything is a bog and a bore. It is kindness that places a screen over the sharp electric rays of perception, kindness that refuses to illumine the deformities and miseries of the intellectual hospital, kindness that waives the classification of one's neighbour on the basis of stupidity, or rather of discernment. Kindness has a fear of privilege; it prefers to be humble and charitable; it strives not to see what stares it in the face, the imperfections, the infirmities, the deformities of the mind, and all its rheumatic disorders and blindnesses. It throws a hood over sagacity in order not to make others needlessly suffer; and, when sagacity has beheld, kindness gets in the first word and draws attention to some pretty shell on the barren sand, a spangle in the commonplace mass, a sprig of sweet marjoram in the sheaf of dry, odourless straw. Its pity assumes an air of approval. It triumphs over its distastes in order to encourage and liberate.

It has often been observed that Vinet praised weak things. It was not because of any illusion in his critical feeling; it was charity. "The smoking flax shall he not quench." And I add: Let us never cause useless sorrow. The cricket is not the nightingale. Why tell it so? Let us enter into the idea of the cricket: this is more novel and more ingenious. It is the counsel of kindness.

The intellect is aristocratic, kindness is democratic. In democracy, the equality of self-loves in an inequality of merits creates a great practical problem. Some people escape from it by muzzling the freedom of their minds with prudence; others by correcting their perspicacity with a kind forbearance. A friendly good will seems to be surer than circumspection. It wounds nothing, it kills nothing. It is the course I have followed.

It is more amusing to strip and whip, as Boileau did; but this is to assume a right that no one possesses. Everybody has a right to live, and every creature after its own kind. Occasions arise when one must help everyone to develop according to his nature.—Even in the strictest intimacy, one can scarcely speak the whole of one's mind. One is bound to keep other people's secrets, even when one has discovered them and not received them in confidence. One is really the master only of one's own personal secrets; one has a right to dispose of these; one may divulge one's follies, one's deficiencies, faults, mistakes; but even this must be done only to give one's interlocutor courage and enlightenment, for one is giving him a hold over oneself, and who knows that later he will not abuse it? Charity is generous; it willingly risks itself, and, in spite of a hundred experiences, one after another, it does not take evil for granted at the hundred and first. One cannot be at once kind and crafty, or serve two masters, selfishness and love. It is good to take chances knowingly, not to resemble the clever ones of this world, who never forget their interest, who think of nothing else. One should be able to be deceived. This is the sacrifice that mind and self-love must make to conscience. This is the account to be opened with the soul, it is what the children of God do.

Was it not Bossuet who said: Only noble souls know how much greatness there is in goodness?

*January 21, 1879.*—Someone has just described to me Bouvier's [1] first lecture (on the Bible). As always, he tries to reconcile science and faith, and the real cosmology with the Genesis of Moses. The theologians cannot be consoled that the Bible of Nature alone has authority for science. But science does not offer an ideal; the religions give the popular ideal, and the popular ideal of life is indispensable. The best religion for us will be the one that gives us most strength and consolation.

Religion at first takes the place of science and philosophy; later it must take only its own place, the intimate emotion of the conscience, the secret life of the soul in communication and com-

[1] Auguste Bouvier (1826–1893), professor in the Faculty of Theology, preacher and writer. Amiel, who held him in high esteem as a friend, collaborated with him in various publications on the history of the University of Geneva.

munion with the divine will and the universal order. Piety is a daily
refreshing of the ideal; it restores the equilibrium of our inner
being, agitated, troubled, diverted from its course, irritated, embittered by the everyday accidents of existence. Prayer is the spiritual balm, the precious cordial that gives us peace and courage. It
reminds us of forgiveness and duty. It says to us: You are loved,
love; you have received, give; you must die, do your work; conquer your anger with generosity; overcome evil with good. What
matters the blindness of public opinion? Supposing you have been
slighted, supposing you have met with ingratitude, you are not
bound to follow vulgar examples, nor are you obliged to be successful. Do what is right for you, come what may. You have a witness,
your conscience; and your conscience is God speaking to you.

*February 1, 1879 (4 p. m.).*—A curious sight awaited me at the
Pont du Mont-Blanc. A whirlwind of several hundred gulls eddying
about downstream from the bridge, plunging into the river, rising
like rockets, crying, beating their wings, snatching in the air the
crumbs that were thrown to them; it was as giddy as a merry-go-
round in the air, without truce and without rest. For two sous
worth of fresh bread, one could amuse oneself for half an hour.
Twelve majestic swans sailed about through this aquatic populace,
annoyed by its feverish turbulence and insolent voraciousness. A
few bold sparrows ventured out on to the abutment of the bridge,
to catch some forgotten crumb. This swarm of gulls was like a
cloud of snow and carried the imagination away to the Norwegian
fiords. The wings are indeed a little grey above and black underneath; but the white dominates. It was like flying hoar-frost.

*February 25, 1879.*—High north wind all night; and now the
snow. Nature has been positively convulsed and frantic of late. The
hurricane of February 20 is to begin again tomorrow; the weather-
bureau in New York predicts it. This fury is coming to us from
Bermuda. The scientist nowadays has the whole planet under sur-
veillance, but, although he can denounce the runaways, he cannot
yet clap them back into prison. He says: Look out ahead there!

Take your precautions! And this is something gained. Evils that are foreseen can be partially allayed and repaired. Shutting down the hatches and clewing up the sails is equivalent to clipping the tempest's claws. The essential thing is not to obstruct an external phenomenon, but to preserve oneself from it. What matter if it hails, so long as one can get the harvest under shelter, or, more simply, if the losses themselves are covered by insurance. It is not necessary to steer the wind, if one can steer oneself in spite of the wind. Let Nature follow her laws, provided that, by neutralizing one of these laws by another, man can shield his desires and forward his ends. Let the wind blow, if, with steam, we can travel in the face of it; if, with electricity, we can dispense with steam; if, with chemistry and mechanics, we wield forces that set at defiance the forces without. The hurricane for us is a broken-winded charger; the telegraph outstrips it by three or four days over spaces that are relatively restricted, such as the breadth of the Atlantic. They can print in San Francisco an address delivered in London eight hours before London hears it. The latest news from Afghanistan comes to us by way of New York, having travelled three times the distance of the direct route.

*March 3, 1879.*—The criterion of sound politics is social utility, the public good, the greatest realizable good; empty, braggart, harebrained politics sets out from the idea of the rights of the individual, abstract rights the extent of which is affirmed, not demonstrated, for the political rights of the individual are precisely what is in question. The revolutionary school always forgets that rights without duties are like a pair of compasses with only one leg. It inflates the individual by filling his mind with himself and what others owe him, by saying nothing of the corollary and extinguishing in him the capacity to devote himself to a general work. The State becomes a shop, and interest is its principle (English utilitarianism); or else it is an arena in which each gladiator works only for his own honour (French radicalism). In both cases, egoism is the motive force of the individual.

The Church and the State should open two complementary careers to the individual. In the State, the individual should merit, that is, win his rights by services; in the Church, he should do good, effacing his deserts by willing humility.

Americanism evaporates the moral substance of the individual, who subordinates everything to himself, believing that the world, society and the State are made for him, to serve him for a punching-bag. There is something repugnant in this disparaging, freebooter's point of view. This absence of human gratitude, of the spirit of deference and the instinct of solidarity chills me. It is an ideal without beauty and without nobility.

A consolation. Equalitarianism counterbalances Darwinism, as one wolf holds another wolf at bay. But both are strangers to duty. Equalitarianism upholds one's right not to be eaten by one's fellow-creature, Darwinism establishes the fact that the big eat the little, adding, so much the better. Neither the one nor the other knows love, fraternity, goodness, pity, voluntary submission, the giving of the self.

All forces and all principles act simultaneously in the world. The result, on the whole, is good. But war is ugly, because it throws all truths out of joint and presents only errors in battle against errors, parties against parties, that is to say halves of beings and monsters against other monsters. An aesthetic nature cannot adjust itself to this spectacle, it wishes to find harmony, not the perpetual grating of dissonances. It is impatient for this union, which is perpetually deferred. It loathes the scene-shifting, it longs for the theatrical illusion; it asks for the meal and wishes to have done with the culinary preparations. Every issue of the daily paper is a photograph of this confusion of Babel, in idea, interest, tendencies. —One must indeed accept noise, hatred, fraud, crime, the ferocity of interests, tenacity of prejudices as the condition of human societies; but the philosopher sighs over it and cannot give it his heart.

*Le combat du volvon avec le vibrion*

nauseates him, for he must needs look at history from above and often hear the music of the eternal spheres.

*March 13, 1879.*—Reading: Hermann Grimm (*Goethe Studied as One of the Great Types of the Poetic Imagination*).

These chemical analyses of genius always make me laugh, for they imply the possibility of remaking what they decompose. And the characteristic of genius and even of life is precisely the coalescence, the fusion of elements that chemistry can only disaggregate. Science, which is admirable in the domain of quantitative, ponderable, measurable things, is absurdly clumsy in the things of the soul, the heart, taste. It is like a blacksmith trying to forge a butterfly's wings or the eyes of a fly. This pedantic heaviness is more characteristic of the German theoreticians than of anybody else.

> *Par la sambleu, Messieurs, je ne croyais pas être*
> *Si plaisant que je suis.*

One must be very naive to believe that one is still doing what one set out to do when one has destroyed the phenomenon which one had set about explaining. One might as well butcher a rabbit to find the secret of life in its stomach. People who undertake the fabrication of talents are in the same boat. What is taught is never anything more than secondary, what is learned is not talent, but the art of using it. No one ever knows anything well except what he has found out for himself. The mature talent kindles budding talents, but by its example, not by precepts.

One understands only what one repeats in oneself, only what one finds in one's own nature. Psychological mimesis is the art of penetrating. Nothing can replace divination, intuition, and the numskulls deceive themselves if they think they can force an entrance anywhere with their counterfeit keys, their ladders and their dark-lanterns. They cannot even understand the first little girl they meet, the merest scrap of a child clinging to its nurse's skirts. The obtuse are obtuse everywhere, armed though they may be with spectacles, scales and scalpels. Do not the grammarians pulling the poets to pieces present a ridiculous spectacle? Incompetence, in a word, is to be found everywhere because the presumption of the dull knows no bounds. In all matters, one must belong to the family, the house, the trade, one must have an instinct and a feeling for the thing to speak of it without nonsense and verbiage.

*March 15, 1879.*—Reading: Stahl *(Les histoires de mon parrain);* Legouvé (a few chapters of *Nos Filles*). These writers have wit, grace, gaiety and charm, as well as courtesy and manners. Their intention is to show that virtue is not so insipid, and that good sense is not so tiresome. They are persuasive moralists and captivating story-tellers. They are working for the elevation of France, and they arouse an appetite for the good. There is a danger, however, in this gracefulness. A sugary morality certainly passes muster, but one fears that it passes muster because of its sugar and that moral feeling gains nothing by it. The sybarites tolerate a sermon that is graceful and delicate enough to flatter their literary sensuality; but it is their taste that is charmed; their conscience is not awakened. They are soothed, but they are not moved; their vanity is satisfied, but their principle of conduct has not been reached.

To moralize by diverting people, to instruct by amusing are both methods that are greatly favoured in ages of weakness, but they are probably both illusions. Enlivening, instructing and moralizing are forms of writing that can be mixed and associated, no doubt; but one must be able to separate them in order to obtain real and full effects. The well-organized child, as a matter of fact, does not like mixtures that depend on artifice and trickery. Duty requires obedience, study demands application, play requires nothing but good temper. To convert obedience and application into a pleasant game is to unman the will and the intelligence. Nature has given the child bones and teeth; why refuse him the opportunity to masticate and toil? Do you not wish him to become a man?

Conclusion. These efforts to make virtue fashionable are laudable enough, but, if they do honour to the writers, they show the moral anæmia of society. There is no reason to make such a fuss about giving unspoiled stomachs a taste for bread.

*March 17, 1879 (11 p. m.).*—Reworked my lecture on Positivism. A feeling of tedium every time I touch upon this sham doctrine, as meagre in new perceptions as in interesting results. This Comte has not a trace of verve, wit, fecundity. He has only one idea, spun out with an unbearable prolixity, and this idea is not exact, it is not new, it is not great. When one takes away from Comte what he has taken from Hume, from Broussais, Saint-Simon, Turgot, nothing is left but the diffuse, pretentious litter of vulgar empiricism. When one has plucked this mock-peacock, one finds merely an ordinary capon, puffed up with itself. It is irritating. And the admiration that people have for the thing and for the man tires one's patience, like every stupid exaggeration.

*March 23, 1879 (noon).*—Reread this note-book. It shocks me with its many repetitions. But these repetitions have a useful side; they are verifications, checks. One who wishes to please avoids them; but one who is concerned only with the truth tolerates them. Barometric, hygrometric notations, etc., are all they are able to be: they follow the variations of the weather and the uniformity of its variations. They represent only what is, and trace out no invented curves. Art strives to do something new, for fear of satiety; observation notes the real as it presents itself.—Perhaps there are one or several constants in these daily variations of thought and feeling: these are to be drawn from them later. Are there seasonal or yearly variations, variations from period to period? An open question. Will I ever have the time to reread these fifteen thousand pages or derive some scientific use from them? It is doubtful. They will at least have helped me to live, like all the other hygienic habits, bathing, rubbing oneself down, sleeping, eating, walking, etc. The principal usefulness of the Journal is in reëstablishing the integrity of the mind and the equilibrium of the conscience, that is, one's inner health. If, in addition, it is instructing or diverting, this is

a good thing, but supererogatory. If it sharpens the analytical temper, if it keeps the art of expression in good repair, so much the
better; but it could dispense with these advantages. If it serves as
a memorandum of one's life, this again is accessory.

*March 31, 1879 (11 p. m.).*—It is hard to change suddenly one's
occupation and way of living and pass from a historical course to
a theoretical course. The momentum one has acquired and the
force of inertia impede this mental inversion. To facilitate the
crisis, I have had all the books I have used this winter taken out
of my room, and I have spent two hours putting in order and filing
all the loose pages that compose the course I have just ended. I
have swept up all the old memories, and I have opened again the
books and the notes relating to my summer course. But here, as
always, struck with a desolating impression, that of my penury and
insufficiency, my emptiness, my antiquated state. I seem to know
nothing any more; I feel as if everything should be turned upside
down, done over again, cut anew and out of whole cloth. On the
other hand, I feel that this would be rash and absurd, that I have
not the time for it, that it is better to use what is ready-made,
perfect what has been sketched out, rectify what has gone stale,
fill out whatever gaps there are. I should really have liked to undertake a few new researches, even though these monographs were not
interrelated; but a course must present a subject in its unity, in
its entirety. So here I am tossed between these two methods which
lead to quite different plans. Which one is better? One of the
methods advances science, the other seems more necessary to students. One way tends to discovery; with the other, one gains an
assured hold over a conquered territory, maps it and occupies it.

*April 1, 1879 (6 p. m.).*—Psychologized all day. Carried the crisis
through, passed into this mode of thought, reawoke in myself the
aptitude, the interest and the memory necessary for this kind of
research. This crisis resembles the phenomenon of conversion. It is
a matter of breaking off one's habits, assuming the vesture of a
new man, in a word, doing the impossible, or what one supposed

to be such. This transformation, which is more than a superficial moulting or a strategic shifting of one's activity, is a violent jolt that shakes us to our foundations. One might liken it to the crisis through which an insect passes in its metamorphosis.

At bottom, it is a moral ordeal. Necessity becomes virtue. One violates one's inclination, desire is subdued by will, inertia is overcome by duty. This is something more than mechanical work changed into heat and electricity. It is the changing of the caterpillar into the butterfly.

*April 7, 1879.*—A full but lacerated life would have been better, perhaps, than an empty and barren life . . . But my life has not been barren or empty; it has been, taken as a whole, the life of a contemplative man, who has made sacrifices to duty and has known many affections. It is true that filial, conjugal and paternal love has not been granted him; but he may have known love and friendship all the better. He has kept passion at arm's length; but sympathy, kindness, disinterested and helpful charity, Platonic love, human warmth of heart have abounded in his life. Will he complain of his portion? No. If others' are more enviable and attractive, his has been that to which the wise aspire. Disinterested activity, sweet affections, leisure and freedom, meditative peace, these are what he has had. His real independence has been greater than that of anyone else. He has never had to submit to another's will, and he has felt himself his own master since he was thirteen years old. The place allowed to his fancy and the free disposition of his time has been enormous. The inner life has opened all its avenues to him. He has been able, for his recreation, to write fifteen thousand pages of reflections in which revery meditates at its pleasure. All this counts for something.

*Easter Monday, April 14, 1879 (8.30 a. m.).*—O joy, I have slept and returned almost to a normal state. The roofs are white, winter has returned, too, but what of that? Health is the real sunshine. Let us quickly gather a few lessons from the harsh experience of these three days.

I am eminently destructible. A slight disorder at one point very quickly jeopardizes the whole machine. I have therefore very little power of resistance, very little vitality, properly speaking.

Once caught in the meshes of pain, I never expect to get out again. I have very little of that force one calls hope; I look for nothing from the future, I appeal to no god of succour, and I have no greater faith in the doctor. I withdraw into a Stoic apathy that is like a gloomy desolation, for all seems lost to me.

Sickness shames me more than anything else; it humiliates me, like a physical defect, like an absurdity, like a swollen eye or a twisted shoulder. This means that I do not count on the compassionate charity of my fellows, and that I fear their commiseration, such as it is.

Sickness incapacitates one, and I have a horror of giving an opening to the mockery of inferiors or equals.

Sickness makes one dependent, and I dread dependence; I am afraid of being a burden, of being troublesome, repulsive, tiresome. I can imagine only one pleasant case, that of a surgical accident, a soldier's wound, cared for by a loving woman; here the ailment is aesthetic and the convalescence delightful. But with all the ugly and disfiguring ailments, the chronic afflictions, my instinct is that of a cat, to conceal myself and disappear.

Sickness is a blow to our freedom and our dignity, and for this reason it is especially dreadful to the man of leisure and ease. To imagine it as sent by a jealous or paternal deity is an ingenious stratagem of the human consciousness, which ennobles it in order to fight with it, as a knight would arm a serf in order to be able to cut his throat. In reality, nature is heartless, without humour or honour, and it pleases her to devour everything that does not, with might and main, defend itself against death.

It is too late to set one's affairs in order if one waits for the signal, sickness; for, if some sicknesses arrest only the outer activity, others strike at once the nerves and even the brain, that is, they suspend thought, clear perception, memory and the sense of justice.

Sickness ought to teach attentive kindness. We must realize that many people are sick without admitting it, that many have their secret thorn, their unknown splinter, their hidden ordeal, the hair-shirt and cross of which others are unaware, and that not to take this into account is to run the risk of being cruel. Even those who are well and cheerful will not always be so, their triumph may well be short-lived. Eternal prosperity is not the property of our species; it is the unique good fortune of one out of ten million mortals. Therefore let us enter whole-heartedly into the human condition. We are members of a suffering race, which is obliged to struggle endlessly against hunger, cold, want, ignorance, brutality, sickness, passion, injustice, and must be content with the least evil and the slightest progress, expecting for everyone defeat and destruction. Let us pay our tribute of pity and labour. Let us collaborate with a patient piety in the work of the species. Let us give a little joy to all these galley-slaves of existence, all these creatures condemned to death. This is our reason for being and our reward as well.

*April 21, 1879.*—Why all this synonymy in the pages of my Journal? The instinct that impels me to this luxuriance must be rather complex. I dare say the desire to refurbish my vocabulary, to note all the details and aspects of the thing, to grope after the essential characteristic, are concomitant causes of this terminological luxuriance. Perhaps this luxuriance has its disadvantage: it disperses the mind and takes away its precision. Perhaps I ought to impose on myself, for two weeks every month, the discipline of excluding all synonymy. Three almosts do not take the place of the exact stroke. This latter is unique. My ordinary method envelops the subject and revolves around it; the other method strikes at the centre and marks the characteristic feature. It would be good to have both methods at one's disposal so as not to be the slave of either or contract any bad habit. It is true that in the Journal the pen does not keep an eye on itself, but capers along at its natural gait; but it would be better if it had all the gaits. Besides, it seems to me that this flexibility is within my powers and, further, within my range of taste. Manner tires me; when I let it have its way, it is because I am lazy. The one style that pleases me is the style of the thing itself. Yes, but the difficulty lies in one's previous habits. Instinct avoids everything that is unknown to it, for breaking one's path is always hard. How many literary forms I have neglected, gay narration, connected reasoning, soaring improvisation, light criticism, eloquence, that is, the substantial and the pleasing! My habitual form is desultory or laborious; it lacks grace and playfulness. Why? Because these qualities are the result of conversation, and Geneva has condemned me to the meditative silence of the monologue.

*April 27, 1879.*—My listlessness is rather acquired than original. Despair is an old story with me; so is the preference of reflection to action. Hamlet's affliction is indeed my affliction, too. It is also the tendency of a whole group of German thinkers, and the Buddhistic basis of Schopenhauer's doctrine. Animal impulsion and will are inferior to thought.

*May 5, 1879.*—It is only in self-defence that I think of the wilful misunderstanding with which people judge me. Were I not on my guard, I should forget every grievance and lose my dignity by doing so. The need to be on the defensive makes me do violence to my nature. By taste, I prefer the good-natured geniality that keeps no record of any unfavourable observation; and, appearances notwithstanding, this Journal is a hygienic process for returning to the indulgent point of view. My pen relieves my pain. Confiding to myself disburdens my heart. And I am never more disposed to open a new account with those who have annoyed me than when I have closed these pages. The truth is, at bottom, that, having small hopes of changing things or people, and liking neither complaint, which is useless, nor reproach, which aggravates the evil, I labour only to change my impression and to recover my balance. Annoyances and chagrins put the soul in the subjective state; soliloquy brings it back to the impersonal state. Is not this the rhythm of my days?

The world agitates me and disturbs me, and I reconquer serenity as best I can, now through contact with true affection, now by meditation. I do not wish to accuse or blame anybody, I do not have to apologize, I aspire only to find calm again and to return to good will. Supposing that I am mistaken about the people and things of which I have occasion to speak; even supposing that the sufferings are illusory and the injuries imaginary; the result would still remain good and legitimate, inasmuch as it means the cure of these little woes and the return to the objective state. Thus it is not a question either of prosecution or defence, for there is neither audience nor tribunal. It is a question of daily therapeutics, or, more simply, ablution. One purifies one's body of the dust of the road; why not purify one's soul of the contact with human uncleanliness? Thus one takes up the march again, having cast behind one everything that is not worth remembering. It is an indirect application of the biblical precept: Let not the sun go down upon your wrath. It is a more prosaic form of the evening prayer.

*May 6, 1879.*—Magnificent day. Impression as of Athens, passing the Place Neuve. Flood of light, joy to the eyes, beautiful architectural forms, under the limpid azure dome. Lightness of being, nervous alacrity, soaring thought. I thought I was young, I felt like a Greek.

> *J'ai sur l'Hymète éveillé les abeilles,*
> *C'est là, c'est là que je voudrais mourir!*

O Pallas Athene, you have appeared to me, and I have been carried away in rapture.

*May 22, 1879 (Ascension Day, 8 a. m.).*—Magnificent and delightful weather. Lightness of being. Gaiety out of doors and indoors. Soothing light, limpid blue of the air, birds warbling; to the very sounds in the distance there is nothing that has not something young and springlike in it. This is a rebirth, indeed. The Ascension of the Saviour of men is symbolized by this blossoming of nature,

rising to meet the sky . . . A salvo of bells. The morning sunbeams
dance on the chairs, on the rugs, bringing to light a garden-bed of
colours. The wood of the floor, the subtle hues of the hangings, the
folds of the curtains smile and offer a bouquet of fresh, velvety
tones, soft and bright, gladdening the eye. The ear and the lungs
likewise have their luxurious feast. The character of all these united
sensations is a sort of bland sweetness. I feel restored to the aesthetic state, from which I have been estranged so long. My soul
looks out through all its windows. Forms, contours, tints, reflections,
tones, contrasts and accords, the interplay and harmony of all these
things strike and ravish it. There are times when it is good to live
on the periphery; it is refreshing. There is joy dissolved in the
atmosphere. It is May in all its beauty. It would be almost a sin
to reject its advances, and to imprison one's heart in cloistral
severity.

In my court-yard, the mantle of ivy has turned green again, the
chestnut is fully clothed in its leaves, the Persian lilac, near the little fountain, has turned red and is about to blossom. Through the
broad openings, to the right and left of Calvin's old school, appears
the Salève over the trees of Saint-Antoine, the Voirons over the
slope of Cologny; and the three flights of steps, well spaced and
rising tier upon tier, that lead between two high ramparts from the
Rue Verdaine to the Terrasse des Tranchées, recall to the imagination some old city of the South, a glimpse of Perugia or Malaga.

*(9.45).*—All the bells of the city are chiming at once. The hour
of worship is approaching. To the picturesque, musical and poetic
impressions are added the historical and religious. All the peoples of
Christendom, all the churches scattered over the planet, are celebrating the glorification of the Crucified . . .

All the bells suddenly stop. Thrilling silence. Expectation and
almost oppression of the soul. This is the moment when worship is
a deliverance; the community belongs to the orator, and gives itself
with him to its God. And what are the other nations doing at this
moment, all those nations that have other prophets and honour

the Divinity in other ways? What are the Jews doing, the Moslems, the Buddhists, the followers of Vishnu, the Parsees? They have other days of devotion, other rites, other solemnities, other beliefs. And yet all have something in common. All have religion, all give life an ideal and expect man to rise above the miseries and the meanness of the present and the selfish existence. All have faith in something greater than themselves, all pray, humble themselves, adore; all see the Spirit beyond Nature, good beyond evil. All bear witness to the Invisible. It is through this that all the peoples are brothers. All men are creatures of longing and desire, anxiety and hope. All would rejoice to find themselves in harmony with the universal order and feel themselves approved and blessed by the Author of the universe. All know suffering and long for happiness. All know sin and beg for pardon.

In the competition of the religions, Christianity has a few advantages: it can purify and spiritualize itself. Reduced to its original simplicity, it is the reconciliation of the sinner with God, through the certitude that God loves in spite of all and that he chastises only from love. If Christianity did not create morality, it has provided a new incentive and a new force for achieving moral perfection. It has given sanctity a savour by associating it with filial gratitude.

*May 23, 1879.*— . . . I know no more inviting banquet of the spirit than to read the depths of a soul and to be initiated into an inner life. Since this is the joy that people expect in paradise, why do they so rarely give it to themselves on earth? Is it that moral brotherhood does not permit divine love, which is indifferent to sex and a stranger to sexual pleasure? This kind of loving has always seemed to me natural and easy, but people are called devourers of hearts, insatiable Don Juans, who demand nothing for themselves, who do not aim at any jealous possession and repudiate a tyrannical, exclusive passion. The affection of the soul seems to be a thing that is unclassified, unknown, unadmitted. Tender, disinterested friendship between the sexes is considered absurd and impossible.

Impossible? This it is not, for I have experienced it ten or twenty times. Absurd? I do not find it so, for it is the dream of the future.

*June 28, 1879 (noon).*—Last lecture of the course, the semester and the year. Good ending. My students applauded warmly, and I feel relieved of a great weight. Managed to condense into three quarters of an hour the material of half a dozen lectures, tied together all my threads, reduced my subject to a spherical unity and ended at the mathematical centre.

*August 6, 1879.*—If, then, the finite being has a tendency to affirm itself, to expand itself, it also has the contrary tendency, that of denying itself. The thirst for existence contains the thirst for destruction. The desire for procreation has for a correlative the taste for death. Thus, in fact, annihilation has its own voluptuousness. Radical egoism is complemented by anti-egoism, autophobia, the antipathy for self. An individual whose keyboard is complete will thus be also his own enemy and his own persecutor, a *héauton-timorouménos,* as Terence calls it. People consider this monstrous, absurd, impossible. They have not considered it carefully. They have closed too quickly the inventory of our secret impulses. Man is more complicated than they imagine. Self-love alone is apparent to our consciousness, whereas self-hatred belongs to the obscurer region. This hatred acts in us independently of us; it is the process by which nature combats the disadvantages of egoism. When this hatred is largely mollified and becomes conscious, it is called disinterestedness, detachment. When this detachment costs something and is the result of effort, it becomes renunciation, resignation, abnegation. These things are virtues, whereas self-hatred is a danger. But every virtue has an instinct for its point of departure. The instinct in question here has for its object the driving back of the self, its limitation, even its suppression. It is the principle of negation, the thirst for death.

*August 23, 1879.*—A rhymester is not a poet; an amateur is not an artist. One must be wedded to one's profession to distinguish oneself in it; one must be the perfect master of one's instrument to be in the running. As for you, you pride yourself on nothing, you try a few things to amuse yourself, but you do not get beyond the preludes, the beginnings, when you have divined the method and grasped the procedure that people follow. Your desire is not to produce but to understand, not to do but to be capable of doing. You are interested not in putting your talents to the proof but in feeling them. Thus all your activities and even your publications are only psychological exercises, analyses of the soul and manipulations of your faculties. The height of my ambition is to be one who knows human nature; it is to feel at ease in all the labyrinths of this unknown land. My mind, as fluid and impersonal as it could well be, would be content were it able to feel at home everywhere, making no claim to be the proprietor anywhere.

Thus I am neither a poet nor a philosopher, a pedagogue, a savant or a writer. I am a critic, more or less, and more or less a psychologist, that is all. And as I detest putting myself forward, the moment that sympathy is absent, I hide from the profane my true gifts, my true desires, and offer only my inoffensive fancies.

*September 9, 1879.*—Brought F. a bundle of letters from her father and mother. It struck me that they did not interest her greatly, considering the ugliness of the paper and the humble circumstances it revealed. Self-love might well have something to gain from noting its rise in the world; but it submits to the aristocratic prejudice and blushes at a modest extraction.

A naturalist has well observed, "I should be prouder of being a perfected monkey than a degenerate Adam". The popular feeling runs the other way. It envies the parvenus, while it makes fun of them. The parvenu himself is usually foolish enough to be ashamed of his origin.—At bottom, it is the two conceptions of the world that are in conflict here: that of Judaism and Gnosticism, and that of contemporary science, the former seeing in the spiritual creation a continual decay, the latter seeing in it a constant evolution, one setting out from a hypothetical perfection, the other tending towards it. Does the excellent lie before us or behind us? Is it something that has been or something that is to be? Is the best past or future? This is the question. Is the new-born child superior to the old man? Is the acorn superior to the oak, the eagle's egg to the eagle itself? This absurd supposition rests on an unconscious premise, that nothing, without defect and without error, is better than being, with errors and defects.

Nothingness is perfect, being is imperfect: this shocking sophism becomes beautiful only in Platonism, because there nothingness is replaced by the Idea, which is, and which is divine.

The ideal, the chimerical, the void should not be set so far above the real, which has the incomparable advantage of existing. Is the million you so easily imagine worth the note for a thousand which I have placed in the savings-bank? An ideal woman would certainly be charming, but she is a phantom; the woman who loves you has her imperfections, but at least you hold her in your arms. One does not live on the food one dreams of, the bread one has in prospect, the affections for which one hopes, intangible shadows.—The ideal kills enjoyment and content by causing one to disparage the present and the real. It is the voice that says No, like Mephistopheles. No, you have not succeeded; no, this woman is not beautiful; no, you are not happy; no, you will never find rest; everything that you see, everything that you do is insufficient, insignificant, overrated, deformed, imperfect. The thirst for the ideal is the goad of Siva, who only quickens life to precipitate death. This incurable desire causes the suffering of the individual and the advancement of the species. It destroys happiness in the interests of dignity. It sacrifices man to mankind. If voluntary suicide is accounted irreligious, unconscious suicide is the divine law, for the noble creatures are those that immolate themselves for a disinterested cause. In other words, God indeed desires suicide, but he desires it for himself alone. One who kills himself is a deserter in his eyes. But that each generation should be consumed for the generation that follows is the rule. Only the last, for which all mankind will have sacrificed itself, or rather will have been sacrificed, will be selfish and will not be happy. Thus universal history becomes a colossal hoax. Thought is only a cause of misfortune, a fatal and even perfidious gift . . .

Well? The only positive good is order, hence the return to order; hence the return to equilibrium. Thought is bad without action, and action without thought. The ideal is a poison if it is not integrated with the real, and, reciprocally, the real becomes vitiated without the perfume of the ideal. Nothing in particular is good without its complement and its opposite. Self-examination is dangerous if it encroaches upon the out-flowing of the self; revery is harmful when it puts the will to sleep; gentleness is bad when it takes away strength; contemplation is fatal when it destroys the character. The too much and the too little are equally contrary to wisdom. Excess is an evil, apathy another evil. Energy in measure, this is duty; attraction in calm, this is happiness!

*September 24, 1879 (3 p. m.).*—Present, an hour ago, at an extraordinary phenomenon. We were making soap-bubbles with my god-daughter.[1] The suds had been renewed, and the bubbles were not dividing very well under the fan; they seemed too watery. One subdivided bubble, however, an inch in diameter, did what I have never seen before. It wandered about close to the ceiling for a long time, without coming down, then it turned pearl-colour, next it became dented and wrinkled in places, and finally seemed to be changed into a captive silk balloon, which floated in the air without losing any of its contents. At a mere motion of our lips and breath, it descended a little, then gently rose. In short, it was solidified, changed into a cocoon, an aerostat. All three of us witnessed it. After about a quarter of an hour, we wished to see the texture of this light balloon. I received it on the fan, where it remained intact, with a shape that was no longer quite spherical. After we had examined and even touched it, I wished to send it off again. Un-

[1] "After dinner, blew soap-bubbles with much success. From one bubble, I formed as many as forty or fifty little bubbles. This game is truly poetic. It demands much sleight-of-hand." (*Journal intime,* June 18, 1880.) See poem XL in the collection *Jour à jour: La bulle de savon.*

happily, the fan was varnished; the balloon stuck at one point and was torn. The tissue, exquisitely fine and silky in its wrinkles, was perfectly dry. Under my finger it became impalpable. How I should have liked to study it under a microscope!

The sum of the matter is that the water had evaporated and the meshless and poreless web of soap had made a complete globe. In short, the bubble had become solid. This metamorphosis threw us all into an awed astonishment, as a sort of miracle. We thought we had exhausted the secrets of Pompholyx, and, after two months of the most varied attempts, here was something new, here was a prodigy. It savoured of religious mystery.

> *Émus, nous croyons voir Brahma,*
> *Brahma jouant avec les mondes.*

One speaks figuratively of a dream assuming a body; here transformation was a literal fact. The bubble was altered. It lost its iridescence, its sphericity, its fragility and its transparency in changing its order of existence. To be born is to consolidate a fluid. What increases the marvel of the phenomenon is that, a moment before it occurred, Berthe said to me: "Oh, make one of those lovely bubbles solid!" The sudden realization of this assumed a fantastic character. One might have thought that magic was not unconnected with it. After it was over, I remembered that my poem began with this verse:

> *Perle que traverse le jour,*

and that it spoke of *contexture,* of *tissue* and *aerostat.* Is a poet a visionary? He fancies he is using only images, and these images become facts; these metaphors are truths. He prophesies unwittingly. He expresses nature somnambulistically. The world we regard as real is only the dream of Maya; and inspired souls are only the unconscious echoes of this cosmogonic dream. The intuitive imagination is a mode of knowledge.

*November 5, 1879.*—It is for the individual, the citizen, to judge parties, leaders, orators and to form an opinion in spite of the importunate sophistries that are clamouring around him. Oratory and the press, far from helping people to see things clearly, do their utmost to entangle people and throw dust in their eyes. Honesty is as rare a bird as impartiality. People do not want to be just; passion has a secret horror of everything that threatens to disturb it. The intelligence does not lead the will, nor does the moral conscience direct the mind; far from it, the will guides the intelligence, and passion steers the will. The intelligence is a means, an instrument, a slave, a domestic animal; it has a master, and this master is the obscure and unreflecting part of man which is called his nature. The liberty of the majority of men scarcely differs from that of the beast: it is the liberty of following one's unconscious impulsions, one's unacknowledged motives. La Fontaine knew this well.—Man is a passion setting in motion a will that drives an intelligence, and thus the organs, which have an appearance of being in the service of the intelligence, are only the agents of passion. Determinism is true of all vulgar beings; inner liberty only exists in the exceptional case and through a victory over oneself. Even one who has tasted liberty is free only at intervals and sporadically: real liberty is not therefore a continuous state, it is not an indefectible and invariable property. The opinion that is commonly held is not the less stupid. One is free only in proportion as one is not the dupe of oneself, one's pretexts, one's instincts, one's nature. One is free only through criticism and energy, that is, through detachment from and government of the self. This presupposes several concentric spheres in the self, the most central being superior to the self, being the purest essence, the super-individual form of our being, our future form, without doubt, our divine type. We are thus in subjection, but susceptible of enfranchisement; we are bound, but capable of releasing ourselves. The soul is in a cage, but it can fly about its cage. Platonism explains very clearly the nature of this emancipation.

*January 2, 1880.*—Feeling of repose, even of quietude. Silence in the house and out of doors. Tranquil fire. Well-being. My mother's portrait seems to smile at me. I am not troubled but happy over this morning of peace. Whatever may be the charm of the emotions, I am not sure that it equals the sweetness of these hours of silent composure, when one has glimpses of the contemplative pleasure of paradise. Desire and fear, sorrow and care do not exist any longer. One feels oneself existing in a pure form, in the most ethereal mode of being, namely the consciousness of self. One feels happy, in accord, without any agitation or tension whatsoever. This is the dominical state, perhaps the soul's state beyond the grave. This is happiness, as the Orientals understand it, the felicity of the anchorites, who struggle and will no longer, who adore and enjoy. I am at a loss with what words to convey this moral situation, for our tongues are aware only of the particular and localized vibrations of life; they are unfit to express this motionless concentration, this divine quietude, this state as of the ocean in repose which reflects the sky and is self-possessed in its own profundity. Things at such moments are absorbed into their principle; multiple memories are resolved in memory; the soul is no longer anything but soul and ceases to feel itself in its individuality, in its state of separation. It is something that feels the universal life, it is one of the sentient points of God. It no longer appropriates anything, it feels no emptiness. No one, perhaps, but the Yogis and the Sufis have deeply known this state of humble delight, combining the joys of being and non-being, a state that is no longer either reflection or will, that is above moral existence and intellectual existence, that is the return to unity, the reëntering into the Pleroma, the vision of Plotinus and Proclus, the desirable aspect of Nirvana.

It is certain that the Occidentals, the Americans especially, feel very differently. For them, a devouring and incessant activity is synonymous with life. They must perforce conquer gold, domination, power; they must trample upon men and subject nature. They must have quantity, detail, movement. They are ravenous for number and do not even conceive the infinite. They cling to the means and do not think for a moment of the end. They confound being with individual being, and the expansion of the self with happiness. That is to say, they do not live by the soul, they ignore the immutable and the eternal, they toil and moil on the periphery because they cannot penetrate to the axis of their existence. They are restless, strenuous, irritable, matter-of-fact because they are superficial. What good is there in all this bustle, uproar, lust and combat? It only leads to stupefaction. Do not people see this on their death-beds? Then why do they not see it sooner? Activity is beautiful only if it is holy, that is, expended in the service of that which does not pass away. The ant-man and the bee-man are very poor specimens of man.

*January 3, 1880.*—A letter from C. R.[1] This kind friend is merciless. He feels that my thanks are not warm enough. He still prefers the collection of 1874 to the one that has just been published. He maintains that to make concessions to the publisher is to sin against the Holy Spirit of poetry, etc.—Sensitive as a woman and tenacious in his impressions, he is a little difficult in correspondence. I try to reassure his hyper-delicate susceptibilities. The solitary life has two major disadvantages: it makes one touchy beyond measure and it dulls one's good sense. My kind C. R. is a sage in his disinterestedness, but he isolates himself too much from the public and the world. That will injure, it already injures his taste, which leans to the side of eccentricity and misanthropy. When I see him clinging to

---

[1] Charles Ritter (1859–1905), an old pupil of Amiel's who called himself his "disciple", and who was one of his most faithful friends. Amiel had thought for a while of bequeathing to him the MS of the *Journal intime*, and of naming him as one of his testamentary executors. "Let me tell you one more thing," wrote Charles Ritter to M. Edouard Schuré in 1883, "and that is my great admiration for Amiel's *Journal*. A revelation, as I live! Who would ever have thought it? You had an inkling of it, perhaps: not I. It is one of the sweetest and most beautiful books I have ever read." Amiel's name frequently appears in the collection of letters: *Charles Ritter, ses amis et ses maîtres*, published by his brother, Eugène Ritter, Lausanne, Payot, 1911.—The published collection of which Amiel speaks here was *Jour à jour, poésies intimes*, Paris, Fischbacher, 1880.

the "Grumbling Epistle" and the "black" pieces, which I have eliminated, I feel worried. He has a weakness for what I consider the
least good among my writings. Which of us is wrong, he or I? Is
the literary revision to which I have subjected my pieces a mistake?
I think I am right poetically, but he may be right psychologically. . . .

It is a curious sensation to be obliged to defend oneself against
one's disciples; it is embarrassing to dash off letters when one sees
them examined under a magnifying-glass, and treated like inscrip-
tions on monuments in which every character has been premeditated
and engraved for all eternity. This disproportion between the word
and its gloss, between one's winged vivacity and severe dissection,
is not conducive to one's ease of mind. One does not dare to be
ingenuous in the presence of a seriousness that attributes importance
to everything. It is difficult to preserve one's unconstraint, if one
must look twice at every phrase and every word.—Wit consists in
taking things in the sense they ought to have, in attuning oneself to
the pitch of people, to the level of circumstances; it consists in
justice, which divines, weighs and appreciates quickly, lightly and
well. Well you knew, O men of Athens, that wit plays, that the
Muse has wings! O Socrates, you knew how to jest!

*February 3, 1880.*—Death of Bersot; sympathetic article by Edmond Scherer (*le Temps*). It was a cancer of the face and pharynx
that carried off this philosopher, who stoically endured this loath-
some malady and toiled to the end without complaint. He was director of the École Normale, and was born in 1816.

*February 6, 1880.*—Read the four addresses pronounced at the
grave of Ernest Bersot. They brought tears to my eyes. There is
much more grandeur in this end of a Stoic than in the end of a
devotee, surrounded with all the superstitious rites of the Church
and the puerile incantations with which the priesthood defends its
credit and its ascendancy. Catholicism allows its business interests
to appear too plainly at every death-bed. Here everything was
manly, noble, moral, spiritual.—The Department of Public Instruc-

tion (Ferry), the Academy of Moral Sciences (Levasseur), the École Normale (Gaston Boissier) and the students (Michel), paid homage to the character of the deceased, his devotion, his constancy, his elevation of mind. "Let us learn from him how to live and die." Such obsequies as this have an antique dignity.—It is a safe wager that *l'Univers,* that tout of the clericals, will have slavered over this ceremony with its drivel, for the sacristan knows nothing but the holy-water sprinkler and cries down everything else. Pah!

*February 7, 1880.*—Frost and fog without a moment's truce, but the world looks fairy-like and has no suggestion of the gloom of which the papers speak in Paris and London.

This silver landscape has a dreamy grace, a fantastic elegance, unknown in the lands of sunshine as in those of soft coal. The trees have an air of belonging to another creation, in which white has taken the place of green. Looking at these lanes, these groves, these clumps, these arcades, this lace-work, these living candlesticks, one has no wish whatever for anything else; their beauty is original and self-sufficient, all the more because the powdered-sugar earth, the sky shading off into mist, the distances, soft and blended, form a scale of tones that charms the eye, a general effect that is full of harmony. Nothing harsh, everything velvety. In my enchantment, I repeated my walk, before and after dinner. One has the impression of a festival, and the subdued tints are, or seem to be, a sort of coquetry of winter, which has laid a wager that it can paint something without sunlight and charm the spectator nevertheless.

*February 9, 1880.*—Bad night ... My throat clogged from hyperviscosity. Owing to this I was very late getting up, blundered through my hygienic routine. A series of confusions. Now I am cold all over, my head is sluggish and my hand numb, and I am coughing like a half-dead horse ... Life flows on, without regard for the damaged ones! When the Achilles tendon gives way, when the back loses its spring, and the memory goes, one is helplessly tossed by the wave of the young, the sound of tooth, the ravenous and the healthy. *Væ victis, væ debilibus* is always the shout of the mob that springs to the assault of the good things of this world. One is always an obstacle to somebody because, however small one makes oneself, one always occupies some space or other, and, little as one envies or possesses, one is the object of somebody's envy and covetousness. Blackguardly world, world of blackguards! To find consolation, one must think of the exceptions, the noble and generous souls, the beings who wish us to endure and not to disappear, to whom we are necessary and who wish us well. And such there are, and what do the others matter!—The traveller crossing the desert feels that he is surrounded by creatures of prey thirsting for his blood. By day, the vultures hover above his head; at night, the scorpions slip into his tent, the jackals prowl around the fires of his bivouac, the mosquitoes dig at his skin with their eager needles, everywhere menace, animosity, ferocity. But over the horizon, beyond the barren sands where, worst of all, hostile tribes and human hordes wander, the traveller remembers a few dear heads, a few eyes and hearts that follow him in his dreams, and he smiles. All things considered, we defend ourselves for a few years more or less, but we are always conquered and devoured; the worm of the tomb never fails us. They who love us sometimes die before us. Destruction is our destiny and oblivion our portion.

> *Nous avons tout prévu pour fuir la mort cruelle,*
> *Mais des plaines de l'air va fondre l'hirondelle . . .*
> *La pauvre libellule, oh! ne l'envions pas!*

How near the gulf is! At the first break in my skin, I become aware of the true situation. My skiff is as delicate as a nutshell, an eggshell, perhaps. If the damage grows a little worse, I can see it is all up with the navigator. A nothing separates me from idiocy, a nothing from madness, a nothing from death. A slight flaw is enough to imperil this whole ingenious, fragile scaffolding called my being and my life. The dragon-fly is not a sufficiently frail symbol; the soap-bubble, in fact, best renders this illusory magnificence, this fugitive apparition of the little self which is all we are.

*February 11, 1880.*—Laprade has elevation, grandeur, harmony, nobility. What is it, then, that he lacks? Naturalness and perhaps wit. Hence this monotonous solemnity, this somewhat bombastic tension, this hieratic air, this statuesque bearing. He takes himself all too seriously; this muse never takes off the buskin, this royalty never removes its crown, even to sleep. The total absence of playfulness, familiarity, simplicity is a defect. Laprade is welded into his armour. Socrates and Plato were full of fun. Laprade is to the ancients what French tragedy is to Euripides, what the wig of Louis XIV is to the hair of Apollo. His majesty is factitious and wearisome. Poet-angels are liable to become bores. They are never able to say: "Nick, bring me my slippers"; one cannot depart from the decorous in their company, descend from the clouds, touch the real; their sustained sublimity exhausts and ends by irritating the simple mortal. If, strictly speaking, there is no affectation in all this, there is at least a kind of theatrical and sacerdotal pose, a professional posture, which is an aesthetic disadvantage. The true is not as handsome as all that, but it is more alive, more pathetic, more varied. Works in marble are cold. Was it not Musset who said: If Laprade is a poet, then I am not one?—The impassive are at least picturesque.

*February 23, 1880.*—All the great religious and political edifices have crime for their foundation, injustice and fraud for their masonry, and human blood for their cement.—And hosannas are always sung later over the results that have been achieved. One will never find a people making amends for its past or giving back a territory it has stolen. Modesty and conscience are things that do not belong either to nations or to churches: they always think that what they do is the will of Providence, and, consequently, that their success absolves them. Selfishness and passion, deceit and audacity preside over all history. Only the characters who are second in command preach justice, the ideal, the good, and stand for self-sacrifice. The devourers rule, the devoured do the work. The strong are the masters, the pure are the victims. The virtues of the latter are the mine which the former exploit. The guilelessness of the stockholders provides the wealth of all the promoters, bigwigs and lazy sleeping partners. Lions and foxes are the masters of the world.

*February 27, 1880.*—Translated a dozen or fourteen little poems by Petœfi. They have a strange tang. The steppes, the Orient, Mazeppa, frenzy are all in these songs, with the lash of the horsewhip behind them. What transports of passion, and what wild outbursts! What grand and savage images! One feels that the Magyar is a centaur, and that only by chance is he a European and a Christian. The Hun, with him, turns into the Arab.

*March 20, 1880.*—Reading: Cahun (*La Bannière bleue*), history of the world in the epoch of Genghis Khan, in the form of Memoirs. It is a Uighur Turk who tells the story. One sees civilization on its dark side, in all its perversity. It is the task of the nomads to sweep this corruption away.

Thus Genghis professes to be the scourge of God, and in fact he achieved the vastest empire known to history, extending from the Blue Sea to the Baltic, and from the tundras of Siberia to the banks of the sacred Ganges. He wrecked the stablest empires of the Ancient World under the hoofs of his horses and with the shafts of his archers. From the commotion into which he threw Occidental humanity, three great things arose: the fall of the Byzantine empire, and hence the Renaissance; the voyages of discovery to Asia, undertaken by both sides of the planet, by da Gama and Columbus; the formation of the Turkish empire and the preparation of the Russian empire. This tremendous hurricane, descending from the high Asiatic plateaus, felled the rotten oaks and the worm-eaten buildings of the whole ancient continent. The descent of the Mongols, those flatnosed yellow men, was a historic cyclone that devastated our thirteenth century and restored it to health. At the two extremities of the known world, it shattered the two great Chinese walls, that which enclosed the ancient Middle Kingdom and that which penned up, in ignorance and superstition, the little world of Christendom.

Attila, Genghis, Tamerlane should count in the memory of men like Caesar, Charlemagne and Napoleon. They stirred and aroused the vast racial masses, ploughed up the ethnic world, caused rivers of blood to flow and renovated the face of things. The Quakers do not know that there is a law of storms in history, just as there is in Nature. Those who curse war are like those who curse the thunder, the tempests and volcanoes; they know not what they do. Civilization tends to rot men, as great cities tend to vitiate the air.

*Nos patimur longæ pacis mala.*

Catastrophes violently restore equilibrium and brutally bring back the order that has not been appreciated. Evil punishes itself. Collapse and ruin take the place of the regulator that has not been found. No civilization can endure more than a fixed amount of abuse, injustice, corruption, shame, crime. When this measure has been reached, the boiler bursts, the palace gives way, the scaffolding falls to pieces; institutions, cities, states, empires crumble into ruins. The evil that an organism contains is a corroding virus that ends by overpowering it, if it is not eliminated. And as nothing is perfect, nothing can escape death.

*March 24, 1880.*—How much more fruitful it is to count the sands of the sea, to ransack etymologies, to study the anatomy of a plant-louse, in short, to busy oneself with real things and escape from the vacuities of opinion, the inanities of belief!—None of these religionists know what truth is, demonstrated, impersonal, permanent truth; they are somnambulists imprisoned in their infatuation, unable to distinguish between a phantom and a body, between a hallucination and a verified fact. One does not discuss things with them, one avoids them, one avoids their conversation, their clutches, their anathemas. It is impossible to convince them, tiresome to follow them, dangerous to contradict them.

*April 18, 1880.*—Why should it be hard for me to die, when I feel myself pushed aside by the whole generation that succeeds me? With the exception of two or three individual attachments, there is no work that needs me. My family, the university, my country, science, literature will scarcely notice my disappearance; and even the tokens of regret will be only a courtesy, a matter of propriety, and not a proof of grief. There is no review, no newspaper, no group, no party that will lose much in losing me. Indeed I am aware of only two hearts in which I shall leave a real void.

I have no great work in hand, I leave no child to be brought up, no principle to be defended. The world will get along very well without me. I have never had the energetic vitality that appropriates things and deifies its Self. It is easier for me than for others to be submissive in the presence of death.

Besides, fifty-eight is a presentable age, which notably exceeds the average life. Your fellow-beings will feel that you have had your share. Look at yourself with the eyes of others. Why should you regret yourself more than you will be regretted? True, you have not been able to "unpack" everything that was in you, you have not known how to adapt yourself to your environment or to find happiness in it, or to give it what would have been pleasing to it. But if your life has had this disadvantage, at least it facilitates your departure. Better to have had a full life, to have expended all the forces of your mind and heart, and to go away full of days. But for each man, the essential thing is to accept his destiny, and to be content with his privations . . .

Fate has deceived you, and sometimes you have sulked over your fate. No more mutual recriminations. One must go to sleep in concord.

*April 25, 1880.*—It is possible that, at the very bottom of my consciousness, there lies a secret discontent, a sadness, a revolt, an anguish, a doubt, which I dare not bring to light or consider. I suspect there is a hurt pride, a broken heart, an insubordination, which is ashamed to declare itself or even perceive itself. Am I neither brave, nor resigned, nor consoled? I have no hope, and I have no wish to contend with fate, or to set others a bad example, or to dash against the impossible, or to lacerate myself over the irremediable. In a word, I am in harmony neither with myself, the world or God . . . Therefore I have not peace, only the semblance of peace. There must be a depth of unacknowledged distress, of mute desolation, indefinable melancholy, beneath my calm and my detachment. Is it that life has broken its word with me? That I have missed happiness? That I have failed in my destiny? Who knows? Have I a tenacious faith in a survival of my being, a compensation for my present lot? Scarcely, indeed not at all. I feel that everything, everything escapes me, and that I shall never be happy, either here below or elsewhere. Whence could I draw my joy, how renew it? My joy rests solely on the affection of a few beings who are as fragile as I. The Christian believes that he is personally beloved by the Eternal and predestined to beatitude. He can brave evils, bereavements and death.

Belief may be more precious than truth. Truth is pitiless, belief is maternal. Science is cold to our aspirations, faith soothes them and restores us.

Is it possible, then, that the most beautiful souls are those who are most subject to error?

*May 10, 1880.*—What does this monologue signify? That revery revolves upon itself like dreams; that aimless soliloquy is a waste of time; that the whole sum of one's impressions do not produce equitable judgment or exact thought; that a journal is good-natured and puts up with verbiage, tiresome repetition, effusiveness, complaint . . .

There is only one good thing about this chatter: it evaporates one's discontent, restores the neutral state and inner balance. A further utility may be that it keeps one's hand in practice, one's literary fingering, as playing scales does with the pianist. These outpourings that have no witness or object are the mind's conversation with itself, the involuntary but not unconscious arpeggios of that Æolian lyre which we carry within us. These vibrations do not execute any piece, they exhaust no theme, achieve no melody, they realize no programme, but they render life in its intimacy. They express not a will but a sensibility, a consciousness that murmurs. And while the will fatigues, this prattling relaxes. Fatigue is born of labour and effort; relaxation comes from play and abandon.

But both are bad when they are ·followed to excess. Stop, then, To work!

*May 19, 1880.*— . . . People used to say that I was made for the domestic life, that I was eminently marriageable, but I was not so at all. I was made only for the affections, the affections of free friendship. I have never had the measure of illusion and enthusiasm that is necessary for risking the irreparable. No engagement in perpetuity has ever tempted me. Perfection alone would have reassured me, and, on the other hand, I was not worthy of perfection . . . I have made use of the ideal itself to secure me from any real captivity . . . For all the common things, good sense seemed to me sufficient. But for marriage, I saw that more was necessary, a stroke of grace, an irresistibility, a rapture, a charm, a summons. O candour! O mysticism! It was poetry that weaned me from prose, it was marriage as I saw it that dissuaded me from marriage. Inadaptibility through mysticism, through inflexibility, through delicacy and disdain is the misfortune or at least the character of my life. I have not been able to come to terms with anything or to adjust myself to anything. Wishing not to disturb either things or myself, I have merely quietly abstained from everything that was not to my taste. Independence has been my refuge, detachment my fortress. Since things could not satisfy me, I have sought to extirpate the desire by which they enslave us. I have lived the impersonal life, being of this world as if I were not of it, thinking much and wishing nothing, resigning all, save liberty.

This state of mind corresponds to what, in women, is called a broken heart; and it resembles this, in fact, for the common feature is despair. When one knows that one will never obtain that which one might have loved, and that one cannot fall back on any-thing less, then one has entered the cloister, so to speak; one has cut the Achilles tendon, shorn the golden hair that makes human life, that is, illusion, an incessant effort towards an end which one believes accessible. One lives by the law of chance, but one no longer has the thirst to live, one has lost the motive for living, the incentive to activity. One is in the state of dreams and con-templation. One is an anchorite and a revenant. One watches from the shore the waves of the great sea and the navigators struggling against the wind. One is no longer of this world, and one can scarcely even understand the naivety of the combatants, who do not foresee their disillusionment and believe that their passions of a day are to endure forever . . .

*May 26, 1880.*—All these ideal things, Country, Church, Na-tion, Humanity, Science, Civilization, Art, are visible only at a dis-tance, when one ceases to distinguish the individuals who represent them. Imagination and enthusiasm submerge all the miseries, the imperfections, the shortcomings of real and actual individuals in the great whole which they are thought to compose. Posterity and the public are two more of those beautiful myths which the mind personifies. The real fills us with irony, disdain or bitterness, and we must poeticize it to make it supportable. In order to see Chris-tianity, one must forget almost all the Christians. To recover a little faith, one must restore the nimbus which experience dissolves and disperses, one must recreate the illusion in oneself.

The critical feeling in you is so lively that all the uglinesses of men, their wretchedness, error and insufficiency leap up before your eyes and catch you by the throat. Everything that is not per-fect makes you suffer. Therefore you must have solitude to recover your balance and become indulgent again. It also helps you to forget the way of this world, in which the tail usually leads the head, force prevails over mind, the will precedes the intelligence, in which the best qualified, the most expert rarely directs, pro-nounces, organizes, executes.—It is your misfortune to be unable to bow to public opinion, to journalism, to universal suffrage, to democracy, because a lesser evil is not a good and a fiction is not a truth. All these principles that men profess are almost as harmful as they are useful, almost as false as true. You recognize, in short, only individual superiorities; collectivities are not organs either of science or wisdom. All fetishes are repugnant to you. But you are aware that this disillusioned temper is a misfortune.

One should never fall out with one's time. On the contrary, one must be grateful to the people who are willing to be legislators, doctors, administrators, teachers, journalists, etc., and tell oneself that without them things would go still worse. Any number compared to infinity becomes nil, but compared to zero it becomes something. One should condemn nothing that acts.

*May 28, 1880.*—The seesaw of the imagination and the reason is a very singular thing. I always begin with an exaggerated sensation, and by seeing things in black; I put things at their worst and anticipate the direst consequences. This is the effect of a character that is little disposed to hope and of a slightly morbid sensibility. But a step out of doors, any little diversion, giving a lecture, a walk, a meal restores my balance. I see things afresh and under another aspect, my impression is completed, my judgment becomes composed. Thus I see the disadvantages of the solitary life, of debility, a frail organization; and I must be on my guard against my first impulse, which is a fear of novelty, a refusal to investigate, irritation at being disturbed, unpleasant presentiments . . .

Do not speak out until you have looked at things three times. Distrust the pessimism of the first and the optimism of the second impression. Arrive at the truth by the elimination of the two consecutive and opposite excesses.

*May 30, 1880.*—Have I not exaggerated my independence? By refraining from touching the walls of my prison-yard, from looking my obstacles in the face, my obligations, my chances for escaping a broken heart, have I not exceeded the right of prudence and the measure of wisdom? You dread not only vain effort, but effort itself. You are weary of a combat that is endless and hopeless. You have ceased to struggle against fate, against sickness, against men, against your nature. You try to exist with the least possible friction. A valetudinarian and a disheartened man can hardly do better. But to be submissive in the presence of death and before the living is not to be heroic; it is to live from the point of view of the cloister, it is to enter the Thebaid, it is to be a bonze or a sufi. This is to exist as little as possible. It is to die to life so as to facilitate the transition to Nirvana.—Well and good, but there is no choice. When strength is gone, one must not keep the ambitions of strength; better even to abdicate in advance. "To know how to part from the state that is parting from us," said Jean Jacques, "is to be a man in spite of fate."

It would be still better to die to sin. Sin is as much not wishing what ought to be wished as wishing what is not good. To renounce may be a form of self-seeking. Pride may well be a culpable pleasure. God desires less our total renunciation than the renunciation of our self-will. He intends us to follow his path and his method rather than our own, to do what pleases him and not what gives pleasure to ourselves.

O God, dost thou dwell in the depths of my consciousness? No. There are discontents there, shames, regrets, sorrows which I dare not even arouse. There are doubts, distresses, fears, confused and unspeakable. The foundation of our virtues is not virtue. I believe that the curse of my life has been the question of sex, everything that is bound up with modesty and sensual gratification. It has tormented my days and my nights, my waking life, my dreams, my childhood, my youth and my maturity. It has troubled my conscience, heated my imagination, frightened my timidity, overwhelmed my heart, impeded my career. This physiological function, for me, has been an unending woe. A precocious marriage, or even libertinism, would have been better than continence, better than celibacy. It is woman who delivers us from impurity, because she delivers us from desire, from day-dreams and temptations. It is horribly dangerous to play the angel when one is a man, and to play the virgin when one is a male.—Nature takes a ferocious revenge from the denial of justice which one has made through cowardice or prudence.

*May 31, 1880 (8 a. m.)*—Let us not be over-nice. Subtle views remedy nothing. One has to live, whether or no. The simplest thing is not to dispute any illusion and to accept the inevitable with good humour. At the theatre one must lend oneself to the assumptions of the theatre and not act like one who is disillusioned and disgusted. Thrust into human existence, one must take it as it is, without tragic horror, without bitter raillery, without unseasonable sulkiness, without exaggerated demands; serene patience and a playful spirit are the better part. We should treat it as the grandfather treats his granddaughter, as the grandmother treats her grandson, entering into the fiction of childhood and youth, even though we ourselves are advanced in years. God himself, in all probability, looks with complacence on the illusions of the human species, when they are innocent. There is nothing evil except sin, that is, selfishness and revolt. As for error, man often changes his error, but he never escapes from it, just as he may travel without stopping but is always somewhere. One is at one point of the truth, as one is at one point of the globe. Ubiquity and omniscience are not attributes of man. Great minds foresee and foreshadow the spherical Mind, which sees everything, knows everything, envelops everything. The Mind of God is in all the modes at once and admits all possibilities at once: thus it escapes error.

Individual minds might be compared to those little spheres which the fan, dividing the soap-bubble, causes to emerge from it. They all tend to the spherical form and all tend to reproduce the colours of the prism and the image of the circumjacent world. They are only an appearance, content to be an appearance, but they realize the law. The substance they contain is almost nothing; it is a drop of water with a few atoms of soap. Their law is to round themselves out under the breath of hope, and to weave for themselves a globe with a grain of truth, developed in every direction by fantasy and illusion. The difference between pompholyxes and men is that the former are not deceived and the latter are almost always deceived. Bubbles are successful, people are not. Bubbles are spherical, people present all the deformities that one can imagine.—On the other hand, vegetables and animals, all finite beings are a series of particular cases between the empty sphere of the bubble and the full sphere of mind, between zero and infinity, between o and ∞. To become individualized is not merely to be separated from the mass, it is usually to wrinkle and shrivel the spherical form, as happens with the cells that compose an organic tissue.

Society alone represents a more or less complete unity. The individual must be content to be a stone in the building, a wheel in the immense machine, a word in the poem. He is a diminishing fraction of the family, the State, humanity, and of all the special groups formed by interests, beliefs, aspirations and work. The most eminent souls are those who are conscious of the universal symphony, those who collaborate in full accord with the vast and complicated concert which we call civilization.

The individual is only a point which becomes a circle, a cell, an organism, a life, a mind and which, through all the momentary particularizations that are necessitated by action, does not lose sight of the sphere, the whole, harmony.—He is permitted to recreate, mentally, in himself all the series, industrial, aesthetic, moral, religious, scientific, juridical, that is, to refashion rapidly his planet and even the cosmos. Every woman who gives birth to a child reproduces in miniature the series of maternities. The mind of the thinker can reproduce, in epitome, the evolution of its race, find in itself again the granite and the eozoön, the solar state and nebulous matter. The labour of humanity up to the moment of his meditation, the result of the ages, becomes the stuff of his meditation, the array of his dream. This is the analogue of the divine omnipresence. That is why the ancient formula of "man created in the likeness of the Eternal" is not untrue. The mind is a diminutive of mind. A sphere of the radius of a millimeter is a sphere, like the celestial sphere. A new-born child is to his father what his father, a simple man, is to a genius, what a human genius is to one of the arch-angelic intelligences, or what the Director of Sirius is to God, to speak in Semitic terms and in the language of piety.

The mind is capable in principle of abolishing all the limitations which it finds in itself, limitations of language, nationality, religion, race, epoch. But it must be said that the more spiritual and omnimodal it becomes, the less hold it has over others, who cease to understand it and do not know what to make of it. Influence belongs to the men of action, and for action nothing is more useful **than narrowness of mind** joined to energy of will. You must be a sword, a hammer or a cannon-ball to move men and attain a goal. The ambitious and the voracious mock the dreamers, who return their mockery with disdainful pity. Dreams are gigantic, while action is a puny thing. To captive minds belong success, renown and profit. This is enough and to spare; but they do not know the delights of liberty and the joys of voyaging in the infinite.—But I do not mean to give the preference to the one rather than to the other, for everyone is happy only after his own nature. Besides, history is made only by specialization and by fighters. Only it is not a bad thing perhaps that amid the devouring activities of the Occidental world a few souls should Brahmanize a little. The European and especially the American is a man but he is not man. The sage, who has meditated on the sphere, wishes to be conscious of man in his completeness, and all Christian civilization, for him, is still only one manner of being, a specimen to be consulted, and not humanity.

*(11 a. m.).*—Are these excursions into the Empyrean a sort of playing truant? Yes and no. Yes, if nothing is to result from them but a passing distraction for my *Wenigkeit*. No, if my profession permits me to think without an aim, since my teaching and my pen will profit from it later.—Aimless thought seems to me an indolent epicureanism, and yet revery is the mother of poetry, sometimes

597

even of discovery; it is a form of prayer, a way of breathing for the soul; it is a dilation of the being, the sport of thought, the delight of the mind.—This means that it may alternate with work, but should not take its place.—You incline to the abuse of revery, because you have a foible for the useless and because, among men, you have an unsatisfied hunger for brotherly communication. The monologue supplements the dialogue. Your natural sociability has been obliged to change its form into a scribbler's seclusion. Rather than hold his peace, a lover would tell the walls about his martyrdom. One prays, in default of a wife, a confidant, a friend; in default of prayer, one opens one's private journal. And page follows page, as, with a woman who regrets her youth, tears follow tears, soundlessly and unseen, unrepressed and without provocation.

Sometimes it seems as if I were watching my life flow away as a wounded man watches the blood flowing from his veins. This resigned apathy, witnessing the destruction of the being, without fighting against fate, suggests Mioritza, the Rumanian shepherd whose sheep preached to him. This is the disadvantage of revery; it is paralyzing in the long run. Experience discourages one. One ceases to be the dupe of hope. One becomes fatalistic like a Moslem, meek as a sheep.—One is cloyed at last with one's indolence, as with everything else, and action, duty, the urgent claim us again in turn. After the sugar, we need the salt; after immobility, walking or gymnastics; after solitude, one must return to one's fellows. Alternation for equilibrium, this is the law.

> *Il est bon de parler et meilleur de se taire,*
> *Mais tous deux sont mauvais alors qu'ils sont outrés.*

*June 1, 1880.*—Reading Stendhal, *La Chartreuse de Parme.* It is a remarkable work. It is even a type, a point of departure. Stendhal opens the series of the naturalistic novels, which suppress the intervention of the moral sense and mock the pretensions of free will. People are irresponsible; they are ruled by their passions, and the spectacle of the human passions is the delight of the observer and the pasturage of the artist. Stendhal is the novelist after Taine's heart, the faithful painter who is neither moved nor indignant, who is amused by everything, the rascal and the slut as well as the good man and the decent woman, but who has neither belief, nor preference, nor ideal. Literature here is subordinated to natural history, to science; it is no longer one of the *humanities,* it no longer honours man with a rank apart; it ranges him with the ants, the beavers and the monkeys. This indifferent non-morality encourages a taste for immorality, for the base has more savour than virtue. Vitriol is more singular than sugar, and poisoning presents more phenomena than simple nourishment.

The vice of this whole school is cynicism, contempt for man, who is degraded to the rank of the brute; it is the cult of force, indifference to the soul, a lack of generosity, respect, nobility, which is visible despite all protestations to the contrary, in other words, inhumanity. One cannot be a materialist with impunity; refined as one's culture may be, one is gross, nevertheless. A free mind is a great thing, surely, but elevation of heart, belief in the good, the capacity for enthusiasm and devotion, the thirst for perfection and sanctity is a still finer thing.

*June 7, 1880.*—I am rereading Mme. Necker de Saussure . . . The *Education progressive* is an admirable work. What measure, what justice, what reason, what gravity! How well observed it all is, how well thought and well written! This harmony between science and the ideal, between philosophy and religion, between psychology and morality is beneficent because it is healthy. This book is a beautiful book, a classic treatise, and Geneva may well be proud of such a production, summing up such a high culture and such a solid wisdom. Here is the true Genevan literature, the central tradition of the region.

*June 21, 1880 (11 a. m.).*—My god-daughter has installed me in her little blue sitting-room; I have spent two hours there and grown to feel quite at ease in it. At first it seemed to me too still, then I became aware of the aesthetic harmony of it. This boudoir, full of attractive forms and creations (for every drawing, every piece of furniture, every book, every knick-knack, every colour has some meaning, is the result of a choice, the mark of a taste, the effect of an effort), this boudoir impresses me as a sanctuary, a poetic, intimate sanctuary, beneficent, composed. The hour one spends alone in a woman's boudoir is an initiation into her life; one has the history of her dreams and a sort of vista on her soul. A young woman who leaves a friend in her sanctuary does him the same favour as if she were lending him the journal of her thoughts. An intruder, a clodhopper, an evil-minded man, a libertine who penetrated fraudulently into the secret cell would certainly give its inhabitant a feeling of profanation. A sort of purification would be desired after this sort of pollution. Virginal modesty extends to the whole interior that is occupied by a young girl, to everything that is personal to her, everything that is especially hers. The breath or even the glance of the unworthy offends and stains everything it touches. The delicate being repulses this shocking familiarity, as it would refuse to drink from the glass that has just been used by a table-companion. Self-respect requires that the veil between the coarse curiosity of the outer world and the mysterious graces of the sanctuary shall not be lifted. The imagination, the heart, innocence are like the ermine. *Noli me tangere* is their device. Purity is their ideal.—This feminine horror of profane proximity is a profound instinct of the sex, which safeguards the freshness and delicacy of virtue. The virgin must fly from all contacts and envelop herself in a nimbus to preserve her magic and her grace. Immaculacy is her duty and gives her her power. It is thus that she keeps herself for love.

The room in which she lives, the room in which she sleeps, are like the outer, protecting envelope of the flower, like the cocoon of the silk-worm. Their tissue must remain intact. It is good to carry the defence of delicacy even to a mystical degree. This force of repulsion is the guardian of modesty and honour. From the sacred to the secret is scarcely more than a step. Mystery is a treasure.

*June 25, 1880.*—A wild storm yesterday afternoon. Thunderclaps, lightning, enormous downpours mingled with hail. Worked at my last two lectures, and took measures to have everything said in the reduced and abbreviated form that time imposes upon me. I find no little charm in solving this problem of teaching, to sacrifice no part of one's vast subject, to fill out one's programme fully and finish at the hour set on the appointed day. This gives the mind the same satisfaction as a "flawless" sonnet. It is the bush on the roof of the newly built house, it is the professorial point of honour, the glory of the vocation. Unless I am greatly mistaken, I shall finish punctually, having tied together all the threads and reassembled all the lines in my peroration and farewell. It seems to me propitious . . .

*June 26, 1880 (noon).*—Finished my course with the precision I desired. The work is well rounded off. I omitted nothing and put everything in its place in this vast and teeming subject.[1] It all came full circle. I am not dissatisfied. To effect it, I subdivided my hours into minutes, calculated my masses, reckoned up my stitches and my points. This oratorical embroidery is a process which I could learn, but it is only a very small fraction of the professorial art. To divide one's material into a given number of lectures is more difficult. To find the proportion of the parts, the normal speed of exposition is not an easy thing. The lecturer can give a series of complete lectures, and in this case the unit is the lecture; in a scientific course he ought to set himself a greater aim, the unity of the subject and the course. His point of view is objective. He does not aim at oratorical success or to please the curious; but he is the priest of his subject, he does the honours of it with gravity and composure. He presupposes in his audience respect and love for

[1] Amiel's teaching, in this summer semester (four hours a week), dealt with the Psychology of Nationalities, a course he had given for the first time in 1861.

science and disdains all the culinary artifices, all the stratagems of the rhetorician. What he wishes to delight is the pure intelligence, the desire to comprehend and contemplate. If I am not mistaken, it seems to me that my course can give this pleasure. The witness of other people at other times helps me to check this impression. My courses have been compared to transparent cathedrals, in which the masses, lines and details are seen in their proportions and bathed in light. Platonic serenity is the tone that befits truth and philosophic exposition.

*June 27, 1880.*—Individual opinion has no value in matters of science. Why does it seem to have one in questions of morality, education, politics, theology? Because here it is more difficult to prove the foolishness of the man who asserts his opinions. The most brazen person would not dare to pronounce on a question of chemistry, astronomy, geology, algebra, the very terms of which he does not understand. But where matters are concerned that are much more difficult and complicated, he recovers his assurance, he thinks himself competent and sets up for a connoisseur . . . What this comes to is that there are mathematical and natural sciences, but that there are no moral sciences. The State and the Church, for instance, are playthings which are much more easy to know than a watch or a top. One must go through a certain apprenticeship to make a lock or a slipper, but when it comes to making laws, it is all plain sailing, requiring no preface or reflection. Here innate knowledge is every man's property, and a whippersnapper is as good as anyone. All the Socratic irony comes to mind in connection with this grotesque infatuation. That everyone should wish to teach himself and try to form a just opinion is a good thing. But, as a rule, opinion is antecedent to investigation; it decides, settles, pronounces without a moment of doubt or modesty. This is the sad absurdity of it. It is the youngest who are the most arrogant; pretensions are in inverse proportion to merits. Democracy has always tended to this result because it effaces systematically differences in age, experience, education and deserts, and because it only cares to

count opinions and those who have them. Democracy exists; it is a
waste of one's pains to note its obliquities and follies. Every regime
has its own, and this regime is still the least evil. The supposition in
this regime is that everybody loves truth, that everyone seeks enlightenment and yields to good reasons. One must act on this
hypothesis. Everything must be pleaded before the public, the
crowd, the multitude. Victory is not to the wisest but to the most
persuasive. To manipulate appearance adroitly was the art of the
sophists; it is always the talent of those who succeed in democracy. "The sophist is superior to others, not because he possesses
more truths (every opinion is as true as every other), but because
he knows the art of winning men over to his way of thinking, to
that which it serves him to make them believe." The Athenians
said this frankly: the popular orator is the master of pleasant illusions; he is the magician who plays with passions and juggles with
principles. His strength is measured by his success.

*(Later.)*—Called on S. and continued yesterday's conversation.
Talked about the maladies that threaten democracy and that derive
from the legal fiction which it makes its basis. The remedy would
be to insist, at all times, on the truth which it systematically forgets, and which would serve as a counterpoise to it: on the inequality of talents, virtues and merits, on respect for age, capacity,
services that have been rendered, etc. Youthful arrogance and jealous ingratitude should be stigmatized as often as possible, when the
institution legally favours them. One should insist upon duty, when
the institution speaks only of the rights of the individual. One
should not concur in the opinion towards which people tend. All
this, it is true, is only a palliative, but in human society one cannot hope for more. Men proceed only by a succession of contrary
errors. They cross truth as the pendulum crosses the perpendicular,
to pass out of it at once.

*June 28, 1880.*—Reading: Mme. Necker de Saussure (finished the
*Étude sur la vie des femmes*). It is beautiful, grave, intelligent, elevated, delicate, finished. A few asperities and mistakes in language

do not count. One feels for the author a respect that is mingled with tenderness, and one says to oneself, this is a rare book, in which everything is sincere and everything true.

*July 1, 1880 (3 o'clock).*—Temperature oppressive. Sirocco. Ennui. Languor. I ought to review my notes and think of tomorrow's examination. Inner aversion, discontent, feeling of emptiness. Is it the conscience murmuring? The heart sighing? The soul eating itself away? The feeling that strength is ebbing and that time is being lost? Whence comes this vague anxiety? Is it grief, a regret, an apprehension? I do not know. But this obscure torment is dangerous; it drives one to sudden, mad decisions. One wishes thus to escape from oneself, to rout the black butterflies and the blue devils, to stifle the importunate voice of what one misses. Discontent is the father of temptations. I understand the multifarious frenzies of sexual pleasure, hashish, alcohol. It is all to gorge the invisible serpent that lurks at the bottom of our well, to gorge it in order to put it to sleep.

And all these vain rages, to what do they testify? To an aspiration. We have a thirst for the infinite, for love, for I know not what. It is an insatiable need. It is God calling or taking revenge. It is happiness roaring at the bottom of the gulf.

*July 3, 1880.*—Spent the evening at the Passerine.—Everyone is full of tomorrow's plebiscite.[1]

*July 4, 1880 (Sunday, 8.30 a. m.).*—The sun is coming out after a heavy rain. Is it a presage on this solemn day? The great voice of the *Clémence* has just rung out. Its mighty peals have gripped my vitals. For a quarter of an hour it continued its moving appeal: "Geneva, Geneva, remember. My name is *Clémence*. Shattered by time as I am, the desire of the people has brought me to life again. I am the voice of the Church and the Fatherland. Genevans, serve God and be united."

[1] A law providing for the separation of Church and State, adopted by the Grand Conseil, was, on this day, referred to the vote of the people of Geneva. It was rejected by a large majority (9,305 votes to 4,044).

*(7 p. m.)*—The *Clémence* rang out again during the last half-hour of the balloting. When it stopped, at five minutes to five, the silence had a terrible gravity, like that which weighs on the crowd awaiting the return of the judge and the capital sentence.—The fate of the Church, the household gods of Geneva, is now in the ballot-box. The counting must have begun.

*(11 p. m.)*—Victory up and down the line; the *ayes* have only two-sevenths of the vote, on an enormous ballot of 13,200 voters. Universal relief. At the Passerine and in the Rue Charles Bonnet, I find everyone full of emotion, joy and thankfulness.[1] Everyone feels that Geneva has had a narrow escape and that the fatherland can count still another deliverance.

At home, my god-daughter wept for joy on learning the result.

*July 5, 1880.*—A day of great emotion.

The *Clémence* rang out twice, once after the official announcement of the results of the plebiscite, and again after noon, as a call to prayer.

The whole city was on tip-toe. It was a holiday. The flags were hung from the windows. The people gathered at the Molard, climbed up to Saint Pierre; service of thanksgiving, procession through the whole city, with the music and banners of 1813. Return to the Molard, where two more speeches were delivered. Universal gaiety.

The most affecting moment was at Saint Pierre. Four or five thousand men, bare-headed, filled the parvis of the cathedral, and J. Cougnard gave this thrilled crowd the patriotic and soldierly address it had been expecting. The soul of old Geneva and the spirit of its forbears were indeed there under the vaults of the temple, which has sheltered, in a way, the whole Republic, as in the days of Athens and Argos . . .

Impression of piety, as in the presence of a mystery. It was as if one had a fleeting glimpse behind the scenes of history and Providence.

[1] The Passerine, the home of the Mercier ladies; the Rue Charles Bonnet, the home of Professor Auguste Bouvier.

There are still words that have a magic virtue with the populace, such words as the State, the Republic, the Fatherland, the Nation, the Flag, and I think even the Church. Culture, sceptical and mocking, does not realize the feeling, the exaltation, even the intoxication which these words inspire in the simple. The blasé do not understand how these appeals that leave them cold thrill the soul of the people. This is their punishment; it is also their infirmity. They are ironical, they are individualists, they are isolated and infertile.

I feel afresh what I felt at the centenary of Jean Jacques. All these little genteel folk, the pious money-changers, the race of the well-bred, who, in their pharisaism, have broken with the crowd, freeze my heart and imagination.

But then, I am always astride of an inner contradiction; I suffer from a double instinctive repugnance, an aesthetic repugnance to every kind of vulgarity, a moral repugnance to coldness of heart.— Thus, personally, I am attracted only to persons who are highly cultivated, distinguished, intellectual, while, on the other hand, nothing is sweeter to me than to throb with the national spirit, the feeling of the crowd. Thus I enjoy only the two extremes, and this separates me from both of them. The refined consider me low; the vulgar think I am over-refined.

*July 6, 1880.*—Magnificent weather. College promotions. Heard the signal of the drums and the band . . . I did not feel enough enthusiasm to go to the celebration . . . Besides I wished to let my impressions of yesterday settle. The need of calm, immobility, composure prevailed . . .

Towards nightfall, I accompanied our three ladies to the Plaine de Plainpalais. Immense crowd, joyous faces. The celebration ended with the traditional fireworks, under a calm sky filled with stars. On the way back, I thought, This is the Republic, just the same. For a week, all these people have been a-flutter. They have camped like the Athenians in the Agora. Since Wednesday, speeches, popular meetings have followed on one another's heels; there are newspapers and pamphlets in every house, harangues in the clubs; on Sunday, the plebiscite; on Monday, gay parades, hymns at Saint Pierre, speeches at the Molard, men's celebrations. On Tuesday, the young men's celebration. On Wednesday, the celebration of the elementary schools, etc., etc.

Geneva is an ever-seething kettle. It is a blast-furnace that never lets its fires die out. To preserve one's peace in all this seething and whirling, one must have a refuge and be able to shut the door.

Vulcan had more than one forge. Geneva is certainly one of the vent-holes of the European mind, one of the anvils on which the greatest number of projects are hammered out, one of the factories where the greatest numbers of novelties are tried that have not yet been patented by the governments. When one reflects that the refugees of all the causes are working here, the mystery is explained a little. But the best explanation is that Geneva, republican, Protestant, democratic, learned and enterprising, has been for centuries a sort of advance-guard, exploring unknown lands, and that it is used to extricating itself from its own difficulties. Since the days of the Reformation, it has been on the *qui vive* and has advanced with a lantern in its left hand and a sword in its right. Its boldness is prudent; it never throws up the sponge or stakes its whole fortune. What pleases me is that it does not yet yield to imitation, that it makes up its own mind. The people who say to it, Do as they do in New York, do as they do in Paris, do as they do in Rome, in Berlin, are still underneath. The parrots and the monkeys cannot persuade it. It lets the doctrinaire who would rend it asunder preach to the desert air; it scents the traps and turns aside from them. I like this mark of vitality. Only what is original has a sufficient reason for living. When the watchwords come from without, then one has only a province . . . Hollow, cosmopolitan formulas undermine small nationalities, just as they ruin the arts and literature. *Isms* are acids that dissolve everything that is living and concrete. With realism, liberalism, romanticism one does not create a masterpiece, or even a work, any more than one makes a child with a physiological theory. Separatism has even less virtue than all the other *isms,* for it is the abstraction of a negation, the shadow of a shadow. *Isms* are not fecund principles, they are hardly even explanatory formulas. They are rather the names of diseases, for they express an element in excess, a dangerous and improper exaggeration. Examples: empiricism, sansculottism, idealism, Voltairianism, radicalism. It is the characteristic of really successful things, as of well-developed beings, that they escape these nosological categories. One who is perfectly well is neither sanguine, bilious nor nervous. A normal republic contains parties and points of view that are opposed, but it contains them in the state of combined salts. A ray of light also contains all the colours, whereas red does not contain a sixth part of light in its fullness.

*July 8, 1880.*—It is thirty years since I read Waagen (on *Museums*); my friend R. R.[1] is reading him now. Every year I observe the same thing: he treads all my paths a generation after me. In 1842, I was mad about painting; in 1845, I studied Krause's philosophy; in 1850, I taught aesthetics, etc. Of the same age as myself, this reincarnation of me arrives at the stage I have left when for me it is ancient history. This impression of distance is a strange thing. At these moments I see myself through the catacombs of my memory and in the layers of historic ashes accumulated under my present soil.

Is not the life of the mind like that of old willow-trees or the imperishable baobabs? Is not the living layer of consciousness superimposed upon hundreds and thousands of dead layers? Dead? That is saying too much, no doubt, but when the memory is sluggish, the past is almost wholly wiped out. To remember that one has known is no rich possession, it is the indication of something lost; it is the number of an engraving that is no longer on its nail, the title of a book that is no longer on its shelf; it is a scar of the memory, a

[1] Rodolphe Rey (1824–1882), author of *Genève et les bords du Léman,* 1868. Amiel spent the winter of 1874–5 in his company at Hyères. Delicate health prevented Rodolphe Rey, with whom, after this, Amiel exchanged a number of letters, from staying in Geneva during the cold and fog.

hilum that distresses one. Such is my mind; it is the empty frame of a thousand images that have been effaced. My mind, taught by these innumerable exercises, is all cultivation, but it has retained almost nothing in its meshes. It is without substance; it is nothing but form any longer. It is fitted for everything and it possesses nothing. It has no knowledge any longer, it has become method. It is etherealized, algebraicized. Life has acted on it as death acts upon others, already prepared it for a further metamorphosis. When I was sixteen, I could see with a blind man's eyes that had just been opened, that is, I could cancel in myself my visual education and abolish distances; now, I can look at existence almost as if from beyond the grave, as if from the other side, *sub specie æterni;* I can feel as if I had risen again; everything is strange to me; I can be outside my body and my individuality, I am *depersonalized,* detached, I have taken wing. My consciousness can become that of a bonze, a sufi, a Brahman. One form only is not quite natural to me, my own.—Is this madness? No. Madness is the inability to regain one's equilibrium after vagabonding in alien forms, after Dantean visits to the invisible worlds, after excursions to the Witches' Sabbath. Madness consists in not being able to judge and stop oneself. And it seems to me that my mental transformations are only philosophical experiences. I am not riveted to any of them. I psychologize. But I do not conceal from myself that these experiments attenuate the thread of good sense, for they dissolve one's prejudices and one's personal interests. One only protects oneself indeed by returning to the world of men and by stiffening one's will. Pure contemplation evaporates the individuality; in order to emerge from dreams, one must suffer and act.

You are a captive balloon; do not allow the string that attaches you to earth to be worn away. You are a man, be a man. It is true that physical pain often and infallibly reminds you that you are not a spirit. But it behooves you also to cling to reality by the other faculties. One must work for one's fellows and willingly bear one's part of the burden of the race. One must share one's possessions, spread one's ideas, and share the ills of others, that is, lend a hand in the steering of the great ship.

You have done this, for you have acted as a professor and citizen. The reaction is taking place. You are falling back into ecstatic meditation, into the immobility of the solitary. There is no great harm in this. The omphalopsychics also has its rights.

Just the same, strengthen your muscles, recover a firmer vitality. Beware of becoming effeminate. It runs too easily into pusillanimity, sterility and hypochondria.

*July 14, 1880.*—In Genevan literature, what is the book I should most like to have written? Perhaps that of Mme. Necker de Saussure or Mme. de Staël's *Germany*. So moral philosophy, after all, is still the best thing for a Genevan. Intellectual gravity is the thing that least ill becomes us. History, politics, economic science, education, practical philosophy are open to us. We have everything to lose in becoming French or Parisian, for then we are only carrying water to the Seine. Independent criticism of the higher type is easier perhaps in Geneva than in Paris, and Geneva must keep in its own path, less enslaved to fashion, the tyranny of taste, to the reigning opinion, to Catholicism, to Jacobinism. Geneva should be to the great nation what Diogenes was to Alexander, the independent thought and free speech which does not submit to prestige and does not gloss the truth. This is a thankless role, no doubt, laughed at and unappreciated; but what of that? . . . In this order of things, one must be content to be alone.

*Montre ce qu'on peut faire en le faisant toi-même.*

Advise nobody, act; and if you do not act, keep your secret. One does not prescribe originality; one realizes it, if one can.

*July 25, 1880.*—Went down to the M. apartment and paid my respects to the works of art. The "Crouching Venus" is the most charming piece in the collection. For contrast of lines, grace of contours, variety of movement, plenitude of form, for chaste seductiveness and felicitous appearance, one could not wish for anything more accomplished. It is the eurythmy of beauty, the poem of the feminine body, the cantata of plastic perfection. From the tips of the hair to the soles of the feet, all is velvety, caressing, elegant, suave, delightful. Aphrodite would be a goddess even by universal suffrage. To her, the golden apple. Even the part one never sees, the part least often sculptured but most massive, the region between the waist and the knees, has ravishing sculptural refinements, rounded and flattened curves and dimples that vivify the surfaces and set the depths quivering. The sanctuary in which budding life is elaborated is a shrine from an exquisite hand, beautiful to contemplate from any aspect. The words that designate all these parts have something low about them, but the eye finds here only superb modelling and delicate charms, unforeseen, unnamable. Sculpture in its silent speech expresses in detail and *con amore* these broad expanses of beauty; it moulds them from the hip to the knee-cap, from the bosom to the flanks, from the flanks to the loins, from the loins to the back; but the spectator is at a loss how to designate with propriety these fractions of the nude, these segments of the torso of Cytheræa. The ear has more numerous susceptibilities than the eye; but the eye itself borrows its modesty from the imagination; it can see Aphrodite in her entirety without a veil, and admire . . . It is never anything but the accesory idea connected with nudity that creates indecency. There is something touching about Eve naked, in the midday sun, on the sward of Eden; but a woman naked in the shadow of her alcove is simply erotic. The nude can be innocent and pure, even in the goddess of pleasure; it is licentious in frivolous beauty; it is revolting in sensual ugliness . . . Fashion has only one reserve, that of calculation; it denies itself only that which would cause it to miss its object. It is the people with ugly feet who insist upon long dresses, the people with imperfect figures that dread bare backs and close-fitting gowns. This is as much as to say that the beautiful is made to be seen, that clothes obstruct the sight. Therefore all art will labour to make clothes the auxiliary of beauty, to make them flattering, transparent or even nil.

Sculpture goes even further, for, in the interest of the aesthetic, it strips feminine beauty even of the intimate growths that nature preserves; it effaces also the last traces of the useful, namely, the two lower hila, already almost concealed, in the living person, in a mysterious pit. In a word, it removes all visceral allusions; it cloaks the physiological laboratory; it hides everything that might inspire repugnance and leaves to be seen only the enchanting.—Nature has another resource; as it wishes love and as beauty is often wanting, it blinds with desire. Sex becomes an attraction by itself; the sexes pursue each other in the shadow, and the imagination, kindled by the senses, supplies all that is lacking. Thus the she-gorilla becomes a Cypris for her gorilla, whom she sees as an Apollo, and, in default of the reality, the momentary spell suffices for the ends of nature.

Art would be the despair of nature if it became a criterion. But everyone shuts his eyes and eats his poor fish with the sauce of the ideal. This is wiser, more practical and more human. One must dream of perfection and accommodate oneself to the imperfect . . . And then, too, what are the imperfections of line and the flesh, beside the imperfections of the heart and mind? A soul that is badly made or badly brought up in a well-made body yields joys that are very brief. There is this, at least, to be said for art, that it gives the illusion and sometimes the presence of the perfect; that is, it rejoices the sense of the divine, consoling it momentarily for the real, which is always imperfect. Art is a vista of a superior world, in which things respond to our aspirations and we say, At last!

*July 28, 1880.*—A long walk this afternoon in the sun, but the air was tonic and wholesome. I return satisfied with my carcass and joyful to have come into communion with nature again. The waters of the Rhone and the Arve, the murmur of the waves, the sternness of the bluffs, the luxuriance of the verdure, the shivering of the leaves, the splendid light of July, the radiant fertility of the fields, the distant clearness of the mountains, the whiteness of the glaciers under the serene blue sky, the cool breeze at the Junction,[1] the coppices of La Bâtie, the shadows of Saint-Georges, everything charmed me, eyes, senses and imagination. I seemed to have returned to the years of strength. I was flooded, dazzled with sensations. I was surprised and grateful. The universal life bore me aloft. The caress of summer went to my heart. I saw again the immense horizons, the bold peaks, the blue lakes, the winding valleys, all the liberties of other days. Yet it was not nostalgia. It was an indefinable impression, without hope, desire, regret, a sort of tenderness, a transport mingled with wonder and admiration. One feels at once joy and emptiness, one sees, through whatever one possesses, the impossible and the unrealizable, one measures at the same time one's riches and one's poverty. In a word, one is and one is not; one feels an inner contradiction because one is in a state of transition. This inexpressible ambiguity is proper to human nature, which is ambiguous because it is flesh becoming spirit, extension changing into thought, the finite glimpsing the infinite, the intelligence tacking its way through love and pain.

Man is the common sensorium of nature, the place in which all values are interchanged. The mind is the plastic medium, the principle and the issue of everything, the material, the laboratory, the product, the formula, the sensation, the expression, the law, that which is, that which does, that which knows. Everything is not mind, but mind is in everything and contains everything. It is the consciousness of being, that is, being to the second power.—If the universe endures, it is because the mind likes to perceive its contents in their richness and in their expansion, in their preparation especially. We, too, find a certain charm in our portraits as children, our childish note-books. But God is not egoistic, he is willing that myriads of myriads of suns should sport in his shadow; he grants life and consciousness to countless multitudes of creatures that participate in

[1] The junction of the two watercourses that unite below Geneva.

being, in nature, and all these animated monads in some way multiply the divinity.

*August 4, 1880.*—I receive the tenth and latest number of the *Feuille centrale de Zofingue* (twentieth year).[1] It is the eternal beginning again of youth, which fancies it is doing something new by always repeating the same thing. Luckily, the poplars, the warblers and the jasmins do not issue magazines, for every spring they would talk anew of their leaves, their songs, their perfumes, assuming that it represented progress.

It is continuity that dominates nature, the continuity of recurrence. Everything is repetition, reconquest, refrain and *ritornello,* and the new is strangely rarer than the known. The rose-bushes never weary of yielding their roses, the birds of building their nests, young hearts of loving, young lips of singing the thoughts and feelings that have served their predecessors a hundred thousand times. Profound monotony in universal agitation, this is the simplest formula afforded by the spectacle of the world. All circles are alike and all existences tend to trace their circle.

How avoid *fastidium?* By shutting one's eyes to uniformity, by looking for the little differences, then by learning to like repetition. Human faces are not identical, and dining every day is not a bore.— The best preservative, however, against satiety and surfeit is work. What one does may weary others, but personal effort is at least useful to the worker. Scrawling and daubing amuse the child who does the scrawling and daubing; the dust that he raises, the nonsense he performs give him the illusion of importance and wit. Therefore, if everyone works, the universal life will have a savour, although it repeats forever the same burden, the same aspirations, the same prejudices and the same sighs. "Every dog has his day" is the device of mortal beings. If they do the same old thing, they themselves are

---

[1] Journal of a society of students of the various cantons of Switzerland, which met annually in the little town of Zofingue. Amiel had been an enthusiastic member from 1838 to 1843.

new; if they imitate, they fancy they invent. They have received, they transmit. *E sempre bene!*

*August 8, 1880.*—This evening, reading aloud. It is a pleasure with intelligent people who understand at a hint and complete one's intentions. But what an art the art of reading is; it includes three or four others, the least of which abounds in difficulties and resources. When I think of the fruit it might have borne in my hands and the obstacles that impede me now (pharyngitis, bronchitis, asthma, etc.), I cannot help sighing.

*August 9, 1880.*—My god-daughter speaks to me again about my reading yesterday. She admires it warmly, and then we talk about this art in itself. She insists that I am equally successful with all the varieties of reading, all types and all styles, that it gives her more pleasure than the theatre, that all my characters, animals or human beings, as well as my landscapes, become living and distinct; that all these roles created by a stroke of the wand produce the illusion of nature and give the impression of a poetic game; that she cannot imagine where I made the acquaintance of all the professions and every kind of character. One serious remark: "One would say that you had made man and the world, or at least that you were there when they were made; you possess them all so well."—Intuition is, in fact, that sympathetic power which divines the soul of things and vibrates in unison with it. Magnetic clairvoyance is not an empty phrase. Everything is in everything, and we can συμφρονεῖν with all existences. The more mind is mind, the more it is omnimodal; the Protean is its privilege and its measure; and it appears to less advanced beings limitless and without configuration. Captive minds are barnyard fowls that cannot follow free minds or approve of them, unless they love them, and when they watch from the shore the swan braving the sea, the eagle conquering space, they say to themselves, We are the true children of the egg, these others are foolhardy creatures. Captive minds, to put it better, are crustaceans shut up in their own special form; they have the same complaint to make of metamorphoses that the tailless fox made of long tails.

Every form of impotence likes to think that it is voluntary abstention; the inferior likes to assume the mask of the superior; the incapable man likes to give himself out as a sage . . .

To taste everything like a critical epicure is merely dilettantism; and twenty dilettanti do not count as much as a single artist. To do one thing is of more value than to talk of a thousand. All the foliage of an apple-tree is not the equivalent of an apple. What endures, what can resist death, especially what is fruitful, this is the essential. Of what consquence, then, are the 16,300 pages of this Journal! A story by Mérimée, an article by Sainte-Beuve, a letter of Doudan's count more, for they are written, published and in a finished style.

*August 20, 1880.*—Languor lets the end come, but it does not make an end, in the active sense of the word. Death itself can become an acquiescence, and thus an act, a moral act. An animal expires, man should consign his soul to his maker and resign his functions with dignity, he should will what God wills. In this way he ennobles pure natural necessity; he moralizes the physiological, he solemnizes what would otherwise be dismal and trivial. Decrepitude and destruction are thus brought into harmony with the higher life; the soul proves its nobility, surmounting the ignoble; the divine shines through its abasement and its tatters. *Incessu patuit Dea.*

*August 24, 1880 (9 a. m.).*—If one waits to act, one does not act; if one waits to rest, one does not rest; if one postpones wisdom, pleasure, reflection, their hour never comes. It is better not to be too proud, but to profit by the present and not count on the future. This was the ethics of Epicurus. To do one's duty at every moment was Zeno's. To follow one's bent or oppose it is the soul's eternal oscillation, moving to and fro between happiness and dignity, because it needs both. It is certain that I am drawing slowly away from Stoicism, and that I am drifting towards the nonchalance of Montaigne. When ambition and hope are dead, when everything is uncertain and fleeting, one takes refuge in benevolent calm and quietude. One wishes not to suffer and to lessen the suffering of others. One aims no longer at genius, heroism, glory; one is content with tranquillity. To feel and to think in one's hermitage, to this all longings limit themselves; one leaves the will to youth and to men with desires. This renunciation of old age is natural when strength is gone and infirmities have arrived. Old age is not an age; it is a privation and mutilation . . .

With the years, I have come to love the beautiful more than the sublime, the smooth more than the rough, the nobility of Plato more than the wild sanctity of the Jeremiahs. All the violences of the barbarians seem to me inferior to the playfulness of Socrates, the serenity of Jesus. I relish well-balanced souls and educated hearts, whose liberty is amiable and free from the rudenesses of the recently liberated slave. It is the tempering of virtues, one by another, that charms me, as it is the fusion of all the delicate nuances that creates the matchless grace of the feminine complexion. Qualities that are exclusive and decided serve only to attest imperfection. Imagine an eye in an ugly face, one beautiful eye; this eye throws into relief the ugliness of the rest.

*August 29, 1880.*—Lively feeling that I am better. I profit by it to resume my neglected exercises and interrupted habits, but a minute toilet bears out what I had quite supposed, that these rude thrashings have shortened the distaff of my days. In one week I have grown several months older; this is easily perceptible in my hair. Those who are about me pretend, in their affection, not to see anything; the mirror is more veracious. This does not detract from the convalescence; but one hears the shuttle of fate, none the less, and one feels that one is running to meet death, despite the halts and truces that are granted.—The most beautiful existence would be that of a river, in which the rapids and cascades would have to be passed only near the source and whose swelling stream would be formed from a succession of rich valleys, all of them summed up in lakes, equally and variously picturesque, and ending, over the plains of old age, in the ocean where everything that is weary comes to seek for rest.—There are few of these existences, full, fruitful, sweet. What use to desire or regret them? It is wiser and more difficult to see one's lot as the best one could have had, and to say that, after all, the most skilful tailor could not make us a jacket that would have fitted us better than our own skin.

*Le vrai nom du bonheur, c'est le contentement.*

*August 30, 1880 (2 o'clock).*—Distant and heavy rumblings of thunder. The sky is grey, without rain; the birds are making little excited cries of fear. It is like the prelude of a symphony or a catastrophe . . .

*Quel éclair te traverse, ô mon cœur soucieux?*

One thing is curious: all the occupations of the neighbourhood (the tinsmith, the wool-carder, the school-master) go straight ahead; even the unloading of boards and other unusual sounds are added to these, and yet these sounds float in silence, in a dead, positive silence which they cannot disguise, a silence that replaces the confused up-roar of the hive at work, observable on a week-day in any town. This silence is extraordinary at this hour, for it is not hot. It sug-gests expectation, meditation, almost anxiety. Are there days when "the still voice of Job" produces more effect than the tempest? When a dull rumbling on the horizon brings to a stop the general concert of voices, like the roaring of the lion, in the desert, when the night falls . . .

*September 2, 1880 (9 a. m.).*—Joy of the eyes. Charming colours are spread out before me. Flowered rug, embroidered furniture, Pompeian fire-guard, black and gold screen, scarlet feather-broom, and, on my mantel, a green spray of heather, a velvety peach, iri-descent balls and crystals, the garland of multicoloured immortelles, under the portrait of my mother, the four armchairs in different styles, all this makes a palette of tones that blend and contrast in ravishing shades.—The sensations of the ear are equally varied and sweet; one is aware of life at a distance, in a perspective which poetizes everything: voices, sounds, murmurings, footsteps, songs, men at work combine in a light music that sets one dreaming. The mere analysis of this acoustic tissue is almost a voluptuous pleasure. All the pulsations of the world's life enter and resound in my consciousness, as all the vibrations of the atmosphere thrill Arachne at the centre of her web. It is delightful. The immense volume of air that my windows command gives its richness to this kaleidoscope of sound, in which nothing recalls suffering, misery, sickness or grief.

A September Thursday is a lucky day. If it has favours for strength, it has graces for languor. I do not fly to the conquest of the world, but the world comes to greet me in my cell. I am not disinherited.

*September 3, 1880.*—The sleeping self has indeed the same axis as the waking self, but the individual has lost many of his qualities and his attributes: he lacks reason, will, morality, humanity. The beast and its appetites remain, together with memory, and all this at the mercy of the imagination, which is perhaps at the mercy of the vital organs and merely translates into images the state of the liver, the lungs, the kidneys, the stomach, the blood and the loins. No, that is saying too little. Dreams are an inner crossroads where all the different agitations of life re-echo: there are dreams of the heart, of the soul, and even of the reason. I made this complete classification many years ago. Why break it up? We spend our days beginning again less well what we have done better and breaking the earlier moulds.

This, as a matter of fact, is the way that humanity proceeds in art and fashion, in thought, in institutions. What it desires is to change. After a relative equilibrium it returns to confusion; after the good style, it makes shift with the mediocre. "On, on; renew, transform; what is forbidden you is to hold to the good, the acquired, the tried. Progress is permitted, but so is decay. Move on, it is the will of nature and the order of fate." From good to better is a fine motto; but improvement is only a matter of chance, perfection is only a possibility. The fatal, inevitable thing is change, not progress.

It is manifest that the individual perfects himself at one point, only to the detriment of other points (sanctification, for instance, through the sacrifice of the will). Why should it be otherwise with the species? Evolution is satisfied if the attribute that assumes the temporary preponderance has some value or rarity.

*September 9, 1880.*—It seems to me personally that with the decline of my active powers I become more intellectual; everything becomes transparent to me, I see types, the *mothers,* the foundation of beings, the meaning of things . . .

My natural tendency is to convert everything into thought. All personal events, all particular experiences are for me pretexts for meditation, facts to generalize into laws, realities to be reduced to ideas. This metamorphosis is the work of the brain, philosophical labour, the operation of the consciousness, which is a mental alembic. Our life is only a document to be interpreted, a substance to be spiritualized, a series of fleeting phenomena to be transformed into a microcosmic outline. Such, at least, is the life of the thinker. He *depersonalizes* himself every day; if he is willing to experience and to do, it is the better to understand; if he wills, it is in order to know the will. He regards himself as a laboratory of phenomena, and asks from life nothing for himself but wisdom. But he wishes also to give joy, to console, to make happy.

What distinguishes him is disappropriation. Sweet as he may feel it to be loved, and though he knows nothing else so sweet, he still seems to himself the occasion of the phenomenon rather than its object. He contemplates the spectacle of love, and love remains a spectacle to him. He does not even believe his body is his own; he feels passing in him the vital whirlwind, which is lent to him for a moment to enable him to perceive the cosmic vibrations. He is only the thinking subject, he retains only the form of things, he does not assume the material possession of anything.

It is this disposition that makes him incomprehensible to all that possesses, dominates, engrosses. In fact, he is as fluid as a phantom, which is plainly seen and yet cannot be grasped, because its solidity and opacity are only apparent. Disappropriation renders him empty and void; he resembles a man, as the manes of Achilles and the shade of Creusa resembled the living. Without having died, I am a ghost. I dream on my feet and wide-awake. Others seem dreams to me, and I seem a dream to others. It is half the state of a visionary. If it were not for suffering and illness, I might doubt that I am positively alive. The apparitions of the risen Christ do not surprise me greatly, for this form of existence, abstracted from weight and floating between corporeity and spirit, is almost familiar to me.

*September 15, 1880.*—Reading: de Vigny (*Le Capitaine Renaud*). Sympathetic author, meditative mind, supple, strong talent, elevation, independence, seriousness, nobility, originality, pride, audacity and grace: he has everything. He depicts well, he narrates well, he judges well, he thinks and he dares. His fault is perhaps a slight excess of self-respect, a quite Britannic reserve and haughtiness, which has a horror of familiarity and is afraid of abandon. But even this tendency is not an eccentricity, it is a trait of character and a refinement of dignity. Only it has been a disadvantage in making the author unpopular by holding the public at a distance, treating it as a babbling mob, as the *profanum vulgus*. Was not Alfred de Vigny rallied finally by Molé and Sainte-Beuve? The Gallic race has never relished the principle of the inviolability of the personal consciousness; it will have none of these Stoics, shut up in their dignity as in a tower and recognizing no master but God, duty or faith. This inflexibility annoys it, and even irritates it. This solemnity humiliates it and makes it impatient. It repudiated Protestantism because of this, and in every crisis it has crushed those who have not yielded to the passionate current of public opinion. In this race, society bends the individual; fashion, tone, taste, the reigning prejudice make the law for all. Liberty is synonymous with revolt. Everyone wishes to be like everyone else, so as not to be chaffed and bullied. State, Church, Usage decide on all matters of conduct; the individual reserves for himself only the insignificant details. Extreme sociability is dearly bought.

*September 17, 1880.*—I cannot conceal from myself that for a dozen years or more I have ceased to be under the spell of sex; I know too well the defects and weaknesses of the idol. I had set it too high, to the detriment of the virile man; I have liked women and sought their company too much. At last impartiality has come. It is never too late to be wise. If I continue to feel a slight preference for the more loving sex, I am less naive, less blind, less credulous, less admiring than before. The veil of Maya has worn thin, and illusion is less necessary to me. My *camaraderie* has enabled me to see truly. I can look at them as they look at one another, as their mothers, fathers and brothers look at them, as the doctor sees them, that is, in all the ways other than the amorous and illusioned way. I am sensitive to their charm, without overrating them; I am touched, moved, grateful, attracted, without being deceived. This is the state I prefer.

*Clarens, September 21, 1880*—The apprenticeship of debility is painful to me. Every year I see the circle of my liberty contracting, and this horrifies me, in spite of myself. It seems to me that I am confused with someone else, that there is a mistake, that everything is going to be cleared up. But no, it is indeed my wrists that are being handcuffed, it is upon me that this cross is imposed; this carcass is indeed mine, and I have no spare one. *Dura lex, sed lex.*

Another experience: to reach the macrocosm one must pass first through the corporeal medium; to be restored to harmony with nature, the self must not be harassed by the organism. Cœnæsthesia raises an opaque fog between the landscape and thought. The mind, bewildered by internal sensations, is no longer vacant for the perception of the outer world. It sees the veil rather than that which lies beyond. Impersonality, contemplative objectivity become impossible for it, and this is what distresses me.—What is insanity? The thickening of this subjective and idiosyncratic curtain that separates the individual from the real world. The nervous state, estranging one from this outside world and conveying it badly, is a step towards insanity.

*Clarens, September 22, 1880 (11 a. m.).*—Wonderful day.—First, a long uninterrupted sleep, then found the sun and the blue sky again. For four hours now I have been bathing in the light, to the joy of my eyes, ears, nostrils and lungs. Roamed about the country-side, found the old paths and scenes, the lake, the hillsides, the or-chards, the mountains, and the crests of Baugy, Planchamp, Tavel, Le Châtelard. Dreamed for a long time at Le Platanée, from whence I surveyed the ravishing panorama of Lake Leman, from the Catogne to the Jura, from Chillon to Coppet, from Évian to Blonay, from the Grammont to the Fully. I was dazzled, full of emotion, intoxicated. Followed the profile of the mountains, the outline of the shore, picked out all the hamlets, steeples, châteaux and villas, en-graved on my memory the effects of shadow and sunlight, the flying mists and sculptured rocks, the thousand and one details enlivening every spot; the thrushes, the flies, the bees, the butterflies, the clumps of chestnuts, the islets of verdure about every country-house; the brooklets, the flowering walls, the gardens bursting into gay colours (gladioli, geraniums, laurel, nasturtiums), the steamers, the locomotives, the carriages, the checker-boards of the slate roofs glistening in the morning sun, the sapphire lake with its golden spangles and the ripples left by boats that had vanished; gulls and crows, distant sails; delightful verdure, red apples, golden grapes, picturesque and soothing undulations of the landscape, invigorating breeze, gaiety of everything, a veritable burst of beauty.—Drowned in impressions, I finally got the upper hand and sang, sang, like a bird, through the meadows and the shady paths, tirelessly, and with a joy in my breast that carried me back to the days of my youth.

*Clarens, September 24, 1880.*—The Dent du Midi rears its snowy battlements opposite me, a generous sunshine floods my two corner windows and is drying all the clothes that were dampened by my morning walk. There is health in these rays, peace in this landscape. My spirits have risen. Besides, my strength is coming back. I have an appetite. I did not sleep badly, the walk was charming. It is pleasantly warm, and I am writing this in my shirt-sleeves. Italian sensations, the joy of a lizard. The joy, too, of independence, perfect leisure. The joy of pure meditation; I hear the silence, as it were, and no one will pass my door. That is the way man is made. He dreads the loneliness of the heart, but he loves solitude for hours together, as he loves uninterrupted sleep. Anything that breaks in upon his thought or his mood is disagreeable to him. An afflux of sensations pleases him only when he has sought it. Well-being is thus the feeling of an unthwarted existence, when neither what is within nor what is without warns us of its presence by any opposition whatever, when the skiff silently rides the river of time. This peaceful navigation is itself a delight, even when it leads nowhere.

*Clarens, October 9, 1880.*—Walk. Tender thoughts and wonder. It was so beautiful, so caressing, so poetic, so maternal! I felt that I was forgiven. The sunlight, the leaves, the sky, the bells said to me: Take heart and strength again, wounded child. These are the days of good will; there is calm here, rest and forgetting. Faults and punishments, anxieties and regrets, cares and wrongs are all but one burden. We do not make distinctions, we ease all woes, we spread peace, we are consolation. Blessings on the weary and heavy-laden, blessings on the afflicted, blessings on the sick, the sinful, on all who suffer in heart, conscience and body. We are the bountiful spring, drink and live! God makes his sun rise on the just and on the unjust. His munificence does not haggle over mercy and grace; it does not weigh them out like a money-changer and number them like a bank-cashier. Come hither, there is enough for all!

*Clarens, October 14, 1880 (11 a. m.).*—The days succeed one another, but they are all different. Yesterday was dismal, grey, damp and cold, as miserable and dreary as could be. This morning the landscape has recovered all its charms. I return from a three hours' walk, overwhelmed with picturesque sensations, moved, electrified, ravished. I sang for more than a league together. How many delightful sensations, memories going back thirty years, thoughts, too, that rose in my mind, while I slowly followed the road that winds from Tavel to Planchamp, from Planchamp to Charnex, from Charnex to Sonzier. Splendid view, lovely effects of the lake and the mountains. Immense horizon, the lake smiling all the time. Shadows and sunlight, bluish waves of heat, dew in the grass, sparkling brooks, the gamut of blue, the gamut of green, iridescence of the leaves, outline of the shores, the twelve notches in the massif opposite, crowned with snow and forming an Alpine girdle; and the symphony of the flocks at Charnex, at Chailly, at Tavel; one or two butterflies still; vintage-wagons, milk-buckets, grape-baskets.—Two odd phenomena: 1., a flock of about a hundred crows high in the air, uttering little cries of joy that had no resemblance to their terrestrial caws; it was their morning hymn; I scarcely believed my eyes and ears, for they were crows, beyond a doubt, simulating song-birds (their song was that of a sparrow-warbler);—2., a flock of about eight cows or heifers, leaving their grass to listen to the passer-by who was singing. They came up and blocked my road. I had to frighten them off with my parasol in order to break through the curious line. This was above Châtelard.—In these two circumstances, animals entered the aesthetic sphere. The crows were celebrating the reappearance of the sun, and the cows were welcoming the music; the zebus were flocking to the Brahman. This idyllic country is the only one for such reminiscences of Eden.

*October 29, 1880.*—If I have not made any great impression on men, I shall have been loved much by women. This testimony is as good as any other. And why have they loved me? Because they find in me what they need, strength of mind, delicacy of heart, gentleness, discretion and frailty. They feel they are understood, enveloped, protected, and if they might have wished me less disinterested and more exclusive, they feel, at least, that they can rely upon me and that I am a real friend. To whom has it is fallen to receive confessions and to be taken for a guide and confidant against himself and against the passion of which he was the object? This has happened to me many times, six at least. One might describe it as a speciality. Since my twentieth year, and my journey to Italy, I have always been somebody's confessor and I have lived on intimate terms with the feminine soul. Widows, wives, young girls, grandmothers have opened to me, of their own accord, the chapel of their secret thoughts. And nationality counted for nothing, for this involuntary vocation began among the Italians, and it was carried on in South and North Germany, in eastern and western Switzerland. I have been a lay director, chosen spontaneously by his penitents. I know almost as much about the life of the sex behind the scenes as an abbé whom everyone pursues and entreats. I know the inmost heart even of women artists, devotees of this or that confession, literary women. I know what they utter and what they conceal, strong and weak, good and bad. Regarding the psychology of women, I thus have precious insights and observations at first hand. But I shield my confidants with Hippocratic, masonic secrecy. I draw upon their confessions only for their own advantage.

Others may share this initiation if they wish to do so and if they are worthy of it. The best in everything is not to be transmitted by instruction. The gift, the instinct, the genius, the divine favour remain private property. Beyond knowledge, which can be communicated, there is a mystery that must be divined. That is why imitators are only parrots. Education is a valuable heritage, but taste, wisdom, invention, perspicacity are not part of it. What a man knows is a wealth that he has received or acquired; but what he is reduces this wealth to nothing, for if he has a base character, a vulgar soul, a cold heart, it makes a nullity of all the rest and multiplies his wealth by zero. And zero times ten thousand, or ten thousand times zero is nothing.

The ideal of an individual does not give his true measure, I mean the ideal he professes to hold and pursue. This ideal may be ostentatious, imaginary, strategic. Millions of people call themselves Christians, and doubtless believe themselves to be so; but what does this matter in any real sense? What they are is the essential thing.

626

*Il n'est bonne dorure, ami, que d'être d'or.*

The ideal that is professed is still in the realm of the apparent; it may be a shift meant for the eye of one's neighbour, a snare for the good faith of the individual himself, who claims the merit of the badge he wears. Exactly the contrary is oftenest the case. The finer the badge is, the less the wearer is worth: this is to be taken for granted. As a rule, the cardinal is not as good as the bishop, the bishop as good as the parish priest, the Pharisee as good as the simple believer, the Greek as good as the Turk. It is extremely dangerous to plume oneself on any moral or religious title whatever. Is there a more intolerable pride than that of the priest who professes humility? Where is there less true charity than in the ecclesiastical world? Less union than in the monasteries? Less humanity than among the fanatics of election and predestination? Tell me on what you pride yourself and I will tell you what you are not.

But how is one to know what an individual is? By his deeds, first, but by something else also, something that is perceived only by intuition. The soul judges the soul by elective affinity, through and beyond words and silence, deeds and all the eye can see.

The criterion is subjective, I admit, and subject to error; but, in the first place, there is none more certain, and then the justness of the approximations is proportional to the moral culture of the judge. Courage is the judge of courage, goodness of goodness, nobility of nobility, loyalty of the upright. One only knows really well what one has or what one has lost, that is, what one regrets, the candour of the child, for instance, the modesty of the virgin, the integrity of honour. The true judge is therefore infinite goodness, and after this the regenerate sinner or the saint, the experienced man or the sage. It is just that our touchstone should be finer in proportion as we are less evil.

The world is the judge of appearances, but the good see the real being. Public opinion is thus only a provisional and frivolous estimate; the judgment of the dead belongs to another tribunal.

*October 31, 1880.*—Letter from S., who astounds me with the work that she despatches every day, and with all she reads, in addition to her five daily classes and many social duties. It is true that, with her excellent memory, her hours and her employment of them count for something in her mind; with me, on the contrary, all I have been able to do or think in a week or a month melts together and rapidly runs to zero. My life itself seems empty to me. The category of time does not exist for my consciousness, and consequently all those compartments that tend to make of a life a thousand-chambered palace break down for me, and I never emerge from the primitive unicellular state. I return of myself into the formless and the fluid, into the vague mode of possibility and omnipossibility, into the νόησις νοήσεως. Is this non-existence? No, it is pure mind in the state of tension, it is virtual existence, it is the globular state. I only possess myself in the state of the monad and the I, and I feel my faculties themselves in process of being reabsorbed into the substance which they have individualized, a little as the amœba sucks in its momentary organs of prehension.—All the benefit of being an animal is repudiated, so to speak; all the proceeds of study and culture are likewise annulled; all crystallization is dissolved again in its bath; the outer sheath of Iris is drawn into the interior of the dew-drop; the consequences return to the principle, effects into the cause, the bird into the egg, the organism into the germ.

This psychological *reimplication* is an anticipation of death; it images the life beyond the grave, the return to Sheol, the vanishing among the phantoms, the fall into the region of the *Mothers* (*Faust*), or rather the simplification of the individual, who, allowing all his accidents to evaporate, exists no longer except in the state of the type, the Platonic idea, the indivisible state of the point, the state of mathematical power, the fecund zero. Is not this the definition of mind? Is not mind removed from space and time just this? Its past and future development exist in it as a curve exists in its algebraic formula. This nothing is an all. This *punctum* without dimensions is a *punctum saliens*. What is the acorn but the oak that has lost its branches, its leaves, its trunk and its roots, that is to say, all its accoutrements, its forms, its particularities, but which is concentrated in its essence, in the figurative form that is able to reconquer everything?

Thus this impoverishment is only a superficial diminution. A man may lose his four limbs and four of his five senses; he is still a man as long as he has his head and heart, less than this, as long as he is a consciousness. To reënter one's eternity is thus indeed to die, but not to be annihilated; it is to become virtual again.

*November 2, 1880.*—Reading: Marc Monnier (*Le demi-galant homme,* eight *feuilletons* in the *Débats,* August, 1880) . . . What impression does Monnier's Neopolitan tale make on me? Mixed. It gives no pleasure to the imagination, although it amuses the intellect. And why? Because the author, who cannot escape his obsession for burlesque and marionettes, goes in too much for irony and is always bantering. Besides, one feels too much that he wishes to inform us about the country, circumstances, customs, and this distracts one from the characters, who are only the pretext for the narration. The gaiety here is not gay, and the sensibility is not touched. One recognizes the school of Victor Cherbuliez and the Voltairian tradition: much malice and wit, small feeling, no naivety. This combination, eminently propitious for satire, for journalism and literary warfare, is much less happy in the novel and story, for wit is not poetry, and the novel, though on the border of poetry, is still within its bounds. The indefinable discomfort which these epigrammatic productions give one is probably due to a confusion of *genres*. We do not like women disguised as men, or the reverse, because we are repelled by the equivocal and have no security with the ambiguous. Hermaphroditism in art is ill-advised. Mockery should not be cloaked in the tender. One cannot achieve humour by the raillery of wit. I even doubt if the droll can rise to the comic, lacking as it does depth and impersonality. There is no real joy in laughing at things and people. It is a chilly pleasure, a dry hilarity: the clown at least shakes his bauble and joins in the game. Clownery is more wholesome because it has a little more goodness in it. The reason why perpetual irony repels us is that it lacks two things: humanity and seriousness. It is a form of pride, since it always sets itself above others; it is frivolous because the conscience cannot contrive to silence it. Or it is egoistical, and egoism is sterile; or else it is an attitude, and this attitude is unpleasant. In short, dissolvents and corrosives may be useful in dyeing, but they are not an aliment. One runs through the ironical books, one only becomes attached to the books that have some *pectus* in them.

*December 8, 1880.*—Read the whole of number 49 of the *Revue critique d'Histoire et de Littérature*. Whenever one encounters erudition, in the proper sense of the word, knowledge at first hand, one becomes aware of the immensity of one's ignorance. Each of the little articles in this collection filled me with a secret shame. And yet what is the use of this prodigious accumulation of learning? What should I do with it if it were mine? If this heap of fertilizer does not yield a flower, does not produce a grain of wheat, does not engender a thought, what is the use of it? The soul needs something else; the mind asks for something better. This bric-à-brac is only a means. Its value is not in itself but in what can be drawn from it. Intemperance of the bookish kind, the indigestion of too much paper even have something unwholesome and delusive about them. Pure erudition is mental gormandizing. It is stupefying, like the gluttonous feasts of Rabelais, but it should not be admired. Let us be modest before this strength of stomach and memory; let us not be jealous. Were a brain to contain all the pages of all the books in a library, what would this add to the spiritual and moral capital of the race? Nothing. The gluttons leave no memory behind them, and this is as it should be. Invention, creation, discovery, originality, thought are thus worth much more than stupid erudition, more even than enlightened erudition. The erudite man knows what others have written, said or done, a fine sort of progress! A mirror is not a landscape, an echo is not a voice, a parrot is not a person.

No matter; to every man his role. Since the artist does not create a museum, the collector renders a service; the curator of collections and even the man who sweeps the hall are useful. They all live by the genius and talent of others, but they also earn their bread. So long as one graduates the ranks, there is room for all activities. But between Homer and the bookworm who prints him or the schoolmaster who mangles him, there are degrees. Erudition is at the bottom of the ladder of knowledge, but it is through this that one must begin.

*(Later.)*—The professor must simplify, but it is proper that he should give his students a sense of the immense wealth and complexity of things, so that the student will have no illusions in regard to his own ignorance. A course is only a diagram; it outlines the indispensable, but it should also open vistas on all the subjects which it only sketches in their general features. The student must not be permitted to confound a summary with the science itself or fancy that he has arrived at the end of study because he has reached the end of the elements. A well-constructed course is not merely an explanatory diagram, but also a suggestive programme; it satisfies a first need of culture and ought to arouse a new appetite. This is the proof that it has nourished the mind, rather than encumbered the memory.

*December 10, 1880.*—Reading: G. Moynier [1] (*Les Lois de la Guerre*), with two reports; three pamphlets in all.

Wrote to the author, to congratulate him. The problem is well stated and well solved. The successes of the practical mind impress me as much as those of art or science. At bottom, all methods come back to method. My principle, which is to catch the spirit of things, puts me at my ease in every kind of activity.—In everything, the irreproachable gives me the same satisfaction; whether it is a passage of Roman law, a military operation, the cut of a garment, a

---

[1] Gustave Moynier (1826–1910), one of the first founders, the promoter and real organizer of the international Red Cross, of which he was the president for forty years.

song of Béranger's, a drawing of Leonardo's, a good reading or true singing voice, the aesthetic impression is of the same nature, that of the propriety of the means to the end, the proportioning of the force to the act. When it carries the day, when what should have been done is done, the mind is content, while the almost, the middling, the drivelling and the lax fill the world.—Yesterday, H. seemed to me idiotic when he was judging poetry; today Gustave Moynier has rejoiced me talking about ambulances and bombardments. The subject is thus almost indifferent, the essential thing is the way in which it is treated. Talent is measured by execution. Tell me what you can successfully perform and I will tell you what your aesthetic value is. The moral has an entirely different criterion; here the intention is the capital thing. The intention in art, on the contrary, is insignificant.

*December 13, 1880.*—How is one to behave when one has bad luck? Keep quiet, and apply oneself with patient meekness, like a novice, to everything one does; in other words, go back to one's ABC's. The question is to relearn how to move successfully and to win back one's courage. Failures bewilder and confuse one; one must recover faith in oneself by succeeding in something, however small. In sum, two simultaneous procedures, tranquil resignation in regard to whatever does not depend upon us, a falling back upon our remaining strength.—Is not this the procedure of the leader of an army in times of reverse? He rallies his disordered troops in a retrenchment camp, and then tries to discipline them by a few skirmishes.—Similarly, in a circus, a horse that has stumbled, a rider who has failed to carry through his act must gradually recover their self-assurance; otherwise they are lost. The moment one no longer thinks one can, one cannot any longer. One must therefore cut short this discouragement, which is demoralization.

*December 25, 1880, Christmas Day ( 10 a. m.).*—Reading of Synoptic Gospels (birth and childhood of Jesus). Felt at once the poetry of the miraculous in Christianity and its difference from true history. But the history of what has been believed to be historic is

632

also a kind of history; it is religious history. Legend is the way in which real events are pictured in the mirror of the naively moved soul; this mirror is never level, and it considerably modifies the images. Tradition is a translation that adds to things everything that they have awakened in the imagination, the soul and the heart of the successive narrators.—The illusion of the apologist lies in confusing the historicity of beliefs with the historicity of facts. It is rather as if one believed that the great air in *William Tell*, written by Rossini, had actually been heard at Altorf in 1308; or as if one invoked this cavatina as a testimony of the authenticity of the vows of Grütli. Tradition, legend, myth have their laws of formation and remain one of the most interesting of psychological phenomena, even while criticism deprives them of their historicity. Faith is a spring of unconscious poetry; the moment one becomes conscious of this poetry, the faith evaporates. This happened to the Greek mythology among the Christian peoples. It happens to everything miraculous, the moment one asks oneself whether it really happened. Science has killed all the sylphs, the undines and fairies. It also kills the gods. And the supernatural in Christianity is threatened with the same fate. The mere attentive reading of the evangelical documents suffices to show that history did not begin for Jesus until his appearance on the scene, and that everything that precedes is a later creation, a glorifying legend born in the community of the believers. —The one thing of which tradition is incapable is the transmitting of the naked truth, that is, historical truth. Its law is to embellish, idealize, explain; and, in the particular case, this was to show that everything had been announced and prophesied by the seers of Israel. The role was outlined to the last detail (see St. Matthew). Jesus knew it and fulfilled it; therefore he is the Messiah. That is the way the Jews understood the divine, and the way the first generations of Christians understood it after them. This puerile literalism is the mark of the Semite. And it must be acknowledged that the Judaic imprint has not yet been effaced from the Occidental mind. Christian orthodoxy is a captivity of the understanding which is by no means near its end. The spiritualistic theologians are always colliding with the narrow, the stubborn and the captious who take metaphors literally and materialize everything.—Christianity has not escaped the fatal destiny of all religions, which is to liberate and enlighten at first, only to become later an obstacle to light and freedom.

*December 27, 1880.*—I am delighted to find that my impression of the day before yesterday regarding the Synoptics coincides with the general results of the great modern criticism. "Strauss", says Biedermann,[1] "has demonstrated that the events in the Gospels were not real facts, but products of the religious imagination, which has unconsciously materialized into external facts this idea of faith that in Jesus the Messiah had appeared."—This seems to me just what I observed four pages back, and I still prefer my shade of distinction, which does not evaporate history itself into an idea.

Biedermann reproaches Strauss for being too negative and for having broken with Chrisianity. The goal, according to him, is: 1, to disburden religion of all mythological elements; 2, to substitute for the obsolete dualism of orthodoxy another point of view: the victory over the world effected by the feeling of a divine sonship.

It is true that another question arises: Would not religion without its particular marvels, without the locally supernatural, without unverifiable mystery, lose its savour and its efficacy? To satisfy the thinking and educated public, is it wise to sacrifice the influence over the multitudes?

> *Las! j'admirais bien plus l'aurore*
> *Quand je connaissais moins les cieux.*

Answer. Pious fiction is still a fiction. Truth still has a higher right. It is for the world to set itself right with the truth, and not the reverse. Copernicus overthrew the astronomy of the Middle

---

[1] A. E. Biedermann (1819–1885), professor of dogmatic theology in the University of Zürich, one of whose articles, translated by Charles Ritter, had just appeared in the *Etrennes chrétiennes,* Geneva, 1881.

Ages; so much the worse! The eternal Gospel revolutionizes all the Churches; what of it! When symbols become transparent, they no longer bind. One sees them as poetry, as allegory, as metaphor; one no longer believes in them.

Yes, but all things considered, there is an inevitable esotericism, since critical, scientific, philosophic culture is only within the reach of a minority. The new faith will have to find its symbols and its pedagogy. For the moment, it has rather an effect of profanity on pious souls; it has a disrespectful, incredulous and frivolous air, and it seems to emancipate one from traditional dogma only to remove seriousness from the conscience. How safeguard the inner trembling, the feeling of sin, the need of forgiveness, the thirst for sanctity, while eliminating the errors that have served these for so long as a support and an aliment? Is not illusion indispensable? Is it not the method of education ordained by Providence? Can one abolish the fairy-tales?

Perhaps the method would be to distinguish deeply between opinion and belief, and between belief and science. A mind that discerns these different degrees can fancy and believe, without being excluded from a further and higher advance. Egypt, India, neo-Platonism, Catholicism have known degrees of initiation. But the Gospel has professed to tear apart the veils, and the profession of democracy is to level the ranks of intelligence. How remove this difficulty? It is quite simple. Science offers itself to everybody; everyone takes and assimilates whatever he can of it, and he then supposes he has as much as everyone else. Vanity is satisfied and justice likewise.

*December 28, 1880.*—There are two ways of classifying the people we know: the first, the utilitarian way, relates to ourselves and distinguishes those who are friends, enemies, antipathetic, indifferent, those who can render us services or harm us, etc.;—the second, the disinterested way, ranks them according to their intrinsic worth, their own qualities or defects, apart from the sentiments which they feel towards us or which we feel for them.

My tendency is towards the second kind of classification. I appreciate men less for the special affection which they show me than for their personal excellence, and I am unable to confuse gratitude with esteem. The auspicious case is that in which one can unite these two feelings. A painful case is one in which we have to be grateful without feeling respect or confidence.

It is not easy for me to believe in the lastingness of accidental states. The generosity of a miser, the good nature of an egoist, the gentleness of a fanatic, the tenderness of a cold nature, the pity of a prosaic heart, the humility of irritable self-esteem interest me as phenomena and can even touch me if I am the occasion of them; but they inspire in me little confidence for the future. I foresee their end too well; I cannot believe in a miracle. All exceptions tend to disappear and return to the rule again. All privileges are temporary, and, besides, I am less flattered than troubled in being the object of a privilege . . .

In vain does the primitive character cover itself with the later deposits of culture and acquisition, it always comes back to the surface, when the years have worn away all that is accessory and adventitious. I admit that there are great moral crises which sometimes revolutionize the soul, but I do not count on them. They are a possibility, they are not a probability. For one's friends, one must choose those who have native qualities and constitutional virtues; to reckon upon borrowed and additional virtues is to build on artificial soil. One runs too many risks.

> *Chacun a son défaut où toujours il revient,*
> *Honte ni peur n'y remédie.*

Exceptions are snares; and especially when they charm our vanity, then is the time when we should suspect them. It is always a temptation to women to stabilize an inconstant lover; to make a proud woman weep with tenderness is enough to intoxicate any man. But these enticements are deceptive. Affinity of nature based on reverence for the same ideal and proportional to the perfection of the soul is the only one that has any value. True love is the love that ennobles the personality, fortifies the heart and sanctifies existence. The loved object should not be a sphinx, but a limpid diamond; then admiration and attachment increase with knowledge. For earthly loves, on the other hand, illusion is indispensable; the moment the lovers see each other as they are, love is dead, and nothing remains but habit, tolerance or resignation.

*O le charlatanisme! il se glisse partout.*

*Ehrlich währt am längsten,* says the German proverb.

*Il n'est bonne dorure, ami, que d'être d'or.*

*December 30, 1880.*—If I have some understanding of other human beings, it is because no impulse is unknown to me, and because I reproduce in myself, by turns, the most diverse existences. At my desk, I can feel all the human passions in succession; but none of them imprisons me, and it is this that saves me. To understand things is to have been in the things and then to have emerged from them; there must be a captivity, then a deliverance, illusion and disillusion, infatuation and disenchantment. He who is still under the spell and he who has not undergone the spell are incompetent. One knows well only what one has believed and then judged. In order to possess, one must have been possessed and then have reconquered one's independence. To understand, one must be free and yet not have been free always. This is the case whether the question is one of love, art, religion, patriotism, etc. Sympathy is the first condition of criticism. Emotion is the pedestal of reason, and the antecedent of justice.—That is why, in Christianity, Jesus, then Mary, have been adored rather than the Father: the faithful desire a humanized God, who has passed through life and suffering, who has known trial, borne his cross and felt seven thrusts of the spear in his heart;

for man then feels that he is better understood in his misery and desolation. An impassive judge frightens one.

*December 31, 1880.*—To foresee and manage one's own decease is very far from agreeable. It even seems as if one were trying to disarm the King of Terrors and take the future into one's own hands. But this is a superstitious preconception. To settle one's debts with one's family and friends, with the public and with one's memory, is merely fitting for a wise man. It is not to oppose God, or even to embarrass anybody. It is, on the contrary, to make one's last toilet and bury oneself with one's own hands, in order to disturb one's neighbours as little as possible. Far from being pretentious or ostentatious, it is simply a matter of discretion towards others and respect for oneself.—So much for the theory, the difficult part lies in the practice. One never finds the right moment for this work of the lawyer and grave-digger.

*January 5, 1881.*[1]—I probably dread shame more than death. Tacitus said: *Omnia serviliter pro dominatione.* I am just the opposite. Even universal domination would be less dear to me than liberty. Dependence, even if it is voluntary, is a burden to me. I should blush to have my mind determined by interest, to yield to constraint, to be the serf of any will whatever. Vanity seems to me a slavery, self-esteem a meanness, utilitarianism a baseness. I detest the ambition that makes one the liegeman of anything or anybody. I wish to be my own master simply, and act only according to my taste.

If I had health, I should be the freest man I know, though a little coldness of heart would be necessary to increase my independence.

Let us not exaggerate anything; my liberty is only negative. Nobody, man or woman, foreigner or compatriot, nobody on earth can give me a command or exact submission of me. How many people

[1] With the year 1881, beginning with the month of January, we enter upon the last period of Amiel's illness. Although he continued to attend to his duties, and kept silent regarding his premonitions, he felt that he was mortally affected, as the following extracts from the Journal show.

are there who can say as much? I have neither creditor, nor guardian, nor chief, nor wife, nor father-in-law, nor partner, nor administrative board, nor housekeeper, nobody who has an advantage over
me or whose consent, authorization or permission I desire to obtain for any purpose whatever. If I am pleased to consult anyone, it
is because I find it agreeable to do so, and I can say, like an absolute monarch, Such is my pleasure.—How about my professorship?
I have, it is true, an administrative superior (the Department of
Public Instruction), but it can neither dismiss nor cashier me, and I
myself can send in my resignation whenever it suits me to do so. I
have a voluntary occupation, and one that cannot hold me in spite
of myself, for I can deprive myself of my stipend. I have no contract that binds me beyond the semester that has begun.—Many
things, however, are not possible for me, and, if I were stupid
enough to seek them, the limits of my freedom would become evident and my pride would suffer. So I am careful not to wish for
them or even call them to mind. I wish only what I am capable of,
and thus I do not strike against any wall, I even conceal from myself the boundaries of my prison-yard. I rather wish for a little less
than I might have, so that I may not even brush against any obstacle or come within sight of humiliation. Renunciation is the safeguard of dignity. We should strip ourselves that we may not be
stripped. He who has given his life away can look death in the face;
what more can death take from him? The abolition of desire and
the practice of charity is the whole method of Buddha and the whole
art of Deliverance.

*(Later.)*—My throat pesters me. It is snowing. So I depend on
Nature and God. But I do not depend on human caprice; that is a
capital point. It is true that my druggist may make a blunder and
poison me, my banker might abscond and reduce me to beggary, as
an earthquake might destroy my property beyond any indemnity.
Absolute independence is thus a pure illusion. But I have a relative
independence, that of the Stoic, who retires into his will and shuts
the gates of this fortress.

*Jurons, excepté Dieu, de n'avoir point de maître.*

The oath of old Geneva remains my motto, and a concurrence of favourable circumstances has permitted me to realize it.

*January 7, 1881.*—The dives that Descartes made out of sight, suddenly stealing away from his friends, relatives and connections in order to go and work in some place that was unknown to them, show that at times man feels an imperious need of belonging to his thought, of ceasing to speak to anyone but himself and barricading his fortress. At these times sociability seems to him a destruction of his personal life. He flees from it as one flees from mosquitoes, ghouls, vampires and all drinkers of blood. He uses his right of self-defence. It is so tiresome to be forever chattering, explaining oneself, excusing oneself, that is, living on the surface; this eternal reaction to persons, that is, to vanity, curiosity, will, exhausts and wearies one; one wishes to occupy oneself with things. Things are silent, calm; they wait for one. One is restored with them, while people use one up. Long live peace and stillness! Hail to the cell that is sealed three-quarters of the day and night! One recovers oneself there.

*January 10, 1881.*—To be affected by the ill-will, the ingratitude, the indifference of others is a weakness to which I may be inclined. It is painful to me to be ignored, to be ill thought of; I lack manly ruggedness, my heart is a little feminine and consequently more vulnerable than it should be. It seems to me, however, that in this region I have grown quite tough and weather-beaten. The malignity of the world bothers me much less than formerly. Do I owe this to philosophy? Is it an effect of age? Perhaps the reason is simply that I have received sufficient evidences of respect, attachment and sympathy to be reassured about myself. The harm that the malevolent do us is to put us in doubt about ourselves; in our modesty, we tell ourselves that they may be right. But if we are able to think that they are mistaken all is saved. One regrets their mistake, one is no longer troubled or desolated. It has taken repeated proofs, and proofs from without, to make me conscious of my worth and to inspire me with some esteem for myself. Otherwise I should readily have believed that my merit was nil and that all my endeavours were meaningless. For the timid, success is necessary; praise raises their morale; admiration is a strengthening elixir. One thinks one knows oneself, but as long as one does not know one's comparative worth, one's standing in society, one does not know oneself sufficiently. In order to act, one has to reckon in some degree with others, feel that one has weight and credit, so as to proportion one's effort to the resistence that is to be overcome. As long as one scorns opinion, one lacks a measure for oneself, one does not know one's relative power. I have disdained opinion too much, while being too sensitive to injustice. These two mistakes have cost me dear. I have refused to impose myself or to push myself, and I have ceased to have any object but my inner freedom.

*Selon qu'il a semé, chacun récolte en moi.*

I should have liked to have goodwill, sympathy, equity, but my pride forbade solicitation, shrewdness, calculation. People have never given me my true place nor quoted me at my true price. I have made it a point of honour to endure this. But I could not prevent myself from observing it. I do not think I have followed a false path, inasmuch as I have been in accord with myself. But self-defence against my environment has used up two-thirds of my strength. In surroundings congenial to my nature, I should have given ten times as much as I have been able to give in Geneva. The want of adaptation has worn me out for nothing. At my death, they will say here, What a pity! And I, too, will think, What a pity! Only the identity of the phrase will cover an ambiguity of meaning. People will throw the blame on me, and my feeling is that they have done me wrong. Many good things will have been prevented: that is the truth of the matter. But whose fault was it? That is the essential point.

I am at peace now. But my career is finished, my strength at an end and my life near its close.

*Il n'est plus temps pour rien, excepté pour mourir . . .*

That is why I can look at it all historically.

*January 15, 1881 (11 p. m.).*—Ran through Pascal again *(Pensées,* Havet's edition, 1852).

I find at once the solution of a little problem that defied the acumen of Fougère and Havet. The Salomon de Tultie who perplexed and annoyed them is none other than the anagram of a pseudonym, namely that of Louis de Montalte, the very name chosen by the author of the *Lettres à un provincial* when these were collected in a volume. The same fifteen letters form both names.

I perceive also the decisive flaw in Pascal's apologetics. It is the same as that which the story of the golden tooth recalls. He assumes as given exactly what is in question, namely, the traditional Catholic dogma. The question is whether or not this dogma is the expression of Christianity, whether it is revealed, whether religious revelation consists of a document ready-made and dropped from heaven. And Pascal did not even suspect what had to be examined. He has not the least particle of the critical and historical sense. Catholicism for him is a sacred whole which he does not analyze or explain. These absolute, peremptory, geometrical minds are utterly incompetent in problems of this order. They know only black and white, the false and the true. This elementary logic is powerless before everything that is living, before that which is metamorphosed and becomes, before historical concretions and spiritual formations . . .

The history and the philosophy of religions, the progress of the exegetical and archæological sciences have totally reshaped the face of things, the meaning of problems, the methods of research, the spirit of responses. Pascal is sincere, but his powerful intelligence was unable to clear itself of the net of a fundamental prejudice.

*January 23, 1881.*—Very passable night, but this morning the

clots of mucus were difficult to expel.—Splendid weather. Sun full
in the windows. With my feet on the andirons, I finish reading the
newspaper . . .

At this moment I feel well, and it seems singular to me that I am
condemned to a brief term. Life feels no kinship with death. This is
doubtless why a sort of mechanical, instinctive hope is forever reborn in us to becloud our reason and cause us to doubt the verdict
of science. Life tends to persevere in the being. Like the parrot in
the fable, it repeats, even at the moment when it is being strangled;

*Cela, cela ne sera rien.*

Thought states things at their worst, but the animal protests.

*Elle ne croit au mal que lorsqu'il est venu.*

Is this such a bad thing? Probably not. Nature wishes the living
to defend themselves against death; hope is identical with the love
of life; it is an organic impulse, subsequently placed under the
shelter of religion. Who knows, God may save us, work a miracle.
Besides, is one ever sure that there is no remedy? Uncertainty is the
refuge of hope. The doubtful is reckoned among the favourable
chances. That which is not against us is for us. Mortal frailty
clutches at every prop. Why complain of it? Even with all its aids, it
is not likely to escape affliction and distress.

The master solution is always to submit to necessity, calling it
the paternal will of God, and to bear one's cross courageously,
offering it to the arbiter of destinies. The soldier does not debate
the orders he has received; he obeys and dies unmurmuring. If he
waited to see what purpose was served by his sacrifice, he would
never know submission.

—Two feet of snow. In London, the Thames frozen; floods in
Belgium, Calabria, Spain. We are going through an ugly phase. I
was thinking this morning that, except for two or three members

of the family, nobody suspects our physical tribulations. And even our intimates do not know of our conversations with the King of Terrors. There are thoughts that have no confidant, sorrows that no one shares. Generosity even requires us to hide them. One dreams alone, one suffers alone, one dies alone; one inhabits alone the closet of six planks. But one is not forbidden to open this solitude to God. The austere monologue thus becomes a dialogue. Aversion becomes docility. Renunciation becomes peace. Sorrowful destruction becomes liberty again.

> *Vouloir ce que Dieu veut est la seule science*
> *Qui nous met en repos.*

Through each one of us pass many opposite impulses. But the moment we recognize where order lies and submit to order, all is well.

> *Comme un sage mourant, puissions-nous dire en paix:*
> *J'ai trop longtemps erré, cherché; je me trompais;*
> *Tout est bien, mon Dieu m'enveloppe.*

Charles Heim [1] died like Epictetus, like Spinoza. Let us try to do the same. The forgiveness of sins through the intermediary and by intercession is a more special and less lofty faith. It is the traditional Christian faith; but it was not the faith of Jesus himself, the great-hearted hero who proclaimed that God was love. If God is love, he has no need of a propitiatory victim, his majesty asks for no substitutional punishment. Orthodox and vulgar Christianity makes Jesus better than God, since Jesus gives his life, though innocent, for the guilty, and since God pardons the guilty only after the shedding of innocent blood. In vain does faith wrap this consequence in the respectful cloud of mystery, the consequence remains and indicts the dogma. Education by dogma may have been neces-

[1] This was the "dear and sweet friend" whose death was noted in the *Journal intime* on December 26, 1868.

sary and may have had its advantages. But there is a vengeance for the contradictory. And if so many free minds have abandoned the Church, it is because the Church has preferred dogma to truth, the temporary to the eternal, the apparent to the substantial and illogical faith to reasonable faith . . .

My pupils can see with what difficulty thought has freed itself, at what a price science and philosophy have had to redeem themselves from their servitude; what religion is, and the position of Christianity among the other religious systems. I do not polemize, I narrate; I do not quarrel, I shed light.

I know that light can scarcely break through prejudice; but, with the apostle, I repeat to people, Judge ye what I say. The truth is, I do not like to offend or violate any fixed custom or any conviction. I say, Be free, but leave me free. I do not indoctrinate, I give the means of pronouncing. I endeavour to be impartial and to convey things justly. This aim is as good as any, it seems to me, and this teaching has its usefulness.

*January 25, 1881 (noon).*—Terrible night. Struggled for three or four hours together with my garrotters and had a close glimpse of death. This continuous assault by the enemy is exasperating. To perish in one's spittle, what a humiliation!

Respite and sleep from three to six in the morning. Gave my lecture notwithstanding, though my voice was muffled; but sustained speaking is exhausting under these conditions. And I can climb my four flights only with effort; my chest aches as if someone had struck me with an iron rod, and the waist-band of my trousers feels like an iron collar.

I cannot well account for those four hours of nocturnal torture; I see them as a sort of nightmare, the reality of which seems hardly certain to me. Is it really true? Is it I who almost expired, by surprise, through treachery, through inadvertence?

*January 29, 1881.*— . . . It is clear that what awaits me is suffocation, asphyxia. I shall stifle.

645

Perhaps I should not have chosen this death; but when there is no option, one must be resigned and say no more.

Spinoza died in the presence of the doctor he had summoned. You must accustom yourself to the idea of dying alone, some fine night, strangled by your laryngitis. This is not as good as the last sigh of a patriarch with his family in prayer about him. It lacks beauty, grandeur and poetry; but Stoicism consists in renunciation. *Abstine et sustine.* You know besides that you have loyal friends; it is better not to torment them. Groans and agitation make the great passage more painful. One utterance takes the place of all the others: Let the will of God be done and not mine!

Leibnitz was accompanied to the cemetery only by his servant. The loneliness of the death-bed and the coffin is therefore not an evil. The mystery is not to be shared. The dialogue between the soul and the King of Terrors demands no witnesses.

It is the living who insist upon cheering him who is passing away. —And, after all, no one knows exactly what is in store for him. What will be will be. There is nothing for us but to say *Amen.*

*February 4, 1881.*—A singular sensation to get into bed thinking that perhaps one will not see the morrow. I had it yesterday strongly enough, and yet here I am. But to be dependent on one's phlegm, on a single clot, this destroys one's ardour for any enterprise. The feeling of excessive frailty facilitates humility, but it makes short work of all ambition;

> *Quittez le long espoir et les vastes pensées.*

A work that depends on a long future seems absurd. One lives now only from day to day;

> *A quoi bon troubler notre vie*
> *Des soins d'un avenir qui n'est pas fait pour nous?*

If one cannot dream of having a lustrum before one, a year, a month of freedom, if one reckons now only on dozens of hours and the coming night is a menace, filled with unknown possibilities, it stands to reason that one renounces art, science and politics and is content to converse with oneself, a thing that is possible to the very end. Inner soliloquy is the sole resource of one who is condemned to death and whose execution is deferred. He gathers himself together in his innermost conscience. He ceases to radiate, he psychologizes. He ceases to act, he contemplates. He still writes letters to those who rely upon him; but he gives up the public and retires within himself. Like the hare, he comes home to die, and this home is his consciousness, his thought. His vestibule is his private journal. As long as he is able to hold the pen and is permitted a moment of solitude, he meditates in the presence of this echo of himself, and he converses with his God.

Yet this is not a moral examination, an act of contrition, a cry for help. It is only an Amen of submission. The preoccupation with sin, the only method of the common faith, has become foreign to me, no doubt because the frenzies of self-will are not in my line. "My child, give me thine heart."

Renunciation and acquiescence are less hard for me than for others, for I desire nothing. My only wish would be not to suffer, but Jesus in Gethsemane believed that he could make the same prayer. Let us unite with him in these words, "Nevertheless not my will, but thine, be done", and wait.

Have I practised sanctification? Not in the strict ascetic sense. I have always tried to recover inner freedom and goodness, but rather from respect for human nature than to obey an external commandment. For many years, the immanent God has been more real to me than the transcendent God, and the religion of Jacob has been more foreign to me than that of Kant or even Spinoza. The whole Semitic dramaturgy has appeared to me as a work of the imagination. The apostolic documents have changed in value and meaning in my eyes. The distinction between belief and truth has grown increasingly clear. Religious psychology has become a simple phenomenon and has lost its fixed and noumenal value. The Christian apologetics of Pascal, Leibnitz, Secrétan seem to me no more convincing than those of the Middle Ages, for they presuppose what is in question: a revealed doctrine, a Christianity that is definite and immutable. It seems to me that what remains from all my studies is a new phenomenology of the mind, the intuition of universal metamorphosis. All particular convictions, decisive principles, confessed formulas, ideas that cannot be fused, are only prejudices, useful in practice, but restrictions of the mind. The absolute in detail is absurd and contradictory. Political, religious, aesthetic, literary factions are anchyloses of thought that are taken for advantages. Every special belief is a rigidity and obtuseness, although this consistency is necessary in its time. Our monad, in so far as it thinks, is freed from the limitations of time, space and historical circumstance; but in so far as it is individual, and in order to do something, it adapts itself to the current illusions and sets itself a definite goal. One is permitted to be man, but it is fitting also to be a man, to be an individual. Our role is therefore double. Only, the philosopher is authorized to develop especially the first, which almost all human beings neglect.

*February 7, 1881.*—Fine sun today. But I have scarcely enough energy to notice it. Admiration and joy presuppose a little respite. And the weight of my head fatigues my neck, the weight of life oppresses my heart; this is not the aesthetic state.

An idea besets me: I have not properly drawn up my will. How many times I have thought of it! But momentary fancies are nothing.—I have thought of various things which I should have written, but the most original and the best in ourselves is that which we most often allow to be lost. We hold ourselves back for a future that never comes. *Omnis moriar.*

*February 8, 1881 (10 a. m.).*—Terrible night. Azraël passed over me at three o'clock in the morning. For fifteen minutes I was between life and death, every second awaiting suffocation. First, several hours of continuous agony. I felt as if a hair were across the glottis, and the spasms to clear it out, powerless in their outbursts,

had left me breathless and almost without any strength. I was afraid
of dropping dead before I could draw up my armchair, dress myself
warmly and sit down in a dressing-gown beside my fire. Impossible
to ask for help, and besides there was no help that anyone could
give me. Any incautious attention rendered to me, any explanation I
might have given, any word I uttered would have been the end of
me. I have never been closer to the last gasp. The situation was
frightful. What saved me was an almost mechanical effort. I swallowed my gargle drop by drop, and it seemed to clear the opening
of the glottis. My breath came back. But the reprieve could not be
a deliverance. It was at this moment of truce that I could have
wished to hold a friendly hand and make the vigil of arms. It was a
solemn hour, and I doubted if I should see the morning.

*February 9, 1881 (10 a. m.).*—Oh ravishing! I have coughed very
little, I breathe, I feel strong. And yet a night in this armchair
would scarcely seem enviable to those who are in health. But to
escape the Thugs for a few hours brings such a feeling of relief that
the aspect of everything changes. Comparing yesterday with today, I
hardly recognize myself. It is as if a dying man were galvanized into
life or had undergone a blood-transfusion.

*(Later.)*—Since January 17, as I see from this note-book, my
nightly battle with my Thugs has been almost unintermittent.
Wretched night, woeful night, abysmal night, merciless night, frightful night, such is the daily bulletin. As long ago as January 25, or
about a fortnight ago, I read these words: Had a close glimpse of
death, almost fainted, etc. So it is not a dream; I have been grap-
pling and wrestling with the dark angel for a long time. Jacob escaped with one night of mysterious combat; with me, the combat
begins afresh almost every night. And so when there is a respite, as
this last time, it is a benediction, an alleluia. The passing of an
agony has the effect of a rebirth. Blessed be a day of rest, blessed be
he who has permitted it and she who has procured it.

*February 14, 1881.*—Assuming that your weeks are numbered,
what should you do to set yourself right with the world? Render to

each his due, attend to the things of justice, prudence, goodness, leave a sweet memory. Try, therefore, not to forget anything useful or anyone who depends upon you.

> *Ne cherche point ton rang sur l'échelle infinie;*
> *Qui fait tout ce qu'il doit n'est jamais le dernier.*

*February 15, 1881.*—This morning, the idea that my days are numbered seems to me fantastic. This magnificent sunshine makes funereal preoccupations almost ridiculous. Besides, the moment I feel a little comfortable, it seems to me that I have never been ill. This way of feeling has awkward effects with the doctor, who always supposes that I am better and livelier than I am.

Be that as it may, gave up, not without a pang, my lecture at the University, and summoned my Æsculapius. Desire to settle my affairs and put things in order. Placed on my mantel-piece, in a glass of water, two camelias which Fida Memor sent me yesterday, with a few stanzas of poetry . . . Letters from Miss Jessie (London), Charles Fournel (Paris); G. Revilliod sends me a greeting from Thebes of the hundred gates (postmarked Luxor). A good little letter from Fida [1] . . . They are like so many wreaths cast upon a grave.

Mentally I am taking leave of all the distant friends whom I shall not see again.

*February 18, 1881.*—Misty weather. Fairish night . . . The emaciation continues, however . . . In short, the vulture is giving me a

---

[1] Miss Jessie H. had been Amiel's pupil in Geneva, in 1863. Greatly attached to her old teacher, who represented for her "poetry and thought", she had stopped in Geneva in 1878 to see him again. After this meeting, they exchanged a few letters.—Charles Fournel, son of the poet of whose *Essais dramatiques* Amiel had published, in 1878, a posthumous selection.—Gustave Revilliod, a rich Genevese patrician who bequeathed to his native city the admirable collections he had made in the course of his travels and assembled in the sumptuous museum of L'Ariana.—*Fida* was one of the names given by the Journal to Fanny Mercier, among such others as Seriosa, Stoica, Gudule and Calvinia.

respite, but he is hovering over his prey . . . The possibility of resuming my official functions and recovering a stable balance seems like a dream to me.

Although my impressions at the moment are not of the world beyond the grave, I feel that I am a captive for good, a chronic invalid. This floating state, which is neither life nor death, has its own sweetness because, if it is a renunciation, it permits thought. It is a painless revery, a peaceful composure. Surrounded with affections and books, free at least to the threshold of my apartment, I ride the current of time as once I glided over the canals of Holland, without jolt or sound. I fancy I am still in *treckschute*. Now and then, I all but hear the gentle lapping of the water cleft by the canal-boat or the hoofs of the draught-horse ambling along the sandy path. There is something fantastic in travelling under these conditions. One is not certain that one still exists and has a foothold on the earth. One remembers the manes, the fleeting shades in the twilight of the *inania regna*. It is the fluid existence.

"What have you in hand? What are you writing?" Auguste Bouvier asked me.—Heavens, nothing.

I watch my impressions go by, my dreams, my thoughts, my memories, like a man who has given up everything. I have withdrawn into my last observatory, the psychological consciousness. I observe the events within myself without arousing them or shunning them. This contemplative immobility is akin to that which one attributes to the seraphim. The individual self does not interest it, but only a specimen of the monad, a sample of the general history of the mind. Everything is in everything, and the consciousness examines what it has before it. Nothing is great or small. The mind is omnimodal and it finds everything good.

In this state, the relations with the body, with the outer world, with other individuals disappear. The *Selbstbewusstsein* [1] returns to

[1] State of a being conscious of itself.

the impersonal *Bewusstsein.* The universe is dissolved in the Trimurti, and the Trimurti in the Parabrahm.

To become a person again requires suffering, duty and will (see *Jour à Jour*).

Should one regret these oscillations between the personal and the impersonal, between pantheism and theism, between Spinoza and Leibnitz? No, for it is one of these states that makes one conscious of the other. Since man is capable of visiting both these realms, why should he mutilate himself?

*(Later.)*—O bliss! Thirty pounds less weight on my chest. I have come back from a walk . . . I was breathing better, I was stronger, I climbed up my four flights with almost no effort of breath. I scarcely knew myself. This was not the same man as day before yesterday. It was like a convalescence. I am as grateful as I am surprised. Is it possible that the vulture has abandoned its prey? That I might be able to resume my lectures? Is it a real improvement that is going to continue, or only a pleasant clearing between two ordeals? Bah! Let us not make conjectures,

*Jouissons du bonheur, jouissons du printemps!*

A bird in the hand is better than two in the bush. What is here is good; to God belongs the rest, even the most immediate future.

*February 22, 1881.*—The movement typical of the mind lies in astronomy: no immobility, but no precipitation; orbits, cycles, advance, but harmony; motion, but order; everything weighs and counter-balances, everything receives and gives back light. Might not this cosmic and divine activity become ours? Is the cannibalism of the war of all against all a superior type of equilibrium? I am loath to think so. The phase of ferocity is considered by some theoreticians the final form. There must be a mistake here. Justice will prevail and justice is not egoism. Independence and goodness must work out a resultant that will be the line we require.

*Hanc veniam petimusque damusque vicissim.*

*March 1, 1881.*—Running through the *Journal*,[1] I have just glanced over the affairs of the world. It is the tumult of Babel. But it is rather a pleasure to make the tour of the planet in an hour and review the human race. It awakens a feeling of ubiquity. A newspaper in the twentieth century will be composed of eight or ten daily bulletins, the political, religious, scientific, literary, artistic, commercial, meteorological, military, economic, social, judicial and financial bulletins, and will comprise only two parts, *Urbs* and *Orbis,* the region and the world. The need to sum things up, to simplify, will generalize the reportorial methods that render series and comparisons possible. We shall end by feeling the pulse of the race and the globe as easily as that of an invalid, and we shall note the palpitations of the universal life as sensitively as we hear the grass growing in the fields, or the sound of the sun-spots, or the gathering of volcanic disturbances. Activity will be converted into consciousness; Ge[2] will perceive herself. And then she will also blush for her disorders, her uglinesses, her miseries, her crimes, and perhaps she will take energetic resolutions in the direction of justice. When humanity has cut its wisdom teeth, it will have the decency to mend its ways and will wish to reduce methodically the portion of evil. The *Weltgeist* will pass from the state of instinct to the moral state. War, hatred, egosim, fraud, the right of the strongest will be regarded as barbarisms of the old days, distempers of growth. Civilized men will replace their pretensions with real virtues. Men will be brothers, peoples will be friends, races will be sympathetic, and they will draw from love as powerful a principle of emulation, invention and zeal as the crude stimulus of interest has provided. Will this millennium come to pass? It is an act of piety to think so.

*March 4, 1881.*—Guizot never knew how to laugh; he never threw aside his harness of sobriety. Therefore he won respect, but he had a pedantic and pedagogical air that was all too virtuous and solemn. Fancy, poetry, art, nonsense, gaiety, good-nature did not exist for

[1] The *Journal de Genève.*
[2] Γῆ, the Earth.

him. This perpetual gravity is an imperfection. *Desipere in loco* is a part of wisdom. Guizot tired the patience of the French, like an Aristides and a Grandison, like a school-master of politics, a dean of the doctrinaire. This Calvinistic rigidity ends by getting on one's nerves. People who go to bed in their armour are not very pleasant. —Thiers once said, Guizot is a great orator, but he is stupid in politics. In other words, he had general maxims but no ideas, character but no invention. These grave manikins make professors of politics but not statesmen. They lack the infusion of finesse and scepticism that produces freedom of mind. In compensation, they are bars of iron.

*March 10, 1881 (noon).—Jacta est alea.* I have just given my instructions to Charles Ritter, and sent him a title-deed, a letter and three notes of introduction, so that he can close the affair. What affair? That of assuring me a few feet of earth in the oasis of Clarens. It would not be so easy, if I were to die here in Geneva. One cannot dispose of one's own body. All sorts of precautions are necessary, indeed, if one is to escape the automatic machinery of the local routine that tramples over every preference and every desire. I shall have done at last all that is possible for the realization of this wish, an old one, now, with me, which the ugly question of the Genevese cemeteries has only made more lively. I shall sleep in a beautiful countryside, brimming over with my recollections; and for forty years those for whom my name will mean something will know where they can give my memory a thought. Slumber in this spot has a peculiar sweetness, and it is easy there for visitors to meditate.—The promiscuous mingling of ashes, the uproar of a great city cannot reach those who sleep at Clarens. *Requiescunt in pace.*

*March 14, 1881.*—Finished Mérimée (*Lettres à Panizzi*, II).

*Votre deuil me prédit mon sort.*

Mérimée died of the illness that torments me: "I cough and I choke". Bronchitis and asthma, leading to an inability to take nourishment, and then to exhaustion. He too tried arsenic, winters in Cannes, baths in compressed air. Everything was useless. Suffocation and inanition carried off the author of *Colomba. Hic tua res agitur,*

*Et dans chaque feuille qui tombe*
*Je lis un présage de mort.*

The dull, grey sky shares the colour of my thoughts. And yet the irrevocable also has its sweetness and its calm. The oscillations of illusion, the uncertainties of desire, the sudden leaps of hope give way to tranquil resignation. It is as if one were beyond the grave. Besides, this week my corner of earth in the Oasis is to be bought. Everything tends to the conclusion, *festinat ad eventum.*

*March 15, 1881.*—The *Journal* is crammed with details about the horrible attempt at St. Petersburg.—A long historical article on the Transvaal proves the perfidy of the British policy in Africa. But one also sees that the accumulation of iniquities at length creates catastrophes that break over innocent heads. Historic justice is usually belated, so belated that it becomes unjust, unless one accepts the Turkish way, which is to strike somebody, after the crime, saying, Too bad if this is not the criminal! The providential theory is founded on solidarity. Louis XVI pays for Louis XV, Alexander II for Nicholas. We make atonement for our fathers, and our grandchildren will be punished for us. Individualism will exclaim that this is a double iniquity. And it will be right, if its principle is true, but is its principle true? That is the point. It seems that the individual part of his destiny is, for any given man, only a part of this destiny. Morally, we are responsible for that which we have desired, but socially our happiness and our unhappiness depend on causes that are independent of our will. Religion replies, Mystery, obscurity, submission, faith. Do your duty; leave the rest to God!

*(10 p. m.)*—Received callers: Bernard Bouvier, who brings me the sympathy of his comrades . . .

*March 16, 1881 (11 a. m.).*—Dismal night. Melancholy morning.

Falling to pieces. My god-daughter remained at my bedside until midnight, and was helping me again, from two to four in the morning, to pass through my *angustiæ*. I am privileged, no doubt, and I do not forget to be grateful. But how cruel for a man is this ignoble decomposition, with its deceptive intermissions! The doctor's two war-horses, digitalis and bromide, seem ineffectual with me. Weary and bored, I watch my own destruction. What efforts to prevent oneself from dying! These defensive operations are too much for me.

Useless and incessant struggle humiliates a manly nature. The thing that the lion can least endure is to be slain by mosquitoes, to do battle with the gnat. The natural man feels the same way. But the spiritual man must learn meekness and long-suffering in patience. The inevitable is the will of God. One might have preferred something else, but the question is to accept the lot assigned to us.

> *Comme un sage mourant puissions-nous dire en paix:*
> *J'ai trop longtemps erré, cherché; je me trompais;*
> *Tout est bien, mon Dieu m'enveloppe.*

*(10 p. m.)*—My sister L. sends me a vase of azaleas, covered with flowers and buds. Fida brings me some roses and violets from Nice. Everybody spoils me; this proves I am ill . . . The weather was superb. But I had no strength for walking, and I came in again very quickly.

*March 19, 1881.*—Disgust, discouragement. The heart is growing worse. Every morning there is some new impairment to be noted. My patience is wearing out.

And yet what affectionate attentions, what anxious care surrounds me . . . Everything in the house is arranged for my comfort, and I am enveloped in none but soothing and restful sensations. I have sunshine and no noise, a fire that burns as if on the altar of Vesta, an excellent table, books in profusion.—*Epicaurès,* I am constantly saying to myself. And yet, without health, of what avail is all the rest? Of what use to me is everything that is granted me? Of what use were the trials of Job? To ripen his patience, to exercise his submission.

Come, one must get out of oneself, one must shake off this melancholy, this disgust. Let us think not of all that is lost, but of all that might still be lost. Let us think again of our privileges. Spoiled child, count them over . . . But, when all is said, I am in a pitiful state.

*March 21, 1881.*—This invalid's life is too Epicurean. For five or six weeks now I have done nothing but mark time, nurse myself or amuse myself, and I feel satiated. What I lack is work. Work is the relish of existence. There is something insipid in life without an aim, life without effort. Indolence leads to languor; languor gives birth to disgust. Besides, the nostalgia of spring is here again. It is the season of vague desires, of obscure uneasinesses, confused aspirations, sighs without an object. One dreams wide awake. One seeks, one gropes, for what, who can say? One cries out for something that has no name, unless it is happiness or death. One is like a man in a fever, who tosses on his bed and cannot find any position that is better than any other. This indefinable anxiety is the effect of the rebirth of things,

> *Le sang remonte à ce front qui frissonne,*
> *Le vieux coursier a senti l'aiguillon.*

To defend oneself against these dangerous exhalations, one must gird one's loins, one must concentrate oneself and, above all, work. You have thrown up the sponge, and, as you are no longer able to do much, you have done nothing. The result is precisely emptiness and ennui. You have no plan, no programme, no work in hand, and you let yourself drift with the days. This looks like patience, like meekness; but it is really apathy. With more will, ambition, courage, you would turn your circumstances to much better account.

*March 28, 1881.*—I cannot work; it is difficult for me to exist.

Let us give a few months to the pampering of our friends, for this phase is good. But afterwards? Better to give place to that which has life, to the active, the productive.

> *Tircis, voici le temps de prendre sa retraite.*

Can it be that I still cling strongly to living? I do not think so. It is health I desire, non-suffering. As this desire is vain, the rest for me has no savour.—Satiety, Lassitude. Renunciation. Abdication. Disgust follows mutilation and impotence. "In your patience possess ye your souls."

*April 3, 1881 (11 p. m.).*—Reading: *Mémoires d'un Sibérien,* by Rufin Piotrowski. Selected and translated by Julien Kladsko, 1870.

Nothing could be more moving than these recollections of a Polish political prisoner, deported to the banks of the Irtich, who contrived to escape from Siberia in 1846. This flight savours of the miraculous. And as for the picture of Siberia, it is enough to horrify one with the Russian regime and lead one to measure the mountain of crimes heaped up by the czars.—If the regicidal attempts are multiplying against the Romanovs, the iniquities of their house must not be forgotten. Muscovy is synonymous with ferocity, and the sovereigns have set the example for the subjects, *lupus lupis.* Monsters have brought forth monsters. The law of retaliation is the only law on a level with this inferior society, which has scarcely emerged from moral barbarism. Historical vengeance is indeed a form of justice. But what an odious history is that of Russia!—The universal indignation against the nihilist assassins is an homage rendered to morality; but czarism has set itself above morality and chosen to subject to it only its numberless victims. But there cannot be two rules, one for the vanquished, the other for the conquerors. Let justice among brigands be what it can. The lookers-on would be very ingenuous if they took sides between the band and its leader. The Russian world is the world of force. Whether authority crushes the conspirators or the conspirators overthrow authority, this is a matter of war. Autocracy and its adversaries have no common law and give one another no quarter.

*April 10, 1881 (Sunday).*—Have gone through a thousand different sensations during the last thirty hours: disappointment with the doctor, a bad night, consciousness of my decay, weakening of my stomach, satiety with everything, even with the anxious care that no longer lets me take a breath by myself, enervation, languor and discomfort.—Spent a few hours with Fida, call at the *Isle d'azur*.

*April 13, 1881 (9 a. m.).*—Favourable crisis. Better night, appetite, strength coming back. The turn came yesterday afternoon. I am surprised and delighted, but I scarcely dare to believe it. Why, having slept but little, have I been feeling gay since dawn? Probably because my stomach has resumed its functions. If they were willing not to overwhelm it, it would always be ready to perform its service. But still everything hangs on a thread, for even now I feel pain in two places, one in the back, the other in the heart. Let us rejoice in the present moment; the future belongs to God.

> *Oh! demain c'est la grande chose;*
> *De quoi demain sera-t-il fait?*

A sad piece of news has come. The kind curé from Lorraine is mortally ill. The doctors give him only two months. When the young go off like this, the veterans have no right to rebel.

*(10 p. m.).*—Reading: a few chapters of *Graindorge.* Part of *Clovis Gosselin,* a novel by Karr. A number of the *Revue critique.*

Wrote to the Abbé Roussel, Aménaïde, Eugène A . . . and P. V . . .[1]

Visit from Doctor B . . . I am not at all satisfied, for I get neither relief nor enlightenment. He does neither my mind nor my body

---

[1] The Abbé Roussel was the "kind curé from Lorraine", the curé of Domrémy, author of a book of poems: *Fleurs des Vosges,* who had given Amiel tokens of his admiration for the poems *Jour à jour;* Aménaïde and Eugène A., two cousins; P. V., a colleague in the University.

any good and really leaves me alone in the homicidal crises day and
night. Bromide, chloral, this is easily said, but it answers to one
point only of the area to be defended and to one difficulty only in
this inch-by-inch battle.

*April 14, 1881 (3 p. m.).*—In eighteen hours, this is the first moment of relief. Wretched evening, horrible night, cruel morning,
such is the balance-sheet. I am exhausted, floored. Here I am back
in the suffocation of February, after twenty experiments of every
kind. The birds of ill-omen are flying about me again. The worst
of my many disappointments is that relative to the doctor. He is
not the man, he is not my man. For three months I have given him
all my trust, but he has obstinately persisted in the minor matters
without making any headway in the essential. The many warnings
have had no effect in putting him on the right track. He cares more
for his opinion than for the truth and for his art than for his patient. It is a pity.

Reading: Karr (*Clovis Gosselin*).

Feeling a little better. I observe for the twentieth time how
quickly discomforts slip out of my memory. Trials, constraints, sufferings, infirmities affect me like old crotchets, bad dreams; they
are not mine, they are not I. They are no sooner gone than forgotten.

This means that my nature has a horror of these distortions and
gaps in one's being. It undergoes suffering but does not recognize
it. It thought it endured blows on its cheek, but it does not believe in the reality of this impression. It rejects from itself every
injury to its liberty, as the glacier repels the impurities that come to
sully it. This instinctive repugnance to the irremediable is allied to
the instinct of personal preservation, the need of integrity. It is
probably identical with hope and synonymous with vital power.

*April 16, 1881 (10 p. m.).*—Reread *Sous les Tilleuls*, by Al-
phonse Karr. Disappointment and discontent. As a novel, it is
wretchedly constructed. As a portrayal of manners, it has neither
place nor date nor truth. A quantity of indelicate and even indecent

scenes. Much idle digression. Naturalness and unconstraint cannot take the place of everything. Fire, wit, humour, satire and even passion are not qualities enough for the novel, which belongs to the epic and objective genre, requires, that is, characters and a theme that can carry on by themselves. Verisimilitude is the law of this kind of work. Well, Karr outrageously violates physical, moral, social probabilities. His fantasy, moreover, is without proportions. In a word, this long novel, which is neither composed nor connected, is an abortive effort of a man of wit. The success of *Sous les Tilleuls* was a matter of date. Today it would fall flat.

*April 17, 1881, Easter.*—The day has been glorious outside. But it has weighed rather heavily on me. I have not had one good hour, either last night or up to this very moment, when ten o'clock is sounding from Saint Pierre. My poor body has impressed itself in every way on my attention . . . Felt keenly today how tiring attentions can be. One can wear an invalid out by crushing him with a continuous indulgence of suggestions and changes. Calm, peace, silence are strong needs of my nature, and perpetual amelioration is a kind of torture. Just as it is not ingesting but digesting that nourishes one, so it is not the multitude of attentions that gives pleasure, but the attentions that are really useful and offered with discretion. Measure and the appropriate should be the motto, even of the sisters of charity. Invalids can be unnerved by the heaping-up of assiduities; what they like is to be divined, not to be manipulated by the zeal of others.

*April 18, 1881 (2 p. m.).*—Atrocious night. The fatal lasso of suffocation is always tightening more and more. And the days are becoming as burdensome and painful as the nights. Languor of flesh and spirit. Miseries without issue and persecution without truce.

I know two Fannies [1] as different as possible in the matter of letters. The second was describing to me this very day how she

[1] His sister Fanny, who had informed him, a few weeks previously, that she had just burned all his letters; and his friend Fanny Mercier (Fida).

understands these trusts and the duty of a pious archivist: "It is good for you to be jealous of yourself, for you protect yourself so little. Too proud to justify yourself, impenetrable sometimes, you are, at other moments, so absolutely unguarded; besides, you are so impressionable that some of the things you write need their context in order to give their real truth." My dear Fida, stoical in some respects, is still too much a woman not to be concerned much and always with gossip and the opinions of her neighbours. She is right from her point of view, but she will never give me the taste for what I disdain, nor respect for what I despise. There are forms of blame and approbation that are not worth the pains of escaping them or seeking them. One who has known independence has no desire to place himself again at the mercy of the world, for the world is fickle, unjust, suspicious and profane.

Felt all day the feebleness of my nothingness. I am reduced to a tenth of what I was. I cannot lift the lightest weight; there is not a particle of strength left in my arm, head or voice. O misery! In ten weeks sickness and especially the doctor have brought me to this annihilation.

*(10 p. m.).*—Reading: Gréville *(La Cité Ménard)* . . . Call from Auguste Bouvier, who presses me in his arms with such strength that he hurts me.

*April 19, 1881 (10 a. m.).*—Oppression, somnolence, for I only slept an hour. The difficulty of breathing has come back.

> *Que vivre est difficile, ô mon cœur fatigué!*

*(3 p. m.).*—An indirect proof of the gravity of my condition is the excess of indulgence that comes to me from all sides. People only pamper the dying. It is easy for me to read in the faces of E. L. and C. L., in the letters of H. and F. B., the shade of sympathy that is addressed to those who are believed to be lost. Today, an old acquaintance, Mme. S. D., writes me a letter of exalted compassion, offering me flowers, music, prayers to enliven and

fortify the invalid and the poet whom she and her household love. If a rivalry of zeal breaks out among my readers, what will become of me? This heart-felt commiseration, which asks permission to become active, is one of the noblest traits of the feminine soul. But what strikes me as most curious is that every woman fancies herself alone in her good intention, and imagines that she is called exclusively and uniquely to save the person in whom she is interested. The idea of coördination, subordination, inferiority never occurs to her, because it would humiliate her. Her ardour is jealous, her goodness is monopolizing, her aspiration is to dominate. Feminine zeal is not maternal; for it, the necessary thing is not that good should be done, but that it should be done by it . . .

*(10 p. m.).*—Wretched all day. Reading: Doudan *(Pensées et fragments).*

*April 20, 1881.*—. . . The thing that astonishes me is that I am still here. After my bath, my rubbing down and breakfast, there is a little rise. The omnibus-hack has felt the whip and trembles. But these vain appearances of strength and courage do not arrest the decay. I am vanishing, passing away. All the elementary functions are impeded. Bankruptcy is inevitable.

*(4 p. m.).*—By various arrangements and attentions, distractions (reading and games), my god-daughter has procured me an hour or two of respite . . .

Reading: finished Doudan, who is all too over-refined, too brilliant, too delicate, too studied. In his *Révolutions du Goût,* he outdoes his own manner. He ought to be compared with Rivarol *(Discours sur la langue française).* But what a consummate jeweller! What a subtle and discriminating critic! What a lover of fine diction!

*(10 p. m.).*—Reading: *Les trois Maupin* (by Scribe and Boisseau).

*April 21, 1881.*—Middling day, ending in a frightful night, the twentieth without sleep.

Reading: Loiseleur *(Controverse sur la Saint-Barthélemy)*; Barrière *(Les faux bonshommes)*.

*April 22, 1881.*—Solemn day. I was dying at dawn. They washed, combed, rubbed and dressed me like a child. But, time being short, I devoted the whole morning to setting my affairs in order. Every step and every gesture wrung from me a groan that I could not repress. Cleared my tables and my desks, gathered together hastily the notes of six university courses, tied up my letters in bundles, set aside the books to be returned, took up and completed my will. In short, I arranged everything as if this were my last day. Extreme fatigue, but relief. These clearing-up times cleanse the soul. And yet these precipitous arrangements are immensely faulty. But I must break off. My writing brings on nausea.

Dictated a few letters . . .

I have been wonderfully watched over and cared for by my goddaughter, who has not left me day or night.

Received from Fida a bouquet and an excellent letter. Many friends have come to ask for news of me . . .

*April 23, 1881.*—It was an attack of bronchitis that overthrew Benjamin Disraeli, Lord Beaconsfield. But he went off gently. Morning wasted. I do nothing but drag myself from chair to chair, seeking air and driving away sleep.

*April 25, 1881 (9 a. m.).*—I still live, but the danger has not diminished and there has been no truce. I cannot sleep yet, or breathe, or eat, or speak; and I exist like a shadow.

Yesterday, Sunday, the last calls came one after another. Everyone thought me at the end of the road. My two sisters and Fida even came back twice. Looks, words, attentions all seemed to be dressed in mourning. I myself was of the same opinion. I could not dress or leave my bedroom. Many fellow-professors came for news.

I was ready for the end during the day, and I was prepared to die in peace. I was wonderfully cared for, watched over, surrounded, assisted every minute. And if I am still here, it is by virtue of a victory over nature. But what an exercise of patience for a poor sick man who has no longer an atom of strength and has not one good hour in twenty-four!

*April 26, 1881.*—The torture continues. Abysmal nights, exasperating days; no sleep, no appetite.

The one good side of my situation is the tokens of interest, which are multiplying.

I have no strength for anything any longer. I do not know where to sit down, I cannot hold a pen. I have neither voice nor muscles left.

*April 27, 1881 (10 a. m.).*—Inexpressible weakness. Here I have been on the rack for twelve weeks, and the anguish, the palpitations leave me no rest. There is nothing but skin on my bones any longer.

A solemn night, this. I was astonished to survive it. What was the use? My god-daughter bravely keeps up the night-watch, and three people are living here simply to care for my sickness.

But the dissolution is proceeding by leaps and bounds, and existence is becoming a torture that has something infernal about it.—I persist in resignation and patience while I am dying of fatigue and want of sleep. A daily cause of nervous exasperation is the universal lameness of my body, which prevents a moment of respite and allows me no rest whatever.

*(4 p. m.).*—The excess of torment has brought about a denouément. Discovered that my lean back was the prey of enemies in ambush, namely, a big round button in the belt of my *Schlafrock,* a large trouser-buckle, a sturdy waistcoat-buckle, the meeting of two suspender-buttons one of which had got on top of the other in the course of my emaciation. These five engraving-tools were ploughing into my back and causing the painful bruise that kept me from breathing.

In this matter, the doctor did not make a single useful conjecture. What proves the sagacity of Hippocrates, however, is the discovery of little, secret causes.

I am likewise persuaded that, by putting an end to the furry cough, an Arab doctor would have saved me twelve weeks of torture, basketfuls of medicines and the fearful wear and tear of life that all this has caused me, in the subsidiary organs, the heart, the stomach, the diaphragm, etc.

*April 28 and 29, 1881.*—Days of such wretchedness that I cannot even bear the weight of a pen. In compensation, there are abundant tokens of sympathy and interest. People send me flowers, jellies, letters, tokens of affection. Sometimes these things come from friends who are quite far away.

My god-daughter makes a list for me of the calls that I receive; she serves me as a factotum, a secretary, a reader. For three months the mother and the daughter have been rivals in zeal, and they will not yet accept any aid or anyone to share the task.

*The Journal stops at this date, with this homage to friendship. After so much suffering and anguish, Amiel entered a slow and silent agony. Extreme weakness gradually overcame him, and he died gently on Tuesday, May 11, towards six o'clock in the morning.*

# INDEX

667